Social Psychology

For our children:
Ainura Mahina (CJ)
Ross and Marlis (KAH)

Sara Miller McCune founded SAGE Publishing in 1965 to support the dissemination of usable knowledge and educate a global community. SAGE publishes more than 1000 journals and over 800 new books each year, spanning a wide range of subject areas. Our growing selection of library products includes archives, data, case studies and video. SAGE remains majority owned by our founder and after her lifetime will become owned by a charitable trust that secures the company's continued independence.

Los Angeles | London | New Delhi | Singapore | Washington DC | Melbourne

Social Psychology
Individuals, Interaction, and Inequality

Karen A. Hegtvedt
Emory University

Cathryn Johnson
Emory University

Los Angeles | London | New Delhi
Singapore | Washington DC | Melbourne

FOR INFORMATION:

SAGE Publications, Inc.
2455 Teller Road
Thousand Oaks, California 91320
E-mail: order@sagepub.com

SAGE Publications Ltd.
1 Oliver's Yard
55 City Road
London, EC1Y 1SP
United Kingdom

SAGE Publications India Pvt. Ltd.
B 1/I 1 Mohan Cooperative Industrial Area
Mathura Road, New Delhi 110 044
India

SAGE Publications Asia-Pacific Pte. Ltd.
3 Church Street
#10-04 Samsung Hub
Singapore 049483

Acquisitions Editor: Jeff Lasser
Content Development Editor: Gabrielle Piccininni
Editorial Assistant: Adeline Wilson
Production Editor: Jane Haenel
Copy Editor: Megan Markanich
Typesetter: C&M Digitals (P) Ltd.
Proofreader: Caryne Brown
Indexer: Michael Ferreira
Cover Designer: Candice Harman
Marketing Manager: Kara Kindstrom

Printed in the United States of America

ISBN: 9781412965040

This book is printed on acid-free paper.

17 18 19 20 21 10 9 8 7 6 5 4 3 2 1

• Brief Contents •

• Detailed Contents •

• Preface •

Although we (Karen and Cathy, as we refer to ourselves throughout the book) dedicate this book to our children—so that they may come to understand what excited their mothers' scholarly interests—we owe a debt to the decades of undergraduate and graduate students who we invited to venture into the world of social psychology. With each teaching of the substance of social psychology, we developed a story, requiring a semester in the telling, of how individuals enter their social world and come to function in groups small and large, intimate and impersonal.

Our training as sociological social psychologists heavily influences the story that we tell. For many years, we used various texts, typically written by psychologists. None, however, captured the important message that we wished to deliver to our students: that what individuals do (how they perceive, emote, behave, and interact) matters for dynamics within and between groups, which in turn reinforces or changes the nature of social inequalities. With the study of social inequality at the heart of the discipline of sociology, we stress how the microlevel of individuals and their interactions have consequences for macrolevel phenomena within social groups. While there are many social psychological processes (e.g., creation of meaning, identity, categorization, cognition, attitudes, emotions, status, power, legitimacy, and justice), our story illustrates the interconnections between these processes. The invitation to write this book ensured that we could share this story beyond the confines of our classrooms.

Prior to the invitation, we had already begun to collaborate on research (see the About the Authors section). Thus, we knew that we could work well together on a coauthored book. We sorted topics according to our fields of expertise and inclinations. We discussed the content of each chapter and how it would contribute to the story we would shape for our readers. We then each authored a set of chapters but relied on the other to review, comment, and revise. One of the biggest challenges was to find an appropriate "voice" for the book that would engage undergraduates but also provide the academic unfamiliar with social psychology with an introduction to important theories and works in the field. Cathy was quicker to catch on to writing for this audience than Karen, who tended to go into "scholarly review" mode. (But, occasionally, Karen caught Cathy reverting to that mode as well!) With the writing and revision of each chapter, we soon harmonized into what we hope readers will find an engaging "voice."

Having "pretested" various chapters in several sections of our "Individual and Society" course (i.e., the undergraduate introduction to social psychology in our department), we have been relieved to hear students enthusiastically praise the wide array of examples we employ to drive home sometimes complex theoretical notions. Indeed, we sincerely believe what a button distributed among our colleagues at an annual meeting of the American Sociological Association said so simply— "Social psychology: it's actually everywhere!" Thus, it was not difficult to generate examples that resonate with our readers, revealing the importance of the processes we analyze as well as the impact of contextual factors on how individuals think, feel, and behave.

Our work as coeditors of *Social Psychology Quarterly* also enhanced the depth of our knowledge of the field and how pieces of it fit together into a larger picture of how microlevel processes help to shape inequalities in groups, informal and formal. Those same editorial duties, however, drew time away from actually composing the chapters. Additionally, we both took on administrative roles during the time we were to be writing the book. While those duties (Karen chairing the department, Cathy acting as a dean in the graduate school) delayed completion of the book, they also provided some of the examples within it. Of course, except for examples in which we referenced our children, we changed names and disguised circumstances to keep our friends and colleagues guessing about how their experiences inspired our examples.

Additionally, we appreciate the support of our colleagues and staff in the department and in the Laney Graduate School as we embarked on this writing project. Elsewhere, we acknowledge the contributions of specific individuals who eased the writing and revising of the chapters. Yet knowing that many of our colleagues see the value of social psychological processes in understanding their own domains of research—for example, cultural processes, crime, health outcomes, family interactions, labor market dynamics, and the like—helped to solidify our determination to produce a work that provides an introduction to the substance of social psychology for scholars trained in other fields as well.

We hope that the story we tell in the following pages will pique the interests of students for years to come and provide them with a framework for understanding their own lives within the context of their social world. A primary goal in our classes is for our students "to take something home" with them. We doubt that they will remember details of the studies we introduce or all of the terminology of social psychologists. Yet we trust that they will come to grasp a number of elements of social psychology that will lead them to consider how their identities and perceptions shape what they do, how the structures in which they are embedded may constrain or facilitate their behaviors, and how these dynamics contribute to reinforcing or ameliorating inequalities in their social groups. In so doing, they will see social psychology everywhere as we do.

• Acknowledgments •

The completion of this text has not been a solitary activity. Of course, we had each other. But we had far more as well. Over the course of nearly 8 years (with a writing hiatus when overwhelmed with editorial and administrative activities), we have relied on a variety of people. The first drafts of early chapters benefited from the close reading of one of our former undergraduate students, Sara Berney, who often highlighted passages where we lost our "voice" for our undergraduate audience and encouraged us to provide more examples! She also started a number of the reference lists. Dr. Lesley Watson, during her time as a graduate student in our department, also provided invaluable feedback on several of the chapters. A current graduate student, Jennifer Hayward, was instrumental in providing feedback on later drafts and the completion of all chapters. She carefully read every chapter, searched down references, provided suggestions to augment our arguments, and painstakingly put up with our craziness when we were in the throes of honing each chapter. Xueqing (Zoe) Wang came to the project in its final two semesters, crafting a compendium of recent studies from which we could ensure inclusion of new research. She, along with another undergraduate, Hilary Druckman, provided feedback from their particular point of view on what worked and what did not in various chapters.

As noted in the Preface, we have appreciated the support of our colleagues in our department and in the graduate school. Special thanks go to Dean Lisa Tedesco of Laney Graduate School, who supported Cathy's time to continue her scholarly work in sociology while in her administrative position. Beyond Emory, a number of our colleagues in our social psychology networks have encouraged our endeavor and have implied to us that they will use the book once it is completed. Thus, we had to get it done!

Additionally, we have benefited from the constructive critiques of reviewers secured by SAGE, including the following:

Abdallah M. Badahdah, *University of North Dakota*

Lindsey Joyce Chamberlain, *The Ohio State University*

David Diekema, *Seattle Pacific University*

Curt G. Sobolewski, *University of Notre Dame*

Moreover, we have sincerely appreciated the support of the editorial staff at SAGE. Because this project was in progress for more years than we really want to count, we saw a couple of editors come and go. Each encouraged us in their respective ways. Our most recent editor, Jeff Lasser, deserves credit for spurring us to the finish line. He, along with his editorial assistant Adeline Wilson, ensured that our chapters were well written and complete.

Finally, thanks go to those closest to us for enduring our absences and obsessions as we ignored them to focus on writing this book. Karen appreciates how her spouse, Patrick, took over tasks like cooking Sunday dinners and schlepping children to various activities so that weekends could be spent composing at the computer. Cathy is incredibly grateful to her spouse, Evie, who was truly understanding of her Sunday afternoons in the office (with their daughter who spent the time laboring over her homework) and thus relinquished their time together on those days. We could not ask for more supportive spouses whose acknowledgment of the truth that social psychology is everywhere (among other things) safeguards balance in and endurance of our relationships.

• About the Authors •

Karen A. Hegtvedt (PhD, University of Washington) is professor and former chair of the Department of Sociology at Emory University. She has published a number of empirical articles and review pieces on topics relating to justice processes. Some of this work examines cognitive processes underlying justice evaluations and other work attempts to integrate issues of power, emotions, and legitimacy into perceptions of and responses to injustice. With Jody Clay-Warner, she coedited a volume of *Advances in Group Processes* focused on justice.

Cathryn Johnson (PhD, University of Iowa) is professor of sociology and senior associate dean of the Laney Graduate School at Emory University. She has published many articles that focus on a variety of group processes. Much of her research examines how legitimacy processes connect to issues of power, emotions, and justice dynamics. She has also coauthored articles on identity dynamics. She has edited a special issue of *Research in the Sociology of Organizations* focused on legitimacy.

For the past 15 years, the authors have collaborated on a number of publications joining Cathy's favorite independent variable—legitimacy—with Karen's favorite dependent variable—perceptions of injustice. That work has involved both basic experimental investigations on how legitimacy constrains responses to injustice and a multimethod study focused on the impact of the perceived legitimacy of university administrators' sustainability efforts on students' environmental behaviors and perceptions of environmental justice. They are currently involved in two strands of research. The first project extends their previous legitimacy and justice research (supported by the National Science Foundation) by examining how justice processes enhance the development of legitimacy. The second project elaborates on their previous sustainability research (supported by the Spencer Foundation) by focusing on how racial identity and experiences with discrimination affect African Americans' environmental behaviors and justice perceptions. Their individual and collaborative work has appeared in *American Sociological Review, American Journal of Sociology, Social Forces, Annual Review of Sociology, Social Psychology Quarterly, The Sociological Quarterly, American Behavioral Scientist, Social Justice Research*, and other journals and edited volumes. In addition to their research collaborations, they recently coedited *Social Psychology Quarterly*. And, on Fridays, they eat fish tacos together.

Introduction to the Interrelated Processes of Social Psychology

In the fall of 1960, a cohort of young women arrived at Spelman College, a historically black women's college in Atlanta, Georgia. These 16-, 17-, and 18-year-old recent high school graduates came from a variety of states, seeking fulfillment of the promise of higher education as a means to better their lives. Their largely middle-class families anticipated that their daughters would adjust to life away from home; attend classes; join campus clubs; choose a major; prepare themselves for future careers; and, perhaps, date Morehouse College men. Their college years began on the eve of the civil rights movement, which would transform not only the history of the United States but also the personal lives of these young African American women.

Foot Soldiers: Class of 1964 documents their freshman-year journey and beyond.[1] Arriving from mixed neighborhoods in the North or from segregated ones in the South, these women identified their entire lives as "colored." For those arriving in the southern city for the first time, signs directing them to "colored only" restaurants, store entrances, and bathrooms were unsettling. For others, such symbols of segregation characterized their lifetime experience. For nearly all, their parents had sternly admonished them not to participate in the sort of protests launched a year earlier in Greensboro, North Carolina, when four African American college students refused to vacate seats at a "whites only" lunch counter.

Despite their parents' seeming acquiescence to the existing system of inequality and instructions to their daughters to focus on their studies and remain distant from the unrest, these young women chose another pathway. Taking cues from upper-class students at their college, they asked, "Why do people hate me? They don't know me." They wondered, Why should people like me be steadily and squarely confronted with discrimination in daily interactions in public places such as stores, restaurants, and other businesses solely for the color of our skin? Ultimately, they joined the coordinated civil rights protests sweeping the American South.

They picketed. They attended sit-ins. They suffered the wrath of Ku Klux Klan members, police, and even less racist whites who simply feared challenges to the long-standing Jim Crow laws. Yet through nonviolent means, they conveyed their determination and commitment to challenge the existing system of racial inequality and to persuade powerholders to make significant changes. In effect, these young women came to recognize the injustice of discriminatory segregation and to question the legitimacy of the system that permitted such discrimination. Their actions, along with those of many others, including high-status (white) people in positions of power, spurred the passage of the Civil Rights Act of 1964.

The story of the Spelman women highlights individual-level processes that combine to shape an understanding of a situation, the actions of single as well as multiple individuals within a particular context, and the consequences of their endeavors that pave the pathway for further social dynamics—and, in the case of the civil rights protest, reshape history. This book focuses on such individual-level processes, embedded in and shaped by the social context, that have consequences for larger groups.

The Spelman freshmen might have thought of themselves in terms of who they are (e.g., colored, high school graduate, Christian) and what they might become (certainly college student, but also, perhaps, teacher, civil servant, nurse, or lawyer). These identities, plus their backgrounds and previous experiences, directed their attention to information in their environment about an array of factors, including the beliefs and actions of others, as well as the places to which they had access and those from which they were prohibited. They may have processed that information in different ways, automatically with little conscious effort by relying on existing beliefs, or in a more controlled fashion, taking into account their goals, weighing arguments from their peers and from their parents, considering the benefits and costs of different strategies of action. Certainly, they were exposed to radical ideas about challenging the system by the upper-class women. In their efforts to be similar to and respected by Spelman juniors and seniors, the young freshmen adopted the upper-class students' beliefs about the unfairness of any system allowing discrimination. The emergence of new attitudes among the freshmen—distinct from those of their parents—may have resulted from explicit acts of persuasion or by subtle influence processes owing to the higher status of the women closer to achieving their degrees.

Moreover, they may have experienced an array of emotions associated with new identities and attitudes: indignation in response to (long-standing as well as recent) encounters with discrimination, excitement about joining the protest movement, or frustration at the slow pace of social change but also hope for securing legal changes ensuring civil rights. New attitudes and felt emotions, in turn, propelled participation in various protests, where encounters with more powerful others (e.g., city administrators, police) unfolded. The protests clearly pitted groups, defined by skin color, against each other. Thus, while individual-level processes may have led to (collective) action, as representatives of different groups, the encounters extended beyond the individual to characterize intergroup dynamics as well.

Identity processes, information processing, attitudes, emotions, behaviors, dynamics of status and power, evaluations of fairness, and intergroup processes capture the individual and his or her relationship to society. This relationship forms the core of the domain of **social psychology**, which *involves the systematic study of the influence of the real, imagined, and implied presence of others on an individual's thoughts, feelings, and behaviors* (Allport 1954). While it is certainly the case that actual others in our environments may encourage us to do some things we ordinarily might not do—like join a protest movement—this definition also allows for the possibility that those not present may have a similar effect. For example, we think about what our rabbi, minister, or imam might want us to do if we witness acts of discrimination. The teachings of our faith or the demands of our moral compass, developed through exposure to the beliefs of our parents, teachers, community leaders, media outlets, and so forth, may influence our actions even though none of the representatives of those groups are present. In this way, influence extends beyond the dynamics between individuals to also include the effect of groups and elements of history and culture (Aronson 2012).

While the definition of social psychology seems to propose a unidirectional impact of other people, resources and opportunities, and cultural frameworks on the individual, as the Spelman example suggests, individuals also influence the social group, the society even, to which they belong. Emphasis in social psychology ultimately rests on the *interaction among individuals, between an individual and a group, or among groups, ensconced in a particular social context, which gives meaning to unfolding behavior.* Research in the area explicates these dynamic processes. Given that people believe, perceive, feel, and act, what social psychology examines pervades many of our routine endeavors. For instance, think about how we meet new people and develop new relationships; defer to our bosses at work; cheer for the home team at a basketball game; stifle our anger toward a teacher scheduling a test the day before Thanksgiving; buy vegetables from the same vendor at the farmer's market even though the number of vendors has expanded; and contribute to reducing our carbon footprint through recycling and conservation activities, which, collectively, helps to reduce the threat of climate change.

Social psychological theoretical approaches pertain to these instances and a wide variety of other concrete social situations. Thus, it should not be difficult to apply the theoretical arguments introduced in the coming chapters to your own experiences and social interactions. For each chapter, we begin with a concrete example, drawn from history, fiction, or current institutional practices. (We also offer an array of additional examples throughout the book, some drawing on our own experiences. For those, we refer to ourselves as Karen or Cathy.) And while each chapter may stand alone, together they weave a story of how individuals come to perceive and act in their social worlds. That weaving involves exploration of key social psychological processes that help us to understand how people construct their realities and ways of doing things in everyday interaction.

Additionally, the story that we develop is one that provides a basis for understanding how even individual actions may contribute to upholding a particular set of social arrangements or, as in the case of the Spelman women, contribute to changing those social arrangements. Our fundamental goal is *to illustrate how individual-level processes contribute to explaining processes of social inequality related to class, race, gender, disability, and so forth within social groups and organizations* (see McLeod, Lawler, and Schwalbe 2014). Generally, we think of **social inequality** as a state of affairs involving an uneven distribution of resources or opportunities in society, creating patterns along lines of socially distinguished groups of people. For example, even though many of the Spelman freshmen in 1960 came from middle-class families, in their everyday encounters, they could readily discern that "colored" people like themselves had fewer opportunities than the white people they encountered. Similarly, being of middle-class standing in terms of family income or wealth is often accompanied by access to particular schools, financial institutions, or even after-school activities to which those who live in poverty are denied. Individuals' positions in a stratified hierarchy in a given society affect how their life changes and how they experience social life.

Sociologists have long discussed causes and consequences of inequality based on income, race, gender, and so forth (Neckerman and Torche 2007). Structural factors, stemming from economic, educational, and political arrangements, that affect competition over resources, conflict between social groups, or even repression of members of certain groups stimulate inequalities. Cultural beliefs regarding what entitles people to resources and opportunities further reinforce these inequalities. As McLeod, Lawler, et al., note (2014:v), inequality also stems from "subtle (and sometimes unconscious processes) of exclusion, othering, and devaluation" and that "sociological social psychologists share a common interest in analyzing how, why, and under what conditions people come to be seen as different and, as a consequence, to be given unequal access to valued society resources." Thus, as we introduce you to the substance of social psychology, we highlight how fundamental individual-level processes help to create and maintain social inequality as well as how they provide means to stimulate social change to address long-standing inequalities. Beyond this fundamental goal, several key themes also pervade the book.

Roots, Overview, and Key Themes

The definition of social psychology presumes that individual-level processes are studied systematically, through social scientific methods. Throughout the book, we refer to patterns of findings that corroborate underlying assumptions of and hypotheses derived from social psychological theorizing in a variety of substantive areas. We offer a primer on such methods in Chapter 2. These methods transcend the roots of social psychology, which is at the intersection of two scientific disciplines. Some areas within social psychology may seem akin to psychology, which emphasizes the individual per se, as exemplified by attention to "internal" processing leading to the development of perceptions, attitudes, emotions, and individual behavior. Psychologists also tend to focus on differences among individuals, owing to personality factors or personal experiences rather than more general group structures or cultural beliefs. The impact of the latter falls under the rubric of a more sociological approach to social psychology. Sociology involves the systematic study of society, including institutions represented in economic, political, and cultural spheres. More sociologically oriented social psychology highlights the importance of social stimuli present in a particular context or implied by larger social factors such as socioeconomic status, minority group status, or social roles. Regardless of the disciplinary source of a particular social psychological process, we seek to elaborate on the connection between the individual and society, where society both influences and is influenced by the individual. Below we offer you a preview of the book. (We do not pause to define every concept, as each chapter will offer such definitions!)

We begin with a focus on what is uniquely human (compared to other animals): how **individuals construct their social worlds** and how they acquire a sense of themselves (Chapter 3). Such construction provides the basis of meaning. The social self, as Chapter 4 illustrates, consists of multiple **identities** based on who we are, to whom we are connected, and what we do. These identities affect how people perceive social stimuli in situations, make choices, and interact with others. Individuals' perceptions also depend upon background factors and existing beliefs, salience of contextual features, and the like. Such **social cognitions** (Chapter 5) along with **attitudes** that capture our positive or negative assessments of stimuli in our environments (Chapter 6) prompt various individual behaviors as well as the way interaction unfolds. We recognize, however, that people are more than perceivers. They also experience an array of **emotions** (Chapter 7), which likewise fuel action, though sometimes what is felt might not be displayed to others for fear of negative consequences. Constraints on emotional expressions may stem from characteristics of the structure of the relationships in which individuals are embedded. Thus, we examine structural features of groups, defined in terms of **status** (Chapter 8) and **power** (Chapter 9) differences in relationships. Such features shape meanings, perceptions, and emotions and also drive behavior. As we will illustrate, status and power processes often reinforce the status quo of relationships—that is, maintaining existing structural relationships. Evaluations of the **legitimacy** (Chapter 10) and **justice** (Chapter 11) of such structures and the interactions that they cultivate may reinforce the status quo or provide a means to challenge it. The dynamics of perceptual, emotional, structural, and evaluative processes move beyond intragroup processes and extend to **intergroup processes** (Chapter 12) as well.

In our explanations of these social processes, we make an assumption about the nature of the individual, an issue beyond the formal definition of social psychology. We recognize individuals as biological creatures who believe, perceive, feel, and act. Given advances in the past 20 years in identifying biological markers and using neuroimaging techniques, when appropriate, we signal linkages to biophysical or neurological processes underlying the means by which people process information, experience emotions, determine fairness, and the like. Beyond our reliance on the systematic research bolstering the understanding of processes involving biological beings, we stress three themes that capture the reciprocal influence between the individual and society and tie together chapters of the book.

There is no single, overarching theory of social psychology. As the description of the chapters of the book suggest, a number of perspectives address different substantive aspects of believing, perceiving, feeling, and behaving. Thus, our first key theme is that those *"areas" of social psychology are interrelated*, and we attempt to present them as such in this book. For example, when the Spelman freshmen took on the new identity of protester or civil rights activist, they deviated from the routine activities that accompany the identity of student and in so doing created implications for racial dynamics in the city of Atlanta. Some chapters focus largely on individual-level internal processes, whereas others emphasize the context in which the individual is embedded, described by the structural elements of the group or dynamics between groups. Both are necessary for an understanding of social dynamics.

Indeed, the second theme stresses that *individuals' thoughts, feelings, and behaviors depend upon the social context*. We frequently note that individuals attend to situational information or are embedded in status and power structures. Of course, it is possible that certain behaviors may be disallowed in particular contexts. While it may be acceptable to break down in tears at a funeral, doing so during a college class might be considered inappropriate. Also, it is important to determine *how* patterns of thoughts, feelings, and behaviors vary by different contextual factors. For example, upper-class women at Spelman may have exerted more influence than parents on the freshmen only if the newcomers to the school wished to gain the respect of the juniors and seniors. If they cared less about what the upper-class women thought of them, then the first-year students may have been more likely to heed the advice of their parents to stay away from the protests. In other words, situational factors *condition* or moderate patterns of beliefs, perceptions, feelings, and behaviors. Such factors may stem from cultural dimensions, and thus, when appropriate, we highlight cross-cultural differences in substantive patterns.

Given our goal of illustrating the impact of individual-level processes on patterns of social inequality related to class, race, gender, disability, and the like, our third key theme is that *social psychological processes act as a micro- or individual-level foundation for macro- or group-level phenomena,* such as group structures, organizational cultures, health inequalities, educational patterns, crime rates, social movements, or large-scale social processes in general. Social psychology identifies mechanisms by which individuals sort themselves into categories relevant to the structure of groups or patterns of beliefs representing how an organization or institution carries out its tasks. Social psychological mechanisms also may account for why certain diseases are more prominent for African Americans than whites or why certain groups of children do better in school than others.

For example, members of resource-disadvantaged racial minority groups, compared to whites, are, on average, exposed to greater stresses, a form of negative emotional response to a situation, often stemming from discriminatory interactions; higher levels of stress suppress immune systems and thereby result in the greater likelihood of particular diseases (see McLeod, Erving, and Caputo 2014). In a similar vein, Lareau (2011) illustrates how the belief systems and opportunity structures of parents, defined in terms of class and race, affect the interaction dynamics between parents and their children, which in turn shape children's outlooks and achievements. Despite the unequivocal goals of all parents to raise happy and healthy children, middle-class parents, regardless of race, have more resources to develop children's skills through organized and supervised activities. They are also more likely to encourage language development and reasoning. In contrast, working-class and poor families rely more heavily on the spontaneous growth of their children, assuming that they will gain what they need by engagement with other children independent of organized activities and through parental directives (rather than reasoning). As a consequence, children of the middle (and upper) class grow better equipped to navigate social institutions and meet the demands for critical thinking skills necessary to achieve in college. Colleges are "middle- to upper-class" institutions, and students from poor and working-class backgrounds have more to navigate as they learn the rules and norms of institutions of higher education. In effect, these examples illustrate how microlevel dynamics carry implications for reinforcing social inequalities.

Segue: Moving From the Content of Social Psychology to the Means of Studying It

The social psychological processes detailed in this book provide different lenses through which you might examine the stories told by the Spelman women in the class of 1964. For example, you might want to focus on how their identities shifted from simply college student to civil rights protestor. Alternatively, you could ask questions about what they were thinking during this time and, in this historical context, how they came to decide to join the protests despite the threat of arrest. Doing so may reveal motivations and information that they considered relevant to their decisions to participate. While the documentary film illustrates the viewpoint of the protest participants, what about students who may have believed strongly in civil rights but failed to participate in any sit-ins? How could their behaviors be so inconsistent with their attitudes? Did they not feel the same anger (and fear) as their peers? Were they constrained by the power that their parents or perhaps school administrators wielded over them? You might further wonder how, over 60 years later, the United States still witnesses discriminatory actions in the workplace, communities, and on the street and spurs students and others to join movements such as Black Lives Matter. What has changed or failed to change to allow the maintenance of inequalities among racial groups? These questions that are focused on a particular historical event, however, transcend the time period. They refer to more abstract issues regarding identity processes, social perceptions, the attitude–behavior relationship, the impact of status or power structures on behavior, intergroup dynamics, and the like. Importantly, thinking abstractly allows consideration of an array of similar concrete issues and the strategies to address them.

As a scientific endeavor, social psychology seeks to bring evidence to bear on questions such as these, posed at both the abstract and concrete levels of analysis. The nature of the question directs attention to the kind of evidence or data relevant to answering it. It is not enough to simply rely upon opinions or hunches, though they may be starting points for thinking about particular issues. Ultimately, it is necessary to do the hard work of collecting and analyzing relevant data. In the next chapter, we outline the scientific method of developing theoretical ideas and testing them using different approaches, including experimentation, surveys, and observations.

Endnote

1. Executive producer: Dr. Georgianne Thomas. Writer, producer, and director: Alvelyn Sanders. It was the winner of the Pan African Film Festival–Los Angeles 2013 Best Short Documentary.

References

Allport, Gordon W. 1954. *The Nature of Prejudice*. Reading, MA: Addison-Wesley Publishing.

Aronson, Eliot. 2012. *The Social Animal*. 11th ed. New York: Worth Publishers.

Lareau, Annette. 2011. *Unequal Childhoods: Race, Class, and Family Life: A Decade Later*. 2nd ed. Berkeley: University of California Press.

McLeod, Jane, Christy Erving, and Jennifer Caputo. 2014. "Health Inequalities." Pp. 715–42 in *Handbook of the Social Psychology of Inequality*, edited by J. McLeod, E. Lawler, and M. Schwalbe. New York: Springer.

McLeod, Jane, Edward Lawler, and Michael Schwalbe, eds. 2014. *Handbook of the Social Psychology of Inequality*. New York: Springer. doi:10.1007/978-94-017-9002-4

Neckerman, Kathryn, and Florencia Torche. 2007. "Inequality: Causes and Consequences." *Annual Review of Sociology* 33:335–57. doi:10.1146/annurev.soc.33.040406.131755

Methods of Developing Social Psychological Knowledge

1964. The rape and stabbing death of 28-year-old Kitty Genovese in front of her Queens, New York, apartment building drew headlines. Although the attack went on for 30 minutes, complete with screams for help, none of the residents at the building reported the incident while it was ongoing.[1]

1983. Gang rape occurred at a bar, with a woman assaulted on a pool table in front of witnesses.[2]

2005. A fraternity pledge died from water intoxication with four fraternity brothers present. They hesitated too long to call an ambulance after the pledge collapsed and had a seizure.

2009. Outside a homecoming dance at a Richmond, California, high school, a 15-year-old was assaulted and raped while people walked by, some of whom even took pictures on their cell phones. Yet none of them reported the incident.

2016. Marques Gaines left a Chicago area bar where he had been drinking and dancing. Assailants punched and knocked him unconscious into a crosswalk outside a 7-Eleven, robbing him of his cell phone and debit card. Pedestrians strolled along the street corner and lingered on the sidewalk, but no one attempted to lift him from the pavement, block the flow of traffic, or call for help until after a taxi ran him over, resulting in his death.

In these five different incidents—years and miles apart, involving both male and female victims—bystanders observed the event and then hesitated or even failed to offer help in a timely fashion. In all cases, perpetrators of the crimes were ultimately punished. Nonetheless, you might ask, How can people just stand by and watch something horrific happen to another human being? That, indeed, was the research question posed by psychologists Bibb Latané and John Darley in the wake of the Kitty Genovese murder and sensationalized media accounts that accompanied it. The development of their classic work on bystander intervention in emergencies (Latané and Darley 1970), augmented by other scholars throughout the years, epitomizes the logic of scientific inquiry and the use of various methodologies to address substantive and theoretical questions of interest to social psychologists.

As the definition of social psychology offered in Chapter 1 emphasizes, to understand the relationship between the individual and society requires systematic study. Of course, we all have hunches about why people act the way they do. For instance, in the wake of the Kitty Genovese murder, some people attributed the commotion to a "lovers' quarrel" or their hesitancy to their "fear of getting involved" or "fear of getting hurt." The first account implies that people did not perceive an emergency situation, whereas the others suggest that individuals weighed threats to themselves or just how much time they would lose if they had to answer police questions. Latané and Darley (1970), of course, considered these intuitive or commonsense explanations but went further by developing a *theoretical argument* and bringing *systematic evidence* to bear upon predictions derived from their argument about the conditions facilitating or hindering provision of interventions. Given what they had observed, they asked this: *Under what conditions* are people likely to help or not help in emergency situations?

In this chapter, we outline steps necessary to producing scientific evidence in social psychology. We apply the logic of such inquiry to the study of helping behavior generally. We use actual empirical research on bystander interventions and helping to illustrate the different methodologies that social psychologists use to investigate people's thoughts, feelings, and behaviors in social situations. We conclude by considering how social psychological research extends beyond commonsense knowledge and provides deeper insight, for example, than the musings of people at a party, the speculations of family members, or the conjectures of workers about why a friend, a cousin, or a boss acted in a particular way.

The Logic of Scientific Inquiry

Imagine reading the initial *New York Times* article on the Kitty Genovese murder or any of the more recent incidents noted at the beginning of this chapter. You may feel stunned that (purportedly) so many people witnessed some element of the attack but did little to intervene. As you discuss the incident with your friends, someone might say, "Ah, do you remember the recent robbery at the convenience store? Two teenagers assaulted the cashier and then absconded with the cash in the register, running out of the store in full view of a dozen people getting off a bus. No one intervened." Someone else might raise another incident, such as the failure of anyone—despite the presence of an array of tourists along the embankment—to aid boaters whose vessel capsizes on the Thames River in London.[3] A third person could extend the discussion to why people don't contribute to charity fundraisers, where such help may assist a local hospital, food bank, or community center. As stories of similar incidents unfold (regardless of their veracity), you have taken the first step in any social scientific endeavor: making **observations**. Latané and Darley (1970) perhaps began with such a process before launching their systematic research program. Figure 2.1 illustrates the basic components of the logic of scientific inquiry.

In the course of our daily lives, we make many observations, which we may later share with family, friends, or even acquaintances met while riding the bus. In effect, we are describing reality as we experienced it. Of course, our observations may be casual and flawed by our expectations and existing beliefs. For example,

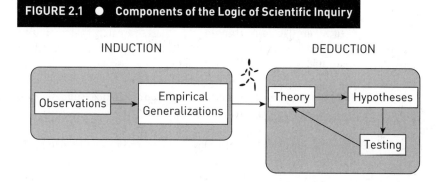

FIGURE 2.1 ● Components of the Logic of Scientific Inquiry

if you have heard that the required statistics course is the toughest course in your major, you may perceive after the first day that the instructor is hard-nosed and the homework arduous. While scientific inquiry begins with observations, it also requires a more *systematic description of reality* involving observations of similar incidents, across time, across locations.

Systematic observations attempt to exclude preconceived notions of the observers that may lead to selective observations, overgeneralization from events, or simple inaccuracy. To examine scientifically whether a professor or course is "tough," for example, might involve comparing the syllabi for that professor (or course) and others; identifying the discipline; and looking at the amount of reading, the number of assignments, the availability of tutorials, and the like. We could also compare professors' classroom policies on things like makeup exams, penalties for late assignments, and so forth as well as their demeanor on the first day of class (friendly? empathetic?) as a means of tapping into whether they are so rigid and inflexible to deserve to be called hard-nosed. Plus, we could ask students to rate the toughness of their professor on a specific scale, not simply rely on the anecdotal evidence of some students. Moreover, we could extend our study beyond our own campus to look at what constitutes professorial toughness in other college settings. In other words, a scientific approach to describing reality ultimately involves gathering observations in a careful, orderly way, minimizing as much bias as possible. And in so doing, we may develop **empirical generalizations**, which refer to relationships between factors across time and across locations grounded in data. For example, we could look to see whether factors like discipline, type of institution, course topic, characteristics of the instructor, or level of the course influence whether professors appear to be tough. We might also see whether the same factors that affect perceptions of toughness at one university (say a large state school) likewise influence perceptions at a small liberal arts college. In so doing, we are looking for patterns that vary in terms of place or location. It might be further interesting to see if the impact of a particular factor changes over time as well. Establishing patterns of variation across time and place in the relationship between factors of interest provides the basis for empirical generalization but not the reasons for the observed relationships.

The logic of scientific inquiry captures two forms of logical reasoning— (1) induction and (2) deduction—that represent different stages in knowledge on a topic. **Induction** characterizes the process involving the movement from casual to systematic observations allowing the emergence of coherent patterns that provide the basis for theorizing (Babbie 2016). Inductive reasoning acts as a starting point in scientific inquiry typically when little is known about the phenomenon under study. This form of thinking stimulates research that may ultimately produce empirical generalizations. Recognition of a pattern, however, does not suffice to explain it.

The next step is for researchers to offer an **explanation** for *why* certain patterns exist. Karl Popper (1963), a renowned philosopher of science, suggests that the process of going from observations to abstract theorizing about a phenomenon constitutes what might be called a great leap of faith (as illustrated by the character in the figure leaping from empirical generalizations to theory!). In some ways, it does not matter where the theoretical ideas came from. What matters is the logic of the explanation, the ability to test predictions derived from it, and the way tests confirm or disconfirm the theoretical ideas. Such reasoning represents **deduction**, which involves the specification of an abstract theory from which hypotheses deduced from it can be tested through further specifically focused observations in a research study (Bryman 2012). Several terms are central to understanding deduction.

A **theory** is a systematic explanation for the observations that link two (or more) aspects of social life (Babbie 2016). For example, a cost–benefit or social exchange approach to helping (see Dovidio et al. 2006) suggests that people are motivated to maximize their rewards (positive material or social outcomes) and minimize their costs (negative material or social outcomes) in social interactions. Accordingly, they are likely to weight the rewards and costs in their decision about whether or not to intervene in a helping situation. Such reasoning calls attention to several important concepts: rewards, costs, and intervention. At the abstract level, **concepts** represent aspects of social reality by naming groupings of observations that share similar features (Bryman 2012). The groupings may suggest underlying variation or distinctions from another grouping. For example, in trying to explain "interventions in emergency situations," a key concept is "intervention." An intervention occurs when an individual does something to change the ongoing situation by providing help to someone in need. Interventions vary in that some people intervene and some people do not in emergency situations. Similarly, the concepts of rewards and costs may vary from low to high. (How these concepts are "observed" for research purposes depends upon the nature of the situation or the nature of the study, as described more in the next section.)

Theories consist of propositions that may outline underlying motivations or identify how concepts are linked. These propositions form the core logic of the theoretical argument. From them, researchers may deduce a **hypothesis**, which represents a testable statement indicating how a set of factors (represented conceptually) are related. For instance, from the social exchange approach to helping, an investigator might hypothesize the following: People are more likely to intervene when rewards for doing so are high and costs are low. In addition, researchers may define the **scope** of their theory, or the conditions under which they expect their hypotheses to hold. A scope condition in assessing the social exchange helping hypothesis is that it may apply only when individuals are physically able to provide the assistance necessary in the situation (if they are not physically capable of doing so, rewards and costs may not matter at all).

Testing a deductive hypothesis requires bringing observations (of various types, through various methodologies) to confirm or disconfirm the hypothesis and, by implication, the explanation offered by the theory. If new observations (not those giving rise to the theoretical ideas in the first place!) provide no support for the hypotheses, researchers may first try to test the hypotheses under different conditions or using different methodologies. Continued lack of support, or falsification, however, inevitably requires reconsideration of the theoretical argument. Next, we use the development of an explanation for "why people fail to intervene in emergency situations" to illustrate movement from induction to deduction.

Bringing Data to Bear on a Hypothesized Relationship

Think about why people may or may not provide help in an emergency situation. What sort of factors does your list include? Are they factors focused on the individual's personality, their friendliness, empathy, or the like? Or do the factors on your list describe characteristics of the situation, like the nature of the help that seems to be needed or the number of people present? As previously noted, Latané and Darley (1970) may have examined various incidents about when people offered help and when they did not. They moved beyond simply suggesting that it is something about individuals—their apathy or lack of empathy (i.e., individual-level explanations)—by focusing on the situations in which bystanders are embedded and the decisions they make (i.e., contextual explanations). Their theoretical argument (Latané and Darley 1970) requires that bystanders (1) notice the situation, (2) interpret it as an emergency, (3) recognize their personal responsibility to help, (4) know how to help, and (5) make the decision to act in spite of potential negative consequences to themselves. While each step has been extensively investigated (see Dovidio et al. 2006), we focus on the third step to illustrate aspects of the logic of scientific inquiry, especially the development of a theory and subsequent testing.

Recognizing personal responsibility for helping (Step 3) is more likely when only one person witnesses the need for help. In thinking about the Kitty Genovese situation, many people were (ostensibly) present. Thus, no one individual may have felt personal responsibility for helping. Latané and Darley (1970) propose that when many people are present in an emergency situation, responsibility to provide help is diffused. That is, individuals believe that others will offer help and they themselves do not need to do so. When each individual absolves himself or herself of personal responsibility, little bystander intervention emerges. With this theoretical reasoning in mind, Latané and Darley (1970) could hypothesize that diffusion of responsibility is negatively related to intervention in an emergency situation.

This hypothesis involves a testable relationship involving two concepts, each of which may vary from low to high or absent to present: (1) diffusion of responsibility and (2) intervention. When a **relationship** exists, variation in one concept coincides with variation in the other. Our diffusion of responsibility and intervention hypothesis also suggests a "direction" of the relationship between the two concepts. A *negative relationship* is one in which an increase in the variation represented by one concept is associated with a decrease in the variation represented by another concept. Thus, the more a situation allows for diffusion of responsibility, the less likely people are to intervene. In contrast, in a *positive relationship*, variation represented by one concept is associated with an increase in the variation represented by another concept. The following hypothesis suggests a positive relationship between feelings of empathy (experiencing the same emotion as others) and helping behavior: Individuals who are high in empathy are more likely to intervene in an emergency situation than those low in empathy (see Batson and Oleson 1991). Another way of stating that hypothesis is: empathy is positively related to interventions in an emergency situation. These hypotheses, of course, are posed at the conceptual level.

To test a hypothesis, researchers must translate the concepts into what can be readily observed or measured. Such translation is called **operationalization**, which allows movement from the abstract level of theorizing to the concrete level of measurement. For example, in assessing how diffusion of responsibility in a helping situation might unfold, researchers might measure how many people are present when emergency situations arise and track whether anyone intervenes with help. The more people present, the greater the diffusion of responsibility. Of course, the nature of intervention must also be operationalized; people might provide direct aid, call 911, find a police officer, or the like, depending upon the nature of the situation. As described more fully below, when investigators study helping behavior using experimental methods, operationalization pertains to what can be manipulated. For example, in early helping behavior studies, researchers created situations in which a target respondent observes someone in distress when no one else is present, representing low diffusion of responsibility, or when five or more people are present, indicating high diffusion of responsibility.

In the hypothesis (and experiment) involving diffusion of responsibility operationalized as the number of people present, that concept and its operationalization create the **independent variable**, or presumed cause, which is assumed to affect a belief, feeling, or behavior. The presumed effect is labeled the **dependent variable**. Despite the language of presumed cause and effect, assessing **causality** between variables requires additional considerations. First, the two variables must be *statistically associated*, meaning that their relationship does not rest upon chance alone but rather signifies a real relationship. Second, the independent variable must precede in time the dependent variable to ensure appropriate *time order*. And third, the observed association between the independent and dependent variables must be *nonspurious*—that is, not caused by some other, perhaps unmeasured, variable to which the two other variables are related.

For example, an oft-cited empirical observation is that ice cream sales are positively related (statistically associated) to drownings. You might ponder why. Are people who drown failing to wait the hour after eating ice cream to return to their water activities? But why are ice cream eaters the only ones to violate the frequent parental dictum to wait that hour? Thinking further, you might ask, When are ice cream sales likely to be the highest? When are drownings likely to be the highest? Both are highly likely when the weather is hot. Thus, the observed positive relationship between ice cream sales and drownings is due to both variables being independently related to outside temperatures and not causally related to each other. The ice cream sales and drowning relationship is spurious and thus fails to confirm causality between eating ice cream and drowning. Generally, investigators may attempt to include and measure factors that they think may account for spuriousness between their focal concepts and associated measures in their analyses so that they can feel confident that their hypothesis tests are sound.

Thus, to bring data to bear upon a theoretically derived hypothesis requires translation from the abstract to the concrete and consideration of other processes that may impinge on the focal relationship. Importantly, hypothesis testing provides evidence that may confirm or disconfirm the underlying theoretical reasoning or the explanation offered for a particular phenomenon. Especially when hypotheses are disconfirmed (i.e., evidence fails to support the proposed relationship), researchers may reconsider their arguments and potentially alter their explanation or specifically identify conditions under which (through further testing) the proposed relationships are confirmed. Next, we examine the different methods of collecting data to test a hypothesis and in so doing consider how researchers employ various means to take into account other processes or factors that may impinge on their hypotheses.

Social Research Methodologies

In previous sections, you took the role of "researcher," beginning with your own observations of helping behavior, then developing an abstract theoretical argument to get at the conditions under which individuals might be likely to lend a hand. Armed with knowledge of previous patterns and with a potential understanding of *why* people might help, you need to determine how to collect further data to test your hypothesis. You would ask yourself, "What methodology might work best in trying to understand why people help others in emergencies?" Should you simply ask people, perhaps in a survey, how likely they are to help others in need? Or maybe you could observe at a busy gathering place, waiting for someone to fall and then watch to see who helps. Doing so might take a lot of time, so instead you may enlist a friend to act out a "falling scenario" and then observe people's responses. Researchers often ponder their methodological options before settling on a particular data collection strategy.

When Latané and Darley (1970) first began their investigations into helping behavior, they had to determine the most suitable way to collect data that would allow them to test their hypothesis. Indeed, the first step for any researcher is to ask, "Given my research question, what sort of data will allow me to address it?" To some extent, the approach to data collection may depend on how much knowledge exists on a topic. As described previously, when scholars know little about a particular social process, they may begin with a series of observations in different types of situations. In contrast, once a theoretical explanation has been developed, they may opt to test derived hypotheses using methods that afford them the greatest amount of control to isolate the predicted relationship. By doing so, they can feel confident that they have minimized the influence of other factors on that focal relationship.

Social psychologists use a range of methods, including the experiment, written surveys, oral interviews, naturalistic observation, and archival investigations. All of these methods may be used to produce **quantitative research,** which involves quantifying the collection and analysis of data (i.e., using numbers!) (Bryman 2012). For example, in a written survey, respondents might be asked to indicate on a numeric scale ranging from 1 to 7 how much they disagree or agree with a particular statement. Researchers may represent the extent of agreement with the statement by pointing to the average of all responses, where a 2.2 would suggest disagreement and a 6.7 strong agreement. The latter three methods, in different ways, may also be the means of developing **qualitative research,** which typically pertains to using words, rather than numbers, to capture the data and its analysis (e.g., Glaser and Strauss 1967; Tavory and Timmermans 2014). For example, in an oral interview, researchers might probe how individuals who have one black parent and one white parent see themselves (i.e., Do they identify as black? White? Biracial?). A qualitative, compared with quantitative, research strategy may require greater interpretation of the data and construction, after data collection, of the nature of the social phenomena under study. Next, we address these fundamental methodologies. We use both quantitative and qualitative studies related to helping behavior to illustrate each methodology.

The Experiment

Imagine being in a situation in which you overhear an epileptic seizure. You know that you are alone and thus may be the only person who can provide aid. What do you do? Now imagine that four other people are likely to have overheard the same seizure in progress. What do you do? This scenario is the basis for one of the first bystander intervention studies conducted by Darley and Latané (1968). These researchers argue that despite humanitarian norms to help people in distress, *situational factors* weaken such norms by decreasing perceived personal responsibility to provide assistance. The number of bystanders, as previously noted, may allow diffusion of responsibility, which reduces the likelihood of intervention. Additionally, Darley and Latané (1968) argue that, with such diffusion, the punishment or blame for not acting is slight, and the inability of bystanders to observe each other makes it easy to assume someone else is taking action. These additional situational conditions allow observers to rationalize their own inaction.

Laboratory Experiments

To test their ideas, Darley and Latané (1968) designed a laboratory experiment. An **experiment** involves the exposure of study participants to specially designed situations and the systematic recording of their reactions. Those specifically designed situations represent manipulation of levels of the independent variable denoted by a hypothesis (while holding constant other factors), whereas the reactions capture the dependent variable. Experiments afford the researcher the means to assess causality because the manipulation of the independent variable unquestionably precedes the measurement of the dependent variable, thereby meeting the time order criterion.

Additionally, a fundamental characteristic of the experiment is **random assignment**, which involves the random or "by chance" (like flipping a coin) allocation of study participants to the experimental conditions constituting levels of the independent variable. Random assignment ensures that each participant has an equal chance of being assigned to any specific experimental condition. As a consequence, individual-level characteristics (such as empathy, shyness, or dominance) are evenly spread out across conditions, ensuring that the groups assigned to particular conditions are equivalent. Such equivalency helps to minimize the impact of factors that might influence measures of the dependent variable, thereby decreasing the likelihood that the observed relationship between the independent and dependent variables is spurious. For example, assume that individuals vary in terms of empathy. If all highly empathetic study participants were in the experimental condition of being the only bystander to an epileptic seizure, researchers would not know whether it was "empathy" or the nature of the condition that produce higher rates of helping than in other conditions.

But, with random assignment, highly empathetic participants are spread across all variations of "number of bystanders present."

Darley and Latané (1968) operationalized the concept of diffusion of responsibility by varying the number of people that the study participant thought could overhear the epileptic seizure of the ostensible victim in need of help.[4] Seventy-two male and female college students participated, and each was randomly assigned to one of three group size conditions: two (consisting of participant and victim); three (participant, victim, and one other); and six (including four others). The experimenter claimed that "he was interested in learning about the kinds of personal problems faced by normal college students in a high pressure, urban environment. He said to avoid possible embarrassment about discussing personal problems with strangers that several precautions had been taken" (Darley and Latané 1968:378). These "precautions" ensure creating a situation that circumscribes the situation in a manner consistent with researchers' theorizing. Thus, study participants remained anonymous within individual cubicles and had no communication with others, so they could not determine how others would respond to the epileptic seizure (the experimenter indicated that he would not be listening in during the initial discussion).

The researchers used prerecorded voices so that all study participants had a similar experience during the discussion. The "victim" spoke first, indicating that he was prone to seizures. After the study participants and the "others" presumed to be in the situation had a chance to talk, the victim began again, but this time, sounding incoherent, he noted that he was having a problem and needed help. At that point, the experimenter began to assess the focal dependent variable: time lapse before helping. Time was measured from the beginning of the victim's fit until the study participant emerged from the cubicle to report the emergency to the experimenter.

The Darley and Latané (1968) study highlights the hallmarks of experimental methodology. The laboratory afforded the researchers a great deal of control. Such control allowed them to isolate theoretically relevant variables of interest and, through random assignment, examine the impact of group size on the likelihood of helping, without concern about how other extraneous factors (those not represented in the hypothesis) might impact the focal relationship. Thus, experiments provide a high degree of **internal validity**, which refers to the extent to which findings regarding a causal relationship are likely to be sound. When experimental procedures capture researchers' intentions, without faulty manipulations, poor measurement, or contamination by extraneous variables, the findings produced are likely to be internally valid. Darley and Latané (1968) found clear support for their hypothesis, with 85% of participants in the "alone" condition providing help, 62% in the three-person group, and only 31% in the group of six. A similar pattern emerges in terms of how many seconds it took study participants to seek help. This effect of group size, as representing diffusion of responsibility, has emerged in many other studies as well. Replication of a study's results through repeated studies signals that findings are **reliable**.

While laboratory experiments such as Darley and Latané's (1968) with high internal validity and potential for replicability are an excellent way to examine causal hypotheses, several concerns do arise. First, one may be reluctant to make sweeping generalizations based on the responses of 72 undergraduates behaving under controlled circumstances. Experimental results tell us little directly about the natural world in which we live. They do, however, allow confirmation or disconfirmation of theoretical ideas, which have bearing upon understanding the social world. The theory acts as a bridge from the laboratory to the "real world" (Zelditch 1969). With this conception of the experiment and the theory driving it, criticisms that experimental situations are artificial grow moot (Webster and Sell 2014). Such artificiality allows incorporation of theoretically presumed causes while eliminating factors that may contaminate the relationship under study. Less artificial situations are more complex and may include other factors that enhance or minimize the impact of the presumed cause on the hypothesized effect.

A second concern is that even in well-designed experiments, threats to internal validity do arise. Study participants are human and thus may not interpret the manipulations in the manner that experimenters had planned. When that happens, results may not really indicate the effect of the independent variable on the dependent variable. Experimenters often include "manipulation checks" at the end of an experiment so they can assess the extent to which they have successfully operationalized their independent variables. Such checks may take the form of questions in a brief survey or asked by experimental assistants at the end of an experimental session. In the helping experiment, a manipulation check would be to ask the participants how many people were in their group to make sure they correctly could recall the size of their group.

Assuming that the manipulations are strong enough, other threats to internal validity include demand characteristics and experimenter effects. **Demand characteristics** take the form of activating study participants' preconceived notions of the study's purpose, which in turn lead them to behave in a certain way (thus, these are sometimes called subject effects). For example, if participants know that they are in a study explicitly about fairness in interpersonal relationships, that study label may entice them to act in what they imagine is the fairest way possible, regardless of the actual experimental conditions. Researchers are thus careful to eliminate any words or actions that may cue participants into particular behaviors. Indeed, the experimenter must circumscribe his or her own behavior to avoid conveying to participants anything about what is expected of them to confirm the hypothesis. Expectations for behavior unwittingly communicated by the person running the study are called **experimenter effects.** For example, a researcher who nods far more to participants in the "alone" condition of a helping study compared to those in the "large group" condition when asked if he or she will be available during the experimental session is unconsciously conveying ease of helping to people in the condition expected to help more. That nodding contaminates the impact of the manipulated factor.

A third concern often voiced about experiments is the use of deception. In the Darley and Latané (1968) experiment, study participants were led to believe that they were in groups of various sizes, when in reality each person was alone in the study. The recorded voices merely projected the image that others were involved in the discussion. **Deception** includes providing false information or withholding information with the goal of leading study participants to believe that something is true when it is not (Sieber 1992). The experimenter deliberately misleads the participants into believing something that is untrue. When used as a means to manipulate independent variables, it has scientific value. But the nature of the deception must be weighed in terms of the harm it might cause to study participants, as discussed further in a subsequent section (see Hegtvedt 2014). Researchers are responsible for anticipating and minimizing such harm.

Debriefing at the end of an experimental session allows study participants to be fully informed of the nature of the deception and to decide whether to allow their data to be included in the study. Moreover, experimenters may use the debriefing to ensure that no harm has occurred or to make sure assistance is provided to those showing psychological distress. When experiments move outside of the laboratory, such debriefing grows less necessary because participants may not know that they are involved at all in a study.

Field Experiments

While the laboratory is the most common venue for experimental research, driven by theory testing, some experiments also may occur elsewhere. **Field experiments** involve the manipulation of factors within natural settings. Piliavin, Rodin, and Piliavin (1969) examined the response of bystanders to a person in distress in a New York subway. They employed the best experimental practices by controlling as many variables as possible. They staged the scene approximately a minute after the train passed the first station, with male victims of similar age and dressed in similar casual clothes, behaving in a similar fashion dropping to the floor in the same location. They manipulated whether the white victim appeared sober (carrying a cane) or drunk (without a cane).[5] In addition to the victims, three observers trained by the experimenter (called confederates) were present, located at strategic viewpoints in the car, to record the responses of subway riders. The experimental team ran 103 trials of the study, each time noting the race, sex, and location of all people on the train, the number who assisted the victim, and how long it took before assistance arrived. They also tried to record comments made by passengers. Unlike the patterns observed in laboratory studies, help was more frequent, often involving more than one person. In nearly 95% of the "sober, with cane" trials, observers provided help, whereas only 50% came to the drunk victim's assistance. Typically, males provided the initial assistance (perhaps because female observers believed that they did not have the physical strength to help a victim to a seat).

In this field study with its high degree of **ecological validity**, where study findings apply to behavior in everyday, natural settings (Bryman 2012), diffusion of responsibility did not unfold. As a consequence, Piliavin and colleagues (1969) developed a model focused on emotional arousal (e.g., fear, disgust, or sympathy regarding the victim, which may be shaped by the victim's personal responsibility for his or her plight) coupled with an evaluation of cost and rewards. The desire to reduce the arousal spurs whether a person will offer help, considering the costs and rewards of each action. Help is most likely when the costs of doing so are low (e.g., no threat of physical harm, ease of effort) and the rewards (e.g., praise from others are high). Helping also emerges when costs of not helping (e.g., self-blame) are high and the rewards from not helping (e.g., being able to get on with one's own activities) are low. (Conversely, people may rationalize not helping when there are high rewards to do so and low costs!) In effect, Piliavin and colleagues (1969) used their field experiment results to elaborate on conditions under which diffusion of responsibility is likely to emerge. In doing so, they augmented reasoning offered by Darley and Latané (1968).

In field experiments, study participants are often unaware that their behavior is under scrutiny. Thus, they are less likely to respond to demand characteristics or experimenter effects. And the ecological validity of such studies may provide the opportunity to generalize findings to populations beyond those immediately present in the study. Moreover, sometimes field experiments can involve social changes that occur because of decisions by an organization or a government. In such cases, researchers do not actively manipulate their independent variable, but may examine behavior before and after the change. For example, to determine whether a "no littering law" has an effect, investigators could measure the amount of trash at a main intersection before and after the law goes into effect. Of course, such naturally occurring field experiments may involve a number of extraneous variables beyond the researchers' control.

In summary, the experimental method is ideal when scholars have a strong theoretical argument for their predictions and desire to test them under controlled circumstances. There are benefits to moving beyond the laboratory, though trade-offs between control and ecological validity emerge. While experiments may provide the surest way to assess causal relationships, they are inappropriate for answering particular research questions, where knowledge may not have yet extended to the development of a strong theoretical argument or where there is a need to assess patterns within a large population, perhaps pertaining to particular substantive or attitudinal issues. For such questions, survey approaches may be appropriate.

Survey Approaches

College students are rarely far from their mobile phones, computers, tablets, and the like, using them to facilitate communication with both near and distant family members, friends, and acquaintances. With the rise in technology-mediated communication, greater opportunity for hurtful online behaviors arises. Often such behavior may lead to harmful consequences for the victims while at the same time may be observed by countless others reading Facebook or Twitter posts. Brody and Vangelisti (2015) ask the following: When do bystanders intervene in instances of cyberbullying? Their work builds on previous research examining assistance provided to victims of (offline) bullying, which suggests that in most cases other people are present (O'Connell, Pepler, and Craig 1999) and that assistance from bystanders, either directly as a means to stop the bullying or indirectly with provision of emotional support, can attenuate the ill consequences of suffering such mistreatment (Matsunaga 2010). And, of course, they draw from theoretical work of Latané and Darley (1970). But to tackle their research question, they used a written survey.

Survey research involves the collection of data by asking people questions. The questions may be written and self-administered either in paper form or via an online platform. In other instances, questions may be asked orally by an interviewer. Typically, researchers use written questionnaires to collect information quickly and efficiently, often involving a large number of respondents, resulting in a body of quantitative data. Interviews, on the other hand, usually involve fewer study participants but offer rich qualitative data because the researcher may ask follow-up questions and probe participants' responses to gain insight on a topic or process under investigation. We first focus on written surveys and then turn to interviews.

Written Surveys

A key characteristic of written survey methodology pertains to how researchers secure a sample of respondents. **Random sampling** involves the inclusion of a "unit" of a population of interest by chance alone. In other words, imagine that you wanted to know something about people's responses to bullying incidents in middle schools in your community. Your population of interest would be middle-school–aged children in schools within the districts in your community. Fortunately, you would not have to survey the entire population! Rather, you could select at random every tenth student (the exact size of the sample depends upon the size of the population and other factors). Such random selection ensures replication of population characteristics (e.g., percentage female or nonwhite), thus creating a **representative sample**.

To thoroughly ensure that such population characteristics are represented in a sample, researchers will perform random selection within each important category of the population. This is called **stratified random sampling**. Sometimes, however, researchers rely on a **convenience sample**, selected for its availability for researchers but that may provide a starting point in the development of knowledge about a particular topic. For example, if you wanted to know how college students at a particular institution view climate change, you could sit out in front of the student center and ask a set of students who come by on a particular day.

Finally, sometimes researchers use **snowball sampling**, which relies on using referrals of initial participants to obtain additional participants, when it is difficult to locate respondents because the desired sample characteristic is uncommon. For example, Khanna (2004) examined factors affecting the nature of the preferred racial identification of white/Asian college students. No list indicates multiracial people who identify as white/Asian individuals, and so they are not easy to locate. Thus, Khanna placed classified advertisements about her study in local university newspapers and some magazines serving multiracial readers and posted a call for participants on multiracial websites and mailing lists. The rest of the participants were found through word of mouth or referrals. Snowball samples are nonrandom, similar to convenience samples.

Random sampling, whether stratified or not, is a means of ensuring the **external validity** of study results, defined as the generalizability of findings beyond the sample to the population of interest or to other settings. Results from convenience and snowball samples, in contrast, cannot be generalized to the population, but as with experimental research, the theoretical argument underlying the hypotheses being tested may provide a bridge to the larger population.

For a first look at how bystanders might respond to cyberbullying incidents, Brody and Vangelisti (2015) used a convenience sample of 265 undergraduate students who completed an online survey.[6] The survey instrument is the means by which investigators measure their independent and dependent variables. As in previous laboratory research, the researchers hypothesized about the effects of the presence of other bystanders and perceived (visual) anonymity on reducing the likelihood of providing help and the positive impact of relationship closeness between the observer and victim on help provision. Thus, through their survey questions, they needed to measure the independent variables of presence of additional bystanders, visual anonymity, and relationship closeness. They also operationalized helping, their dependent variable, in different ways. Other questions allowed them to control for factors that may influence how participants respond as bystanders, such as their personal experiences with cyberbullying, the extent that they perceived the victim to be hurt by the cyberbullying incident, and gender.

The researchers asked study participants to recall an incident, occurring in the past 6 months, that involved the online bullying via Facebook of someone they knew. Based on the recalled episode, a series of questions captured details and measured the independent variables. Responses to the question of

"Approximately how many other people witnessed the bullying episode?" provided a means to measure the number of additional bystanders. Several questions captured visual anonymity. Participants indicated agreement on a 7-point Likert scale (where 1 represented strongly disagree and 7 strongly agree) whether they thought that others (victim, perpetrator, additional observers) "were aware of me," "knew I was there," "recognized my presence," and "could see that I was online." **Likert scaled responses** are a frequently used means to measure attitudes or perceptions represented by degree of agreement with a series of statements. Multiple Likert items may be combined or added together to create a **composite scale** or score for a particular underlying concept. In this case, the researchers created a scale of visual anonymity (to do so, they had to reverse-code the items before combining so that higher numbers corresponded to higher perceived visual anonymity). Multiple item scales may have greater **reliability**, indicating the degree to which the measure of a concept appears to be stable. Brody and Vangelisti (2015) also created a scale from the multiple items indicating closeness to the victim—for example, "How close are you to this person?" and "How important is your relationship with this person?" Responses could range from 1 = not at all to 7 = very much.

Reported bystander behavior was measured through various questionnaire items. The researchers modified an existing scale consisting of Likert agreement items (Salmivalli and Voeten 2004). For example, respondents indicated their agreement with items such as "I told the perpetrator to stop their behavior," which suggests active defending of the victim and items like "I stayed outside the situation" to capture passive responses. Additionally, they included items that tapped into different types of support that people might lend, such as emotional or network-based by connecting the victim to people who can provide help.

When using survey questions to measure concepts, researchers take care to phrase items in a precise way to solicit the most accurate representations of what they are trying to study. Typically, it is easier for respondents to answer short, straightforward questions that *avoid jargon* rather than long questions—especially those using words that may be unfamiliar. For example, the visual anonymity scale includes clearly and simply worded items that pertain to a wide array of possible ways in which bystanders might perceive each other. Providing the option, "were aware that I might be virtually present at the same time" is far more cumbersome than simply "were aware of me." Similarly, a single global item asking, "How likely did others know of your presence?" might produce results different from the scale of *multiple, focused items*. In addition, *response categories must "match" the questions*. For example, the relationship closeness items use a "not at all" to "very much" scale rather than the "agreement scale," to ensure a match with how the questions are worded. Variations in phrasing or response scales may affect the meaning of the question to respondents or create confusion, potentially generating results that are misleading or not replicated in other studies.

Survey researchers also may be sensitive to the level of measurement of each item (which affects the extent of variation potentially captured and the nature of the statistical analyses that might unfold). **Nominal measures** refer to variables having distinct, often mutually exclusive, categories associated with them. Typical examples are political party affiliation, college major, or religious affiliation. In Brody and Vangelisti's (2015) study, gender is considered a nominal measure. **Ordinal measures** suggest more or less of a particular variable, such as agreement with a statement measuring political liberalness or support for a particular policy. Likert scales noted previously represent ordinal measures. The actual "distance" between marking a 2 versus a 5 on such a scale may not signify standardized units that carry the same meaning, but a 2 indicates far less agreement than a 5, which surely implies greater agreement. In contrast, the actual distance between variables that represent **interval measures** is meaningful, relying on standard intervals between responses. For example, measures of "age" that use "years" constitute an interval measure, where a 40-year-old respondent is twice as old as a 20-year-old one.

In development of their survey study, Brody and Vangelisti (2015) grappled with the best way to measure the concepts represented in their theoretical hypotheses. Although all concepts were measured at the same time, their theoretical argument indicates what factors are likely to affect helping. Their results confirmed their hypotheses that a higher number of bystanders and increased visual anonymity decreased active defending of the victim (and increased passive behaviors), whereas closeness to the victim increased such behaviors (and decreased passive responses). Visual anonymity decreased and closeness to the victim increased emotional and network support as well, but number of bystanders influenced only network support. In the support analyses, researchers included the control variables (e.g., gender, own experiences with cyberbullying) to rule out other potential influences on why respondents lent support.

While written survey approaches compared to experimental strategies are generally a weaker means by which to assess causal relationships, researchers may employ statistical techniques to assess theorized patterns of causality. Sometimes, such as when surveys are employed in the study of social problems, researchers will collect data at multiple points in time, involving the same study participants. Such **longitudinal surveys** provide greater opportunities for researchers to assess causal relationships by meeting the criterion of "time order." For example, an investigator interested in the relationship between self-esteem and juvenile delinquency might collect data at the beginning of high school and then yearly until graduation. That would mean that the level of self-esteem during the freshman year could be used to predict juvenile delinquency during subsequent years.

Of course, a study of juvenile delinquency or even of helping behavior raises a general issue about surveys: the extent to which individuals reply truthfully to questions. Typically, self-reports of one's attitudes and behaviors are relatively honest assessments—to the extent allowed by memory—unless the questions pertain to highly personal information, especially that which may be illegal or embarrassing. Faulty recall (even to simple questions like "How frequently did you access Facebook in the last week?") and the tendency to provide socially desirable responses plague survey research. Yet the strengths of such a strategy often outweigh such weaknesses, especially when researchers anchor their studies in previous research and carefully construct their survey instruments. Survey research is ideal for efficiently collecting a large amount of data that allow for the description of a population (assuming a random sample) and patterns regarding attitudes and behaviors within that population. The use of oral questions within a subset of a population may allow for probing of patterns revealed by large-scale surveys or the creation of knowledge about underlying processes.

Oral Interviews

This chapter opens with a number of actual situations in which bystanders failed to provide assistance to individuals who were victims of horrendous assaults.

If you wanted to delve into bystanders' perceptions of why they did not assist and how those reasons might stem from their belief systems or previous experience, a strategy would be to employ in-depth **interviews** (e.g., Glesne 2015; Gubrium et al. 2012). Essentially a conversation between two people, interviews involve a researcher asking a series of questions to a member of a group of interest. The questions may be structured so that all interviewees are asked the same open-ended questions, or semistructured, such that while most questions are asked of all study participants, the researcher may ask additional questions to probe answers given to initial queries or to pursue insights arising in the course of the interview.

For example, Einolf (2011) drew on narrative interviews with 88 respondents from a larger study, the Midlife in the United States (MIDUS), to examine how religion influences the likelihood that people will engage in helping acts. By closely reading the narratives, he identified six themes characterizing individuals' religious beliefs and values: (1) the importance of religion as an aspect of one's own identity, (2) increased commitment to religious life during adulthood, (3) perceptions of the relationship between religion and helping, (4) inspiration found in Jesus' example and sacrifice, (5) religious definitions of morality, and (6) belief that it is one's life mission to carry out God's mission. While these themes emerged from the body of narratives, each interviewee did not necessarily talk about every one. Einolf was curious as to whether talking about a particular aspect of religious life (represented in the various themes) would impact how frequently individuals provided help in the form of volunteering and contributing to religious and secular charities. Thus, he combined data coded from the narratives for each respondent with other data available from responses to MIDUS surveys on volunteering and donating. His correlational analyses indicated that the first four themes were positively related to helping behavior. He then returned to the narratives to characterize the most highly prosocial individuals in the sample. For those individuals, religious themes were very prominent. From his qualitative analyses, he showed how people use language to learn and internalize religious values and how individuals come to act on those values by providing help of various kinds.

Narratives of the sort that Einolf (2011) used typically involve general questions that allow the respondent to tell a story. The interviewer guides the story through additional prompts. In such cases, researchers are interested in how people create meaning in their lives. Of course, in-depth interviewing may pertain to a variety of research questions. For example, the method is well suited to addressing issues of identity (e.g., Khanna 2011; Wilkins 2012), stigma (e.g., Snow and Anderson 1987), and emotions (e.g., Lois 2003; Wingfield 2010). In such cases, the interviewer begins with a research question, which helps to direct development of the set of open-ended questions that will be posed to study participants. Yet he or she is not constrained by the questions on the interview guide. Indeed, flexibility is a fundamental characteristic of this methodology, allowing interviewers to ask follow-up questions and probe responses further. Typically, interviews are audio recorded and later transcribed. The transcriptions provide the raw data for analysis.

Researchers may rely upon electronic tools (e.g., computer programs like MAXQDA or ATLAS.ti) to help organize information derived from the transcriptions. These tools help identify themes or words that frequently emerge in study participants' responses. Often, researchers will begin by "looking for" particular themes based on their research questions, but they also allow themes to emerge organically from the data (see Glesne 2015 regarding coding, organizing, and analyzing interview data). For example, Einolf (2011) may have presumed that something about Jesus' teachings would be relevant to helping behavior among Christian respondents, so he may have first looked for such references. In contrast, it may be that the commitment to religion over one's adult life emerged as a theme unanticipated by Einolf (2011). Organization of themes provides the basis for the important activity of the qualitative researcher: interpretation of the meanings within interviews and across interviews. The goal is to achieve understanding about why people behave in a certain way (e.g., why they help, how they defend an identity) or why they hold a particular set of beliefs, values, or identities. In other words, in-depth interviewing allows researchers to get at processes underlying actions and thoughts.

While the flexibility in asking questions and the depth of analysis exceeds that possible when using survey or experimental methodologies, interviews are typically limited to small samples (often achieved through snowball sampling). The intent is not to generalize the results from these samples but to provide insight that may contribute to building theories and expanding understanding of a phenomenon. Interviewers must be careful, like experimenters, not to influence the responses of their study participants. A key concern is how the position of the interviewer vis-à-vis the respondent may influence how forthright and honest responses may be.

The **positionality** of a researcher collecting qualitative data refers to the investigator's reflection on his or her own placement in the social contexts and power or status structures relevant in the situation and how that placement may engender subjective viewpoints, which may affect data collection and interpretation (England 1994). For example, a white researcher interviewing a black study participant about his or her racial identity might be conscious of being more privileged compared to the person being interviewed; in turn, the interviewee may view the white researcher with skepticism and distrust. Interviewers should recognize the potential impact of their positionality both during and after the interview. Establishing trust with the study participant while maintaining a degree of detachment so as not to cue the respondent in some way are hallmarks of a thoughtful interviewer. Investigators aware of their own subjectivities are likely to be careful to recognize how they may enter into interpretations of the data as well. And, as with written surveys, interviewees may be more inclined to provide responses that put themselves in a favorable light. In studying behavior, one means of avoiding the social desirability that may plague responses to written and oral questions may be to directly observe behavior.

Observation

When we were young sociologists, one of the most startling things that we realized as we were sitting in the lobby of the hotel hosting our annual professional meetings and observing the dynamics of people around us was that we were not alone in the hazard of our trade: Others were observing us! We all "people watch" from time to time—in parks, airport waiting areas, bars, malls, and the like. These casual observations are usually just a way to pass the time and are rarely informed by preconceived notions of what might unfold. Sometimes, however, what people observe through casual observations might provide the basis for further investigation.

A key distinction between observational and survey research is that the former focuses on actual behavior, whereas the latter relies on self-reported behavior, which may be influenced by faulty recall or social desirability. Of course, not all behaviors are observable (e.g., criminal activities, sexual acts). As a consequence, observational approaches are limited to what can be seen, typically in public places or places to which an investigator has been given special access (e.g., a work organization, a unique religious group, high school classrooms).

The **observation strategies** of social psychologists involve gathering data directly by observing particular behaviors of interest (e.g., lending assistance), coding them into categories (e.g., direct help by administering to someone in need, indirect help by calling others to help), and classifying characteristics of the surrounding situation (e.g., number of people present, gender of victim and helper, time of day, location). They may be highly structured or less so, with noninvolvement or involvement by the researcher in the group under observation. Structured observations, described first in the next paragraphs, typically involve **nonparticipant** observers who are not engaging in the social situation and behaviors under scrutiny. The usual goal of such endeavors is to produce quantitative data regarding the behaviors observed. In contrast, less structured observations may be more likely when a researcher acts as a **participant**, engaged in the activities of the group being observed, often with the intent to develop qualitative data.

Structured, Nonparticipant Observation

Jiobu and Knowles (1974) extend Latané and Darley's (1970) interest in the impact of norms on helping, controlling for situational factors. In their study, rather than focusing on providing assistance to a victim in need, they focus on the prosocial activity of making charitable contributions as a form of helping. They argue that social expectations regarding helping are likely to be stronger around nearness to holidays characterized by giving (such as Christmas) than at other times of the year. To empirically examine this prediction about the strength of norms on people's contributions to charity, they devised a **structured observation** study, using a set of predetermined categories to code the behavior observed in a natural setting. On the four Wednesdays between Thanksgiving and Christmas from 9:30 a.m. to 9:00 p.m., they witnessed and coded people's willingness to "give" to the Salvation Army kettle in the central business district of a small midwestern city (population about 88,000).[7]

Two similarly aged and dressed Salvation Army workers took turns sitting in the booth where the kettle was located, steadily ringing a handbell but not engaging in any interaction with people passing by. The kettle sat on the sidewalk, near a department store, with plenty of room for pedestrian traffic. This setup ensured that the researchers controlled on a number of situational factors that could affect contributions: day of week, nature of solicitations, ease of accessing the kettle, and nature of stores near the kettle. Thus, they could focus on the increased strength of the norm of closer to Christmas (their independent variable) on giving behavior (their dependent variable) measured by two unobtrusive observers. One observer recorded donor characteristics (e.g., gender, age), and another coded the number of people passing by. With this information, the researchers calculated (1) the percentage of pedestrians who gave (conceptualized as the "extensity of giving") and (2) and the average contribution on each day ("intensity of giving").

Results provided mixed support for their hypothesis. While the average number of people giving dropped off as Christmas approached (perhaps because some of the people had already given), the average contribution was the highest on the last Wednesday before Christmas. In other analyses, the researchers did note that situational factors, such as the wind chill index and volume of pedestrians present, also affected the percentage of donors, with numbers decreasing with colder weather and more people present. The latter finding is consistent with previous evidence for diffusion of responsibility. Thus, results from this observational study dovetail with those from laboratory and survey research.

Nonparticipant observational studies focused on securing quantitative data typically employ structured coding schemes, with predetermined categories, to track behaviors of interest. Such coding schemes specify the behaviors to be observed and include instructions about which behaviors are allocated to particular categories (Bryman 2012). They must have a clear focus and be easy to use, or observers may get overwhelmed with trying to keep up with all that is going on in a situation! Yet even with a structured coding scheme, observers ultimately use their judgment to determine what fits and does not fit into a category.

Observers make decisions about what to include and what to exclude in terms of their observations. These decisions extend beyond the actual observation process to include considerations of when and where observations will take place and who will be included. Because these are, to some extent, judgment calls, researchers must be aware of how their own biases may influence them and try to minimize their effects. Often, observers are trained to follow the outlined procedures and to understand what fits within each category of a coding scheme. Observers may be assessed to make sure that their own coding is consistent over time, ensuring **intra-observer reliability**. Another strategy for minimizing potential biases emerging in structured observations is to include two or more observers, focused on the same actions, and to assess consistency across observers. Such consistency captures **inter-observer reliability.** Assessment of such reliability presumes use of a structured coding scheme, which may, at least initially, be absent in other forms of observational approaches.

Less Structured, Participant Observation

When the researcher is a participant in the group under observation, he or she engages, to various degrees, in the same activities of study participants and communicates with them informally and sometimes formally through in-depth interviews. Participant observers may immerse themselves in an organization or community for a long period of time, getting to know the people and flow of their interactions. Such placement may be characterized as **field research**. Rather than the structured observation of the donation study, they rely upon less structured observations, often detailed in **field notes** chronicling the activities of the people observed, their conversations, responses to informal questions, and the overall processes unfolding. Investigators may attempt to reveal the meanings that the participants attribute to their behaviors. An **ethnography** is the written account organizing the observations and interpretations.

For example, Adler and Adler (2004) draw upon 8 years of participant observation and interviews in their examination of workers in five luxury resorts in Hawaii. In their book, *Paradise Laborers*, they seek to understand how the global economy impacts the lives of people whose occupation is to provide services to vacationers (a form of help, you might say, though not in response to an emergency situation!). They observed characteristics of the workforce and, with permission of resort management, began with informal conversations with the workers about what they do, their views on their jobs and future opportunities, and factors affecting whether they remain in resort employment. A small number of workers functioned as **informants**, individuals occupying particular positions to provide background information and help the researchers to both organize their work and understand their findings. Adler and Adler (2004) also completed extensive interviews with 90 workers. Four ethnicity- and gender-diverse groups, each with different approaches to the services that they render as well as their futures, emerge: new immigrants holding unskilled positions with little pay; Hawaiian locals, often young but with few occupational alternatives in their island homeland; college-educated middle class (mostly male) managers, whose stints at the resorts may be stepping-stones; and young, largely white, adults from the mainland seeking an adventure-filled interlude in their lives. Through their observations and both short and long interviews, Adler and Adler (2004) reveal the different occupational cultures, worker lifestyles, and mobility patterns of the groups.

Such in-depth study often begins with an orienting question. Adler and Adler (2004) initially believed that the nature of the ownership of the resorts—by U.S. or international corporations—might affect the dynamics. Yet once their study was under way, they came to see that such a contrast was far less impactful than the nature of the employee groups themselves. Thus, especially in comparison to quantitatively focused research methodologies, ethnographies allow for greater flexibility in the data collection phase of a project. Sifting through relevant information to identify patterns of behavior remains one of the biggest challenges. And, as with structured observations and oral interviews, the positionality and biases of the researchers in shaping the behaviors they observe, the people with whom they talk, and so forth are a concern.

Concerns About Observational Strategies

As with demand characteristics in experimental research, investigators using observational strategies must be aware of how their presence, if known, may affect the behavior of the people and the interactions that they are studying. This "reactivity" of those observed may then represent atypical behaviors, which raise concerns about whether researchers are investigating what they had conceptualized. Such reactivity may emerge early in a study, but often study participants become acclimated to the presence of an observer and busy with other activities, and thus their behavior grows typical (McCall 1984). Nonetheless, researchers using observation strategies must be sensitive to the potential for reactivity.

The benefits of observation of actual behaviors must be balanced with the drawbacks of the influence of biases of researchers and the reactivity of those being observed. Also, as with experimental research, often the observation involves a narrow field of study participants, which leads to concerns about the generalizability of the results. Again, researchers must consider why observation is the most effective means of addressing the research question of interest. Through observation, they may reveal patterns of behaviors. While structured observations rarely can reveal the intentions underlying behaviors, less structured ethnographic work provides one means of delving into such intentions when observation is also accompanied by other methods, as evidenced in *Paradise Laborers* (Adler and Adler 2004). Indeed, qualitative researchers often may draw upon multiple sources of data so that they may cross-check their findings. Such a process is called **triangulation**. Adler and Adler (2004) also had access to work policies and job descriptions and procedures developed by resort management. Review of such policies, descriptions, and procedures, which may influence social dynamics and workers' mobility, falls under the rubric of archival research.

Archival Methods

Unlike experimental, survey, or observation research in which study participants may respond, consciously or unconsciously, to the process of being involved in the research endeavor, archived materials as a source of data are not "reactive" to the fact that they are being examined. **Archival methods** refer to various strategies of analyzing (or reanalyzing) existing information, including documents, texts, pictures or videos, songs, websites, or statistics, collected or produced by others and often for purposes other than research. As with other methodologies, the goal is to reveal patterns of behavior currently or historically. To achieve that end, investigators rely on their research questions to direct them to certain forms of information and develop coding schemes (much as in observation research) to capture representations of particular variables of interest. Such endeavors are unobtrusive because they allow for "methods of studying social behavior without affecting it" (Babbie 2016:323).

Recall the description of what Latané and Darley (1970) might have done in the wake of the news stories about the Kitty Genovese murder: look for other recorded incidents of whether bystanders provided help to victims. One means of doing so would have been to search newspapers for published accounts of assaults and murders, categorizing the content of each by aspects of the situation as reported. **Content analysis** involves a detailed review of the documents, written or visual (as in various forms of media). To the extent that researchers attempt to quantify content of documents (broadly defined) in a systematic and replicable manner by coding information into predefined categories, their goal is quantitatively oriented. (Their interpretations, in some cases, may be considered qualitative.) Those categories depend upon the research question and relevant theoretical ideas about the social behavior under examination as well as the operational definitions of central variables. They may identify the actors present, various types of behaviors, references to particular themes, or even the use of specific words (or images). Categories should be mutually exclusive (i.e., no overlaps between categories representing different concepts or variables) and exhaustive (i.e., all possible categories represented in the coding scheme) (Bryman 2012).

To perform a content analysis, researchers must select a sample of the documents to be examined. (It would be impossible to review the contents of every newspaper published in the United States, across all the years of publication!) The sampling frame might specify which media sources, the time period covered, or the unit of analysis (e.g., individual behavior or rates of behavior aggregated over a larger unit such as a county). Once the sample has been determined, coders trained in the designed categorization scheme review the information provided in the selected documents to allow quantification of the behavior at issue. And, as in the case of structured observation research, employing multiple coders and assessing how consistently they use the coding scheme ensures intercoder reliability.

Content analysis affords the researcher the opportunity to study an issue over time in an economical fashion. The method is well suited to identifying descriptive patterns and revealing relevant factors that may influence a behavior, though it is less suitable for explaining why a pattern emerges. Unlike other methodologies, it allows readily for the correction of errors. When manipulations in an experiment fail or when survey questions are poorly phrased, the researcher would need to relaunch the study with appropriate corrections. But with content analyses, researchers can go back and recode their documents. The completeness of coding schemes and clarity of coding instructions also ensures the feasibility of replication and follow-up studies.

Assuming that such an archival method is appropriate for the research question, investigators do, however, need to be aware of the extent to which the documents they have sampled are complete and created by individuals who themselves were not biased in their record-keeping. For example, the contents of newspaper articles may be colored by the political leanings of the publisher. Or, in the case of historical documents, there may be gaps in recording owing to degradation of materials over time or even destruction of some periods of data due to fire or flood (really!). And the coding scheme created by a researcher relies on interpretation and may also introduce biases owing to what the investigator chooses to code or not code. Thus, though content analysis focuses on nonreactive records, the method is not without potential contamination by biases of various sorts.

Another form of archival methods involves the compilation and **analysis of existing statistics**, a decidedly quantitative undertaking. Government agencies, corporations, religious organizations, nonprofit groups, and the like often collect routine data about a variety of things (e.g., characteristics of populations, rates of crime, number of dwellings with more than one bathroom, levels of contributions, disease rates). Researchers relying on existing statistics often bring together different sources to answer distinct questions. Those questions rarely pertain to specific individual behaviors but may capture what individuals, at an aggregated level, may do.

For example, Whitehead (2014) examines the impact of population density on two general forms of helping behavior: (1) volunteering time with charitable organizations and (2) making monetary contributions to such organizations. He argues that people who live in cities, with higher population density (the number of people living in a designated unit of area like a square mile), often experience high sensory overload and thus spend less time on each activity. Thus, city dwellers may be less likely to volunteer than those living in more rural areas. He also proposes that the relationship between population density and volunteering would be stronger than the one between population density and monetary gifts, which may be more tied to income.

To empirically examine these ideas, he brought together statistics regarding: number of residents per square mile in each state in 2010 (from the U.S. Census Bureau), the volunteer rate by state (compiled by the Corporation for National and Community Service for 2011); IRS Statistics of Income regarding the average contribution to charitable organizations in 2011, state-level income tax rates for 2011 (from the Tax Policy Center), and the median household income for 2011 (from the U.S. Census Bureau). Note that all of the statistics collected pertain to relatively the same period of time. His analysis used statistical correlations to assess whether there was any relationship between state-level population density and measures of volunteerism and monetary charitable giving. (Such a strategy does not allow for assessing whether population density *caused* the levels of different forms of helping.)

Results of this study using existing statistics confirmed Whitehead's (2014) expectation that in states with higher population densities, people volunteered less often—and that relationship was stronger than the one between population density and charitable giving. Interestingly, however, monetary gifts were not positively related to higher incomes (regardless of how measured). The study highlights the importance of recognizing different population-level antecedents to particular types of helping behavior (at the state level).

With use of existing statistics, researchers must be wary of whether they accurately represent what they claim to report (Babbie 2016). While Whitehead's

(2014) population density measure may have been accurate, the nature of the volunteer rate may depend upon what the Corporation for National and Community Service "counted" as relevant forms of volunteerism and whether they relied upon data from nonprofit groups or perhaps some sort of survey that they conducted. And, although Whitehead's (2014) study involves a snapshot in time, research using existing statistics needs to consider if and how record-keeping systems may have changed over time. Nonetheless, given the availability of statistics from a wide variety of sources, this archival method may be useful in answering particular questions about social behaviors at the aggregated level, especially over time or even cross-culturally (assuming similar measures can be obtained from sources in different countries). Researchers, however, must recognize the potential for using their results in a manner that constitutes an **ecological fallacy**, or inferences about individual behaviors from aggregated data. For example, while Whitehead (2014) could make claims about patterns of population density and volunteering rates in states, he cannot say that individuals who live in high-rise apartment buildings are less likely to engage in volunteer activities than those in single-family dwellings. To address that issue, researchers might survey people who live in different types of residences about their volunteer activities.

Archival methods, like previously discussed experimental, survey, and observation strategies, have advantages (like nonreactivity of the data) and disadvantages (e.g., potential for the ecological fallacy). As stressed earlier in the chapter, which method researchers choose depends upon the nature of their knowledge of the topic and the research question at issue. And regardless of the methodology, all researchers must be sensitive to how their approach ensures protections for the rights and well-being of their study participants. More generally, no researchers should go into the field without considering the ethics of their approach.

Ethical Issues

In most of the helping studies used to illustrate different methodological approaches to studying social psychological processes, investigators had either active contact with their study participants by inviting them into a laboratory or to complete a questionnaire, or passive contact through observing their behavior in public places. The contact between researchers and their study participants can be described as a form of interaction. And, importantly, as initiators of the interaction, scholars, throughout all stages of their research endeavor—from design, to data collection, to data handling and storage, to dissemination of results through publications—must be cognizant of treating their study participants in an ethical, respectful manner, demonstrating regard for their rights and well-being. Professional associations prescribe ethical procedures in research, as do various governmental organizations charged with enforcing federal regulations about the ethical conduct of research.[8] Here, we describe key features of research that ensure ethical treatment of study participants (see Babbie 2016; Bryman 2012; Hegtvedt 2014).

Regardless of the methodology chosen to address a research question, researchers must keep in mind that their study participants are not merely "research material" or objects to be examined. Such objectification may allow investigators to grow insensitive to the potential harms that may be produced, even unintentionally, from their studies. Instead, researchers should be mindful that study participants are human beings who think, feel, and behave just as they do. Additionally, to the extent that a researcher has something that study participants desire (e.g., money, access to a particular treatment or grade), he or she may be in a position to coerce or exploit participants. As with objectification, the potential to exploit may lead to callous treatment of study participants. With these considerations in mind, investigators should anticipate and minimize the variety of **potential harms** that may befall those who join in their studies.

Harm may be of various types, and vary in both intensity (how bad is it?) and likelihood of occurring (is it rare or highly likely?). Typically, rare in social psychological research is physical harm, such as injury. More common are psychological harms, often in the form of some sort of embarrassment, anxiety, distress, or loss of self-esteem or confidence. For example, failing to help a victim in need, even if others are present, may challenge an individual's view of himself or herself as a good person, leading to feelings of guilt for not providing assistance or loss of self-esteem. Social harms may also arise when studies ask participants to reveal private facts about themselves that could potentially compromise their reputation or even threaten their freedom. For example, revelation of responses to surveys of self-reported criminal activities might lead to inquiries by law enforcement officials. It is incumbent upon researchers to design study procedures that minimize the intensity and likelihood of anticipated harms.

Several common procedures built in during the design stage of a study and implemented during data collection help to lower risks of harms owing to participation. First, researchers should ensure that participation is **voluntary**, which includes both agreement to be involved in the study and the right to stop participation at any time during the study. No one should feel obligated to be in a study for fear of repercussions from the researcher or the institution conducting the study. For example, if students enrolled in introductory psychology, sociology, or social psychology classes are required to be part of a "subject pool" and participate in studies as part of their grade, voluntariness is jeopardized unless students are given a choice of whether to be part of a subject pool and a choice of studies in which to participate. (Departments that run subject pools are required to give students alternative assignments that require a similar amount of time as, say, a particular experiment that they may choose instead.)

Second, participants must offer **informed consent**, which is the process by which a researcher conveys information about the study (who is conducting it and for what purpose, what participation involves, how long it takes, potential harms and benefits, means to ensure anonymity or confidentiality, any compensation, etc.) (Dunn and Chadwick 2012). Typically, informed consent occurs before the study begins, but in some cases, informed consent continues to be sought in the middle or at the end of the study. And while elements of the information conveyed is consistent across methodologies involving active contact between researcher and participants, the nature of the process varies depending upon the study population, the substantive content of the data being gathered, and means of data collection. For example, in the typical laboratory experiment, the researcher will offer a written document describing the previously noted information about the study and ask the participant to sign the document to signal consent. In many surveys, participants read a description of the study, and the actual completion of the questionnaire (online or on paper) signals their consent. For collection of interview data, especially with what might be considered a vulnerable population (e.g., gang members, HIV positive individuals), study descriptions may be offered orally and oral consent accepted.

Third, in any type of consent procedure, researchers must make efforts to protect the **privacy** of their study participants as a means of warding off psychological or social harms. One way to ensure privacy is to indicate that the data collected will be **anonymous**—no names will be associated in any way to the data provided. Assurances of anonymity are common in much survey and structured observation research in public settings. Oftentimes, however, researchers will know the names of their study participants (indeed, they may have signed a consent document!). And knowing the names is important for collecting follow-up data or triangulating with other data sources. In such cases, investigators may create identification codes so that they can link sources of data (e.g., surveys of high school students and archival data on their academic performance). When investigators can link names to the data collected, it is incumbent upon them to hold these records **confidentially**. Doing so focuses on handling of data in a manner that avoids breaches in confidentiality, which is a major threat for psychological and especially social harms (Citro, Ilgen, and Marrett 2003; Sieber 1992). In addition to creating identification codes, researchers might provide separate storage for and limited access to master files that link codes with names, use password-protected computers and computer files, and only present data in aggregate form so that the responses of no one person are singled out. For qualitative endeavors using quotes from interviews, pseudonyms help protect respondents' privacy.

Although such precautions guard the well-being of study participants, additional concerns arise in experimental research that involves deception. Recall that in the Darley and Latané (1968) study, participants heard voices, presumably of other students involved in the study, and one of those ostensibly suffered a seizure in the course of the experimental session. Both of these study procedures were designed intentionally to create variation in group size and the need for help, respectively. And yet, the prerecorded voices were of **confederates**, research assistants instructed to act in a particular way by the experimenter and unbeknownst to the study participants, including sounding as if a seizure was in process. Darley and Latané (1968) deceived their study participants by providing false information, with the intention of misleading them to believe something that was not true (no one was suffering a seizure!). Many scholars have debated the potential harms to study participants, researchers, as well as professions that may be wrought by the use of deception (e.g., Cook and Yamagishi 2008; Hertwig and Ortmann 2008; Korn 1997; see Hegtvedt 2014 for a summary).

In effect, deception deprives study participants of their right to determine their willingness to participate in full knowledge of what to expect in the situation because informed consent procedures omit initial mention of deceptive practices. Such full disclosure prior to the participation would jeopardize the validity of the findings regarding the impact of independent variables created through deception. In such cases, further informed consent is sought at the end of the experiment, after the study participant has been fully informed of the intentions of the study and debriefed about the deception. At that point, assessment of whether the participant feels any distress or embarrassment at being "duped" is necessary, with researchers providing remedies for such distress and allowing participants to drop out of the study as well. Beyond the individual level, there is concern that the use of deception may stimulate suspicion about and negative inclinations toward the research endeavor, which may spill over to nondeceptive studies and thereby threaten the viability of social research in general. Little evidence, however, confirms this potential threat to the credibility of social research.

Typically, the benefits of deception must be weighed in terms of harms to individual study participants or society more generally. Deception should be used only when no alternative procedures are feasible to ensure a study's validity or address a particular issue. In addition, study designs must minimize risk of harm to study participants. Many deceptions are relatively harmless (e.g., creating false expectations about procedures), whereas others may involve false feedback that results in damage to individuals' self-evaluations. In the latter type of situation, researchers must provide a means of restoring a positive sense of self.

Beyond the ethical obligations that researchers have to their study participants, they must also consider concerns arising after data are collected, in the process of analyzing and publishing their findings. For both of these steps in the research endeavor, investigators must signal the extent to which they are being honest about how they treated the data, interpreted the data, and conducted the statistical analyses that reveal the results that appear in published articles. Dishonesty may take the form of excluding particular cases because they do not "fit" the pattern expected, adding or changing participants' responses, or failing to include potential confounding variables in their analysis (which may reduce the observed impact of focal factors). The bottom line is this: Researchers should not fabricate their data or their results!

Additionally, they should report negative findings—those that do not support the hypothesized relationships—and reveal shortcomings and limitations of their own work. Within psychology today, there is much debate about the extent to which findings from studies can be replicated (e.g., Maxwell, Lau, and Howard 2015; Simmons, Nelson, and Simonsohn 2011). When new studies fail to produce patterns of findings consistent with existing published work, the veracity of the findings and the soundness of the data collection procedures and analysis may be called into question. Such challenges may compromise scientific knowledge and faith in the community that produces it. Thus, it is important that scholars clearly report their data collection practices and procedures, as well as their statistical techniques, so that others may attempt to replicate the findings, thereby strengthening confidence in existing scientific knowledge. Moreover, conforming to the ethical standards of the scientific community signals researchers' integrity and ensures the public's confidence in the scientific endeavor.

Segue: From the Means of Collecting Data to the Patterns Revealed

As illustrated in Chapter 1, social psychologists pursue a wide variety of topics related to the understanding of social behavior. Their pursuit, however, differs from that of the casual observer of interaction dynamics insofar as they attempt to bring systematic evidence to bear upon the issues that they study. Using research in the domain of helping behavior, here we have provided an overview of the logic of scientific inquiry and the means by which investigators collect data. The use of any one strategy—experiment, survey, interview, structured/less structured observation, or archival materials—depends upon the existing level of knowledge on a particular topic, the purpose of the research itself (i.e., to explore patterns in a particular place, at a particular time or to test hypotheses derived from deductive theory), and the particular question under scrutiny. Strengths and weaknesses of each method shape which method is chosen for which research question. There is no "one size fits all" in social psychological research.

Subsequent chapters of this book present theories, supported by empirical research, that provide a basis for understanding how individuals influence and are influenced by their social worlds. Throughout, you will encounter studies that further illustrate the methodological tools of social psychologists. To move beyond commonsense understandings, feel free to employ the refrain "show me the evidence." Our intent is to present such evidence.

Endnotes

1. The headline for the original *New York Times* story read, "37 Who Saw Murder Didn't Call the Police." Yet further inquiries revealed inconsistencies: Few may have seen the attack, though many may have heard it; two people claim to have called the police in the pre–911 era, but no record exists; and one woman went to Kitty's aid as she died. Stephanie Merry raised such issues in "How Everyone Got the Infamous Kitty Genovese Case All Wrong" (*Washington Post*, June 29, 2016). The 2015 documentary, *The Witness,* illustrates William Genovese's attempt to set the record straight about his sister's murder and raises questions about the veracity of the original reporting. Nonetheless, the original reporting spurred social psychological research.

2. The 1988 film *The Accused*, starring Jodie Foster, depicts this incident in New Bedford, Massachusetts.

3. These are fictitious incidents.

4. The researchers also created variations in the composition of the three-person group, with the other present bystander either a male, female, or male who said he was premed.

5. They also included conditions in which the victim was black. Plus, they were prepared to have one of the study team members act as a model, providing help if no one else did after a particular interval. The models, however, rarely had to act.

6. Brody and Vangelisti (2015) report two studies. Here, we describe Study 1. Their second study combines elements of experimental design by creating vignettes in which the three central independent variables of Study 1 (few/many bystanders; high/low visual anonymity, close/acquaintance relationship with victim) are manipulated to create eight versions of an online bullying incident. Each of 379 respondents in a convenience sample read one scenario and completed measures of the same dependent variables as in Study 1.

7. Originating in 1891, the Salvation Army kettle, bright red in color, was a means to collect small contributions to provide holiday meals to needy individuals. Today, contributions during the holiday season help to allow the Salvation Army to continue its assistance to people in need through the entire year.

8. Codes of ethics are available from the American Psychological Association (http://www.apa.org/ethics/code/index.aspx) and the American Sociological Association (http://www.asanet.org/membership/code-ethics). The U.S. Office for Human Research Protections (https://www.hhs.gov/ohrp) is responsible for overseeing the operation of university-based Institutional Review Boards, which implement procedures for the review of research involving human study participants and ensuring compliance with the Code of Federal Regulations Title 45 Part 46.

References

Adler, Patricia A., and Peter Adler. 2004. *Paradise Laborers: Hotel Work in the Global Economy.* Ithaca, NY: Cornell University Press.

Babbie, Earl. 2016. *The Practice of Social Research.* 14th ed. Belmont, CA: Thomson/Wadsworth.

Batson, C. Daniel, and Kathryn C. Oleson 1991. "Current Status of the Empathy-Altruism Hypothesis." Pp. 62–85 in *Prosocial Behavior.* Vol. 12, *Review of Personality and Social Psychology,* edited by M. S. Clark. Newbury Park, CA: Sage.

Brody, Nicholas, and Anita L. Vangelisti. 2015. "Bystander Intervention in Cyberbullying." *Communication Monographs* 83:94–119. doi:10.1080/03637751.2015.1044256

Bryman, Alan. 2012. *Social Research Methods.* 4th ed. Oxford, England: Oxford University Press.

Citro, Constance, F., Daniel R. Ilgen, and Cora B. Marrett. 2003. *Protecting Participants and Facilitating Social and Behavioral Sciences Research.* Washington, DC: National Academy Press.

Cook, Karen S., and Toshio Yamagishi. 2008. "A Defense of Deception on Scientific Grounds." *Social Psychology Quarterly* 71:215–21. doi:10.1177/019027250807100303

Darley, John M., and Bibb Latané. 1968. "Bystander Intervention in Emergencies: Diffusion of Responsibility." *Journal of Personality and Social Psychology* 8:377–83. doi:10.1037/h0025589

Dovidio, John F., Jane A. Piliavin, David A. Schroeder, and Louis A. Penner. 2006. *The Social Psychology of Prosocial Behavior.* Hillsdale, NJ: Erlbaum.

Dunn, Cynthia M., and Gary Chadwick. 2012. *Protecting Study Volunteers in Research.* Boston: Centerwatch.

Einolf, Christopher J. 2011. "The Link Between Religion and Helping Others: The Role of Values, Ideas, and Language." *Sociology of Religion* 72:435–55. doi:10.1093/socrel/srr017

England, Kim V. L. 1994. "Getting Personal: Reflexivity, Positionality, and Feminist Research." *The Professional Geographer* 46:80–89. doi:10.1111/j.0033-0124.1994.00080.x

Glaser, Barney G., and Anselm L. Strauss. 1967. *The Discovery of Grounded Theory: Strategies for Qualitative Research.* Chicago: Aldine Publishing.

Glesne, Corrine. 2015. *Becoming Qualitative Researchers: An Introduction.* Upper Saddle River, NJ: Pearson Education.

Gubrium, Jaber F., James A. Holstein, Amir B. Marvasti, and Karyn D. McKinney. 2012. *The SAGE Handbook of Interview Research: The Complexity of the Craft.* Thousand Oaks, CA: Sage. doi:10.4135/9781452218403

Hegtvedt, Karen A. 2014. "Ethics and Experiments." Pp. 23–51 in *Laboratory Experiments in the Social Sciences,* 2nd ed., edited by M. Webster Jr. and J. Sell. Amsterdam: Elsevier. doi:10.1016/B978-0-12-404681-8.00002-9

Hertwig, Ralph, and Andreas Ortmann. 2008. "Deceptions in Social Psychological Experiments: Two Misconceptions and a Research Agenda." *Social Psychology Quarterly* 71:222–27. doi:10.1177/019027250807100304

Jiobu, Robert M., and Eric S. Knowles. 1974. "Norm Strength and Alms Giving: An Observational Study." *The Journal of Social Psychology* 94:205–11. doi:10.1080/00224545.1974.9923207

Khanna, Nikki. 2004. "The Role of Reflected Appraisals in Racial Identity: The Case of Multiracial Asians." *Social Psychology Quarterly* 67:115–31.

Khanna, Nikki. 2011. *Biracial in America: Forming and Performing Racial Identity.* Lanham, MD: Lexington Books.

Korn, James H. 1997. *Illusions of Reality: A History of Deception in Social Psychology*. Albany: University of New York Press.

Latané, Bibb, and John M. Darley. 1970. *The Unresponsive Bystander: Why Doesn't He Help?* New York: Appleton-Century-Crofts.

Lois, Jennifer. 2003. *Heroic Efforts: The Emotion Culture of Search and Rescue Volunteers*. New York: New York University Press.

Matsunaga, M. 2010. "Testing a Mediational Model of Bullied Victims' Evaluation of Received Support and Post-bullying Adaptation: A Japan-U.S. Cross-cultural Comparison." *Communication Monographs* 77:312–40. doi:10.1080/03637751003758235

Maxwell, Scott E., Michael Y. Lau, and George S. Howard. 2015. "Is Psychology Suffering from a Replication Crisis?" *The American Psychologist* 70:487–98. doi:10.1037/a0039400

McCall, George J. 1984. "Structured Field Observation." *Annual Review of Sociology* 10:263–82. doi:10.1146/annurev.so.10.080184.001403

O'Connell, Paul, Debra Pepler, and Wendy Craig. 1999. "Peer Involvement in Bullying: Insights and Challenges for Intervention." *Journal of Adolescence* 22:437–52. doi:10.1006/jado.1999.0238

Piliavin, Irving M., Judith Rodin, and Jane Piliavin. 1969. "Good Samaritanism: An Underground Phenomenon." *Journal of Personality and Social Psychology* 13:289–99. doi:10.1037/h0028433

Popper, Karl. 1963. *Conjectures and Refutations: The Growth of Scientific Knowledge*. London, England: Routledge.

Salmivalli, Christina, and Marinus Voeten. 2004. "Connections Between Attitudes, Group Norms, and Behaviour in Bullying Situations." *International Journal of Behavioral Development* 28:246–58. doi:10.1080/01650250344000488

Sieber, Joan. 1992. *Planning Ethically Responsible Research: A Guide for Students and Internal Review Boards*. Newbury Park, CA: Sage. doi:10.4135/978 1412985406

Simmons, Joseph P., Leif D. Nelson, and Uri Simonsohn. 2011. "False-positive Psychology: Undisclosed Flexibility in Data Collection and Analysis Allows Presenting Anything Significant." *Psychological Science* 22:1359–66. doi:10.1177/0956797611417632

Snow, David A., and Leon Anderson. 1987. "Identity Work among the Homeless: The Verbal Construction and Avowal of Personal Identities." *American Journal of Sociology* 92:1336–71. doi:10.1086/228668

Tavory, Iddo, and Stefan Timmermans. 2014. *Abductive Analysis: Theorizing Qualitative Research*. Chicago: University of Chicago Press.

Webster, Murray, Jr., and Jane Sell. 2014. "Why Do Experiments?" Pp. 5–21 in *Laboratory Experiments in the Social Sciences,* edited by M. Webster Jr. and Jane Sell. Amsterdam: Elsevier. doi:10.1016/B978-0-12-404681-8.00001-7

Whitehead, George I. 2014. "Correlates of Volunteerism and Charitable Giving in the 50 United States." *North American Journal of Psychology* 16:531–36.

Wilkins, Amy C. 2012. "Becoming Black Women: Intimate Stories and Intersectional Identities." *Social Psychology Quarterly* 75:173–96. doi:10. 1177/0190272512440106

Wingfield, Adia Harvey. 2010. "Are Some Emotions Marked 'White Only'? Racialized Feeling Rules in Professional Workplace." *Social Problems* 57:251–68. doi:10.1525/sp.2010.57.2.251

Zelditch, Morris, Jr. 1969. "Can You Really Study an Army in the Laboratory?" Pp. 528–39 in *Complex Organizations*, edited by A. Etioni. New York: Holt, Rinehart and Winston.

The Individual in a Social World

What is Monday, and where did it come from? How do you experience Monday? What Monday may mean in one culture, such as the first day of the workweek, may mean something entirely different in other cultures or not exist at all. It is Cathy's least favorite day of the week and has been for quite some time. In some pop music, Monday is often associated with being blue, rainy or stormy, lonely, manic, or sleepy! Maybe she was deeply influenced by all those songs that dissed Mondays.

In many societies, people learn how to organize their activities and interactions around the notions of hours, days, weeks, months, years, and seconds. Clocks, calendars, and schedules are all culturally defined objects that help people in particular cultures to "keep time" and be "on time" (Flaherty 1999). Most, if not all, of us take for granted these categories of time (and names of days and months, thanks to the ancient Romans and Greeks!) and accept the fact that they structure our day-to-day and weekly activities and interactions. Of course, some of us see ourselves as people who are "on time" and don't keep people waiting, while some of us are "always" late. And sometimes we are "fashionably late," at least for certain occasions.

Our notions of time are related to our daily habits, including when we have to get up; when we eat breakfast, lunch, and dinner; and when we are expected to sleep and for how long (at least for school and many jobs). How many hours do you think you should be sleeping during the night (for those who don't work at night)? Did you think 8 hours? Eight straight hours seems to be a commonly held notion of the "right" amount of sleep for good health and good performance. Some reports show that nearly one third of all working adults get 6 or fewer hours of sleep at night. And some occupations are more prone to sleep deprivation than others.

But this idea that we should have 8 straight hours of sleep is actually a relatively new idea, dating back to the invention of the light bulb in the late 1800s (Isaacson 2015). Indeed, historian Roger Ekirch (2001, 2006) found consistent descriptions of a segmented sleep schedule in preindustrial works of literature, including diaries and instruction manuals. Before the Industrial Revolution, it was common for people to sleep for a few hours, stay up for another few hours, and then sleep for several more hours. The period of awakened consciousness between these two phases of sleep at night allowed for self-reflection, getting a jump on the day's activity, chatting with neighbors, and making love, and was not interpreted as middle-of-the-night insomnia. Some neuroscience research supports this idea, showing that when there is no artificial light, people often wake up in the middle of the night, reflecting a sign of normal brain functioning (Wehr 1992). The invention of electric lights seems to have led to many cultures' adoption of later bedtimes, the continuous 8-hour sleep idea, and fewer overall hours of sleep or rest.

In addition, different cultures sleep in various ways. For example, David Randall (2012) noted that napping at your desk in China and India is common. Very short naps (which can include deep sleep) seem to improve our cognitive performance, depending on such factors as duration (Milner and Cote 2009). Randall (2012) notes that the gradual acceptance that sequential sleep hours are not required for good health or good job performance has led some companies, such as Google, to allow employees to take naps at work.

Obviously sleep is essential, but the way we think about what is "good sleep" and whether we are "good sleepers" changes and varies over time and place (Ekirch 2001, 2006). These various taken-for-granted categories and conceptions of time across cultures compel us to ask two fundamental questions: (1) How do individuals socially construct their worlds? (2) In those social worlds, how do individuals acquire a sense of self?

To answer these questions, here and in Chapter 4, we draw upon one of the major prominent theoretical perspectives in sociological social psychology, the symbolic interactionist perspective. The beauty of **theoretical perspectives** in general, as we shall see in this book, is that they provide a lens through which we may see our social world. Specifically, theoretical perspectives in sociological social psychology are a set of assumptions about social behavior that provides a particular point of view. These assumptions are neither true nor false. They are either more or less useful to us in furthering our understanding of the social world in which we live. We hope, as social scientists, that our perspectives are useful to us in doing three things: (1) directing us to useful and interesting questions that, if answered, help us know more about our social world than we did before; (2) providing us with guidelines and strategies for approaching and examining social life—that is, providing effective ways of studying our social world; and (3) telling us what concepts and processes are important and helpful in describing and explaining social phenomena. The knowledge that we gain by drawing upon these theoretical perspectives guides us in developing solutions to social problems and issues of inequality.

In this chapter, we will address the first two questions stated previously—two central questions that scholars who draw upon the symbolic interactionist perspective strive to answer. We will learn about the **symbolic interactionist perspective** by seeing how symbolic interactionists study social life and what important concepts and processes they use to inform and increase our knowledge about how we navigate through day-to-day interaction with each other.

How Do Individuals Socially Construct Their Worlds?

What distinguishes humans from other animals, if anything? How do we recognize and name things around us? How do we learn to name ourselves, and how do we acquire and negotiate aspects of ourselves in day-to-day interaction? In this first section, we explore how humans develop "mind" and how minded behavior distinguishes humans from other animals. As we shall see, mind is not an entity but rather a process.

Is There a Distinguishing Difference Between Humans and Other Animals?

George Herbert Mead (1863–1931), an American philosopher and social psychologist at the University of Chicago in the early 1900s, is one of the renowned scholars associated with the symbolic interactionist perspective. One of Mead's key questions during his time was this: Is there a distinguishing difference between humans and other animals?

Mead addressed this and many other questions in the early part of the 1900s—a time when a prominent perspective of human behavior—behaviorism—was central in psychology. One key premise of this psychological approach is the idea of the stimulus–response process. A stimulus is anything in the person's environment that provokes an action or response. Stimuli could be anything from types of foods, money, threats in the environment, or particular words. Behaviorism suggests that much of our behavior is learned as a result of gratification or punishment associated with particular stimuli. During Mead's time, there was an extreme form of behaviorism that viewed human consciousness as something that could not be studied. Rather social scientists were called upon to study only observable behaviors and their connection to observable stimuli. Mead believed differently. He believed that the stimulus–response process was not an adequate account of human conduct.

One reason for Mead's opposing view is that he was heavily influenced by pragmatism, an American philosophical tradition developed during the early decades of the 20th century. Pragmatists, such as Charles Peirce, William James, and John Dewey, were concerned with the process of thinking and how it influences the actions of individuals. Pragmatism views thought as a process that allows humans to adjust, adapt, and achieve goals in their environment. In his work, *Mind, Self, and Society* (a compilation of his lectures by his graduate students), Mead (1934) argues that there is something missing between a stimulus in the environment and an individual's response to that stimulus. He does acknowledge that much of human behavior is indeed simply a reaction to a stimulus either in the environment or to our own physiology. For example, we may see a friend eating an ice cream sundae on a hot summer day and salivate and then proceed to buy one immediately! We may see a mountain lion on our hiking trail, start to panic, and go in the other direction. And surely we can think of many times when we are driving and then realize that we have not been paying attention at all to the traffic lights and street signs, but fortunately we have been driving correctly! We are often on autopilot. There are times, however, when we do more than simply react. This missing piece helps us to answer what may be unique about humans.

For Mead the unique feature of humans is **mind**. Mind is not a thing or an entity but rather is the process of manipulating symbols (Mead 1934; Meltzer 2003). "[Mind] is really a verb, not a noun" (Strauss 1978:xiv)—it is a process of using what Mead referred to as significant symbols. A **symbol** is an abstract representation of something that may or may not exist in tangible form. Organizations use symbols all the time to represent themselves. For example, the apple symbol (with a bite out of it so that a small logo would still look like an apple and not a cherry, as noted by creator Rob Janoff) representing the Apple logo is an easily recognized brand logo in the world, as are the Olympic rings. The golden arches represent McDonald's, and Mickey Mouse ears signify Disney. The American Medical Association (AMA) symbol features the single snake of the Staff of Asclepius (the Greek god of healing). *American Medical News* (amednews.com) states that the AMA has used several versions of the serpent and the staff logo over the years but now, since 2005, has adopted a new, more stylized design in order to make a statement about the transformation of the AMA as "inviting and unifying, and most importantly, signals a new energy and vitality of the organization." (The logo also changed colors from teal to purple to change its symbol for a new AMA, as the color purple signifies the nobility of medicine's standards and ethics.) Organizations try to convey quite a lot with their symbols (see Glynn 2002).

Words are also symbols. The word *desk* is a symbolic representation of a class of objects that are constructed of hard substances and designed to serve certain purposes, such as a workspace. And the word *embarrassment* represents something intangible—a feeling with which we are all familiar (often perhaps too familiar!)—or something we cannot touch. Inherent in the idea of symbols is the fact that for something to be a symbol, it has to have meaning that is shared among others. If you are in a movie theater and someone yells fire!, this word has the same effect on you as it has for everyone else in the theater who knows English. The vocalization of this word calls up the same thing in you as it does in others (Mead 1934). So symbols are **shared meanings**. Will your reaction to someone yelling fire be the same as others in the theater? Fundamentally, yes, in the sense that all of you in the theater will try to evacuate the building, but there will be some variation in terms of feelings of panic and consideration of others when trying to exit. Overall, however, all will have a similar goal as a result of the shared meaning of this spoken symbol.

The beauty of symbols is that we can use them to transcend the concrete to have experiences not rooted in time or space. These abstractions allow us to remember, fantasize, plan, as well as have vicarious experiences that others tell us about. When we fantasize, for example, we are manipulating symbolic images. Think of all the times you have played out a conversation in your head with someone else either before or after it has occurred. It could be in regard to going on a job interview, asking someone out on a date, or trying to settle an argument with someone dear to you. We spend quite a bit of time rehearsing or planning these conversations, and we can do so because we can manipulate symbols in our heads. Also, vicarious experiences (e.g., hearing a friend's story about her trip to South America) provide us the opportunity to learn by observing, listening to, and conversing with other people. The process of manipulating symbols is important because it gives us the ability not to have to experience everything ourselves to comprehend what someone else is experiencing. It is the key element for transmitting culture (i.e., the ways of doing things).

Mind, then, allows us to be free of our immediate situation. We can rehearse potential courses of action, inhibit our impulses to assess consequences of our actions, or bring in anticipated futures and our remembered pasts into our current contemplation. We can solve complex problems (Weigert and Gecas 2003).

Although symbols have shared meanings for some collective group of people, we know that sometimes a particular symbol will elicit one meaning for one group of people and a totally different meaning for another group of people. For example, snails in France are a delicacy yet considered a pest in Korea (Kim, Park, and Park 2000). Jodi O'Brien (2006), in her book, *The Production of Reality*, provides a beautiful example of how objects may have various meanings to different groups of people:

> In rural Central American villages, religious festivals are an important part of the local culture. A documentary film crew was around to record one of these events in another country. The film shows brightly colored decorations, music, dancing, and a variety of delicious and special foods made for the festival. The special treats are clearly a highlight for everyone, especially the children, who crowd around the stands. In the middle of one crowd of children waiting for a treat is a very large stone bowl. A large stone pillar rises out of the center of the bowl. The pillar seems alive. It is completely covered by shiny black beetles crawling around and over each other. The person in charge takes a tortilla, spreads some sauce on the inside, grabs a handful of live beetles, and fills the burrito with them, quickly folding the tortilla so that the beetles cannot escape. Playfully pushing the beetles back into the tortilla between bites, a gleeful child eats the burrito with relish. Would you be willing to try a beetle burrito? Is a strip of burnt cow muscle (also known as a steak) inherently any more desirable than a beetle burrito? (O'Brien 2006:2)

In this example the same stimulus, live beetles, elicits different subjective interpretations and, as a result, different responses. Importantly, the way a person responds to a stimulus depends on how a person *interprets* the stimulus. Our reactions depend on how we define the situation. If a person just now came up to you and kissed you on the cheek, what would be your reaction? It could be wonderful, or it could be disgusting! And some of us may wince at the idea of getting our noses pierced; others will think it is awesome. What is interesting, then, is not the actual stimulus but the meanings that individuals and groups assign to the stimulus. It is the process of assigning meaning that determines how people will act. When former senator Hillary Clinton became teary-eyed at a presidential campaign rally in 2008, was she seen as weak, manipulative, strong, or compassionate? In 2016, former secretary of state Hillary Clinton ran again for president. If she had become teary-eyed again, would she have been seen as weak, manipulative, or compassionate against Donald Trump? The answer depends on *who* is interpreting the act, *when,* and in *what context* (which involves social cognition processes as discussed in Chapter 5).

We typically, then, do not respond directly to our physical environment, but instead, most of our responses to others stem from our interpretation of stimuli or cues around us. These cues could be such things as gestures, physiological features, or adornments (e.g., clothing and jewelry) of others. When we interpret and then respond based on that interpretation, we are said to engage in "minded behavior" (Mead 1934; Meltzer 2003). When we consider alternatives and then adjust our responses, this activity is "mind." Mind is the activity that makes it possible for us to engage in deliberate conduct. Mind is social.

For Mead and symbolic interactionists in general, then, *humans are symbol-using creatures who interpret their world.* Interpretation involves the process of thinking. Our interpretation of things and cues in the environment is affected by our own thought processes (i.e., our own perceptions, biases, and views of the world) (Blumer 1969). In the beetle burrito story, for example, many people who grew up in the United States would not be willing to try this "delicacy" like the children in rural Central American villages! Not surprisingly, then, in response to behaviorists, Mead (1934) argued that although an activity such as thinking is unobservable, it is still behavior. When confronted with stimuli, humans often do not simply see them and respond but rather actively seek and select certain cues, based on past experiences, anticipated futures, interests, and needs. Therefore, they are "doing" something (Couch 1989; Meltzer 2003).

In addition, animals, such as primates, are capable of using symbols (see Hewitt 2003 for a discussion of the difference between natural signs that animals learn and symbols that humans can manipulate). Gorillas, for example, are quite capable of learning a certain set of symbols used in American Sign Language (e.g., see Koko and the Gorilla Foundation). Humans, however, are **complex symbol users** relative to other animals in that they create religions, philosophies, cities, and medical treatments, to name a few. Humans can create symbols that stand for other symbols.

Also, we, as humans, can think about our pasts and futures in a much more complex fashion (Couch 1989). Cathy sometimes thinks about her cats—and surely they do "think" and respond to her vocalizations (well sometimes anyway!). And if she begins to open a can of cat food, that sound represents to them that food is coming. They have learned this meaning of this particular sound over time. They also can let her know when it is time to eat by incessant pawing at her face in the morning. As well, when she pets them, they purr. And dogs can learn to "sit" (unlike cats most of the time because perhaps they simply do not have the inclination to follow your commands!). But dogs cannot teach each other the meaning of the command sit to their friends, even though they are individually capable of learning this command (Hewitt 2003). They also cannot fantasize about what they may be doing in 5 years. They are unable to produce a symbol at will if the thing or event they signify is not present. Humans, however, can talk about a dog that is not present, and in so doing, use this symbol even though the referent is not present. Other animals, then, are limited in the meanings they can share with us.

How Do We Learn Symbols?

Herbert Blumer (1969), one of Mead's students, wrote the book *Symbolic Interactionism*, which provides the foundation of this theoretical perspective. He articulated three basic assumptions. The first assumption states that *humans act toward a "thing" (e.g., an event, a sign, a behavior, a tradition, a material object) on the basis of the meaning they assign to the thing.* For example, the way that one approaches a computer varies for different people based on the meaning of that object. For some, it is used for word processing; for others, it provides an opportunity to create computer programs; and yet still, others use it for online trading of stocks and bonds, and for others it is just a hard object. How we relate to computers depends on the meanings we have learned from the kinds of experiences we have had with computers. Think about grass: Grass is not the same thing for cats and cows (Meltzer 2003). Also, do you know what the word *triskaidekaphobia* means? This word refers to a fear of the number 13. Notice how some buildings do not have floor number 13, and airplanes do not have row 13. Some say this fear comes from the belief that because Judas may have been the 13th apostle, the number 13 is cursed.

Another example is "the bottle" in the film *The Gods Must Be Crazy* (Uys 1980), released in 1980. It follows the story of Xi, the leader of a small group of Bushmen in the Kalahari Desert whose tribe has no knowledge or experience beyond their own local world. One day an empty Coke bottle is tossed out of a plane flying overhead by the pilot and falls to earth unbroken. Xi finds the bottle—this unusual hard object—and brings it back to the group. Of course, this object is considered an empty Coke bottle and a piece of trash by the pilot (today it is often viewed as an object to be recycled). For the Bushmen, however, who had never seen this object before, the bottle acquired many different meanings created through interaction. For example, it was seen as a tool for curing snakeskin, a musical instrument to make tones by blowing into the object, and a useful thing for making decorations on cloth. But there was only *one* Coke bottle, and as a result, people began to fight over it, and later in the film, it was even used as a dangerous weapon to bonk one another on the head. In fact, later in the story, Xi calls it "the evil thing." This example shows that our interpretation of a thing, event, or situation affects our response toward it, not the object itself.

The second assumption is that *meanings of "things" are socially derived*. That is, the meanings of objects, events, and behaviors are created through social interaction among individuals and groups of individuals (Blumer 1969). Meanings, therefore, are not in objects themselves. Rather, through interaction with others, people learn to conceptualize a person, place, or thing and attach meaning to it. Clearly, this occurred in the Coke bottle example. This process is known as **naming** (O'Brien 2006). To name something is to know it. We name things and then respond according to the implications carried by the name. Is your own spit something, for example, you would swallow once it is out of your body? Probably not. Typically, many of us have an aversion to bodily fluids that have left the body, like spit. The word *spit* elicits an evaluative response (e.g., ick!), and then a course of action is followed, such as avoiding the spit. We have learned to assign meaning to the fluid and respond to the meaning, not the object itself (O'Brien 2006:67). Through naming, we learn symbols. We have learned names for all kinds of animals, flowers, and religions as well as the days of the week and the meanings of these things we have named will vary across time and place. In the beginning of the chapter, we discussed Monday. We learn to categorize all the days of the week in our culture and what constitutes a weekend. (Notably, Britain was the first country to create "standard time" in the mid-1800s where time was set throughout a region to one standard time. Why? Railways! The railways could not function well with inconsistencies of local mean time and so forced a uniform time on the country. The railroads in the United States and Canada instituted standard time in time zones in 1883.)

This process of naming involves the process of categorization (Hewitt 2003). We create and use categories to group things in a way that makes them related to one another and gives them order, like a mental filing system (O'Brien 2006). Once something is named, we also learn from others how to react toward it—what to do and what not to do with it.

Importantly, we need others to help us learn those symbols; we cannot learn them on our own. For example, Helen Keller, who became deaf and blind during infancy, could not have learned symbols without her teacher, Anne Sullivan. Learning language (set of symbols) is an interactional process. The first word that

Helen learned was *water*, finger spelled in her hand. How did she learn that this cool, wet something pouring over her hand was named water? Anne had to get Helen to recognize that she and Helen were attending to this cool, wet something together, at that same time (called **joint attention**). Once Helen was aware that they had a **shared focus** on the object (the cool, wet something), Helen could then learn to name this object by Anne's finger spelling *water* in her hand (Couch 1989). Keller described the experience of learning her first symbol at the age of 7 in this way:

> We [Anne Sullivan—her teacher] walked down the path to the well-house, attracted by the fragrance of the honeysuckle with which it was covered. Someone was drawing water and my teacher placed my hand under the spout. As the cool stream rushed over one hand she spelled into another the word W A T E R, first slowly, then rapidly. I stood still, my whole attention fixed upon the motion of her fingers. Suddenly, I felt a misty consciousness as of something forgotten—a thrill of returning thought: and somehow the mystery of language was revealed to me. I knew that W A T E R meant the wonderful cool something flowing over my hand. That living word awakened my soul; gave it light, hope, joy, set it free!! There were barriers still, it is true, but barriers that could in time be swept away. (Keller and Macy 1903)

We take this naming process for granted, but when there are barriers to this process, such as in Helen Keller's case, it is very difficult. Helen Keller overcame those barriers with the help of her teacher and later graduated from Radcliffe College in 1904. Notably, however, some children such as severely autistic kids have trouble focusing on an object with another person at the same time—that is, they have difficulty in joint attention with another person. This, in turn, affects their language acquisition and expression in interaction and has lasting effects throughout adulthood (Couch 1989; Mead 1934). Mind (i.e., the process of manipulating symbols) comes about only through interaction (Blumer 1969; Mead 1934; Meltzer 2003).

Words are symbols that denote the meaning of something else and are conveyed through writing, speaking, and signing. Words assign meaning to our experiences. Make a list of as many emotions as you can. Then read your list out loud to others. They should be able to understand them, such as the words *grief, happiness, embarrassment, jealousy, pity, sadness*, etc. Now select a word that is well understood by others around you. Attempt to communicate this emotion to someone next to you through direct physical contact. Do not use words. Select other emotions. Which ones can you successfully convey without words, and which ones need words for others to understand? It may be possible to convey anger or fright through touch, but how, for example, would you convey bitterness, jealousy, melancholy, or envy? Many emotions on your list convey a much wider range of emotion than you could communicate effectively without using words (O'Brien 2006). There are as many emotions as there are words to describe them, and as we shall see in the emotions chapter (Chapter 7), there are some different labels for distinct emotions across different cultures.

In addition, the meanings of words are not benign—they are often associated with additional ideas and experiences. For example, being left-handed used to be defined in Western cultures as not simply having more dexterity in the left hand than in the right but also as clumsy, tactless, awkward, and maladroit, while being right-handed was defined as being helpful, skillful, and reliable, in addition to using the right hand more easily than the left (see these associations in a wide range of languages). For example, many children as late as the 1960s were not allowed to write with their left hands in school in the United States. Indeed, the right side has been considered the good side in many practices and beliefs of many cultures (e.g., in Roman and Greek traditions, Jewish and Christian traditions). And consider these common expressions: "He's your right-hand man." "You have two left feet!" "That comment was out of left field."

Another example that meanings of words are not benign is seen in a story noted in Malcolm X's (1969) autobiography. A fellow prison inmate of Malcolm X showed him a dictionary of different meanings associated with terms *black* and *white*: black—opposite of white, dark-complexioned, without light, dark, dirty, evil, wicked, sad, dismal and sullen; white—having the color of pure snow or milk, pure, innocent, having a light-colored skin, and Caucasian. And what do we say people have when we think they are courageous or have guts? "They have balls!" But why not say, "They have ovaries!"

The second assumption that meanings of things are socially derived also implies that meanings of things are not fixed. Rather, they change through the course of interaction and over time. Through social interaction, meanings of things are negotiated—new meanings arise, old meanings are reaffirmed or change. How has our view of smoking cigarettes and marijuana changed over the past 70 years? How about adoption of children or our perceptions of divorce? In the scene mentioned previously with the Bushmen in the Kalahari Desert example, the empty glass Coke bottle was first assigned positive meanings through interaction as a useful tool and a musical instrument, but its meaning changed over time to the evil thing that created conflict. After all, the gods sent only one of them.

Finally, the third assumption of symbolic interaction is that *meanings of things are "handled in, and modified through, an interpretative process used by the person in dealing with the thing [s]he encounters"* (Blumer 1969:2). This means that the use of the meanings of things by an individual occurs through a process of interpretation (as mentioned earlier). In this process, the individual first indicates to himself the meaning of the thing, and then he "selects, checks, suspends, regroups, and transforms meanings in the light of the situation in which he is placed" (Blumer 1969:5). This means that the individual uses the meanings she has for things to guide and direct the action taken in the situation.

For example, the meaning we attribute to a particular odor depends on our interpretation of that odor in a particular context. If we "sense" an odor as foul smelling due to body sweat and we are in a gym or a locker room, for example, we typically find this acceptable because we associate body sweat with locker rooms. If we sense this same odor on someone on a first date, we may not be so forgiving and chalk it up to our date's lack of hygiene. This does not bode well for a second date in the future. You may love the smell of fresh-baked chocolate chip cookies because it reminds you of happy memories—for example, being young and after school coming home to fresh-baked cookies. This associative relationship between the odor of fresh-baked cookies and its source generates an interpretation of the odor—a loving sensation of that odor! Sensory judgments are associated with cultural values, and evaluative interpretation of odors depend on how we have learned to make sense of the odor within particular contexts (Waskul and Vannini 2008; see also Vannini, Waskul, and Gottschalk, 2013).

Summary

The symbolic interactionist perspective is a social constructionist argument, suggesting that individuals actively shape their reality through social interaction (Berger and Luckmann 1966). The beliefs we adopt about things around us create our own reality. In addition, it is important to understand people's interpretation of "things" in order to understand why they behave the way they do. Behavior is, in part, based on the definition of the situation. Whether people are interacting face-to-face or having an imagined dialogue in their heads, much of human behavior is directed toward understanding how to respond to others in specific contexts (Blumer 1969).

In quest of a clearer understanding of human behavior in social contexts, a key component of the research in symbolic interaction focuses on the development, maintenance, and negotiation of the self and identities in interaction (the topic of Chapter 4). To prepare for our discussion of identities, we will first examine how the social self emerges. The same kind of categorical thinking and knowledge is applied to the self as it is to the things external to the person (Hewitt 2003).

How Does the Social Self Emerge?

Do you remember what your parents said were your first words when you were a toddler? The first thing that children typically name is some object in the environment such as a ball, a cat, or a person, such as dada. It is never their own proper name, *me*, or *myself*. Why? Because during the period when they first learn significant symbols, children are not capable of seeing themselves as an object, separate from other objects—a requirement for the development of the social self. That is too complicated initially. Selfhood, in this case, is the awareness that one is separate from all other things and people. It is a process by which we see ourselves "from the outside"—that is, from other people's point of view.

How Do I "Know" Myself?

If every time you tell a joke no one laughs, will you think you are funny? Are you funny? If you want to be the next winner of *The Voice* because you feel that you are a talented singer but no one thinks you can sing, will you see yourself as a good singer? Or perhaps you are not a good singer, but others around you encourage you despite your lack of talent. Cathy has recently been listening to ukulele players at a local bar or restaurant at open mike night. Most of the musicians are talented ukulele players and decent singers. But one young man, although a solid ukulele player, simply does not sing well at all. But every time he sings several songs, the crowd applauds loudly. No one is going to tell him that he sings poorly. Needless to say, he must think he is a good singer indeed!

A sociologist who influenced Mead's work, Cooley (1902), suggested that a necessary way to know yourself is to see yourself in action and watch how other people react to your behavior. You see in their reactions the meaning of your behavior. You learn to take the perspective of others toward yourself. As you interact with others—particularly significant others who are close to you such as parents, caregivers, and siblings—you begin to see yourself from the viewpoint of others. Indeed, family members are often the child's most significant others (Cooley 1902; Erickson 2003). This process is called the **looking-glass self**: The reactions of others serve as mirrors in which people see and evaluate themselves, just as they see and evaluate other objects in their social environment. In Cooley's (1902) view, we imagine how our behavior appears to others, we imagine how others evaluate our behavior, and we feel pride or shame about others' evaluations of us. Based on our interpretation of others' reactions, we develop feelings and ideas about ourselves. Importantly, for a social self to emerge, it needs a mirror (other people) that reflects its image.

There are several important points thus far to note. First, *self-conception is a social process and arises in social interaction.* What makes us human depends on and is only achieved through interaction with others. For Cooley (1902), primary groups such as family, peers, and sometimes other groups such as religious groups are most important for the initial development of the self. Second, *self-conception is based on how we think others see us*, not on how they actually see us. In fact, we may be inaccurate about how we think others see us and misjudge others' perceptions, but we can only imagine ourselves as we imagine how others see us. We are sure you can think of a friend who seems totally clueless or is totally off the mark about how somebody else actually views him or her. Regardless, these inaccurate views influence a person's self-view.

Perceptions of how we think others see us are referred to as **reflected appraisals**, perceptions of how others actually see us are called **actual appraisals**, and perceptions of self are called **self-appraisals**. Empirical evidence shows that there is a moderate correlation between reflected appraisals and self-appraisals more so than between actual and self-appraisals (Felson 1985). Reflected appraisals are most important in the development of the self-concept when there are no clear criteria or objective feedback as a basis for self-views. For example, perceptions of one's own physical attractiveness or popularity are more likely to be influenced by how you think others view you (i.e., by reflected appraisals) than perception of oneself as a math student (grades and teacher evaluations provide tangible feedback) or as an athlete (performance and evaluations by coaches). As we shall see, reflected appraisals are important when we examine the development of racial identities in the next chapter.

Third, our *self-conception, although fairly stable, is also mutable—it can change over time.* How? New relationships (such as a romantic partner or mentor), new achievements (such as mastering a new sport), and new experiences (such as going into the Peace Corps) can change the way you view yourself. Also events, such as aging, illness, or social relocation, throughout one's life may reconstruct the self (Weigert and Gecas 2003). The genesis of an individual's self, then, continues throughout his or her lifetime. Karp, Holmstrom, and Gray (1998), for example, examine how college students' views of themselves change over time as they transition from the high school years through the college years. It is an important time period because individuals are going out on their own for the first time, leaving home. It is a time where many students leave their old-town identities behind to some extent and have a chance to reinvent themselves over time. College provides an opportunity to develop and enact new aspects of the self often consistent with the person they wish to become. How has the college experience or a new work experience changed your self-conception, if at all, so far?

How Do We Learn to Take the Perspective of Others?

Can you remember yourself as an infant? What are your first memories of yourself, and how old were you? Most likely, you are not able to remember any of your experiences before the age of 2 and, as mentioned previously, your first words were not *me* or *myself*. This is because you were not aware of being separate from others before this age. Therefore, you do not have any "thing" or "self" to hang your memories onto because it had not emerged by this time. This is not to say that you were not human before the age of 2 but rather your sense of the social self had not fully emerged.

Like Cooley, Mead (1934) recognized that you can acquire a sense of self only in interaction with others. Babies do not naturally develop into human adults without interaction (Couch 1989). Unfortunately, there are cases of extreme isolation of children where these children never completely developed because of the detrimental effects of long-term social isolation. For example, in one case a child, Anna, spent the first six months of her life in a children's home and then lived with her mother and grandfather in an abusive situation for 5.5 years. Anna was kept in an attic-like room, receiving very little attention and interaction, and survived on milk for 4 years. When she was found at age 6, she had little strength, could not speak, and had little affect (e.g., little expression of emotion, and did not smile or laugh). She received treatment and, over time, was able to attain the skills comparable to a 2.5-year-old mental level, before she died of a blood disorder at the age of 10 (Davis 1947).

In another famous case, in 1970 a 13-year-old girl, Genie, was discovered in California. She had been in isolation since the age of 2 by an abusive father and a mother who was also abused. Genie had been locked in a room, tied to a potty chair most of the time, and was rarely spoken to by anyone. She survived on baby food and cereal. When she was found, she could not speak or stand upright. She scored only as well as a 1-year-old on intelligence tests. Genie underwent intensive training at a children's hospital that continued with foster parents and scientists. Genie was able to learn some signs and acquire some speech, but it was very limited. Today, she lives in a residential home for adults and does not speak or sign. The story is more complicated than this, but suffice it to say, this extreme lack of interaction and human touch has devastating effects on the development of language and, in turn, on the emergence of self.

The self arises in interaction, and this emergence is dependent upon close contact. The longer the isolation, the more difficult it is to overcome the effects. Neurologists, for example, find that interactions with others (i.e., the sight, touch, smell, and intense involvement through language and eye contact) affect the number and sophistication of neuron links within the brain that, in turn, are the key to creativity and intelligence later in life (for an interesting discussion of the importance of maternal contact for associated behavioral and responses to stress in rat offspring, see Weaver et al. 2004, "Epigenetic Programming by Maternal Behavior"). In addition, the number of words an infant hears each day is one of the key predictors of competence and intelligence, along with emotional encouragement (Hart and Risley 1995). Human infants are very interested in people and their behaviors, and social interaction is key to activating children's ability to learn (Meltzoff et al. 2009). In addition to the experience of severe physical, emotional, and social neglect, Anna and Genie, no doubt, heard very few words as young children.

Most children, thankfully, do acquire a social self, and Mead provided more detail than Cooley about how this happens. Do infants blush? Do they get embarrassed? Do they feel shame or guilt? No, they do not. Why? What is necessary in order to feel embarrassment or guilt? To answer these questions, we take a look at Mead's stage approach—a contingency model in the sense that individuals must pass through one stage before going on to the next stage. Importantly, the key to his stages is the process of learning to role-take. **Role-taking** involves learning to adopt the perspective of others by imagining being in their position—that is, seeing yourself from another's perspective. We do this all the time as seen by the conversations we have in our heads. We anticipate another's response to our behavior, and then plan how we will respond to them. Infants, then, do not blush or feel embarrassment or guilt because they do not have a social self yet—they cannot take the perspective of another person at this point (Shott 1979). (We will discuss role-taking emotions, such as embarrassment and guilt, in Chapter 7.)

Before individuals can role-take, they must have learned to manipulate symbols (i.e., acquire the process of mind). During the first stage, the **preparatory stage**, children imitate behavior and gestures. At this point, they do not have a sense of self separate from others (i.e., the self is not yet an object), but they do begin to learn to use symbols as discussed previously. This ability to use symbols is necessary before moving into the **play stage**. In this stage, children learn to take the role of particular others. They pretend to take on the roles of particular people, either real or imagined, such as teacher, firefighter, mom, dad, baby, Supergirl, or Batman—that is, as Mead (1934) suggests, they play at being something like a mom or superhero. They try out different roles, one at a time, and learn the appearance and behaviors associated with each role (Stone 1981). In doing so, they try to enact the behaviors of that role, such as pretending to give communion in the role of priest. Or they may tie a towel around their shoulders in the form of a cape to become a superhero. For several years, Cathy's daughter, Ainura, pretended to be "Purple Power Supergirl" (with cape and accessories). She, too, remembers fondly her Superman cape, and of course being a captain of a submarine. (Of course, as we know from Edna in the *Incredibles* film, capes are no longer fashionable for superheroes.)

In the play stage, children also learn that a number of possible roles exist, yet they do not realize that roles are intertwined with other roles. For example, they do not understand that their father is also an uncle, a brother, a son, and a musician or that the mail carrier is also a mother and a softball player. Their play involves only a single role relationship like hide-and-seek. In this game, you only need to know who is *it* and who *is not it*. In general, children in this stage view their relationships from a "me" point of view as they relate to one other person. There is Mom and me, Dad and me, my sister and me, etc. Finally, kids in this stage have a difficult time keeping complex rules of games in their heads. Have you ever watched 3- and 4-year-olds play soccer? They have a really difficult time knowing which way to run, whom to kick the ball to, and even where their "team's" goal is located! Often they play in teams of three players to keep it simple, and even then it is often chaos but fun chaos nevertheless!

In the final stage, the **game stage**, children learn more complex role-taking abilities. Now they can imagine the roles of several people reacting toward them *at the same time*. They can imagine the viewpoints of several others at the same time. Mead (1934) provides the example of baseball, wherein in order to play, you have to keep in mind several different roles at once. Baseball, as well as many other games and activities like playing out relationships among characters on favorite TV shows, requires cooperation and coordinated action because the players have to assume the role of all the players at once. In addition, during the game stage, children are capable of learning the rules of complex games as a result of this complex role-taking. As well, they begin to understand that some roles are related to other roles and that the same person can be in many relationships at the same time. They also learn that there are categories for types of relationships in general, such as the father–daughter relationship, and that other people have these relationships too besides themselves. Cathy remembers discovering that her great aunt Edna was actually her dad's aunt. In effect, she learned a new category and relationship—the great aunt category and the great aunt–great niece relationship (Cathy was quite scared of her growing up until she was in her late teens!).

The final part of the game stage is the ability to role-take the perspective of the larger community, referred to as the **generalized other**. Here, children learn the expectations of social groups to which they belong (such as teams, neighborhoods, church groups) and eventually more abstract groups as well such as "society-at-large." Children begin to care about what *they* think and how *they* would view them if they engaged in a particular behavior. *They* refers to those groups that people belong to but also refers to a community of strangers that they do not know. For Mead, the generalized other serves as a form of self-control and ensures cooperation from society's members. The community exercises control over the conduct of individuals because we care what others think, even others that we do not know. Society gets in our heads—and here is the link between self and society. Self-criticism is really social criticism. And the experience of sympathy is possible only when we have learned to role-take; likewise, feelings of guilt, shame, and pride depend upon role-taking skills (Shott 1979). Little toddlers do not care what strangers think—that is, why they can have tantrums right in the middle of a store and roll around on the ground! They do not care, but most adults do care what strangers think. If adults did not care, interaction in public places would look very different. Adults have internalized the communal norms and values (the generalized other), which affects their behavior. Of course, children approaching 8 or 9, and then even more so in middle school, begin to really care what others think, particularly their peers (see Adler and Adler 1998). The generalized other is seeping in and continues as children grow.

Although Mead focused heavily on the socialized side of the self, he also claimed that there is a spontaneous and impulsive side of the self. He argued that the self is composed of two aspects: the **Me** and the **I**. The Me, based on the view of significant others and the generalized other, is a set of attitudes toward the self. It is the socialized side of the self—the part that takes into consideration the views of others and society. "What would they think of me!?" The I is the spontaneous, active, and sometimes impulsive side of the self. Have you ever said to yourself, "I can't believe I just did that!" The I and the Me have an internal dialogue with one another. For example, Cathy was at a church service a number of years ago sitting in one of the back rows, and a few church members were performing a short skit up near the alter. For some reason, unbeknownst to her, she laughed out loud at a line said by one of the performers. Unfortunately, she was the only one who laughed at this time, in an otherwise silent room of people. Everyone in the church turned around and looked at her. Me, the socialized side of herself, could reflect on what she (the I) had just done. The I and the Me allow for self-reflexivity— her Me looked back upon herself and reflected on what her I had just done. Poor her!

What Other Processes Are Involved in the Emergence of the Social Self?

The emergence of the self does not simply involve the reflected appraisals process. It is more complex, as noted by Cooley (1902; Weigert and Gecas 2003) and symbolic interactionists today. Although how we think others see us is important, we are also **active agents** in the development of our selves. We actively seek to understand and affirm who we think we are. For example, as we shall see in the next chapter, as boys and girls learn about their gender, they actively seek out what it means to be a boy or a girl (Cahill 1989).

In addition, **social comparison processes** are at play in the emergence and continued development of our social selves. Leon Festinger (1954:117), a central figure in social comparison processes, stated, "There exists, in the human organism, a drive to evaluate his opinions and abilities." Often, people draw upon social comparisons with others when they evaluate themselves in terms of their own abilities and opinions. **Social comparisons** are defined as "the process of thinking about information about one or more other people in relation to the self" (Wood 1996:520–21). According to the theory, people learn about and assess themselves through comparisons with other people, particularly when they cannot rely on objective measures in their self-evaluations. So, for example, an aspiring actress may try to assess her acting abilities by comparing her own abilities to those of other aspiring actresses around her.

Festinger's (1954) original theory focused on comparison of one's opinions and abilities. People also make social comparisons to evaluate their own emotions, personality traits, and self-concepts (Suls and Wheeler 2000). Two important questions that more recent social comparison theorists ask are the following: (1) What motivates us to make social comparisons with others besides self-evaluation? (2) What are some types of comparisons that people make?

Besides self-evaluation (the central motive in Festinger's [1954] theory), other motives for making social comparisons are to create a positive view of the self (i.e., self-enhance), to build self-esteem, and to improve oneself (Hogg 2000; Tajfel and Turner 1986; Wood 1989). Specifically, some research shows that individuals make **downward comparisons**, where they compare themselves to less fortunate others, for self-enhancement and self-esteem motivations. For example, a student may compare her SAT scores to students with lower scores to increase her self-esteem. In contrast, sometimes individuals make **upward comparisons**, where they compare themselves to someone deemed socially better in some way, for self-improvement. For example, an aspiring singer compares himself to professional singers as a way to motivate himself to improve his skills.

A relatively new development in social comparison theory is the differentiation between realistic and constructive social comparisons (Goethals and Klein 2000). **Realistic social comparisons** as self-evaluations are based on "actual information about social reality" (Goethals, Messick, and Allison 1991:154). That is, people compare themselves to real others (e.g., family members, friends, peers, coworkers) to evaluate themselves. In contrast, **constructive social comparisons** as self-evaluations are based on "'in-the-head' social comparisons based on guess, conjecture, and rationalization" about social reality (Goethals et al. 1991:154). In this case, individuals may ignore social reality and instead fabricate, make up, manufacture, and construct persons for comparison. For example, Wood, Kallgren, and Preisler (1985), in a study of social comparisons made by cancer patients, found that, at times, cancer patients invented comparison targets—that is, they compared themselves to cancer patients that they imagined as less fortunate to make themselves feel better about their situation. Sometimes people may use realistic social comparisons when they are seeking objective self-appraisal (e.g., to gauge class rank when deciding what colleges to apply to) and use constructive social comparisons for self-serving purposes (e.g., to maintain self-esteem; Goethals et al. 1991). There may be times, however, when people want an objective evaluation but use constructive evaluations to make that evaluation. This may be most likely when they do not have the real comparison data they need or when that information is too costly to obtain (Goethals and Klein 2000).

Finally, scholars study the association between downward and upward social comparisons and health outcomes such as anxiety and depressive symptoms, negative self-evaluations, and positive self-esteem (Steers, Wickham, and Acitelli 2014; Tesser, Millar, and Moore 2000). One study examined how a sample of college students may use social comparisons on Facebook, such as comparing the number of likes or comments other people have posted on their updates to those of their peers (Steers et al. 2014). People could also use others' updates to compare themselves to a friend's failing grade, acceptance into a prestigious college, new and exciting relationship, or received award. They found that students who spent a great deal of time on Facebook (including just viewing) were more likely to compare themselves to others and, in turn, experienced more depressive symptoms. Spending more time on Facebook on a daily basis may allow for more opportunity to make social comparisons to peers. Often people's status updates are positive, showing only an idealized view of the self and their experiences or activities. When people view these status updates, this may increase their negative feelings.

In addition to social comparisons, we can also come to know ourselves from our own accomplishments of our efforts. When we can master something or make something happen, referred to as **self-efficacy**, we feel a sense of control, and this, in turn, affects how we see ourselves (Gecas and Schwalbe 1983). Imagine a child who just learned to walk or built a large tower of blocks—it feels good! Of course, she still looks for others' positive responses and evaluations of her newly acquired skills. For example, after a child masters something like rolling a ball to another person, she waits for her audience to give her high praise for that glorious feat. People have different opportunities to acquire mastery depending on their circumstances—for example, some occupations allow for more flexibility in developing new abilities than other occupations (e.g., a trauma surgeon versus a coffee barista).

Once the self is formed, it is possible to resist others' evaluations because they conflict with our prior self-conception. We can also selectively choose with whom we hang out in order to manage conflicting evaluations from others. This strategy for the development and protection of the self is called **selective association**. Some gay and lesbian Christians, for example, actively select their audiences that they associate with in order to protect themselves from negative evaluations, either from conservative Christians or from non-Christian gay men and lesbians who feel negatively toward Christianity. (Also, see O'Brien [2004] for a discussion of how gay and lesbian individuals negotiate the conflict between Christianity and homosexuality.)

Finally, there is an extensive literature that examines **cross-cultural differences** in the conception of the self. Much of the research on the self has developed from and been applied to a Western notion of the self—that is, a self that is perceived as autonomous, independent, and bounded. This notion, however, is challenged by some cross-cultural research. For example, Luriia (1974), in a study of peasants in a remote area of Uzbekistan in the early 1930s, found that when the people were asked to describe themselves, they often provided events that had occurred in their lives, descriptions of their neighbors, and evaluations of the groups to which they belonged instead of a list of attributes or dispositions. Tellingly, they spoke about their evaluations of their groups in terms of "we" rather than "I."

In addition, Markus and Kitayama (1991) suggest that people in Asian cultures, such as in Japan, and those in Western cultures, such as in the United States, may hold different views of the self, others, and the interdependence of the two. An American view, for example, stresses, "the attending to the self, the appreciation of one's differences from others, and the importance of asserting the self" (Markus and Kitayama 1991:224). The Japanese, in contrast, emphasize, "attending to and fitting in with others and the importance of harmonious interdependence between them" (Markus and Kitayama 1991:224). The so-called Western view, referred to as the **independent self**, perceives the individual as independent, self-contained, and autonomous—one who comprises a unique set of traits, abilities, motives, and values as well as behaves primarily as a result of these internal attributes. People construe themselves as individuals whose behavior is made meaningful mainly by reference to one's own thoughts, feelings, and actions rather than by reference to the thoughts, feelings, and actions of others. This view is seeing the self as an autonomous, independent person. Others around us are important but primarily because they are sources that can verify and confirm our sense of self (i.e., reflected appraisals).

In contrast, the **interdependent self**, claimed to be exemplified in Asian, African, and Latin American cultures as well as in some southern European cultures, is characteristic of seeing oneself as part of ongoing social relationships. The emphasis is not on being distinctive from others but rather on how to fit in with other people and be connected in particular contexts, to fulfill and create obligations in relationships, and to become part of various interpersonal relationships in different social contexts. The self, then, is very context-dependent. The focus is not on the "inner self" but the relationships of the person to other actors (Esyun, Shumpei, and Creighton 1985; Markus and Kitayama 1991). Other actors are assigned much more importance and will carry more weight when one decides one's own behavior in social contexts.

These two construals of the self are illustrated with the following sayings. "In America, 'the squeaky wheel gets the grease.' In Japan, 'the nail that stands out gets pounded down'" (Markus and Kitayama 1991:224). Another illustration is found in a comparison between an American company and a Japanese supermarket. "A small Texas corporation seeking to elevate productivity told its employees to look in the mirror and say 'I am beautiful' 100 times before going into work each day. Employees of a Japanese supermarket that was recently opened in New Jersey were instructed to begin the day by holding hands and telling each other that 'he' or 'she is beautiful'" (Markus and Kitayama 1991:224). These cultural differences in how the self is construed are also seen in the meaning of words in different languages. For example, the word *wa* in Japanese means the harmonious ebb and flow of interpersonal relations; it is said that it is important not to disturb the *wa*. And according to Esyun and colleagues (1985), in Japan selfness is confirmed only through personal relationships and is seen as a fluid concept that can change through time and across situations according to these relationships.

In American culture, too, there are subcultures in which the theme of interdependence is central to how the self is construed (Markus and Kitayama 1991). For example, Quakers value and promote interdependence, as do many small towns or rural communities. And women may be more likely than men on average to lean toward the interdependent self, depending on their social group memberships. As we shall see in later chapters, these construals of the self sometimes have consequences for cognitive processes and behavior in social situations.

A fairly recent cross-cultural study compared the emotions experienced by a sample of college students in Japan and in the United States as they thought about a variety of daily life situations they have experienced (e.g., good interactions with family members, participation in a sports activity, class got canceled, took an exam, late for an appointment, argument with a friend, and skipped class) (Kitayama, Mesquita, and Karasawa 2006). The authors found that the American students experienced an individually oriented emotion, pride, more strongly in positive situations than the Japanese students, while the Japanese students felt more strongly with friendly feelings. American students also felt more strongly the individually oriented emotion, anger, in negative situations than the Japanese students. This study provides some evidence that cross-cultural differences in the conception of the self seem to also affect the intensity of reported emotions in positive and negative situations. Individuals with independent selves may experience more intensely individually oriented emotions such as anger, pride, and frustration, while individuals with interdependent selves may experience more intensely relationship-oriented emotions such as friendly feelings and sympathy. In Chapter 7, on emotions, we will discuss in detail how culture affects the experience and expression of emotions.

How Do We Present Our Selves to Others in Interaction?

What do professional wrestlers, presidents, and prostitutes all have in common? Erving Goffman (1959), a sociologist who was heavily influenced by social anthropologists, provides us with a particular answer. They all are like actors on the stage in a theater, attempting to manage particular impressions of themselves that they present to their audiences (another person or a group of people). All three categories, then, consist of people who work, both consciously and unconsciously, at their presentations of selves to others in face-to-face interaction (and in the media). Professional wrestlers manage their performances with great precision, and so do politicians and prostitutes. All are concerned, for example, about their dress and appearance, their use of body language, tone of voice, and their choice of words.

In fact, Goffman (1959) views all of us as impression managers who often use carefully calculated tactics designed to make a particular impression on others. For example, when we go for a job interview or on a first date, we are particularly concerned about how we come across to others. We often try to present a socially acceptable image to others, and in many situations, this entails being seen as likable and competent. Intentional use of tactics to manipulate the impression others form of us is called **impression management** (see also Chapter 5 on social cognition and the notion of emotion management in Chapter 7). When we use techniques of impression management, we are trying to influence the definition of the situation by attempting to control the information about ourselves that others have of us. Impression management involves the impressions given (i.e., the impressions we believe that we are giving) and the impressions given off (i.e., the impressions that others in the interaction have of us). Social interaction, then, is viewed as a kind of drama where we are, in a sense, giving a performance in front of an audience (another person such as a dating partner or potential coworkers at a job interview).

In order for the performance to occur, the actor prepares her **appearance** or her personal front (Goffman 1959). This may involve choice of clothes, grooming, habits like chewing gum, personal possessions displayed, accent, vocabulary, body movements, adornments, gestures, posture, and facial expressions, to name a few (remember the example regarding odor earlier in this chapter?). Through our appearance, we indicate the kind of person we are. Of course, appearance also includes, age, size, gender, and indicators of race and ethnicity, for example. The performer also may manipulate the **setting** in which the interaction is to take place. For example, if an actor is planning a party, he works on the scenery and props, such as decorations, food or drinks, and selection of music that will be used by his audience at the party to convey a particular impression and mood. Think of a dentist's office. What are the props and scenery used to convey competence? Finally, the performance involves the **manner/demeanor** adopted by the actor such as one of deference, assertiveness, politeness, or aggressiveness. All three elements are used to create the desired image and definition of the situation. Goffman suggests that in performances actors tend to present idealized versions of themselves and underplay those aspects of self that appear incompatible with that version.

Besides manipulating appearance, setting, and demeanor, people may also use **ingratiation tactics** to give off a particular impression—that is, use tactics to get someone to like them. For example, they may pretend to share the other person's views on issues even though they privately disagree. Or they may use flattery in order to enter into the good graces of their audience. Finally, they may exaggerate their own admirable qualities or, in contrast, "play dumb." For example, Orenstein (2000) found that many girls believed that boys like it when they act helpless. Cathy remembers her mother always telling her to let the boy win when she played games or sports. She happened to be pretty good at pool because she had a pool table in the basement, and her dad and she would often play after dinner. When she invited her first "boyfriend," Steve, over, of course, they played pool. Following her mom's sage advice, she let him win—over and over again. Weeks passed, and one day Steve and Cathy went over to her friend Terry's house who had a pool table. They played teams: Steve and Cathy against Terry and her boyfriend. Cathy completely forgot about letting Steve win, and instead, she played pool as she usually did. Needless to say, Steve was dumbfounded. She was caught in her own performance. The good news was that Steve couldn't have cared less that she could beat him in pool!

In the previously given example, Cathy felt very embarrassed because her whole performance had been disrupted! Goffman (1959) identified the fragile nature of performances and the embarrassment or shame actors feel when their performances are disrupted. He noted that it takes very little to throw off a performance, such as the young teenager who acts "cool" and then trips. Goffman said that actors **lose face** when they fail to give off the desired impression. When performances are thrown off or interrupted, we try to **save face** (Goffman 1969). For example, we may give accounts of why the performance is thrown off. For example, Cathy told Steve that her mom told her to let him win! Blame Mom! Goffman stated that we may use **defensive practices** such as apologies or excuses, as in the previously given example. As well, the audience often can help the actor out by using **protective practices**. For example, they may ignore the performance altogether (e.g., by not mentioning that one's pants zipper is unzipped during a lecture) or use some kind of tact in the situation to let the actor off the hook. They may also simply forgive the actor for her transgressions. The audience's support for an actor's performance is somewhat self-serving because helping others to save face also makes interaction easier to maintain for the actor and the audience. If we, as the audience, help others to save face, they are more likely to help us when we need support in interaction.

Many performances and their preparation require regions, or places set off in some degree by barriers of perception. The front region, or *front stage*, is where the actors present their performance for the intended audience, such as a living room for a party, a sanctuary of a church for a wedding, or a seating area of a restaurant for dining. In contrast, the back region, or *back stage*, is where the actors prepare, rehearse, and rehash performances. This stage is off-limits to the audience, such as a kitchen of a restaurant, or boardrooms of a corporation. Some spaces can be both front and back stages but at different times, such as a living room for a party. You can see the wonderful putting on and taking off of character as you watch waitpersons go through the kitchen doors of a restaurant. Sometimes back stages are exposed, such as when political or religious scandals are revealed to the audiences.

Much of our interaction with others does have some element of performance. For example, think of the performance of self that takes place in job interviews. We are very conscious of what impressions we give off to others, particularly in situations where we do not know the audience well yet want to make a good impression.

Segue: The Symbolic Interaction Approach and Identity Processes

Symbolic interactionists recognize the importance of learning symbols— language and other means of communication through interaction with others. In this interaction, we engage in the process of naming. In doing so, we approach our world as a set of categories of things. We learn what sorts of things are similar to each other such as flowers, animals, foods, holidays, days or months, and rituals. Importantly, we learn to refer to ourselves in terms of these categories, giving us a social self.

In the next chapter, we continue to draw upon the symbolic interactionist perspective to explore how people categorize themselves and others based on all types of characteristics such as race, ethnicity, age, social class, as well as physical appearance and types of qualities such as being fat, lazy, good-natured, and tenacious. Specifically, we address two more fundamental questions of symbolic interaction: (1) How do individuals socially construct their own identities? (2) And, in turn, how do these identities affect social interaction?

Suggested Readings

Chan, Cheris Shun-ching. 2013. "Doing Ideology Amid a Crisis: Collective Actions and Discourses of the Chinese Falun Gong Movement." *Social Psychology Quarterly* 76(1):1–24.

de Waal, Frans B. M. 2005. "A Century of Getting to Know the Chimpanzee." *Nature* 437:56–59.

Lin, Chun-Chi, and Susumu Yamaguchi. 2011. "Effects of Face Experience on Emotions and Self-Esteem in Japanese Culture." *European Journal of Social Psychology* 41(4):446–55.

Peräkylä, Anssi. 2015. "From Narcissism to Face Work: Two Views on the Self in Social Interaction." *American Journal of Sociology* 121(2):445–74.

Stroebaek, Pernille S. 2013. "Let's Have a Cup of Coffee! Coffee and Coping Communities at Work." *Symbolic Interaction* 36(4):381–97.

Ueno, Koji, and Haley Gentile. 2015. "Moral Identity in Friendships between Gay, Lesbian, and Bisexual Students and Straight Students in College." *Symbolic Interaction* 38(1):83–102.

Wei, Junhow. 2016. "'I'm the Next American Idol': Cooling Out, Accounts, and Perseverance at Reality Talent Show Auditions." *Symbolic Interaction* 39(1):3–25.

References

Adler, Patricia A., and Peter Adler. 1998. *Peer Power: Preadolescent Culture and Identity*. New Brunswick, NJ: Rutgers University Press.

Berger, Peter L., and Thomas Luckmann. 1966. *The Social Construction of Reality*. New York: Doubleday.

Blumer, Herbert. 1969. *Symbolic Interactionism: Perspective and Method*. Berkeley: University of California Press.

Cahill, Spencer. 1989. "Fashioning Males and Females: Appearance Management and the Social Reproduction of Gender." *Symbolic Interaction* 12:281–98. doi:10.1525/si.1989.12.2.281

Cooley, Charles H. 1902. *Human Nature and the Social Order*. New York: Scribner's.

Couch, Carl J. 1989. *Social Processes and Personal Relationships*. Dix Hills, NY: General Hall.

Davis, Kingsley. 1947. "Final Note on a Case of Extreme Isolation." *American Journal of Sociology* 52(5):432–37. doi:10.1086/220036

Ekirch, A. R. 2001. "Sleep We Have Lost: Pre-industrial Slumber in the British Isles." *The American Historical Review* 106(2):343–86. doi:10.2307/2651611

Ekirch, A. Roger. 2006. *At Day's Close: Night in Times Past*. New York: W. W. Norton.

Erickson, Rebecca J. 2003. "The Familial Institution." Pp. 511–38 in *Handbook of Symbolic Interactionism*, edited by L. J. Reynolds and N. J. Herman. Walnut Creek, CA: AltaMira.

Esyun, Hamaguchi, Kumon Shumpei, and Mildred R. Creighton. 1985. "A Contextual Model of the Japanese: Toward a Methodological Innovation in Japan Studies." *Journal of Japanese Studies* 11:289–321. doi:10.2307/132562

Felson, Richard B. 1985. "Reflected Appraisal and the Development of Self." *Social Psychology Quarterly* 48(1):71–8.

Festinger, Leon. 1954. "A Theory of Social Comparison Processes." *Human Relations* 7:117–40. doi:10.1177/001872675400700202

Flaherty, Michael G. 1999. *A Watched Pot: How We Experience Time*. New York: New York University Press.

Gecas, Viktor, and Michael L. Schwalbe. 1983. "Beyond the Looking-glass Self: Social Structure and Efficacy-based Self-esteem." *Social Psychology Quarterly* 46:77–88. doi:10.2307/3033844

Glynn, Mary A. 2002. "The Emergent Organization: Communication as Its Site and Surface." *Administrative Science Quarterly* 47:169–72. doi:10.2307/3094898

Goethals, George R., and William P. Klein. 2000. "Interpreting and Inventing Social Reality: Attributional and Constructive Elements in Social Comparison." Pp. 23–44 in *Handbook of Social Comparison: Theory and Research*, edited by J. Suls and L. Wheeler. New York: Kluwer. doi:10.1007/978-1-4615-4237-7_2

Goethals, George R., David M. Messick, and Scott T. Allison. 1991. "The Uniqueness Bias: Studies of Constructive Social Comparison." Pp. 149–73 in *Social Comparison, Contemporary Theory and Research*, edited by J. M. Suls and T. A. Wills. Hillsdale, NJ: Erlbaum.

Goffman, Erving. 1959. *The Presentation of Self in Everyday Life*. Garden City, NJ: Doubleday Anchor.

Goffman, Erving. 1969. *The Presentation of Self in Everyday Life*. New York: Doubleday Anchor.

Hart, Betty, and Todd R. Risley. 1995. *Meaningful Differences in the Everyday Experience of Young American Children*. Baltimore, MD: Brookes.

Hewitt, John P. 2003. "Symbols, Objects, and Meanings." Pp. 307–48 in *Handbook of Symbolic Interactionism*, edited by L. T. Reynolds and N. J. Herman-Kinney. Lanham, MD: Rowman & Littlefield.

Hogg, Michael A. 2000. "Social Identity and Social Comparison." Pp. 401–21 in *Handbook of Social Comparison: Theory and Research*, edited by J. Suls and L. Wheeler. New York: Kluwer. doi:10.1007/978-1-4615-4237-7_19

Isaacson, Betsy. 2015. "Our Sleep Problems and What to Do About It." *Newsweek*, January 30.

Karp, David, Lynda L. Holmstrom, and Paul S. Gray. 1998. "Leaving Home for College: Expectations for Selective Reconstruction of Self." *Symbolic Interaction* 21(2):53–76.

Keller, Helen, and John A. Macy. 1903. *The Story of My Life*. New York: Doubleday.

Kim, Uichol, Young-Shin Park, and Donghyun Park. 2000. "The Challenge of Cross-cultural Psychology: The Role of Indigenous Psychologies." *Journal of Cross-Cultural Psychology* 31:63–75. doi:10.1177/0022022100031001006

Kitayama, Shinobu, Batia Mesquita, and Mayumi Karasawa. 2006. "Cultural Affordances and Emotional Experience: Socially Engaging and Disengaging Emotions in Japan and the United States." *Journal of Personality and Social Psychology* 91(5):890–903. doi:10.1037/0022-3514.91.5.890

Luriia, Alexander R. 1974. *Ob Istoricheskom Razvitii Poznavatel' Nykh Protsessov*. Moscow: Nauka.

Malcolm X. 1969. *The Autobiography of Malcolm X*. New York: Random House.

Markus, Hazel R., and Shinobu Kitayama. 1991. "Culture and the Self: Implications for Cognition, Emotion, and Motivation." *Psychological Review* 98:224–53. doi:10.1037/0033-295X.98.2.224

Mead, George H. 1934. *Mind, Self, and Society: From the Standpoint of a Social Behaviorist*, edited by C. W. Morris. Chicago: University of Chicago Press.

Meltzer, Bernard N. 2003. "Mind." Pp. 253–66 in *Handbook of Symbolic Interactionism*, edited by L. J. Reynolds and N. J. Herman. Walnut Creek, CA: AltaMira.

Meltzoff, Andrew N., Patricia K. Kukhl, Javier Movellan, and Terrence J. Sejnowski. 2009. "Foundations for a New Science of Learning." *Science* 325(5938):284–88. doi:10.1126/science.1175626

Milner, Catherine E., and Kimberly A. Cote. 2009. "Benefits of Napping in Healthy Adults: Impact of Nap Length, Time of Day, Age, and

Experience with Napping." *Journal of Sleep Research* 18(2):272–81. doi:10.1111/j.1365–2869.2008.00718.x

O'Brien, Jodi A. 2004. "Wrestling the Angel of Contradiction: Queer Christian Identities." *Culture and Religion* 5(2):179–202. doi:10.1080/143830042000225420

O'Brien, Jodi A. 2006. *The Production of Reality: Essays and Readings on Social Interaction.* 4th ed. Thousand Oaks, CA: Pine Forge Press.

Orenstein, Peggy. 2000. *Flux: Women on Sex, Work, Kids, Love, and Life in a Half-changed World.* New York: Doubleday.

Randall, David. 2012. "Rethinking Sleep." *New York Times*, September 23, p. SR1.

Shott, Susan. 1979. "Emotion and Social Life: A Symbolic Interactionist Analysis." *American Journal of Sociology* 84:1317–34. doi:10.1086/226936

Steers, Mai-Ly N., Robert E. Wickham, and Linda K. Acitelli. 2014. "Seeing Everyone Else's Highlight Reels: How Facebook Usage Is Linked to Depressive Symptoms." *Journal of Social and Clinical Psychology* 33(8):701–31. doi:10.1521/jscp.2014.33.8.701

Stone, Gregory P. 1981. "Appearance and the Self: A Slightly Revised Version." Pp. 187–202 in *Social Psychology through Symbolic Interaction*, 2nd ed., edited by Gregory P. Stone and Harvey A. Farberman. New York: Macmillan.

Strauss, Anselm L. 1978. *Negotiations: Varieties, Contexts, Processes, and Social Order.* San Francisco, CA: Jossey-Bass.

Suls, Jerry, and Ladd Wheeler, eds. 2000. *Handbook of Social Comparison: Theory and Research.* New York: Kluwer. doi:10.1007/978–1–4615–4237–7

Tajfel, Henri, and Turner, John C. 1986. "The Social Identity Theory of Intergroup Behavior." Pp. 7–24 in *The Psychology of Intergroup Relations*, edited by S. Worchel and W. G. Austin. Chicago: Nelson-Hall.

Tesser, Abraham, Murray Millar, and Janet Moore. 2000. "Some Affective Consequences of Social Comparison and Reflection Processes:

The Pain and Pleasure of Being Close." Pp. 60–75 in *Motivational Science: Social and Personality Perspectives*, edited by E. T. Higgins and A. W. Kruglanski. New York: Psychology Press.

Uys, Jamie [Director]. 1980. *The Gods Must Be Crazy.* DVD. Retrieved February 12, 2016 (http://repositori.filmoteca.cat/handle/11091/1763).

Vannini, Phillip, Dennis Waskul, and Simon Gottschalk. 2013. *The Senses in Self, Society, and Culture: A Sociology of the Senses.* New York: Routledge.

Waskul, Dennis D., and Phillip Vannini. 2008. "Smell, Odor, and Somatic Work: Sense-Making and Sensory Management." *Social Psychology Quarterly* 71(1):53–71. doi:10.1177/019027250807100107

Weaver, Ian C. G., Nadia Cervoni, Frances A. Champagne, Ana C. D'Alessio, Shakti Sharma, Jonathan R. Seckl, Sergiy Dymov, Moshe Szyf, and Michael J. Meaney. 2004. "Epigenetic Programming by Maternal Behavior." *Nature Neuroscience* 7:847–54. doi:10.1038/nn1276

Wehr, Thomas A. 1992. "In Short Photoperiods, Human Sleep Is Biphasic." *Journal of Sleep Research* 1(2):103–7. doi:10.1111/j.1365–2869.1992.tb00019.x

Weigert, Andrew J., and Viktor Gecas. 2003. "Self." Pp. 267–88 in *Handbook of Symbolic Interactionism*, edited by L. J. Reynolds and N. J. Herman. Walnut Creek, CA: AltaMira.

Wood, Joanne V. 1989. "Theory and Research Concerning Social Comparisons of Personal Attributes." *Psychological Bulletin* 106:231–48. doi:10.1037/0033–2909.106.2.231

Wood, Joanne V. 1996. "What Is Social Comparison and How Should We Study It?" *Personality and Social Psychology Bulletin* 22:520–37. doi:10.1177/0146167296225009

Wood, Wendy, Carl A. Kallgren, and Rebecca M. Preisler. 1985. "Access to Attitude-Relevant Information in Memory as a Determinant of Persuasion: The Role of Message Attributes." *Journal of Experimental Social Psychology* 21:73–85. doi:10.1016/0022–1031(85)90007–1

Identity Processes

An old custom in rural northern Albania, in existence for over 500 years, allowed a woman to "become" the "man" of the family. This swapping of genders was considered appropriate because it was a way of addressing the shortage of men due to their deaths from blood feuds and wars. As a result of these deaths, many clans were without male heirs to rule the family. This custom, orally handed down, allowed certain women to become the head of the family and live as men—although they also had to take a vow of lifetime virginity. These sworn virgins kept their "female" names but dressed like men, cut their hair short, and sat and drank like men and were given the same authority and obligations as men (e.g., the obligation to avenge deaths of family members). Until fairly recently, the role of women in rural northern Albania was extremely limited to taking care of children and the home. Not surprisingly, women also were considered much less valuable than men. Sworn virgins, in contrast, were given all the privileges of men such as the right to own property, carry a weapon, move freely about, pray with the men at the mosque, and make decisions for their clan members. As one woman stated, "Back then, it was better to be a man because before a woman and an animal were considered the same thing." These women did not undergo any sex-change surgeries—that is an entirely different situation than this custom. Instead, they "became men" in order to support their clan members, particularly their female members who would have been stigmatized if they did not have a "man" as head of their family. These women were accepted in public, socializing with other men, and were often adulated. Approximately 40 sworn virgins still remain. Today, there is more gender equality in Albania, and female-headed households are less stigmatized; hence, this custom is fading because it is no longer necessary (Bilefsky 2008).

This story provides a good illustration of how we, as humans, actively construct our social realities and identities within particular contexts. In this case in rural northern Albania, women had the opportunity to "become men" as a result of war and feuds and the meanings of being men and women in this society. As they took on this role as "man" (and head) of the family, they changed how they appeared to and behaved toward others. Also, their position of power changed, granting them the same rights and resources as men. This story also highlights the idea that how we view ourselves and how others view us is a fluid and flexible process, and these views often affect how we behave with others in everyday interaction. And this story compels us to ask the following questions: How do individuals socially construct their identities? How do individuals' identities affect the choices they make and their interaction with others? In this chapter, we continue to draw upon the symbolic interactionist perspective to understand how individuals form and negotiate their identities in an ever-changing social world.

How Do Individuals Socially Construct Their Identities?

On a sheet of paper, answer the following question: Who am I? Respond as if you are giving the answer to yourself and not to someone else. List anything that comes to mind. Now list the most important descriptions that you have listed about yourself. Have any of these descriptions of who you are changed over time? If so, how and why?

Who Do You Say You Are?

Often, this "Who am I?" activity is administered by asking individuals to answer this question 20 times using a paper with 20 empty lines. It is referred to as the Twenty Statements Test (TST), developed by Kuhn and McPartland (1954). Typically, people's responses to this question can be categorized into four groups: (1) **physical characteristics** (e.g., I have brown hair and a big nose; I am tattooed); (2) **social roles or group memberships** (e.g., I am a sister, son, Catholic, friend, soccer player, woman, Haitian); (3) **personal qualities, attributes, feelings, or self-evaluations** (e.g., I am shy, creative, ambitious, sensitive, happy, boring); and (4) **some general or holistic description of self** (e.g., I am one with the universe). Review each of your responses and try to place them into these categories.

Interestingly, there are some cross-cultural differences in responses to the "Who am I?" test. Individuals with a more interdependent self may be more sensitive to the social context, aware of others' constraints on their behavior, and more conscious of how they fit into the set of relationships in that context than individuals with an independent self (Kanagawa, Cross, and Markus 2001). As discussed in Chapter 3, the interdependent self is characteristic of seeing oneself as part of ongoing relationships and is often seen as exemplified in Asian, as well as other, cultures; the independent self, the so-called Western view, is characterized as seeing oneself primarily as an autonomous independent person.

In a study by Kanagawa et al. (2001), a sample of Japanese and American students were asked to answer the question "Who am I?" and randomly assigned into four different contexts. In the first condition, the students answered this question in the experimenter's office (authority condition), where the experimenter was one of the professors who conducted this study. In the second condition, they completed the TST in a small room and the instructions for the "Who am I?" question were provided by audiotape (solitary condition). In the third condition, they completed the task in groups of 20 to 50 other students (group condition). In the fourth condition, they were paired with another student to complete the task, and one student was randomly chosen in each pair to serve as the experimenter who would pose the "Who are you?" questions to their partners (peer condition). In the authority, group, and peer conditions, the experimenter was not able to read the participants' responses.

Japanese self-descriptions varied across situations more than the American self-descriptions, although the American students, on average, did show some sensitivity to the type of situation. The Japanese students, on average, tended to write less about their psychological attributes and more about the immediate situation in the peer condition than in the other conditions. In addition, they described them-selves more negatively in the authority condition with a faculty member than in the other conditions and described their abilities more in the solitary condition than in the other conditions. The Americans also varied in the responses across conditions but not to the same extent. In the authority condition, for example, they described themselves in terms of their goals and aspirations more often than in the group condition. The authors concluded that individuals with interdependent selves (i.e., Japanese) were more likely to consider the context when asked the "Who am I?" question than individuals with independent selves (more so the Americans) (Kanagawa et al. 2001).

What Are Identities?

The responses that you give on the TST often reflect the identities you hold. **Identities** are defined as self-definitions that represent the various meanings attached to oneself by self and by others (Gecas and Burke 1995). Identities are also "internalized role expectations" (Stryker and Burke 2000:286–87). The mean-ings of identities are derived from existing social roles (e.g., student, surgeon, uncle), social categories (e.g., racial, gender, nationality), group memberships (e.g., Catholic, soccer player), or personal qualities or attributes (e.g., competent, moral; also referred to as person identities) (Burke and Stets 2009; Gecas and Burke 1995). The meanings of identities are also derived from the social roles that individuals are *not* associated with, called counter roles (Stryker and Burke 2000). For example, the meanings associated with being a Democrat develop not only from specific beliefs and behaviors that are associated with this political orienta-tion but also through the meanings of the counter role of Republican.

Usually, we can place our set of identities into a hierarchy of importance to us, referred to as an **identity salience hierarchy** (Stryker 1980). For example, iden-tifying as a professor, mother, partner, friend, science fiction lover, and as reli-gious are more important to Cathy than identifying as a volunteer at her child's school or a tennis player. In addition, we have some identities that are more often invoked or called upon in our everyday interactions than others. Cathy enacts her partner, professor, friend, and mother identities more often on a regular basis than other identities she holds. Also, identities have assigned meanings attached to them, and these meanings can change over time. For example, what it means to be a father today is different from what it meant to be a father 50 and 100 years ago in the United States. Today, fathers have more responsibility for child care, for example, although there is still a gender gap in the division of labor in the home (Hochschild 1983; Wharton 2011). Also, 30 years ago, the concept of a U.S. Supreme Court justice implied a man, but today this association has relaxed some-what, where people can also imagine a woman in this position (Smith-Lovin 2007; and thanks to having three women justices currently on the Supreme Court!).

As well, identities and their meanings are historically and culturally specific. For example, the meaning of being gay or lesbian varies dramatically in different cultures (compare Sweden, the United States, Russia, China, and Iran, for exam-ple). Also, the meaning of same-sex marriage, and marriage in general, in the United States (and a number of other countries, such as Brazil and Argentina) has changed dramatically over time. Although the movement to obtain civil marriage rights and benefits for same-sex couples began in the 1970s in the United States, it was not until 2003 that Massachusetts issued marriage licenses to same-sex couples—the first state to do so. Between early 2003 and the summer of 2015, through state legislation, lower court decisions, and popular referendums, 37 states (and Guam and District of Columbia) had legalized same-sex marriage to some degree. In 2012, the U.S. Supreme Court, in *Windsor v. United States*, ruled that Section 3 of the Defense of Marriage Act (DOMA) that defined marriage as a union of one man and one woman for purposes of the federal law violated the Fifth Amendment. And on June 26, 2015, the U.S. Supreme Court ruled in *Obergefell v. Hodges* that denial of marriage licenses to same-sex couples is in violation of two clauses of the Fourteenth Amendment of the U.S. Constitution. As a result, all 50 states (and U.S. territories and the District of Columbia) must now recognize all same-sex marriages in any state. The United States is the 21st country to legalize same-sex marriage. These rulings have enormous implications for the meaning of marriage and for the everyday lives of millions of same-sex couples and the lesbian, gay, bisexual, and transgender (LGBT) community at large.

Identities, then, according to symbolic interactionists, are socially constructed. We assign meanings to these identities, and these identities are accomplished and revised in social contexts, as we shall see.

On the "Who am I?" test, did you put down that you are a woman or a man? Did you put down anything about your race, ethnicity, or nationality? How about if you are heterosexual? LGBTQ? Able-bodied? Did you have anything about your social class? Many people in the United States who are white, heterosexual, or middle- or upper class do not list these descriptions. On the other hand, gay men and lesbians, and persons of color, for example, are more likely to list these categories when they describe themselves. Why is this so?

Identities and their associated meanings are not only personal (e.g., I'm a good daughter) but they are also tied to the larger social structure—that is, they are tied to the already existing economic, political, occupational, religious, as well as race and gender constructions (Smith-Lovin 2007; Stryker 1980). For example, there are already existing belief systems that prescribe what a good daughter is and should do, based on gender, the occupational structure, family dynamics, as well as possible other belief systems such as religious and racially based systems. In addition, we doubt that you made up any identity on your own. Meanings of your identities have already been constructed (but they can change over time as previously mentioned) and are already available as a result of the social structure. Mead (1934) and Cooley (1902) recognized that society is not a blank slate but rather a complex of constructs and histories that shape, though not completely determine, our experiences in interaction (Stewart 2003). Some identities have more specific meanings than others—such as gardener versus father.

Getting back to our question of why individuals who are white, heterosexual, or middle- or upper class in the United States may not list these descriptions—individuals who identify with categories or roles that are less highly valued in the larger society and have fewer resources or less power are much more aware of their identities than those who are in powerful positions within the larger society. For example, if you are heterosexual, you most likely are not thinking about it much because it is assumed that people, in general, are heterosexual. It is the common category—the status quo. But if you are gay or lesbian in American society, up until June 2015 you were not in a position to take your rights for granted. Even now, there is no federal law that prohibits discrimination against members of the LGBTQ community in terms of employment, housing, or public accommodations. As well, if you are white in American society and a U.S. citizen, you might not be thinking as much about race or ethnicity, compared to individuals who are black, Hispanic, Native American, Asian, or recent immigrants. Whites continue to hold the most resources and wealth, on average, in the United States and hold the most economic and political power. As we shall see, what identities are important to us and others around us depends on the historical and cultural context in which we live.

How Do Identities Form, and How Do We "Do" Identities?

In order to illustrate how identities form and how we play them out in interaction, we discuss three identities: (1) gender identity, (2) racial and ethnic identity, and (3) cyberspace identities.

Gender Identity

Imagine that you see a person walking down the street, but you are not sure if this person is a man or a woman. What do you do? Most of us cannot help but try to figure it out. We look for cues in the person's appearance such as clothing, hairstyle, and facial hair. We also look at the body language and mannerisms such as the way the person is standing, gesturing, sitting, walking, or interacting with others (and if we are close enough, their tone of voice). When these cues fail us, we really are not sure what to do. It is similar to the old skit about Pat on *Saturday Night Live*. Is Pat a woman or a man? We cannot tell. But why do we care in the first place? Does it really matter what gender a person is? One reason we strive to know someone's gender is that we think this information will help us know how to interact with him or her. This reduces our uncertainty, making the interaction more smooth and predictable.

Indeed, gender is a fundamental aspect of the self and exists in relationships with other people and in their interactions. It is also one of the most common responses on the TST (Howard and Hollander 1997; Stewart 2003). Specifically, **gender** refers to what it means to be a woman or girl or a man or boy in terms of the "appropriate" and expected behaviors and characteristics assigned to each category. Symbolic interactionists argue that, just as with all objects, gender is socially constructed. We assign what it means to be a woman or girl or a man or boy, and it is accomplished in social contexts in everyday interaction (West and Zimmerman 1977). Children learn these meanings as they grow up through interaction with others. They carefully observe others in regard to their appearance, body language, and their actions. Young children do not differentiate men from women and boys from girls through anatomical characteristics. Rather, they learn these categories through appearance such as hairstyle, clothing, and decorations on the body (Cahill 1989). For example, they may associate a beard with a man and a ponytail with a woman.

Children also learn the appropriate behaviors, appearances, social skills, and characteristics associated with being a boy or a girl in different contexts. They learn these things from parents, teachers, siblings, relatives, caretakers, peers, and through the media. For example, children learn how to present themselves in how they walk, the looks they give, the way they cross their legs, how they stand, and the makeup they do or do not wear. Girls learn how to tilt their heads and sway their backs as seen in movies, magazines, and TV shows; Goffman 1976). They learn what is appropriate to wear and not to wear as well as how to act (Couch 1989). That is, they learn how to "do" gender in different settings (West and Zimmerman 1977). They learn the "right" toys, hairstyles, colors, bodily movements, volume of voice, and interests for their gender (Cahill 1989; Stone 1962). What is inherently "girlish" about the color pink? Nothing, but we have associated pink with femininity. Venture into a toy store lately? The meanings associated with the genders are strikingly evident in toy stores (pink-and-blue packaging) as well as girls' and boys' clothing sections in department stores. Even birthday cards are distinguished for boys and girls—boys are supposed to receive cards with bold colors and with characters and things that only boys should appreciate (e.g., superheroes, trucks, and trains); girls are supposed to receive cards with pastel colors and "girl" interests (e.g., princesses, ponies, and flowers). (Target recently moved away from gender-based signs in their toys and home and entertainment sections. And they removed the use of pink, blue, yellow, or green paper on their back walls of their shelves. Labels make a difference.)

As they learn these gendered meanings, children are very aware of the reactions of others as they negotiate gendered meanings in interaction. In fact, it is difficult to escape others' reactions (both negative and positive) because they have a powerful effect on how they feel and view themselves as boys or girls and how they behave. You can imagine the brutal reactions of children toward boys, for example, who play dress-up after a certain age. Things have changed a bit, however. Although parents in a U.S. sample still responded negatively to the possibility of their toddler sons playing with "feminine" toys, such as Barbie, skirts, tights, frilly clothing, or nail polish, they were more comfortable with the idea of playing with toys tied to caregiving and family activities, such as doll houses, tea sets, and play kitchens (Kane 2006; Kroska 2014).

Girls and boys, however, are not passive learners. Children learn by doing (Corsaro 1992). They actively participate in the negotiation of what it means to be a boy or a girl and also engage in their own meaning-making (Cahill 1986, 1987, 1989; Denzin 1977; Stewart 2003). They also develop and test different strategies to use in order to align their actions with adults and other children. For example, Thorne (1993) reveals how gender identity is negotiated in her study of playground behavior of elementary school girls and boys. She showed how these children, "construct 'the girls' and 'the boys' as boundaried and rival groups through practices that uphold a sense of gender as an oppositional dichotomy" (Thorne 1993:158). That is, they create boundaries between each other in their interactions such as creating competitions in the classroom or on the playground between each other (girls against the boys). They also participate in cross-gender chasing, such as in girls-chase-the-boys where, again, they become separate teams. In addition, however, sometimes certain practices can neutralize or even challenge the significance of gender. For example, boys would join the girls in jump rope or other activities, and girls would join boys in their games (often, however, on the periphery of the game).

Importantly, and alluded to previously, the enactment and construction of gender depend on the context. Girls playing with boys, on average, are more passive (e.g., more hesitant to grab the toys) than girls playing with other girls. Is passivity a trait of girls? No, because if it were, girls would be passive across contexts (Maccoby 1990). We will see in later in Chapters 8 and 9 that many "gender differences" in behavior are more a result of the context and depend on other characteristics of the situation such as the differences in power (i.e., who gets their way despite resistance from others) and status (i.e., who is thought to be worthy and highly valued) among individuals in particular contexts.

As children seek out what it means to be a girl and a boy, they form a gender identity—a self-definition of being a woman or girl or a man or boy that represents the various meanings attached to oneself by self and by others in regard to gender. As children's gender identities form, they learn two important social constructs: (1) **femininity** and (2) **masculinity**. What are the meanings of these two constructs? What are their associated characteristics? Masculinity in American culture is often characterized as being dominant, aggressive, less emotional, active, confident, competent, adventurous, logical, individualistic, and hard as well as working with things. Femininity is often characterized as being submissive, weak, emotional, passive, hesitant, less competent, not risky, illogical, cooperative, and soft as well as working with people. Studies of socialization in grade school and high school reveal how children learn what is acceptable behavior, skills, and attributes for girls and boys. For example, boys are more likely rewarded for athletic ability, toughness, sexual prowess and aggression, and competitiveness more so than girls (Eder and Parker 1987; Messner 2009; Pascoe 2011), while girls are more likely to be rewarded for attractive appearance, a romantic interest in boys, academic success, and sexual nonpermissiveness (Kreager and Staff 2009; Kroska 2014; Milkie 1999; Simon, Eder, and Evans 1992).

In essence, all individuals possess masculine and feminine qualities in varying degrees. What is important, however, is that masculinity and femininity are not equally valued in our society. Rather, our society, as well as in most societies, more highly values masculine than feminine characteristics in general. When men and women and boys and girls exhibit counternormative displays of gender, they are discouraged by others, and sometimes more brutally treated (Moss-Racusin, Phelan, and Rudman 2010). Who is much more mercilessly teased on the playground: a masculine girl or a feminine boy? (See Pascoe [2011] for a discussion of masculinity in high school.) Threats to masculinity are especially discouraged because masculinity is more highly valued in society (Moss-Racusin et al. 2010; Rudman et al. 2012; Schrock and Schwalbe 2009). As we shall see in later chapters on status and power hierarchies, this difference in value leads to negative consequences for women and men both on an interactional level and in the larger social structure, such as in the job market, politics, and family dynamics.

Children learn the meanings of gender that are available in their culture and during the historical period in which they live. Meanings associated with gender and gender identity change over time and vary across cultures. For example, in the late 19th century, early 20th century, and even into the 1960s and 1970s in some areas of the United States, it was assumed that girls and women should not exert themselves too much in sports. In fact, girls were restricted in their physical exercise in some schools. For example, during the 1960s in some regions of the United States, girls were not allowed to dribble the basketball more than three times before passing and could only play on one half of the court! Why?!! One very popular reason was that it was believed that too much physical exertion could interfere with fertility (Lever 1978)! Today, this limitation is no longer practiced due to changing beliefs about the relationship between femininity, fertility, and sports. Sports are still very gendered, and sports played by boys and men are still more highly valued than sports played by girls and women across high schools, colleges, and nationally, but the value of women's sports has increased since the 1960s!

The meanings of gender, then, are contextual; they change over time and are continually constructed in everyday interaction. Take, for example, the development of a recent gender process: **gender fluidity**. This is a process whereby gender identity and its expression (through dress, mannerisms, tone of voice, body language, etc.) shift between masculinity and femininity and can change every day or every few hours, depending on the situation. Gender fluidity is not the same as transgenderism or sexual preference. In addition to being historically and culturally specific, self-meanings about gender are affected by an individual's own interactional history with others and of his or her own structural position within the larger society—such as occupational, race, and educational positions (Stewart 2003). These meanings influence who we think should do what types of jobs; what jobs we believe we personally should do; how the division of labor should be constructed in the family (e.g., who does child care, housework; earns money); and who should be in powerful positions in the educational, occupational, political, and religious structures in society.

In addition to gender, race and ethnicity are key social constructions that influence our interactions and the identities we develop and negotiate throughout our lifetime. As with gender, the meanings of race and ethnicity and their enactment in interaction vary across time and space.

Racial and Ethnic Identity

Just as children learn about, take on, and do gender, a similar process occurs in forming and negotiating a racial and/or ethnic identity. Race and ethnicity are also key aspects of the development and negotiation of the self in everyday interaction. They influence how children come to see themselves, how they think others see them, and how they interact with others. Both race and ethnicity are social categories, and just as with gender, the meanings of these categories are socially constructed.

Race is viewed as a fairly modern phenomenon (a notion that was invented in the 1700s). It may be defined as socially created categories used to categorize people according to arbitrary measures, often depending upon the objective of the classification (Khanna 2004). For example, in 1930 the U.S. Census Bureau classified Mexican as a race. This category was eliminated in 1940, and Mexicans were then classified as white. In 1950, the Chinese, Japanese, and Filipino were classified separately in the Asian or Pacific Islander category. All other Asian or Pacific Islanders were grouped together under the Other Race category. From the 1970s to 2000, the racial categories changed where Black became Black or African American, Asian became its own separate category after splitting from the new category, Native Hawaiian, or other Pacific Islander. Also, for the first time, in 2000, respondents were and continue to be allowed to check more than one race, which is, in effect, allowing for a multiracial category. In comparison, the Brazilian Institute of Geography and Statistics classifies the Brazilian population in five categories based on skin color: white, black, pardo (brown), yellow, and indigenous, and embedded within this classification is a profusion of skin tones. For example, some Brazilians describe themselves as "coffee and milk," and others with brown–black skin claim to be negro formiga (ant black). Whereas the one-drop rule makes a very "white-looking" American a black as long as there is a black ancestor, there is less precision in the Brazilian classification, leading to a profusion of claimed skin tones. (See Monk [2016] for an excellent examination of "race" and "color" in Brazil and their association with inequality; the author found that skin color has a stronger effect on educational attainment and occupational status than census race–color categories. This means that race and color should be considered analytically distinct concepts because they are empirically distinct.)

When scholars state that *race is a social category*, then, this means that boundaries between races are subjective and that people create arbitrary rules for racial classifications. These arbitrary rules change over time, often to suit political needs. For example, the one-drop rule enforced during the Jim Crow system from 1877 to the mid-1960s was that if you had one drop of "black blood" this "made you" black. Although 70% to 90% of African Americans are actually multiracial, this rule suggested that if you have even one very distant relative that is black, you were then classified as black. The purpose of this rule was to ensure that anyone with black ancestors would not be able to vote, own private property, or receive educational opportunities that whites were afforded. On the other hand, the blood quantum laws enforced by the U.S. government stated that in order for an individual to be classified as Native American, they must prove that they are at least one quarter Native American. One reason the U.S. government used this higher requirement of one-quarter minimum for Native American classification (higher than the one-drop rule for African Americans) was that it effectively limited the amount of resources and benefits given to Native Americans. Today, the "amount of blood" required depends on the specific Native American nation, but the point is it is an arbitrary, yet political, decision. Japanese Americans who were one-sixteenth Japanese were placed in camps during World War II—why this arbitrary requirement?

In comparison to race, **ethnicity** applies to cultural characteristics and refers to people who identify with one another on the basis of common ancestry and cultural heritage. It is derived from the Greek word *ethos*, meaning people or nation. Ethnicity encompasses a sense of belonging that can center on such things as country of origin, food, dress, family names and relationships, language, music, and customs. Examples of ethnicities are Chinese, Egyptian, Nigerian, Mexican, Hawaiian, Greek, and Russian.

Racial and ethnic identities are often conceptualized along several dimensions. An **internal racial or ethnic identity** is that identity that the individual believes about his or her own race or ethnicity—that is, how individuals see themselves (Harris and Sim 2002). An **external racial or ethnic identity** is how the individual believes that others perceive his or her racial or ethnic identity. Sometimes internal and external racial identities may conflict with one another. For example, some people may view a white/Asian individual to be white, even though the individual perceives himself to be Asian. Sometimes scholars also discuss **expressed racial or ethnic identity**. This type refers to the words and actions that convey beliefs about an individual's race (this may also be referred to as a public racial or ethnic identity; Harris and Sim 2002). For example, a person may claim that she is biracial (e.g., black and white) on U.S. census forms but may internally identify as black. These different types of racial or ethnic identity raise important issues for how this identity is formed and negotiated in interaction.

Can you remember any lessons or sayings that you may have learned about race or ethnicity as a child? Forming racial and ethnic identities is an important aspect of socialization. As with gender, children learn about racial and ethnic concepts and identities through their families, neighborhoods, community activities, schools, peers, and media. For a long time, social psychologists and psychologists believed that children were incapable of using abstract concepts like race until at least the age of 7 (Van Ausdale and Feagin 1996). Van Ausdale and Feagin questioned this assumption and showed that even children between the ages of 3 and 6 are able to create and assign meaning to racial and ethnic concepts. They addressed the following question: How do children use racial and ethnic understandings in everyday interactions? Through extensive observations of 58 children in a large preschool for 11 months, they documented the interactions between children of several different racial or ethnic backgrounds, including black, white, biracial, Asian, and Latino/a. The first author was a teacher's aide during this time period and also recorded her observations.

They found that indeed children used these concepts in at least five ways during their interactions with each other. First, ethnicity was used to exclude others from play. For example, a white child and a white/Latino/a child excluded a Chinese child from playing with them by stating that only people who speak Spanish could come into their playhouse. They associated race and ethnicity with language use. The Asian child could not speak Spanish but ironically nor could the white child, but this apparent contradiction was dismissed by the 4-year-olds, not surprisingly! Second, racial and ethnic concepts were also used to include others in order to engage each other in play and teach them about these identities. For example, a 5-year-old Chinese girl would bring a book on the Chinese language and would engage other kids in the learning of the Chinese characters. This girl was aware that learning Chinese is a distinct experience relative to the other children. Third, some children used these concepts to define themselves. In these cases, often physical differences were associated with differences in cultural tastes such as food. Some children brought different types of ethnic food to preschool, and this food was associated with their racial or ethnic identity.

Children also used racial and ethnic ideas to define others, typically by exploring the differences in skin color, hair differences, and facial characteristics. For example, several of the kids thought that one of the authors of this study was Indian because she wore her dark hair in a braid. Finally, children used these concepts at times to control other children, showing that some kids even at this age have an inkling of the racial power differences in the United States. For example, a 4-year-old white girl was trying to convince a 4-year-old black boy that he could not possibly have a white rabbit at home because he is black and "blacks can't have whites." Also, a 4-year-old white girl made it very clear that only white Americans could pull the wagon on the playground. Here, the children have some awareness that power and authority are granted to whites. Children attach meaning to racial and ethnic concepts (through association with language, food, physical characteristics, and racial nuances such as power differences) in both positive and negative ways at an early age through interaction with others. This affects their awareness of their own racial or ethnic identities, others' identities, and the larger power differences based in race and race relations (Van Ausdale and Feagin 1996, 2001).

Lewis (2003), in her ethnographic study of three elementary school communities with varying racial compositions, examines how grade school children *negotiate racial categories* in everyday interaction as they learn where they fit into an already existing racial scheme and how they see themselves relative to others. Over a course of a year, Lewis spent about 35 hours a week in the schools and also conducted 85 interviews with school personnel, parents, and children. Like Van Ausdale and Feagin, Lewis (2003) observed that children used cues such as skin color and language as markers of difference between racial groups. Other racial markers like names, accents, and dress were used to define difference and, hence, create racial boundaries. These racial classifications then were used as a way to include and exclude others, ranging from simply ignoring others to using violence against one another. In addition, she found that, as with gender, children also "do race" in that race is, in part, about performance (Goffman 1977) that is produced in interactions. Lewis provides the following example:

> Another example of the importance of both language and performance came up one day while I was driving three African American boys from West City (Darnell, Malik, and Thompson) to watch a basketball game. I explained to them that I had never been to the school we were headed to but that my understanding was that it was a pretty "fancy" place. Malik assured me that it would not be a problem, "Don't worry, Ms. Lewis, Darnell knows how to talk White." Here, Malik, with Darnell and Thompson nodding in agreement, illustrated that he not only understood that certain ways of talking were racialized but also that these speech modes were ones he and his friends could perform to perhaps better blend into an alien space. (Lewis 2003:292–93)

Recently, there has been a burgeoning amount of work in the study of **multiracial identity formation**. This is good news, given that 9 million people (about 3% of total population) in the United States reported a multiracial background in the 2010 U.S. census, and this number is predicted to rise significantly by 2050 (Lee and Bean 2004).

This work on multiracial identity builds upon earlier work on the *fluidity of ethnic identity*. Fluidity, in this context, refers to the idea that individuals have some flexibility in the way they identify their ethnic identity to others and to themselves. For example, Waters (1990) showed that people have the opportunity to change their ethnic identity in different contexts, such as embracing a Greek heritage at a Greek family wedding, but downplaying this ethnicity at school. Ethnic identification may also change over time during particular events, such as going to college, having children, or nearing one's end of life. For example, when people have children, they may be more likely to embrace an ethnic identity that they had previously forgone because they may realize the importance of handing down this ethnic identity and the cultural knowledge associated with this identity to their children. In Cathy's case, she has a German, English, Irish, and Swiss heritage, but she must admit that she does not embrace any of these ethnicities. Her grandmother could speak German and cook many German dishes, but her mother did not. Why? Perhaps because her parents were beginning their family during World War II—where being German was not something to embrace at the time.

For many, racial identity is stable across contexts, but it is interesting to examine accounts of those who may be considered, either by themselves or by others, as multiracial. Multiracial may be defined as how people define themselves (internal), how they are identified by others (external), how they express themselves in public (public), how their ancestors are identified, or any combination of these. Harris and Sim (2002) used data from a school-based health survey consisting of a U.S. representative sample of adolescents from Grades 7 to 12 (the Adolescent Health data set). Unique to their study, they examined four measures of race: (1) an in-school survey measure that consisted of a private, self-reported response about their racial identity,

(2) a home survey measure where an interviewer asked them about their racial identity with or without another family member present, (3) a measure that asked them for the best single race that describes them, and (4) their parent-based race.

Harris and Sim (2002) found that one third of the respondents with known multiracial ancestry did not report having a multiracial identity. Therefore, having parents of different races does not automatically mean that individuals will claim a multiracial identity. Importantly, they also found that the context in which racial identity was asked affects individuals' reporting of their internalized racial identity. For example, black/white youth were more likely to identify as multiracial or white when a family member was not present than when a family member was present. On the other hand, white/Asian and white/American Indian youth were more likely to identify as Asian and American Indian when the family member was not present in the interview. In addition, context in terms of neighborhood and region of country affected their responses. For example, Asian/white youth living in a predominately white neighborhood were more likely to identify as white than those living in a predominantly Asian neighborhood. And white/black youth living in the South were less likely to select white as their single best race than white/black youth in other regions. This regional effect may be due to the fact that the one-drop rule is rooted in the South (Harris and Sim 2002). These results illustrate the fluidity of race and that perceived racial identity depends on the context. Harris and Sim wonder how these patterns in racial identity may change as the adolescents in this sample age.

In addition, Khanna (2004), building upon Harris and Sim's (2002) notion of the **flexibility of racial identity**, addressed the following question: What are the factors that shape racial identity for multiracial Asians? Asians have the highest outmarriage rates of any racial minority in the United States—that is, they are more likely to marry outside of their race than other racial minorities. Khanna (2004) draws upon Cooley's (1902) **reflected appraisals** idea that how they think others view them will affect how they view their own racial identity (see Chapter 3 for an in-depth discussion of reflected appraisals). In a survey of 100 white/Asian–identified individuals, the author found that phenotype (physical appearance), in terms of how you think others see your appearance, has a strong effect on racial identification. Respondents who think they appear more Asian than white are much more likely to identify as Asian than those who think they appear white. In addition, one's cultural exposure to and knowledge of one's nonwhite heritage, in terms of food and language in particular, and others' reactions to the respondents' cultural knowledge in terms of language, food, and customs strongly affected racial identity. The more exposure and positive feedback toward that exposure, the more likely the respondents were to identify as Asian. Other factors, such as socioeconomic status, Asian parent (either mom or dad), gender of respondent, and time family spent in the United States were not as important as others' reactions to phenotype and cultural knowledge in the formation of racial identity for these multiracial individuals.

Are some multiracial individuals afforded more flexibility in their racial identification than others? Harris and Sim (2002) found that 75% of white/black youth identified as black when asked, "What is the single best race that describes you?" On the other hand, about 50% of the white/Asian youth identified as Asian (Khanna [2004] also found this fairly equal split), and only 13% of the white/American Indian youth identified as American Indian. The authors speculated that there are stricter social rules (e.g., the one-drop rule) and political reasons for black/white individuals to identify as black rather than as white. American Indian/white youth who have little ancestral, cultural, or phenotypical (physical appearance) connection to American Indians will more likely identify as white. Asian/white youth, at least in this sample, have the most flexibility in racial identity in terms of which race they most identify. Also, Khanna (2011), in a qualitative study consisting of biracial black/white individuals in the South, found that, although the majority of respondents publicly identified as multiracial (33 out of 40), a majority claimed black as their internalized identity (24 out of 40). This, again, is in contrast to Asian/white individuals who have more flexibility in their choice of internal racial identity.

Other central nonracial identities—gender, religion, and socioeconomic status—also affect choice of racial labels. Biracial college women (biracial in this case meaning individuals who identify their parents with different races) are more likely than biracial college men to identify as multiracial. This is so for Asian/white, white/Latino/a, and black/white college students, but the greatest gender difference is between black/white students, indicating more rigidity of the black/white boundary for black men (Davenport 2016). Biracial college students who practice "ethnic" religions are more likely to identify with only one racial group compared to those who do not. For example, Catholic white/Latino/a students are more likely to identify as Latino than students who do not identify as Catholic. Black/white students who are Baptist are less likely to identify as white than their non-Baptist counterparts. And students from a more affluent background and neighborhood are more likely to identify as white than those who come from a less affluent background (Davenport 2016). Racial labels that individuals claim are impacted by the social groups in which they belong.

As noted previously, the meanings attached to racial labels will continue to change over time, as well as the political meanings associated with race. As we shall see in later chapters, the difference in perceived value of racial categories lead to often profound negative consequences for persons of color; in everyday interaction; and in economic, educational, political, and legal institutions.

Cyberspace Identities

With the age of the Internet, individuals have opportunities to create, present, and manage identities in particular contexts online, such as in online chats, Facebook, Twitter, Pinterest, and forums for all types of interests (such as music and science fiction). As with gender and race, we can "do" our cyberselves. Waskul (2007) examines how individuals present themselves in online chats. Cyberspace is an interesting context for Waskul; he claims that "computer-mediated communication has created a new realm of social being or what he terms *cyberselfhood*" (Waskul 2007:119).

As mentioned in Chapter 3, our interaction is often like being on stage—we are all actors performing with and for one another, with particular lines of conduct, props, and sets (Goffman 1959). We often manage how we appear to others in order to come across as someone desirable. Somewhat contrary to face-to-face interaction, in some online contexts individuals have more freedom to choose their identities and attributes to display, as well as their names. In addition, visual cues that reveal something about each other's social characteristics (such as gender, race, ethnicity, physical attractiveness, age, and social class) that are readily apparent in face-to-face interaction are not apparent online. Examples of these cues are clothing, skin color, adornments on the body, and other physical characteristics.

Online, however, these taken-for-granted cues are unavailable. Bodies are assumed to be associated with individuals, but bodies are not physically present (Kendall 2000; Waskul 2007). As a result, people have the opportunity to make choices about what they reveal to others about themselves in online communication and the descriptions they use about themselves. They also must interpret and evaluate other peoples' identity information and descriptions of themselves.

For example, on many forums, screen names are used to provide information about the self and make claims about the individual's identities, particularly in initial stages of communication. "MrMaine," for example, is a name that indicates the person is male and from Maine (Waskul 2007). Other screen names may reveal interests such as "SciFiLover," a name that reveals someone who loves science fiction. This love of science fiction, in turn, is often associated with other characteristics, such as computer geek, male, and young (even though this stereotype of people who enjoy science fiction is not wholly accurate, just like any stereotype, as discussed in Chapters 5 and 12). These names provide people with an outward cue that affects how others communicate with him or her, based on available cultural assumptions about these identities. As forum members interact, they may also choose to reveal other aspects about themselves, called **self-claims**, such as their occupations, age, or marital or relationship status. In fact, as a result of communication, members reveal something about who they are. In addition to these self-claims, other cues such as expressions of opinions, interests, activities, and the tone used in communication (i.e., humorous, sarcastic) also reveal who they are to others online. Often, these self-claims are not contested to any significant degree. The cyberself is thus presented, negotiated, and validated in communication with others online. And the cyberself "is always whatever is passing for a self at the moment in an electronic computer-mediated context" (Waskul 2007:124). Participants, then, create a "working consensus" about who they are, and this, in turn, allows for further interaction.

Kendall (2000), in her study on an online interactive text-based forum, provides an interesting example of self-claims. She states that because of the online demographics, participants in her study assumed that people they encountered were white. In fact, 6% of the forum members were Asian American. Kendall describes one of the members, a Chinese American male, as deciding to refer to himself as white, even though some of the other forum members knew that his parents emigrated from China. He labeled himself white in this context because he equates whiteness with nerdiness, a characteristic that many of the participants claimed to be. The point here is that this online context sometimes gives people some choices about what to reveal and how to reveal themselves to others.

There is a burgeoning literature on presentation and expression of the self on the Internet. For example, some research suggests that the Internet is a place where individuals can express identity-important aspects of their selves that are not often or easily expressed to others, often more so than in face-to-face interaction (Bargh, McKenna, and Fitzsimons 2002). It may be that the Internet facilitates self-expression for some people more than face-to-face interaction, particularly when meeting a new acquaintance. On the Internet, people are free of the expectations and constraints that accompany typical social interaction, and the costs and risks of sanctions in face-to-face interactions are also reduced (Bargh et al. 2002). This opens up the possibility of more frank self-disclosure. Consistent with this idea, research shows that people who believe they are better able to express their "real me" online are more likely to form close relationships with people over the Internet than those who believe they express their "true" selves in non-Internet relationships (McKenna, Green, and Gleason 2002).

Each of us has a set of identities that are important to us. In the next section, we examine how these identities affect choices in our lives and our interactions with others.

How Do Identities Affect the Choices We Make and Our Interactions With Others?

To address this question, we examine some of the key identity processes that shape our interactions with others. We also see how the identities we hold affect, in part, the choices we make and the interests we hold, such as what types of classes to take, what careers to pursue, whom to date, and where we desire to live. We will also discuss how, at times, we are motivated to make identity claims by announcing who we are *not* rather than who we say we are.

What Are Some of the Key Identity Processes That Shape Interactions?

There are several key identity processes that will help us better understand how our identities, particularly the important ones, affect the choices we make and how we negotiate our interactions with others. The first key premise is that *we interact with people in terms of the meanings these identities have for us and others in interaction*. These meanings will vary for different people, in different contexts, at different times. When Cathy is playing pool in a bar, her identity as a professor is not very important, but her identity as a "pool shark" is important. Now, if a student of hers walks into the bar, she might be presenting both the pool shark and the professor identities, and her behavior may change slightly as a result of her student's presence. Your identity as son or daughter is very relevant in some contexts (say, while at home visiting your parents) but may not be relevant at a party at school.

When individuals present different identities in different contexts, we refer to them as **situated identities** (Alexander and Wiley 1981; McCall and Simmons 1966; Vryan, Adler, and Adler 2003). Our situated identities emerge from our joint actions and meaning of cues (e.g., social characteristics, behaviors, and declarations) during our interactions. Examples of situated identities that may emerge in different contexts are customer, defendant, diner, tourist, or student (Vryan et al. 2003). We enact these identities along the culturally defined expectations attached to these identities, and these expectations vary in their looseness or strictness, depending on the context (or definition of the situation). A defendant, for example, is expected to answer the lawyers' and judge's questions at particular times, and there is little flexibility in these expectations. A tourist at a national park, on the other hand, may have more leeway in the choice of her behavior within that context. Importantly, situated identities are easily changeable from one context or interaction to another (e.g., you may shift from a student to an athlete, to a friend) and may even do so during a single interaction. Are there any identities that seem almost always salient across situations? Gender, perhaps? How about race?

Second, *we often try to confirm our most important identities in interaction*. Often, people want their identities validated by others in interaction to give them a social reality—to make their identities "real" (Wicklund and Gollwitzer 1982). For example, it is important to Cathy that she believes that others perceive her as a good mom. So sometimes she will do activities she really does not want to do—such as volunteering at her daughter's school when she is really busy. She also wants to be seen as a good professor. She likes it when she gets positive feedback from students to confirm this identity. If she has had a bad day and seemed disorganized, she will make sure to make up for it in the next class period.

Burke (1991) and Stets (Burke and Stets 2009; Stets and Burke 2000) developed **perceptual control identity theory** (also called **identity theory**) to explain, in rich detail, how people negotiate their identities in everyday interaction. (For an excellent review of research in identity, see Owens, Robinson, and Smith-Lovin 2010; for an excellent book on new directions in identity theory, see Stets and Serpe 2016.) They assume that often people want to have their already formulated identities verified in interaction (the *self-verification assumption*; see also Swann et al. [1987]). Burke (1991) views identity as an ongoing interactional process, wherein individuals in interaction monitor their identities by comparing their perceptions of the feedback they receive about themselves with their own conception of their identities. The major objective is to maintain **consistency** between how they view themselves in terms of their claimed identities (referred to as the identity standard) and their perceptions of feedback they receive from others in situations. A major assumption is that people want to self-verify (called **self-verification**) and maintain congruency in their identities.

Importantly, "any discrepancy between perceived self-in-situation meanings and identity standard meanings . . . reflects a problem in verifying the self, and as a result of this the individual experiences negative emotional arousal" (Stets and Burke 2002:139). In other words, it does not feel good to perceive an inconsistency between how you see yourself and how you think others see you. This is particularly true if the identity in question is important to you, if the other person or group that is providing feedback is significant to you and you care about what they think, if this is an identity that you are dependent upon (i.e., such as an occupation), and if this inconsistency persists over time. If this inconsistency persists, the individual can experience an **identity interruption**, causing discomfort and distress (Burke 1991). As a result, the individual may respond by adjusting his behavior in an attempt to bring the situation back into balance. That is, people often modify, adjust, and negotiate their behavior in order to regain consistency.

For example, if a self-proclaimed very "masculine" individual perceives that a newly found friend views him as only moderately masculine, then he will adjust his behavior so that he tries to change the self-in-situation meanings that he perceives the other to have of him (Stets and Burke 1994, 1996). He will act even more masculine than usual to change the other's point of view. This adjustment process is often automatic, but if the discrepancies continue, it can lead to an increasing amount of distress. In this case, he will be highly motivated to realign his identity, but if not successful, he may try to change his identity—that is, he may change the meanings of his identity, shed the identity, or change to a new identity if possible (Burke 2006).

Much of our behavior is motivated by confirming our identities. Interestingly, this is so even when they are negative. Cathy is not a good cook (unlike Karen!), and she never has been. For some people, that is a real problem, but thankfully to her partner, it is not! She does not want to become a good cook—in fact, she does not like cooking. And she has no problem verifying this side of herself to others. She would not want others to even think she had the potential to be a good cook because then she would be expected to cook. Robinson and Smith-Lovin (1992) found support for this self-verification process. In their study, people who perceive that they are terrible public speakers chose to interact with individuals who were more negative in their evaluation of their speechmaking skills than those who were more positive in order to confirm their identity as a poor speechmaker (see also Swann et al. 2000 for similar support).

Khanna (2011) provides another example of individuals desiring to move toward consistency. Imagine how a biracial black/white individual with a strong white identity who is perceived as black may adjust his behavior by "acting" or "dressing" white. He may also try to distance himself from other blacks, embrace the white side of the family, and avoid interests and activities that may be deemed as "black." In this way, the individual is doing **identity work**. Identity work consists of a " . . . range of activities to create, present, and sustain identities that are congruent or supportive of their self-concept" (Snow and Anderson 1987:1348). For example, individuals may create, find, or arrange physical settings or props to present an identity. If an individual wants others to see her as Hawaiian, she may display Hawaiian art and other Hawaiian artifacts in her home or invite friends over for a Hawaiian style dinner. Or individuals may work on their physical appearance to display their identities. For example, a white/ Chinese woman may dye her hair black in order to portray a particular image. And individuals may engage in selective association with other individuals or groups that support their identities. Gay Catholics, for example, may join a local gay or lesbian Catholic group where members accept simultaneously their Catholic and gay identities.

Finally, some research suggests that in *some situations, individuals want to enhance rather than confirm their self-concepts in interaction.* **Self-enhancement** refers to presenting a positive self-concept to others in the hopes of getting positive feedback and treatment from others (Swann et al. 1987). For example, Snow and Anderson (1987) discuss how individuals who are homeless assert positive aspects of themselves through verbal construction or **identity talk**. Identity talk is an important form of identity work by which people construct, negotiate, and assert their own self-attributed identities. The authors found that many homeless individuals, a group that is visibly stigmatized, used identity talk as a means of self-enhancement. Membership in this "low-status" group is problematic because it is difficult to hide the fact that one is homeless, and it is consistently looked down upon by many in society. Yet Snow and Anderson (1987) found that these individuals—particularly those who had not been on the street for very long—are motivated to protect and support a positive self-concept. For example, some individuals distanced themselves from the homeless as a general category by stating "I'm different" from others on the street. Others distanced themselves from the role of a street person, talking more about their day labor jobs and how they deserve better and also how they would soon be off the streets. Still others who had been homeless for longer periods of time embellished their stories of previous and current experiences. For example, some exaggerated their claims of past and current wages; others embellished their experiences in the military. These forms of identity talk were attempts to present a positive identity to yield a measure of self-respect and dignity. We will discuss the negotiation of lowly valued group identities in detail in Chapter 12 when we examine intergroup relations.

How May Our Identities Be Related to the Choices We Make in Our Lives?

The choices we make often reflect the identities we hold (Stryker 1980). To illustrate this point, we discuss a study by Lee (1998), who asked the following question: Why are women in the United States disproportionately underrepresented in most scientific and technological disciplines compared to men (science, math, and engineering are referred to as SME disciplines)? There have been changes in the percentage of women over the past 30 years in SME disciplines—particularly in terms of earning bachelor's degrees—but there is still a wide gender discrepancy when examining advanced (masters and doctorate) degrees. Specifically, Lee asked this: Why do *qualified* women drop out at a higher rate than qualified men during the crucial period between the latter part of high school and the first several years of college? During this period, women are more likely to abandon their interest in these disciplines than men.

The most common explanations for this discrepancy are important ones: lack of role models for young girls in these disciplines, gender bias in the classroom in science and math classes where boys are more encouraged to pursue these areas than girls, lack of encouraging social networks (i.e., fewer opportunities for girls to be supported by family, and school counselors more likely to encourage boys to take advanced classes in these areas). Also, scholars argue that the way in which educators cultivate the learning environment for science and math is more conducive to boys than girls. All these explanations play a role in the gender discrepancy we still see in SME disciplines (e.g., chemistry, math, physics, and engineering). Lee (1998) contributes to these arguments by taking a symbolic interactionist approach to addressing this question.

Lee examined high school juniors and seniors who have distinguished themselves in science and math and show an interest in SME careers. He argues that students who see themselves as "future scientists" are more likely to choose classes or programs in science and math, compared to students who do not see themselves this way. Importantly, he suggests that there is a link between the interests that students have in subjects or disciplines and their self-concepts rooted in gender identity. He found that the girls in his study are more likely, on average, to face a discrepancy between their self-view as girls and their view of scientists than boys do. Scientific careers are perceived as more "masculine"—specifically, these careers are seen as fitting individuals who are individualistic, less emotional, logical, and who like to work with things instead of people. As a result, girls, on average, have less interest in pursuing careers in SME than boys because they face a larger discrepancy between how they see themselves (more cooperative, emotional, and working with people) and how they see "future scientists" and professionals in these areas. This is so, even though these girls are highly qualified to pursue these areas. On the other hand, boys are much less likely to face this discrepancy between their self-concept rooted in gender identity and how they see future scientists and professionals. Boys are more likely to see themselves as individualistic and working with things, and this "matches" their perception of scientists. You can imagine that for other disciplines that are perceived as feminine, such as nursing, boys will face a larger discrepancy than girls and hence lose interest in "feminine" disciplines.

Lee (1998) argues, then, that students are interested in and choose disciplines that often match their self-concepts. The choices we make and the interests we hold often reflect the identities we have of ourselves—in this case, gender identity and our career choices. We have already shown that self-concepts and gender identity are socially constructed. What we think of as masculine and feminine is created and maintained and can be changed in interaction (although this is not easy to do). One implication of Lee's study is that perceptions of these disciplines and the skills associated with them as masculine need to be changed.

More recently, scholars suggest that high school girls are more likely than high school boys to create new same-sex friendships at these SME summer camps. These friendships, in turn, created more opportunities for change in the importance of "future scientist" identity and also opened up exposure to a wide range of identities (Lee 2002). It may be that girls are more influenced by these same-sex friendships than boys and, as a result, have a tendency to opt out of math and science classes in high school because their friends are not as likely to be in these classes (Kroska 2014).

Finally, in a similar line of research, some scholars draw upon identity theory to address how science-training programs for undergraduates in university settings increase the degree to which students maintain an interest in science careers throughout their undergraduate careers and into graduate school. Research shows that science-training programs not only provide academic support but also facilitate the development of positive relationships with other students. This positive interaction, in turn, increases students' salience of their science identities. As a result of these positive relationships with other science students, participants in these programs build a stronger science identity and, in turn, they are more likely to choose a STEM (science, technology, engineering, and math) major and persist in that major during their undergraduate careers (Merolla et al. 2012). This is important because this research shows that providing social structures, in this case science-training programs, is tied to individuals' identities, through developing relationships, which in turn positively affect choices of courses, major, and retention in these majors. This is important because, as mentioned previously, a central concern in higher education is the increased participation and success of students of color and women in the STEM fields. The better we understand under what conditions these training programs facilitate future participation and success, the more likely it is we will see an increase in the diverse set of students in STEM fields in undergraduate and graduate education.

"Who Am I Not?" and How May This Affect My Interactions With Others?

We asked you to think about who you are, but now we want you to answer who you are not. What types of things would you say if asked this question?

We should not only study identity processes in terms of **self-identification** (e.g., "Who am I?") but also in terms of who we say we are not ("Who am I not?"), or in terms of **self-disidentification** (McCall 2003). When people describe themselves in terms of who they are not, they create a **not-me**. It is not a negative identity but rather a disidentification, such as I am not a Republican or I am not a cook. Or if I tell someone I am a lesbian, I may also claim that I am not a man hater, just in case I get the sense that he or she equates the two. Individuals negotiate both their claims of "who I am" and "who I am not" in interaction with others as situations arise. Self-disidentification is a form of **reactive identity work** in interaction (McCall 2003). That is, people who disidentify with a particular identity are confronting and countering a representation they perceive that others have of them. For example, a biracial individual who is perceived as black by others, but actually views herself as biracial, may work to counter that perception.

A good example of a "Who am I not?" claim in action is illustrated in a study by Killian and Johnson (2006; see also Killian 2006). Killian studied identity negotiation processes of North African immigrant women in France and interviewed 45 women in 1999. These Muslim women are a low-status, visible ethnic minority in France who often must manage an identity that is looked upon unfavorably in their host country of France. Algeria, Tunisia, and Morocco were all colonies of France. Tunisia and Morocco were decolonized relatively peacefully, but the Algerians fought a violent 8-year war with France that ended colonial rule in 1962. In response to their low-status positions, some of these women actively resist the labels that are imposed upon them by French society, including that of immigrant. In fact, a portion of the sample claimed in the interviews that they were not immigrants. This was surprising, given that these individuals moved from one country to another country and plan to stay. Why would they resist the identity of immigrant?

A major reason for this rejection is that they perceive this label as something negative. In fact, some of these women redefined what it means to be an immigrant by viewing immigrants as people who do not adapt well to their host country, have moved to France for economic reasons and typically take low-status jobs, and who are of lower socioeconomic status in general. Some of the women, then, said that they were not immigrants because they see themselves adapting well in France, and have come to France for more than just economic reasons. Importantly, the only women who are able to resist the label of immigrant are those who have the resources to do so. That is, these are women who are well-educated, speak French well, and are exposed to French cultural ideas. They refused the immigrant social category in order to construct a positive identification of someone who is well-adjusted, at ease, and is not poor. They redefined what it means to be an immigrant—at least for them.

In addition, Killian and Johnson (2006) revealed how some of these women engage in identity work to affect how others perceive them in general (Snow and Anderson 1987). For example, some engage in identity talk, as shown in this passage:

> "Even when I take a trip, I have a French passport, et cetera. I remember a trip I took to Cyprus were the person asked me where I was from and I said, 'From France; I'm French.' 'No, you're not French.' 'Yes, I don't look French because I'm of Algerian descent.' And he said, 'Ah yes, I understand now.'" (Killian and Johnson 2006:69)

They also manage their appearances to fit others' expectations. For example, some women reported being very careful to always appear clean and well-dressed in public (and often in a Western or French style). They also make sure that their children are well-behaved in order to protect themselves from racism. Finally, some women strive to interact with people who are better educated (e.g., selective association) because they believe that highly educated people are less likely to hold stereotypes.

We have seen previously that individuals do have some flexibility in their adoption and negotiation of their identities (such as gender, racial, and cyber identities), but there are also constraints on these processes. For example, Killian and Johnson (2006) showed that only North African women with the resources and a high level of education could reject the identity of immigrant in France. And our example in the beginning of this chapter reveals that the Albanian women who took on this role as "man" (and head) of the family were granted similar rights and resources as men for the survival of their clan, but they also had to remain virgins and take on the appearance and behaviors of men.

As we shall see in the chapters ahead, sociological social psychologists, as well as sociologists in general, examine social interaction from two sides of the same coin: the freedom and agency of the individual to make choices but also the constraints on behavior as a result of the social structures and cultural rules that already exist.

Do We All Have Equal Access to Identity Claims?

No, we do not all have equal access to identity claims! People are in **social structural locations** that are unequal in terms of available and accessible resources (e.g., unequal access to a good education and high-paying occupations; political power in local, state, and national arenas; and wealth). These locations often limit opportunity for certain groups of people to take on particular social identities and social roles (Stryker 1980; Stryker and Burke 2002). For example, children who do not receive a solid education in the early years will have a difficult time going into particular occupations, such as positions in the STEM fields or high-paying professional careers.

Importantly, symbolic interactionists argue that who a person becomes is profoundly dependent on the networks in which he or she is embedded. **Social networks** include the connections people have with other people through important institutions such as their family and relatives, friends, family friends, schools, neighborhoods, geographical location (e.g., big cities or small rural areas), and life or romantic partner (Smith-Lovin 2007). Your social networks are shaped by the social places you occupy (e.g., which neighborhoods you grew up in, what schools you have gone to, programs you have participated in, and what opportunities you have been afforded). These social places are referred to as **proximal social structures**, and they affect what identities you will and will not acquire and your behavior as it is tied to these identities (Merolla et al. 2012). Your access to these proximal social structures depend, in large part, on your social structural location.

The bottom line here is that who you become is a reflection of who you know. Most importantly, *"what we do depends much more on where we are and who we are with than who we are"* (Barker 1968; Smith-Lovin 2007:106). Are you likely to become a Hollywood director? You may have the necessary talent but not the connections necessary to have the opportunity to become a Hollywood director.

Similarly, people with lots of money or wealth are much more likely to meet other people with lots of money or wealth than people who have much less money or wealth.

What Are Stigmatized Identities?

Some identities are associated with stigma (i.e., stigmatized), and this stigma process varies across contexts, cultures, and time. Goffman (1963:3; same Goffman discussed in Chapter 3) defined a **stigma** as "an attribute that is deeply discrediting," and this attribute is associated with negative and undesirable characteristics. Goffman (1961) did ethnographic work in a mental hospital and wrote an influential book, *Asylums* and, in part, based his views about stigma on the experiences of people labeled with mental illnesses. Notice that his definition seems to imply that a stigma lies within the individual, something she possesses.

Although Goffman did focus on some consequences of stigma, a more recent **enriched definition of stigma**, building on Goffman's work, conceptualizes stigma as having four interrelated components. First, *"people distinguish and label human differences"* (Link and Phelan, 2001:367). As we will see in Chapters 5 and 8, categorization is central to our cognitive processes, and people consistently distinguish between differences, such as cat or dog lovers (or both!), and obvious distinctions such as blind and sighted people or black, brown, and white people. Second, *the labeled difference gets linked to negative stereotypes* (overgeneralized beliefs that are applied to all people in a particular category—see Chapter 12 for details). For example, dominant beliefs link incompetence or dangerousness to people with mental illness and gluttonous and undisciplined to people who are seen as obese.

Third, people who are labeled are perceived in distinct categories and are separated from others such that *people separate themselves from labeled individuals, creating "us" and "them."* Examples are found based on sexual orientation, nationality, and religion who may be considered fundamentally different kind of people than "us."

Fourth, *labeled individuals face disapproval, rejection, exclusion and discrimination* (Link and Phelan 2001). (We will examine discrimination carefully in Chapter 12.) We focus here on how people labeled must negotiate disruptions in their social and personal relationships. When people are labeled, separated from others, and linked to undesirable and negative characteristics, a rationale is created to justify devaluing them and excluding them. They face disruption in their social and personal relationships. They may also face exclusion in the workplace, neighborhoods, or by their families. For example, people with mental illnesses or who have been in prison are often seen as dangerous or incompetent, which affects their ability to attain work. Importantly, stigma is dependent on power differences between groups. Lower power groups have little access to social, political, and economic power (Link, Phelan, and Hatzenbuehler 2014; power will be discussed in detail in later chapters).

Much work focuses on how people negotiate **stigmatized identities**— identities that carry stigma—in everyday interaction. For example, individuals who struggle with weight gain and perceive that they are being treated unfairly at work or in other public places as a result of their weight are more likely to self-identify as being overweight. They perceive themselves as heavier if they have perceived being treated unfairly by others as a result of their weight, compared to others who do not face mistreatment. In addition, they are more likely to have physical health problems above and beyond the effect due to body weight alone. A sense of being marginalized because of one's weight can lead to steeper health declines than for those who are considered obese but do not perceive mistreatment (Schafer and Ferraro 2011).

Finally, *people also seek to resist stigma.* For example, some people who have mental illnesses are able to deflect, impede, or refuse the stigma and the associated negative characteristics or stereotypes (Thoits 2011). They may say this is only a small, unimportant part of their person or that mental illness does not apply to them. This protects the self, much as some people who are homeless do when they use identity talk mentioned previously. They may also challenge the stigma by trying to change people's beliefs and behaviors. For example, they may try to behave in ways that contradict the negative associated stereotype or try to educate others to move away from the stereotype, confront others who are mistreating them, and finally engage in advocacy and activism (Thoits 2011). Challenging is not easy to do on an individual level, nor is it easy to be successful in actually changing stereotypical views. But group-based resistance, such as the civil rights movement and the gay and lesbian movement, have had some success. Collective action can, in the long run, alter the balance of power between stigmatizing high power groups and stigmatized low power groups. It is a difficult process, with fits and starts, but it is possible (see Link et al. 2014 for an excellent discussion on stigma).

We have not forgotten about group identities! In Chapter 12, we discuss group identities and group identification. People identify as members of groups, such as a member of a sorority, a club, a neighborhood community, or more general groups, such as an ethnic group or a fan of particular genre of music, such as indie rock. This identification of a group membership can be very weak to very strong, and people will feel and act according to the norms of the group based on this identification. We will also discuss how people compare their own group with other groups and their motivation to enhance a positive impression of the groups in which they belong. And we will examine the dynamics of intergroup relations, power, and conflict and their relation to social inequality.

Segue: The Symbolic Interaction Approach, Identity Processes, and Social Cognition

In the next chapter, on social cognition, we discuss, in a more complex way, how individuals create and use categories to process new information they receive about others or about themselves in social interactions. Specifically, we examine how individuals perceive social stimuli and, in doing so, process information in their environment. We then examine how individuals form impressions of one another and also assess the causes of others' and their own behavior in situations. These cognitive processes provide the basis for the meanings that symbolic interactionists presume are central to maintaining successful (cooperative) social interaction. They also provide the basis for conflicting meanings, such as the contradictory meanings of the Confederate flag, as seen in the ongoing debate before and after the 2015 mass shooting at the Emanuel African Methodist Episcopal Church in downtown Charleston, South Carolina.

Suggested Readings

Brown-Saracino, Japonica. 2015. "How Places Shape Identity: The Origins of Distinctive LBQ Identities in Four Small U.S. Cities." *American Journal of Sociology* 121(1):1–63.

Granberg, Ellen M. 2011. "'Now My "Old Self" Is Thin': Stigma Exits after Weight Loss." *Social Psychology Quarterly* 74(1):29–52.

Hughes, Michael K., Jill Kiecolt, Verna M. Keith, and David H. Demo. 2015. "Racial Identity and Well-being among African Americans." *Social Psychology Quarterly* 78(1):25–48.

Khanna, Nikki A., and Cathryn Johnson. 2010. "Passing as Black: Racial Identity Work among Biracial Americans." *Social Psychology Quarterly* 73(4):380–97.

Legewie, Joscha, and Thomas A. DiPrete. 2014. "The High School Environment and the Gender Gap in Science and Engineering." *Sociology of Education* 87(4):259–80.

Monk, Ellis P., Jr. 2016. "The Consequences of 'Race' and 'Color' in Brazil." *Social Problems* 63(3):413–30.

Wilkins, Amy. 2012. "Stigma and Status: Interracial Intimacy and Intersectional Identities among Black Men." *Gender and Society* 26(2):165–89.

Willer, Robb, Christabel L. Rogalin, Bridget Conlon, and Michael T. Wojnowicz. 2013. "Overdoing Gender: A Test of the Masculine Overcompensation Thesis." *American Journal of Sociology* 118(4):980–1022.

References

Alexander, Norman, and Mary G. Wiley. 1981. "Situated Activity and Identity Formation." Pp. 232–45 in *Social Psychology: Sociological Perspectives*, edited by M. Rosenberg and R. Turner. New York: Basic Books.

Bargh, John A., Katelyn Y. A. McKenna, and Grainne M. Fitzsimons. 2002. "Can You See the Real Me? Activation and Expression of the 'True Self' on the Internet." *The Journal of Social Issues* 58(1):33–48. doi:10.1111/1540-4560.00247

Barker, Roger G. 1968. *Ecological Psychology: Concepts and Methods for Studying the Environment of Human Behavior*. Stanford, CA: Stanford University Press.

Bilefsky, Dan. 2008. "Albanian Custom Fades: Woman as Family Man." *New York Times*, June 25, pp. 13–16.

Burke, Peter J. 1991. "Attitudes, Behavior, and the Self." Pp. 189–208 in *The Self Society*

Interface: Cognition, Emotion, and Action, edited by J. A. Howard and P. L. Callero. New York: Cambridge University Press. doi:10.1017/CBO9780511527722.011

Burke, Peter J. 2006. *Contemporary Social Psychological Theories*. Stanford, CA: Stanford University Press.

Burke, Peter J., and Jan E. Stets. 2009. *Identity Theory*. New York: Oxford University Press.

Cahill, Spencer. 1986. "Language Practices and Self Definition: The Case of Gender Identity Acquisition." *The Sociological Quarterly* 27:295–311. doi:10.1111/j.1533-8525.1986.tb00262.x

Cahill, Spencer. 1987. "Children and Civility: Ceremonial Deviance and the Acquisition of Ritual Competence." *Social Psychology Quarterly* 50:312–21. doi:10.2307/2786816

Cahill, Spencer. 1989. "Fashioning Males and Females: Appearance Management and the Social Reproduction of Gender." *Symbolic Interaction* 12:281–98. doi:10.1525/si.1989.12.2.281

Cooley, Charles H. 1902. *Human Nature and the Social Order.* New York: Scribner's.

Corsaro, William A. 1992. "Interpretive Reproduction in Children's Peer Cultures." *Social Psychology Quarterly* 55(2):160–77. doi:10.2307/2786944

Couch, Carl J. 1989. *Social Processes and Personal Relationships.* Dix Hills, NY: General Hall.

Davenport, Lauren D. 2016. "The Role of Gender, Class, and Religion in Biracial Americans' Racial Labeling Decisions." *American Sociological Review* 81:57–84. doi:10.1177/0003122415623286

Denzin, Norman K. 1977. *Childhood Socialization: Studies in the Development of Language, Social Behavior, and Identity.* San Francisco, CA: Jossey-Bass.

Eder, Donna, and Stephen Parker. 1987. "The Cultural Production and Reproduction of Gender: The Effect of Extracurricular Activities on Peer-Group Culture." *Sociology of Education* 60:200–13. doi:10.2307/2112276

Gecas, Viktor, and Peter J. Burke. 1995. "Self and Identity." Pp. 41–67 in *Sociological Perspectives on Social Psychology*, edited by K. Cook, G. A. Fine, and J. House. Boston: Allyn & Bacon.

Goffman, Erving. 1959. *The Presentation of Self in Everyday Life.* Garden City, NJ: Doubleday/Anchor.

Goffman, Erving. 1961. *Asylums.* Garden City, NY: Doubleday Anchor.

Goffman, Erving. 1963. *Stigma.* Englewood Cliffs, NJ: Prentice Hall.

Goffman, Erving. 1976. "Gender Advertisements." *Studies in the Anthropology of Visual Communication* 3:69–154.

Goffman, Erving. 1977. "The Arrangement between the Sexes." *Theory and Society* 4:301–33.

Harris, David R., and Jeremiah J. Sim. 2002. "Who Is Multiracial? Assessing the Complexity of Lived Race." *American Sociological Review* 67(4):614–27. doi:10.2307/3088948

Hochschild, Arlie Russell. 1983. *The Managed Heart: Commercialization of Human Feelings.* Berkeley: University of California Press.

Howard, Judith, and Jocelyn Hollander. 1997. *Gendered Situations, Gendered Selves: A Gender Lens on Social Psychology.* Thousand Oaks, CA: Sage.

Kanagawa, Chie, Susan E. Cross, and Hazel R. Markus. 2001. "'Who Am I?' The Cultural Psychology of the Conceptual Self." *Personality and Social Psychology Bulletin* 27:90–103. doi:10.1177/0146167201271008

Kane, Emily W. 2006. "'No Way My Boys Are Going to Be like That!' Parents' Responses to Children's Gender Nonconformity." *Gender & Society* 20(2):149–76. doi:10.1177/0891243205284276

Kendall, Lori. 2000. "'Oh No! I'm a Nerd!' Hegemonic Masculinity on an Online Forum." *Gender & Society* 14(2):256–74. doi:10.1177/089124300014002003

Khanna, Nikki. 2004. "The Role of Reflected Appraisals in Racial Identity: The Case of Multiracial Asians." *Social Psychology Quarterly* 67:115–31. doi:10.1177/019027250406700201

Khanna, Nikki. 2011. "Ethnicity and Race as 'Symbolic': The Use of Ethnic and Racial Symbols in Asserting a Biracial Identity." *Ethnic and Racial Studies* 34(6):1049–67. doi:10.1080/01419870.2010.538421

Killian, Caitlin. 2006. *North African Women in France: Gender, Culture and Identity.* Stanford, CA: Stanford University Press.

Killian, Caitlin, and Cathryn Johnson. 2006. "'I'm Not an Immigrant!': Resistance, Redefinition, and the Role of Resources in Identity Work." *Social Psychology Quarterly* 69:60–80. doi:10.1177/019027250606900105

Kreager, Derek A., and Jeremy Staff. 2009. "The Sexual Double Standard and Adolescent Peer Acceptance." *Social Psychology Quarterly* 72(2):143–64. doi:10.1177/019027250907200205

Kroska, Amy. 2014. "The Social Psychology of Gender Inequality." Pp. 485–514 in *Handbook of the Social Psychology of Inequality*, edited by J. D. McLeod, E. J. Lawler, and M. Schwalbe. New York: Springer.

Kuhn, Manford H., and Thomas S. McPartland. 1954. "An Empirical Investigation of Self-Attitudes." *American Sociological Review* 19(1): 68–76. doi:10.2307/2088175

Lee, James Daniel. 1998. "Which Kids Can 'Become' Scientists? Effects of Gender, Self-Concepts, and Perceptions of Scientists." *Social Psychology Quarterly* 61(3):199–219. doi:10.2307/2787108

Lee, James Daniel. 2002. "More Than Ability: Gender and Personal Relationships Influence Science and Technology Involvement." *Sociology of Education* 75:349–73. doi:10.2307/3090283

Lee, Jennifer, and Frank D. Bean. 2004. "America's Changing Color Lines: Immigration, Race/Ethnicity, and Multiracial Identification." *Annual Review of Sociology* 30:221–42. doi:10.1146/annurev.soc.30.012703.110519

Lever, Janet. 1978. "Sex Differences in the Complexity of Children's Play and Games." *American Sociological Review* 43:471–83. doi:10.2307/2094773

Lewis, Gregory B. 2003. "Black-white Differences in Attitudes toward Homosexuality and Gay Rights." *Public Opinion Quarterly* 67:59–78. doi:10.1086/346009

Link, Bruce G., and Jo C. Phelan. 2001. "Conceptualizing Stigma." *Annual Review of Sociology* 27:363–85. doi:10.1146/annurev.soc.27.1.363

Link, Bruce G., Jo C. Phelan, and Mark L. Hatzenbuehler. 2014. "Stigma and Social Inequality." Pp. 49–64 in *Handbook of the Social Psychology of Inequality*, edited by J. D. McLeod, E. J. Lawler, and M. Schwalbe. New York: Springer.

Maccoby, Eleanor E. 1990. "Gender and Relationships." *The American Psychologist* 45:513–20. doi:10.1037/0003-066X.45.4.513

McCall, George J. 2003. "The Me and the Not-Me." Pp. 11–25 in *Advances in Identity Theory and Research*, edited by P. J. Burke, T. J. Owens, R. Serpe, and P. A. Thoits. New York: Springer. doi:10.1007/978-1-4419-9188-1_2

McCall, George J., and Jerry Laird Simmons. 1966. *Identities and Interactions.* New York: Free Press.

McKenna, Katelyn Y. A., Amie S. Green, and Marci E. J. Gleason. 2002. "Relationship Formation on the Internet: What's the Big Attraction?" *The Journal of Social Issues* 58(1): 9–31. doi:10.1111/1540-4560.00246

Mead, George H. 1934. *Mind, Self, and Society: From the Standpoint of a Social Behaviorist*, edited by C. W. Morris. Chicago: University of Chicago Press.

Merolla, David M., Richard T. Serpe, Sheldon Stryker, and P. Wesley Schultz. 2012. "Structural Precursors to Identity Processes: The Role of Proximate Social Structures." *Social Psychology Quarterly* 75(2):149–72. doi:10.1177/0190272511436352

Messner, Michael A. 2009. *It's All for the Kids: Gender, Families, and Youth Sports.* Berkeley: University of California Press.

Milkie, Melissa A. 1999. "Social Comparisons, Reflected Appraisals, and Mass Media: The Impact of Pervasive Beauty Images on Black and White Girls' Self-Concepts." *Social Psychology Quarterly* 62:190–210. doi:10.2307/2695857

Monk, Ellis P., Jr. 2016. "The Consequences of 'Race' and 'Color' in Brazil." *Social Problems* 63(3):413–30.

Moss-Racusin, Corrine, Julie Phelan, and Laurie Rudman. 2010. "When Men Break the Gender Rules: Status Incongruity and Backlash against Modest Men." *Psychology of Men & Masculinity* 11:140–51. doi:10.1037/a0018093

Owens, Timothy J., Dawn T. Robinson, and Lynn Smith-Lovin. 2010. "Three Faces of

Identity." *Annual Review of Sociology* 36:477–99. doi:10.1146/annurev.soc.34.040507.134725

Pascoe, Cheri J. 2011. *Dude, You're a Fag: Masculinity and Sexuality in High School.* Berkeley: University of California Press.

Robinson, Dawn T., and Lynn Smith-Lovin. 1992. "Selective Interaction as a Strategy for Identity Maintenance: An Affect Control Model." *Social Psychology Quarterly* 55:12–28. doi:10.2307/2786683

Rudman, Laurie, Corrine Moss-Racusin, Julie Phelan, and Sanne Nauts. 2012. "Status Incongruity and Backlash Effects: Defending the Gender Hierarchy Motivates Prejudice against Female Leaders." *Journal of Experimental Social Psychology* 48:165–79. doi:10.1016/j.jesp.2011.10.008

Schafer, Markus H., and Kenneth F. Ferraro. 2011. "The Stigma of Obesity: Does Perceived Weight Discrimination Affect Identity and Physical Health?" *Social Psychology Quarterly* 74:76–97. doi:10.1177/0190272511398197

Schrock, Douglas, and Michael Schwalbe. 2009. "Men, Masculinity, and Manhood Acts." *Annual Review of Sociology* 35:277–95. doi:10.1146/annurev-soc-070308-115933

Simon, Robin W., Donna Eder, and Cathy Evans. 1992. "The Development of Feeling Norms Underlying Romantic Love among Adolescent Females." *Social Psychology Quarterly* 55:29–46. doi:10.2307/2786684

Smith-Lovin, Lynn. 2007. "The Strength of Weak Identities: Social Structural Sources, Situation, and Emotional Experience." *Social Psychology Quarterly* 70:106–24. doi:10.1177/019027250707000203

Snow, David, and Leon Anderson. 1987. "Identity Work among the Homeless: The Verbal Construction and Avowal of Personal Identities." *American Journal of Sociology* 92:1336–71. doi:10.1086/228668

Stets, Jan E., and Peter J. Burke. 1994. "Inconsistent Self-views in the Control Identity

Model." *Social Science Research* 23:236–62. doi:10.1006/ssre.1994.1010

Stets, Jan E., and Peter J. Burke. 1996. "Gender, Control, and Interaction." *Social Psychology Quarterly* 59:153–220.

Stets, Jan E., and Peter J. Burke. 2000. "Identity Theory and Social Identity Theory." *Social Psychology Quarterly* 63(3):224–37. doi:10.2307/2695870

Stets, Jan E., and Peter J. Burke. 2002. "Identity Theory and Social Identity Theory." Pp. 367–83 in *Handbook for Self and Identity*, edited by M. Leary and J. Tangey. New York: Guilford Press.

Stets, Jan E., and Richard T. Serpe, eds. 2016. *New Directions in Identity Theory and Research.* New York: Oxford University Press. doi:10.1093/acprof:oso/9780190457532.001.0001

Stewart, Mary White. 2003. "Gender." Pp. 761–85 in *Handbook of Symbolic Interaction*, edited by Larry T. Reynolds and Nancy J. Herman-Kinney. New York: Rowman & Littlefield.

Stone, Gregory P. 1962. "Appearance and the Self." Pp. 86–118 in *Human Behavior and Social Processes*, edited by A. M. Rose. Boston, MA: Houghton Mifflin.

Stryker, Sheldon. 1980. *Symbolic Interactionism: A Social Structural Version.* Menlo Park, CA: Benjamin/Cummings.

Stryker, Sheldon, and Peter J. Burke. 2000. "The Past, Present, and Future of an Identity Theory." *Social Psychology Quarterly* 63(4):284–97. doi:10.2307/2695840

Stryker, Sheldon, and Peter J. Burke. 2002. *Symbolic Interactionism: A Social Structural Version.* Caldwell, NJ: Blackburn.

Swann, William B., John J. Griffin, Steven Predmore, and Bebe Gaines. 1987. "The Cognitive-Affective Crossfire: When Self-consistency Confronts Self-Enhancement." *Journal of Personality and Social Psychology* 52:881–89. doi:10.1037/0022-3514.52.5.881

Swann, William B., Laurie P. Milton, and Jeffrey T. Polzer. 2000. "Creating a Niche or Falling in Line: Identity Negotiation and Small Group Effectiveness." *Journal of Personality and Social Psychology* 79:238–50. doi:10.1037/0022-3514.79.2.238

Thoits, Peggy A. 2011. "Resisting the Stigma of Mental Illness." *Social Psychology Quarterly* 74:6–28. doi:10.1177/0190272511398019

Thorne, Barrie. 1993. *Gender Play: Girls and Boys in School.* New Brunswick, NJ: Rutgers University Press.

Van Ausdale, Debra, and Joe R. Feagin. 1996. "Using Racial and Ethnic Concepts: The Critical Case of Very Young Children." *American Sociological Review* 61(5):779–93. doi:10.2307/2096453

Van Ausdale, Debra, and Joe R. Feagin. 2001. *The First R: How Children Learn Race and Racism.* Lanham, MD: Rowman & Littlefield.

Vryan, Kevin D., Patricia A. Adler, and Peter Adler. 2003. "Identity." Pp. 367–90 in *Handbook of Symbolic Interactionism,* edited by L. J. Reynolds and N. J. Herman. Walnut Creek, CA: AltaMira.

Waskul, Dennis D. 2007. "Cyberspace and Cyberselves." Pp. 119–128 in *Inside Social Life,* 5th ed., edited by Spencer E. Cahill. Los Angeles: Roxbury Publishing Company.

Waters, Mary C. 1990. *Ethnic Options: Choosing Identities in America.* Los Angeles: University of California Press.

West, Candace, and Don Zimmerman. 1977. "Woman's Place in Everyday Talk: Reflections on Parent-Child Interaction." *Social Problems* 24:521–29. doi:10.2307/800122

Wharton, Amy S. 2011. "The Sociology of Arlie Hochschild." *Work and Occupations* 38(4):459–64.

Wicklund, Robert A., and Peter M. Gollwitzer. 1982. *Symbolic Self-Completion.* Hillsdale, NJ: Erlbaum.

Intraindividual Processes

Social Cognitions

Elizabeth Bennet and Mr. Darcy, fictional main characters in Jane Austen's classic novel *Pride and Prejudice*, meet at a country "ball" (a community dance in the 18th century). She is a spirited, intelligent young woman, one of five daughters of a gentleman whose wealth is limited and whose estate will be inherited by a distant male relative. He is a handsome landowner from Derbyshire whose income exceeds £10,000 a year (a fortune in the 18th century). At the ball, Darcy comments to his one friend that Elizabeth "is tolerable, but not handsome enough to tempt *me* [to dance]" (Austen [1813] 1981:7). Upon overhearing this and observing Darcy's treatment of others at the assembly, Elizabeth concludes he is proud, haughty, and in want of inviting manners.

These initial impressions shape how each character interprets the behavior of the other. And, were it not for the introduction of new information that profoundly differs from these "first impressions," the story of Elizabeth and Mr. Darcy would have been short, mundane, and hardly the stuff that engenders a place in the canon of English literature.[1] The new information drives the narrative, just as people in their daily interactions revise their opinions of classmates or coworkers, altering their behavior and interaction to "fit" with what they perceive and expect of others. The ways in which individuals process, organize, structure, and retrieve information to make sense out of themselves, others, and situations is called **social cognition** (see Fiske and Taylor 2013; Howard and Renfrow 2003; Kunda 1999; Moskowitz 2005).

Emerging largely in psychology, social cognition provides a basis for the meanings of social objects that symbolic interactionists presume are central to successful interaction. This chapter responds to the question: What role does cognitive processing play in shaping behavior? People possess conceptual systems that **represent their knowledge** about the world, consisting of a "collection of category representations, with each category representing a different component of experience," including objects, actions, groups, roles, relations, and internal states, such as emotions and motivations (Barsalou 2008:236). These representations support a variety of cognitive activities, including ongoing perception and categorization of people, storage of information in memory, and inferences about one's own and others' behaviors based on perception and memory. Existing representations guide the processing of new information and individual behavior, thereby affecting how interaction unfolds (Howard and Renfrow 2003).

In *Pride and Prejudice*, a representation of social class underlies Darcy's perception. He knows that Elizabeth's family and friends are much less wealthy than he is, and this knowledge shapes his evaluations of the beauty of the women and induces his disdain toward the locals at the country ball. And while Darcy's income, coupled with his handsome features, initially excites admiration, his snubbing of so many shifts opinion to disgust. Sometimes these cognitive processes are under conscious control, while at other times they seem to be automatic or spontaneous (see Moors and De Houwer 2006). They may also seem to be systematic as "rational" models suggest, or they may appear colored by mental shortcuts or biases. In this chapter, we examine the processes of making judgments about people and their behavior that *help perceivers to predict others' behaviors, which in turn helps to direct and control their own behavior.* Such judgments are critical to the understanding of social interaction.

This chapter reviews the multifaceted ways that intraindividual cognitive processes unfold and how they shape what happens in groups. Individuals draw from previously stored and organized information to process new information about others in a given context. In addressing how humans perceive social stimuli, we first look at processes underlying social cognition, which provide a basis for conceptualizing the kind of "processors" that humans are. Then we focus more specifically on questions regarding how people form impressions and assess the causes of behavior—two cognitive processes with consequences for interaction. The chapter concludes with a focus on how cognitions affect behavior. What evolves from these cognitive processes provides a basis for subjective evaluations in groups (see Chapter 12), akin to the symbolic interaction notion of shared meanings, which drive the nature of further interaction.

Cognitive Processing: How Do Humans Perceive Social Stimuli?

Nearly 60 years ago, Fritz Heider (1958) argued that people attempt to analyze their social environments, much as scientists do. As "naïve psychologists," we use "principles" to attain an understanding of self and others and behavior unfolding in a situation. In *Pride and Prejudice*, many scenes depict Elizabeth, her mother, and her sisters commenting on the behavior of others in their circle of friends and attempting to explain why they behaved in a certain way—much as college students might do today when discussing who hooked up with whom after a social event. In comparison to systematic, scientific principles, the ones we naïvely use to interpret social behavior may be flawed or biased. And often we are simply unaware that we are invoking principles at all. Thus, social cognition researchers no longer liken perceivers to scientists. Instead, they ask how situations draw people's attention and how people process the information. By doing so, they create an image of the types of perceivers we are.

Although this chapter largely focuses on the social aspects of these cognitive processes, since the 1990s cognitive researchers have also begun to examine the neural basis for cognitive and social processing (see Adolphs 2009; Fiske and Taylor 2013; Smith and Kosslyn 2007). Determining how the brain matters in social cognition is possible through the use of functional magnetic

FIGURE 5.1 ● Basic Brain Structure

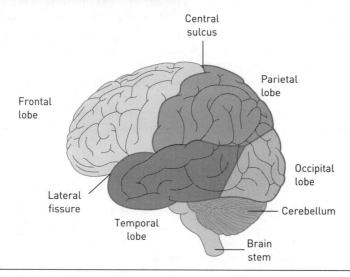

Central
sulcus

Parietal
lobe

Frontal
lobe

Occipital
lobe

Lateral
fissure

Cerebellum

Temporal
lobe

Brain
stem

Source: Garrett, B. (2015). *Brain & behavior: An introduction to biological psychology* (4th ed.). Thousand Oaks, CA: Sage.

resonance imaging (fMRI) techniques, which show the brain at work and complement other biophysical measurement techniques. fMRI methods involve exposing subjects to stimuli while they are in the magnetic resonance imaging (MRI) machine and measuring blood flow to different regions of the brain. Figure 5.1 exhibits different lobes of the brain. Studies show the activation of different neural systems for various aspects of social perception.

The medial prefrontal cortex, which appears at the tip of the frontal lobe shown in Figure 5.1, appears to be particularly important in cognitions about social stimuli pertaining to interaction (Amodio and Frith 2006). Parts of the temporal lobe are also involved in the processing of social information. For example, the superior temporal sulcus, which separates the superior gyrus and middle gyrus of the temporal lobe, is involved in judgments of intent. Exposure to faces or objects within a person's area of expertise elicits response from the fusiform gyrus portion of the brain, located at the bottom of the temporal and occipital lobes (Gauthier et al. 2000; Kanwisher, McDermott, and Chun 1997). And, as discussed more in Chapter 7, an interior portion of the brain—the amygdala (not shown)—plays a role in intense emotional experiences (Phelps 2007). Sometimes, however, affective and cognitive neural circuits involve the same regions (Davidson, 2003; Murphy, Nimmo-Smith, and Lawrence 2003).

Researchers have also determined that different parts of the brain direct automatic processing of stimuli compared to controlled (Lieberman 2007). The brain is the hardwired processing center that allows us to take in and make meaning of the multitude of stimuli encountered each day and to drive our behavior with others, regardless of sociohistorical time or location. The context, however, highlights what draws people's attention and begins the process of categorization to make sense of interaction dynamics.

Situational Cues and Categorization Processes

At an 18th century ball, a big-band-era nightclub, a modern rave, or even a wedding, a diverse array of people may gather for dancing, food, drink, and conversation. An attendee at such a function might be overwhelmed by the stimuli—the people, the "action," the smells, the room temperature, and so on. To make sense out of the situation, perceivers must attend to elements of the situation and encode information by transforming the stimuli into mental representations (Fiske and Taylor 2013). In doing so, they simplify the barrage of stimuli to create meaning from the social context. How people simplify involves consideration of both situational features and the cognitive process of categorization, which sifts incoming stimuli.

Gestalt psychology (see Köhler 1930; Lewin 1935), from which the modern study of social cognition derives, suggests that most aspects of a situation constitute the background against which perceivers judge a "figure" or the object of perception within the context, such as a person who does something of note (e.g., a soloist at a concert) or behaves in an unexpected way (e.g., a minister break-dancing at a wedding). The meaning of a "figure," however, depends upon the context. The rowdy drunk at a rave might receive only passing attention, but the same figure at a wedding might disrupt the ceremony, and lead to generating excuses for the person's behavior, and a "story" to be replayed at future weddings. Akin to the premises of symbolic interaction, social cognition dictates that the way that people perceive is partly determined by the context in which observed behavior occurs. "Situated cognition" suggests that perceivers sample from and combine multiple representations stored in memory to derive an inference about a particular stimulus (Barsalou 1999, 2008; Smith and Semin 2004). For example, how you would approach a woman weeping at a wedding or at a funeral would differ because the representation of the situation combines with the representation of the focal figure. Cues inherent in the situation include elements of it that are salient or that have priming effects.

What Gets Noticed

In a given situation, the figure and other features may be **salient**, standing out in some ways against other aspects of the situation and independent of the perceiver's expectancies or goals. These attention-grabbing stimuli are those that may be novel, intense, sudden, moving, repetitive, or related to the perceiver's goals in the situation (Fiske and Taylor 2013). For example, highly skilled dancers on the dance floor or a rowdy drunk may stand out at a party. In addition, people tend to pay greater attention to negative information. Given routine expectations for positive outcomes, negative information is more diagnostic in a situation because it violates expectations (Skowronski and Carlston 1989) and raises concerns with risks and losses that people want to avoid (Kahneman and Tversky 1984). For example, at a political rally, the candidate is more likely to notice an attendee with a menacing look than one who is smiling.

Contextual elements, moreover, may **prime** the activation of existing representations. Higgins (1996) defines priming as experiences or procedures that bring a particular category to mind and in doing so heightens the likelihood that information in the situation will be processed in terms of it. Perceivers are typically unaware of the prime or its effects on their responses. Priming is a largely automatic process that enhances accessibility of a representation stored in memory, often without the perceiver consciously connecting the two. The strength of the prime depends on how recently and frequently the category has been encountered. For example, if during a squabble a couple's favorite song begins to play, the music might evoke a positive representation about the relationship, which in turn produces an amicable resolution to the argument. For the song to act as a prime, however, requires that the couple can hear the music and that it has been paired in the recent past with positive relationship feelings. The prime may also activate other information associated with the initial representation (e.g., the song recalls memories of events that the couple enjoyed).

Typically, when a representation is made accessible owing to priming, an individual uses it to interpret other information in the situation. This is called **assimilation**—the "fitting" of new information into what has been accessed. For example, if you have just been watching the Summer Olympics swimming events (the prime) and you encounter a new person at the park where your local pool is located, you might assume that he or she is a swimmer. Assimilation (Moskowitz 2005) is likely to occur when the primed construct seems applicable to an ambiguously defined person (the new person at the pool) or a particular act under observation. In such instances, there is some room for constructing a judgment, especially when there are no social or physical constraints, like rules prohibiting swimming or the new person sporting a full body cast. For a prime to be effective, the perceiver is typically unaware that it may be influencing his or her judgment. (Awareness of a potentially biasing influence inhibits assimilation!)

Sometimes, however, priming may backfire. Awareness of a blatant prime and its link to a particular stimulus may lead to **contrast effects**—that is, movement away from the judgment implied by the prime (Lombardi, Higgins, and Bargh 1987). For example, if Jessica talks about how cute the Phi Alpha fraternity boys are (which acts as a prime) and then sets her friend Rachel up on a date with a young man from that house (which constitutes a stimulus), Rachel may be conscious of how Jessica has primed her. When the blind date arrives, she may find him less attractive than she would have if she had not been primed! Contrast effects tend to occur when the actual stimulus does not overlap much with the primed category (Herr 1986). If a prime is very extreme (e.g., Jessica rates all Phi Alpha members a 10—the highest on the attractiveness scale), then perceivers are unlikely to find similarities between it and the focal stimulus, resulting in judgments opposite to that implied by the accessible category (e.g., Rachel sees her blind date, who objectively might be a 7, as a 3—far from the 10 she anticipated). Both conscious and unconscious primes thus anchor judgments of incoming stimuli, with assimilation resulting when stimuli features match those of the primed category and contrast when they do not.

Categorizing Social Information

The processes of assimilation and contrast, though typically discussed in the context of the effects of priming, are also relevant to **categorization processes** central to social cognition. Categorization entails placing perceived situational stimuli into groups of conceptually equivalent "objects"—ones sharing key characteristics—thereby organizing (and assimilating) incoming stimuli with information existing in memory. **Categories** are mental representations of classes or groups of abstract or concrete things, events, or people that structure knowledge and are stored in memory (Markman and Ross 2003). They may overlap with each other (e.g., "neighbors" may also be "friends") or be nested (e.g., "nurses" can be found among "hospital workers") and may be organized hierarchically (e.g., health care workers vary in rank: doctors, nurses, orderlies). Although categorization may result in loss of accuracy, it provides an initial basis from which to make *inferences*, which in turn shape the pursuit of a line of action. The activation of a category, sometimes the result of priming, culminates in the interaction between stimulus cues and perceptions of how they match the stored representation (Higgins 1996). For instance, while visiting a hospitalized friend, if you categorize the person dressed in scrubs examining your friend as a nurse, you may interact with her differently than you would if you categorized her as a doctor. Once a stimulus is categorized, further knowledge becomes available because the initial category activates associations stored in memory (Smith and Kosslyn 2007).

For example, when Darcy sizes up the women at the dance, he engages in categorization: attending to the beauty and manners of the local young women; comparing them to features in his category of "appealing women," stored in memory; and deciding whether the new women fit his category. He may also ask himself, "Am I trying to impress anyone here?" or "Are these women of my social class?" These questions situate the categorization process. Answering no to both questions may facilitate finding the women to fall short of his standards for "appealing women," thus permitting him to not ask any of the young ladies present to dance. Categorization, in effect, involves a reiterative process of matching features of a stimulus to features of existing categories.

Although categorization processes typically proceed without conscious awareness (Moskowitz 2005), the process is a means to actively construct reality and thus is a step underlying the construction of meaning described in symbolic interaction. Moreover, members of cultural and social groups are likely to share the general content of categories (Morris and Peng 1994). For example, what constitutes the features of the category of "attractive people" is likely to be similar for members of the same racial and socioeconomic groups and, perhaps, distinct across such groups. Category knowledge emerges by perceiving and creating representations of individual members of a category and then integrating those representations (Smith and Kosslyn 2007). For example, a child encounters people who teach different things— colors at preschool, prayers at church, strokes at the swimming pool. He comes to recognize that what all these people do is similar, leading him to create a representation of "teacher," which he uses to judge others who instruct. Routes to the formation and integration of categorical knowledge include prototypes, exemplars, and schema.

Forming Categories, Organizing Information, and Interpreting Events

A **prototype** is "a representation detailing a typical category member, summarized by the set of most common features that are most probable to be found in a category member" (Moskowitz 2005:164). Prototypes capture, as abstractions, the central tendencies of characteristics or the properties that are most likely true of members of a particular group. They are, however, drawn from experience and thus to the extent that people have different experiences, the content of prototypes may vary. For example, a prototype for the category of "teacher" is likely to take on different features for an instructor in elementary school than one in college. For both, a teacher imparts information and provides skills training, yet the college teacher relies less on repetition and art projects to convey knowledge than the elementary school teacher. Despite this potential variation in content, proto-types function in perception to allow people to generate missing information and to make inferences (Cantor and Mischel 1977).

The second idea proposed for the formation of categories focuses not on abstractions but on specific examples of actual members—that is, **exemplars** (Medin 1989). Information constituting the cognitive representation stems from characteristics compiled based on an individual's perception of real people who represent a particular category. For example, if people use George R. R. Martin and Stephen King as exemplars for their category "fiction writers," then the cat-egory is likely to include characteristics such as white, male, best-selling, and rich (which could be misleading, given that most authors are lucky to eke out a living based solely on their writing!). Exemplars may vary in terms of their extensiveness. Plus, for certain frequently encountered categories, people tend to store more details. For example, the category "teacher" is likely to be described in greater detail than a less frequently encountered category such as "senator" (Smith and Zarate 1992). The greater variability in exemplars compared to pro-totypes suggests that inferences drawn from an exemplar may be different than one drawn from a prototype (Murphy and Medin 1985). In most situations, both prototypes and exemplars provide the perceiver with a point of comparison of an actual instance to a category, however formed. Thus, the ongoing perception reflects the extent to which the current stimulus is similar to or different from the category stored in memory.

Prototypes and exemplars epitomize the accumulation of properties of a category, with little attention to how they are organized. **Schema**, cognitive structures that *organize* information by identifying the attributes of a category (formed either from prototypes or exemplars) and the relations among those attributes (Fiske and Taylor 2013), are a form of background knowledge. Schema may pertain to a sequence of events in familiar situations, to roles, interpersonal relationships, and even to the self. They are conceptually driven and abstract and thus hold across many particular instances. Importantly, in addition to containing information relevant to categorizing, they include information relevant to understanding events surrounding the invocation of a particular category (Smith and Kosslyn 2007). For example, a schema for the category of "teacher" contains information relevant to processing observations about people serving in a variety of schools, on the playing field, or in a kitchen. By guiding the way that new information is processed, schema set up expectancies for the behavior of self and others. Thus, even though you had never set foot in a college before your freshman year, you already had an idea of how to talk to your professor and knew that talking to him or her might unfold in a different manner than talking to your friends. Perceivers tend to see and remember infor-mation about people in a manner consistent with their schema (e.g., Rogers, Kuiper, and Kirker 1977).

A classic example of how this occurs was illustrated in a study by Hastorf and Cantril (1954) regarding hot-tempered reactions to a relatively rough football game between Dartmouth and Princeton. Students at the respective universities watched a movie of the game and while doing so identified "dirty" plays com-mitted by each team. Results showed that although Dartmouth study partici-pants counted an equal number of infractions for each team, Princeton students indicated that twice as many dirty plays were committed by Dartmouth players as by Princeton players. The findings show both how *an identical event can be differentially interpreted* and, especially in the case of the Princeton study

participants, how one's negative schema about another team produces a potentially biased estimate of negative behaviors.

Similarly, in *Pride and Prejudice*, Mr. Wickham, a soldier who is handsome, possesses pleasing manners, and who was, ostensibly, denied an inheritance prom-
ised by Mr. Darcy's father, charms the Bennet sisters. The categories to which
Mr. Wickham belongs (i.e., soldier, attractive in appearance and manners, victim) evoke schema that the young women positively evaluate and, possibly, with
which they sympathize. Thus, they are quick to judge all of his behavior positively and ignore (at least initially) less favorable or scandalous information. As
Snyder and Swann (1978) show, people tend to seek information that confirms
their schema-based expectancies and to neglect information that disconfirms such
expectancies. This pattern, called the **confirmation bias**, indicates a tendency
to confirm initial expectations and beliefs. The bias leads perceivers toward perceptual "sharpening" for schema consistent information (e.g., when the Bennet
sisters welcome stories from their neighbors about how charmingly Wickham has
behaved) and perceptual "flattening" of schema inconsistent information (e.g.,
when Elizabeth wants to ignore news of the debts that Wickham has incurred).
Both perceptual sharpening and flattening affect impression formation and intergroup processes (see Chapter 12).

Important to intergroup processes are categorizations of individuals as representatives of groups. A **stereotype** refers to beliefs about the features, opinions, and expected behaviors of a group that may be generalized to individuals
belonging to the group. Allport (1954) noted that stereotypes often begin with a
kernel of truth based on an experience or observation. How beliefs shaping the
stereotype build, however, may be subject to cognitive errors, biases, and lack of
revision so that the resulting stereotype includes information that may not accurately describe the majority of group members and may reflect ideological beliefs
rather than the diverse reality of the people to whom the stereotype is applied.
For example, the stereotype of the southerner evokes an image of white people
(see Griffin, Evenson, and Thompson 2005) who may additionally be characterized as uncouth, poor, stupid, and lazy. Such a characterization hardly represents
the diversity—in terms of race, class, intelligence, effort expenditure—found in
the South today. Like prototypes, exemplars, and schema, stereotypes invoked in
the process of categorization have consequences for behavior, and, in the case of
stereotypes, the behavior may be discriminatory (see Chapter 12).

Categorization processes are quite robust in filtering social stimuli and reinforcing existing representations. Thus, it is difficult to break down representations
stored in memory. Several conditions, however, may thwart routine categorization (Fiske and Taylor 2013). Perceivers are less likely to succumb to their existing
representations as a basis for cognitions about their own and others' behavior
when (1) categorical information is weak; (2) the content of the representation is
so extreme that all incoming information appears contrastive; and (3) (behavioral)
information diluting the impact of the existing representation is clearly relevant
to the judgment being made—that is, there is compelling contradictory evidence.
For example, imagine that you expect everyone at a science fair to be geeky, so
into their science projects that they ignore hygiene, appearance, and social cues.
Yet you discover well-dressed individuals who make eye contact when speaking
and enthusiastically answer questions in lay terminology. In other words, the
evidence is overwhelming that these competitors at a science fair do not fit your
extreme view of being wholly geeky. Change in representation content stems

from integration with new information and reconciliation with information in other activated categories.

A dynamic process of perception emerges from the confluence of situational cues and categorizations (Smith and Kosslyn 2007). Although categories contain lots of different information, not all of it is activated when a category is accessed. Rather, perceivers draw information from categories that gain their attention and seem relevant in the situation. That information, moreover, may also pertain to goals, motivations, and emotions—not necessarily simply properties of a category. And, as situations vary, the information drawn from existing representations also varies. In this way, *perceivers actively construct what is meaningful in their situations using information that represents people, objects, motivations, goals, and settings.* By doing so, they figure out how they should behave and how others are likely to behave, which affects subsequent social dynamics and relationships. Although focused on the cognitive system rather than the interaction context, this process is consistent with the tenets of symbolic interaction. Parties involved in interaction may produce different interpretations of the same situation (as was true for observers of the Princeton versus Dartmouth football game) because information activated from accessible categories may vary across the people interacting.

Yet perceivers generally face some uncertainty regarding what representation to use for interpreting social stimuli. Which stimuli become central, likewise, may create uncertainty. Individuals reduce uncertainty by using filtering principles to minimize the representations that could pertain to their focal stimuli.

Filtering Principles Shaping Patterns of Cognitions

In (consciously or unconsciously) deciding which mental representations best fit a given stimulus's attributes, people do not compare all possible categories or schema to the stimulus (because it would be complicated and take forever!). Instead, they simplify by relying on guidelines for producing a "rational" inference about the stimulus, given uncertainty (Moskowitz 2005). Thus, people employ filtering principles: heuristics, anchors, and framing processes.

Heuristics

Tversky and Kahneman (1974, 1982) outlined three **heuristics**, which are basically cognitive shortcuts that allow perceivers to get a sense of a situation without considering all available information. Although individuals are unlikely to use heuristics when the stakes are high or when they are held accountable for their inferences (Fiske and Taylor 2013), they may use them when they are in situations in which they have had lots of practice or when they cannot use judgment processes involving a thorough and accurate assessment of all stimuli and systematic application of all potential cognitive representations (Liberman 2001). As a consequence, perceivers are unwitting accomplices in the errors produced by heuristic processing. Importantly, these are neither motivated biases nor evidence of irrational behavior.

The **representativeness heuristic** (Tversky and Kahneman 1974) proposes that categorization reflects the extent to which a focal stimulus represents or is similar to the category to which it belongs. When information about the stimulus is indicative of the larger category, then the representative heuristic is not misleading. For example, an animal is likely to be a porcupine if it appears to have defensive spines or quills on its body and tail. In contrast, information about social categories may be less diagnostic for any one member of the category (Kunda 1999). For example, Mr. Darcy may presume "country girls" are plain, uneducated if not slow-witted, and tractable. But in doing so, he wholly underestimates Elizabeth, who is attractive, intelligent, and of strong opinions. Although there is a high probability that Elizabeth is like country girls, solely relying on the representative heuristic is misleading.

Reliance on representativeness may also lead perceivers to ignore **base-rate information**, which refers to the statistical pattern representing the frequency or probability of a particular event or attributes of an individual occurring (Kahneman and Tversky 1973). A classic example of the *underuse* of base-rate information entails a car buyer who ignores the high consumer reports ratings of a model and opts against buying that model because an acquaintance who once owned the same car said it was constantly undergoing repairs. The car buyer allows the vivid example of his friend's lemon of a car to represent all cars of that model, thereby underusing the base-rate information on the car's reliability. In terms of social judgments, people may rely more on what a set of categorical and trait descriptors suggests than on the actual statistical probability that an individual belongs to a particular group. For example, if a man is described as wealthy, athletic, Republican, and suave, then we might agree that it is likely he belongs to a country club even though the percentage of male Republicans belonging to such institutions is small. Although base-rate information that is causal in nature or highly salient draws more attention, reliance on representativeness remains an oft used cognitive shortcut (Kunda 1999).

Related to the representativeness heuristic are three other processing "errors" (Fiske and Taylor 2013). These errors pertain to the failure of individuals to think in statistical terms. First, people are likely to ignore "sample size," even though characteristics of small samples may differ from those of larger samples, which provide more reliable estimates of population features. For example, the experience of two or three of your friends with regard to owning a Corvette may not represent the same experiences of 1,000 other Corvette owners. Second, whenever a behavior is influenced by chance (e.g., a person's extremely high [or low] score on a test reflects both ability and good [or bad] luck), the next instance of that behavior is likely to be less extreme owing to "regression to the mean." And, third, the "conjunctive fallacy" suggests that, in assessing a person, inferences that combine multiple outcomes are less likely to be true than those suggesting only one. For example, consider the following: a bearded, scholarly man whose beliefs in social equality underlie his activism in disadvantaged communities might be inferred to be a "professor" or an "activist," but it would be less likely that he would be both. Enriching details may increase representativeness, but they reduce the probability of the joint outcomes.

Just as the representativeness bias results in leaping to conclusions that a person who shares some characteristics with typical members of a group belongs to that group, the **availability heuristic** (Tversky and Kahneman 1974) suggests that people jump to conclusions based on what comes readily to mind. When the ease of remembering reflects the actual higher frequency of something occurring, this heuristic is useful. Thus, it is probably easier to bring to mind images of high-ranking male military officers than female ones because there are more male officers. The availability heuristic is misleading when what quickly comes to mind is independent of frequency. For example, a child fears the rides at Disney's Animal Kingdom park because what comes quickly to mind are the startled faces of those riding the Dinosaur ride at the park.

Tversky and Kahneman's (1982) last shortcut is the **simulation heuristic**, indicating that perceivers mentally simulate why people (themselves included) are doing something. Simulation outcomes form the basis for interpreting the person and his or her behavior. Simulations may involve counterfactual thinking of the sort—"if only she had acted in a different manner"—which suggests what could have been the case. A turning point in *Pride and Prejudice* is when Elizabeth's parents allow her youngest sister to go to Bath, a city housing many soldiers; there she elopes with Mr. Wickham, leaving her parents to wonder what would have happened if they had not permitted her to go to Bath. On a more trivial level, if you are trying to get to an appointment during rush hour, you might opt for the freeway; should you get caught in a traffic jam that causes you to miss the appointment, you might wonder what would have happened had you driven your normal surface streets route. Use of the simulation heuristic tends to intensify emotional reactions to a situation (e.g., you are more frustrated for taking the freeway as you sit in rush hour traffic than you might have been had you driven your normal route). And when it is easy to imagine people behaving in alternative ways, the simulation heuristic affects impressions that are formed. For example, Elizabeth could readily imagine Darcy acting more politely at the first dance; his failure to so act exacerbated how negatively she viewed him.

Although inconsistent with visions of individuals as naïve scientists, the use of heuristics is often functional. Judgments based on these shortcuts may be acceptable to both the perceiver and others. Plus, they are achieved without the expenditure of large amounts of mental effort.

Anchors and Framing

Similarly, **anchors**—perceptual reference points—help reduce ambiguity in a situation and simplify perceptions (Fiske and Taylor 2013). For example, when Steven Colbert gives John Oliver's show "five stars," you might think Oliver put on a great performance. If, however, Colbert is using a 10-star scale, then the show was only so-so. The 10 on the scale anchors your perception of a five-star rating. Often, however, anchors are not as clear-cut or objective as that. In such cases, perceivers may use themselves—their dispositions and behavior—as anchors to judge others' behaviors (Epley et al. 2004; Fong and Markus 1982). Thus, for example, if Karen's extremely extroverted son, Ross, were to use himself as an anchor in judging the demonstrativeness of others, he may see them all as relatively shy, even though by objective standards—or even the anchors used by others—they are not. Seemingly irrelevant situational factors may also function as anchors. For example, teachers who verbally describe on the first day of class dire consequences for failure to turn in assignments on time might be seen as tougher than those who hold the same standards but do not articulate it verbally. In effect, anchors enhance the accessibility of particular schema and thus shape perceptions.

How problems are presented more generally also affects how people perceive them and ultimately the decisions that they make. The **framing** of decisions or choices activates different representations that provide the basis for interpreting relevant information. In particular, framing decisions in terms of the gains or losses that will result affects how people respond even if the actual outcomes are basically the same (Kahneman and Tversky 1984). Imagine choosing among public health programs to combat a deadly flu that may kill 600 people: with Option A, 200 lives will be saved; with Option B, there is a one-third probability that

600 lives will be saved and a two-thirds probability that no people will be saved; with Option C, 400 people will die; and with Option D, there is a one-third probability that no one will die and a two-thirds probability that 600 people will die. Even though the outcomes are exactly the same for all Options, when framed in terms of lives saved (gains), people typically choose Option A, not B. When framed in terms of lives lost, people tend to select Option D, not C, even though these two options produce similar outcomes (Tversky and Kahneman 1981). Such a pattern of choice, illustrated in a wide variety of settings, demonstrates that people avoid risks when dealing with potential gains but take risks with potential losses (Levin, Schneider, and Gaeth 1998).

The use of framing, anchors, and heuristics are means by which perceivers simplify the information available to them to make sense out of a situation. Their use may result in misleading inferences, especially in the absence of sufficient evidence to make more informed inferences. These processing information shortcuts, coupled with reliance on salient or primed situational cues and categorization processes, signify a particular image of the perceiver.

Image of Perceivers

Given that processes underlying social cognitions produce inferences that may only approximate what a more scientific approach would suggest, perceivers might be called biased. Such a label, however, would be misleading. Instead, as research on social cognition has accumulated, various images of perceivers have been offered (Fiske and Taylor 2013).

In the 1980s, scholars were fascinated with the rapid processing of social information by relying on categories, schema, and heuristics. They labeled perceivers as *cognitive misers*, who conserved their cognitive resources by relying on stored representations and shortcuts. In the 1990s, researchers brought in consideration of perceivers' goals, motives, or needs, which led to an image of *motivated tacticians*. The tactician tries to sort through situational information to allow maintenance of flexibility and efficiency. Individuals flexibly allocate their cognitive resources for attending to and processing stimuli to conserve mental energies for assessing other information (Sherman 2001; Uleman, Newman, and Moskowitz 1996). Flexibility allows for times when people are motivated by personal goals (e.g., looking for a date), when the situation demands accuracy and more detailed processing (e.g., interviewing a job candidate), or when emotions overcome all else (e.g., cheering on the home team). Efficiency involves using mental resources in a way that corresponds with the needs of the perceiver and situation.

Whether perception appears to be automatic while at other times it appears to be more controlled depends upon cues in the social context. Bargh (1994) describes **automatic processing** as determined directly from the stimuli, not under volitional control, using little mental energy, and without awareness of what is occurring. Such nonconscious processing of information may arise owing to practice, repetition, or habit (Bargh 1990). In addition, social forces—for example, politeness rituals, deference rules—may also trigger automatic responses. In contrast, **controlled processing** suggests the ability of the perceiver to direct and regulate his or her cognition, perhaps in pursuit of incentives or a goal (Wegner and Bargh 1998). Imagine walking across campus and you suddenly feel yourself smiling as you approach a close friend. What you might miss in the situation is that your close friend is hanging out with your sworn enemy (which might, if more thought was given to your response, elicit a more perplexed expression or even stimulate an angry response). Automatic processing of the situation results in the initial smile. Later encounters, however, may be characterized by more controlled processing about the close friend's association with your nemesis. With the turn of the 21st century, what we know about how people perceive has led to the label of *activated actors*. For such actors, the situation activates perceptions that do not just reflect individuals' deliberate "thinking" but their unconscious thoughts and affective concerns as well.

Summary

The process by which humans perceive social stimuli is obviously complex. When Darcy walked into that ballroom in the countryside, he had to process a lot of information about the people there, how they lived their lives, what the occasion meant to them, and the like. What drew his attention most depended upon possible priming (foreknowledge of the families that would be attending) as well as his experiences previously, which may have activated assimilation and contrast processes. And, of course, as previous examples have suggested, his existing categories, defined by prototypes or exemplars, fueled the schema he used to understand the situation. What he saw may have differed from Elizabeth's impressions because of the content of their categories and the use of different filtering principles, which may have narrowed the myriad of social stimuli they encountered. Some of their processing of information may have been conscious and controlled, while much of it was probably automatic. While the account of Darcy and Elizabeth is fiction, all of us have found ourselves entering new situations and trying to make sense of them. The processes of categorization and invoking comparisons to "what we know," such as those suggested by cognitive heuristics, allow us to make sense out of the new situation.

Recall the example of encountering your friend with your sworn enemy. You may have wondered about your friend's new acquaintance. In doing so, you may form impressions of this newcomer and at the same time wonder why your friend is hanging out with her. Such questions capture two key elements of social cognition: (1) the processes of impression formation and (2) attribution regarding the causes of a person's behavior. Heider (1958) argued that behavior is a function of both the **person** behaving and the social **environment** in which the person is embedded—that is, behavior = f (person + environment). As the foregoing suggests, however, people are not simply naïve scientists who objectively process information. Rather, their perceptions are subjective, determined both by the shortcomings of automatic processing and their own goals in the situation. Consideration of the involvement of the perceiver is reflected in recent models of impression formation and remains implicit in approaches to attribution.

How Do People Form Impressions of Others?

The introduction to this chapter recounted a scene in *Pride and Prejudice* in which the main characters are forming the first impressions of each other. Regardless of whether the impressions were accurate (they were not, as later information in the novel suggests), they provided an initial guide for action and interaction. Much as symbolic interactionists would suggest, psychologists have long asserted that individuals construct knowledge of others in order to provide a meaningful way in order to anticipate future behavior (James [1907] 1991). An **impression** refers to "a perceiver's organized cognitive representation of another person" (Hamilton, Katz, and Leirer 1980:123). Like the formation of any social cognition, the formation of an impression involves attending to, processing of, retrieving from memory, and organizing information. Perceivers rely on both their direct experience with a person and their existing expectancies, based on their representations, biases, goals, moods, and the like, to form an impression, which in turn may alter stored existing knowledge and shape current behavior. Impressions may emerge from thoughtful, controlled processing but also quite frequently from automatic, spontaneous inferences (see Uleman, Saribay, and Gonzalez 2008).

Basic Models

Just as Elizabeth and Mr. Darcy sized each other up at the ball, freshman college students form impressions of individuals and groups in their first encounters with roommates and others at dorm or fraternity parties. Information available to perceivers includes what is readily observable such as appearance (physical features, posture, attire, perceived attractiveness) and behaviors (verbal, nonverbal gestures). How that information is interpreted depends upon the context in which it is embedded and the viewpoint of the perceiver. For example, a female dressed in a sheer, cleavage-baring, sleeveless blouse with a micromini skirt and spiked sandals may seem out of place at work but in sync with others at a cocktail party. An employer might judge a worker dressed in that way as unprofessional, which could jeopardize promotion chances. In contrast, a male partygoer might judge the woman to be "hot" and invite her on a date.

Early work on impression formation focused on **bottom-up, data-driven** information processing in which perceivers combined specific pieces of details about another person to form a cogent image of the whole. In particular, emphasis rested on modeling how individuals combine personality traits, largely ignoring other characteristics used to form impressions, the context, and the perceiver's own subjectivity. Asch (1946) presaged the schema concept by arguing that in forming impressions of other people, perceivers attempt to unify the individual elements to bring them in line with the overall impression.

A classic example of Asch's configural approach to impression formation involves the differentiating effects of the characteristics warm and cold when included in a list of other characteristics (intelligent, skillful, industrious, determined, practical, and cautious). A person described by characteristics including warm is more positively evaluated on other attributes compared to someone described as cold. Dubbed central traits, the characteristics of warm and cold change the meaning of other traits, bringing them in-line with a largely positive or negative, respectively, evaluation. Spreading the valence of evaluation of some traits to others suggests a "halo effect" (positive traits enhance the evaluation of other traits) or a "horn effect" (negative traits detract from other traits; Nisbett and Wilson 1977).

Regardless of type of information, typically perceivers weigh more heavily the information that they first receive (Fiske and Taylor 2013). The **primacy effect** suggests that initial information spurs impressions, decreasing the impact of later information on the final judgment. In effect, people tend to maintain already established beliefs even in the face of contradictory evidence. For example, Elizabeth's image of Mr. Darcy was so negative that when she toured his estate months after meeting him, she could hardly countenance hearing his house-keeper describe him in glowing terms. For many voters in the 2008 presidential primary, their initial impression of Barack Obama as politically inexperienced was hard to overcome. Situational factors, however, may modify the impact of the primacy effect. Tetlock (1983) showed that if perceivers are held accountable for the impressions they form, they grow more vigilant in processing information and more cautious in drawing conclusions from incomplete information. Thus, managers conducting job interviews—especially if higher administrators are depending upon them—are likely to collect all information before forming an impression of the applicant. And, given the importance of the 2008 election, voters seemed to scrutinize information about the candidates throughout the election, not simply relying on the first descriptions they heard.

Data-driven models of impression formation generally require greater cognitive effort than do **top-down, theory-driven** approaches that capitalize on categorical processing of information about a target. Information based on appearance that denotes various social categories (e.g., gender, race, age) activates associated representations and propels the impression. Such strategies emerge when cognitive resources are restricted owing to time pressures that limit the length of deliberations or to working on many tasks at once (i.e., high cognitive load) or on complex or difficult tasks (Moskowitz 2005). For example, an elementary school teacher who is overwhelmed by tasks that keep his 35 new students challenged may quickly form an impression of a student who fails repeatedly to turn in homework as lazy; the teacher does not have the time to devote to finding out if there is something else (e.g., a language barrier, lack of supplies in the family) that interferes with homework completion.

While the top-down use of categories reduces the complexity of the impression formation task, as noted previously, perceivers have a tendency to see information consistent with their expectancies. Consequently, top-down processing may result in impressions reflecting the extent to which perceivers are familiar with the relevant categories if not their biases about those categories (Darley and Gross 1983; Wyer and Srull 1989). For example, thinking of political candidates only in terms of their gender or race ignores information more appropriate to the offices that they are seeking, like their knowledge of lawmaking and familiarity with issues facing their constituencies. The 2008 presidential primary pitted a female candidate against an African American candidate, both of whom were highly competent, in contrast to what some believe that these categories represent. A key question is this: When do people use top-down methods of forming an impression rather than a bottom-up process?

Dual Process Models

Dual process models (Brewer 1988; Chaiken, Liberman, and Eagly, 1989) address this question. Such models recognize that the context and perceivers' goals may determine the extent to which people rely upon data-driven (bottom-up) or theory-driven (top-down) approaches to impression formation. Generally, these models describe a move from the ease and automaticity of top-down processing to more systematic and controlled, bottom-up processing when situational or motivational conditions create aversive psychological tension. To relieve tension, perceivers shift from theory-driven to data-driven processing of information about others. Situations in which a high degree of inconsistency exists between information stored in existing representation and the target person's (unexpected) behavior produce more systematic processing. Such a condition forces reexamination of both incoming data and the contents of one's category.

Motivational conditions involve perceivers' desires to be accurate in their impressions, make a point, fulfill goals, or maintain particular self-images. Accuracy in impressions is valued when the situation holds perceivers responsible and accountable for their impressions or involves perceivers who depend on others and are fearful of having their impressions invalidated (Moskowitz 2005). Also, when people use their cognitions to prove a particular point or to create an image of another person in terms of what they want to believe is true to support their own interpersonal needs, they may act in ways to ensure that the desired impression emerges (Chaiken et al. 1989). A key example of this sort of motivated impression formation occurs during political campaigns when opposing candidates try to cast their opponents in a negative light to win votes. The desire to maintain a particular image of oneself also drives how people form impressions of others. Akin to self-confirming processes described by symbolic interaction, forming impressions may be colored by motivations to defend self-relevant knowledge and beliefs (Chaiken et al. 1989), to verify a self-concept (Swann 1990), and to enhance self-esteem (Sedikides 1993). Thus, even though people may pursue a systematic, bottom-up impression formation strategy, motivations lead them to selectively attend to and evaluate information about others.

Brewer's (1988) dual process model explicitly considers how perceiver's motivations aid the switch between automatic and controlled processing. In any situation, without conscious thought, perceivers recognize the entrance of a new person. This first step in automatic processing, labeled *identification*, initiates the categorization process. Which category is activated depends upon characteristics of the context (e.g., the purpose, others present), the perceiver (e.g., his or her mood, easily accessible categories), and most certainly the target (e.g., physical features, behavior). The impression will rely on top-down processing unless the target in some ways is seen as relevant to the perceiver's current goals. Such "self-relevance" activates controlled processing, which unfolds in various ways, depending upon whether the perceiver views the other person as someone important to know. If the other is deemed important to know, the perceiver focuses on getting to know the other person from the bottom up. Labeled *personalization*, this process involves assessing personal characteristics and behaviors rather than general categories. If the perceiver does not regard the other as someone with whom to become self-involved, then further top-down categorization continues until the stimulus person "fits" a known category. Should that never occur, the perceiver may decide that the person is unique— possibly an exception to a schema— resulting in what Brewer (1988) labels individuation.

Imagine looking to buy your first condominium. You visit various condo complexes, and at one, you meet someone who lives next door to the unit you have just seen. Your encounter stimulates automatic information processing to form an impression—the neighbor is male, late 20s, possibly biracial, and dressed conservatively. Unless you decide to bid on the condo, your impression is unlikely to go beyond that categorical information. Should you decide to purchase the condo, that neighbor becomes more relevant to you. On subsequent encounters, you may share basic information—where you work, the schools you attended, mutual friends, favorite activities. Finding commonalities on that information may lead you to grow more involved with the neighbor to the extent that you get to know him as a friend (or more) and not simply the representative of some category or group. A lack of commonalities, however, would lead you into an iterative process of finding a category into which he fits—computer geek, for example. His biracial appearance, however, may fail to fit any existing category (e.g., in your experience, computer geeks are usually nerdy white boys); thus, the person is designated as an exception.

Brewer's (1988) dual process model emphasizes perceivers' needs and goals as central to the switch to more effortful cognitive processing. Chaiken et al. (1989) offer a model that likewise distinguishes between an effortless "heuristic" processing approach and a more effortful "systematic" approach. This model relies heavily on premises about how people usually process information rather than on their personal motivations related to others in a situation. Chaiken et al. (1989) assume that perceivers typically prefer to process information about others in a way that requires the least amount of effort (and thus employs categorization and heuristics). When one does not feel "sufficiently confident" in a judgment or when there are situational pressures for accuracy, accountability, or personal involvement, heuristic processing gives way to systematic processing. Generally, to the extent that people grow aware of these automatic processes or realize that they exert unwanted influence on their assessments (e.g., an open-minded, tolerant person begins to pronounce bigoted or prejudicial judgments), motivation shifts toward more effortful processing of social stimuli. While social categories may initially "anchor" impressions, they are pliable. Adjustments occur as necessary, owing to personal motivations or situational demands (Trope 1986; Trope and Alfieri 1997). Undoing first impressions (especially those based on implicit evaluations) requires new information implying an opposite evaluation and reframing initial information (Mann and Ferguson 2015). For example, Darcy's costly efforts to suppress and rectify the scandal of Elizabeth's youngest sister's ill-advised elopement and his refusal to claim credit for his efforts cast him as caring and modest rather than inconsiderate and proud. That new information allows Elizabeth to see him as "good" and reframes her initial observations of his behavior at the country ball in terms of self-protection and shyness rather than haughtiness.

Summary

Impression formation processes highlight two pathways: (1) the automatic, top-down, category-driven process and (2) the systematic, bottom-up, data driven strategy. While situational forces and cognitive processing inclinations of perceivers often encourage reliance on top-down impression formation strategies, perceivers' goals and motivations about others encourage shifts toward use of bottom-up strategies. When one looks at more detailed information about another person, information received first and central traits may exert greater influence.

Impressions, generally, flesh out the "person" factor in Heider's (1958) heuristic equation of what contributes to causal inferences. The models of attribution processes discussed next recognize that the "person" is an essential component but construe the person more narrowly than impression formation models, limiting conceptualization of the person to an "actor" who produced an observed behavior within a specific situation.

What Determines People's Inferences About the Causes of Social Behavior?

To understand social situations, perceivers commonly search for the causes and reasons for events. Perceivers ask why an event occurred to determine their own reactions to it (Heider 1958). For example, Elizabeth puzzles over the failure of her sister Jane's suitor, Mr. Bingley, to visit them when they were all in London, imagining that Mr. Bingley did not have affection for her sister or that others failed to convey to him that Jane was in close proximity. Such a situation remains common today when friends ponder why one of them did not get a callback from a prospective girlfriend or boyfriend. In these examples, Elizabeth and the group of friends engage in a social inference process called attribution. Generally, social inferences involve observing someone's action, reflecting on the action to assess its nature and meaning, and then considering the possibility of other interpretations (see, e.g., Lieberman et al. 2002). Both reflection and consideration of other interpretations may involve a high degree of automaticity (Todd et al. 2011), though initial formulations of attribution processes suggest a thoughtful undertaking.

The Nature of Attributions

An **attribution** is an inference about the cause of someone's action. Elizabeth's first response suggests that she believes that it is something about Mr. Bingley—his lack of affection for her sister—that accounts for his failure to contact her. This is an **internal attribution**, which takes as its focus the actor or person—his or her stable disposition, character, and abilities, as well as temporary states such as effort, moods, motives, or goals. The second explanation, in contrast, suggests something beyond Mr. Bingley's character or mood as the reason he fails to contact Jane. **External attributions** focus on contextual features, social constraints or pressures, or even uncontrollable forces (e.g., luck). In interaction situations especially, external attributions may include what others in the situation have done (or not done).

While Heider's (1958) formulation couples internal attributions with intentional causes and external ones with unintentional causes, Weiner (Weiner et al. 1972) offers additional attribution dimensions. Within internal and external loci, he distinguishes causes that are **stable** and do not change from situation to situation from those that are unstable and may change across situations. Further refining Heider's attachment of elements of intentionality to locus of cause, Weiner (1979) introduces variation in **controllability**: the extent to which the actor or others in the situation can exert control over their behavior. These three dimensions of attributions (locus [internal and external], stability, controllability) combine to create unique causal attributions.

For example, in achievement situations, an attribution to an internal, stable, and controllable source would focus on a person's routine level of effort; attribution to innate ability or aptitude would also be internal and stable but uncontrollable. Temporary effort is an unstable yet controllable cause, whereas one's mood on test day is both unstable and uncontrollable. Among external causes, typical uncontrollable causes include task difficulty (a stable feature of the stimulus) and luck (an unstable situational consideration). The controllability dimension for external attributions may imply something about others; for example, teacher biases in grading (stable, yet potentially controllable) or unusual help from others (controllable, yet unstable) might account for a given grade. Although Weiner (1986) applies these dimensions beyond achievement, analyzing potential causes by these dimensions may not always be possible.

What is important, however, is to recognize that attributions shape future behaviors and interactions. And, beyond ascertaining the locus of cause, determining stability or controllability may in some situations be critical for formulating appropriate behavioral strategies. For example, Elizabeth's attribution about why Mr. Bingley failed to visit Jane conditions her responses to him in future encounters and how she talks to her sister about him. An internal attribution to his lack of love (stable, uncontrollable) may soften her response to him. In contrast, should Mr. Bingley have simply refused to alter his social calendar to visit Jane (stable, controllable), Elizabeth might snub him when they meet again. In contrast, nearly any external attribution for his behavior would allow her to converse with him with the aim of reinforcing his affection for her sister. The nature of the external attribution, however, might affect her response to the friends biased against her sister (controllable, stable features of those friends).

Although the attribution process is common in social interaction, efficient perceivers do not make attributions about every witnessed behavior. To do so would be overwhelming. Instead, people tend to engage in the attribution process when situations are novel or outcomes, especially negative ones, are unexpected (Wong and Weiner 1981). Under such circumstances, perceivers are more apt to notice a behavior and be concerned about processing it appropriately to avoid potential costs of failing to do so. In addition, mental representations that filter and organize information may not exist or may require elaboration. For example, students hardly wonder why a professor writes on the dry erase board; if the same professor, however, used finger paints on the wall to present an overview of the lecture, students might certainly ask why he or she is doing that. Another condition that may stimulate the attribution process is simply being asked by another observer why a person behaved in a certain way. For example, your parents might ask you to explain why your brother or sister stayed out until 2:00 a.m., will not talk to them, or refuses to go to a school-sponsored event. While you might think that these actions are typical of your stubborn sibling, when your parents ask you the reasons for the behavior, you may initiate a conscious process of trying to determine why he or she is treating your parents in that way.

Scholars have suggested various mechanisms for determining the causes of another person's behavior. Some involve basic schematic processing while others require consideration of a variety of information in the situation. Even if the systematic, thorough processing may produce a "rational attribution," in reality the shortcomings of cognitive processing and other biases often lead to deviations from the systematic approach. Regardless of the attribution process, the results provide guidance for perceivers in their future interactions with the actor.

Schematic Attribution Processing

As noted previously, when individuals process information in a social context, they cannot possibly take into account all the information present, let alone information to which they do not have access. Consequently, perceivers invoke categorical or schematic processing or use cognitive shortcuts in order to come to some judgment that propels interaction. Kelley (1972, 1973) reasoned that people might also rely on shortcuts in determining the causes of another person's behavior when information is incomplete or when the situation requires economical and fast causal analysis. **Schematic processing** of causal relations relies upon notions of how particular causes and effects are related to each other. For example, if a baseball comes through your window and you see a child with a bat nearby, you might reasonably assume that the child's swing of the bat at the ball caused the breakage. Hitting balls with bats in the vicinity of windows readily "goes with" the possibility of shattering glass. When perceivers observe a particular effect, the schema they consciously or unconsciously invoke suggests a particular cause. Such schematic attribution typically involves the observation of the enactment of a single behavior, by a single actor, within a specific context. Sometimes, however, multiple potential causes might be relevant to an observed behavior. Kelley offers two principles for sorting among causes.

The **discounting principle** suggests that perceivers "discount" the influence of any one particular cause when other potential or sufficient causes exist. When there are other potential causes, multiple schema pertain to the observed effect—thereby diminishing the power of any particular cause. For example, should a bird slam into the same window to which the baseball was hurtling, multiple causes are present. To the extent that multiple potential causes include both those specific to the actor and those characterizing the situation, the presence of a potential external cause decreases the likelihood that an observer internally attributes the actor's behavior. This is especially true if the external cause in some way facilitates the actor's behavior. For example, if a driver arrives at her destination in record time, it may be because she has excellent driving skills (an internal cause) or because it is 5:00 a.m., the roads are empty, and the lights all blink yellow rather than cycle through green and red (external causes). The absence of other cars and the lights setting facilitate the speedy arrival, reducing the emphasis on the driver's skills.

A combination of two types of causes characterizes the **augmentation principle**. Facilitative causes are those that aid in the enactment of a certain behavior, whereas inhibitory causes work against the occurrence of a particular behavior. Kelley (1972, 1973) suggests that when there is both a plausible facilitative cause and plausible inhibitory cause present in a situation, perceivers are more likely to attribute the behavior to the actor who overcomes constraints to produce the behavior. The actor's abilities, effort, motivation, and the like are responsible for surmounting obstacles epitomized by the inhibitory causes. Overcoming the inhibitory cause augments the connection between something about the actor and the behavior. For example, a record-breaking performance of an athlete who competed while ill would be attributed more strongly to the athlete's prowess rather any other potential cause. That ultimately Mr. Darcy marries Elizabeth Bennet, despite her lowly connections, lack of fortune, and protests of his powerful aunt, suggests that his love and passion for her overcomes these external constraints.

While both of these principles inherently simplify the attribution process, the discounting principle exerts greater influence than the augmentation principle on attributions (Hansen and Hall 1985). Despite the differential use of these two principles, schematic causal processing usefully describes how perceivers may infer causes in the absence of complete information. Other attribution models require consideration of a wide variety of information.

Systematic Attribution Processing

Two models of attribution processing presume that perceivers have access to a variety of information and systematically analyze it as a means to discern "why" an actor behaved in a particular way. Even though the models are complex, the intention was to illustrate how rational thinkers might determine the causes of another person's behavior, which would give the perceiver some idea of how to interact with the other person. The first model, offered by Jones and Davis (1965), focuses on analysis necessary to ascertain whether an actor's behavior "corresponds" to an underlying disposition—that is, a presumed internal cause. In contrast, in the second model, Kelley (1967, 1972) details how information about the actor, the situational stimulus, and other people produces either an internal or external attribution for the actor's behavior.

Correspondent Inference Theory

Jones and Davis's (1965) correspondent inference theory proposes that perceivers focus on the consequences or effects of an act to determine why an actor behaved in a certain manner. With knowledge of the consequences, perceivers attempt to ascertain a reason that the person acted in a particular way, focusing on underlying intentions and the actor's ability to bring about the observed consequences. Consequences that are desirable or produced owing to social constraints tell the perceiver little about the actor's intentions and the like. Likewise, if many behavioral pathways could have created the same consequences, the perceiver again has little useful information. In contrast, behavior that is less desirable, counternormative behavior, or produces "noncommon" effects (i.e., those associated with a distinct behavioral pathway) is likely to signal to the perceiver that the behavior corresponds to some internal disposition of the actor. Of course, assessing noncommon effects involves a great deal of cognitive energy aimed at reviewing the consequences of both the chosen and unchosen actions. In contrast, recognition of situational constraints simplifies the assessment, but is unlikely to suggest that the behavior is intentional or stems from an underlying disposition.

To illustrate elements of correspondent inference theory, imagine a new worker in an organization who peppers conversations with foul language. In such an instance, the behavior is undesirable; counternormative; and in comparison to typical office behavior, produces a noncommon effect in the situation and thus may lead the perceiver to make a correspondent inference. Jones and Davis (1965), however, note that such systematic analysis of information may be disrupted if the actor's behavior is relevant to perceivers in some way that would bring them pleasure (or pain). In such instances, the actor's behavior carries "hedonic relevance" to the perceiver and may color the perceiver's interpretations of the information. Recognition of such relevance presages current emphasis on the impact of the perceiver's goals and motives in social cognition.

Correspondent inference processes focus on the way a perceiver might systematically go about connecting something about an actor to his or her behavior. It uniquely recognizes that perceivers themselves may have a stake in the outcome of their analysis. While the theory requires consideration of situational information, it does not allow for the possibility of external attributions. Kelley's covariation model, in contrast, considers information necessary to derive either an internal or external attribution.

Kelley's Covariation Model

Kelley's (1967) covariation model assumes that perceivers are neutral and systematic analyzers of information, intent on making accurate attributions (and are thus not influenced by hedonic relevance). The model itself draws from the logic of statistical analysis in which there are three factors (types of information described next) that create distinct configurations to produce different attributions for an observed action. (Some of the "results" of the combination of factors, however, may not be as definitively "external" or "internal" as others.) The covariation model applies in situations in which the perceiver has access to multiple instances of behavior—both by the actor and by others. Covariation involves the co-occurrence of the behavior under scrutiny and other events. For example, in *The Simpsons*, if Lisa gets Homer out of every predicament he finds himself in, then there is high covariation; in contrast, if sometimes Lisa succeeds in saving Homer's reputation and other times she fails, then there is low covariation. In this example, the goal of an investigator would be to determine the cause of Lisa's record of success by examining various potential causes and assessing with which, over time, Lisa's success varies.

Kelley (1967, 1972) identifies three types of information that shape perceivers' attributions. Two types of information pertain specifically to the actor. **Distinctiveness** information indicates how the same person acts toward different "entities." An entity may be a person, a thing, an event, or generically some stimulus that elicits a reaction. An entity high in distinctiveness is one that elicits a reaction like none elicited by other similar entities. In other words, the actor's behavior toward this particular entity is distinctive and does not generalize to other entities. In contrast, an entity low in distinctiveness encourages a response much like other similar entities. The reaction to such an entity does generalize to other entities. For example, when a high school student raves about a particular teacher, an observer might wonder if this particular instructor elicits raves while no other teacher does (and thus is a highly distinctive entity) or if this teacher as well as others elicit raves (thus suggesting that the entity is not that distinct). Distinctive entities are more likely to lead to external attributions—it is something unique about a particular entity that caused the student to rave, not something unique about the student.

Perceivers may also ascertain **consistency** information about the actor's behavior. If the actor behaves in the same way toward the specified entity over time, then his or her behavior is highly consistent. Information about behavior that is low in consistency suggests that the actor's reaction to the entity is unstable over time. A student may repeatedly rave about a particular teacher or alternate between raving and complaining—the former is consistent behavior and the latter is not.

In addition to the behavior of the actor, the perceiver may consider how other people respond to the same entity in the situation, creating **consensus** information. Consensus is high when others respond similarly to the entity; consensus is low when others respond to the entity in ways distinct from those of the focal actor. For example, if the student's friends also sing the praises of the particular teacher, high consensus exists in appraisals of the teacher. In contrast, if only the focal actor lauds the specific instructor, then there is little consensus. When others and the focal actor respond similarly, then it is likely that the actor's behavior is due to something about the entity (e.g., extraordinary teaching skills) or the situation.

According to Kelley's (1967, 1972) model, the systematic perceiver would assess each type of information, determining if it was "high" or "low." In effect, consideration of two levels of the three types of information produce eight (2 × 2 × 2) potential attributions. Fiske and Taylor (2013) outline the eight combinations, noting that in some instances the resulting attribution is clear while in other instances it is ambiguous. For example, a student who always raves about a particular teacher and whose friends similarly rave about that teacher (high distinctiveness, high consistency, high consensus) suggests an external attribution to the entity—the person is simply a spectacular teacher! Also clear is an internal attribution to the actor when there is low distinctiveness, high consistency, and low consensus (e.g., the student raves about many teachers and does so consistently while no one else seems to gush about the teacher). An attribution is more ambiguous under informational conditions of low distinctiveness, low consistency, and high consensus, such as when a student praises many teachers, not just a particular one, but does so sporadically while others are apt to praise the targeted teacher consistently. Here, the types of information provide contradictory evidence for internal or external attributions, and thus the perceiver may be unable to specify what causes the particular student's behavior.

Given that the example implies a dynamic between two people—a teacher who interacts with a student whose interpretation of the teacher's behavior may result in praise—it illustrates some of the complexities that operate with regard to attributions in social situations. As Fiske and Taylor (2013) point out, sometimes information leads to a combination of causes. For example, when a student always raves about a particular teacher (high distinctiveness and consistency) but no other students do so (low consensus), the cause of the actor's behavior may be something about the dynamic between this particular student and teacher. The student may appreciate the teacher's quirky sense of humor or tangents into Roman history that other students disdain. So the student's praise for the teacher is owing to something about his or her own tastes (an internal attribution) as well as the teacher's behavior (an attribution external to the actor whose behavior is under examination). The typical internal or external locus of cause dichotomy often falls short in interactive or interdependent relationships (see Fletcher 1983; McRae and Kohen 1988). The "interaction" per se may be a potential cause shared by the actor and others, including the perceiver, in the situation.

Empirical evidence supports some aspects of Kelley's covariation model but also suggests some revisions to it (e.g., Chen, Yates, and McGinnies 1988; McArthur 1972; Orvis, Cunningham, and Kelley 1975). For example, consistency information appears to impact perceiver's attributions more than distinctiveness (Kruglanski 1977), and perceivers often underuse consensus information, perhaps owing to the difficulty in assessing whether "others" are similar or dissimilar to the perceiver (e.g., Kassin 1979; Kruglanski et al. 1978; Olson, Ellis, and Zanna 1983). The cumbersomeness of rigorous processing of multiple types of information often leads people to do so only when they analyze an unexpected or unusual event (Hilton and Sugolski 1986). Plus, sometimes perceivers do not have sufficient information to assess the combinations of the three types of information, or they rely on additional information (that others or researchers may be unaware of) and thus offer attributions that may seem "rational" but appear inconsistent with Kelley's (1967, 1972) model (e.g., Cheng and Novick 1990; Hewstone and Jaspers

1987). With sufficient information, perceivers who also consider the actor's motivations and goals seem to produce more precise attributions (Sutton and McClure 2001). Although the model excludes perceiver's motivations, people may base their attributions of other people's behavior on their own motivations and beliefs about causes and effects (Kelley and Michela 1980).

The theoretical approaches to attribution formation that essentially describe how neutral, systematic observers would go about establishing what causes another person's behavior are called normative models. Yet evidence of so-called errors in processing—deviation from the predictions of these normative models—is abundant. The efficient, flexible perceiver that has emerged in social cognition studies might make spontaneous attributions or fail to consider all pieces of potentially relevant information because he or she has established a "likely" cause based on categorical or heuristic processing. And perceivers' own motivations may affect how they evaluate the causes of not only their own behavior but the behavior of others as well.

Errors and Biases in Attribution Processing

People are rarely the objective and systematic perceivers as the normative attribution models suggest. Rather, the attributions perceivers typically produce in daily life reflect unintentional errors in information processing and perhaps subjectively biased analysis of situations. In judging the behavior of another person, the most general and typical error involves the overreliance on dispositional attributions. For example, when Elizabeth learns that Darcy intentionally kept Mr. Bingley from her sister Jane, she immediately attributes such action to his proud, haughty disposition. When judging their own behavior, in contrast, individuals not only have access to more information than an observer but also may be motivated to present themselves in a good light. For example, Darcy defends his actions with regard to Bingley and Jane by saying that he did not detect Jane's affection toward his friend and thus acted nobly by protecting Bingley from heartache. In other words, Darcy externalizes his behavior (in effect, blaming Jane) and casts himself positively.

Errors

Perceivers' tendency to overattribute another person's behavior to his or her personal characteristics is hardly surprising. As already discussed, Gestalt psychologists argue that behavior engulfs the field. Consequently, it is the behavior of another actor that perceivers take to be the most salient aspect of the situation. In addition, cultural dictates (see Choi and Nisbett 1998; Morris and Peng 1994) in Western societies that emphasize individualism lead individuals to presume that people are responsible for their own, freely chosen behavior, and thereby condition perceivers to look to the actor's dispositions as the cause of the behavior. In more collectivist cultures, such emphasis on the person as a causal force is minimized.

Even if perceivers take into account the context, they may underestimate its role owing to lack of familiarity with situational constraints or unrealistic expectations for the actor's behavior (Moskowitz 2005). Those expectations, moreover, may reflect perceivers' own estimates of how people should behave in the situation, and any failure to behave as expected may lead to a dispositional attribution. For example, a group of new workers in an organization may not yet be familiar with the norms of the organization but nonetheless presume professional standards; thus, a coworker's use of foul language would violate their presumption and result in an internal attribution about the verbal unruliness. Alternatively, perceivers may simply initially assume internal causes for an actor's behavior and fail to adjust accordingly as they notice more about the situation. Cognitive busyness, which depletes perceiver's mental energy, would exacerbate the tendency to go with a dispositional attribution despite situational cues suggesting otherwise.

The notion of **spontaneous trait inference (STI)** suggests such an underlying assumption. Uleman and colleagues (1996) describe an STI as a "snap judgment" focused on the traits of an actor to account for his or her behavior. The judgment lacks the conscious awareness of or intent on the part of the perceiver. Because the perceivers are unaware that they formed such inferences, researchers have developed clever means to test for the possibility of such spontaneous inferences. For example, to the extent that individuals form an STI, their reaction time to information consistent with the inferred traits is much lower than when STIs have not formed. Essentially, such trait inferences anchor subsequent judgments.

The dominancy of individualism likewise may account for Jones and Davis's (1965) initial emphasis on the correspondence between behavior and underlying dispositions. In a test of that model, Jones and Harris (1967) found that even when perceivers knew of external pressures (i.e., the lack of choice), they attributed an actor's behavior to traits or dispositions. For example, if a new family moves into a neighborhood of small cottages, you may presume that they like cozy living even though rumors suggest that they needed to downsize their home due to hugely reduced income during an economic turndown. Thus, they did not prefer a small home, but that was the only housing within their budget constraints. This attribution pattern reflects two related biases. The **fundamental attribution error** (Ross 1977) combines the tendency for perceivers to overestimate dispositional factors and underestimate situational ones as causes of an actor's behavior. And, the **correspondence bias** (Gilbert and Malone 1995) is the propensity to draw correspondent trait inferences from situationally constrained behavior. As previously implied, such biases are more common in Western than in Asian societies. The fundamental attribution error, moreover, has greater impact on evaluations of behavior of others whom perceivers do not know well compared to those with whom they are close (Idson and Mischel 2001).

The extent of knowledge of the actor and its effect on the operation of the fundamental attribution error parallels differences in how an actor and observer view the actor's behavior. The **actor–observer bias** (Jones and Nisbett 1971) suggests that actors tend to explain their own behavior in situational terms, whereas observers of the actors tend toward dispositional explanations. Actors have greater access to information about themselves and must negotiate aspects of the situation to produce their behavior. Thus they more clearly assess "consistency" information and "distinctiveness" information insofar as situational factors are likely to be more salient for them. In contrast, for observers, an actor's behavior is the most salient thing about the situation. For example, during a football game, the quarterback may appear to be going in for the long pass necessary to get the first down and at the last minute run with the ball, yet gaining little yardage. A spectator, focused on the quarterback's behavior may yell an obscenity, attributing the change in plans to the player's stupidity. In contrast, the player may have seen all available receivers get tackled; thus, his decision to run with the ball was wise, despite having failed to make a first down. Had the spectator put herself in the quarterback's position, she may have been less likely to attribute the failure to the quarterback. That attributions to situational factors are more common for actors than observers, however, does not guarantee that they are more accurate. While actors may have access to more information about themselves and the situation, they may also be motivated to present themselves in particular manners.

Although, according to Kelley's (1967) model, consensus information should increase the tendency to make external attributions, perceivers often underuse it or personally construe it (Mullen et al. 1985). The **false consensus effect** is the tendency to see one's own beliefs and behaviors as typical and therefore to assume that others would have reacted in the same manner as oneself (Ross, Green, and House 1977). As a consequence of personalizing consensus information, perceivers may contrast an actor's behavior with this false information and view that behavior as deviant or inappropriate, resulting in an internal attribution. For example, Karen washes bedsheets every 2 weeks and thus believes that others are likely to do so as well (if not more frequently). When she learns that one of her students did not change his sheets for an entire semester, she immediately thinks his slovenly nature "caused" this behavior. In reality, however, it may be typical for college students to launder sheets only once a semester. False consensus also provides perceivers with a basis for underemphasizing the role of dispositions in assessments of their own behavior; they see themselves as behaving like others, and such consensus suggests that some situational stimuli are responsible for the behavior. This effect indicates that people create their own social realities, which has implications for processing social information and the dynamics of interaction. The misleading construal of the typicality of one's own behaviors, however, constitutes an error rather than a bias in social cognition.

Biases

Errors in attribution processing function to simplify incoming information and, as a consequence, may be decreased under conditions calling for greater attention to the situation (Krull 1993), greater accountability (Tetlock 1983), and the like. In contrast, biases in making attributions generally involve self-serving goals and thus may be more difficult to alter when perceivers are invested in their self-images. Generally, people are egocentric in their perceptions, seeing themselves as more central to events than they really are (Greenwald 1980) and are motivated to see themselves positively (Tesser 1988). Most work on biases focuses on attributions for the perceiver's own behavior, although, especially in social situations, self-attributions may have implications for the attributions of the behavior of an interaction partner.

The **self-serving bias** (Bradley 1978) addresses self-promotional behavior, often to protect self-esteem or defend one's ego. This bias leads perceivers to selectively process self-relevant information. Processing information about the self is often motivated by skepticism about negative information, which leads individuals to examine critically negative information and to accept readily positive information (Ditto and Lopez 1992). By embracing information favorable to one's self-image and avoiding information negative to that image, perceivers are likely to make internal attributions for positive outcomes and external attributions for negative ones. In effect, the self-serving bias allows individuals to take credit for good results from their behaviors and to blame other sources for bad results. The latter is a form of an **ego-defensive** attribution in which perceptions of others are created to ensure one's own positive self-image. For example, imagine an adolescent boy telling a joke at the dinner table; when his mother fails to laugh, he blames her lack of understanding or narrow sense of humor for the silence resulting from his joke. He does not consider the possibility that his joke was lame or his delivery flat. To do so would reflect badly on him; thus, instead he attributes the silence to external factors, constructing a perception of his mother's traits in a way that accounts for the lack of laughter. Insofar as the self-serving bias allows confirmation of a positive self-image, it is similar to other cognitive processes that lead perceivers to maintain consistency in category-relevant information.

The pattern of attribution stemming from the self-serving bias, however, contrasts under certain conditions with the pattern based on divergent perspectives (Sicoly and Ross 1977). Divergent perspectives suggest that an actor makes external attributions for his or her behavior. The self-serving bias indicates that would be true for negative outcomes. For positive outcomes, in contrast, actors perceiving their own behavior are likely to make internal attributions. The contrasting effects suggested by these attribution strategies call attention to considering perceiver's motivations and situational conditions. Whether a perceiver seeks self-assessment with a goal of accurate evaluation, self-verification with a goal achieving control by promoting a stable and consistent self, or self-enhancement may depend upon interactional circumstances (Moskowitz 2005). For example, in situations requiring accuracy or self-verification, people may be more accepting of negative feedback in areas in which they perceive themselves to have deficiencies. People also respond differentially to information about themselves if it is given by dating partners compared to family or friends (Swann, Bosson, and Pelham 2002).

Self-serving goals may extend beyond analysis of one's own behavior to analysis of the behavior of close associates. As we will discuss in Chapter 12 on intergroup processes, people tend to view the groups to which they belong in a positive light (and to contrast their own group with other groups, often leading to denigration of the out-group) (Tajfel and Turner 1986). These processes have implications for attributions regarding the behavior of in-group members such as family and friends. The **ultimate attribution error** (Pettigrew 1979) is the tendency to attribute the positive behaviors and outcomes of own group members to dispositional causes and to externalize the causes of their negative behaviors and outcomes. In other words, a perceiver would credit his or her family members and friends for their positive outcomes and find an excuse (an external cause) for their negative ones. For example, when a friend flunks a test, the last thing you might say to him or her is "You are really dumb." Instead, you might attribute the failure to the toughness of the test or the professor's unfair grading strategy.

Given how rapidly people must process incoming information, it is hardly surprising that resulting appraisals deviate from normative models. The errors are a way to simplify information, for example, by relying only on dispositional attributions for a person's actions without concern for potentially impactful situational factors. Similarly, casting a favorable light on interpretations of our own behavior or that of people close to us allows retention of a positive self-image, which has implications for our self-concept (see Chapter 3) and, ultimately, how we behave.

Summary

Determining the causes of a person's behavior is no simple feat. Yet we frequently make attributions. For example, as parents, we (the authors) have discussed various

times when we have tried to understand why our children have acted in particular ways: Why did she fail to turn in an assignment in a timely fashion? How
could he miss the soccer bus yet again? What was the drama in the friendship
group all about—did my daughter do something offensive, or are others to blame
for the rift? Admittedly, as social psychologists, we know what information is necessary to systematically derive an attribution, given information about our children and about the context—think here about Kelley's (1967) covariation model.
Yet do we always collect information about the entity eliciting the behavior, the
consistency of the behavior over time, and whether others behave in the same
manner? No. We might if the behavior at stake was egregious or if our child was
terribly upset and we were trying to help him or her cope with the situation.

The covariation model (Kelley 1967) and correspondent inference theory
(Jones and Davis 1965) are normative models offering explanations for how rational processors might make an accurate attribution about the cause of someone's
behavior. In the absence of the information required by the models, perceivers
rely upon schematic processing (Kelley 1972), assessing what presumed causes
produce particular effects. Even then, assessments may be blurred by errors or
biases (Ross 1977). We might find ourselves making more external attributions for
negative behavior and more internal attributions for positive behavior about our
children's behavior. The result of the cognitive processing, however enacted, has
important implications for how behavior unfolds.

How Do Cognitions Affect Behavior?

Heider (1958) recognized that perceptions mattered both in terms of understanding one's social world and in terms of providing a basis for anticipating one's own
actions and those of others. Decades later, Fiske (1992) simply, yet profoundly,
stated that "thinking is for doing," and Smith and Semin (2004) offer the premise "cognition is for action" in their melding of a biological approach with the
inherently situated nature of social action. In the latter case, they argue that
cognition evolved to facilitate adaptive action taking place in social contexts.
And stated in words that could also be spoken by a symbolic interactionist, Fiske
and Taylor (2013:421) conclude that "behavior depends on how people define a
situation and adopt relevant personal goals, showing considerable flexibility. . . .
Sometimes . . . [proceeding] consciously by making explicit goals and plans; . . .
[other times goal pursuit] occurs automatically." In other words, perceptions matter for behavior— in both the short and long terms—and, as discussed previously,
those perceptions may be shaped by both thoughtful, deliberate processes and
automatic, spontaneous ones. Moreover, information garnered through interactions provides the substance of perceptions in the situation and the content of
longer-lasting schema. Thus, while cognitions may drive behavior, behavior also
drives cognitions. (Chapter 6 illustrates this bidirectionality more explicitly with
regard to the attitude–behavior relationship.)

The cognition–behavior relationship emerges in discussions about individuals'
motivations and goals—forms of cognitions about a situation—that encapsulate
what is desired or what is defined as the purpose of an action. People often choose
among alternative goals, recognizing whether the situation will allow pursuit of
those goals, and following the implied course of action (Gollwitzer and Moskowitz
1996; Gollwitzer and Sheeran 2006). For example, a critical point in *Pride and*

Prejudice is when Mr. Darcy learns that Elizabeth's younger sister Lydia has run off with Mr. Wickham, a man Darcy long knew to be unscrupulous yet whose worthlessness Darcy did not make known to others. Darcy's perception of his indirect role in the scandal directs his choice among his alternative courses of action. By attributing responsibility to himself for failing to make Wickham's character known, he chooses to try to rectify the situation with resources at his disposal, rather than do nothing. That course of action, moreover, alters Elizabeth's perception of him, securing their future romantic relationship.

Less conscious cognitions also stimulate behavior as in the case of priming, described previously in this chapter. The mere presence of an environmental cue relevant to an existing category may trigger a behavior without conscious thought (Dijksterhuis and Bargh 2001). For example, have you ever been headed to the mall, but upon reaching a particular intersection, turned as if headed to work or school? Likewise, interactions with employers, teachers, or other superiors may be guided by our representations for deferential behavior and enacted without much conscious thought. Situational cues may trigger a representation that includes a particular type of behavior—for example, rooting for the home team at a baseball game.

Other evidence for the effect of cognition on behavior comes from work on the **self-fulfilling prophecy** (Merton 1957). A self-fulfilling prophecy occurs when one person possesses (false) expectations of another person's behavior, which leads the first person to act in a certain way toward the second person and thereby leads the second person to act in a manner that confirms the first person's expectations. The now classic study by Rosenthal and Jacobson (1968) involved the manipulation of teachers' expectations about a subset of their students. Teachers were told that this subset consisted of the "bloomers" who would be likely to make significant performance and intellectual gains in the course of the year. Although these so-called bloomers were randomly assigned to the subset and in reality did not differ in systematic ways from the other students, after several months their school performance and IQ scores had improved notably. Presumably, the teachers acted in a different way toward these students, creating a warmer learning climate, providing more feedback, and allowing them extra opportunities in the class to ask and answer questions. In effect, teachers transmitted their higher expectations to these students who then acted in ways to confirm the expectations.

Of course, self-fulfilling prophecies may also focus on negative behaviors. For example, Bart Simpson often gets a bad rap. Even when he is trying to do something good, others (his sister Lisa or parents, Marge and Homer) expect him to screw up, and inevitably he does. Bart or any target of false expectations, however, could act in a way to dispel them (Neuberg 1989). That is, the target's behavior is directed at reshaping the perceptions of another.

Likewise, the realm of impression management focuses on how a person presents himself or herself in a particular way to create a particular image of himself or herself in the eyes of another person (Goffman 1959; Nezlek and Leary 2002). Applying for jobs, picking someone up in a bar, and meeting the future in-laws are situations in which a focal actor (the job applicant, the date hound, the son-in-law-to-be) wants to make a positive impression on another (the potential employer, the cute person at the bar, the mother-in-law-to-be). While there are various strategies of impression management (see Fiske and Taylor 2013; also Chapter 3), the point is that the actor acts on his or her cognition, which reflects what the actor thinks that the others want to see, and that behavior shapes the cognition of another. The dynamics of impression management (like most of interaction) involve sequencing of perceptions and behavior for both self and others.

Such sequencing recognizes the role of cognitions in determining individuals' subjective experiences in interaction. Although cognition may be viewed as an intrapersonal process distinct from the interdependent process described by some symbolic interactionists (Stryker and Gottlieb 1981; see Chapter 3), there is a growing emphasis on its role in interaction. As Moskowitz (2005:546) suggests, "Interpersonal perception is a dance of mutual construal and prediction . . . directed by goal-driven, expectancy-riddled, schema-based cognitive processes, both effortful and automatic, that allow us to perceive what others are like, just as they are perceiving us, and guide us through the dance that is the interaction sequence."

Moreover, social cognition has implications for processes within and between groups (see Chapter 12). Collective cognitions develop through interaction and affect subsequent interaction (Howard and Renfrow 2003). For example, although using different labels, Snow, Rochford, Worden, and Benford (1986) argue that the sharing of interpretative frames—similar cognitions about a situation—may motivate social movement participation. And, generally, when scholars link structural or objective circumstances of groups to behaviors, they call upon cognitive or perceptual processes to explain the linkages. For example, as discussed in Chapter 8, theoretical arguments about the effects of status on influence processes rely upon perceptions of competence associated with status positions. Likewise, in understanding why people respond to injustice (Chapter 11), the subjective perception of injustice, not objective circumstances per se, shape how people respond. DiMaggio (1997) argues that culture and cognition are closely related. To the extent that culture affects how information is processed, retained, and used in making inferences, cultural practices and behaviors provide further evidence of the cognition–behavior linkage.

Segue: Social Cognitions Feed Attitude Processes

Perceivers are asked to do a lot: attend to information, encode new information, access existing information, develop a perception from these information pieces, and ultimately act upon what they have perceived. They do this to make sense of situations and develop a sense of control by understanding their own and others' behavior as well as anticipating how to behave in the future. Underlying perceptual processes—impression formation and attribution strategies— are sometimes relatively automatic and spontaneous yet other times deliberate and controlled. With processing errors and self-serving biases, contradictions between what is accurate and what is subjectively believed to be true emerge. A report in our local newspaper indicated that crime in a number of neighborhoods was down, yet people were crying out for greater police presence. Why the outcry? A single shooting death of a bartender at a well-known restaurant was the salient (and very negative) event that rallied neighborhood residents, not accurate statistics about violent crime. They asked, "Why did this happen? What could prevent it from happening in the future?" They worried that it could happen to someone they loved.

What matter are people's perceptions, and those perceptions—impressions of others or causal inferences—depend upon information available in the situation, its fit with existing category information, perceivers' own goals, and characteristics of the context, including the other people in it. To the extent that perceivers attend to different information, invoke different representational information, or possess different goals in the situation, the resulting subjective impression or attribution will vary between people. Processes of social cognition may be used to justify positions in social groups, in society. Imagine how the advantaged in society claim credit for their accomplishments and cast dispersions on the disadvantaged, arguing that they are lazy or incompetent; otherwise, they too would be advantaged. To the extent that the disadvantaged are treated in ways to "keep them down," self-fulfilling prophecy notions would suggest that they come to believe that they deserve their disadvantage. Thus, while typically viewed as an intraindividual process, social cognitions play a role in maintaining social inequality.

With variation in perceptions of the same phenomenon, sometimes people will try to convince others to share their perception. Change may depend upon identifying new information or reshaping existing representations. Advertising, political campaigning, legal briefs, and the like are ways that people try to shape others' perceptions. In social psychology, the study of such change originally focused on attitudes. As the first intraindividual cognitive processes studied (Allport 1935), attitudes capture favorable or unfavorable evaluations of objects, people, places, or ideas. We turn to the development, change, and impact on behavior of such evaluations in Chapter 6.

Endnote

1. Given the pivotal role of impressions in this novel, it is hardly surprising that Austen's initial title for this work was *First Impressions* (Drabble 1985).

Suggested Readings

Adams, Gabrielle S., and M. Ena Inesi. 2016. "Impediments to Forgiveness: Victim and Transgressor Attributions of Intent and Guilt." *Journal of Personality and Social Psychology* 66:866–81.

Brambilla, Marco, Patrice Rusconi, Simona Sacchi, and Paolo Cherubini. 2011. "Looking for Honesty: The Primary Role of Morality (vs. Sociability and Competence) in Information Gathering." *European Journal of Social Psychology* 41:135–43.

Hunzaker, M. B. Fallin. 2014. "Making Sense of Misfortune: Cultural Schemas, Victim Redefinition, and the Perpetuation of Stereotypes." *Social Psychology Quarterly* 77:166–84.

Hussak, Larisa, J., and Andrei Cimpian. 2015. "An Early-emerging Explanatory Heuristic Promotes Support for the Status Quo." *Journal of Personality and Social Psychology* 109:739–52.

Simon, Dan, Douglas M. Stenstrom, and Stephen J. Read. 2015. "The Coherence Effect: Blending Cold and Hot Cognitions." *Journal of Personality and Social Psychology* 109:369–94.

References

Adolphs, Ralph. 2009. "The Social Brain: Neural Basis of Social Knowledge." *Annual Review of Psychology* 60:693–716. doi:10.1146/annurev.psych.60.110707.163514

Allport, Gordon W. 1935. "Attitudes." Pp. 798–844 in *Handbook of Social Psychology*, edited by C. Murchison. Worcester, MA: Clark University Press.

Allport, Gordon W. 1954. *The Nature of Prejudice*. Reading, MA: Addison-Wesley.

Amodio, David M., and Chris D. Frith. 2006. "Meeting of Minds: The Medial Frontal Cortex and Social Cognition." *Nature Reviews. Neuroscience* 7:268–77. doi:10.1038/nrn1884

Asch, Solomon E. 1946. "Forming Impressions of Personality." *Journal of Abnormal and Social Psychology* 41:258–90. doi:10.1037/h0055756

Austen, Jane. [1813] 1981. *Pride and Prejudice*. New York: Bantam Books.

Bargh, John A. 1990. "Auto-Motives: Preconscious Determinants of Social Interaction." Pp. 93–130 in *Handbook of Motivation and Cognition: Foundations of Social Behavior*, Vol. 2, edited by E. T. Higgins and R. M. Sorrentino. New York: Guilford Press.

Bargh, John A. 1994. "The Four Horsemen of Automaticity: Awareness, Intention, Efficiency, and Control in Social Cognition." Pp. 1–40 in *Handbook of Social Cognition*, edited by J. R. S. Wyer and T. K. Srull. Hillsdale, NJ: Erlbaum.

Barsalou, Lawrence W. 1999. "Perceptions of Perceptual Symbols." *Behavioral and Brain Sciences* 22(4):637–60. doi:10.1017/S0140525X99532147

Barsalou, Lawrence W. 2008. "Cognitive and Neural Contributions to Understanding the Conceptual System." *Current Directions in Psychological Science* 17(2):91–95. doi:10.1111/j.1467-8721.2008.00555.x

Bradley, Gifford W. 1978. "Self-Serving Biases in the Attribution Process: A Reexamination of the Fact or Fiction Question." *Journal of Personality and Social Psychology* 36(1):56–71. doi:10.1037/0022-3514.36.1.56

Brewer, Marilynn B. 1988. "A Dual Process Model of Impression Formation." Pp. 1–36 in *Advances in Social Cognition*, Vol. 1, edited by T. K. Srull and R. S. Wyer. Hillsdale, NJ: Erlbaum.

Cantor, Nancy, and Walter Mischel. 1977. "Traits as Prototypes: Effects on Recognition Memory." *Journal of Personality and Social Psychology* 35:38–48. doi:10.1037/0022-3514.35.1.38

Chaiken, Shelly, Akiva Liberman, and Alice H. Eagly. 1989. "Heuristic and Systematic Information Processing Within and Beyond the Persuasion Context." Pp. 212–52 in *Unintended Thought: Limits of Awareness, Intention, and Control*, edited by J. S. Uleman and J. A. Bargh. New York: Guilford Press.

Chen, Hong-Jen, Brian T. Yates, and Elliott McGinnies. 1988. "Effects of Involvement on Observers' Estimates of Consensus, Distinctiveness, and Consistency." *Personality and Social Psychology Bulletin* 14:468–78. doi:10.1177/0146167288143005

Cheng, Patricia W., and Laura R. Novick. 1990. "A Probabilistic Contrast Model of Causal Induction." *Journal of Personality and Social Psychology* 58:545–67. doi:10.1037/0022-3514.58.4.545

Choi, Incheol, and Richard E. Nisbett. 1998. "Situational Salience and Cultural Differences in the Correspondence Bias and Actor-Observer Bias." *Personality and Social Psychology Bulletin* 24:949–60. doi:10.1177/0146167298249003

Darley, John M., and Paget H. Gross. 1983. "A Hypothesis-Confirming Bias in Labeling Effects." *Journal of Personality and Social Psychology* 44:20–33. doi:10.1037/0022-3514.44.1.20

Davidson, Richard J. 2003. "Seven Sins in the Study of Emotion: Correctives from Affective Neuroscience." *Brain and Cognition* 52:129–32. doi:10.1016/S0278-2626(03)00015-0

Dijksterhuis, Ap, and John A. Bargh. 2001. "The Perception-Behavior Expressway: Automatic Effects of Social Perception on Social Psychology." *Advances in Experimental Social Psychology* 33:1–40.

DiMaggio, Paul. 1997. "Culture and Cognition." *Annual Review of Sociology* 23:263–87. doi:10.1146/annurev.soc.23.1.263

Ditto, Peter H., and David F. Lopez. 1992. "Motivated Skepticism: Use of Differential Decision Criteria for Preferred and Nonpreferred Conclusions." *Journal of Personality and Social Psychology* 63:568–84. doi:10.1037/0022-3514.63.4.568

Drabble, Margaret, ed. 1985. *The Oxford Companion to English Literature.* Oxford, England: Oxford University Press.

Epley, Nicholas, Boaz Keysar, Leaf Van Boven, and Thomas Gilovich. 2004. "Perspective Taking as Egocentric Anchoring and Adjustment." *Journal of Personality and Social Psychology* 87(3):327–39. doi:10.1037/0022-3514.87.3.327

Fiske, Susan T. 1992. "Thinking Is For Doing—Portraits of Social Cognition from Daguerreotype to Laserphoto." *Journal of Personality and Social Psychology* 63:877–89. doi:10.1037/0022-3514.63.6.877

Fiske, Susan T., and Shelley E. Taylor. 2013. *Social Cognition.* New York: Random House. doi:10.4135/9781446286395

Fletcher, Garth J. O. 1983. "The Analysis of Verbal Explanations for Marital Separation: Implications for Attribution Theory." *Journal of Applied Social Psychology* 13:245–58. doi:10.1111/j.1559-1816.1983.tb01738.x

Fong, Geoffrey T., and Hazel Markus. 1982. "Self-Schemas and Judgments About Others." *Social Cognition* 1:191–204. doi:10.1521/soco.1982.1.3.191

Gauthier, Isabel, Pawel Skudlarski, John C. Gore, and Adam W. Anderson. 2000. "Expertise for Cars and Birds Recruits Brain Areas Involved in Face Recognition." *Nature Neuroscience* 3:191–97. doi:10.1038/72140

Gilbert, D. T., and P. S. Malone. 1995. "The Correspondence Bias." *Psychological Bulletin* 117:21–38. doi:10.1037/0033-2909.117.1.21

Goffman, Erving. 1959. *The Presentation of Self in Everyday Life.* New York: Doubleday.

Gollwitzer, Peter M., and Gordon Moskowitz. 1996. "Goal Effects on Thought and Behavior." Pp. 361–99 in *Social Psychology: Handbook of Basic Principles*, edited by E. T. Higgins and A. Kruglanski. New York: Guilford Press.

Gollwitzer, Peter M., and Paschal Sheeran. 2006. "implementation Intentions and Goal Achievement: A Meta-Analysis of Effects and Processes." *Advances in Experimental Social Psychology* 38:69–120.

Greenwald, Anthony G. 1980. "The Totalitarian Ego: Fabrication and Revision of Personal History." *The American Psychologist* 35:603–18. doi:10.1037/0003-066X.35.7.603

Griffin, Larry J., Ranae J. Evenson, and Ashley B. Thompson. 2005. "Southerners All?" *Southern Cultures* 11:6–25. doi:10.1353/scu.2005.0005

Hamilton, David L., Lawrence B. Katz, and Von O. Leirer. 1980. "Organizational Processes in Impression Formation." Pp. 155–77 in *Person Memory: The Cognitive Basis of Social Perception*, edited by R. Hastie, T. M. Ostrom, E. B. Ebbeson, R. S. Wyer, D. L. Hamilton, and D. E. Carlston. Hillsdale, NJ: Erlbaum.

Hansen, Ranald D., and Christine A. Hall. 1985. "Discounting and Augmenting Facilitative and Inhibitory Forces: The Winner Takes Almost All." *Journal of Personality and Social Psychology* 49:1482–93. doi:10.1037/0022-3514.49.6.1482

Hastorf, Albert H., and Hadley Cantril. 1954. "They Saw a Game: A Case Study." *Journal of Abnormal and Social Psychology* 49:129–34. doi:10.1037/h0057880

Heider, Fritz. 1958. *The Psychology of Interpersonal Relations.* New York: Wiley. doi:10.1037/10628-000

Herr, Paul M. 1986. "Consequences of Priming: Judgment and Behavior." *Journal of Personality and Social Psychology* 51:1106–115. doi:10.1037/0022–3514.51.6.1106

Hewstone, Miles, and Jos Jaspers. 1987. "Covariation and Causal Attribution: A Logical Model of the Intuitive Analysis of Variance." *Journal of Personality and Social Psychology* 53:663–72. doi:10.1037/0022–3514.53.4.663

Higgins, E. Tory. 1996. "Knowledge Activation: Accessibility, Applicability, and Salience." Pp. 133–68 in *Social Psychology: Handbook of Basic Principles*, edited by E. T. Higgins and A. W. Kruglanski. New York: Guilford Press.

Hilton, Denis J., and Ben R. Slugoski. 1986. "Knowledge-Based Causal Attribution: The Abnormal Conditions Focus Model." *Psychological Review* 93:75–88. doi:10.1037/0033–295X.93.1.75

Howard, Judith A., and Daniel G. Renfrow. 2003. "Social Cognition." Pp. 259–81 in *Handbook of Social Psychology*, edited by J. DeLamater. New York: Plenum.

Idson, Lorraine C., and Walter Mischel. 2001. "The Personality of Familiar and Significant People: The Lay Perceiver as a Social-Cognitive Theorist." *Journal of Personality and Social Psychology* 80(4):585–96. doi:10.1037/0022–3514.80.4.585

James, William. [1907] 1991. *Pragmatism*. Reprint, Buffalo, NY: Prometheus Books.

Jones, Edward E., and Keith E. Davis. 1965. "From Acts to Dispositions: The Attribution Process in Person Perception." *Advances in Experimental Social Psychology* 2:219–66.

Jones, Edward E., and Victor A. Harris. 1967. "The Attribution of Attitudes." *Journal of Experimental Social Psychology* 3:1–24. doi:10.1016/0022–1031(67)90034–0

Jones, Edward E., and Richard E. Nisbett. 1971. "The Actor and the Observer: Divergent Perceptions of the Causes of Behavior." Pp. 79–94 in *Attribution: Perceiving the Cause of Behavior*, edited by E. E. Jones, D. E. Kanouse, H. H. Kelley, R. E. Nisbett, S. Valins, and B. Weiner. Morristown, NJ: General Learning Press.

Kahneman, Daniel, and Amos Tversky. 1973. "On the Psychology of Prediction." *Psychological Review* 80:237–51. doi:10.1037/h0034747

Kahneman, Daniel, and Amos Tversky. 1984. "Choices, Values, and Frames." *The American Psychologist* 39:341–50. doi:10.1037/0003–066X .39.4.341

Kanwisher, Nancy, Josh McDermott, and Marvin M. Chun. 1997. "The Fusiform Face Area: A Module in Human Extrastriate Cortex Specialized for Face Perception." *The Journal of Neuroscience* 17(11):4302–11.

Kassin, Saul M. 1979. "Consensus Information, Prediction, and Causal Attribution: A Review of the Literature and Issues." *Journal of Personality and Social Psychology* 37:1966–81. doi:10.1037/0022–3514.37.11.1966

Kelley, Harold H. 1967. "Attribution Theory in Social Psychology." *Nebraska Symposium on Motivation* 14:192–241.

Kelley, Harold H. 1972. "Attribution in Social Interaction." Pp. 1–26 in *Attribution: Perceiving the Causes of Behavior*, edited by E. E. Jones, D. E. Kanouse, H. H. Kelley, R. E. Nisbett, S. Valins, and B. Weiner. Morristown, NJ: General Learning Press.

Kelley, Harold H. 1973. "Processes of Causal Attribution." *The American Psychologist* 28:107–28. doi:10.1037/h0034225

Kelley, Harold H., and John L. Michela. 1980. "Attribution Theory and Research." *Annual Review of Psychology* 31:457–501. doi:10.1146/ annurev.ps.31.020180.002325

Köhler, Wolfgang. 1930. *Gestalt Psychology*. London, England: Bell.

Kruglanski, Arie W. 1977. "The Place of Naive Contents in a Theory of Attribution: Reflections on Calder's and Zuckerman's Critiques of the

Endogenous-Exogenous Partition." *Personality and Social Psychology Bulletin* 3:592–605. doi:10.1177/014616727700300408

Kruglanski, Arie W., Irit Z. Hamel, Shirley A. Maides, and Joseph M. Schwartz. 1978. "Attribution Theory as a Special Case of Lay Epistemology." Pp. 299–334 in *New Directions in Attribution Research*. Vol. 2, edited by J. H. Harvey, W. Ickes, and R. F. Kidd. Hillsdale, NJ: Erlbaum.

Krull, Douglas S. 1993. "Does the Grist Change the Mill? The Effect of the Perceiver's Inferential Goal on the Process of Social Inference." *Personality and Social Psychology Bulletin* 19:340–48. doi:10.1177/0146167293193011

Kunda, Ziva. 1999. *Social Cognition*. Cambridge, MA: MIT Press.

Levin, Irwin P., Sandra L. Schneider, and Gary J. Gaeth. 1998. "All Frames Are Not Created Equal: A Typology and Critical Analysis of Framing Effects." *Organizational Behavior and Human Decision Processes* 76(2):149–88. doi:10.1006/obhd.1998.2804

Lewin, Kurt. 1935. *A Dynamic Theory of Personality: Selected Papers*. Translated by D. K. Adams and K. E. Zener. New York: McGraw-Hill.

Liberman, Akiva. 2001. "Exploring the Boundaries of Rationality: A Functional Perspective on Dual-Process Models in Social Psychology." Pp. 291–305 in *Cognitive Social Psychology: The Princeton Symposium on the Legacy and Future of Social Cognition*, edited by G. B. Moskowitz. Mahwah, NJ: Erlbaum.

Lieberman, Matthew D. 2007. "Social Cognitive Neuroscience: A Review of Core Processes." *Annual Review of Psychology* 58:259–89. doi:10.1146/annurev.psych.58.110405.085654

Lieberman, Matthew D., Ruth Gaunt, Daniel T. Gilbert, and Yaacov Trope 2002. "Reflexion and Reflection: A Social Cognitive Neuroscience Approach to Attributional Inference." *Advances in Experimental Social Psychology* 34:199–249.

Lombardi, Wendy J., E. Tory Higgins, and John A. Bargh. 1987. "The Role of Consciousness in Priming Effects on Categorization: Assimilation Versus Contrast as a Function of Awareness of the Priming Task." *Personality and Social Psychology Bulletin* 13:411–29. doi:10.1177/0146167287133009

Mann, Thomas C., and Melissa J. Ferguson. 2015. "Can We Undo Our First Impressions? The Role of Reinterpretation in Reversing Implicit Evaluations." *Journal of Personality and Social Psychology* 108:823–49. doi:10.1037/pspa0000021

Markman, Arthur B., and Brian H. Ross. 2003. "Category Use and Category Learning." *Psychological Bulletin* 129:592–613.

McArthur, Leslie Z. 1972. "The How and What of Why: Some Determinants and Consequences of Causal Attribution." *Journal of Personality and Social Psychology* 22:171–93. doi:10.1037/h0032602

McRae, James A., and Janet A. Kohen. 1988. "Changes in Attributions of Marital Problems." *Social Psychology Quarterly* 51:74–80. doi:10.2307/2786986

Medin, Douglas L. 1989. "Concepts and Conceptual Structure." *The American Psychologist* 44:1469–81. doi:10.1037/0003-066X.44.12.1469

Merton, Robert K. 1957. *Social Theory and Social Structure*. New York: Free Press.

Moors, A., and J. De Houwer. 2006. "Automaticity: A Theoretical and Conceptual Analysis." *Psychological Bulletin* 132:297–326. doi:10.1037/0033-2909.132.2.297

Morris, Michael W., and Kaiping Peng. 1994. "Culture and Cause: American and Chinese Attributions for Social and Physical Events." *Journal of Personality and Social Psychology* 67:949–71. doi:10.1037/0022-3514.67.6.949

Moskowitz, Gordon B. 2005. *Social Cognition*. New York: Guilford Press.

Mullen, Brian, Jennifer L. Atkins, Debbie S. Champion, Cecelia Edwards, Dana Hardy, John E. Story, and Mary Vanderklok. 1985. "The False Consensus Effect: A Meta-Analysis of 115 Hypothesis Tests." *Journal of Experimental Social Psychology* 21:262–83. doi:10.1016/0022-1031(85)90020-4

Murphy, Fionnuala C., Ian Nimmo-Smith, and Andrew D. Lawrence. 2003. "Functional Neuroanatomy of Emotions: A Meta-Analysis." *Cognitive, Affective & Behavioral Neuroscience* 3(3):207–33. doi:10.3758/CABN.3.3.207

Murphy, Gregory L., and Douglas L. Medin. 1985. "The Role of Theories in Conceptual Coherence." *Psychological Review* 92:289–316. doi:10.1037/0033-295X.92.3.289

Neuberg, Steven L. 1989. "The Goal of Forming Accurate Impressions during Social Interactions: Attenuating the Impact of Negative Expectancies." *Journal of Personality and Social Psychology* 56(3):374–86. doi:10.1037/0022-3514.56.3.374

Nezlek, John B. and Mark R. Leary. 2002. "Individual Differences in Self-Presentational Motives in Daily Social Interaction." *Personality and Social Psychology Bulletin* 28(2):211–23. doi:10.1177/0146167202282007

Nisbett, Richard E., and Timothy D. Wilson. 1977. "Telling More Than We Can Know: Verbal Reports on Mental Processes." *Psychological Review* 84:231–59. doi:10.1037/0033-295X.84.3.231

Olson, James M., Robert J. Ellis, and Mark P. Zanna. 1983. "Validating Objective Versus Subjective Judgments: Interest in Social Comparison and Consistency Information." *Personality and Social Psychology Bulletin* 9:427–36. doi:10.1177/0146167283093013

Orvis, Bruce R., John D. Cunningham, and Harold H. Kelley. 1975. "A Closer Examination of Causal Inference: The Roles of Consensus, Distinctiveness, and Consistency Information." *Journal of Personality and Social Psychology* 32:605–16. doi:10.1037/0022-3514.32.4.605

Pettigrew, Thomas F. 1979. "The Ultimate Attribution Error: Extending Allport's Cognitive Analysis to Prejudice." *Personality and Social Psychology Bulletin* 5:461–76. doi:10.1177/014616727900500407

Phelps, Elizabeth A. 2007. "The Neuroscience of a Person Network." *The American Journal of Bioethics* 7:49–50. doi:10.1080/15265160601064223

Rogers, Timothy B., Nicholas A. Kuiper, and William S. Kirker. 1977. "Self-Reference and the Encoding of Personal Information." *Journal of Personality and Social Psychology* 35:677–88. doi:10.1037/0022-3514.35.9.677

Rosenthal, Robert, and Lenore Jacobson. 1968. *Pygmalion in the Classroom: Teacher Expectation and Pupils' Intellectual Development.* New York: Holt, Rinehart and Winston.

Ross, Lee. 1977. "The Intuitive Psychologist and His Shortcomings." *Advances in Experimental Social Psychology* 10:173–220.

Ross, Lee, David Green, and Pamela House. 1977. "The 'False Consensus Effect': An Egocentric Bias in Social Perception Processes." *Journal of Experimental Social Psychology* 13:279–301. doi:10.1016/0022-1031(77)90049-X

Sedikides, Constantine. 1993. "Assessment, Enhancement, and Verification Determinants of the Self-Evaluation Process." *Journal of Personality and Social Psychology* 65(2):317–338. doi:10.1037/0022-3514.65.2.317

Sherman, Jeff W. 2001. "The Dynamic Relationship between Stereotype Efficiency and Mental Representation." Pp. 177–90 in *Cognitive Social Psychology: The Princeton Symposium on the Legacy and Future of Social Cognition*, edited by G. B. Moskowitz. Mahwah, NJ: Erlbaum.

Sicoly, Fiore, and Michael Ross. 1977. "Facilitation of Ego-Biased Attributions by Means of Self-Serving Observer Feedback." *Journal of Personality and Social Psychology* 35:734–41. doi:10.1037/0022-3514.35.10.734

Skowronski, John J., and Don E. Carlston. 1989. "Negativity and Extremity Biases in Impression Formation: A Review of Explanations." *Psychological Bulletin* 105:131–42. doi:10.1037/0033–2909.105.1.131

Smith, Edward E., and Stephen M. Kosslyn. 2007. *Cognitive Psychology: Mind and Brain.* Upper Saddle River, NJ: Pearson Prentice Hall.

Smith, Eliot R., and Gün R. Semin. 2004. "Socially Situated Cognition: Cognition in Its Social Context." *Advances in Experimental Social Psychology* 36:53–117.

Smith, Eliot R., and Michael A. Zarate. 1992. "Exemplar-Based Model of Social Judgment." *Psychological Review* 99:3–21. doi:10.1037/0033–295X.99.1.3

Snow, David A., E. Burke Rochford, Jr., Steven K. Worden, and Robert D. Benford. 1986. "Frame Alignment Processes, Micromobilization, and Movement Participation." *American Sociological Review* 51(4):464–81. doi:10.2307/2095581

Snyder, Mark, and William B. Swann. 1978. "Hypothesis Testing in Social Interaction." *Journal of Personality and Social Psychology* 36:1202–12. doi:10.1037/0022–3514.36.11.1202

Stryker, Sheldon, and Avi Gottlieb. 1981. "Attribution Theory and Symbolic Interactionism: A Comparison." Pp. 425–58 in *New Directions in Attribution Research*, Vol. 3, edited by J. H. Harvey, W. Ickes, and R. F. Kidd. Hillsdale, NJ: Erlbaum.

Sutton, Robbie M., and John McClure. 2001. "Covariational Influences on Goal-based Explanation: An Integrative Model." *Journal of Personality and Social Psychology* 80:222–36. doi:10.1037/0022–3514.80.2.222

Swann, William B. 1990. "To Be Adored or to Be Known? The Interplay of Self-Enhancement and Self-Verification." Pp. 527–61 in *Handbook of Motivation and Cognition: Foundations of Social Behavior*, Vol. 2, edited by E. T. Higgins and R. Sorrentino. New York: Guilford Press.

Swann, William B., Jennifer K. Bosson, and Bret W. Pelham. 2002. "Different Partners, Different Selves: Strategic Verification of Circumscribed Identities." *Personality and Social Psychology Bulletin* 28(9):1215–28. doi:10.1177/01461672022812007

Tajfel, Henri, and Turner, John C. 1986. "The Social Identity Theory of Intergroup Behavior." Pp. 7–24 in *The Psychology of Intergroup Relations*, edited by S. Worchel and W. G. Austin. Chicago: Nelson-Hall.

Tesser, Abraham. 1988. "Toward a Self-Evaluation Maintenance Model of Social Behavior." *Advances in Experimental Social Psychology* 21:181–227.

Tetlock, Phillip E. 1983. "Accountability and Complexity of Thought." *Journal of Personality and Social Psychology* 45:74–83. doi:10.1037/0022–3514.45.1.74

Todd, Andrew R., Daniel C. Molden, Jaap Ham, and Roos Vonk. 2011. "The Automatic and Co-Occurring Activation of Multiple Social Inferences." *Journal of Experimental Social Psychology* 47:37–49. doi:10.1016/j.jesp.2010.08.006

Trope, Yaacov. 1986. "Self-Enhancement and Self-Assessment in Achievement Behavior." Pp. 350–78 in *Handbook of Motivation and Cognition*, edited by R. M. Sorrentino and E. T. Higgins. New York: Guilford Press.

Trope, Yaacov, and Thomas Alfieri. 1997. "Effortfulness and Flexibility of Dispositional Judgment Processes." *Journal of Personality and Social Psychology* 73:662–74. doi:10.1037/0022–3514.73.4.662

Tversky, Amos, and Daniel Kahneman. 1974. "Judgment under Uncertainty: Heuristics and Biases." *Science* 185:1124–31. doi:10.1126/science.185.4157.1124

Tversky, Amos, and Daniel Kahneman. 1981. "The Framing of Decisions and the Psychology of Choice." *Science* 211:453–58. doi:10.1126/science.7455683

Tversky, Amos, and Daniel Kahneman. 1982. "Judgments of and by Representativeness." Pp. 84–98 in *Judgment Under Uncertainty: Heuristics and Biases*, edited by D. Kahneman, P. Slovic, and A. Tversky. New York: Cambridge University Press. doi:10.1017/CBO9780511809477.007

Uleman, James S., Leonard S. Newman, and Gordon B. Moskowitz. 1996. "People as Flexible Interpreters: Evidence and Issues from Spontaneous Trait Interference." *Advances in Experimental Social Psychology* 28:221–79.

Uleman, James S., S. Adil Saribay, and Ceila M. Gonzalez. 2008. "Spontaneous Inferences, Implicit Impressions, and Implicit Theories." *Annual Review of Psychology* 59:329–60. doi:10.1146/annurev.psych.59.103006.093707

Wegner, Daniel M., and John A. Bargh. 1998. "Control and Automaticity in Social Life." Pp. 446–96 in *The Handbook of Social Psychology*, 4th ed., Vol. 1, edited by D. T. Gilbert, S. T. Fiske, and G. Lindzey. New York: McGraw-Hill.

Weiner, Bernard. 1979. "A Theory of Motivation for Some Classroom Experiences." *Journal of Educational Psychology* 71:3–25. doi:10.1037/0022-0663.71.1.3

Weiner, Bernard. 1986. *An Attributional Theory of Motivation and Emotion.* New York: Springer-Verlag.

Weiner, Bernard, Irene Frieze, Andy Kukla, Linda Reed, Stanley Rest, and Robert M. Rosenbaum. 1972. "Perceiving the Causes of Success and Failure." Pp. 95–120 in *Attribution: Perceiving the Causes of Behavior*, edited by E. E. Jones, D. E. Kanouse, H. H. Kelley, R. E. Nisbett, S. Valins, and B. Weiner. Morristown, NJ: General Learning Press.

Wong, Paul, and Bernard Weiner. 1981. "When People Ask 'Why' Questions, and the Heuristics of Attributional Search." *Journal of Personality and Social Psychology* 40:650–63. doi:10.1037/0022-3514.40.4.650

Wyer, Robert S., and Thomas K. Srull. 1989. *Memory and Cognition in its Social Context.* Hillsdale, NJ: Erlbaum.

Intraindividual Processes
Attitudes

I believe a leaf of grass is no less than
the journey-work of the stars.

—Walt Whitman

If a leaf of grass is the careful crafting of the stars, imagine what a collection of such "leaves" signifies. The American lawn stands out, from in-town neighborhoods, to suburban subdivisions, to the area immediately surrounding rural houses. An expanse of lush, green grasses, trimmed low, contributes to the charm and the aesthetic of individual homes and the communities in which they are embedded. Simply put, Americans generally have a positive attitude toward—or maybe even a crazed love affair with—lawns (and sometimes all that goes with them—riding mowers, fertilizers, holiday decorations) (Steinberg 2006). The rise of the lawn in the hearts of Americans coincides with the post-war years and the growth of suburbs, where houses were often purchased by returning veterans with loans from a government grateful for their service. Thus, social conditions in the 1950s paved the way for this favorable, perhaps even passionate, evaluation of what was then (and is still now) a species ill suited to much of the United States.

Despite this lack of suitability, townships and cities from northern Maine to Miami, from the heartland of the Midwest to the shores of the Pacific, from the rainy Northwest to the arid Southwest, boast both private and public expanses of lawn. Yet as drought conditions bear down upon parts of the country, maintenance of such carpets of green has been challenged. As California approached its fourth year of a drought in the summer of 2015, Governor Jerry Brown ordered a 25% reduction in water use and called for 50 million square feet of lawns to be ripped out as a means of conserving water. Such environmental conditions defy Americans' positive attitude toward lawns. The challenge, of course, is to get people to change their attitudes about lawns—or at least about the suitability of lawns in ecosystems lacking sufficient water resources to support the human population and native flora and fauna. After all, lawns are largely ornamental—a comfortable landscape for running barefoot or picnicking—but not necessary. Other forms of landscaping using indigenous plants may be just as lovely.

The task of California government authorities was to persuade residents to change their minds about their landscaping. In Nevada, a state located largely in the Mojave Desert (with average yearly rainfall of fewer than 5 inches), that change has been a work in progress since 1999 (Glionna 2015). Under the area's Water Smart Landscapes Program, representatives have made persuasive pitches to community residents and followed up with cash incentives provided by local water authorities to eliminate water-dependent yards and public places. Authorities, environmentalists, and water-savvy neighbors sing the anthem of "Don't feed it [the lawn]. Replace it!" The water authorities have sponsored landscaping contests and provided homeowners with garden designs, free of cost. As a consequence, Nevada residents have relinquished their feelings of entitlement to the green grass that characterized childhood homes in water-rich states and have come to adopt desert landscaping. Through both persuasive communications and enticements to change behaviors, Nevada residents have altered their attitudes toward lawns. Governor Brown hoped that similar tactics would help in California, where annual rainfall, especially in the southern portion of the state, is less than 15 inches a year (compared to 50 in Atlanta and New York).

The push by municipalities to squelch certain attitudes and encourage others regarding water conservation illustrates key social psychological processes pertaining to attitude formation and change as well as the relationship between attitudes and behaviors. As one of the first intraindividual, cognitive processes studied (Allport 1935), **attitudes** refer to favorable or unfavorable evaluations of objects (including people, places, ideas, or things) (Eagly and Chaiken 1993). Like the more general notion of cognitive representation, attitudes affect what is perceived, attended to, and remembered in social contexts. Early research on attitudes, however, focused simply on how attitudes change and how they influence behavior. A positive attitude toward lawns clearly would affect lawn care strategies (regular mowing, use of fertilizers) as well as afternoons of playing croquet or running through the lawn sprinkler.

Generally, we reveal our attitudes in daily interaction whenever we state liking or disliking for something (e.g., a particular food, a movie, a person). Revealing one's attitude—or even indifference—may be met with arguments from others who either reinforce or try to change the initial attitude. Waxing on about the lushness of one's lawn in drought-stricken Los Angeles in the summer of 2015 would likely have been met with scorn or shaming by others. Sometimes the link between attitudes and behavior is strong (such as when we like a political candidate and then vote for him or her), whereas other times it is weak (such as eating a hated food to avoid insulting the cook). Attitudes, like perceptions of people, affect how we interact with others, although the effects are not always direct or obvious.

As noted previously, Americans' love of lawns arose largely in the mid-20th century with the rise of housing subdivisions. In that instance, social conditions facilitated the appearance of lawns. Individuals came to "like" lawns because of their association with the prosperity of home ownership and the pleasing appearance they offered. Thus, at the simplest level, attitudes emerge implicitly from associations. In other instances, people explicitly debate issues, shaping opinions. For instance, imagine an office staff debating whether the actress Hilary

Swank is "hot."[1] When voting on Swank's appeal, half of the staff agrees that she is indeed hot, whereas the other half contends she is not, allowing this seemingly trivial matter to evolve into a heated yet absurd debate (the stuff of sitcoms), which would rest once a majority votes for or against Swank's "hotness." Formal presentations by representatives of each side, complete with visual aids, ensue to persuade at least one person to switch sides. Here, a simple matter of a difference in attitudes is shaping the dynamics in the workplace for a day. An attitude is an inner state that represents an evaluative tendency, with various objects (e.g., a person, a concrete item, an issue, a policy, a situation) as the focus of the evaluation. As an internal state, an attitude is not readily observable. What is observable, however, is the object eliciting the attitude (e.g., pictures of Hilary Swank), called the referent, and responses to the attitude object (e.g., how the staff argued their points).

Eagly and Chaiken (1993), in their classic review of the psychology of attitudes (see also Albarracín and Vargas 2010; Crano and Prislin 2008; Perloff 2008) described three types of observable responses or attitude expressions: (1) cognitive, (2) affective, and (3) behavioral. **Cognitive** responses focus on the thoughts and beliefs that individuals have about the object. For example, in the office example, the extent to which Hilary Swank's face reveals symmetry (arguably an attractive facial feature) constitutes a cognitive response by linking the object to its various attributes. **Affective** responses are tuned to feelings, emotions, moods, and the like evoked by and expressed toward the object. When asked why he did not think Hilary Swank was hot, a male worker might respond, "It's a gut thing," illustrating how his emotion colored his attitude. **Behavioral** responses pertain to actions taken toward the object. Here, think of how one staff member might get another to imagine Hilary seducing him in the office, as a means to encourage a switch (even if temporary) to the "she's hot" camp. Given the range of responses to an attitude object, it is no surprise that attitudes have been central to attempts to explain behavior and interaction dynamics for over 80 years. Only more recently have attitudes come to be seen as one of the bedrocks, focused on the evaluation of particular stimuli, for information represented in categories. Like mental representations more generally, attitudes—especially strong ones—filter what people will attend to in a situation, encode, and remember.

The approaches we will discuss first identify cognitive, affective, and behavioral sources shaping attitude development. Those sources also characterize differences in approaches to attitude change. For some people, appeals to fear (an affective concern) may undermine existing attitudes, whereas for others new information (a cognitive concern) stimulates attitude change. We recognize the complex role of behavior in relation to attitudes as well. Some arguments suggest attitudes affect behavior, whereas others recognize the reverse.

How Do Attitudes Develop?

You probably have some experience with lawns. Perhaps they surrounded your home, providing a cushiony place to play tag or kick around a soccer ball. You may have been charged with raking leaves from them in the fall and mowing them in the summer. You may have never been asked directly whether you like lawns, but the dreamy look you get when thinking about blades of grass tickling your toes or the grunts you express when asked to contribute to lawn maintenance indicate your attitude (positive or negative, respectively) toward lawns. In contrast, it is likely that you have been asked why you like a particular national political candidate or college major. While you may have had direct experiences with lawns or with courses in your major, how you decided on a candidate to support is unlikely to involve direct learning. Attitudes form through both direct experience with an attitude object and indirect experience, such as when information about the object comes through the media or other people. For both types of experience, formation processes differentially stress cognitive, affective, or behavioral elements. And what forms attitudes hints at what changes them.

Attitude Formation Processes

In recalling your childhood, do you remember a favorite blanket, stuffed toy, or activity or even how you formed your first friendship? Most likely, you developed attitudes toward toys, activities, and people through direct experience. The emergence of a particular object as a favorite may stem simply from **mere exposure** (Zajonc 1968), which suggests that the repeated exposure to an object increases the favorability of the attitude toward that object. This process is relatively nonconscious. Learning to like something occurs not by processing information about it but by simply being exposed to it. Development of attitudes through mere exposure is limited, with liking increasing only to a point. And if there is an initial dislike, repeated exposure may exacerbate the initial unfavorable attitude rather than create a favorable one (Bornstein 1989). For example, when Karen would walk to the park each morning with her then toddler son Ross, they would pass a very tall, narrow palm tree, which was distinct from most other trees in the area. Her son claimed this tree and, whenever he passed it, would exclaim enthusiastically (even years later) "My tree!" clearly signifying a favorable attitude, largely owing to familiarity.

One could argue that Ross liked the tree because he associated it with going to the park, a pleasurable experience. Such associative learning typifies classical and operant conditioning, which, as key mechanisms of socialization (see Grusec and Hastings 2007; Shaffer 2005), also account for attitude formation (see Banaji and Heiphetz 2010). **Classical conditioning** was illustrated in the landmark experiment (by Russian physiologist Ivan Pavlov) on salivation in a dog, highlighting how the repeated pairing of an unconditioned stimulus (food) with a conditioned neutral stimulus (a metronome beat) may lead to the expression of the unconditioned response (salivation) in the absence of the unconditioned stimulus. In other words, the metronome beat begins to elicit salivation and thus is called a conditioned response.

Classical conditioning focuses on how "pairings of pairings" result in the learning of attitudes (Staats and Staats 1958). The initial pairing consists of the repeated experience of positive or negative affect (resulting, for example, from unconditioned stimuli like a tender touch or a physical punishment, respectively) and words such as *good* or *bad*. With subsequent pairings (or "higher-order" pairings) of these words (now functioning as unconditioned stimuli) with other stimuli, people develop reactions to or attitudes toward those stimuli that are on par with positive or negative affect first experienced. For example, when a child who has been conditioned to associate the word *bad* with a negative feeling repeatedly hears the word *bad* to describe dogs, fire engines, or a minority group, she will develop negative attitudes toward those entities. Classical conditioning of attitudes implies that learning occurs without conscious thought. Yet recent formulations, labeled evaluative conditioning, take into account cognitive processes connecting unconditioned and conditioned stimuli (Walther and Langer 2008).

Likewise, operant conditioning principles shape attitudes in a seemingly automatic way (Insko 1965). **Operant conditioning** pertains to situations in which the consequences of an action affect repetition of the action in the future (Skinner 1953). When a favorable consequence follows a behavior (i.e., it is reinforced), the likelihood that the response will recur increases. In contrast, when an unfavorable consequence follows a behavior (i.e., it is punished), the likelihood of recurrence decreases. Distinct from classical conditioning, operant conditioning requires that individuals must first "act" by expressing an opinion—even a neutral one. What follows the expression then dictates whether the person retains or begins to question the attitude. Los Angeles homeowners who expressed a love for well-watered lawns during the drought were sometimes shamed in videos posted on YouTube. Such "punishment" is designed to reduce violations of water restrictions, brought on by positive attitudes, entitling homeowners to green lawns.

Similarly, consider friends discussing favorite movies. Someone might say, "I don't know what my favorite movie is." If friends respond, "You've got to be kidding. It is impossible *not* to have a favorite," they are delivering a punishment by chastising the person's indecisiveness, making it unlikely that he or she would express such a neutral opinion in the future. In contrast, when someone says, "My favorite movie is *Citizen Kane*," verbal agreement or praise of that movie may solidify the attitude, whereas ridicule of the choice may inspire attitude change. In other words, social reinforcement strengthens the attitude (or frequency of its expression), whereas social punishment weakens it (or likelihood of its expression). Generally, classical and operant conditioning forms attitudes without cognitive deliberations. Other formation approaches, especially those involving indirect experience, allow cognitions to play a central role.

Bem's (1967, 1972) **self-perception theory** likewise emphasizes behavior as a starting point for shaping one's behavior, but as the label suggests, perception and cognition also play a role. The main premise of self-perception theory is that people infer their attitudes from their own behavior. In this way, actors are like observers who focus on observable clues about another person's inner state. For example, a child might contend that she does not like vegetables (what kid would claim to like them?). Yet if that child observed how ravenously she consumed green beans and broccoli at dinner, she would conclude that she did indeed like (some) vegetables. Her parents, as observers, would concur. As Bem (1972) noted, the inference of an attitude from a behavior *presumes the absence of other possible causes for the behavior*. In other words, had the child expected that her grandmother would pay her $5 for consuming vegetables, she could not infer a positive attitude from her consumption of them. The presence of other plausible causes leads to the discounting of an internal preference—an attitude—for a particular object.

A **balance theory** (Heider 1958; see also Newcomb 1968) approach to attitude formation (and change) also proposes a central role for cognitions. Unlike conditioning approaches, balance theory incorporates how other people influence a person's attitudes. And distinct from Bem's self-perception theory, the theory presumes that individuals are motivated to achieve consistency, a psychologically pleasing state. Using symbolic language to describe relationships between the focal perceiver (p), another person (o), and an object (x) about which an attitude may be directed, Heider (1958) analyzes how "balance" and "imbalance" exist in a three-element structure. Balance suggests consistency in the liking or "sentiment relations" among elements in the structure (i.e., p and o's relationship, and each person's relationship with the object x).

A balance theory approach to the development of an attitude involves consideration of the perceiver's cognitions about (1) own liking or disliking of the other person and (2) the other person's liking or disliking of the attitude object (see Figure 6.1). To the extent that the perceiver likes the other and the other likes the attitude object, then the perceiver is likely to also form a positive attitude toward the object. For example, if Harry likes Sally, and Sally really likes Ethiopian food, Harry is likely to (at least try) to like such food as well. In such a situation, all relationships are positive and the structure is balanced because the product of the multiplication of each sign (positive or negative) of the relationships in the structure (here: +, +, +) is also positive. Alternatively, if Harry really cannot stand Sally, and Sally still likes Ethiopian food, Harry may develop a negative attitude to that type of food (the " –, +, –" configuration produces a positive sign, signifying balance). Likewise, if two people really love science fiction (two positive relationships toward the attitude object), they may also develop a positive attitude toward each other. In effect, attitude formation stems from the drive for the pleasing state of balance. Imbalance implies inconsistency and may shape attitude change.

Balance theory represents a relatively simplistic approach to attitude development. In addition to the valence of each relationship, the strength matters (Judd and Krosnick 1989). Stronger relationships between people undergird the formation of attitudes more than weak relationships, such as when a romantic relationship leads to liking new hobbies, whereas an acquaintance relationship does not.

Summary

Approaches to attitude formation consider both unconscious, automatic processing and more conscious, possibly systematic processing, much like social

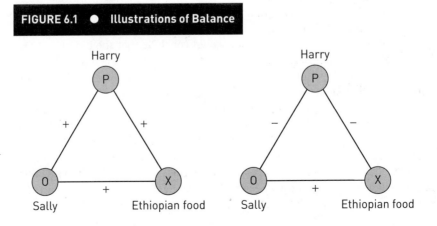

FIGURE 6.1 ● Illustrations of Balance

cognition more generally. Attitudes developed through mere exposure, classical conditioning, and operant conditioning require direct experience but not much of a person's cognitive resources. In contrast, self-perception and balance approaches suggest that individuals are thinking and reflecting about why they hold a favorable attitude toward some object. Balance theory, in particular, highlights individuals' motivations and the effect of another person on the perceiver.

More generally, social influence—exercised in many ways—is a central force in shaping attitudes. The interpersonal aspects of how attitudes develop may be implicit and passive, such as when one reads a newspaper columnist's argument for a new city policy and the reader has only indirect experience with the city policy. In contrast, the interpersonal dynamics may be quite explicit and active, as in the case of a husband, who, having attended private schools himself, has formed his opinion through direct experience, attempts to convince his spouse that their children should do likewise. His attempts at persuasion are very active, yet the wife's emerging attitude toward private schools, with which she has no experience, forms from indirect experience. In both examples, a communicator (the columnist or the husband) provides information about an object, person, or issue in an intentional attempt to affect the nature of the attitude held by the target of the communication. Persuasion of this sort may shape a new attitude or stimulate change in an existing attitude. Indeed, in much of the persuasion literature, the distinction between attitude formation and change blurs (Eagly and Chaiken 1993).

How Do Attitudes Change?

The mechanisms discussed previously describing how attitudes form are also embedded in theories addressing attitude change. The now classic work on communication and persuasion by Hovland, Janis, and Kelley (1953) at Yale University relied heavily on a reinforcement paradigm. Highlighting the importance of incentives in shaping attitudes, their perspective introduced concerns with how aspects of the communicator, the target, and the nature of the arguments, especially their emotional content, might reinforce an advocated position. In so doing, their work provided the basis for later models that examine distinct pathways—automatic and controlled—to attitude change. While incentives constitute the key motivational factor in the work of Hovland and colleagues, the desire for consistency among cognitions about attitude objects is the central focus in an alternative attitude change theory, cognitive dissonance (Festinger 1957). While proposed as a theory of attitude change, cognitive dissonance has also drawn attention to the role of behavior and self-processes (see Cooper 2007). Although these two theoretical traditions differ in many ways, both identify aspects of cognitive processing that underlie attitude change and imply ways that individuals may resist attitude change.

Considering the Communication, the Communicator, and the Target

As it has evolved, the attitude change approach initiated by Hovland et al. (1953) has grown to emphasize the cognitive responses of recipients of persuasive communications (see Albarracín and Vargas 2010; Perloff 2008). Hovland and his colleagues (1953) focused on how message learning influences attitude change. The component steps of message learning (presentation, attention, comprehension, acceptance, and retention), however, require the perceiver to actively process information. Effective communications result in the intended persuasion and induce perceivers to generate favorable cognitive responses to the communicator or to the message being conveyed. In effect, such positive responses are rewarding, which underscores the perspective's origins in reinforcement theory.

Persuasion is successful if all of the steps of message learning ultimately result in behavior consistent with the changed attitude. Ironically, attempts to determine the likelihood of the occurrence of each step, from attention, to comprehension, to acceptance (e.g., McGuire 1985) demonstrate how difficult it is to change a person's attitudes and behaviors through exposure simply to a message. For example, after the 2003 invasion of Iraq, many college campuses held open debates on whether the United States should have invaded the country. If you were unsure of your position on this issue and you listened to a speech advocating that the invasion was the right thing to do, several factors would affect whether you would accept and retain the arguments. These factors include (1) the manner in which the argument was presented (e.g., provided all reasons for the invasion, but failed to provide counterarguments for why we should not have invaded), (2) the extent to which you attended to the message (e.g., concentrated on the rhetoric only when not scoping out the crowd), and (3) your understanding of the arguments (e.g., how chemical weapons are produced). If the presentation was imperfect, your attention strayed, and you failed to understand the chemistry allowing certain weapons to wreak mass destruction, then you may form a weak attitude favorable to the war, which might be tough to retain (especially if you also listen to antiwar arguments) and certainly would not enhance the likelihood that you would volunteer for a tour of duty. Reception (a combination of attention and comprehension) of a communication typically mediates between presentation factors and acceptance of the message.

The more listeners of persuasive communication generate cognitive responses, even idiosyncratic ones, the more likely they are to receive and reflect on the message (Greenwald 1968). Such thoughts do not merely represent the content of the message but how a person is incorporating the message into existing beliefs and knowledge. Greater cognitive responses, especially more favorable ones, increase the likelihood of attitude change.

The work of Hovland and colleagues, McGuire, and Greenwald provides the theoretical basis for sorting a raft of studies focusing on how features of the communication, the communicator, and the target audience influence attitude change. These studies, in turn, shape the foundations of two process models that recognize both automatic and controlled pathways to attitude change.

Features of the Communication

In trying to persuade your parents to let you go to an all-night concert, you may give a great deal of thought to what you are going to say and how you are going to say it. These features of the persuasive communication or message constitute the "presentation" step in Hovland and colleagues' (1953) formulation and have been extensively investigated (see Perloff 2008). A clear image emerges regarding the most effective structuring of the argument, whereas the impact of the content depends upon a variety of factors.

The structure of the argument focuses on (1) the introduction of the two sides (i.e., supporting and opposing) of any issue, (2) the strength of the arguments, (3) the message length, and (4) the usefulness of drawing conclusions. *Two-sided arguments*, in which the communicator offers arguments supporting his or her position and arguments that not only recognize the opposition's viewpoint but also refute it, are clearly superior (Allen 1998; O'Keefe 1999). Most audiences recognize that there are two sides to any argument; thus, overlooking those opposing arguments makes a communicator appear a bit suspect. For example, when Governor Brown attempts to dissuade Californians from using water to maintain their lawns, he should be aware of how his state's citizens are so attached to them as well. Introduction of opposing arguments reassures listeners that the speaker recognizes that there is opposition but that he or she has weighed different positions before advocating one side. Plus, by refuting opposing arguments, the communicator can offer cogent reasons for why his or her side is preferable. Governor Brown may note how passion for lawns emerged, the abundance of past water supplies, and individuals' fond familiarity with green expanses but indicate that those conditions do not entitle people to use precious water to maintain landscapes during a drought. He may further emphasize the need to divert water supplies to the Central Valley, the state's agricultural heartland, to ensure food supplies. In doing so, the audience is likely to recognize the speaker's honesty and thoughtfulness, which enhance views of his or her credibility.

Argument strength refers to the extent to which the speaker's arguments are good—comprehendible for the audience, clearly relevant to the issue, and internally consistent. *Message length* focuses on the sheer number of arguments for a particular position. Among people who are motivated to process the information that they are hearing, strong and long arguments increase the likelihood of attitude change (Petty and Cacioppo 1984). Likewise, it appears to be good to end an advocacy by *drawing conclusions*, which eliminate any confusion about where a speaker stands on the issues (Cruz 1998). Thus, in trying to convince your parents to let you go to that all-night concert, you want to make sure to foresee their counterarguments; determine ways to refute them; and generate multiple, strong arguments for your side, which may be readily summarized. (And in so doing, not only obtain their permission to attend the concert but also their respect for your oratory skills and application of social psychological knowledge!)

Complementing the structure of a "good argument" is its content—specifically what audience members perceive about it. In general, perception may depend upon the content of the argument, including its framing, use of evidence, extremity of positions described, and stimulation of emotional responses. *Framing* emphasizes what is called to the perceiver's attention. Sequencing elements of an argument may invoke a desired schema, which frames the content. For example, think about instances in which celebrities (and politicians) try to convince you that they are sincerely apologizing for their misbehavior. To the extent that wording of their apologies evokes cultural schema about atonement or reparations for mistakes, then listeners are more likely to be convinced of their sincerity (Cerulo and Ruane 2014). Similarly, the framing of policy messages in terms of provision of positive outcomes (rather than avoidance of negative ones) enhances the likelihood of agreement (Bertolotti and Catellani 2014).

Evidence includes factual statements originating from a source other than the speaker and may include examples, case studies, or quantitative information. For evidence to have the desired impact, perceivers must process how it supports a particular position and use it in evaluating their own position. The provision of evidence is more likely to produce attitude change than the failure to provide evidence (Reynolds and Reynolds 2002). Yet, as noted in Chapter 5, perceivers tend to underuse base-rate or statistical information, opting instead to concentrate on vivid examples. Such examples are concrete or proximal in a temporal, spatial, or sensory way, and thus evoke images that draw listeners' attention. As a consequence, vivid case histories, rather than general observations, can often appear to be very persuasive (Green and Brock 2000; Taylor and Thompson 1982) though not always resulting in attitude change (Collins et al. 1988). Sometimes vivid examples fail to create attitude change because they distract perceivers from processing the general arguments that ensure comprehension (Frey and Eagly 1993). An optimum strategy for a persuasive communication is to use both evidence and examples (Perloff 2008). For example, former vice president Al Gore's (2006) book and movie, *An Inconvenient Truth*, strikes the right balance between statistics and images of global warming (e.g., devastating effects of hurricanes, melting glaciers) to evoke attitude change.

Of course, in advocating his position on global warming, Gore should also take care to moderate the extremity of his arguments to avoid "turning off" his audience. Were he to call for an end to all fossil fuel emissions in the next 2 years or argue that the United States ought to use only nuclear sources to meet all its energy needs by 2025, he might be met with much disbelief. As a consequence, many audience members would discount his argument and continue to believe that the threat of global warming is overblown. This example typifies the impact of *extremity of positions*. Social judgments comparing one's existing attitudes to those advocated may facilitate or hinder attitude change. If a message differs a great deal from one's personal position, it may fall outside of the "latitude of acceptance" and into the "latitude of rejection" (Sherif and Hovland 1961). An existing attitude acts as an anchor or reference point for new information. Incoming messages relatively close to the existing attitude (within the latitude of acceptance) are likely to be assimilated or incorporated into the listener's set of attitudes, producing attitude change. In contrast, incoming messages highly discrepant with an existing attitude are likely to fall into the "latitude of rejection," having been contrasted with the listener's set of attitudes. Although these "latitudes" are conceptual constructs and not directly measurable, attitude change is most likely with the presentation of arguments that are only moderately discrepant from those represented in the audience. Given the subjectivity of the perceiver (and, as noted in Chapter 5, the tendency to incorporate new information into existing schemas), communicators must get a feel for an audience's current beliefs before constructing the content of their arguments.

Getting familiar with an audience's existing attitudes not only may help to shape how extreme—in the evaluative sense—an attitude change presentation may be but may also assist in anticipating the consequences of *emotional arousal* in a message. Think of advertisements to prevent HIV/AIDS or lung disease that depict the devastating toll such illnesses take on physical well-being. Often such advertisements try to scare someone into new attitudes and behaviors. Such fear appeals may motivate attitude change when perceivers accept a communicator's reassuring recommendations and the fear arousal dissipates (Hovland et al. 1953).

In that way, fear reduction—through acceptance of a new attitude—is reinforcing. Thus, fear arousals have a positive effect on attitude change (Eagly and Chaiken 1993; Mongeau 1998; Perloff 2008).

It may be difficult to determine what sort of message inspires fear in an audience because of subjective variation in fear thresholds (Boster and Mongeau 1984). Reading "No one thinks that they will try to tear off their own skin. Meth will do that" may deter drug use in some people while others will simply not believe it (until they become crystal methamphetamine users). These thresholds are akin to the anchors that affect cognitive processing of communications. Fear appeals fail if individuals perceive the proposed advice to be ineffective in diverting threat or impossible to carry out. For fear to stimulate attitude change, perceivers must believe several things (Rogers 1983). They must recognize that the problem described in the message could do serious harm and that they are vulnerable to the problem. Denying that "bad things" could happen to them negates the impact of fear arousal on attitude change (Weinstein 1980). Thus instilling a high, rather than a moderate or low, level of fear tends to have the greatest impact because people have more difficulty activating the "bad things cannot happen to me" defense (Janis 1967). Additionally, people must believe that they have the skills needed to perform the recommended coping strategies. During the California drought, campaigns to conserve water that stimulate fear of failures in the food supply and economic havoc may be effective because citizens can imagine the harms (crop failures), their vulnerability (to higher produce prices), and their capability (by reducing their water usage) to ward off the negative consequences.

While one can tweak a message—as politicians do repeatedly before making a speech—to attempt to increase attitude change, the tweaking process is likely to take into consideration what is likely to work with a particular audience. And how the message resonates with an audience is likely to depend upon the messenger.

Features of the Communicator

Abraham Lincoln and the Gettysburg Address. Martin Luther King Jr. and the "I Have a Dream" speech. John F. Kennedy and "Ask not what your country can do for you . . ." Hillary Rodham Clinton and "Human rights are women's rights." These well-known people delivered speeches that are now considered classic. Had your local grocery store clerk, mail carrier, or adolescent cousin delivered the message of these speeches, would they have found their way onto a famous quote website? Probably not. These speeches garnered respect and delivered impact partly because of who delivered them. These communicators could arguably be said to be "experts," given their formal (e.g., achieved occupations, such as "attorney") or informal (e.g., extended experience) credentials, which enhances the extent to which audiences see them as credible.

Certain characteristics of communicators convey rewards to listeners (Hovland et al. 1953). Experts' statements are presumed to be truthful, corresponding to facts or reality, and, as such, are inherently reinforcing. Expertise, along with trustworthiness, constitutes the *credibility* of the communicator (Eagly, Wood, and Chaiken 1978). While expertise focuses on knowledge relevant to a topic, trustworthiness implies that a communicator is likely to convey honest beliefs and will act with integrity and responsibility toward others. A communicator who expresses good will—understanding and empathy for the issues of concern to the audience—also conveys credibility (McCroskey and Teven 1999). The credibility of a source does not rely upon the communicator's authority position or personal characteristics per se. Instead, it is something that the audience perceives, which leads them to believe in what the communicator says. As a consequence, the credibility of the same communicator may vary depending upon the audience. For example, Hillary Clinton may have had more credibility with female than male voters in the 2016 primaries. Greater communicator credibility, including its component parts, is positively related to attitude change (see Chaiken 1986; McGuire 1985). In a similar vein, communicators viewed as *efficacious*—likely to bring proposed outcomes to fruition—have more impact on altering attitudes as well (Clark, Evans, and Wegener 2011).

In contrast to the weighty character of communicator credibility in affecting attitude change, more superficial characteristics of the communicator also are influential. The general "social attractiveness" of a speaker, represented by his or her status, likability, similarity to audience members, or appealing physical appearance, also exerts an impact. As Chapter 8 details, people with higher status or prestige are likely to be perceived as more competent and thus exert greater influence in group discussions, resulting in attitude change. Individuals who are liked, owing to their personalities, fame, or the like, have better success in changing attitudes. Listeners presume that both *high status* and *likable* communicators will bestow social rewards if they bring their attitudes in line with what is advocated. For example, the opinions of a social clique leader may carry more weight on a teenage female's attitudes toward particular fashion styles than those of a brother. To secure that social approval, individuals are motivated to attend to and comprehend the messages delivered by high status and likable others.

The clique example also pertains to the impact of *similarity* and *physical attractiveness* on attitude change (Chaiken 1979; see also Eagly et al. 1991). To perceive oneself as similar to a communicator increases the likelihood of positive affect toward that person. When people, through social comparisons, perceive themselves as similar to an advocate of a particular position, they may come to believe that as "similars" they should adopt the same position (Berscheid 1966). For example, if a teenage girl wants to have higher status in her clique, she may be able to achieve that by emulating the leader, including sharing her attitudes. Oftentimes, clique leaders are very attractive. People tend to pay attention to attractive speakers, increasing the likelihood that listeners actually process the message. Also, individuals may associate a message with the attractiveness of the speaker or want to identify with an attractive speaker.

In addition to real and perceived aspects of the communicator, how the communicator delivers a message may impact the resulting extent of attitude change. A mail carrier may be unlikely to have the same oratory skills as Martin Luther King Jr. Likewise, some politicians or religious leaders are far better at holding the attention of an audience—regardless of the substance of their message—than are others. It is, however, not the rate of speech itself that affects attitude change. Rather, it is how speakers demonstrate their awareness of their audience's willingness and ability to comprehend their message. The extent to which communicators are in sync with the needs of their audience for various speech styles (e.g., directness of points, use of metaphors, emotionally charged words) may communicate credibility, which, in turn, enhances attitude change (Perloff 2008). During his 2008 presidential campaign, Obama was lauded for his ability to pitch his messages in ways understood by his varied audiences.

Features of the Audience

When Marlis, Karen's daughter, was in second grade, her teacher invited parents in to talk about their careers. Karen wanted to convince the children that it was fun to be a professor! In shaping her arguments, she described college teaching and research in ways that might resonate with second graders. And, like using props in her lectures, she wore her academic regalia—cap, (black) gown, and (purple and gold) doctoral hood. She failed, however, to foresee what truly captured their attention: the fact that universities differ in the color of their gowns and hoods. While the author may not have persuaded them of the fun of being a professor, the students might have begun to consider future college preferences based on university colors. This example highlights the importance of anticipating the reaction of a particular audience to a given message. As already noted, messages must fall within the latitude of acceptance to inspire attitude change. In a related vein, successful communication involves recognition of the current experience and existing beliefs of audience members as well as their individual-level attributes.

Within the situation, to the extent that audience members are comfortable (e.g., fed, relaxed), they are more likely to be swayed by a communication (Janis, Kaye, and Kirschner 1965). More generally, a positive mood tends to increase the likelihood of attitude change (Petty et al. 1993). In contrast, if audience members feel that there is going to be an attempt to persuade them to change their attitudes, they may respond negatively to protect their existing beliefs. Such anticipation allows audience members to develop counterarguments and resist attitude change (Chen et al.1992; Petty and Cacioppo 1977). For example, imagine a college student who has reformed her lifestyle to "live green, live sustainably" returning home to her isolated suburban subdivision where driving is the dominant means of transportation and little attention is paid to recycling and conservation. Anticipating that her family and neighbors may scoff at her newly formed environmentally friendly attitudes and behaviors, she may devise a strategy to engage in civil debate or simply to avoid discussing her new lifestyle choices entirely.

Audience experience may vary across individuals. Although few would argue that some people are simply more persuadable than others, self-esteem and need for cognition affect the likelihood of attitude change. People with high *self-esteem* may feel conflict when encountering attitudes distinct from their own. They are likely able to process communications and thus may be persuaded to change, but equally likely, they may hold onto what they currently believe, owing to confidence in their convictions. And while it may seem that people with low self-esteem may already doubt their beliefs and thus be susceptible to convincing arguments, such people may be preoccupied with their own problems and thus fail to attend to arguments. As a consequence, those most susceptible to attitude change are people who have moderate levels of self-esteem—a group that is also likely to differ on many other factors as well (Wood and Stagner 1994).

Need for cognition refers to people's tendency to engage in and enjoy effortful and even abstract thinking (Cacioppo et al. 1996). Because of this enjoyment, people high in need for cognition are likely to process persuasive communications and thus may be persuaded by good arguments. In contrast, the attitudes of those low in need for cognition may be shaped more by cues in the situation—for example, communicator's credibility or attractiveness.

The impact of individual-level factors on attitude change reiterates a theme inherent in the discussion about factors affecting the success of persuasion attempts: Often a *combination of factors* produces attitude change. Although factors that reinforce attitude change increase its likelihood (Hovland et al. 1953), *when* such factors are likely to result in long-term rather than short-term attitude change requires a focus on the *process* of attitude change.

Dual Process Models of Attitude Change

While persuasive communication models of the 1950s corresponded to the emphasis during that decade on behavioral reinforcement, the dual process models of attitude change reflect the cognitive movement of the 1960s. A key distinction between the two frameworks is emphasis in the process models of the role of the perceiver's own mental reactions to a persuasive communication. Yet as Chapter 5 illustrated, people often use shortcuts in their cognitive assessments of situational stimuli, and sometimes their processing seems automatic. Such observations provide the basis for process models of attitude change that recognize that some situational factors stimulate the cognitive processing of arguments while others do not.

Consider the following: As California suffered the worst drought in recent memory, state authorities campaigned to reduce water usage. They used various mediums (e.g., TV ads, radio reminders, newspaper articles) and community meetings to convey their message to the public. Nonetheless, residents in tony communities like Beverly Hills continued to maintain lush green lawns and even waste water by letting sprinklers run in the heat of the day, allowing water to spill over concrete sidewalks, and turning hoses on those who criticize their practices. Why did the authorities fail to sway Beverly Hills residents to practice prudent water-saving behaviors?

The **elaboration likelihood model (ELM)**, offered by Petty and Cacioppo (1986; Petty and Wegener 1999; Petty, Wheeler, and Tormala 2003), focuses on the extent to which audience members elaborate on—think about or mentally modify—the arguments laid out in persuasive communications. To the extent that elaboration is likely, attitude change is instigated through a **central route** that requires careful consideration of the message, the communicator's ideas, and how they relate to one's own existing beliefs. Given the strength of their feelings of entitlement to green lawns, perhaps Beverly Hills residents failed to elaborate. Alternatively, in the absence of elaboration, people rely on simple cues, such as the communicator's physical attractiveness, style of speech, or expertise as well as situational features such as the room's comfort, audience excitement, soothing background music, or tasty buffet. Cues that convey pleasantness and become associated with the message stimulate the **peripheral route** to attitude change. Peripheral processing relies on cognitive shortcuts or heuristics to pave the way for attitude change. It is doubtful that state authorities could stage a community meeting for Beverly Hills residents that could sway such wealthy denizens through the peripheral route, unless donors stepped forward to cater the affair and attractive movie starts acted as communicators.

Although both routes may lead to attitude change, two factors enhance the likelihood of the central route. The first factor, **motivation**, focuses on how much people perceive that the arguments are relevant to themselves, having implications for their own lives. Presumably, state authorities' messages regarding water conservation should be relevant to all California residents, though they may be less meaningful to residents of water-rich states. While relevance depends upon a person's goals and needs, also contributing to motivation is the individual-level factor need for cognition, discussed previously. Some people simply enjoy effortful, abstract thinking.

The second factor, **ability**, refers to the extent to which people are able to process the message, given situational factors and existing knowledge. Under conditions of distraction (e.g., other people talking, blaring music, more pressing concerns) that block expression of the dominant cognitive response, individuals are unable to process messages. Lack of knowledge about a topic or lack of confidence in one's knowledge also detracts from one's ability to process incoming arguments. Most residents of tony neighborhoods are likely to have the knowledge necessary to understand state rules about water use during a drought.

Both motivation and ability are necessary for attitude change to emerge through a central route. Change from peripheral processing tends to be "relatively temporary, susceptible to counterpersuasion, and unpredictive of behavior" (Petty and Wegener, 1999:43). If you go to a political event because barbeque will be served, it is likely that you might only peripherally process the candidate's message, resulting in little conviction toward the candidate's platform. Processing persuasive communications via the central route results in attitude change that is more enduring, resistant to other counterarguments, and predictive of behavior. Elaboration of incoming messages relies on the quality of the messages and existing attitudes. The key is the extent to which the message generates more favorable (or unfavorable) thoughts than existed previously. Processing, however, varies depending upon whether the message touches on personally relevant outcomes (e.g., vacation locations) or core values (e.g., capital punishment). The former may elicit so-called rational processing (though perhaps contaminated by cognitive shortcuts), whereas the latter may elicit more biased processing. In either case, the ELM requires that a change in cognitive structure occur to produce long-lasting attitude change. Failure at any stage in the elaboration results in maintenance of the existing attitude.

The premise of ELM—that perceivers are "economy minded" in terms of their efficient approach to processing social stimuli—resonates also with the two-pathway **heuristic–systematic model (HSM)** developed by Chaiken (1987; Chen and Chaiken 1999; Todorov, Chaiken, and Henderson 2002). The HSM presents a systematic approach, similar to the central route, and a heuristic approach, akin to peripheral processing, characterized by perceivers' reliance on cognitive shortcuts to evaluate message arguments with little effort. Distinct from ELM, HSM allows that both systematic and heuristic processing may co-occur when motivation and ability for argument scrutiny are high. The HSM framework also delineates multiple motivations. Besides need for accuracy, perceivers may be motivated to defend their own interests or attitudes or to formulate impressions of others in the service of social goals.

Motivations specified by ELM and HSM indicate how actively involved a perceiver might be in processing arguments intended to alter one's attitudes. In contrast, the cognitive dissonance approach to attitude change is independent of persuasive communications, focusing instead on the motivation to hold consistent beliefs and behaviors.

"Dissonance" as a Precursor to Attitude Change

The classic formulation of **cognitive dissonance theory** (Festinger 1957) focuses on the inconsistency between two cognitions that may pertain to a person's beliefs, attitudes, behaviors, or knowledge about oneself or others. For example, Rob might argue that Stanford is his favorite university—his cognition about the university is very positive. Yet Rob's behavior might imply otherwise—he fails to apply to attend Stanford. In such a case, Rob's cognitions about that particular university and his behavior are inconsistent. Such inconsistency or dissonant cognitions (typically between an existing attitude and a behavior) create an aversive, unpleasant state that people are motivated to eliminate by pursuing strategies such as (1) changing one or both of the dissonant cognitions to make them more consistent or (2) adding cognitions.

The first strategy may involve attitude change or the elimination of a behavior that is the source of a discrepant cognition. For example, Rob might decide that Stanford is not his favorite university or he may put in a last-minute application to that institution. The second strategy allows for justification or rationalization of the behavior or the existing attitude to bridge the gap between the initial cognitions. It also allows trivialization of the inconsistent behavior or the discrepancy itself. Thus, Rob may justify his failure to apply by noting that none of his friends with stellar academic records got into Stanford, tuition costs are prohibitive, or he wants to be in a "real" city, not just a "suburb." Both strategies reduce dissonance, and people usually pursue the easiest one. Often it is change in the cognition about the attitude that is least effortful.

When people attempt to deal with being "dumped," they are, in effect, eliminating dissonance between knowing that they liked someone and knowing that the person they liked curtailed their relationship. By "focusing on the negative" about the former lover, one shifts liking the person to disliking. People might add cognitions about the importance of work, not romance, to ensure future happiness. Likewise, advice to get outdoors and admire the ocean, a lake, a mountain, or the like adds cognitions about the "bigger things out there" and the beauty of life and nature, beyond the confines of the nastiness that may have occurred in the relationship. Being dumped in a relationship, however, may not involve **free choice**—a critical component of the extent to which dissonance theory is useful in predicting attitude change.

In the case of a relationship breakup, one person has made the choice to dump the other. But did he or she choose freely? Were there family pressures to find another partner? Brehm (1956) focuses on the consequences of dissonance resulting after an individual has made a decision (i.e., postdecisional dissonance). Largely because there are pros and cons for any options, after making a decision, people try to convince themselves that they selected the right option. Such rationalization pertains to decisions involving interpersonal actions as well as solitary ones (e.g., making a purchase of some type; taking a particular route home from school) and typically involves adding cognitions about the positive characteristics of the chosen option. Dissonance reduction like this mostly occurs when the decision has been made freely between equally valued alternatives. In the absence of free choice—like when family members adamantly oppose a new boyfriend or girlfriend or when the purchasing choice is between a very desirable item and a not-so-desirable one so that the choice is clear—dissonance is less likely to emerge and thus less likely to stimulate reduction strategies to bolster a new attitude.

The element of choice is implied in the classic "**induced compliance**" experiment by Festinger and Carlsmith (1959). Focusing on how counterattitudinal advocacy might lead to changes in an initial attitude, the study examined the effects of the size of the inducement to express views counter to one's existing attitudes. An inducement might be the promise of a reward or the threat of a punishment that provides a person with cognitions consistent with or justifications about advocating against their own beliefs. As a consequence, an inducement decreases the likelihood of stimulating dissonance and subsequent attitude change. Participants in the Festinger and Carlsmith (1959) study were asked to help out a research assistant by introducing an experimental task to new participants. Nearly all agreed to do so, despite their own experience of the task as boring. They were paid either $1 or $20 to engage in the counterattitudinal behavior of telling new subjects that the task is enjoyable. The $1 was sufficient to induce the advocacy but insufficient to justify expressing counterattitudinal views. In contrast, the $20 sufficed as a clear justification for arguing against one's existing attitudes. In a postexperiment interview, participants who had been paid $1 for praising the task clearly evaluated it more positively than those paid $20. In other words, their attitude toward it grew more positive owing to the lack of justification for the counterattitudinal advocacy.

In a similar vein, a classic persuasion technique, which is the "**foot-in-the-door**" strategy, relies on people freely choosing to perform a small favor as a step in eliciting even greater attitude or behavior change (Freedman and Fraser 1966). By getting people to agree to do a small favor (e.g., sign a petition supporting sustainability efforts on campus) they are likely to develop a cognition about themselves as committed to a particular viewpoint (e.g., a positive attitude toward sustainability) and thus more likely to comply when asked to do something more to support the effort (e.g., save recyclable cans and plastic and take those collected to a central location). Failure to comply with subsequent or even larger requests would be inconsistent with their existing cognition and would create dissonance. Acquiescing to the small favor provides justification for subsequent, more involving behaviors; such justification wards off dissonance.

Factors other than freedom of choice and lack of justification that stimulate dissonance related to counterattitudinal advocacy include commitment to the counterattitudinal behavior, the irrevocability of a decision, aversive consequences (especially foreseeable ones), personal responsibility for bringing about an aversive event, and various combinations of factors on the arousal of dissonance (Cooper 2007; Eagly and Chaiken 1993). Yet when people can attribute their negative arousal—their dissonance—to some aspect of the situation, they are less likely to engage in attitude change (Cooper and Fazio 1984). For example, if you recognize that you have signed a sustainability pledge but are not recycling because there are no receptacles within miles, then the dissonance stems from contextual circumstances and is unlikely to affect your positive attitude toward sustainability. When a person feels personally responsible for aversive events (e.g., failing to recycle or lying about the enjoyment of a task), attitude change is more likely.

Such change may be a means to preserve **self-consistency** and a positive self-concept (Aronson 1968; Thibodeau and Aronson 1992). Dissonance is greatest in situations that threaten the self-concept (and such situations typically involve personal responsibility for actions and aversive consequences of those actions). For example, in the Festinger and Carlsmith (1959) study, dissonance would stem from the discrepancy between cognitions about oneself as honest and the cognition that one was dishonest with another human being (without sufficient rewards or threats of punishment to justify the lying). Generally, lower rewards or a lower likelihood of punishment diminishes the possibility of external justification, which in turn creates greater need for internal justification to maintain a positive self-concept (Aronson 2012).

Consider the woman who breaks up with her boyfriend. She might think of herself as a nice, caring person, yet her action hurt someone else. To maintain a positive view of herself in the absence of any rewards for breaking up, she may enumerate reasons for the breakup, such as "He never really understood me" or "The relationship was not going anywhere." In effect, self-justifications reflect attitude changes stimulated by threats to self-consistency. Explanations or justifications that people develop must be acceptable not only to themselves (the private sphere) but to others as well (the public sphere) (Schlenker 1982). Additionally, the attitude change may reaffirm the self, not simply eliminate inconsistency in cognitions (Steele 1988).

The actual cognitive processes underlying dissonance processes are relatively universal, but to the extent that the nature of the self varies cross-culturally, so does the substance of what stimulates dissonance. The more interpersonal the consequences from a person's behavior, the more aversive and dissonance-producing it is for people from interdependent or collectivist cultures (e.g., Asian) compared to those from independent cultures (e.g., United States, Canada) (Hoshino-Browne et al. 2005). The dissonance aroused by inconsistency among cognitions about existing attitude(s) and behavior are shaped by self-construals as well as normative standards of judgments representing what most people in a group or culture perceive to be negative behavior.

Despite differences in underlying motivations, persuasive communications approaches and cognitive dissonance theory highlight the role of cognitions in attitude change. These elements play a role in the means by which individuals attempt to resist attitude change as well.

Resistance to Attitude Change

In 1985, the Coca-Cola Company launched "the new taste of Coca-Cola," aka New Coke, a product designed to replace its original soda. Even with an extensive marketing campaign, consumers clamored to retain the original product. The company relented, relabeling it Classic Coke to distinguish it from New Coke, which remained only briefly on market shelves. Coke consumers had not been swayed by the marketing drive and were, in effect, resistant to attitude change. From the persuasive communication literature, it appears that the campaign for New Coke did not involve enough credible communicators or that the pitch fell outside of the audience's latitude of acceptance. Cognitive dissonance theorists would argue that a favorable attitude toward New Coke would require getting people to taste it (i.e., create a cognition about a behavior inconsistent with an existing attitude), experience dissonance, and then generate cognitions supporting it. Given a strong preference for Classic Coke, however, people may not experience dissonance and instead focus on cognitions to support the existing attitude. To understand such resistance requires more than explanations for study results that disconfirm a predicted attitude change. "People have available to them psychological processes that facilitate resistance to persuasion and that can hamper even well designed persuasive efforts" (Eagly and Chaiken 1993:559). Specifically, resistance to persuasion involves defending an existing attitude from persuasive attack (see Knowles and Linn 2004).

The **inoculation approach** (McGuire 1964) was the first notable theory of resistance to attitude change. Just as health inoculations or immunizations involving administration of a weakened dose of a virus to stimulate antibody production to guard against development of a full-fledged case of a disease, the theory proposes that by exposing people to weak arguments in opposition to their current attitude, they develop defenses against a full-blown persuasive attack. For example, imagine that you hold very liberal political attitudes even though nearly all of your family members are politically conservative. In anticipation of a trip home, you start watching a conservative news channel to brush up on conservative stances to anticipate and ward off arguments that your parents might launch at you to alter your liberal views. You are creating a "refutational defense."

Inoculation may work because it fills both motivational and cognitive gaps. In the absence of having beliefs threatened, individuals have little motivation to launch a defense, lack informational sources to refute opposing arguments, and do not practice defending their own positions. With inoculation, people see their attitudes challenged and thus are motivated to fill the gaps in their knowledge to develop a defense. Another motivational component of resistance is **reactance** (Brehm 1966; Brehm and Brehm 1981), which emerges when events thwarting freedom to express certain beliefs or engage in certain behaviors encourage people to act in ways that restore the belief or behavior. Reactance hinders attitude change and may also foment change in a direction opposite to that proposed in persuasion attempt. For example, if college students hold beliefs that premarital sex is okay in the context of a long-term, monogamous relationship but hear a message advocating total abstinence until marriage, they may feel that their views are threatened and as a result come to hold even more liberal views (e.g., premarital sex is permissible, regardless of the length of the relationship). Thus, it is no wonder that highly coercive efforts to change attitudes may backfire (Eagly and Chaiken 1993).

The ability to resist also depends upon cognitive factors. Arguments falling outside of a person's latitude of acceptance may be readily deflected, as previously noted. Plus, more resistant to change are strong attitudes, which are characterized as particularly important and accessible to an individual; related to other attitudes; and based on personal investments in the belief and emotional commitment to it (Eagly and Chaiken 1993; Petty and Krosnick 1995). For example, if Peggy has a strong, positive attitude toward sustainability, routinely engages in recycling and conservation, and supports organizations like the Sierra Club, she is likely to be fairly resistant to arguments that climate change is a hoax.

Thinking about one's attitude also may make it more extreme because, in doing so, individuals produce other cognitions that are consistent with the existing attitude (Tesser 1978). The desire for consistency, in turn, reinforces linkages between beliefs that may make the attitude more extreme, thereby further enhancing resistance to attitude change attempts (because a change in one belief or attitude would reverberate through the linkages, increasing the costs of attitude change) (Bassili 1996). Resistance to attitude change additionally relies on cognitions that allow for bolstering initial attitudes, making arguments counter to persuasive messages (as inoculation theory suggests), and derogating message sources (Wegener et al. 2004).

Perceiving and reflecting on the process of resistance adds attribution-like inferences about why a person holds certain attitudes (Tormala 2008). When situational factors allow people to positively assess their resistance, the certainty with which they hold the attitude and their subjective conviction that their attitude is correct and clear in their minds increases. In contrast, when situational factors lead to negative appraisals of resistance, attitude certainty decreases. For example, let's say you are opposed to a proposed university policy that would require students to take comprehensive exams to graduate in a particular major. Your roommate argues passionately why such exams would be a good thing. If you resist these arguments because you could hardly hear your roommate's voice over the loud music playing in the room, you might appraise your resistance behavior negatively; you really did nothing but not hear the arguments. On the other hand, if you refuted each of your roommate's arguments systematically, you might be quite pleased with how you resisted persuasion, which strengthens your initial conviction. Positive appraisals for resistance that increase attitude certainty may also enhance attitude–behavior correspondence, a central issue regarding how cognitions affect interaction.

Summary and Linking Attitudes to Social Cognition

Although the attitude concept does not suggest the breadth that is implied by the concepts of mental representation or schema, they share a critical function: helping perceivers to sort through information in a situation that may be relevant to other beliefs, behavior, or interpersonal dynamics. Though focused on evaluation (unlike representations of categories), this knowledge function of attitudes provides a basis for making sense of the world. Attitudes also function to help someone achieve rewards and avoid punishments; adjust to social groups (i.e., shared attitudes pave the way to acceptance into other groups); communicate an identity; express values; and protect oneself from unpleasant emotions (Maio and Olson 2000).

Understanding attitude development and change provides some depth, albeit narrowly focused, on issues implied in the social cognition realm. The mechanisms by which attitudes are learned—conditioning principles, balance, or inferences from behavior—may also apply to how people develop the content of their social schemas. These mechanisms, moreover, are embedded in attitude change approaches, which highlight the complementary roles of motivation and cognition. Motivations may vary from seeking rewards, ensuring cognitive consistency, or avoiding the consequences of an aversive event. The extent to which individuals cognitively process messages or sort through inconsistencies in their cognitions about their beliefs and behavior depends upon these motivations, as well as their self-images and contextual circumstances. A complex interplay among factors may account for the failure of even a well-designed (per existing research) persuasive communication or blaring cognitive inconsistencies to change an attitude or to ensure lasting change in an attitude. Yet what is known of attitude change may be useful in understanding how representations change as well.

Approaches to attitude change differentially emphasize evaluative, cognitive, and behavioral elements. Persuasion and process models focus largely on cognitive issues, with hints of the role of emotions. Cognitive dissonance theory and its descendants suggest that behavior—at least cognitions about it—may stimulate attitude change. One reason that laws are necessary and effective is that they change structures, which in turn demand changes in behavior despite existing attitudes. The behavioral change may create inconsistent cognitions leading to attitude change. For example, by complying with laws that disallow discrimination (e.g., Civil Rights Act of 1964, the Americans with Disabilities Act, hate crime legislation), people come to interact with others toward whom they may hold negative attitudes—thus creating inconsistency in cognitions, which may erode the negative attitudes and allow, over time, more positive attitudes toward those target groups. Of course, such change will rely on beliefs that behavior was freely chosen.

Resistance to attitude change reverse engineers the attitude change models as well as introduces some new considerations. Being able to defend one's existing attitude contributes significantly to resisting messages encouraging attitude change. Largely, attitude change and resistance approaches do not specifically address one of the key reasons for the long history of attitudes research in social psychology: attitudes—those internal, unobservable evaluative beliefs—are presumed to predispose people to behave in particular ways.

Reciprocal Influences: To What Extent Are Attitudes Related to Behavior?

Someone holding liberal political attitudes is more likely to vote for Democratic rather than Republican political candidates. Liking sports should lead someone to become an athlete or spectator. Bigoted racial attitudes or a negative schema for people of color may engender participation in discriminatory acts or worse. Each of these examples suggests that the attitude or schema that one holds provides a basis for a certain type of behavior. But the reverse may be true as well, as suggested by cognitive dissonance theory. A person votes Democratic and then justifies the behavior by espousing liberal rhetoric. A child is put into a soccer program at age 5 and develops a passion for the game and other team sports as well. A group of white people have historically denied, sometimes through laws, another group characterized by darker skin color access to restaurants, jobs, or the like so that they come to see people of color as less skilled and even less human, thus justifying inhumane treatment (see Chapter 12). There are innumerable examples of how attitudes or schema may affect behavior and how behavior may shape attitudes and schema. The attitude–behavior relationship has a long history of empirical scrutiny.

Marketing researchers ask people about how much they like a product for the simple reason that it helps them decide how much to produce. If individuals hold a positive attitude to, for example, a particular brand of frozen waffles, then they are likely to buy them. If people have a negative attitude toward droughts, they should act in ways to alleviate damage from droughts. Such scenarios suggest attitude–behavior consistency. Yet as the opening example of this chapter suggests, people do not always act in ways that seem in step with their attitudes. Indeed, the attitude–behavior relationship is more complex than marketing research suggests (see Ajzen 2012; Ajzen and Fishbein 2005). The realization of that complexity emerged in the 1930s, around the same time that Allport (1935) was promoting the importance of the concept.

Factors Affecting the Attitude–Behavior Relationship

LaPiere (1934) first examined the attitude–behavior relationship by playing on prejudices of the era. As a California resident, he observed negative attitudes toward Chinese immigrants, fueled by the Depression and scarcity of jobs. Using a multimethod research approach, he tested the proposition that such negative attitudes should lead to negative, discriminatory behaviors toward Chinese people. In the first part of his study, he traveled around the United States with a young Chinese couple. He observed how they were treated at the restaurants and hotels they visited. LaPiere was surprised to find that all places, with the exception of one, accommodated the couple. Later, using a mailed questionnaire, he asked proprietors of the establishments that they visited if they would serve a Chinese couple as guests. About 92% of the respondents indicated that they would *not* do so. Clearly, there was an inconsistency in their actual behavior toward the Chinese couple and their espoused attitude to serving such a couple.

For over 30 years, debate raged about whether attitudes could predict behavior (Wicker 1969). As studies cumulated, two things grew clear. First, survey evidence indicated consistency between attitudes and behaviors (Fishbein and Ajzen 1975; Kim and Hunter 1993). And, second, the pattern of findings suggested (just as research on persuasion and cognitive dissonance showed) that the attitude–behavior relationship depends on other factors as well. Persuasion attempts work, if a listener processes the message actively. Cognitive dissonance is aroused if there is free choice. Likewise, attitude–behavior consistency depends upon certain situational characteristics, personal factors, and attitude qualities (Fazio and Roskos-Ewoldsen 1994).

For example, LaPiere may have found greater attitude–behavior consistency if he had considered that the acceptance of a Chinese couple at an establishment reflected social constraints—the person at the front desk did not want to make a scene. Even if the desk attendant held Chinese people in disdain, he or she may have not categorized the couple traveling with a distinguished Caucasian professor in the same stereotyped fashion. In effect, there was a mismatch between a general attitude about a large category of people and a more specific attitude about the particular (educated) Chinese couple. And his study may have been plagued by a methodological problem: the person responding to the questionnaire may not have been the same person who encountered the traveling group at an establishment.

Thus, the question becomes this: *When* do attitudes predict behavior? To the extent that the situation constrains behavior in any way—owing to existing norms, role expectations, or even the mindless enactment of behavioral scripts—the attitude–behavior relationship appears weaker (Perloff 2008). For example, bank tellers may have a negative attitude toward people who arrive with jars of coins; by not rolling the coins before they reach the teller, these people require more time and patience of bank tellers. Bank tellers, however, are likely to "grin and bear it," showing little negative emotion and providing the same services to these people as they do to all other banking customers. In other words, they do not act in a negative fashion, despite their negative attitude. As a service industry, banking involves norms of politeness that tellers must follow and the requirement of attending to the needs of bank customers. In some ways, the effect of situational constraints on the attitude–behavior relationship is similar to their effect on attribution analysis: to the extent that such constraints exist, a person's behavior is less likely to be attributed to internal dispositions, which attitudes, especially strongly held ones, might represent.

In the absence of social constraints, however, the extent to which people hold strong, univalent attitudes (Lord, Lepper, and Mackie 1984; see Petty and Krosnick 1995) affects the attitude–behavior relationship. When individuals are passionate about something, the attitude persists over time and is readily accessible. Thus, not surprisingly, they are likely to take actions indicating that passion to others. A prime example of the relationship between strong attitudes and behaviors are people who strongly oppose abortion rights and picket the clinics that perform pregnancy terminations, despite the possibility of arrest or other harms associated with engaging in such protest. Likewise, environmentalists with strong water conservation attitudes may spend their spare time documenting and shaming water wasters in posh neighborhoods during a record drought. In contrast, if people hold ambivalent attitudes, representing a mixture of positive and negative feelings toward an attitude object, they are less likely to act on them (Conner and Armitage 2008; Conner and Sparks 2002). Ambivalent attitudes draw people in different directions. For example, one could love living abroad yet also abhor the idea of being a "camp counselor" to undergraduates and thus refrain from directing a summer study program in Europe. High levels of attitude ambivalence weaken the attitude–behavior connection.

The source of an individual's attitude also affects the strength of the attitude–behavior relationship. Like strong attitudes, when attitudes are learned through direct experience they are more stable and able to withstand counterpressures. Thus, attitudes learned through direct experience compared to indirect experience have a greater impact on behavior (Fazio and Zanna 1981; Millar and Millar 1996). When people directly encounter the attitude object, it stimulates strong feelings or thoughts regarding the object. For example, meeting a lawmaker and listening to his or her policy proposals requires a listener to process the message in a manner distinct from what occurs when a friend tells about his or her encounter with the same lawmaker. Indeed, when people extensively process information from a persuasive communication, they form persistent attitudes that inevitably drive behavior (Pierro et al. 2012).

Individuals may also vary in the extent to which they attempt to make sure that they act in a manner consistent with their attitude. Snyder (1987) differentiates between people who monitor their behavior to make sure that it conforms to what is expected in a given situation to fit in with others (high self-monitors) and those who are less concerned about displaying socially correct behavior (low self-monitors). High self-monitors are more attuned to social constraints in the situation. As a consequence, their attitudes and behaviors appear to be less consistent than low self-monitors (Snyder and Kendzierski 1982). For example, a young man opposed to underage drinking would be more likely to decline alcoholic beverages offered at fraternity parties if he is a low self-monitor than if he is a high self-monitor. The high self-monitor would go along with the norms of a fraternity party and, thus, imbibe despite his attitude.

While situational and individual level factors moderate the strength of the attitude–behavior relationship, its strength may also be misestimated due to issues regarding measurement of attitudes and behaviors. Typically, attitudes are measured in terms of scales that aggregate multiple questionnaire items, whereas only one behavior may be observed. Yet one attitude might predict multiple behaviors, each of which stems from multiple factors, including attitudes. For example, if you like rock music, you may listen to a rock radio station, download rock tunes, go to rock concerts, and learn to play rock guitar. Whether you purchase rock music or concert tickets, however, also depends on your finances. Though it is tough to predict a single behavior from attitudes, the correlation between an aggregated group of related behaviors and an aggregated group of attitude items is much stronger (Eagly and Chaiken 1993). Several models synthesize various findings illustrating the complexities in the attitude–behavior relationship.

Models of the Attitude–Behavior Relationship

One of the first models to systematize the study of the attitude–behavior relationship emphasized the importance of using compatible measures (Ajzen and Fishbein 1977). Emphasis rested on measuring attitudes and behaviors at similar levels of generality (i.e., a global evaluation of an attitude object and global behaviors relating to the object) or specificity (evaluation of a single object within given circumstances, perhaps even toward a specific behavior, and the specific behavior itself). A general attitude might be something like "I like baseball," and general behaviors may include all activities related to baseball (e.g., attending a game, reading reports of games, collecting baseball cards), whereas a specific attitude might be "I like baseball games between the Braves and the Yankees" and a specific behavior could be attendance at a Braves–Yankees games. The model elaborates on the notion of compatibility by noting that every behavior has elements of (1) action, (2) a target of the action, (3) a context in which the action may occur, and (4) a time frame for the action. Likewise, every attitude pertains to something about the action, target, context, and time. Each of the four elements may range from very specific to quite general. What is important to consider is the extent to which the range of the four elements for behavior corresponds to the range of the four elements for the attitude. To ensure a strong attitude–behavior relationship, the "ranges" for each element across the attitude and the behavior must be equivalent.

Taking into consideration attitude and behavior measurement issues complements an understanding of *when* attitudes predict behavior. The theory of reasoned action (Fishbein and Ajzen 1975) and the theory of planned action (Ajzen 1985, 1991) attempt to explicate how it is that attitudes influence behavior. These theories answer the following question: *Why* do attitudes affect behavior? They do so by focusing on relatively specific attitudes and behaviors, presuming that individuals analyze the costs and benefits of the behavior and consciously deliberate their action. A number of studies confirm their predictions (see Ajzen and Fishbein 2005; Sutton 1998).

The **theory of reasoned action** argues that the attitude toward the behavior, along with the subjective norm for the behavior, affect a person's behavioral intention, which then predicts behavior. The *attitude toward the behavior* entails beliefs about the consequences of the behavior and evaluation (positive or negative) of them. The *subjective norm*, or perceived social pressure to undertake or avoid the behavior, includes a belief component about how specific others think someone should behave and a willingness to comply or not comply with them to gain positive consequences or avoid negative ones. The attitude and subjective norm jointly predict whether a person might put a behavior into effect. Assuming that the behavior is under the person's control, the behavioral intention should correlate strongly with actually performing the behavior. Consider the chances that a young woman will ask a particular man out on a date. If she believes that dating him will lead to positive outcomes, she may ask him out. If friends, however, worry that she will get her heart broken and urge her to avoid him, then she may comply with their wishes, in which case her attitude will not affect her action. In contrast, if they promote the match and she likes him, then she is more likely to intend to ask him out and will do so.

The **theory of planned behavior** takes into consideration instances in which there is variation in the extent to which individuals have control over the behavior in the situation. If, for instance, the young woman in the previously given example does not have the young man's phone number or e-mail address and she must wait until he shows up at a local café, regardless of her attitude, her behavioral intention may not correlate strongly with her actual behavior.

As you might have noted, these models focus on the role of behavioral intention as a mediator, yet its measurement is often very similar to that of the behavior itself (Fazio, Powell, and Williams 1989). Such intentions may be shaped by factors other than the attitude and subjective norms, such as moral obligation, self-identity, past behavior or habit, resources and skills necessary to perform the behavior, and the cooperation of others (see Eagly and Chaiken 1993). And sometimes, as automatic processes reviewed in Chapter 5 suggest, attitudes may affect behavior, even in the absence of such conscious deliberation.

Situating the attitude–behavior relationship more squarely in the realm of cognitive processing, one model draws attention to a spontaneous or automatic pathway (Fazio 1986, 1990). This model stresses the activation from memory of a general or global attitude toward a target owing to cues in the situation. A strong link between the attitude object and the person's evaluation of it stimulates the automatic activation. Thus, the model relies on strong attitudes and emphasizes the accessibility of those attitudes. Once activated, the attitude selectively shapes perceptions of the attitude object, just as schema influence processing of situational information. People are likely to perceive characteristics of the attitude object as congruent with their attitude, even if doing so involves distortions. This perception, coupled with social norms in the situation, leads to a definition of the event, which in turn directs behavior. The link between the definition of the event and behavior likewise occurs without conscious processing.

This automatic pathway depends heavily on global attitudes, yet as described earlier, such general attitudes do not always predict behavior (see Ajzen and Cote 2008; Eagly and Chaiken 1993). Undoubtedly, just as with other cognitive processes, some situations tend to stimulate a more deliberate process and others a more automatic process. Deliberate processes like those depicted by reasoned action and planned behavior (but see also Fazio and Towles-Schwen 1999) occur when people are motivated and have the opportunity to engage in thoughtfulness. In the absence of such conditions, accessible, strong attitudes are apt to shape behavior spontaneously.

Summary

California state officials recognized the need to conserve precious water resources during the record drought. Given the presumed link between attitudes and behavior, one means of achieving that goal was to alter the love affair with expansive, green lawns (i.e., positive attitudes). Yet as the preceding section suggests, the relationship between attitudes and behaviors is complex. Attitudes predict behavior *when* they are learned through direct experience, strongly held and univalent, can be behaviorally expressed in the absence of any situational constraints, and are measured at the same level of specificity.

Models predicting *when* attitudes are likely to affect behaviors draw upon conscious deliberation of situational elements or rely upon more automatic processing, assuming accessibility to the attitude and the related behavioral schema. To some extent, the evaluative nature of attitudes, which infuses them with affect, may account for why they appear to have a greater impact on behavior than social cognitions more generally (Eagly and Chaiken 1993).

Segue: Moving From Attitudes to Affect

As part of social cognition, attitudes move beyond mental representations that provide a means to encode information about objects, people, or events in memory. Along with beliefs about a particular phenomenon, attitudes suggest a positive or negative evaluation, leading people to represent their attitudes in terms of feelings. For example, a person may be "in love with" a particular political candidate, indicating a strong, favorable attitude toward that person. Alternatively, individuals may claim to "hate" Muslim immigrants, representing a strong, negative attitude toward a group of people. Such stances go beyond one's knowledge of a candidate's platform or of the tenets of an immigrant's religion or reasons for departures from a home country. They invoke an affective component not necessarily represented in many of our cognitions, representations, or schema about inanimate and animate objects in our worlds.

This chapter has illustrated social psychological approaches to formation and change in attitudes. A common theme is that the strength of attitudes matters, both for how attitudes might be changed and for when attitudes impact on behavior. For example, strong, favorable attitudes toward the importance of individual effort and hard work as a means to success in America may stymie recognition of barriers that prevent some people (e.g., those of lower class, of color) from achieving higher levels of education or economic success. Such attitudes may reinforce the status quo, even one that increases inequality in society. In contrast, attitudes that the system is not providing equal opportunities for Americans, regardless of class, race, or gender, may lead to movements to enact social changes. Discussion in Chapter 12 of prejudice and discrimination revisits aspects of the relationship between attitudes and behaviors as well as its role in promoting inequality between groups. Additionally, examination of prejudice contrasts the impact of explicit attitudes (the topic of this chapter) and implicit attitudes leading to nonconscious biases.

Although a mundane issue compared to social inequality, strong positive attitudes toward lawns may allow flouting of watering restrictions, whereas similar attitudes toward water conservation may encourage challenges to those failing to adhere to water restrictions. When neighbors in Southern California conflict over those water restrictions, as illustrated in the YouTube "shaming" videos, they go beyond playing out the positive or negative evaluations inherent in their attitudes. They stimulate emotional responses to particular situations and particular behaviors. In the next chapter, we investigate how such affective responses derive from and influence social interaction.

Endnote

1. Example inspired by *The Office,* season 5, episode 12.

Suggested Readings

De Leeuw, Astrid, Pierre Valois, Icek Ajzen, and Peter Schmidt. 2015. "Using the Theory of Planned Behavior to Identify Key Beliefs Underlying Pro-Environmental Behavior in High-School Students: Implications for Educational Interventions." *Journal of Environmental Psychology* 42:128–38.

Miklikowska, Marta. 2016. "Like Parent, Like Child? Development of Prejudice and Tolerance towards Immigrants." *British Journal of Psychology* 107:95–116.

Rebellon, Cesar J., Michelle E. Manasse, Karen T. Van Gundy, and Ellen S. Cohn. 2014. "Rationalizing Delinquency: A Longitudinal Test of the Reciprocal Relationship between Delinquent Attitudes and Behavior." *Social Psychology Quarterly* 77:361–86.

Van Kleef, Gerben A., Helma van den Berg, and Marc W. Heerdink. 2015. "The Persuasive Power of Emotions: Effects of Emotional Expressions on Attitude Formation and Change." *Journal of Applied Psychology* 100:1124–42.

References

Ajzen, Icek. 1985. "From Intentions to Actions: A Theory of Planned Behavior." Pp. 11–39 in *Action-Control: From Cognition to Behavior*, edited by J. Kuhl and J. Beckman. Heidelberg, Germany: Springer. doi:10.1007/978-3-642-69746-3_2

Ajzen, Icek. 1991. "The Theory of Planned Behavior." *Organizational Behavior and Human Decision Processes* 50:179–211. doi:10.1016/0749-5978(91)90020-T

Ajzen, Icek. 2012. "Attitudes and Persuasion." Pp. 367–93 in *The Oxford Handbook of Personality and Social Psychology*, edited by K. Deaux and M. Snyder. New York: Oxford University Press.

Ajzen, Icek, and Nicole G. Cote. 2008. "Attitudes and the Prediction of Behavior." Pp. 289–312 in *Attitudes and Attitude Change*, edited by W. D. Crano and R. Prislin. New York: Psychology Press.

Ajzen, Icek, and Martin Fishbein. 1977. "Attitude-Behavior Relations: A Theoretical Analysis and Review of Empirical Research." *Psychological Bulletin* 84:888–918. doi:10.1037/0033-2909.84.5.888

Ajzen, Icek, and Martin Fishbein. 2005. "The Influence of Attitudes on Behavior." Pp. 173–221 in *The Handbook of Attitudes*, edited by D. Albarracín, B. T. Johnson, and M. P. Zanna. Mahwah, NJ: Erlbaum.

Albarracín, Dolores, and Patrick Vargas. 2010. "Attitudes and Persuasion." Pp. 394–427 in *Handbook of Social Psychology*, edited by S. T. Fiske, D. T. Gilbert, and G. Lindzey. Hoboken, NJ: Wiley. doi:10.1002/9780470561119.socpsy001011

Allen, Mike. 1998. "Comparing the Persuasive Effectiveness of One-and-Two-Sided Messages." Pp. 87–98 in *Persuasion: Advances Through Meta-Analysis*, edited by M. Allen and R. W. Preiss. Cresskill, NJ: Hampton Press.

Allport, Gordon W. 1935. "Attitudes." Pp. 798–844 in *Handbook of Social Psychology*, edited by C. Murchison. Worcester, MA: Clark University Press.

Aronson, Elliot. 1968. "Dissonance Theory: Progress and Problems." Pp. 5–27 in *Theories of Cognitive Consistency: A Sourcebook*, edited by R. Abelson, E. Aronson, W. McGuire, T. Newcomb, M. Rosenberg, and P. Tannenbaum. Chicago: Rand McNally.

Aronson, Elliot. 2012. *The Social Animal*. New York: Worth Publishers.

Banaji, Mahzarin R., and Larisa Heiphetz. 2010. "Attitudes." Pp. 353–93 in *Handbook of Social Psychology*, edited by S. T. Fiske, D. T. Gilbert, and G. Lindzey. Hoboken, NJ: Wiley.

Bassili, John N. 1996. "Meta-Judgmental Versus Operative Indexes of Psychological Attributes: The Case of Measures of Attitude Strength." *Journal of Personality and Social Psychology* 71:637–53. doi:10.1037/0022-3514.71.4.637

Bem, Daryl J. 1967. "Self-Perception: An Alternate Interpretation of Cognitive Dissonance Phenomena." *Psychological Review* 74:183–200. doi:10.1037/h0024835

Bem, Daryl J. 1972. "Self-Perception Theory." *Advances in Experimental Social Psychology* 6:1–62.

Berscheid, Ellen. 1966. "Opinion Change and Communicator-Communicatee Similarity and Dissimilarity." *Journal of Personality and Social Psychology* 4:670–80. doi:10.1037/h0021193

Bertolotti, Mauro, and Patrizia Catellani. 2014. "Effects of Message Framing in Policy Communication on Climate Change." *European Journal of Social Psychology* 44:474–86. doi:10.1002/ejsp.2033

Bornstein, Robert F. 1989. "Exposure and Affect: Overview and Meta-Analysis of Research, 1968–1987." *Psychological Bulletin* 106:265–89.

Boster, Franklin J., and Paul Mongeau. 1984. "Fear-Arousing Persuasive Messages." Pp. 330–75 in *Communication Yearbook*, Vol. 8, edited by R. N. Bostrom. Beverly Hills, CA: Sage. doi:10.1080/23808985.1984.11678581

Brehm, Jack W. 1956. "Postdecision Changes in the Desirability of Alternatives." *Journal of Abnormal and Social Psychology* 52:384–89. doi:10.1037/h0041006

Brehm, Jack W. 1966. *A Theory of Psychological Reactance*. San Diego, CA: Academic Press.

Brehm, Sharon S., and Jack W. Brehm. 1981. *Psychological Reactance: A Theory of Freedom and Control*. San Diego, CA: Academic Press.

Cacioppo, John T., Richard E. Petty, Jeffrey A. Feinstein, and W. Blair G. Jarvis. 1996. "Dispositional Differences in Cognitive Motivation: The Life and Times of Individuals Varying in Need for Cognition." *Psychological Bulletin* 119(2):197–253. doi:10.1037/0033-2909.119.2.197

Cerulo, Karen A., and Janet M. Ruane. 2014. "Apologies of the Rich and Famous: Cultural, Cognitive, and Social Explanations of Why We Care and Why We Forgive." *Social Psychology Quarterly* 77:123–49. doi:10.1177/0190272514530412

Chaiken, Shelly. 1979. "Communicator Physical Attractiveness and Persuasion." *Journal of Personality and Social Psychology* 37:1387–97. doi:10.1037/0022-3514.37.8.1387

Chaiken, Shelly. 1986. "Physical Appearance and Social Influence." Pp. 143–77 in *Physical Appearance, Stigma, and Social Behavior: The Ontario Symposium*, Vol. 3, edited by C. P. Herman, M. P. Zanna, and E. T. Higgins. Hillsdale, NJ: Erlbaum.

Chaiken, Shelly. 1987. "The Heuristic Model of Persuasion." Pp. 3–39 in *Social Influence: The Ontario Symposium*, Vol. 5, edited by M. P. Zanna, J. M. Olson, and C. P. Herman. Hillsdale, NJ: Erlbaum.

Chen, Hong Chyi, Richard Reardon, Cornelia Rea, and David J. Moore. 1992. "Forewarning of Content and Involvement: Consequences for Persuasion and Resistance to Persuasion." *Journal of Experimental Social Psychology* 28(6):523–41. doi:10.1016/0022-1031(92)90044-K

Chen, Serena, and Shelly Chaiken. 1999. "The Heuristic-Systematic Model in its Broader Context." Pp. 73–96 in *Dual Process Theories in Social Psychology*, edited by S. Chaiken and Y. Trope. New York: Guilford Press.

Clark, Jason K., Abigail T. Evans, and Duane T. Wegener. 2011. "Perceptions of Source Efficacy and Persuasion: Multiple Mechanisms for Source Effects on Attitudes." *European Journal of Social Psychology* 41:596–607. doi:10.1002/ejsp.787

Collins, Rebecca L, Shelley E. Taylor, Joanne V. Wood, and Suzanne C. Thompson. 1988. "The Vividness Effect: Elusive or Illusory?" *Journal of Experimental Social Psychology* 24:1–18. doi:10.1016/0022-1031(88)90041-8

Conner, Mark, and Christopher J. Armitage. 2008. "Attitudinal Ambivalence." Pp. 261–88 in *Attitudes and Attitude Change*, edited by W. D. Crano and R. Prislin. New York: Psychology Press.

Conner, Mark, and Paul Sparks. 2002. "Ambivalence and Attitudes." *European Review of Social Psychology* 12:37–70. doi:10.1080/14792772143000012

Cooper, Joel. 2007. *Cognitive Dissonance: Fifty Years of Classic Theory*. London, England: Sage.

Cooper, Joel, and Russell H. Fazio. 1984. "A New Look at Dissonance Theory." *Advances in Experimental Social Psychology* 17:229–62.

Crano, William, and Radmila Prislin. 2008. *Attitudes and Attitude Change*. New York: Psychology Press.

Cruz, Michael G. 1998. "Explicit and Implicit Conclusions in Persuasive Messages." Pp. 217–30 in *Persuasion: Advances Through Meta-Analysis*, edited by M. Alien and R. W. Preiss. Cresskill, NJ: Hampton Press.

Eagly, Alice H., Richard D. Ashmore, Mona G. Makhijani, and Laura C. Longo. 1991. "What Is Beautiful Is Good, But...: A Meta-Analytic Review of Research on the Physical Attractiveness Stereotype." *Psychological Bulletin* 110:109–28. doi:10.1037/0033-2909.110.1.109

Eagly, Alice H., and Shelly Chaiken. 1993. *The Psychology of Attitudes*. Fort Worth, TX: Harcourt Brace Jovanovich.

Eagly, Alice H., Wendy Wood, and Shelly Chaiken. 1978. "Casual Inferences About Communicators and Their Effect on Opinion Change." *Journal of Personality and Social Psychology* 36:424–35. doi:10.1037/0022-3514.36.4.424

Fazio, Russell H. 1986. "How Do Attitudes Guide Behavior?" Pp. 204–43 in *Handbook of Motivation and Cognition: Foundations of Social Behavior*, edited by R. M. H. Sorrentino and E. Tory. New York: Guilford Press.

Fazio, Russell H. 1990. "Multiple Processes by which Attitudes Guide Behavior: The MODE Model as an Integrative Framework." *Advances in Experimental Social Psychology* 22:75–109.

Fazio, Russell H., Martha C. Powell, and Carol J. Williams. 1989. "The Role of Attitude Accessibility in the Attitude-to-Behavior Process." *The Journal of Consumer Research* 16:280–88. doi:10.1086/209214

Fazio, Russell H., and David Roskos-Ewoldsen. 1994. "Acting As We Feel: When and How Attitudes Guide Behavior." Pp. 71–93 in *Persuasion*, edited by S. Shavitt and T. C. Brock. Boston: Allyn & Bacon.

Fazio, Russell H., and Tamara Towles-Schwen. 1999. "The MODE Model of Attitude-Behavior Processes." Pp. 97–116 in *Dual-Process Theories in Social Psychology*, edited by S. Chaiken and Y. Trope. New York: Guilford Press.

Fazio, Russell H., and Mark P. Zanna. 1981. "Direct Experience and Attitude-Behavior Consistency." *Advances in Experimental Social Psychology* 14:161–202.

Festinger, Leon. 1957. *A Theory of Cognitive Dissonance*. Stanford, CA: Stanford University Press.

Festinger, Leon, and James M. Carlsmith. 1959. "Cognitive Consequences of Forced Compliance." *Journal of Abnormal and Social Psychology* 58:203–10. doi:10.1037/h0041593

Fishbein, Martin, and Icek Ajzen. 1975. *Belief, Attitude, Intention, and Behavior: An Introduction to Theory and Research*. Reading, MA: Addison-Wesley.

Freedman, Jonathan L., and Scott C. Fraser. 1966. "Compliance Without Pressure: The Foot-in-the-Door Technique." *Journal of Personality and Social Psychology* 4(2):195–202. doi:10.1037/h0023552

Frey, Kurt P., and Alice H. Eagly. 1993. "Vividness Can Undermine the Persuasiveness of Messages." *Journal of Personality and Social Psychology* 65:32–44. doi:10.1037/0022-3514.65.1.32

Glionna, John M. 2015. "Nevada Has Already Learned Lawn Lesson." *Los Angeles Times*, May 10.

Gore, Al. 2006. *An Inconvenient Truth: The Planetary Emergency of Global Warming and What We Can Do about It*. Emmaus, PA: Rodale Press.

Green, Melanie C., and Timothy C. Brock. 2000. "The Role of Transportation in the Persuasiveness of Public Narratives." *Journal of Personality and Social Psychology* 79(5):701–21. doi:10.1037/0022-3514.79.5.701

Greenwald, Anthony G. 1968. "Cognitive Learning, Cognitive Response to Persuasion, and Attitude Change." Pp. 147–70 in *Psychological Foundations of Attitudes*, edited by A. G. Greenwald, T. C. Brock, and T. M. Ostrom. New York: Academic Press. doi:10.1016/B978-1-4832-3071-9.50012-X

Grusec, Joan E., and Paul D. Hastings, eds. 2007. *Handbook of Socialization*. New York: Guilford Press.

Heider, Fritz. 1958. *The Psychology of Interpersonal Relations*. New York: Wiley. doi:10.1037/10628-000

Hoshino-Browne, Etsuko, Adam S. Zanna, Steven J. Spencer, Mark P. Zanna, Shinobu Kitayama, and Sandra Lackenbauer. 2005. "On the Cultural Guises of Cognitive Dissonance: The Case of Easterners and Westerners." *Journal of Personality and Social Psychology* 89:294–310. doi:10.1037/0022-3514.89.3.294

Hovland, Carl I., Irving L. Janis, and Harold H. Kelley. 1953. *Communication and Persuasion*. New Haven, CT: Yale University Press.

Insko, Chester A. 1965. "Verbal Reinforcement of Attitude." *Journal of Personality and Social Psychology* 2:621–23. doi:10.1037/h0022485

Janis, Irving L. 1967. "Effects of Fear Arousal on Attitude Change: Recent Developments in Theory and Experimental Research." *Advances in Experimental Social Psychology* 3:166–224.

Janis, Irving L., Donald Kaye, and Paul Kirschner. 1965. "Facilitating Effects of 'Eating While Reading' On Responsiveness to Persuasive Communications." *Journal of Personality and Social Psychology* 1:181–86. doi:10.1037/h0021644

Judd, Charles M., and Jon A. Krosnick. 1989. "The Structural Bases of Consistency Among Political Attitudes: Effects of Political Expertise and Attitude Importance." Pp. 99–128 in *Attitude Structure and Function*, edited by A. R. Pratkanis, S. J. Breckler, and A. G. Greenwald. Hillsdale, NJ: Erlbaum.

Kim, Min-Sun, and John E. Hunter. 1993. "Relationships among Attitudes, Behavioral Intentions, and Behavior." *Communication Research* 20(3):331–64. doi:10.1177/009365093 020003001

Knowles, Eric S., and Jay A. Linn. 2004. *Resistance and Persuasion*. Mahwah, NJ: Erlbaum.

LaPiere, Richard T. 1934. "Attitudes Versus Actions." *Social Forces* 13:230–37. doi:10.2307/25 70339

Lord, Charles G., Mark R. Lepper, and Diane Mackie. 1984. "Attitude Prototypes as Determinants of Attitude-Behavior Consistency." *Journal of Personality and Social Psychology* 46:1254–66. doi:10.1037/0022-3514.46.6.1254

Maio, Gregory R., and James M. Olson. 2000. "Emergent Themes and Potential Approaches to Attitude Function: The Function-Structure Model of Attitudes." Pp. 417–42 in *Why We Evaluate: Functions of Attitudes*, edited by G. R. Maio and J. M. Olson. Mahwah, NJ: Erlbaum.

McCroskey, James C., and Jason J. Teven. 1999. "Goodwill: A Reexamination of the Construct and Its Measurement." *Communication Monographs* 66:90–103. doi:10.1080/03637759909376464

McGuire, William J. 1964. "Inducing Resistance to Persuasion: Some Contemporary Approaches." *Advances in Experimental Social Psychology* 1:191–229.

McGuire, William J. 1985. "Attitudes and Attitude Change." Pp. 233–346 in *The Handbook of Social Psychology*, 3rd ed., edited by G. Lindzey and E. Aronson. New York: Random House.

Millar, Murray G., and Karen U. Millar. 1996. "The Effects of Direct and Indirect Experience on Affective and Cognitive Responses and the Attitude-Behavior Relation." *Journal of Experimental Social Psychology* 32(6):561–79. doi:10.1006/jesp.1996.0025

Mongeau, Paul A. 1998. "Another Look at Fear-Arousing Persuasive Appeals." Pp. 53–68 in *Persuasion: Advances Through Meta-Analysis*, edited by M. Allen and R. W. Preiss. Cresskill, NJ: Hampton.

Newcomb, Theodore M. 1968. "Interpersonal Balance." Pp. 28–51 in *Theories of Cognitive Consistency: A Sourcebook*, edited by R. P. Abelson, E. Aronson, W. J. McGuire, T. M. Newcomb, M. J. Rosenberg, and P. H. Tannenbaum. Chicago: Rand McNally.

O'Keefe, Daniel J. 1999. "Variability of Persuasive Message Effects: Meta-Analytic

Evidence and Implications." *Document Design* 1: 87–97. doi:10.1075/dd.1.2.02oke

Perloff, Richard M. 2008. *The Dynamics of Persuasion: Communication and Attitudes in the 21st Century.* 4th ed. New York: Erlbaum.

Petty, Richard E., and John T. Cacioppo. 1977. "Forewarning, Cognitive Responding, and Resistance to Persuasion." *Journal of Personality and Social Psychology* 35:645–55. doi:10.1037/0022-3514.35.9.645

Petty, Richard E., and John T. Cacioppo. 1984. "The Effects of Involvement on Responses to Argument Quantity and Quality: Central and Peripheral Routes to Persuasion." *Journal of Personality and Social Psychology* 46:69–81. doi:10.1037/0022-3514.46.1.69

Petty, Richard E., and John T. Cacioppo. 1986. *Communication and Persuasion: Central and Peripheral Routes to Attitude Change.* New York: Springer-Verlag.

Petty, Richard E., and Jon A. Krosnick, eds. 1995. *Attitude Strength: Antecedents and Consequences.* Mahwah, NJ: Erlbaum.

Petty, Richard E., David W. Schumann, Steven A. Richman, and Alan J. Strathman. 1993. "Positive Mood and Persuasion: Different Roles for Affect Under High- and Low-Elaboration Conditions." *The Journal of Social Psychology* 64:5–20.

Petty, Richard E., and Duane T. Wegener. 1999. "The Elaboration Likelihood Model: Current Status and Controversies." Pp. 37–72 in *Dual-Process Theories in Social Psychology*, edited by S. Chaiken and Y. Trope. New York: Guilford Press.

Petty, Richard E., Christian S. Wheeler, and Zakary L. Tormala. 2003. "Persuasion and Attitude Change." Pp. 353–82 in *Handbook of Psychology*, Vol. 5, edited by T. Milton and M. J. Lerner. Hoboken, NJ: Wiley.

Pierro, Antonio, Lucia Mannetti, Arie W. Kruglanski, Kristen Klein, and Edward Orehek. 2012. "Persistence of Attitude Change and Attitude-Behavior Correspondence Based on

Extensive Processing of Source Information." *European Journal of Social Psychology* 42:103–11. doi:10.1002/ejsp.853

Reynolds, Rodney A., and J. Lynn Reynolds. 2002. "Evidence." Pp. 427–44 in *The Persuasion Handbook: Developments in Theory and Practice*, edited by J. P. Dillard and M. Pfau. Thousand Oaks, CA: Sage. doi:10.4135/9781412976046.n22

Rogers, Ronald W. 1983. "Cognitive and Physiological Processes in Fear Appeals and Attitude Change: A Revised Theory of Protection Motivation." Pp. 153–76 in *Social Psychophysiology: A Sourcebook*, edited by J. T. Cacioppo and R. E. Petty. New York: Guilford Press.

Schlenker, Barry R. 1982. "Translating Actions into Attitudes: An Identity-Analytic Approach to the Explanation of Social Conduct." *Advances in Experimental Social Psychology* 15:194–248.

Shaffer, David R. 2005. *Social and Personality Development*. 5th ed. Belmont, CA: Wadsworth.

Sherif, Muzafer, and Carl I. Hovland. 1961. *Social Judgment: Assimilation and Contrast Effects in Communication and Attitude Change*. New Haven, CT: Yale University Press.

Skinner, Burrhus F. 1953. *Science and Human Behavior*. New York: Macmillan.

Snyder, Mark. 1987. *Public Appearances/Private Realities: The Psychology of Self-Monitoring*. New York: Freeman.

Snyder, Mark, and Deborah Kendzierski. 1982. "Acting on One's Attitudes: Procedures for Linking Attitudes and Behavior." *Journal of Experimental Social Psychology* 18:165–83. doi:10.1016/0022-1031(82)90048-8

Staats, Arthur W., and Carolyn K. Staats. 1958. "Attitudes Established by Classical Conditioning." *Journal of Abnormal and Social Psychology* 11:187–92.

Steele, Claude M. 1988. "The Psychology of Self-Affirmation: Sustaining the Integrity of the Self." *Advances in Experimental Social Psychology* 21:261–302.

Steinberg, Ted. 2006. *American Green: The Obsessive Quest for the Perfect Lawn*. New York: W. W. Norton.

Sutton, Stephen. 1998. "Predicting and Explaining Intentions and Behavior: How Well Are We Doing?" *Journal of Applied Social Psychology* 28 (15):1317–38. doi:10.1111/j.1559-1816.1998.tb01679.x

Taylor, Shelley E., and Suzanne C. Thompson. 1982. "Stalking the Elusive 'Vividness' Effect." *Psychological Review* 89:155–81. doi:10.1037/0033-295X.89.2.155

Tesser, Abraham. 1978. "Self-Generated Attitude Change." *Advances in Experimental Social Psychology* 11:289–338.

Thibodeau, Ruth, and Elliot Aronson. 1992. "Taking a Closer Look: Reasserting the Role of the Self-Concept in Dissonance Theory." *Personality and Social Psychology Bulletin* 18(5):591–602. doi:10.1177/0146167292185010

Todorov, Alexander, Shelly Chaiken, and Marlone D. Henderson. 2002. "The Heuristic-Systematic Model of Social Information Processing." Pp. 195–212 in *The Persuasion Handbook: Developments in Theory and Practice*, edited by J. P. Dillard and M. Pfau. Thousand Oaks, CA: Sage. doi:10.4135/9781412976046.n11

Tormala, Zakary L. 2008. "A New Framework for Resistance to Persuasion: The Resistance Appraisals Hypothesis." Pp. 213–36 in *Attitudes and Attitude Change*, edited by W. D. Crano and R. Prislin. New York: Psychology Press.

Walther, Eva, and Tina Langer. 2008. "Attitude Formation and Change through Association: An Evaluative Conditioning Account." Pp. 87–110 in *Attitudes and Attitude Change*, edited by W. D. Crano and R. Prislin. New York: Psychology Press.

Wegener, Duane T., Richard E. Petty, Natalie D. Smoak, and Leandre R. Fabrigar. 2004.

"Multiple Routes to Resisting Attitude Change." Pp. 13–38 in *Resistance and Persuasion*, edited by E. S. Knowles and J. A. Linn. Hillsdale, NJ: Erlbaum.

Weinstein, Neil D. 1980. "Unrealistic Optimism about Future Life Events." *Journal of Personality and Social Psychology* 39(5):806–20. doi:10.1037/0022–3514.39.5.806

Wicker, Allan W. 1969. "Attitudes Versus Actions: The Relationship of Verbal and Overt Behavioral Responses to Attitude Objects." *The Journal of Social Issues* 25:41–78. doi:10.1111/j.1540–4560.1969.tb00619.x

Wood, Wendy, and Brian Stagner. 1994. "Why Are Some People Easier to Influence Than Others?" Pp. 149–74 in *Persuasion: Psychological Insights and Perspectives*, edited by S. Shavitt and T. C. Brock. Boston: Allyn & Bacon.

Zajonc, Robert B. 1968. "Attitudinal Effects of Mere Exposure." *Journal of Personality and Social Psychology Monograph Supplement* 9(2):1–27. doi:10.1037/h0025848

7

Beyond Cognition
Affect and Emotions

July 6, 2005. Glued to their information sources, Londoners nervously awaited the announcement from the International Olympic Committee in Singapore. Who would host the 2012 Olympics? At lunchtime, the surprising news arrived: London had edged ahead of Paris, the favored city, to win the bid! Then prime minister Tony Blair is said to have "punched the air and danced a 'jig' when he heard the result."[1] In less jubilant terms but wholly in keeping with traditional British demeanor, he eventually commented, "Well done," which was followed by explosions of confetti.[2] Others gathered in central London at Trafalgar Square shared with reporters how their hearts pounded as the announcement was made. To say that the crowd in the square as well as those glued to their news sources was jubilant and excited is nearly an understatement. The city simply erupted with joy and pride—until the very next day.

July 7, 2005, 9:00–10:00 a.m. The hurried rush of commuting came to a virtual standstill. The news reported that a "power surge" had stopped several of London's underground trains. What really had happened underground became known above ground at 9:47 a.m.: a bus exploded in Tavistock Square, near two of the major closed underground stations (Euston and King's Cross). It was the fourth bomb explosion of the morning, the others occurring about an hour earlier on different underground routes. Just like the day before, Londoners tuned into their news sources. This time, however, there was no excitement—simply horror and outrage. People cried in each other's arms. Fifty-two people (plus the four bombers) died, and 700 were injured. Londoners responded to the dire consequences of this terrorist attack, or "unprovoked act of evil," with calm and courage, which harkened back to their resolve in the face of Nazi bombings during World War II.[3] People cleared the streets, returning to their homes or those of friends; businesses shuttered for the day; city streets were eerily silent, except for the periodic sound of the sirens of racing emergency vehicles. By the next morning, ways to honor the victims were emerging: flowers at King's Cross and near the cordoned-off Tavistock Square, books of condolences at foreign embassies, candlelight vigils; moments of silence, and flags at half-staff. Other nations expressed shock, sympathy, sorrow, and solidarity with the British people, who showed great tenacity in denying the terrorists' success.[4] Then London mayor Ken Livingstone, though visibly shaken during his speech that day, called the act "cowardly" and vehemently stated, "You will fail" to divide Londoners, weaken their freedom, and destroy their harmony with one another.[5]

A commentator for the London paper, *The Guardian*, wrote on July 8, "Has any city ever before experienced such a radical mood swing?" and noted, "It made for a dizzying 24 hours; a plunge from high to low that has shaken the city's nervous system."[6] The experiences of Londoners on those two fateful days in July 2005 capture a wide array of emotions. Joy, pride, anger, fear, horror, and sorrow are emotions experienced in response to some stimulus event or social context. Describing Londoners' courage or other nations' solidarity also implies affective states—but ones that may be more enduring and only weakly tied to a particular situational stimulus. The affective or emotional side of social life is often contrasted with the ostensibly more "rational" information processing that characterizes social cognition. Yet, as discussed in Chapter 5, social cognition is influenced by motivations, information availability, and even affective states. And as we will look at in this chapter, affect and emotion do not simply refer to the irrational dictates of the heart but are also shaped by cognitions and beliefs. Like cognitions and attitudes, feelings clearly play a role in the dynamics of behavior and interaction.

Indeed, emotions serve several functions. The first is that emotions *motivate us into action*. As classical sociologist Karl Marx suggested, alienation, the separation of the lower classes from the products of their labor owing to capitalistic economic arrangements, may stimulate class rebellion. Emile Durkheim likewise drew attention to emotional reactions to religious movements as a means of enhancing group solidarity. Think of your own experience when you opened the e-mail (or letter) announcing your admission into the school of choice; your joy may have led you to immediately contact your parents and friends. In contrast, road rage or anger owing to driving infringements may lead to conflict escalation and violent responses. Thus, emotions stemming from structural arrangements or simply daily activities may fuel actions.

Second, *emotions provide clues to help us to understand our world*, including providing a basis for inferring one's own and others' attitudes. For example, at the 2010 Winter Olympics women's hockey award ceremony, the women from Finland seemed jubilant, even though they did not win the gold; unexpectedly winning the bronze was sufficient for their elation. In contrast, the U.S. women appeared sad—despondent even—with their second-place finish because they had expected to beat the Canadian team that placed first. The emotions of these athletes tell us something about the backstories to the competition. And our observation of these emotional expressions indicates something about the athletes' attitudes toward winning and losing. Related to understanding our social world, *emotions aid us in being members of social groups*. The nature of a person's expressed emotions signals to others how they should respond to that person. For example, observing a crying child may lead others to provide comfort. Or consider whom you might approach at a fraternity party—the person wearing a happy expression or someone with a dour expression? In effect, emotions provide the glue that binds individuals together. Feeling or expressing the same emotion as people around us highlights ties to others. For example, Londoners' collective responses to the Olympics bid and to the bombings offered a basis for emphasizing a shared identity.

Finally, *emotions function as a means of self-control, which may facilitate social control* (Goffman 1956, 1959). For example, imagine waiting in a long line at a store to buy a candy bar; you realize that business is so brisk that you could just walk out with it, but you do not. Why not? If you generally uphold the law, you might feel ashamed were you to shoplift. That emotion limits your behavior and may constrain the behavior of others as well, ensuring social control.

Related to these functions is this central question: How do affective feelings arise and impact social behavior? Premises of the theories we will examine draw from perspectives in social cognition and symbolic interaction. We first distinguish among the affective states called emotions, moods, and sentiments. Then we examine physiological, social, and cultural factors that shape emotional feelings, followed by forces that influence the expression of felt emotions. We end by looking at how emotions drive interaction generally and how emotional experiences and expressions contribute to the existence and maintenance of social solidarity and inequality.

What Distinguishes Emotions From Other Affective States?

You ace an exam. Your parents have just informed you that you cannot attend the "party of the year." One day, you find yourself humming pleasantly and smiling at everyone on your way to school. After dating the same person for 2 years, you say, "I love you." Each of these events elicits some feeling: joy, anger, a good mood, a sentiment. All of these feelings convey something about your affective state. Generally, **affect** refers to a deep, evaluative orientation—positive or negative—toward an object, person, action, or situation. As a generic term, it encompasses a range of emotions, moods, and sentiments (Smith-Lovin 1995).

Distinguishing Emotions, Moods, and Sentiments

Our focus in this chapter is on emotions. While there are many definitions of **emotions**, most suggest four components (Thoits 1989). First, emotions involve some sort of *appraisal or evaluation* of an object, a person, an event, a situation, or the like. For example, Londoners appraised "winning the 2012 Olympics." Second, emotions are accompanied by changes in *physiological or bodily sensations*. Recall that individuals in Trafalgar Square mentioned that their hearts "pounded." Third, *expressive gestures* go with felt emotions. Such gestures may be quite overt—for example, "dancing a jig" in response to felt happiness—or they may be subtler, such as when the corners of the lips turn up in joy and down in sadness. The attachment of a *cultural label* to combinations of the first three components of an emotion constitutes the fourth element. Not all four components need to be present for an emotion to be felt. For example, children clearly experience emotions, but they may not be able to articulate the source of the emotion or even provide an appropriate label. Together these components support the widely held assumption that emotions result from the complex interplay of neurological, cognitive, social structural, and cultural forces (Turner and Stets 2005). This chapter details how theoretical approaches to emotion differentially emphasize one or more of the components.

In contrast to how emotions result from particular situational events, **moods** are affective states, internal to a person, without a clear source and thus more impactful across situations (Smith-Lovin 1995). Moods are distinct from emotions in terms of *intensity* (how deeply felt) and *duration* (how long the feeling lasts); they are of lower intensity and yet of longer duration than emotions (Doan 2012). The person humming and smiling may appear to be in a good mood. Alternatively, you may have experienced what is implied by "waking up on the wrong side of the bed," which leads to a bad mood or a dismal outlook for the day's activities. Despite difficulty in determining the source of a mood in natural situations, social psychologists have manipulated moods to study their effects on cognition and social behavior (Fiske and Taylor 2013).

The broadest category of affect involves **sentiments**, which capture enduring evaluations typically pertaining to social relationships or identities. Socially constructed feelings of liking, loving, or hating that transcend the situational context constitute sentiments (Gordon 1981). Attraction processes fueled by the sentiment of liking may lead to loving, which involves a more intense feeling and deep attachment to and caring for another person (Rubin 1973). In contrast, hating may stimulate prejudice (see Chapter 12). We invoke sentiments when "we like dark chocolate" or "cannot stand anchovies." Sentiments shape social dynamics as they direct whom individuals are likely to approach and whom they might avoid. For example, if you are fan of a particular basketball team (i.e., possessing a positive sentiment toward this team), you are more likely to strike up a conversation with other fans of this team than fans of their archrival.

Next, we examine the emergence and consequences of emotions. To understand such processes requires consideration of their dimensions and types as well.

Dimensions of Emotion

Given the range of human emotions, one way to categorize them is by various dimensions (see Thamm 2007). The most prominent dimension is the **valence of the emotion**: positive–negative or pleasant–unpleasant, representing different ends of a continuum. When Londoners felt happy, pleased, or content about winning the Olympics bid, Parisians who lost the bid were feeling unhappy, sad, or blue. A given stimulus rarely evokes emotions at both ends of the evaluation continuum. Positive and negative emotions differ in terms of how they operate (Cacioppo and Gardner 1999) and their complexity (Ellsworth and Smith 1988a, 1988b).

Culture also plays a role in the extent to which people experience positive emotions. Westerners generally report having more positive than negative emotions, whereas Japanese people feel positive and negative emotions equally (Mesquita and Karasawa 2002). And, among European Americans, positive emotions help assuage feelings of depression, whereas that pattern does not emerge for Asian immigrants to the United States (Leu, Wang, and Koo 2011). In social situations, negative emotions may garner more attention than positive ones (similar to how noncommon behaviors or negative outcomes tell more about a person's disposition, as noted in Chapter 5) and may be shaped by a greater number of factors. For example, the meanings of negative emotions such as sadness, anger, disgust, anxiety, and shame depend more on whether the emotion is directed at self or other; experienced by an occupant of a powerful or weak position; and so forth than do positive emotions such as satisfaction, contentment, pride, and joy.

A second common dimension refers to the **degree of arousal** that accompanies the emotion (Russell 2003). Arousal connotes the level of engagement, animation, or liveliness suggested by an emotion. For example, feelings of surprise indicate greater arousal than do feelings of serenity. In addition to evaluation and liveliness, a third dimension is **potency**, which suggests the degree to which a given emotion indicates powerfulness in stimulating action or directing attention. In the list of negative emotions just listed, anger would be considered a more powerful emotion than sadness or anxiety.

These dimensions provide a basis for sorting an array of emotions and reflect dimensions of meaning (as represented in the semantic differential measurement tool) (Osgood, Suci, and Tannenbaum 1957), which underlie one of the theories of emotional experiences discussed later. Although cultural differences in emotional experiences may reflect variation in the dimensions (Mesquita, Frijda, and Scherer 1997), unique biophysical bases for particular emotions suggest the potential universality of some emotions, across all cultures and countries. Such emotions are often characterized as "primary."

Primary and Other Emotions

People, regardless of culture or position in a society, experience many types of emotions. Stimulated by the 19th century work of Charles Darwin (1872), **primary emotions** are presumed to be hardwired or innate, anchored in human biology (specifically neuroanatomy) as a consequence of evolution. Such emotions have enhanced fitness and survival (Izard 1977; Plutchik 1980; Turner 2014). For example, fear gives way to flight from enemies, and anger propels people to destroy obstacles blocking survival. Because of evolution, primary emotions tend to be experienced among all humans and thus considered cross-culturally universal. They are also distinguished from other types of emotions that stem from a combination of primary emotions or social definitions of the situation, which are largely learned within a cultural context (Kemper 1987; Matsumoto and Hwang 2012; Turner 1999).

Lists of primary emotions (see Turner 2000) always include fear and anger as well as some form of happiness (joy, pleasure, satisfaction) and sadness (sorrow, depression). Sometimes surprise and disgust are also identified as primary. These emotions are grounded in physiology, early to emerge in individual human development, cross-culturally universal, and impactful in social relations (Kemper 1987). Claims for universality emerge from a variety of studies. Some focus on facial expressions (see Ekman and Rosenberg 1997) in which people are asked to act out facial expressions in response to scenarios, photographs, or videos describing situations meant to evoke emotions like surprise, sadness, or anger. If you are asked to indicate sadness in response to a loss (of a parent, child, close friend), it is highly likely that the corners of your lips will turn down, and your brows may lower. You would not be alone in this facial expression—people of different cultures likewise exhibit the same lip and brow movements.

Beyond facial expression, universality stems from observations that primary emotions are present in other primates, involve distinctive physiological sources, are provoked by events universally experienced (e.g., loss of a loved one; receipt of something unexpected), produce coherent autonomic and expressive responses, and emerge quickly and automatically rather than through deliberate appraisal of an event (Ekman 1992). For example, if you—or someone from Kenya, Ecuador, or Korea—were very hungry and a person offered you a banana, you would feel happy in response to that offering. (A hungry great ape would also feel the same!) Likewise, if a tiger starts to charge and threatens harm, people, regardless of nationality, are likely to feel fear.

Of course, beyond these primary emotions, we experience many more feelings: annoyance, bitterness, calm, dread, envy, fury, guilt, hope, ire, jealousy, pride, resignation, scorn, thrill, worry, et cetera, et cetera. Some of these are variants of the primary emotions, felt with less intensity (e.g., annoyance for anger) or greater intensity (e.g., thrill for happiness) (Turner 2014). Others may reflect a combination of primary emotions under different socially defined situations (Kemper 1987). For example, feelings of shame emerge when an individual gets angry at himself or herself for a particular behavior. What makes a person feel shame, however, depends upon the meaning and potential negative repercussions of the behavior in a particular cultural or social group. For example, Karen once absentmindedly booked a return flight for a day after the first day of class; she figuratively kicked herself for making the error, briefly apologized to her department chair for the oversight, and arranged for a teaching assistant to cover the first class. She was embarrassed by the error but felt no shame. In contrast, when a similar thing happened to a Japanese colleague, his shame was intense; to ward off negative repercussions, he wrote a detailed letter of apology to his university. Karen's behavior in the context of an American university hardly merited angst; in contrast, in the context of a Japanese university, the same behavior elicited feeling of shame for letting down the school's authorities.

Nonprimary emotions may stem from the pairing of two, three, or more primary emotions, and they may reflect different "ratios" of the pairings (Kemper 1987; Turner 2000). For example, a greater proportion of fear, combined with happiness, may produce awe, whereas more happiness than fear may give rise to wonder. Or a combination of sadness, anger, and fear may produce guilt when sadness (owing to self disappointment for failing to meet expectations) dominates; in contrast, shame may emerge if anger at oneself dominates.

Even though, like primary emotions, other emotions involve patterns of chemical and neural responses (Damasio 2003), situational conditions eliciting the emotions and expressions of the emotions are more cross-culturally variable. Thus, many nonprimary emotions are characterized as socially constructed (as discussed in Chapter 3). With such social construction, a fundamental issue arises: how do cognitions fit into what begins as a result of biological neuroanatomical processes? As noted in Chapter 5, brain processes clearly affect cognition; likewise, they impact emotion. Cognition and emotion constitute separate, but interacting mental functions, involving separate but interacting brain systems (LeDoux 1996). Understanding the neurology of emotions may augment theorizing about social dynamics (Turner 2000). Next, we examine how these two components underlie explanations for how we feel what we feel.

Why Do People Feel What They Feel?

A crying baby cannot articulate why he is feeling a particular way, so parents rush in to diaper, feed, and comfort the child. A crying teenager is another matter: Is she depressed about being excluded from a particular group? Is she ecstatic to have made the varsity team? Or have her parents embarrassed her beyond belief? Crying is a biophysical signal that accompanies the experience of a variety of emotions. Yet what emotion an individual feels depends upon what he or she discerns from the situation, or in other words, cognitions about the situation (including cultural notions) and about himself or herself. Biological neuroanatomy, cognitive processes, and cultural rules combine to create variation in the experience of emotions. Theoretical arguments regarding why people feel what they feel draw, in different measures, from these diverse sources. Below, we first examine the neuroanatomical basis and briefly discuss the role of culture before turning to theoretical approaches.

The Neuroanatomical Basis of Emotional Experiences

Recent advances in neuroscience (noted in Chapter 5) provide the basis for a somewhat informed picture of the biological systems involved in producing emotion. When a situational object, person, or event stimulates an emotion, individuals may not be initially aware that they are emitting an emotion (Franks 2007; Turner 2000). Such unawareness stems from the unconscious activation of a part of the brain called the subcortex (see Figure 7.1), which is sometimes called the "ancient emotion center" owing to its existence in mammals before the development of the neocortex (of which the prefrontal lobe, noted in Chapter 5 as responsible social cognitions, is a part). The subcortex consists of structures that store emotional memories (the hippocampus), pick up on sensory inputs and mediate emotional activation (thalamus and hypothalamus), activate fear and anger (the amygdala), and integrate emotional responses (also the amygdala). To the extent, however, that other people observe the emotion and respond to it, individuals grow conscious of their emotions (LeDoux 1996). In effect, activation of the subcortical brain regions stimulates neuropathways to the prefrontal lobe of the neocortex region, which enables humans to use language and develop culture that allows for labeling of the sensation, turning it into a conscious feeling.

To experience an emotion involves activation of four body systems (LeDoux 1996; Turner 2000). First, the feedback system of the **autonomic nervous**

FIGURE 7.1 ● Basic Brain Structures Involved in Emotion

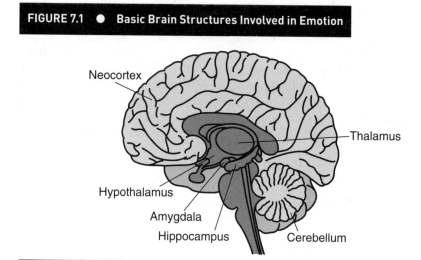

Neocortex

Thalamus

Hypothalamus

Amygdala

Hippocampus

Cerebellum

Source: Kuther, T. L. (2017). *Lifespan Development: Lives in Context.* Thousand Oaks, CA: SAGE.

system, engaging both the subcortex and neocortex, interacts with three other systems to stimulate emotional experiences. Second, the system of **neurotransmitters,** released by the brain (e.g., acetylcholine, dopamine, adrenaline, noradrenaline, serotonin), and **neuroactive peptides,** produced by the endocrine system (governed by parts of the brain such as the hypothalamus and pituitary), create combinations of transmitters and peptides that are associated with the experience of different emotions (Funkenstein 1955). For example, acetylcholine has been associated with satisfaction and depression, adrenaline with fear, and anger with noradrenaline (see Kemper 1987). Third, the **endocrine system** regulates the flow of hormones through the body. And, fourth, the **musculoskeletal system**, controls body movement involving striated muscles, especially those responsible for facial gestures, which communicate to others a person's emotions.

These four systems work in concert to stimulate an emotion, based on situational circumstances. The emotion may remain unconscious until the neocortex cues a cultural label. For example, imagine going up to your door, finding it unexpectedly unlocked, and walking into your darkened apartment; when you flip the light switch, nothing happens. Your heart pounds (a consequence of the autonomic nervous system, fueled by adrenaline) as you back away from the entrance (a musculoskeletal response). Before you become consciously aware of what danger may lurk in your apartment, you have experienced bodily sensations associated with fear. Should your friends switch on a light and yell "surprise!" you may transform your conscious feeling of fear to one of surprise (a cultural label), assuming that other underlying bodily systems that cue both emotions are similar. In effect, the cultural label applied to the sensation shifts the emotion, though the underlying body systems may remain the same (see Turner and Stets 2005).

Although the process of creating emotional experiences involves multiple body systems, particular regions of the brain may contribute to the experience of certain emotions. As noted previously, the amygdala is deemed the center for fear and anger (Phelps 2006). It also helps route emotional arousal to the prefrontal cortex (Franks 2014). Positive emotions like happiness may stem from the anterior cingulated cortex, whereas sadness and related emotions are related to the posterior cingulated cortex, along with neurotransmitters and hormones (Turner and Stets 2005).

Importantly, recent neuroscience reveals that the experience of emotion is more complex than simply finding a brain center that controls feelings. Regions of the brain that are involved in bodily sensations and patterns of arousal (the subcortex) and ones that control language, culture, and cognitions (the neocortex) are both relevant to understanding emotional experiences and, possibly, emotional expressions. The next section briefly examines the impact of culture, which shapes cognitions, on emotions in social situations.

Culture and the Experience of Emotions

Beyond the intertwined neuroanatomical systems that produce our feelings, we label what we experience. As noted previously, the valence of an emotional experience is generally positive or negative. The experience may also vary in terms of its **intensity** (ranging from mild to intense) and **duration** (relatively fleeting to lasting). These dimensions of feelings may be shaped by the context in which they emerge. Cultural contexts play a role in defining how people experience a particular emotion. An emotion culture consists of beliefs about what people are supposed to feel, given the nature of their social group and the situation in which a particular emotion arises (Gordon 1981, 1990; also see further regarding emotional expression).

In the course of socialization, people learn the **feeling rules**, which represent cultural standards pertaining to what people ought to feel in a given situation (Hochschild 1979, 1983). These rules dictate the valence of an emotion as well as its intensity and duration. For example, finding a penny might make you mildly happy, but that happiness may not last very long. In contrast, getting into a favored college or graduate program might produce intense happiness (especially if the acceptance was not expected) and last a relatively long time. With the passage of time since the stimulus event, the intensity of any emotion is likely to wane. For example, the death of a loved one may produce intense grief for weeks or months, but eventually the intensity decreases as other experiences and emotions create distance from the pain of the loss. A group's emotional culture also defines how various group members should experience an emotion; it may be more acceptable for some people to feel a particular emotion evoked by a situation more intensely and with longer duration than other group members. For example, grief should be most intense and long-lasting among the close family members and social intimates of the deceased but weaker and of shorter duration for coworkers, neighbors, and acquaintances (Lofland 1985).

By learning the feeling rules of their cultural group, individuals are propelled (consciously or unconsciously) toward emotion labels that they believe fit their bodily sensations. Generally, people's interpretations and labeling of the sensations are influenced by cultural values and beliefs (Matsumoto and Hwang 2012). Plus, emotion words are inextricably tied to language (Russell 1991), and language is a shaper of the reality of a particular emotional experience (Illouz, Gilon, and Shachak 2014). Although most cultures have a word for emotion and have terms that represent distinct emotions, cultures vary in how they make fine-grained distinctions among emotions, resulting in specific meanings (see Matsumoto and Hwang 2012). Thus, it is possible that the same physiological arousal and situational conditions may evoke different labels and experiences of varying levels of intensity and duration by people of distinct cultural groups. For example, the experience of emotions associated with the self varies depending upon the nature of the culture. In collectivistic cultures (e.g., Japan, China) characterized by an interdependent sense of self, people report experiencing more strongly socially engaging emotions like respect and sympathy compared to individuals from individualistic countries (e.g., United States, Canada), for whom reports of emotional experiences regarding an independent sense of self relied more strongly on socially disengaging emotions like pride or frustration (Kitayama, Mesquita, and Karasawa 2006).

Thus, the subjective experience of an emotion stems from neuroanatomical processes as well as cultural ones, which help to shape the cognitions individuals have about the experience. Theoretical perspectives focused on how people feel take into consideration both sets of processes, but greater emphasis seems to rest on cognitive factors.

Cognitive and Social Elements
Underlying Emotional Experiences

As Karen watched the 41 sixth graders in her daughter's class walk down the center aisle at the conclusion of their graduation ceremony, she noticed many tear-stained faces—largely worn by the girls but also by a few boys. Each had stood in front of the crowd of 300 plus and given a 1-minute speech. One student's free-verse speech summed it up: "This is it!" The students were "leaving" their "home" of 7, 8, or even 9 years (for those who started as 3-year-old preprimary students). They were scattering to different middle schools. They were clearly aroused by the situation. This was it. But were they sad to be leaving or excited by the prospect of summer break and the newness of their next educational adventure? The theories discussed next highlight how cognitions about different aspects of social situations stimulate emotions and the labels people give to what they are feeling.

The Two-Factor Approach

Imagine that you are on a first date with someone who has long caught your attention. After a wonderful evening of conversation, dinner, and a movie, your date and you reach the end of the evening where it is time to say good night. In keeping with a Hollywood-style script, a perfectly romantic scene unfolds in which you experience your first kiss with this person.

Think about your physiological response to the first kiss and the moments surrounding it. Is your heart aflutter? Do you have butterflies in your stomach? Perhaps your hands are a bit sweaty.

Now, imagine later that night, being asleep (alone) in your home when something wakes you suddenly in the middle of the night. You sit up in bed and hear the sound of shattering glass, and you realize someone is breaking into your home. What is your physiological response to this situation? Your heart may be racing, you may have a sinking feeling in the pit of your stomach, and you may feel sweat beading on your brow. In other words, your physiological sensation may be akin to how you felt on the verge of a first kiss. Both situations evoke physiological arousal, but the conditions surrounding the arousal are quite distinct. The first kiss may elicit a feeling of bliss, and the break-in may stimulate fear. The combination of physiological arousal and situational cues is central to an early theory addressing emotional experiences.

In a now classic experiment, Schachter and Singer (1962) combined two factors: (1) **physiological arousal** and (2) **cues in the social situation** to allow interpretation of the arousal. Building on the work emerging in social cognition at the time, they argued that just like inferring attitudes from behavior, people look to situational cues to surmise what their experience of a physiological sensation may mean. When individuals are emotionally aroused yet unsure of what they are feeling, they turn to a wide variety of situational cues, including the behavior of other people in the situation in order to interpret what they are feeling. The Schachter and Singer model combines elements of self-attribution and social comparisons.

To test their ideas about inferring one's emotions, they experimentally manipulated physiological arousal and the emotional displays of another person in the situation. Study participants were in one of four arousal conditions: injected with (1) a placebo causing no physiological effects ("no arousal"); (2) epinephrine (adrenaline), which increases heart rate, face flushing, and possibly trembling, and given an explanation of these physiological effects ("informed"); (3) epinephrine and given no explanation of the physiological effects ("ignorant"); or (4) epinephrine and misinformed about the effects by being told that the injection would cause headaches or numbness ("misinformed"). Schachter and Singer expected that participants who had no explanation for their physiological arousal or were misinformed about it (Conditions 3 and 4) were more likely to search the situation for cues about what they should be feeling. Those who had no arousal (Condition 1) or were correctly informed (Condition 2) had no reason to look to others to determine the emotional experience.

The experimental task involved completing a questionnaire that included many intimate and inappropriate items. Study participants were paired with another student who ostensibly also had an injection but who in reality was a "confederate" of the experimenter, instructed to act in a particular way. The confederate's actions provided the means to manipulate the emotional displays of others as a basis for social comparison and self-attribution about one's own emotional state. The confederate acted either in a euphoric way (all arousal conditions), using questionnaire pages to make paper airplanes; crumpling papers and shooting baskets; and twirling a hula hoop; or in an angry way (arousal Conditions 1–3), ripping the questionnaire in a fit of rage. After exposure to the confederate's behavior, study participants answered questions about how they felt. Results clearly demonstrated that participants ignorant of the source of their arousal felt greater anger than people in other conditions. For those in the euphoria condition, participants who were misinformed felt happier than those who were ignorant. Yet both groups were on average happier than participants who were not aroused or who were correctly informed about the arousal. Thus, the results largely confirm Schachter and Singer's predictions.

A major concern about the study (see Cotton 1981; Reisenzein 1983) regards the issue of arousal. Schachter and Singer's presumption that the same arousal (called undifferentiated) can account for emotions as widely distinct as euphoria and anger has been challenged. As the previous discussion of the neuroanatomical basis of emotions would suggest, the original assumption of undifferentiated arousal was inaccurate. As we know now, arousal is typically "differentiated," owing to different neurotransmitters and other biophysical functions. Relatively unchallenged is Schachter and Singer's claim that social situations shape the experience of emotion. The following approaches to emotional experience take this claim as a starting point and then focus on distinct elements of social situations that stimulate feelings.

A Structural Approach

Some of you may be familiar with the hospital sitcom *Scrubs*, which appeared on TV for 9 years (2001–2010). The show told the tale of the maturing of a set of residents (John Dorian [J.D.], Christopher Turk, and Elliot Reid) under the tutelage of an attending physician (Dr. Perry Cox), the chief of medicine (Dr. Bob Kelso), and the head nurse (Carla). These staff members were located on different rungs of the hierarchy at the fictive Sacred Heart Hospital, where an array of types of interactions unfolded, accompanied by emotional responses to those dynamics. Many episodes found Dr. Cox belittling (by calling Dr. Dorian "Nancy," "Susie," or "Mary") or berating the residents (especially those in surgery—"the cutters") for their failure to diagnose or properly care for the patients. Such treatment by Dr. Cox left the residents feeling disappointed and maybe a little depressed. Occasionally, however, J.D. or one of his peers would do something right, and Dr. Cox would (begrudgingly) offer (tempered) praise, resulting in producing happiness (and perhaps a little surprise) in the resident. While actors are playing roles and following a script, the emotions they depict in response to incidents in the hierarchically structured environs of a hospital correspond to what would be expected based on Kemper's (1978, 1990, 2007, 2014) structural approach to emotions.

Kemper argues that feelings arise from power and status outcomes in interaction. As fundamental aspects of group structure (see Chapters 8 and 9), power and status differences between individuals, and gains and losses of each in the course of interaction affect how people feel in a situation. Kemper defines **power** as the ability to realize one's own will by overcoming resistance by others and gaining their compliance. Basically, power allows a person to tell others what to do and to employ (sometimes coercive) tactics to ensure that they do it. Over time within a group or within an organized hierarchy, power differences (e.g., between authorities and subordinates) stabilize. In effect, people occupy positions of relative power. For example, J.D. was Dr. Cox's subordinate; nurses, orderlies, and janitors were subordinate to all doctors.

While power may involve an element of coercion, status does not. **Status**, according to Kemper, emerges when individuals defer to others voluntarily.[7] Such acts of deference bestow regard, admiration, and the like upon another person, resulting in high status. In *Scrubs*, the nurse Carla had high status; she was knowledgeable and experienced and thus able to show residents what to do and minimize the errors from ineptness. Consequently, the residents often deferred to her even though she was "just a nurse" and not powerful. Even Dr. Cox held Carla in high regard.

The structural approach to emotions examines emotions associated with stable power and status relations and changes in power and status relations, both anticipated and resulting from ongoing interaction. As detailed next, individuals who claim positions of power or status, or who gain or anticipate gaining power or status in interaction are more likely to experience positive emotions, whereas those who occupy lower positions or who lose or anticipate losing power or status are more likely to experience negative emotions.

Feelings that emerge when levels of power and status are stable and constant in a situation are **structural emotions** (Kemper 2007). If power is adequate, individuals feel safe or secure, creating contentment; if status is adequate, they are likely to feel satisfied, contented, or happy. An official who has won reelection by a landslide is likely to feel these positive structural emotions. In contrast, excessive power may lead to feelings of guilt while excessive status may result in shame or embarrassment. An older sibling who gets her younger sibling to do her household chores may feel guilty if she uses blackmail (i.e., exerts power) to coerce the younger sibling or feel shame if she relies upon the sibling's admiration for her. In contrast, insufficient power creates feelings of fear or anxiety and insufficient status may lead to sadness, depression, or even anger. In *Scrubs*, J.D. was always anxious about Dr. Cox's evaluations of his performance. And he never felt that he could win Dr. Cox's respect, making him sad.

Consequent or **situational emotions** capture feelings that arise from gains or losses of power or status in ongoing interaction (Kemper 2007; see Kemper 1991 for an empirical test). At a general level, losses in power or status correspond to a lack of confidence, and gains represent increases in confidence. Of course, how people define what happens in interaction depends, in part, on their existing relative power or status position and what they anticipate from the situation (Kemper 2007; see also Turner and Stets 2005). For power, unexpected losses result in fear and anxiety, whereas unexpected gains in power produce a modicum of satisfaction. For example, when Dr. Cox made J.D. the lead doctor on a patient's case, J.D. experienced an unexpected gain in power (he now could get nurses and others to do his bidding on the particular case) and felt satisfied. Expected gains in power facilitate the development of self-confidence.

For status, expected and unexpected gains result in satisfaction, which, in turn, enhances positive sentiments between the giver and recipient of the regard and facilitates the emergence of group solidarity. For example, although J.D. and fellow resident Elliot competed for Dr. Cox's attention, when J.D. praised Elliot for her treatment of a patient, he gave and she received status, thereby cementing their friendship. Unexpected status losses, however, are complicated by the attributions individuals make for the losses. When individuals blame themselves for the losses, they may feel shame, embarrassment, or depression, if the loss is of some magnitude. When they blame the losses on others, anger is the likely response. For example, in one *Scrubs* episode, the Janitor disrupted J.D.'s blossoming romantic relationship with Elliot, causing J.D. to lose status (in Elliot's eyes). Because J.D. blamed the Janitor (not himself) for things going awry in his romance, he felt angry at the status loss (and retaliated by putting paint in the Janitor's cleaning supplies!).

The core of Kemper's argument attempts to address a fundamental question about how position in the power and status structure affects emotional experiences. Such inquiry potentially provides a basis for understanding how emotions contribute to maintaining or undermining inequalities in society. Evidence that men, typically considered higher status, report experiencing more positive emotions than presumably lower-status women confirms Kemper's expectations (Simon and Nath 2004). Yet data regarding his predictions about status and anger indicate a more complex pattern than simply lower status individuals experiencing more anger. People with low occupational status and those with high report experiencing high levels of anger; those of middle occupational status report the lowest levels of anger (Collett and Lizardo 2010). One reason for this distinct pattern may be that individuals of higher occupational status often encounter subordinates over whom they seek to exercise emotional dominance to maintain their position. Although inconsistent with Kemper's theorizing, the higher levels of anger among the high status may be a way to confirm their identities, which is a key mechanism described by theories of emotional experience described below. Chapter 9 also examines emotions resulting from power processes involved in social exchange.

Identity Approaches

Doctors treat and perhaps even cure patients. Police detectives solve crimes. Parents support and protect children. When doctors fail to treat or cure, when detectives leave crimes unsolved, or when parents repeatedly miss their children's soccer games, we might say that they have failed in their respective roles. Insofar as it is likely that individuals in these roles have taken on the identity of a doctor, detective, or parent, failing to fulfill the identity appropriately may lead to feeling negative emotions. Identity approaches to the experience of emotions stem from the perspectives described in Chapter 4. At the heart of such approaches are notions of shared meanings and individuals' desires to confirm the meanings of their identities (and those of others). Here we discuss two approaches: affect control theory and identity theory.

Affect control theory (ACT; Heise 1977, 2002; Lively and Heise 2014; Robinson, Smith-Lovin, and Wisecup 2007; Smith-Lovin and Heise 1988) argues that adequate or inadequate performances in identity roles stimulate emotional arousal. ACT depends upon culturally shared, affective meanings of identities, behaviors, settings, and emotions to predict what emotion individuals might experience in a situation. Fundamental assumptions of the theory indicate that "people act to maintain the affective meanings that are evoked by a definition of the situation" and emotions are "signals about how well the situation [is] maintaining self-identity meanings" (Robinson et al. 2007:179–80). Essentially, emotions are cultural labels applied to feelings in particular situations. Affect rather than cognition is central to shaping behavior.

The major theoretical premise suggests that people attempt to match their fundamental interpretations of identities, behaviors, and settings to what is actually occurring in a situation. This matching may occur in reference to one's own identity and behavior or in terms of the observed identity and behavior of another person. In either case, the matching process stimulates emotions in self or in response to another. To assess this matching process requires consideration of empirically based categorization (e.g., Morgan and Heise 1988) of the affective meanings of components defining a situation: identities, behaviors, settings, and emotions. These affective meanings involve three dimensions, similar to those describing emotions generally. Evaluation (E) assesses goodness or badness. Potency (P) captures power or weakness. And activity (A) refers to the extent to which the identity, behavior, etc., is animated—ranging from passive to very lively. The empirical EPA ratings (derived from asking members of different populations to rate components of situations on each dimension) are used in mathematical formulas (see Heise 2014; MacKinnon 1994; Smith-Lovin and Heise 1988) to predict, for example, the type of emotion that should be experienced by a person with a particular identity ("mother") in a particular situation ("abusing a child").

Constituting the baseline for matching are **fundamental sentiments**, culturally established affective meanings of identities, behaviors, and emotions that transcend situations. They are socially constructed and relatively enduring. For example, a "mother" is expected to be fundamentally nice, somewhat powerful, and relatively lively—regardless of the situation. People also judge the affective meanings of components of a situation characterizing an ongoing social event. These judgments constitute **transient impressions** of combinations of a behavior, identity, emotion, or setting. When a "mother" acts "nice," the transient impression of the behavior that arises is consistent with the fundamental sentiment about that identity.

In contrast, when a "mother" acts "mean" or "abusive," the behavior is out of sync with the identity. The transient impression and fundamental sentiment do not match, creating a discrepancy or inconsistency called a **deflection**. The discrepancy is between the affective meaning of the behavior ("abuse" is generally negative) and the affective meaning of the identity ("mother" is generally positive). Increasing discordance between the fundamental sentiment and the transient impression is likely to lead to greater emotional arousal.

Emotions indicate how a person is feeling in response to a comparison between the meaning captured by a transient impression and that represented by the fundamental sentiment. Because people strive to confirm their sentiments, the emotions evoked should bring some consistency to their definition of the situation. Disconfirmation of a sentiment generally results in negative emotions. For example, the "mother" who "abuses" her child may feel "awful" and observers may feel "repulsed." The emotion signals how the mother experiences the situation and how observers respond. The deflection stimulates restorative action. The "mother" may "apologize" or "soothe" her child—behaviors that are more consistent with the fundamental identity in terms of their goodness, powerfulness, and liveliness. Observers may want to see that the "mother" feels "remorse" for her actions. Repeated disconfirmations of a fundamental sentiment may force change in that sentiment or a redefinition of the situation. Thus, ACT, through its mathematical formulas, attempts to predict what emotions people will feel under certain circumstances (see Heise and Calhan 1995; Heise and Weir 1999).

Also, ACT addresses how people respond to individuals who fail to express the appropriate emotion. For example, study participants offer different "sentences" to fictive criminals, depending upon whether the criminals display emotions consistent with their identities (Robinson, Smith-Lovin, and Tsoudis 1994; Tsoudis and Smith-Lovin 1998). ACT expects perpetrators with fundamentally good identities to feel remorse and those with negative or stigmatized identities to show neutral emotions. Study participants gave lighter sentences to and thought less negatively about perpetrators who showed remorse. They also seemed to take into account the emotions of the victim. Victims with "good" identities who displayed devastation aroused empathy and led study participants to give stiffer sentences than those given when the victim was "stigmatized" and showed little emotion. These studies show how affective meanings of the identities and behavior of others influence observers' responses.

In addition to ACT, perceptual control **identity theory** (Burke 1991, 1996) offers an explanation of emotional experience that revolves around the self-verification processes described in Chapter 4. Basically, lack of self-verification of an identity stimulates negative emotions, whereas verification produces positive emotions (see Stets and Trettevik 2014). Variation in the strength and intensity of emotional responses corresponds to the extent to which more salient identities—the ones that are more likely to be played out across different situations—are verified or not. For example, a bad review (i.e., negative feedback) for a theatrical performance will evoke greater dismay and disappointment for a professional actor than for a high school student with a small part in a school performance. For the professional, the "actor" identity is likely to be of greater salience than for the high schooler. Contextual factors, however, may affect the direction and degree of the discrepancy between the identity and situational feedback, thereby affecting the nature of evoked emotions (Stets 2003, 2005).

Identity theory also suggests that negative emotions experienced as a result of failing to meet identity expectations will create stress, motivating people to find ways to change or eliminate their bad feelings (Stets and Trettevik 2014). Individuals might act in different ways to get feedback that verifies the meaning of their identity.

The professional actor may take more acting lessons so that his next performance is more convincing. Alternatively, people might change their perceptions of the feedback they have received. For example, the professional actor with the bad reviews may condemn the theater critics as hacks and not take seriously what they have said. If neither the behavioral or cognitive strategy results in more positive feelings, a person may consider changing the meaning of his or her identity altogether. What is important here is how the emotions experienced based on identity processes generate individual behavior, which in turn may affect the dynamics of social interaction.

Summary

For those two fateful days in July 2007, Londoners experienced an array of emotions, ranging from ecstatic owing to having won the Olympics bid to intense sadness and sorrow owing to the bombings. Those feelings involved physiological arousal, stimulated by distinct neuroanatomical processes, resulting in cultural labels that capture the distinct feelings. Although people across cultures are likely to experience the primary emotions of happiness when receiving positive (especially unexpected) outcomes and sadness when encountering losses, British cultural dictates about being "unemotional" may have produced what people in other countries might describe as "restrained" glee or "understated" grief. The experience of emotion combines both physiological and cognitive components— the latter of which may capture cultural diversity.

The theories reviewed previously capture these components. Schachter and Singer's (1962) results show that people take cues from others in a situation to label the emotion stemming from physiological arousal. Kemper's structural theory of emotions attends to the role of stable and changing power and status. ACT and identity theory reiterate the importance of identities in social interaction and how the confirmation or disconfirmation of a salient identity evokes an emotion. Yet whether individuals actually express what they feel to others depends on additional considerations. In the next section, we examine rules about what emotions should be displayed and how people manage the emotions that they experience.

What Influences Displays of People's Feelings?

Social situations shape not only feelings but also expressions of these feelings. For example, a server in a restaurant may be very angry at one of his customers but not express his anger. In addition, in certain situations, we may express an emotion that we really do not feel. For example, a friend may display joy for her friend who has done well on an exam yet actually instead feel envious. Importantly, we need to distinguish between the **experience of emotions** and the **expression or display of felt emotions**. In this section, we examine cultural and structural factors that affect displays of people's feelings toward others in interaction.

A Cultural Approach to Emotional Displays

A **cultural approach** to emotions addresses what factors affect display of emotions. Every society reveals an emotion culture that consists of a set of ideas about how people are supposed to feel and how they should express those feelings in particular situations. This emotion culture indicates to its members the appropriate feelings and emotional responses in various contexts. Two works lay the foundation for this cultural approach to emotions.

Goffman's Dramaturgical Approach and Emotions

Recall Goffman's idea of impression management discussed in Chapter 3 (labeled the **dramaturgical approach**). Goffman views humans as impression managers who use carefully calculated tactics to make a particular impression on others. We often try to present a socially acceptable image to others, which involves being seen as likable and competent. Goffman suggests that we use techniques of impression management to influence the definition of the situation by attempting to control the information about ourselves that others have. Impression management involves (1) the impressions given (what we believe that we are giving) and (2) the impressions given off (what impressions of us that others in the interaction develop). Social interaction is viewed as a kind of drama where individuals are giving a performance in front of an audience (such as a potential employer, an athletic coach, or a committee). Actors manipulate their appearance, setting, and demeanor—all of which are essential for their performance.

Actors' performances, however, involve not only what they say or the props and tactics they use but also their **displays of emotions or expressive cues** in the social interaction. The audience expects that actors will display emotions that are appropriate and consistent for the performance. They expect consistency between the behavior and emotional displays of the actor in order to understand the expectations for interaction in a particular situation. For example, imagine your friend saying to you, "I'm not upset!" as he continues to cry. Something is off here, and of course, you don't believe his words. You will give more weight to your friend's emotional display than to his spoken words to determine what is happening and how to respond. In fact, Goffman states that expressive displays and nonverbal cues (e.g., eye-rolling, sarcastic tone, quivering voice, or incessant rubbing of hands) communicate a more accurate picture of the performance than what is spoken, because these displays or cues are often more difficult to control than what is said verbally. Imagine a friend being utterly tactless at dinner with your parents and later expressing remorse while simultaneously apologizing for his thoughtless behavior. You may believe he is sincere because the emotional display matches the apology. If he apologizes but does not display the appropriate emotion, his performance may be disrupted. We have all heard "I'm sorry" from others in certain situations, yet we don't believe it!

In addition, given Goffman's analysis of the fragile nature of performances (described in Chapter 3), he mainly focused on the emotion of embarrassment, a mild form of shame. When an actor does not or cannot successfully present a self, talks inappropriately in the situation, expresses inappropriate emotions, or is unable to uphold the desired definition of the situation, the actor is said to lose face. In response, the audience may react by expressing negative emotions and sanctioning the actor, eliciting embarrassment in the actor (a role-taking emotion described in Chapter 3). The actor then has a chance to repair the situation through the use of apologies or accounts and thereby allow for the return to the smooth flow of interaction.

Gordon's Emotion Cultures

Although Goffman paid some attention to emotions, Gordon (1981), as mentioned earlier, introduces explicitly the importance of culture in assessing emotional dynamics. Gordon argues that the power of culture (the way of doing things) is evident in the **vocabularies, words, or labels** denoting emotions; the **views and beliefs** that people hold about emotions; and the **rules or norms** about what people should feel in situations and how emotions should be expressed. This complex of vocabularies, beliefs, and rules or norms is referred to as the **emotion culture** of society (Gordon 1990). Emotion cultures vary across societies and subcultures within a society, can change through time, and are learned through socialization processes.

An illustration of a word or label used to denote an emotion is seen in the Japanese word *oime*. This word is defined in English as a feeling of being psychologically indebted to another person. This label is distinctive to Japanese culture (Parkinson, Fischer, and Manstead 2005). *Oime* is perceived to be more negative than sadness or anger because it refers to unmet obligations with others, underscoring the importance of maintaining balanced and harmonious relationships in Japanese culture (underscoring the interdependent self-concept). (See Smith [2015] for 154 words describing different emotions around the world!). An example of beliefs about emotions is the saying "Keep a stiff upper lip," often associated with British culture and referring to suppressing the display of emotion, particularly in the face of misfortune.

Emotion norms may evolve over time, as exemplified by Cancian and Gordon's (1988) study of how the expression of love and anger in marriage changed from 1900 to 1979 in the United States. They conducted a content analysis of a sample of articles on marriage in women's magazines (like *McCall's*) and general magazines (like *Reader's Digest*). They found that these magazines revealed a positive change in the beliefs about the acceptance of more open expression of anger as the 20th century progressed. In the early part of this century and through the conservative era of the 1950s, women were encouraged to control their expressions of anger in their marriages because these displays could lead to divorce or desertion. By the mid-1960s, however, wives were advised to express their anger and allow their partners to do so as well. Expressing disagreements became normalized, and sharing of positive and negative feelings became a necessary part of love in relationships. This shift toward the expression of anger was consistent with the emergence of more equal power between husbands and wives. Love grew associated with self-assertion rather than self-sacrifice (suppressing wives' own desires and feelings to uphold the husbands' wants and needs). Cancian and Gordon (1988) show how structural events, such as the political and social liberation periods, the rise of psychotherapy, and historical events such as World War II shaped emotion norms regarding love and anger.

Hochschild's Cultural Analysis of Emotion Management

Drawing from Goffman and Gordon (and others, e.g., Darwin 1955; Ekman 1973), Hochschild (1979, 1983) argues that societies reveal an emotion culture that consists of beliefs about what people are supposed to feel in various kinds of situations and whether they should express those feelings in particular circumstances. Through socialization and in interaction, individuals learn appropriate feelings and expressions for various contexts. As previously noted, they learn feeling rules indicating cultural standards about what people ought to feel in a given situation. Such rules specify the valence, the intensity, and the duration of what to feel. Recall the example about how intensely and for how long we should feel grief after a loved one's death.

Additionally, learned **display or expression rules** define often unspoken norms regarding what individuals may express in social interaction. These norms may circumscribe displays of feelings. For example, we learn the appropriate ways of expressing grief after the death of a loved one and how long we should display our grief with people close to us, with acquaintances, and in public spaces. There are also expression rules about sympathy.

When do you express sympathy, and when do you hold back? Focusing on such displays in the United States, it seems that individuals maintain "sympathy margins" with each other, and this margin is stronger in close relationships than in acquaintance relationships (Clark 1997). That is, people are expected to display more sympathy and more strongly respond to others' display of sympathy with people close to them than with people they do not know very well. Also, expression rules suggest a lack of reciprocity of expressed sympathy by friends may devastate a relationship just as making false claims to get sympathy may be quite annoying. There is, then, a fine balance between how much sympathy should be expressed by each actor in relationships, depending on the nature of the relationship.

Parents and caregivers teach these rules to ensure that children engage in acceptable and appropriate behavior (Brody 2000). Children often break feeling and expression rules, reminding us of the eminence of these rules in our day-to-day interaction. You can imagine how often parents remind their kids that it is not appropriate to have a temper tantrum (an expression of anger or frustration) in public. Individuals learn cultural beliefs about emotional expressions as they mature and take on various social roles (Gordon 1990; Hochschild 1979).

As with feeling rules, expression rules vary cross-culturally. For example, in the United States in many contexts, people are expected to smile in general encounters, but in Poland, people are expected to smile only as a sincere expression of happiness (Wierzbicka 1999).

What happens when how you feel does not match what you should be feeling, according to these rules? How does this conflict impact the display of your feelings? For example, an employee whose boss eliminates some of her responsibilities may feel angry, but it may be inappropriate for her to express anger toward her boss because to do so may threaten her job security or future opportunities; her boss, in contrast, may have no such constraints on his display of anger toward subordinates. Employees often mask, hide, or suppress their emotions to create an appropriate emotional display (Erickson and Ritter 2001). Hochschild (1979) argues that when individuals feel something different from that expected on the basis of feeling rules, they may engage in **emotion management** to create or change in degree a more appropriate feeling. Emotion management refers to the cognitive and behavioral strategies that people use to bring their felt and expressed emotions into line with culturally mandated feeling and display rules. Feeling and display rules then underlie emotion management.

To engage in emotion management, sometimes we try to change our emotions by changing the outward expressions of our feelings. In doing so, we are trying to act as if we feel a certain way and also often expecting that we might eventually feel this way. Hochschild (1979) refers to this process as **surface acting**. For example, even if we are anxious about our work situation, we might act as if we are happy by smiling or at least by controlling the nervous tapping of our feet. In other situations, we may actually work on changing the feeling itself, referred to as **deep acting**. For example, we try to psych ourselves up before going out with friends even though we feel sad. We try to really "fall in love" with a very nice person even though we don't feel that way. Or we muster up some gratitude for a gift we do not like. We may either work, then, to **suppress a feeling** by trying to block or weaken a feeling we "should not" feel or to **evoke a feeling** we wish we had or wish we felt more intensely.

Surface and deep acting involve various types of emotion management techniques: cognitive, bodily, and expressive. **Cognitive techniques** involve changing ideas or thoughts to alter the feeling around them. For example, a person tries to stop loving his ex-wife by remembering all the times that she has forgotten his birthday or concentrating on all the irritating things about her while forgetting the things that he loved about her. He may also call upon friends to support and reinforce his negative feelings. In cognitive work, individuals change their appraisal of the situation to change their feelings. Second, people may hope to change their feelings by working on their body (**bodily techniques**). For example, an athlete may take deep breaths to calm down, or a student may run a few laps after a poor exam performance to suppress frustration. Finally, people may employ **expressive techniques** by activating expressive gestures to try to change inner feelings. You may stifle a cry when you are upset, for example, and start to sing to your favorite music in the hopes of feeling happy before going out with friends. Some of the most common emotion management techniques are catharsis, seeking support from others, hiding feelings, taking direct action, and reinterpreting the situation (Thoits 1990).

People do not only manage their own emotions but also the emotions of others in interaction. For example, Cahill and Eggleston (1994) examine how wheelchair users manage their own emotions as well as the emotions of others (termed "walkers") in public. Through participant observation, conversational interviews, and autobiographical accounts of wheelchair users, they found that sources of conflict arise when "walkers" ignore wheelchair users, treat them as invisible, or overextend their help and sympathy. Because these actions often elicit negative emotions, wheelchair users manage them by using humor to alleviate awkwardness and anxiety felt by themselves and walkers. For example, walkers may feel uneasy when they see a wheelchair user struggling to negotiate a doorway. As a result, the wheelchair user may make themselves the butt of a joke to ease the tension. Another technique is to express poise and grace when children blurt out questions about why a person is in a wheelchair. Of course, sometimes wheelchair users mask their resentment when others offer unnecessary help. Instead, they may express gratitude, though they do not privately feel it.

Emotions in the Workplace Emotion management often arises in the workplace (see Wharton 2014). For example, in Hochschild's (1983) classic study of Delta Air Lines, flight attendants were expected to sustain a pleasant demeanor dictated by feeling and display rules, even in the face of disruptive and rude customers. In fact, many jobs in service industries (e.g., in restaurants, stores, hotels, etc.), middle-class occupations, and professional jobs require specific ways of feeling and display of feeling (Sloan 2004). Hochschild (1983) notes that as some jobs require different degrees of mental and physical labor, so too do jobs require various amounts of **emotional labor,** or emotion management done for a wage. In this case, officials in institutions such as companies, schools, prisons, and stores, tell workers what to feel and how to express their feelings toward others. Included in many jobs is having the "right" feelings and expressions of them to influence the emotions of others (e.g., customers or clients).

Some institutions have become very sophisticated in promoting the techniques of deep acting, such as Delta Air Lines in Hochschild's study, a company that competes by having the best service. You can think of many other companies that train their workers to feel a particular way and express these feelings toward the customers in order to make them feel "good" and "comfortable." No doubt, Starbucks employees, for example, go through emotion training, as well as camp counselors and employees hired in chain restaurants such as Denny's.

Hochschild (1983) notes that there are costs to emotional labor, particularly if this labor is routinely required over time. Workers who have high demands on their emotional labor are often forced to engage in behaviors that arouse negative emotions. One cost may be the experience of burnout on the job because it becomes difficult to distinguish between the self and the work role: In this case, their sense of self is disrupted. Another cost may be feelings of inauthenticity directed toward the self if workers become estranged from their own feelings. This estrangement from their feelings may also lead to a denial of their emotions in other domains of their lives, such as in intimate relations. Finally, workers may become very cynical toward their job.

For example, medical schools teach students techniques of emotion management, such as learning to manage their disgust, fear, and embarrassment when interacting and treating patients (Smith and Kleinman 1989). Students find out what emotions are appropriate and inappropriate to feel and express not through written rules or textbooks but through observing students' and teachers' reactions to patients. For example, they pick up how to use humor to relieve anxiety, disgust, or embarrassment, and they use scientific or technical talk to distance themselves from their patients. A third-year male medical student stated, "You can't tell what's wrong without looking under the hood. It's different when I'm talking with a patient. But when I'm examining them it's like an automobile engine. . . . There's a bad connotation with that, but it's literally what I mean" (Smith and Kleinman 1989:61). A consequence of this emotion management over time is that some students became estranged from their own feelings, which affects the quality of their interactions in their personal relationships. (See also Cahill [1989] for an examination of emotion management and mortuary science students.)

Emotional labor, however, does not always lead to negative consequences (Wharton 1999). For example, cynicism toward one's job can be a healthy response to the demands of emotional labor. Also, workers in jobs that require emotional labor are no more likely to experience burnout than workers engaged in less emotional labor. Plus, the amount of contact with clients/customers is not necessarily associated with how often workers felt that they could not be themselves at work or had to fake how they really felt at work (Wharton 1993). Yet, consistent with Hochschild's work, workers who face the demand of "handling people well" and managing feelings of agitation or anger, which both require constraining emotional displays, tend to indicate that they had to fake how they really felt at work more often than workers without these demands (Erickson and Ritter 2001; Erickson and Wharton 1997).

Although most emotional management, paid or otherwise, focuses on intrapersonal strategies, **interpersonal emotion management strategies** allow workers to influence others' emotions (Francis 1997; Lively 2008; Staske 1998). Coworkers play a vital role in individuals' ability to manage their own emotions or engage in emotional labor (Lively 2000; Lively and Powell 2006; Lively and Weed 2014). When individuals get angry with someone else at work, they often go to their coworkers for social support, helping each other to manage their emotions, rather than expressing their anger directly toward the person who stimulated the emotion. Such mutual support is regarded as reciprocal emotional management. For example, Lively (2000, 2008) finds that paralegals manage their emotions by venting and blowing off steam together to control their anger toward the attorneys. Such relationships provide a space where paralegals can feel safe in expressing their negative emotions, gripe, and moan with one another, using each other as safety valves. Venting helps to redefine the situation together. Your own experience may also illustrate reciprocal emotion management. College students may get frustrated with a professor who graded an exam unfairly or is severely unorganized in class, yet they are unlikely to express this frustration or anger toward the professor. As a result, they vent to each other, thereby providing mutual support and study together as best they can.

A Social Structural Approach to Emotional Displays

The cultural approach suggests that people learn display rules through interaction that dictates what, where, for how long, and how feelings should be expressed in particular contexts (in addition to feeling rules). In many contexts, who may display what feeling is strongly dictated by the relative position of each individual in the interaction, the nature of the relationship, and the context of the interaction. For example, in the United States individuals are more likely to express anger directly toward family members at home than toward people at work (such as bosses, customers, or coworkers) (Lively and Powell 2006). According to a **social structural approach** to emotional displays, complementing the cultural view, individuals face constraints on their expression of emotions in some contexts, while being afforded opportunities to express their feelings in other contexts. As with the experience of emotions, here we provide some examples of how relative status and power (concepts and processes detailed in Chapters 8 and 9) influence constraints on and opportunities for emotional displays in interaction.

In work settings, **relative status** refers to differences between individuals in terms of perceived worthiness, prestige, and social value within a particular context.[8] For example, a worker in a company may have higher status than her fellow coworkers because she is perceived to be more competent and have more skills; likewise, a church member who consistently volunteers for committees may have more status than one who attends services irregularly. Individuals are less likely to express anger directly toward a person with higher status than themselves than toward a person who is of equal or lower status (Lively and Powell 2006). In addition, individuals with higher status in an interaction are often allowed more opportunities to express negative emotions toward others than individuals with lower status; lower-status individuals, on the other hand, are more constrained in regard to display of negative emotions toward high-status individuals.

In addition to status, individuals often vary in terms of the **relative power** they have in a situation. Relative power refers to the level of resources an individual has compared to another person in the situation that allows him to get others to do what he desires, despite others' resistance. For example, managers, doctors, professors, and judges all have more power than subordinates, patients, students, and prosecutors. Like relative status, relative power of the individuals in an interaction can dictate who can express what feelings. For example, employees may feel angry about failing to receive a deserved pay raise, but they hide that anger around their boss for fear of losing their jobs. In contrast, individuals in more powerful positions may express their anger toward individuals with lower power without fear of retribution (Schieman 2007). Imagine raising your voice in anger toward one of your professors or to your boss—not too likely. Indeed, displays of anger and negative emotions in general, as illustrated in the next several chapters, can be used as a means of controlling others.

How Do Gender and Race or Ethnicity Influence Experience and Display of Emotions?

We have discussed why people feel what they feel and what factors influence display of emotions. Here, we look at the impact of gender and race or ethnicity on emotion processes.

Do you have any stereotypes about how you think women and men experience and express emotions? Cultural beliefs in the United States about gender and emotion *assume* that men and women differ in their experience and expression of some emotions. For example, men are believed to experience and express anger more frequently than women in general, while women are thought to experience and express sadness, anxiety, and positive emotions more frequently (Shields 2002; Stearns and Stearns 1986; Timmers, Fischer, and Manstead 2003). Also, because women are believed to be more emotional than men in general, they are also believed to express emotion more often than men. Certainly, individuals learn gender-specific cultural beliefs about emotions over time (see Alexander and Wood 2000). These cultural beliefs influence individuals' interpretations of and responses to everyday interactions. As a consequence, insofar as cultural norms deem it appropriate in various contexts for women to express sadness more than men and for men to express anger more than women, gender differences may also emerge in observed expressions of emotions. But do they?

Despite these taken-for-granted beliefs about gender differences in experience and display of emotions, empirical evidence is mixed. In regard to experience, evidence from psychological studies shows that women report experiences of joy, empathy, sadness, shame, and embarrassment more frequently than men, while men report greater feelings of pride and contempt than do women (Brody and Hall 2000). Women also indicate greater happiness than do men (Alexander and Wood 2000). Yet survey results (Simon and Nath 2004) involving a probability sample of U.S. residents show that men report more positive emotions than women. Women report more negative emotions than men, although when socioeconomic factors such as income are taken into account this difference disappears.

Based on Kemper's structural approach to emotions, gender differences in feelings may emerge only because women are more likely to have less status and power in situations in general. If so, the expectation would be that women experience more negative emotions (e.g., sadness, fear, anger) than men on average. The identity approaches might indicate that specific identities, identities with greater salience, and identities to which people have stronger commitments might carry greater weight in terms of arousing emotions. To understand the emotional experiences of men and women, then, requires consideration of situational circumstances as well as the identities invoked by the people interacting within the situation.

Mixed results underlie gender differences in emotional display as well. Some studies find that women report that they are more likely to express their emotions in general than men (e.g., Alexander and Wood 2000; Brody and Hall 1993; Rosenfield 1999; Simon 2002; Simon and Nath 2004). For example, women more than men on average disagree with the statements that they (1) keep their emotions to themselves or (2) try not to worry anyone else when they feel anxious. Other studies, however, find similarities for men and women in the likelihood of expressing emotions. For example, men's and women's emotional expressions (except for agitation) at work seem to be fairly similar (Erickson and Ritter 2001), and, when relative status is controlled, they are equally likely to express their emotions at home and at work (Lively and Powell 2006).

In regard to anger, some studies, using samples of men and women in the United States, find that men are more likely to report expressing anger (consistent with cultural beliefs) (e.g., Ross and Van Willigen 1996), yet other studies show that men and women experience anger at about the same frequency and have similar patterns of suppressing these feelings (see Simon and Lively 2010; Simon and Nath 2004). These studies do find, however, that women characterize their anger as more intense and of longer duration than that of men.

Interestingly, women report more symptoms of depression than men (Kessler 2003), and their more intense and persistent feelings of anger are involved in the difference in symptoms of depression between men and women (Simon and Lively 2010; Simon and Nath 2004). Unequal status at work and in the family exposes women to greater risk of anger-eliciting social interactions. Women also report that they are more likely to talk with others about their angry feelings than are men. In contrast, men are more likely to report coping with their feelings of anger by drinking and taking pills (Simon and Lively 2010).

These mixed results on gender and emotions stem, in part, from (1) how self-reports of emotions were measured (e.g., retrospectively or online as occurring), (2) what emotion is considered, and (3) the extent to which analysis takes into account contextual factors. *Taking into account the social context is crucial for understanding specific emotional responses in given situations* (e.g., Lively and Powell 2006; Schachter and Singer 1962; Shields et al. 2007; Smith-Lovin 1995; Thoits 1989, 1990). Relative status and power in relationships within the family and at work, as well as the duration and intimacy of on-the-job interactions, help to shape emotional experiences and expressions.

Beyond the impact of gender on workplace emotions is consideration of how emotions are experienced by racial and ethnic minorities (e.g., Harlow 2003; Kang 2003). For example, black women professors often face white students' perceptions that they are mean, cold, and intimidating, placing them outside the bounds of the stereotype of women as nurturing and caring. These professors manage this situation by doing emotional work to achieve a professional demeanor (Harlow 2003).

More generally, Wingfield (2010) argues that feeling rules and performances have different implications for black professionals than white professionals, and this reinforces racial difference. In professional settings, the structure of workplace culture revolves around white, middle-class norms, and these norms extend to feeling and display rules. For example, usually it is expected that emotions such as calmness and congeniality are appropriate for the workplace, while anger and frustration are tolerable but only under specific conditions.

Two important findings emerged from Wingfield's semistructured interviews with African American professionals, representing a variety of occupations, who were typically one of a few African Americans in their specific workplaces (tokens in the workplace). First, these black workers experience marginalization and heightened visibility (as a result of being a token), which leads to emotions of anger and frustration regarding racial issues that emerge in the workplace. Second, paradoxically, the feeling and display rules in this work context (expectations of always being pleasant and congenial) disallow expressions of anger or frustration for fear that doing so would lead to being labeled the angry black man or woman, further social isolation, and poor performance evaluations. For example, a female manager commented, "What I'm mostly trying to do is feel comfortable. I don't lose my temper or anything like that, I don't control emotions like that, but really to relax and participate and get involved without the weight I carry of feeling different and being looked at as though I'm different. . . . I have to do this if I'm going to be the cool, calm manager I need to be" (Wingfield 2010:257). Similarly, a black male professional noted, "There's different things, that you want to say but you can't. Or you could, but you might not be there long. And that's one of the struggles of being black in the workplace. You have to humble yourself, kind of like modern day sharecropping" (Wingfield 2010:260).

As Wingfield (2010:265–66) states, "Tokenism operates such that black professionals are scrutinized not only for what they *do*, but how they *feel*. This establishes an emotional culture that is built on racial inequality—feeling rules that are applied generally are harder for blacks to follow, and the rules that are selectively applied are done in a way that leaves black professionals with fewer opportunities to express emotions."

In the next section, we explore how affective states (such as felt emotions and moods) may influence or regulate interaction. We end the chapter with a discussion of how emotions, experienced and expressed, contribute to the existence and maintenance of both social solidarity and social inequality.

How Do Affective States Influence Social Interaction?

Affect and Cognition

You have just learned that your best friend has lied to you. How do you react? Do you feel your heart begin to race or your stomach start to ache? Is your head filled with a million thoughts on why he might have lied to you? Do you think there could be a mistake and it cannot be true? Do you feel anger, hurt, or both? In this event, what comes first: the emotions you feel or your thoughts about what caused this situation? Is it possible that you experience emotions and thoughts simultaneously?

Research in emotions struggles with the role of cognitive processes in affective processes (Fiske and Taylor 2013). In our lived experiences, affect and cognition often occur simultaneously. Indeed, this separation is something of a fiction, but for analytic convenience, we divide social cognition and affect and discuss their reciprocal influences on each other.

There are many examples of theories that posit that **cognition influences affect**. For example, Schachter's two-factor theory discussed previously suggests that emotions are mediated by cognitive activity. In addition, using the attributions approaches (Chapter 5), Weiner (1985) shows that specific emotions follow from specific casual attributions. When a favorable outcome (such as a high test score or winning a race) is attributed to oneself and is seen as controllable, pride follows. When we attribute a negative outcome to another person and it is also viewed as controllable, anger follows. Also, using social comparison theory, if a student compares her test score with other students with lower test scores, this may also lead to feeling pride.

Also, affect may be a consequence of a perceptual or cognitive discrepancy (Fiske and Taylor 2013; Mandler 1990). A person's mental representation of a nun, for example, is violated when she overhears several nuns cussing, evoking arousal. Whether a person feels a positive or negative emotion depends on the cognitive interpretation set off by this arousal. For devout Catholics, it may be perceived as inappropriate, evoking negative emotions. For others, it may be perceived as novel and somewhat amusing.

Similarly, perceptual control identity theory, as described previously, suggests that emotions stem from a discrepancy between how people think others view them in a situation and their own identity standard meanings. When there is continuous congruence between the two, positive emotions arise, but when there is consistent incongruence, negative emotions arise (Burke 1991). In a study of newly married couples during their first three years of marriage, when spouses confirmed one's self-view, positive emotions were invoked, and the experience of negative emotions such as distress and depression was reduced. But when spouses continually disconfirmed one's self-view, negative emotions were evoked (Burke and Stets 1999). In a recent study, scholars found that when individuals with a high moral identity, in terms of seeing oneself as being highly just and caring, perceive that others in a situation do not view them as a moral person, this lack of verification is likely to lead to feelings of guilt and shame (Stets and Carter 2012). If you think you are a moral person, but you perceive feedback from others to the contrary, you are more likely to feel guilt or shame in the situation.

On the other hand, sometimes **affect influences cognition**, such as evaluations, judgments, and decisions. For example, cheerful people seem to like just about anything better such as themselves, their health, other people, the future, and even politics than those not so cheery (Bodenhausen et al. 2001; Crano and Prislin 2006; Zajonc 1998). Good moods can foster positive evaluations of things. People in good moods are also more likely to remember pleasant events (e.g., Singer and Salovey 1988). But do people in bad moods dislike most things? The evidence is more mixed for negative moods, but sometimes negative moods do lead to corresponding negative evaluations. For example, negative moods intensify the perception that negative events are likely to happen in the future

(Johnson and Tversky 1983). Also, people who feel depressed are more likely to judge other people according to negative traits than people in a neutral mood (Erber 1991).

Finally, affect and cognition may be independent of each other, at least under certain conditions. Have you ever made important life decisions more from an emotional base than a cognitive one? Many of our life choices seem to be based on our feelings, rather than follow from a "rational" point of view. A classic example is decisions we may make in choosing romantic partners. Yet sometimes our affective processes operate independently from our cognitive processes (Zajonc 1980). This **separate systems view** suggests that affective and cognitive processes run along parallel paths and really do not influence each other much, under certain conditions. Specifically, affect is conceived as more basic than cognition, and affective reactions are more primary. For example, many people "fall in love," choosing romantic partners based on affect rather than on a cognitive list of pros and cons—feelings are not straightforwardly influenced by totaling up a partner's pros and cons. You may feel strongly about someone but cannot remember the reasons why you feel this way! This approach argues, then, that affective reactions are inescapable, possibly independent of cognition, and are present in a more demanding way than simple knowledge. Yet given that cognitions can be unconscious, rapid, automatic, and irrational, similar to affect, it is possible that preconscious cognitions may precede emotions (Epstein 1983; Lazarus 1990).

Mood and Behavior

Good moods often lead people to help one another (Fiske and Taylor 2013). Many things can lead to good moods, such as being given a treat like fresh-baked chocolate chip cookies, listening to desirable music, finding money on the street, receiving a free sample, experiencing good weather, being told one is helpful, and smelling roasted coffee (Penner et al. 2005). When people are in a good mood, they are more likely to help someone pick up dropped papers, donate to a charity, give positive advice, or make a phone call for a stranger. The effect of mood on behavior occurs regardless of people's age, social class, race, or ethnicity. Interestingly, people in good moods tend to be more sociable and are more cooperative negotiators, using less contentious tactics with others in the interaction. You may notice this in yourself. When you are in a good mood, you see the world a bit more positively and are more likely to respond positively to others. Why?

It may be that people in good moods are more likely to focus their attention on their own good fortune, and this, in turn, promotes kindness toward others. Another possibility is that people in good moods have improved social outlooks. In this case, they are more likely to focus on human goodness or feelings of community, which, in turn, enhances prosocial values and behavior. Finally, it could be that people in good moods want to maintain their good moods. As a result, people who are in cheery moods are less likely to help if it will ruin their mood and more likely to help if they expect positive rewards (Fiske and Taylor 2013).

People in happy moods are more likely to be flexible in their decision-making than people in bad moods (Fiske and Taylor 2013). It may be that happy people interpret their good mood as everything is going well. A caveat is that people in good moods may often act too quickly and impulsively when they are not personally involved in the decision-making, but when they are involved, they are more thoughtful than people in bad moods.

The picture for the impact of bad moods on helping others is less clear than for good moods (Fiske and Taylor 2013). People in bad moods are more likely to help others than those in neutral moods, but it may be out of a sense of guilt. And some evidence shows that people in bad moods are also likely to help in order to relieve their negative mood. Thus, whether those in bad moods help depends upon the circumstances of the situation.

Though we know that moods influence various types of behaviors, how moods emerge becomes an important question. One source is the experience of emotions, of particular types, perhaps over time. For example, when does an individual's feeling of anger become such that the individual sees himself as an angry person (someone who experiences persistent anger)? Emotions are more likely to endure into a mood when the emotional reactions are intense (Doan 2012). Sometimes, emotions persist for long periods, leading to what Scheff (1990) calls a "feeling trap" and then become moods. Also, emotions are more likely to become moods through recurring reflection (Doan 2012). For example, sometimes people who experience trauma reflect on their past events, and the reflection continues over time. This reflection can affect emotions felt in the present and lead to persistent moods. This recurrent reflection can heighten or maintain a highly intense emotional reaction.

We often think of emotions on the individual level as something individuals experience, go through, and express, but we also know that people can experience and express emotions collectively, such as when Londoners experienced happiness when their city was chosen to host the Olympics and then sadness when the terrorist attacks occurred the very next day. The next section examines how the experience and expression of emotions with others in groups promotes a sense of belonging to these groups.

Emotional Experiences and Displays: Promoting Group Solidarity

When people experience and share feelings with one another at the same time, these collective feelings contribute to the maintenance of groups and society at large by creating a sense of **group solidarity**—a feeling of "we-ness" with group members (a connection between the individual and the group) where the group is larger than the sum of the individuals comprising it. Think of a particularly moving religious or spiritual service or a high-energy sporting event such as a soccer or football game. The group or crowd experiences a collective feeling, something beyond any one person's experience. Durkheim ([1912] 1965), a renowned French sociologist, theorizes about the relationship between rituals and emotion, building on his ethnographic accounts of rituals performed by Aborigines in central Australia. Much of his work focused on religious ritual, arguing that ritual is the key mechanism that holds a society together. Importantly, Durkheim says that rituals evoke emotional arousal in group members. The group and the sacred totem objects of the group arouse intense emotion during ritual interaction, which in turn are at the basis of group solidarity. Groups come together occasionally to engage in ritual to renew their sense of group membership and affirm the "goodness" of their sacred objects.

Goffman (1967) extends Durkheim's theory of religious ritual to other types of rituals in interaction such as passing greetings like "How are you? Fine, and how are you? Fine. Thank you." Characterizing these informal interaction rituals are a shared focus of attention, an affirmation of solidarity, and the symbols of solidarity, in this case the relations between the actors themselves. Much of our daily interaction is ritualistic (or patterned), and there are clear social norms and constraints that dictate our behavior in these rituals. Without these informal ritual interactions, interaction would be chaotic, but with them a certain rhythm of interaction is maintained—acting as a glue to maintain order in society.

Building on Goffman and Durkheim, Collins (1990, 2004) offers a **theory of interaction ritual chains**, which requires rituals to involve "two or more people in the physical presence of each other; a mutual awareness shared by participants and a common focus of attention, whether it is on the group itself, an activity, or a particular symbol; and a common emotional mood, although this mood can change or grow during the ritual itself" (Summers-Effler 2007:136). When all these factors are present, such as at a religious ceremony, the potential for actors to experience rhythmic coordinated behavior emerges, creating **collective effervescence**, which refers to group-focused solidarity and individual-focused emotional energy. **Emotional energy**, produced by a feeling of belonging and heightening a sense of excitement, motivates people to participate and carry on ritual interaction.

According to Collins (1990), emotions are present in any social interaction, and often individuals desire a common shared mood in interaction. Sports teams psych themselves up to create a similar feeling of enthusiasm. Party hosts and partygoers seek to create a common upbeat, happy, and carefree atmosphere. Political organizations create and arouse collective feelings of empowerment and excitement for their candidate among their members. A sense of group solidarity stems from coordination of these common feelings among members. On the other hand, in the absence of shared connections to other group members, little emotional energy emerges. Emotional energy carries from interaction to interaction and increases when an individual experiences a successful interaction ritual and decreases when the rituals fails or one goes too long without engaging in ritual activity. Collins suggests that actors seek to maximize their experiences of emotional energy. They move from interaction to interaction, where their levels of emotional energy keep adjusting, and thus create chains of interaction rituals.

The key point is that emotional energy (common and shared feelings) is necessary for the development of group solidarity, which when buttressed by the experience of collective emotion often leads to action. For example, consider the relationship between emotions and political and social action. Emotions represent a key element that drives people to participate in political and social activism. Keeping members together, involved, and motivated is an important part of social movement activities and participation in general. For example, Summers-Effler (2005) studied the emotional experiences of people who live and work in Catholic worker houses. These people serve the poor in inner cities by (1) running a house to host "guests" that would typically otherwise be homeless, (2) providing meals to people in the neighborhood, (3) maintaining a clothing pantry, and (4) running an after-school tutoring program for neighborhood youth. Summers-Effler (2005) argues that to face the struggle to get continued support and the daily challenges involved in their work, they need emotional rituals to give them strength and resilience. One example of a formal ritual is their weekly community gathering, consisting of a community dinner at the Catholic worker house and a formal ritual of liturgy wherein community members reaffirm, with praise, the importance of these workers, to the community at large. This attention and praise, in turn, provides an emotional boost to the workers fostered by the community members, thereby encouraging them to continue their invaluable work in the community. These rituals foster the continued experience of positive emotional energy to help to maintain group solidarity, and drive sustained action (Summers-Effler 2005; see Turner and Stets 2005).

Goodwin and Jasper (2007) also describe how social movements use emotional expectations to recruit members. For example, activists transform **deactivating emotions** and moods, such as guilt, resignation, and depression, into **activating emotions**, such as anger and pride. Deactivating emotions discourage action; activating emotions encourage action. Members must have a sense of agency and see themselves as change agents to be motivated into action. With regard to the internal dynamics of social movements, they note, for example, the importance of creating and maintaining positive bonds and at the same time recognize that extremely tight bonds among some of the participants may alienate other participants, causing conflict and/or disaffiliation with the movement. (For an engaging study of emotion and immigrant collective action, see Klandermans, van der Toorn, and van Stekelenburg 2008.)

Subsequent chapters highlight other ways that emotions can create a sense of group cohesion from social exchange processes (Chapter 9) and from perceptions of and responses to injustice (Chapter 11). Plus, emotions play a role in intergroup dynamics as well (Chapter 12).

Segue: Emotions, Status, Power, and Inequality

In this chapter, we saw how emotions lead to action and social change, yet they can also hamper efforts to effect social change, resulting in perpetuating social inequality (Fields, Copp, and Kleinman 2007; Foy et al. 2014). Cultural rules dictate what people are supposed to feel and express in situations and who is allowed to feel and express them. Cultural rules are determined, in part, by relative status and relative power in social hierarchies. Some people have to manage their emotions in certain contexts more than others (as a result of relative status, power, or identities they hold), and this may reinforce their position of disadvantage. When people of higher status or power in a group are allowed to express negative emotions to control, sanction, and influence group decisions and lower status or power members are restricted in their displays of emotions signaling conflict or resistance, the existing status order goes unchallenged. Extensive emotion management by structurally disadvantaged group members may also carry negative consequences, such as high levels of stress and worry.

Emotions, then, play a pivotal role in sustaining existing status and power hierarchies. They also help uphold ideologies that justify the advantages of the most powerful and the disadvantages of the less powerful. Subsequent chapters addressing status, power, legitimacy, justice, and intergroup processes (Chapters 8, 9, 10, 11, and 12, respectively) in groups and organizations reiterate the importance of emotion processes.

Endnotes

1. Oliver, Mark. 2005. "London Wins 2012 Olympics." *Guardian*, July 5. Retrieved May 4, 2009 (www.guardian.co.uk/uk/2005/jul/06/olympics2012.olympicgames1).

2. Honigsbaum, Mark. 2005. "Patriotism and Pop Mark Victory Celebrations." *Guardian*, July 6. Retrieved May 4, 2009 (www.guardian.co.uk/uk/2005/jul/07/olympics2012.olympicgames).

3. *Guardian*. 2005. "In the Face of Danger." July 8. Retrieved March 22, 2017 (www.guardian.co.uk/world/2005/jul/08/terrorism.jul71).

4. Wikipedia. "Response to the 2005 London Bombings." Retrieved March 22, 2017 (https://en.wikipedia.org/wiki/Reactions_to_the_2005_London_bombings).

5. BBC. 2014. "Mayor Condemns 'Cowardly' Act." September 24. Retrieved March 28, 2017 (http://www.bbc.co.uk/london/content/articles/2005/07/08/livingstone_speech_feature.shtml).

6. Freedland, Jonathan. 2005. "London Defined: In Extremis, a City's Character Is Revealed." *Guardian*, July 8. Retrieved March 22, 2017 (www.guardian.co.uk/politics/2005/jul/08/jul7).

7. Chapter 7 shows that while Kemper's definition of power resonates with that of Weber ([1924] 1978) and others, his definition of status is a bit different than that in the dominant theory of status processes (e.g., Berger and Webster 2006). The focus on willing acts of deference cast Kemper's use of status as consistent with the notion of regard, rather than prestige, which characterizes other definitions of status.

8. This definition of status is distinct from that offered by Kemper (1978) and is more consistent with that used in the dominant theory about status processes (e.g., Berger and Webster 2006).

Suggested Readings

Cottingham, Marci D., and Jill A. Fisher. 2016. "Risk and Emotion among Healthy Volunteers in Clinical Trials." *Social Psychology Quarterly* 79:222–42.

Doan, Long, Lisa R. Miller, and Annalise Loehr. 2015. "The Power of Love: The Role of Emotional Attributions and Standards in Heterosexuals' Perceptions of Same-Sex Couples." *Social Forces* 94:401–25.

Hopcroft, Rosemary L, and Dana Burr Bradley. 2007. "The Sex Difference in Depression across 29 Countries." *Social Forces* 85:1483–1507.

Rivera, Lauren A. 2015. "Go with Your Gut: Emotion and Evaluation in Job Interviews." *American Journal of Sociology* 120:1339–89.

Sloan, Melissa M., Ranae J. Evenson Newhouse, and Ashley B. Thompson. 2013. "Counting on Coworkers: Race, Social Support, and Emotional Experiences on the Job." *Social Psychology Quarterly* 76:343–72.

Tettevik, Ryan. 2016. "Identities, Goals, and Emotions." *Social Psychology Quarterly* 79: 263–83.

Vaccaro, Christian A., Douglas P. Schrock, and Janice M. McCabe. 2011. "Managing Emotional Manhood: Fighting and Fostering Fear in Mixed Martial Arts." *Social Psychology Quarterly* 74:414–37.

References

Alexander, Michele G., and Wood, Wendy. 2000. "Women, Men, and Positive Emotions: A Social Role Interpretation." Pp. 189–210 in *Gender and Emotion: Social Psychological Perspectives*, edited by A. H. Fischer. New York: Cambridge University Press. doi:10.1017/CBO9780511628191.010

Berger, Joseph, and Murray Webster, Jr. 2006. "Expectations, Status, and Behavior." Pp. 268–300 in *Contemporary Social Psychological Theories,* edited by Peter J. Burke. Stanford, CA: Stanford University Press.

Bodenhausen, Galen V., Thomas Mussweiler, Shira Gabriel, and Kristen N. Moreno. 2001. "Affective Influences on Stereotyping and Intergroup Relations." Pp. 319–42 in *Handbook of Affect and Social Cognition*, edited by J. P. Forgas. Mahwah, NJ: Erlbaum.

Brody, Leslie R. 2000. "The Socialization of Gender Differences in Emotional Expression: Display Rules, Infant Temperament, and Differentiation." Pp. 24–47 in *Gender and Emotion: Social Psychological Perspectives*, edited by A. H. Fischer. New York: Cambridge University Press. doi:10.1017/CBO9780511628191.003

Brody, Leslie R., and Judith A. Hall. 1993. "Gender and Emotion." Pp. 447–460 in *Handbook of Emotions*, edited by M. Lewis and J. M. Haviland. New York: Guilford Press.

Brody, Leslie R., and Judith A. Hall. 2000. "Gender, Emotion, and Expression." Pp. 338–49 in *Handbook of Emotions*, 2nd ed., edited by M. Lewis and J. M. Haviland-Jones. New York: Guilford Press.

Burke, Peter J. 1991. "Attitudes, Behavior, and the Self." Pp. 189–208 in *The Self Society Interface: Cognition, Emotion, and Action*, edited by J. A. Howard and P. L. Callero. New York: Cambridge University Press. doi:10.1017/CBO9780511527722.011

Burke, Peter J. 1996. "Social Identities and Psychosocial Stress." Pp. 141–74 in *Psychosocial Stress: Perspectives on Structure, Theory, Life Course, and Methods*, edited by H. B. Kaplan. Orlando, FL: Academic Press.

Burke, Peter J., and Jan E. Stets. 1999. "Trust and Commitment Through Self-Verification." *Social Psychology Quarterly* 62:347–66. doi:10.2307/2695833

Cacioppo, John T., and Wendi L. Gardner. 1999. "Emotion." *Annual Review of Psychology* 50(1):191–214. doi:10.1146/annurev.psych.50.1.191

Cahill, Spencer. 1989. "Fashioning Males and Females: Appearance Management and the Social Reproduction of Gender." *Symbolic Interaction* 12:281–98. doi:10.1525/si.1989.12.2.281

Cahill, Spencer E., and Robin Eggleston. 1994. "Managing Emotions in Public: The Case of Wheelchair Users." *Social Psychology Quarterly* 57:300–12. doi:10.2307/2787157

Cancian, Francesca M., and Steven L. Gordon. 1988. "Changing Emotion Norms in Marriage: Love and Anger in U.S. Women's Magazines Since 1990." *Gender & Society* 2:308–42. doi:10.1177/089124388002003006

Clark, Candace. 1997. *Misery and Company: Sympathy in Everyday Life*. Chicago: University of Chicago Press. doi:10.7208/chicago/9780226107585.001.0001

Collett, Jessica L., and Omar Lizardo. 2010. "Occupational Status and the Experience of Anger." *Social Forces* 88:2079–2104. doi:10.1353/sof.2010.0037

Collins, Randall. 1990. "Stratification, Emotional Energy, and the Transient Emotions." Pp. 27–57 in *Research Agendas in the Sociology of Emotions*, edited by T. D. Kemper. Albany: State University of New York Press.

Collins, Randall. 2004. *Interaction Ritual Chains*. Princeton, NJ: Princeton University Press.

Cotton, John L. 1981. "A Review of Research on Schachter's Theory of Emotion and the Mis-attribution of Arousal." *European Journal of Social Psychology* 11:365–97. doi:10.1002/ejsp.2420110403

Crano, William D., and Radmila Prislin. 2006. "Attitudes and Persuasion." *Annual Review of Psychology* 57:345–74. doi:10.1146/annurev.psych.57.102904.190034

Damasio, Antonio R. 2003. *Looking for Spinoza: Joy, Sorrow, and the Feeling Brain.* Orlando, FL: Harcourt.

Darwin, Charles. 1955. *The Expression of Emotions in Man and Animals.* New York: Philosophical Library.

Darwin, Charles. 1872. *The Origin of Species by Means of Natural Selection: Or, the Preservation of Favoured Races in the Struggle for Life and the Descent of Man and Selection in Relation to Sex.* New York: Modern Library.

Doan, Long. 2012. "A Social Model of Persistent Mood States." *Social Psychology Quarterly* 75:198–218. doi:10.1177/0190272512451157

Durkheim, Emile. [1912] 1965. *The Elementary Forms of the Religious Life.* Reprint, New York: Free Press.

Ekman, Paul. 1973. *Darwin and Facial Expression: A Century of Research in Review.* New York: Academic.

Ekman, Paul. 1992. "An Argument for Basic Emotions." *Cognition and Emotion* 6:169–200. doi:10.1080/02699939208411068

Ekman, Paul, and Erika Rosenberg. 1997. *What the Face Reveals: Basic and Applied Studies of Spontaneous Expressions Using the Facial Action Coding System (FACS).* New York: Oxford University Press.

Ellsworth, Pheobe C., and Craig Smith. 1988a. "From Appraisal to Emotion: Differences among Unpleasant Feelings." *Motivation and Emotion* 12:271–302. doi:10.1007/BF00993115

Ellsworth, Phoebe C., and Craig Smith. 1988b. "Shades of Joy: Patterns of Appraisal Differentiating Pleasant Emotions." *Cognition and Emotion* 2:301–31. doi:10.1080/02699938808412702

Epstein, Seymour. 1983. "A Research Paradigm for the Study of Personality and Emotions." Pp. 91–154 in *Nebraska Symposium on Motivation 1982: Personality—Current Theory and Research,* edited by R. A. Dienstbier and M. M. Page. Lincoln: University of Nebraska Press.

Erber, Ralph. 1991. "Affective and Semantic Priming: Effects of Mood on Category Accessibility and Inference." *Journal of Experimental Social Psychology* 27(5):480–98. doi:10.1016/0022-1031(91)90005-Q

Erickson, Rebecca J., and Christian Ritter. 2001. "Emotional Labor, Burnout, and Inauthenticity: Does Gender Matter?" *Social Psychology Quarterly* 64:146–63. doi:10.2307/3090130

Erickson, Rebecca J., and Amy S. Wharton. 1997. "Inauthenticity and Depression: Assessing the Consequences of Interactive Service Work." *Work and Occupations* 24(2):188–213. doi:10.1177/0730888497024002004

Fields, Jessica, Martha Copp, and Sherryl Kleinman. 2007. "Symbolic Interactionism, Inequality, and Emotions." Pp. 155–78 in *Handbook of the Sociology of Emotions,* edited by J. E. Stets and J. H. Turner. New York: Springer.

Fiske, Susan T., and Shelley E. Taylor. 2013. *Social Cognition.* New York: Random House. doi:10.4135/9781446286395

Foy, Steven, Robert Freeland, Andrew Miles, Kimberly B. Rogers, and Lynn Smith-Lovin. 2014. "Emotions and Affect as Source, Outcome and Resistance to Inequality." Pp. 295–324 in *Handbook of the Social Psychology of Inequality,* edited by J. D. McLeod, E. J. Lawler, and M. Schwalbe. New York: Springer. doi:10.1007/978-94-017-9002-4_13

Francis, Linda E. 1997. "Ideology and Interpersonal Emotion Management: Redefining Identity in Two Support Groups." *Social Psychology Quarterly* 60(2):153–71. doi:10.2307/2787102

Franks, David D. 2007. "The Neuroscience of Emotions." Pp. 38–62 in *Handbook of the Sociology of Emotions*, edited by J. E. Stets and J. H. Turner. New York: Springer.

Franks, David. 2014. "Emotions and Neurosociology." Pp. 267–81 in *Handbook of the Sociology of Emotions*, Vol. 2, edited by J. E. Stets and J. H. Turner. New York: Springer. doi:10.1007/978–94–017–9130–4_13

Funkenstein, Daniel. 1955. "The Physiology of Fear and Anger." *Scientific American* 192:74–80. doi:10.1038/scientificamerican0555–74

Goffman, Erving. 1956. "Interpersonal Persuasion." Pp. 117–93 in *Group Processes*, edited by B. Schaffner. New York: Josiah Macy Foundation.

Goffman, Erving. 1959. *The Presentation of Self in Everyday Life*. Garden City, NJ: Doubleday/Anchor.

Goffman, Erving. 1967. *Interaction Ritual*. New York: Doubleday.

Goodwin, Jeff, and James M. Jasper. 2007. "Emotions and Social Movements." Pp. 611–35 in *Handbook of the Sociology of Emotions*, edited by J. E. Stets and J. H. Turner. New York: Springer.

Gordon, Steven L. 1981. "The Sociology of Sentiments and Emotion." Pp. 562–92 in *Social Psychology: Sociological Perspectives*, edited by M. Rosenberg and R. H. Turner. New York: Basic Books.

Gordon, Steven L. 1990. "Social Structural Effects on Emotions." Pp. 145–79 in *Research Agendas in the Sociology of Emotions*, edited by T. D. Kemper. Albany: State University of New York Press.

Harlow, Roxanna. 2003. "'Race Doesn't Matter, But...': The Effect of Race on Professors' Experiences and Emotion Management in the Undergraduate College Classroom." *Social Psychology Quarterly* 66:348–63. doi:10.2307/1519834

Heise, David R. 1977. "Social Action as the Control of Affect." *Behavioral Science* 22:163–77. doi:10.1002/bs.3830220303

Heise, David R. 2002. "Understanding Social Interaction with Affect Control Theory." Pp. 17–40 in *New Directions in Sociological Theory*, edited by J. Berger and M. Zelditch. Boulder, CO: Rowman & Littlefield.

Heise, David R. 2014. "Cultural Variations in Sentiments." *SpringerPlus* 3(1):170. doi:10.1186/2193–1801–3–170

Heise, David R., and Cassandra Calhan. 1995. "Emotion Norms in Interpersonal Events." *Social Psychology Quarterly* 58:223–40. doi:10.2307/2787125

Heise, David R., and Brian Weir. 1999. "A Test of Symbolic Interactionist Predictions about Emotions in Imagined Situations." *Symbolic Interaction* 22:129–61. doi:10.1525/si.1999.22.2.139

Hochschild, Arlie R. 1979. "Emotion Work, Feeling Rules, and Social Structure." *American Journal of Sociology* 85:551–75. doi:10.1086/227049

Hochschild, Arlie R. 1983. *The Managed Heart: Commercialization of Human Feelings*. Berkley: University of California Press.

Illouz, Eva, Daniel Gilon, and Mattan Shachak. 2014. "Emotions and Cultural Theory." Pp. 221–43 in *Handbook of the Sociology of Emotions*, Vol. 2, edited by J. E. Stets and J. H. Turner. New York: Springer. doi:10.1007/978–94–017–9130–4_11

Izard, Carroll E. 1977. *Human Emotions*. New York: Plenum Press. doi:10.1007/978–1–4899–2209–0

Johnson, Eric J., and Amos Tversky. 1983. "Affect Generalization and the Perception of Risk." *Journal of Personality and Social Psychology* 45:20–31. doi:10.1037/0022–3514.45.1.20

Kang, Miliann. 2003. "The Managed Hand: The Commercialization of Bodies and

Emotions in Korean Immigrant–Owned Nail Salons." *Gender & Society* 17(6):820–39. doi:10.1177/0891243203257632

Kemper, Theodore D. 1978. *A Social Interactional Theory of Emotions*. New York: Wiley.

Kemper, Theodore D. 1987. "How Many Emotions Are There? Wedding the Social and Automatic Components." *American Journal of Sociology* 93:263–89. doi:10.1086/228745

Kemper, Theodore D. 1990. "Social Relations and Emotions: A Structural Approach." Pp. 207–37 in *Research Agendas in the Sociology of Emotions*, edited by T. D. Kemper. Albany: State University of New York Press.

Kemper, Theodore D. 1991. "Predicting Emotions from Social Relations." *Social Psychology Quarterly* 54:330–42. doi:10.2307/2786845

Kemper, Theodore D. 2007. "Power and Status and the Power-Status Theory of Emotions." Pp. 87–113 in *Handbook of the Sociology of Emotions*, edited by J. E. Stets and J. H. Turner. New York: Springer.

Kemper, Theodore D. 2014. "Status, Power, and Felicity." Pp. 155–77 in *Handbook of the Sociology of Emotions*, Vol. 2, edited by J. E. Stets and J. H. Turner. New York: Springer.

Kessler, Ronald C. 2003. "Epidemiology of Women and Depression." *Journal of Affective Disorders* 74(l):5–13. doi:10.1016/S0165-0327(02)00426-3

Kitayama, Shinobu, Batja Mesquita, and Mayumi Karasawa. 2006. "Cultural Affordances and Emotional Experience: Social Engaging and Disengaging Emotions in Japan and the United States." *Journal of Personality and Social Psychology* 91:890–903. doi:10.1037/0022-3514.91.5.890

Klandermans, Bert, Jojaanneke van der Toorn, and Jacquelien van Stekelenburg. 2008. "Embeddedness and Identity: How Immigrants Turn Grievances into Action." *American Sociological Review* 73:992–1012. doi:10.1177/000312240807300606

Lazarus, Richard S. 1990. "Constructs of the Mind in Adaptation." Pp. 3–20 in *Psychological and Biological Approaches to Emotion*, edited by N. L. Stein, B. Leventhal, and T. Trabasso. Hillsdale, NJ: Erlbaum.

LeDoux, Joseph. 1996. *The Emotional Brain: The Mysterious Underpinnings of Emotional Life*. New York: Simon and Schuster.

Leu, Janxin, Jennifer Wang, and Kelly Koo. 2011. "Are Positive Emotions Just as 'Positive' across Cultures?" *Emotion (Washington, D.C.)* 11:994–99. doi:10.1037/a0021332

Lively, Kathryn J. 2000. "Reciprocal Emotion Management: Working Together to Maintain Stratification in Private Law Firms." *Work and Occupations* 27:32–63. doi:10.1177/0730888400027001003

Lively, Kathryn J. 2008. "Status and Emotional Expression: The Influence of 'Others' in Hierarchical Work Settings." Pp. 287–300 in *Social Structure and Emotion*, edited by J. Clay-Warner and D. T. Robinson. Burlington, MA: Elsevier.

Lively, Kathryn J., and David R. Heise. 2014. "Emotions in Affect Control Theory." Pp. 51–75 in *Handbook of the Sociology of Emotions*, Vol. 2, edited by J. E. Stets and J. H. Turner. New York: Springer. doi:10.1007/978-94-017-9130-4_4

Lively, Kathryn J., and Brian Powell. 2006. "Emotional Expression at Work and at Home: Domain, Status, or Individual Characteristics?" *Social Psychology Quarterly* 69:17–38. doi:10.1177/019027250606900103

Lively, Kathryn J., and Emi A. Weed. 2014. "Emotion Management: Sociological Insight into What, How, Why, and to What End?" *Emotion Review* 6:202–7. doi:10.1177/1754073914522864

Lofland, Lyn H. 1985. "The Social Shaping of Emotion: The Case of Grief." *Symbolic Interaction* 8:171–90. doi:10.1525/si.1985.8.2.171

MacKinnon, Neil J. 1994. *Symbolic Interaction as Affect Control*. Albany: State University of New York Press.

Mandler, George. 1990. "A Constructivist Theory of Emotion." Pp. 21–44 in *Psychological and Biological Approaches to Emotion*, edited by N. L. Stein, B. Leventhal, and T. Trabasso. Hillsdale, NJ: Erlbaum.

Matsumoto, David, and Hyi Sung Hwang. 2012. "Culture and Emotion: The Integration of Biological and Cultural Contributions." *Journal of Cross-Cultural Psychology* 43:91–118. doi:10.1177/0022022111420147

Mesquita, Bahtia, Nico H. Frijda, and Klaus R. Scherer. 1997. "Culture and Emotion." Pp. 255–97 in *Basic Processes and Human Development*. Vol. 2, *Handbook of Cross-Cultural Psychology*, edited by P. Dasen and T. S. Saraswathi. Boston: Allyn & Bacon.

Mesquita, Bahtia, and Maymi Karasawa. 2002. "Different Emotional Lives." *Cognition and Emotion* 16:127–41. doi:10.1080/0269993014000176

Morgan, Rick L., and David Heise. 1988. "Structure of Emotions." *Social Psychology Quarterly* 51:19–31. doi:10.2307/2786981

Osgood, Charles E., George J. Suci, and Percy H. Tannenbaum. 1957. *The Measurement of Meaning*. Urbana: University of Illinois Press.

Parkinson, Brian, Agneta Fischer, and Antony S. R. Manstead. 2005. *Emotion in Social Relations: Cultural, Group, and Interpersonal Processes*. New York: Psychology Press.

Penner, Louis A., John F. Dovidio, Jane A. Piliavin, and David A. Schroeder. 2005. "Prosocial Behavior: Multilevel Perspectives." *Annual Review of Psychology* 56:365–92. doi:10.1146/annurev.psych.56.091103.070141

Phelps, Elizabeth A. 2006. "Emotion and Cognition: Insights from Studies of the Human Amygdala." *Annual Review of Psychology* 57:27–53. doi:10.1146/annurev.psych.56.091103.070234

Plutchik, Robert H. 1980. *Emotion: A Psycho-evolutionary Synthesis*. New York: Harper & Row.

Reisenzein, Rainer. 1983. "The Schachter Theory of Emotion: Two Decades Later." *Psychological Bulletin* 94(2):239–64. doi:10.1037/0033-2909.94.2.239

Robinson, Dawn T., Lynn Smith-Lovin, and Olga Tsoudis. 1994. "Heinous Crime or Unfortunate Accident? The Effects of Remorse on Reponses to Mock Criminal Confessions." *Social Forces* 73:175–90. doi:10.2307/2579922

Robinson, Dawn T., Lynn Smith-Lovin, and Allison K. Wisecup. 2007. "Affect Control Theory." Pp. 179–202 in *Handbook of the Sociology of Emotions*, edited by J. E. Stets and J. H. Turner. New York: Springer.

Rosenfield, Sarah. 1999. "Gender and Mental Health: Do Women Have More Psychopathology, Men More, or Both the Same (and Why)?" Pp. 349–60 in *Handbook for the Study of Mental Health: Social Contexts, Theories, and Systems*, edited by A. V. Horwitz and T. L. Scheid. Cambridge, England: Cambridge University Press.

Ross, Catherine E., and Marieke Van Willigen. 1996. "Gender, Parenthood, and Anger." *Journal of Marriage and the Family* 58(3):572–84. doi:10.2307/353718

Rubin, Zick. 1973. *Liking and Loving: An Invitation to Social Psychology*. New York: Holt, Rinehart and Winston.

Russell, James A. 1991. "Culture and the Categorization of Emotions." *Psychological Bulletin* 110:426–50. doi:10.1037/0033-2909.110.3.426

Russell, James A. 2003. "Core Affect and the Psychological Construction of Emotion." *Psychological Review* 110:145–72. doi:10.1037/0033-295X.110.1.145

Schachter, Stanley, and Jerome A. Singer. 1962. "Cognitive, Social, and Physiological Determinants of Emotional State." *Psychological Review* 69:379–99. doi:10.1037/h0046234

Scheff, Thomas J. 1990. *Microsociology: Discourse, Emotion, and Social Structure*. Chicago: University of Chicago Press.

Schieman, Scott. 2007. "Anger." Pp. 493–515 in *Handbook of the Sociology of Emotions*, edited by J. E. Stets and J. H. Turner. New York: Springer.

Shields, Stephanie A. 2002. *Speaking from the Heart: Gender and the Social Meaning of Emotion.* New York: Cambridge University Press.

Shields, Stephanie A., Dallas N. Garner, Brooke Di Leone, and Alena M. Hadley. 2007. "Gender and Emotion." Pp. 63–86 in *Handbook of the Sociology of Emotions*, edited by J. E. Stets and J. H. Turner. New York: Springer.

Simon, Robin W. 2002. "Revisiting the Relationships among Gender, Marital Status, and Mental Health." *American Journal of Sociology* 107:1065–96. doi:10.1086/339225

Simon, Robin W., and Kathryn Lively. 2010. "Sex, Anger and Depression." *Social Forces* 88:1543–68. doi:10.1353/sof.2010.0031

Simon, Robin W., and Leda E. Nath. 2004. "Gender and Emotion in the United States: Do Men and Women Differ in Self-Reports of Feelings and Expressive Behavior?" *American Journal of Sociology* 109:1137–76. doi:10.1086/382111

Singer, Jefferson A., and Peter Salovey. 1988. "Mood and Memory: Evaluating the Network Theory of Affect." *Clinical Psychology Review* 8(2):211–51. doi:10.1016/0272-7358(88)90060-8

Sloan, Melissa M. 2004. "The Effects of Occupational Characteristics on the Experience and Expression of Anger in the Workplace." *Work and Occupations* 31:38–72. doi:10.1177/0730888403260734

Smith, Allen, and Sherryl Kleinman. 1989. "Managing Emotions in Medical School: Students' Contacts with the Living and the Dead." *Social Psychology Quarterly* 52:56–69. doi:10.2307/2786904

Smith, Tiffany Watt. 2015. *The Book of Human Emotions.* New York: Little, Brown and Company.

Smith-Lovin, Lynn. 1995. "The Sociology of Affect and Emotion." Pp. 118–48 in *Sociological Perspectives on Social Psychology*, edited by K. Cook, G. Fine, and J. House. Boston: Allyn & Bacon.

Smith-Lovin, Lynn, and David R. Heise. 1988. *Analyzing Social Interaction: Advances in Affect Control Theory.* New York: Gordon & Breach.

Staske, Shirley A. 1998. "The Normalization of Problematic Emotion in Conversations between Close Relational Partners: Interpersonal Emotion Work." *Symbolic Interaction* 21:59–86. doi:10.1525/si.1998.21.1.59

Stearns, Carol Z., and Peter N. Stearns. 1986. *Anger: The Struggle for Emotional Control in America's History.* Chicago: University of Chicago Press.

Stets, Jan E. 2003. "Emotions and Sentiment." Pp. 309–38 in *Handbook of Social Psychology*, edited by J. DeLamater. New York: Kluwer Academic/Plenum.

Stets, Jan E. 2005. "Examining Emotions and Identity Theory." *Social Psychology Quarterly* 68:39–56. doi:10.1177/019027250506800104

Stets, Jan E., and Michael J. Carter. 2012. "A Theory of the Self for the Sociology of Morality." *American Sociological Review* 77:120–40. doi:10.1177/0003122411433762

Stets, Jan E., and Ryan Trettevik. 2014. "Emotions in Identity Theory." Pp. 33–49 in *Handbook of the Sociology of Emotions*, Vol. 2, edited by J. E. Stets and J. H. Turner. New York: Springer. doi:10.1007/978-94-017-9130-4_3

Summers-Effler, Erika. 2005. "The Role of Emotions in Sustaining Commitment to Social Movement Activity: Building and Maintaining Solidarity in a Catholic Worker House." Pp. 135–49 in *Emotions and Social Movements*, edited by H. Flam and D. King. New York: Rutledge.

Summers-Effler, Erika. 2007. "Ritual Theory." Pp. 136–54 in *Handbook of the Sociology of Emotions*, edited by J. E. Stets and J. H. Turner. New York: Springer.

Thamm, Robert A. 2007. "The Classification of Emotions." Pp. 11–37 in *Handbook of the Sociology of Emotions*, edited by J. E. Stets and J. H. Turner. New York: Springer.

Thoits, Peggy A. 1989. "The Sociology of Emotions." *Annual Review of Sociology* 15:317–42. doi:10.1146/annurev.so.15.080189.001533

Thoits, Peggy A. 1990. "Emotional Deviance: Research Agendas." Pp. 180–203 in *Research*

Agendas in the Sociology of Emotions, edited by T. D. Kemper. Albany: State University of New York Press.

Timmers, Monique, Agneta Fischer, and Antony Manstead. 2003. "Ability Versus Vulnerability: Beliefs about Men's and Women's Emotional Behavior." *Cognition and Emotion* 17:41–63. doi:10.1080/02699930302277

Tsoudis, Olga, and Lynn Smith-Lovin. 1998. "How Bad Was It? The Effects of Victim and Perpetrator Emotion on Responses to Criminal Court Vignettes." *Social Forces* 77:695–722. doi:10.2307/3005544

Turner, Jonathan H. 1999. "Toward a General Sociological Theory of Emotions." *Journal for the Theory of Social Behaviour* 29(2):133–61. doi:10.1111/1468-5914.00095

Turner, Jonathan H. 2000. *On the Origins of Human Emotions: A Sociological Inquiry into the Evolution of Human Affect*. Stanford, CA: Stanford University Press.

Turner, Jonathan H. 2014. "The Evolution of Human Emotions." Pp. 11–31 in *Handbook of the Sociology of Emotions*, Vol. 2, edited by J. E. Stets and J. H. Turner. New York: Springer. doi:10.1007/978-94-017-9130-4_2

Turner, Jonathan H., and Jan E. Stets. 2005. *The Sociology of Emotions*. New York: Cambridge University Press. doi:10.1017/CBO9780511819612

Weber, Max. [1924] 1978. *Economy and Society*, Vols. I and II, edited by Guenther Roth and Claus Wittich. Reprint, Berkeley: University of California Press.

Weiner, Bernard. 1985. "An Attributional Theory of Achievement Motivation and Emotion." *Psychological Review* 92:548–73. doi:10.1037/0033-295X.92.4.548

Wharton, Amy S. 1993. "The Affective Consequences of Service Work." *Work and Occupations* 20:205–32. doi:10.1177/0730888493020002004

Wharton, Amy S. 1999. "The Psychosocial Consequences of Emotion Labor." *The Annals of the American Academy of Political and Social Science* 561:158–76. doi:10.1177/0002716299561001011

Wharton, Amy S. 2014. "Work and Emotions." Pp. 335–58 in *Handbook of Sociology of Emotions*, Vol. 2, edited by J. E. Stets and J. H. Turner. New York: Springer.

Wierzbicka, Anna. 1999. *Emotions Across Language and Cultures: Diversity and Universals*. New York: Cambridge University Press. doi:10.1017/CBO9780511521256

Wingfield, Adia Harvey. 2010. "Are Some Emotions Marked 'White Only'? Racialized Feeling Rules in Professional Workplaces." *Social Problems* 57:251–68. doi:10.1525/sp.2010.57.2.251

Zajonc, Robert B. 1980. "Feeling and Thinking: Preferences Need No Inferences." *The American Psychologist* 35:151–75. doi:10.1037/0003-066X.35.2.151

Zajonc, Robert B. 1998. "Emotions." Pp. 591–634 in *Handbook of Social Psychology*, 4th ed., Vol. 1, edited by D. T. Gilbert, S. T. Fiske, and G. Lindzey. New York: McGraw-Hill.

Status Processes in Groups

We both like the *Harry Potter* books. Not only does the author, J. K. Rowling, tell a gripping story from beginning to end, the *Harry Potter* saga also illustrates nicely how status processes, discussed in this chapter, affect behavior in face-to-face interaction. Cathy asked her 10-year-old daughter at the time to tell her who has more status at Hogwarts School of Witchcraft and Wizardry: squibs, pure-bloods, muggle-born, or half-bloods? That is, which category of people are thought to be better, more competent, and more worthy by the Hogwarts students and faculty in general? She said that it would go in this order from high status to low status: pure-bloods (people who possess magical powers and whose parents are both wizards–witches), half-bloods (people who possess magical powers and have one parent who is a wizard or witch and one parent who is a muggle [i.e., not a wizard or witch]), muggle-born (people who possess magical powers even though their parents are not wizards or witches), and squibs (people who do not possess magical powers despite having parents who are both wizards–witches). In this case, wizard–witch (or magical birth) and muggle (nonmagical birth) are two states of a characteristic that are differentially valued at Hogwarts, where those of magical birth are perceived as more valuable, worthy, and competent than nonmagical born. In addition, however, possession of magical powers is also perceived as an important characteristic, and is related to perceptions of worthiness and competence.

These perceptions of status can be seen through the eyes of Malfoy, a pure-blood student, in his disdain for Hermoine, a muggle-born student. He does not see her as a worthy student at Hogwarts. But muggle-born like Hermoine have higher status and worth than squibs like Argus Filch (the caretaker of Hogwarts) because they possess a specific characteristic even though they are muggle-born—they have magical powers that squibs do not have. These powers are an important and relevant skill to possess at Hogwarts School of Witchcraft and Wizardry.

There are other status distinctions found at Hogwarts. For example, Dumbledore, the headmaster of the school and the most influential wizard, has the highest status and garners the most respect as the pure-blood wizard who runs Hogwarts. Also, professors at the school have higher status as a group than the students. Interestingly, another character, Hagrid, is part wizard and part giant. He occupies a unique place at Hogwarts, as he is well loved by Dumbledore. Although pure-bloods like Malfoy and Malfoy's father have little respect for Hagrid, having Dumbledore's respect increases Hagrid's status in the eyes of a majority of students.

In contrast to the context of Hogwarts, in the regular, mundane world, those without wizardry heritage or magical powers are thought to have the most worth, while wizards and witches are highly disdained, as clearly professed by Harry's aunt and uncle, Petunia and Vernon Dursley. Petunia and Vernon do not like Harry at all and believe that his magical powers are evil. Harry is given little respect in the Dursley household and treated much like a servant. Dudley, the Dursleys' son and a muggle without magical powers, is treated like a spoiled prince. Perceived status varies, then, across contexts.

This example sets the stage for our discussion of how status processes affect interaction in groups. **Status** is defined as "a position in a set of things that are rank-ordered by a standard of value" (Ridgeway and Walker 1995:281). In this chapter, we focus on the relative rankings of status between individuals in groups. Those who have high status in a group are perceived to be more *worthy and highly esteemed* than members who have low status. We examine how status processes explain much about individual behaviors in groups, how status inequality in groups can be reduced, and how characteristics acquire status value in the first place. Our purpose is to show how status processes often operate in groups to perpetuate and maintain social inequality in society.

Before we examine how status affects interaction, we begin with a definition of the concept, *group*, followed by a discussion of group conformity. Within groups, members exert influence with each other; they also often pressure each other to comply with particular beliefs or actions. This influence and group pressure process was first studied in terms of its consequences: conformity in groups. Later, emphasis shifted to an examination of how status processes in groups affect influence and compliance.

How Are Groups Defined?

We are born into groups; we learn to name things in the world around us, to play, and to work in groups throughout our entire lives. Much of our waking life is spent in groups, be it in dyads with just one other person, in small groups with a few people, or in large groups, such as dorm or sorority or fraternity house meetings. But what are they? Is a bunch of people in a movie theater or individuals in an elevator a group? What about a sports team or a set of friends who go out to dinner?

A **group** is defined as interaction involving at least two people (Forsyth 2014). In addition, groups have the following attributes. First, there must a **conscious identification of membership**—that is, the group members think of themselves as belonging to the group, and the other members also recognize them as members (Lickel et al. 2000). Second, the members must **interact** with one another, thereby communicating and influencing one another. This communication may be face-to-face, or through other means, such as a chat room or Skype. Third, members have **shared goals**, requiring some level of interdependence with one another in order to attain those goals. The goals may be very diffuse, such as hanging out at a club, or very specific, such as working on a class project. And finally, the members **share a set of expectations, rules, or norms** that limit their behavior and guide their actions (Cartwright and Zander 1968). That is, group norms regulate interaction and often coordinate behavior.

Examples of groups are a set of friends going to a concert together, a committee working on a project, and individuals at a community action meeting. Thus, groups are not just a collection of individuals; they have a patterned set of relations and behaviors. Individuals in an elevator, then, are not a group by the attributes just named, but if they got stuck in an elevator together, they most likely will become a group!

Much of the research on interaction in groups focuses on **small groups**, defined as having anywhere from 2 to 20 members. In addition, much of the early work in groups focused on conformity in groups.

What Is Conformity, and Why Do People Conform in Groups?

Conformity is defined as a change in behavior or beliefs as a result of real or imagined group pressure. Typically, conformity is said to occur when a group member adheres to the group norms and standards (that is, expected ways of behavior in the group) (DeLamater and Myers 2007). Is conformity bad? Is it good? Is it neither? It depends. Conformity is often associated with a negative connotation in the United States, as it seems contrary to the notion of independence and individuality. Who wants to be called a conformist? But in most of our everyday interaction we conform to norms that tell us how we are expected to behave in certain situations, and this is often a good thing.

For example, there are specific norms that students follow in classrooms, and if they do not, this disrupts class dynamics. Chaos would ensue if people failed to conform to interaction norms, such as those pertaining to waiting in grocery lines, adhering to traffic lights, or conducting meetings. On the other hand, sometimes people's conformity in groups has negative results. For example, a peer group may pressure one of its members to bully someone on the playground or on social media. Or we may throw our glass bottle away in the trash rather than recycle because everyone else around us is doing so, even though we would have recycled if we were alone. Finally, some conformity is neither good nor bad—it just is— such as when a group of 10-year-old boy soccer players sport the same haircut (although this behavior may also increase their identification with the group!).

Why do people conform in small groups working on a task together? Two sets of early laboratory studies set the stage for understanding why people conform under certain conditions. The first set of studies was conducted by Sherif (1935, 1936) in his *autokinetic experiments*. In the first part of the study, participants entered individually into a darkened room in a laboratory to participate on a perceptual task that involved estimating how far a pinpoint of light moves on the wall. This task involves a physical phenomenon called the *autokinetic effect* (which means "moves by itself"). It occurs when an individual stares at a pinpoint of light in a darkened room, and it looks as if the light is moving in an erratic fashion, but it never actually moves (because of the way our eyes are shaped). Sherif first asked participants to estimate how far the light moved over a series of trials when they were alone in the darkened room. This set of estimates provided the basis for a stable range for each individual. Individuals' ranges varied considerably from one another, from a few inches to a foot or more. In effect, Sherif used an **ambiguous task** in his studies, where the correct answer is uncertain.

After establishing a stable range, Sherif had each participant join a group of people and once again asked each individual to estimate the movement of the light. For each group, Sherif saw that a common standard emerged. As a result of the uncertainty of the task, group members began to use each other's estimates as a basis for defining the situation. In fact, each group developed its own arbitrary standard, and members used this frame of reference in their judgments. Then a week or so later, the participants came back to the laboratory setting alone and were asked to once again estimate the light's movement. The participants used the group standard for their own individual judgments, showing that the group norm still influenced them even though time had passed.

In the Sherif studies, participants were uncertain of the "correct" response and, therefore, used information provided by group members to shape their own response. This type of influence is called **informational influence** and occurs when a group member accepts information from other group members as evidence of reality. Group members use information from others when they are uncertain about the situation and there are no objective standards to guide judgment. Often, informational influence leads to **internalization**; as a consequence of being motivated by the desire to be right, individuals come to actually believe in what the group has influenced the individual to do, and are motivated by the desire to be right. People experience informational influence in contexts where they do not know how to solve complex problems, and rely on others' help, or in crisis situations when decisions must be made quickly. In these cases, people rely on group members who are perceived to be more knowledgeable about the task or decision, as these "experts" are seen as credible. Contexts such as religious groups, self-help groups, political groups, and peer groups provide information to address complex issues and consequently exert change in behavior or beliefs of group members.

The second set of studies is Asch's (1951, 1955, 1957) *line estimate conformity studies*. Asch created groups in a laboratory setting, consisting of eight members, and asked them to perform a task that was very easy and "objective" in the sense that 99% of the time people chose the correct answer when they were alone. The line judgment task involved projecting a standard line and three comparison lines and then asking the participants to judge which one of the comparison lines matched the standard line. Unlike Sherif's ambiguous task, this task was a simple and **unambiguous task** in that the answers were straightforward. Importantly, also in these studies, the experimenter had instructed all but one of the group members on which comparison line to choose. The focal participant (otherwise referred to as the naïve participant) did not know that the other group members were "confederates" working for the experimenter. These confederates all publicly announced an incorrect answer before the participant chose an answer. The task consisted of 18 trials; the confederates gave a correct response on 6 of the trials and incorrectly responded on the other 12 trials. Naïve participants likely knew the correct answer, but they had heard all the other members give a different answer. This situation created pressure on the participant to conform to the incorrect answers.

Indeed, results showed that that in the 12 trials, nearly one third of the participants' responses were incorrect, compared to the individual error rate of less than 1%. Overall, 75% of the participants gave at least one incorrect answer across the 12 trials. This was somewhat surprising, given that the task was unambiguous and the stakes were not high. Interviews were conducted, asking participants why they had conformed. The majority of participants focused on the discrepancy they felt between the group majority's judgment and their own. Most of them complied publicly with the majority but privately disagreed with their view. Some, however, wondered if they had misunderstood the instructions, and some even questioned their eyesight. Many of the participants conformed to the

opinions of the other group members mainly in order to avoid being embarrassed, ridiculed, or laughed at by the majority. They wanted to be accepted by
the majority—or at least not publicly rejected.

This type of influence is referred to as **normative influence**. Members
conform to the expectations of the other group members in order to avoid punishments or receive social rewards that are contingent on abiding by these expectations (Janes and Olson 2000). Often, normative influence leads to compliance.
Compliance occurs when a group member's behavior conforms to the behavior
of the other group members, even though he or she privately disagrees (i.e., there
is no change in his or her private opinion). Compliance is motivated by an individual's desire to gain rewards or avoid punishments; it is often only as long-lived
as the promise of reward or the possibility of punishment.

There are three caveats:

1. Replications of Asch studies over time in the United States show that levels of conformity steadily declined from the 1950s through the 1980s. In
   addition, cross-cultural studies show that levels of conformity are higher
   in countries that are characterized as more collectivist cultures (e.g., Japan)
   with emphasis on shared goals than individualist cultures (e.g., United
   States) with emphasis on personal goals (but see Bond and Smith [1996] for
   discussion of limitations of these results). More recent studies show that the
   relationship between culture, preference, and behavior is complicated. For
   example, in one study Japanese participants conformed to the majority only
   when the negative social implications for not conforming were clear; when
   they were not clear and they believed their behavior had no implications for
   others, they had a preference for nonconforming behavior (Hashimoto, Li,
   and Yamagishi 2011).

2. Although nearly one third of the participants' responses were incorrect in Asch's
   studies, this also means that about two thirds of the time participants resisted
   group pressure. Also, 25% of the participants consistently never went along
   with majority. We sometimes overemphasize conformity and de-emphasize
   nonconformity behavior (for a discussion of this trend, see Griggs 2015).

3. Some scholars suggest that because some of Asch's participants said they
   were uncertain of their answers, this indicates that these participants did
   not experience normative influence but rather were motivated to adopt the
   same opinions as others in their group (Turner et al. 1987; see Chapter 12
   for a discussion of ingroup–outgroup identification).

In summary, the two types of influence suggest different motivations for conformity. Under informational influence, people want to reduce their uncertainty
and have a better understanding of the situation. Under normative influence,
people often are motivated to conform in groups when they want to be positively
evaluated by the group and/or avoid rejection, and want to have good relationships with others (Hogg and Cooper 2003).

What Are Some Factors That Affect Conformity in Groups?

As a result of this early work on conformity, Asch and other scholars investigated factors that affect whether or not individual members conform in groups.

Importantly, the punchline of all the conformity studies is that **group-level factors** (i.e., specific features of the group, such as the size of the unanimous majority or the status of a group) are much more important than individual-level factors (such as personality characteristics like shyness or intelligence) in predicting conformity.

Imagine that you are in a seminar on American novelists in the second half of 20th century. The class consists of a total of 10 students. The professor asks the class, what American novelist wrote *The Joy Luck Club*? You know this answer: Amy Tan. Before you can answer, however, the other nine students suggest that it is another American novelist, Maxine Hong Kingston. You may begin to doubt your answer, particularly because all the other students suggest Kingston. Suppose that eight students said Kingston, while one other student answered Gish Jen. In this second situation, one other student holds a different answer than the majority besides you. In which context would you be more likely to stand up to group pressure and say, with confidence, Amy Tan?

The Asch studies addressed these types of situations. Indeed, Asch examined the effect of a **unanimous majority** on conformity, where all the group members disagreed with the one lone member. A unanimous majority, even when the task is unambiguous and straightforward, creates strong pressure to conform. A second group factor that affects conformity pressure is the **size of the unanimous majority**. Specifically, as the size of the unanimous majority increases, so too does the strength of conformity pressure and, thereby, also the actual conformity by the individual. Specifically, the pressure to conform is much greater when you have three people who oppose you versus only one other person. Typically, this conformity pressure increases until the majority size reaches three to five members and then levels off (Asch 1955).

Third, group members are less likely to conform when there is a **breach in the majority** opinion than when the group's majority is unanimous. That is, if there is just one other person who holds a different opinion than the majority, even if this opinion is not the same opinion as the minority member (like the Amy Tan example mentioned previously), this reduces the pressure to conform. Why? This breach raises doubt in the majority opinion, and has a liberating effect on the behavior of the members (Allen and Levine 1969). An interesting case related to this factor was a U.S. Supreme Court justice ruling in the case of *Williams v. Florida* (1970). In this case, the Supreme Court ruled that juries composed of 6 jurors were equivalent to jurors composed of 12 jurors in terms of things such as verdict ratio, quality of the deliberations, and the ability of dissenters to resist the pressure of the majority. Social scientists criticized this ruling. The Asch studies were cited, stating that a minority of 1 against 5 faces more conformity pressure than a minority of 2 against 10 because in the latter there is a breach in the majority, allowing for a greater possibility for resistance to majority opinion compared to a unanimous majority context. A number of studies argued that a 6-person jury was fundamentally different from a 12-person jury, in part, because of the potential difference in conformity pressure between the two contexts.

Fourth, conformity pressure is stronger in **groups that have high status**. High-status groups are attractive because they are highly prestigious; people are highly motivated to stay in these groups. As a result, they are more likely to conform to group norms in high-status than low-status groups.

Finally, one important individual-level factor that affects conformity in groups is the individual's perceived level of expertise or **perceived competence**

relative to the other group members on the group task. Members who perceive themselves to be more competent and skilled at the group's task relative to the other group members are more likely to resist conformity pressure than those perceived as less skilled, even in situations where multiple less competent people are exerting pressure (Melamed and Savage 2013). Resistance is based on the degree to which they believe themselves to be more competent than other group members (Ettinger et al. 1971). People who perceive themselves as competent at the group's task rely less on the judgment of others. As we shall see in this chapter, however, perceptions of competence that people have of themselves relative to others often stem from a number of social factors external to the group.

What Is the Process of Groupthink?

Groups sometimes make very poor decisions. Unfortunately, in many cases, poor decision-making occurs in very powerful and high-status groups, and these decisions have broad and powerful consequences. For example, the decision by the United States to escalate the Vietnam War is an example of faulty decision-making with extraordinary consequences. Other examples include the decision to invade Iraq in 2003, based on inconclusive information about Iraq's possession of weapons of mass destruction, and the space shuttle *Columbia* disaster in 2003, partly due to a failure to recognize the relevant concerns for safety brought to attention by NASA engineers. Why would such smart people make such gross errors in judgment?

Janis (1982) suggests that a process of groupthink may have, in part, produced these poor decisions. **Groupthink** refers to faulty thinking by group members when their desire to get along with one another and the leader of the group is greater than their desire to evaluate potential solutions realistically. Evaluating reasonable alternatives is overwhelmed by the pressures for unanimity within the group. Members do not want to question group consensus; as a result, they ignore differing opinions and alternatives and fail to weigh carefully the pros and cons of the decision. And the leader is often overly directive, sharing his or her opinion first rather than initially hearing the opinions of the group, including important minority opinions (those ideas that differ from the majority).

In the case of the Iraq War, no weapons of mass destruction and production facilities were discovered. The U.S. Senate Select Committee on Intelligence (a bipartisan committee) reviewed the evidence and concluded that groupthink was an important factor in this poor decision-making. The committee presumed that Iraq had these weapons; as a result, when they received conflicting evidence, they ignored it, and when they received ambiguous information they interpreted it as showing conclusively the existence of a weapons program. Some also argue that President Bush surrounded himself with people who had ideas and opinions similar to his own instead of people who offered varying or dissenting opinions.

Groupthink draws attention to the availability and processing of opposing viewpoints and contradictory information. More generally, current studies of conformity examine underlying cognitive processes, such as those discussed in Chapter 5. This work includes research on the effects of unconscious priming processes (Pendry and Carrick 2001) and encoding processes in memory (Hoffman et al. 2001). For example, in an experiment, Pendry and Carrick (2001) examined how much participants conformed through a process of priming by exposing their participants to either a "punk" stimulus (representing nonconformity), an "accountant" stimulus (representing the orderly conformist), or no priming stimulus. They used a task somewhere in between Asch and Sherif's in terms of degree of ambiguity—counting the number of beeps they heard. When participants actually heard 100 beeps, the confederates reported between 120 and 125 beeps. Interestingly, the accountant-primed participants conformed to the confederates' estimates of the number of beeps much more often than the participants in the punk-primed condition and in the no stimulus condition. It may be that being exposed to nonconformists in groups could increase more individualized thinking and behavior.

Group conformity studies enhanced our understanding of when and why group members change their opinions and behavior in groups. More recently, scholars pay attention to group structures that lead to influence in groups. In this chapter, we discuss one of these structures: status structures.

Status Processes in Groups

We focus on the relative rankings of status between individuals in groups. Those who have high status in a group are perceived to be more worthy and highly esteemed than members who have low status. But how can you tell that an individual in a group has more status than another individual? What are some *observable signs of status*?

Cathy is a fairly passionate science fiction fan. She reads quite a bit of science fiction (from science fiction authors such as Orson Scott Card, George R. R. Martin, Marge Piercy, and Ursula K. Le Guin) but also is an avid fan of science fiction shows and films (such as *Babylon 5, The X-Files, Fringe, V, Alien, The Terminator, District 9, The Matrix,* and *Avatar*). A few years ago, she ran across a blog for fans who attend one of the largest comic/science fiction/fantasy conventions in the United States, called Comic-Con International. Many science fiction and comic book fans participate in this convention. While online, she read a fan's blog attending the annual Comic-Con in San Diego, 2009. This fan lamented that going in "standard" dress instead of dressing up as a character does not earn you "street cred with the dorks at the Con," nor does it let you interact with them on the same level. The fan vowed to attend next year's Comic-Con in either "full spandex Spiderman" or "Stormtrooper" outfits.

This blog entry illustrates the importance of dressing up in costume as a symbol of status at this convention. From this fan's perspective, if you dress up as Spiderman at the convention instead of standard dress, people will respond to you with a bit more respect than if you do not dress up. Status has much to do with whether or not you are wearing a costume in this particular context. Of course, wearing a Spiderman costume to a board meeting probably will not serve the same purpose, unless it is a board meeting of a comics company. In this context, then, an observable sign of status is the costume.

There are many other observable signs of status. You may detect a person's high status by how articulate she is in her speech, the confidence in her tone, or the fact that she talks the most in the group. You may also notice that her opinions are more positively evaluated and that she uses direct eye contact as she speaks with other group members. It may be that this person indicates something about themselves that also indicates status. She may declare that she has a degree from Princeton, implying high intelligence. Or she may note that she happens to know how to do the group task and has done it before. Or it may be that you notice other characteristics that are related to status, such as the person's gender, race, education, or social class. Finally, it becomes clear to you that this member has the most influence in the group.

In this section, we will discuss how status structures develop in groups, including key observable signs of status, drawing upon classic and recent studies in status research. **Status structures,** or hierarchies, are "rank-ordered relationships between actors" (Ridgeway and Walker 1995:281). We then explore the consequences of these structures for interaction and decision-making. We will then examine how status structures are maintained and why they are difficult to change. Finally, we will see how characteristics, such as gender or race, may acquire status value—that is, how one category of people is believed to be more worthy and competent in general than another category of people. Importantly, if we understand how status processes operate in groups, we will better understand how social inequality is perpetuated and maintained, and can be changed, in societies. You will find yourself in many types of groups, at work, school, and in your community throughout your life. Understanding how status operates will help you recognize when members of your group are not heard when they should be heard and help you to use procedures in your groups to make good decisions for your group and beyond, rather than poor ones with negative consequences.

Early Studies on Status Structures

While Asch began his conformity studies in the 1940s, in the same decade, Robert Bales (1950) was conducting his seminal studies of interpersonal behavior in small groups. Bales recorded interaction in initially leaderless decision-making groups of three to seven members over multiple-hour periods. All group members consisted of white male sophomores at Harvard University (at this time, a majority of group studies focused on white men or boys only). These sophomores were invited to participate in groups to discuss human relations problems (e.g., a case may involve an adolescent who has committed a serious crime but who comes from a disruptive background; after reading about the adolescent's history, the group must reach a decision about how this kid should be treated). In effect, Bales's groups were considered **homogeneous groups** because the members were very socially similar on a number of characteristics, such as gender, race, age, and socioeconomic status (including educational level, income, and occupational prestige). Bales audio recorded these discussions and then analyzed the patterns of conversation in the groups, noting who talked, to whom they talked, and what they were saying. Specifically, he recorded the following categories for each group member: offering opinions or ideas, asking questions, making positive statements such as agreeing or complimenting, and making negative statements such as disagreeing or showing tension.

Bales discovered that even in these homogeneous groups without formally designated leaders, status structures (also referred to as status hierarchies) developed quickly within the groups, where several members acquired more status than other members. That is, members could be ranked on who was perceived as more worthy and esteemed compared to other group members. These hierarchies stabilized and guided continued interaction. In these hierarchies, one or two of the members in the groups talked more than other members, and their ideas were taken more seriously and were more likely to be adopted by the group than ideas of other members. Also, those members who initiated the most participation in the beginning of the group interaction were more likely to continue this participation throughout the interaction.

Bales's studies were extremely important because they provided systematic empirical evidence of patterned inequalities that arise in groups. Specifically, he found that those members who *participated more* in group discussions were also more likely to be *given opportunities to participate* by other members; *receive positive evaluations of their ideas*; and, importantly, gain *influence* compared to the other group members (Bales 1950, 1970; Correll and Ridgeway 2003). These four behaviors were all positively correlated with one another. That is, members who talked more also received more positive evaluations of their opinions, and gained more influence than other members. These behaviors are considered four key *observable signs of status*. Bales's work stimulated research that focuses on how status structures develop, are maintained, and change in groups, as well as how these structures affect members' behavior and the decisions adopted by groups.

While Bales examined status structures in homogeneous groups, other studies also in the 1950s and 1960s examined status structures in **heterogeneous groups**, where members differed on social characteristics such as gender, occupation, and age. Strodtbeck, James, and Hawkins (1957), for example, examined status processes in mock juries. People randomly chosen from a list of those who were eligible to vote in a northeastern city were asked to participate in groups of 12 and deliberate on actual cases (social scientists are typically not allowed to observe actual juries). Specifically, Strodtbeck et al. (1957) examined who participated the most in these groups, who were perceived as most helpful in the jury deliberations, and who was picked jury foreperson. The members differed on two social characteristics: (1) gender and (2) occupation (i.e., professionals, clerical workers, skilled laborers, unskilled laborers). Strodtbeck et al. (1957) found that men and jurors who were in the most highly prestigious occupations also participated more, were seen as the most helpful, and were most likely to be picked jury foreperson.

Importantly, this study, and many other studies at the time, illustrated that members with higher status in the larger society tend to end up with higher status in groups as well. This process is called the **process of status generalization**. In the jury study, for example, men and professionals had an advantage in these mock juries even though gender and occupation were not related to the jury's task of determining outcomes for plaintiffs. The social characteristics of gender and occupation mattered in determining members' perceptions of who they thought to be the most worthy and competent members. Early research also showed that this process of status generalization is more likely to occur when (1) no member has any special skills relevant to the group task, (2) the members have no other information about the members other than their social characteristics, and (3) they have no prior history of interaction.

Scholars recognized that this process of status generalization is a very important problem for groups. It may be that, for example in the Strodtbeck et al. (1957) case, women and members other than professionals were equally or more competent and yet their opinions were not valued. Imagine a neighborhood meeting where neighbors gather to talk about zoning issues or parents talk about school policies at a PTA meeting. Whose opinions will most likely be heard and adopted?

Indeed, much research over the past several decades continues to show that, in specific groups, members who possess a more valued state of a social characteristic in a particular society (e.g., men, whites, and middle or upper class) are likely to be perceived as more competent and worthy in general than members who possess a less valued state (e.g., women, blacks, Latino/as, or poor or working class). As a result, members who are perceived as more worthy are more likely to offer their opinions and be more influential in decision-making groups and thus become high-status members in the group.

How Do Status Structures Develop, and How Are They Maintained?

Scholars, initially in the 1970s and continuing today, examined the many classic studies of status structures conducted in the 1950s and 1960s and developed and tested theories that explain how status structures develop and how they are maintained. In doing so, they also explained *why* the process of status generalization occurs consistently in many types of task groups in many different contexts such as in schools, businesses, political organizations, health care organizations, and religious organizations.

Expectation States Theory

In particular, Berger and colleagues developed **expectation states theory (EST)** specifically to address how status structures develop and are maintained in groups, with particular attention to the more commonly occurring heterogeneous groups. As you recall, heterogeneous groups are those groups where members differentiate on at least one social characteristic (e.g., gender, age, or race) such as in the mock jury studies (Berger et al. 1977; Berger, Rosenholtz, and Zelditch 1980). These scholars examine task groups (instead of primary groups such as families and friendship groups), where members are *task-focused* and are *open to taking into account each other's opinions* (they are collectively oriented and want the group to do well on the group task). Examples of task groups are committees, student government organizations, lab teams, and political groups.

In this theory, Berger and others argue that in every society there are **diffuse status characteristics** that people possess. These characteristics have at least two states where one state is more highly valued (i.e., thought to be more worthy and esteemed) than the other in society. Examples are gender, age, race, education, sexual orientation, and physical attraction in the United States (Berger et al. 1980; Lovaglia et al. 1998; Webster and Driskell 1978). Importantly, the status value of social characteristics is historically and culturally dependent. In some cultures, for example, race may not be a status characteristic, while in others race is one. In addition, there is cultural variation in the status value of particular states of diffuse status characteristics. For example, the status value of age groups varies cross-culturally. In the United States, for example, "middle-age" is seen as the most highly valued, while in other societies, "elders" are the most highly valued. Also, as discussed in the introduction of this chapter, at Hogwarts being muggle-born is considered low status compared to half-bloods and pure-bloods, but in the nonmagical world, muggles have the highest status.

Diffuse status characteristics become important in groups only when they become **salient** in the group—that is, when they provide usable information to the members. Characteristics become salient when members differentiate on the characteristic. For example, gender becomes salient in a mixed-sex group where both men and women are interacting (in a mixed-race group race will become salient). They also become salient when the task is related to the characteristic. For example, gender becomes salient when the group is working on a gender-stereotyped task (such as sewing or changing oil) because it is related to the status characteristic: gender. What tasks can you think of that are not related to gender?

Associated with diffuse status characteristics are implicit general expectations for competence, called **performance expectations**. They are expectations that members form for their own and each other's performance on the group task. They are rough estimates of how well the members think each other will perform on the task, relative to themselves. Key to EST is that members who have a more highly valued state of a diffuse status characteristic are assumed by themselves and other members in the group to be more competent in general *at most things* than those who have a less valued state of that characteristic. The theory presumes an association between states of social characteristics and general competence beliefs; this association is a key **stereotyping process**. For example, if people believe in general that blacks are less competent than whites on most tasks, or even if people think that other people think that blacks are less competent than whites even if they themselves do not believe this, this has clear consequences for interaction in groups.

Specifically, the association between diffuse status characteristics and beliefs about general competence affects behavior in the group. Members for whom people have higher performance expectations (owing to their perceived greater task competence) relative to others in the group will talk more, receive more positive evaluations, receive more attention from others, and be more influential than those members for whom there are lower performance expectations. This differentiated pattern in behavior creates the status hierarchy, where those who talk more and are given more opportunities to participate are also more influential. As a result, they are also seen as more worthy. And, because they are perceived as more worthy, they continue to participate more, get more positive evaluations, and continue to be more influential.

EST explains the link between diffuse status characteristics, the widespread cultural beliefs that particular states of these characteristics are associated with competence beliefs, the behaviors in the group that lead to the development of the status hierarchy, and the perpetuation of the hierarchy. This process describes a **self-fulfilling prophecy**. Recall in Chapter 5 that the self-fulfilling prophecy occurs when one person has expectations (often based on inaccurate information) of another person's abilities and behavior, which leads the first person to act in a way toward the second person, leading the second person to act in a manner confirming the first person's expectations. (For an interesting study on the fulfilling nature of stereotypes regarding physical attractiveness where the perception that "beautiful" people are "good" people, see a classic article by Snyder, Tanke, and Berscheid [1977].) In regard to status processes, certain group members are expected to be more competent at the task; other members act toward them as if they are more competent. These members then talk more, receive more positive feedback and attention, and are more influential in the group; as a result, they are perceived as higher in the status hierarchy, and so the cycle continues.

This process occurs even though a particular group task is unrelated to these diffuse status characteristics—that is, even when these characteristics are not associated with ability on the specific task. In fact, there is **a burden of proof** that must take place in order for the status characteristic to be dissociated from the task (Berger et al. 1980). Members have to be explicitly told that a particular characteristic is not relevant to ability on the task. For example, in some studies the researcher will specifically state that women and men or blacks and whites perform equally well on a particular task. This explicit claim is used to disrupt the association between a status characteristic and competence beliefs.

Example: A Case of Gender

Several years ago, Harvard Business School revealed that female students were participating less in classes on average than men, and when they spoke, they did so in a tentative manner. Also, the professors were more likely to forget their participation than that of male students. Female students were also much less likely to win prestigious awards. These patterns occurred even though female students had test scores and grades similar to those of the male students. Why?! Look up the response by the first female president, Dr. Drew Gilpin Faust. She created a strategy for reducing this inequality at Harvard Business School. For example, professors were asked to use software tools so that they could instantly check their patterns of whom they called on and who participated. Sessions on respect and civility were also conducted. Why do these patterns occur in the first place?!

EST has the answer. Given that gender is a diffuse status characteristic in society, there are widely held cultural beliefs that men are perceived to have greater value and worth than women and, therefore, are believed to be generally superior and competent at most things relative to women (Fiske et al. 2002; Wagner and Berger 1997). When gender is salient in a situation, gender status beliefs cause men and women to expect or expect that others will expect men to be more competent than women, all else being equal. These expectations for competence shape men and women's assertiveness, judgments of each other's ability, and actual performance (Ridgeway and Smith-Lovin 1999; Wagner and Berger 1997; Wood and Karten 1986). Indeed, many studies show that women participate less and get less influence in task groups, on average, than men (even at Harvard Business School!). This cycle continues unless this process is interrupted.

What happens when a member has a specific skill relevant to the group task? Do diffuse status characteristics still matter? For example, who would you expect to be more influential in a group that is working on a math task: a female math major or a male history major? Will the female math major be more influential?

EST helps us address these questions. It states that there are also **specific status characteristics**, defined as characteristics that are associated with specific skills that are relevant to the task. Examples are math ability when the group task is a math problem or skill at ice hockey when the task is a hockey game. These specific status characteristics are associated with specific performance expectations relevant to the specific task at hand. Having a specific skill in say, math, says nothing about ability on other tasks, such as conducting a legal task, fixing cars, or negotiating a marital conflict. In the *Harry Potter* story, an example of specific status characteristic is one's magical abilities, such as using charms or potions. (In the Harvard Business School example, no specific status characteristics were activated in a large classroom setting.)

According to EST, group members use information from both diffuse and specific status characteristics to form expectations of each other's competence. Specific status characteristics are more important than diffuse status characteristics in determining the status hierarchy because they are more directly relevant to the immediate group task. Information on specific status characteristics is weighted more heavily than information on diffuse status characteristics. For example, having specific math skills is more relevant to perceptions of competence than being a woman or a Latina when the group is working on a math task. Importantly, however, information on diffuse status characteristics is still used to form performance expectations rather than being considered irrelevant, even though it should be. In the example just given, according to EST, the female math major will have more influence than the male history major when working on a math task.

Consider two dyads. In the first, a female math major is working with a male sociology major on the same math task. Once again, we expect that both members will perceive the woman as more competent at the specific task than the man; as a result, she will participate more and be more influential at the task. In the second, there is a male math major and a female sociology major working together on the same math task. In this group, the man will be seen as more competent. In addition, however, the male math major in the second group will be seen as more competent in his group than the female math major in her group. Why? Because the male math major with the female sociology major has the advantage of higher status in terms of both the specific ability of math and of gender. The female math major with the male sociology major, however, has the advantage of higher status in terms of the specific skill but has a disadvantage in terms of gender. Here, EST states that people will act as if they are combining the information from both specific and diffuse status characteristics, called the **combining principle** (Berger et al. 1980; Wood and Karten 1986).

Illustrations of this combining principle occur in everyday interaction. For example, many people do not just see a doctor but see a black doctor or a woman doctor; they do not just see a president but see a black president. They do not just see a Supreme Court judge in Sonia Sotomayor. They see a Latina Supreme Court judge.

The theory makes an important point that these expectations about competence do not have to be conscious in order to operate in the group (Webster and Foschi 1988). In fact, often if you ask group members if people should have higher status in groups because of their race, gender, occupation, or age, for example, they will say absolutely not! The process described previously often occurs outside of people's conscious awareness. Much empirical evidence shows, however, that people act *as if* these status characteristics do matter in decision-making behavior in groups (Berger et al. 1980; Wagner and Berger 2002). These studies indicate that the cultural expectations associated with these characteristics continue to significantly affect our perceptions of who seems the most competent in the group. Status hierarchies are very stable as a result of these subtle stereotypic processes and are very difficult to change. (See Ridgeway and Nakagawa 2014 for an in-depth discussion of all assumptions of the status theories.)

As group members form expectations about each other's task performance for themselves compared to another (we can call them first-order expectations), they also anticipate how other group members will judge their own expected performance. Group members' perceptions of what others in the group expect in regard to their performance are called **second-order performance expectations** (Troyer and Younts 1997; Webster and Whitmeyer 1999). They are group members' rough estimates of how others in the group view their standing in the group.

It is like a working consensus, even though this is not necessarily what the group members want or deserve.

Often first-order and second-order expectations align, but sometimes they do not. That is, sometimes a member perceives that others rank her expected performance capacity differently than she ranks her own performance capacity. There is a conflict between how she thinks of her own performance capacity (i.e., competence at the task) and how she views others' ideas about her performance capacity. When second-order performance expectations about what others expect contradict a member's own first-order expectations, the second-order expectations are more likely to shape the member's behavior in the group. This means that a member's perception of what others expect about her performance has a greater impact on that member's deferential and assertive behaviors than her own view of her performance (as compared to others in the group; Kalkoff, Younts, and Troyer, 2011; Ridgeway and Nakagawa 2014; Troyer and Younts 1997).

In summary, as empirical work in status characteristic theory shows, diffuse and specific status characteristics and their relationship to performance expectations are key in explaining how status structures develop and are maintained in groups. Another factor that affects the development of status structures is resources that people possess.

Reward Expectations Theory

Do you think wealthy people are more competent and intelligent than folks in the middle or working classes? Is someone who owns a large home and a luxury car smarter than someone who owns a modest home and a compact car? Are people who earn higher salaries more competent in general at most things than those who earn lower salaries? How about employees who have corner offices with windows compared to employees with less desirable offices?

Berger and colleagues also developed from EST the **reward expectations theory**, which addresses these types of questions (Berger, Wagner, and Zelditch 1985). It argues that many people assume that people with more resources are also more competent in general than those with comparatively fewer resources—or at least they assume that others assume that this is true. This strong association between possession of resources and competence occurs even when resources (such as money, cars, or titles) have nothing to do with actual ability or skills.

Specifically, this theory argues that the possession of rewards or resources is another factor that can influence performance expectations (i.e., perceptions of competence), even when these resources are irrelevant to the group task. Rewards or resources include monetary rewards like salary, pay, and income as well as symbolic rewards such as an office with windows, a prime parking space, real estate, or an honorary title. Studies show that group members who are given more resources than other members are perceived as more competent at the group task, even though these resources are *not* explicitly connected to the group task.

For example, Cook (1975) showed that members who were paid more than other members were perceived as more competent even though pay was not related to their performance or the group task. Group members presumed that those who were paid more by a third party also had greater task ability, and those who were paid less were presumed to have less ability (Harrod 1980; Stewart and Moore 1992).

In our culture, those who have higher incomes and more wealth are assumed to have these resources because they are assumed to be more competent than those with lower incomes and less wealth. Of course, this is often not the case. There are many structural barriers to acquiring wealth, historically rooted, for particular groups in the United States, such as inheritance laws (e.g., see Cross [1985]), which have nothing to do with competence. Also, some very wealthy people are not necessarily competent and smart. (This may be one reason that a number of voters perceived Donald Trump as competent to address economic issues—his perceived wealth is associated with the ability to help others increase their own likelihood of prospering.)

In addition to monetary rewards, rewards that have purely symbolic status value (and are not exchangeable like monetary rewards) affect expectations for performance and, hence, the development of the status hierarchy (Hysom 2009). Hysom (2009) showed this process in his experimental study, where participants worked with a partner on a group task, called the contrast sensitivity task. In this task, members saw a series of slides that have portions of black and portions of white on each slide. They were asked to select one of two black-and-white patterns as having more white area. In reality, each pattern has equal proportions of black and white. For each slide, participants made an initial choice and then learned of their partners' choice. The participants were instructed to then reconsider their initial choice and make a final choice, based on this information.

Once they were finished with the task, the experimenter told the participants that an unusual situation had developed. A famous Nobel Prize winner, a Harvard professor, would be visiting their campus soon to consult with the laboratory staff regarding this study. Half the participants were told that they had been chosen to attend an "exclusive private reception" with this professor as well as meet other important guests such as a past U.S. president and a former UN ambassador. The other half were told that they would not be permitted to attend the reception. Importantly, this *symbolic reward was never explicitly connected to how well the participants performed on the task*. Even so, the participants used this information to infer their own and their partner's competence on the task. Indeed, on a subsequent task after learning about the reception, group members who received the symbolic reward were not as easily influenced by their less-rewarded partners. Participants acted as if this exclusive reward was associated with task ability, even though there was never any explicit connection made between the two.

What Is the Role of Emotions in Status Structures?

Group members not only offer opinions, share ideas, and make decisions; in many situations, they also experience felt emotions and sometimes display those emotions to other group members. Have you ever felt angry toward another person in a group because he or she dismissed your idea? Have you ever felt grateful or pleased because your idea was adopted by the group? Have you been in groups that fall apart because members cannot get along or in groups where members feel a close bond to one another? Groups can fall apart if members feel more negative emotions, such as anger, frustration, or resentment than positive emotions, such as satisfaction and pleasure (Bales 1970; Ridgeway and Johnson 1990). Vice versa, groups may stay together longer because there are more felt positive than negative emotions among group members.

Not surprisingly, just as high-status members talk more, receive more positive feedback and attention, and are more influential than low-status members, they also often have different experiences in their felt and expressed emotions. High-status members are more likely to experience positive emotions than low-status members, who are more likely to feel negative emotions (Lovaglia and Houser 1996; Lucas 1999). High-status members have more opportunity to receive positive feedback about their ideas and have more influence and, therefore, are more likely to experience pleasure and happiness. Low-status members, in contrast, are less likely to receive positive feedback and achieve influence; therefore, anger or depression may result. These findings are consistent with Kemper's (1991) work mentioned in Chapter 7; receiving and gaining high status leads to positive emotions of happiness, satisfaction, and often also pride, while receiving low status leads to negative emotions such as anger.

In addition, some research focuses on the emotional reactions of low- and high-status members in groups and how these reactions help maintain the status structure. Specifically, group members with lower status who receive negative feedback about their ideas from other group members are more likely to experience feelings of sadness or even depression rather than annoyance or anger. Even if they do feel anger or frustration, they are less likely to express it toward higher-status members. In contrast, high-status members who receive negative feedback about their opinions are more likely to feel annoyance or anger. Also, they are more likely to express these negative emotions toward lower-status members because they are freer to do so. The expression of negative emotions, then, is one way that high-status members control the interaction and decision-making outcomes (Ridgeway and Johnson 1990). (See Chapter 7 for discussion of how relative status affects the emotional experiences and expressions of people at work and in families [e.g., Lively and Powell 2006]; see Webster and Walker [2014] for a thorough discussion of emotions and status processes.)

What Are Some Consequences of Status Structures for Behavior in Groups?

Status structures are based on these consensually accepted status beliefs about competence, where one category is thought to be better, more worthy, and competent than another category. These status beliefs that are associated with diffuse status characteristics have far-reaching effects. First, as with the consequences of groupthink described previously, groups often make bad or less than optimal decisions in their groups as a result of this association. Group members with diffuse status advantages are likely to be more assertive and influential in decisions and become leaders than members with diffuse status disadvantages. Yet this consequence often leads to *inefficient decision-making* because members who are in fact more competent are not always those who are listened to and most influential (Wagner and Berger 2002; Webster and Foschi 1988). Rather, status-disadvantaged members may be the most competent, yet their opinions are undervalued, overlooked, or ignored.

Second, members who have lower status in society and who are, therefore, status disadvantaged in the group, must work harder and perform better than status-advantaged members to attain status in the group. They have the extra burden of "proving" themselves competent and worthy. For example, women are held to higher performance standards than men in many situations. People evaluate the contributions of men and women differently in groups; women have to perform better than men to get the same evaluations as men. Obviously, this **double standard** can take a heavy toll, and be physically and emotionally draining (Foschi 1996, 2000; see also Jackson, Thoits, and Taylor [1995]) in regard to black workers in white-dominated workplaces).

Third, these status beliefs create *biases in organizational and labor market practices* (Ridgeway 1997, 2011). For example, in regard to gender status, these beliefs create a *preference of male workers* in the workplace. Often, employers rank male workers as more highly desirable than female workers. When employers interact with applicants during the hiring process, this interaction evokes sex categorization. That is, the employers do not interview or read the résumé of a "gender-neutral" worker. Also, employers often begin the hiring process by either implicitly or explicitly seeking potential workers of a given sex. As a result of this sex categorization of applicants, status beliefs become salient in the hiring process as employers assess applications, interview job candidates, and talk with others in the organization in the hiring process. As discussed previously, gender-status beliefs contain general assumptions that men are more competent than women in general at most things and of course assumptions that men are more competent than women at stereotypically male tasks. As a result, employers often will have a preference for male workers (from auto repair shops to Wall Street), or at least believe that their customers or clients have this preference. These biased preferences affect hiring of women in many professions.

In addition, gender-status beliefs may affect employers' judgments of applicants' potential productivity. Male workers appear better or more qualified than equally qualified female workers. As a result of the double standard, two workers, one male and one female, who would perform equally well are judged to be different and are paid accordingly, based on this perceived difference in potential productivity (Ridgeway 1997, 2011).

Even on eBay auction transactions, women sellers receive a smaller number of bids and lower final prices than do men sellers, and this is so even when they are equally qualified and are selling the exact same product (Kricheli-Katz and Regev 2016)! Examining data of transactions of the most popular products by private sellers between 2009 and 2012, researchers found that women sellers received about 80 cents for every dollar a man received, on average, even though they were selling the new identical product. They attribute the gap to the fairly successful ability of buyers to discern the gender of users, given that eBay does not reveal the gender of users, as a policy. People are more likely to assign a lower value to products sold by women than by men (Kricheli-Katz and Regev 2016). Not surprisingly, women buyers, on average, are more likely to pay more for the same products than men!

Another biased process in the workplace is described in the **motherhood penalty** (Benard and Correll 2010; Correll, Benard, and Paik 2007; Ridgeway and Correll 2004). Being a parent leads to disadvantages in the workplace for women, but men benefit in the workplace from having children. Mothers are less likely to be hired than women who are not mothers and less likely to be promoted, on average. In contrast, fathers are perceived as more committed to paid work and are offered higher starting salaries on average than childless men. Why? Scholars explain this pattern by noting that motherhood is a status characteristic. Mothers are evaluated as less competent and less committed to paid work than nonmothers. These cultural beliefs about mothers and fathers and about family wages still shape the allocation of rewards in the workplace (Benard and Correll 2010; Correll et al. 2007; Ridgeway and Correll 2004).

There are numerous consequences of status structures and status beliefs for interaction in groups and in the workplace, several of which we have mentioned previously. There are times when status structures have positive consequences. Having a clear status hierarchy in an emergency room or in the courtroom, for example, is important for smooth operations. In and of themselves, status hierarchies are not "bad." Negative consequences occur when these status beliefs erroneously associate entire categories of people with levels of competence.

How Can Status Inequality in Groups Be Reduced?

How can we create situations where all members' contributions are equally recognized in groups? How can people who possess status characteristics that are associated with less esteem acquire higher status in groups?

One way low-status members may be heard is by presenting their ideas and opinions in a way that demonstrates that they have the group's interests at heart, rather than a way that demonstrates selfishness. In other words, if these individuals **act group-oriented**, rather than self-oriented, they are more likely to get influence in groups. When a member presents herself as group-oriented, she stresses the importance of cooperating and working together in a group; she presents her ideas for the good of the group, rather than in a way that makes it seem as if she is only looking out for herself. Indeed, Ridgeway (1982) found that when female members with male partners presented themselves as self-oriented, they were not very influential, but when they presented themselves as group-oriented, they were equally influential on their male partners. To acquire status in groups, then, low-status members must not act too uppity when presenting their ideas; they must instead show that they are expressing their ideas for the sake of the group (Ridgeway and Nakagawa 2014).

This strategy can be a pain in the butt, but it is often effective. You may use this technique sometimes (not always consciously) with older siblings, parents, bosses, or professors—you find yourself treading lightly when you disagree with them and want them to see a situation your way. That is, when you offer an opinion that is contrary to their own, you pad your arguments, making sure not to seem too abrasive so that they will listen to your opinion. In addition, Carli (1990, 1991) found that this strategy does work but can create a dilemma in certain situations. For example, she found that when women in all-female groups used a more tentative style with the other female members, they were not very influential, but when they were tentative with their male partners, they were influential. *Tentative speech* includes disclaimers (phrases used while presenting an idea that soften your idea such as, "I'm not really sure, but . . .", "You know more than me about this, but . . .", "I'm no expert, but . . .") and qualifiers (adverbs used to soften the opinion such as maybe or perhaps). Carli shows that women face a dilemma in mixed-sex groups when they want to influence both men and women in the same group.

In an opinion piece in the *Washington Post* (Petri 2015), the author illustrates how a woman would have to say famous quotes during a meeting. For example, for the famous quote by Franklin D. Roosevelt, "The only thing we have to fear is fear itself," a woman in a meeting would have to say the following (catch all the tentative language!):

> I have to say—I'm sorry—I have to say this. I don't think we should be as scared of non-fear things as maybe we are? If that makes sense? Sorry, I feel like I'm rambling.

When low-status members use a group-motivated style, it helps them get influence in the group (Shackelford, Wood, and Worchel 1996). In addition, members award status to other members who demonstrate group orientation when they make contributions to the group task despite a personal cost (e.g., time and effort; Willer 2009). A member who contributes to the group's goals signals his or her motivation to help the group. As a result, other group members award esteem to that member, and, in turn, this member continues to contribute to the group's goals and also views the group more positively (Willer 2009).

A second way for low-status members to acquire status in groups is to **satisfy the burden of proof requirement**. One way to do this is to provide all group members with information that contradicts the performance expectations inferred from the diffuse status characteristic (Berger et al. 1980). But how do you do that? One way is to show to both the low- and high-status members that the low-status members have more relevant skills at the task than the other members. Recall that information on specific status characteristics (possession of skills or abilities relevant to specific group task) is weighted more heavily than information on diffuse status characteristics, although all information is combined. Such weighted combining reveals that a black doctor in a mixed-race medical setting will be more strongly affected by his occupational status than his race, but race will still have an effect on perceptions. It also implies, however, that a black doctor will have higher status than some whites in this medical setting if he is higher than they are on relevant skills.

An example of satisfying the burden of proof requirement is shown in some classic studies by Cohen and her colleagues (Cohen 1982; Cohen and Lotan 1997; Cohen and Roper 1972). They conducted studies in junior high schools and created a situation where they taught black students how to build a radio and then showed them how to teach another student to build a radio. In effect, the researchers created two specific status characteristics that were inconsistent with the students' perceptions of the diffuse status characteristic: race. The researchers then had the black students teach the white students how to build a radio, thereby establishing the superiority of the black students relative to the white students. Finally, they also told the students that the skills involved in building the radio and teaching others to build it were relevant to another task, a decision-making game. When the students played this game, there was more equality between black and white students in terms of who exercised influence over the decisions. Importantly, this study and subsequent studies show that for this strategy to work, the performance expectations of both low- and high-status members must be changed simultaneously. This technique will not work if you change expectations of the low-status members only (Ridgeway and Nakagawa 2014).

Third, and related to the second technique, when the usual expectations for members with given diffuse status characteristics is challenged, this experience can transfer to the way people treat the next person they encounter with that characteristic. Studies show that when men work with women who are clearly more competent than themselves, this causes them to have somewhat higher performance expectations for the next woman they encounter (Markovsky, Smith, and Berger 1984; Pugh and Wahrman 1983; Wagner, Ford, and Ford 1986). This process is referred to as the **transfer effect**; members bring this challenging information about competence into new interactions. Studies show that this effect diminishes over each transfer if there is not renewed information about competence for status-disadvantaged members, but this effect does provide hope that cultural beliefs about the association between diffuse status characteristics and competence can be moderated over time.

Finally, if you **legitimate** a person in a position, such as a leader, supervisor, or manager of a group, this will help reduce the biased effects of status characteristics associated with low competence beliefs. If a person is legitimated, this means that she is backed up and supported by those above her and given the necessary resources to get her job done and the work of her subordinates. Those above her express that she is the right person to be in the leadership position. Legitimacy typically comes from some higher authority and can aid in reducing status inequality. In Chapter 10, we will see how legitimacy and status processes affect leadership and decision-making in groups and organizations.

Summary

As the previous section on status structures shows, status processes involve a stereotyping process where social characteristics are associated with broad cultural assumptions about who is competent and worthy and who is less competent and worthy. These status beliefs have astounding implications for behavior and decision-making in groups and in organizations. For example, assumptions about who is more worthy and competent affects labor market processes such as who gets hired in types of jobs, who is promoted in their jobs, and who has access to opportunities to get ahead on the job. These processes also operate in classrooms, mortgage lending offices, courtrooms, and doctors' offices, to name a few, as well in corporate boardrooms. Status beliefs are one critical mechanism that underlies the maintenance and perpetuation of social inequality. In order to continue to address how social inequality can be reduced, we have to understand how status processes create and sustain inequality (Ridgeway 2014; Ridgeway and Nakagawa 2014). In the next section, we examine how characteristics acquire status value.

How Do Characteristics Acquire Status Value in the First Place?

How does a social characteristic that distinguishes individuals, like gender or race, become a characteristic with status value instead of just a mere difference? The problem with diffuse status characteristics is not the "characteristic" part of the equation but the status part of the equation. For example, if people perceived that blacks, whites, Latino/as, and Asians have similarities and differences, this would not be an issue. The problem is that people assume that people in one category (in this case, whites) are superior, more worthy, and more competent than people in other categories (in this case blacks and Latino/as). (This recalls our discussion in Chapter 4 about the social constructs of masculinity and femininity where "masculine" qualities are assumed to be more worthy and "better" than "feminine" qualities in general). The same can be said for other diffuse status characteristics, such as gender, occupation, physical attraction, and sexual orientation, to name a few. How, then, do social characteristics that distinguish people acquire this status value?

Ridgeway (1991, 2006, 2011; Correll and Ridgeway 2003) provides a theoretical explanation for how these recognized social differences become accepted indicators of social status in society so that some categories of people (e.g., whites, men) are perceived as more worthy and competent than other categories of people (e.g., blacks, women). She developed **status construction theory** to explain how the transformation of a mere difference into a widely accepted status characteristic may occur through repeated interactions. If we understand the structural conditions under which status beliefs arise around particular characteristics, then we can see how changes in the social structure can potentially alter these status beliefs over time.

Ridgeway (1991; Blau 1977) argues that there are four structural conditions, all sufficient, that facilitate this transformation. First, there must *be cooperative interdependence between people in the two categories of a social difference*. This means that people from both categories of a social characteristic in the population regularly interact with one another to achieve what they want or need. For example, in our society men and women regularly interact in a cooperatively and interdependent fashion to achieve their needs and goals.

Second, there must be an economic or other such advantage of one category in a population over the other category—that is, one category has more resources (the resource-rich) than another category (the resource-poor), on average. This means that there is a *resource inequality between the categories*. For example, women and people of color are resource disadvantaged relative to men and whites in many societies (e.g., based on wealth, income, and power). Other factors on which one category of people might be advantaged over another could be control of technology or moral evaluations (Webster and Hysom 1998).

Third, the *population is divided into categories that are readily distinguishable*, such as gender, race, or ethnicity. People can identify what category of the social characteristic members are in as they interact with one another. And fourth, there is a *correlation between the resource level and the category of the characteristic*. For example, in a society like the United States, the resource-rich individuals tend to be disproportionately male and white, and resource-poor individuals tend to be disproportionately female and black or Latino/a.

Under these conditions, a process takes place through repeated interactions. As described previously, in virtually all contexts in which people work on a shared task, a status hierarchy is likely to emerge among participants in these interactions in which some members are more active and influential and are thought to be better at the task than others (Berger et al. 1977; Berger et al. 1980). Ridgeway (1991) argues that resource advantage, however gained, is a biasing factor that provides one category of people (let's refer to them as As) with an advantage over the other category (let's refer to them as Bs) in gaining influence and esteem in their group encounters (Berger et al. 1985).

According to reward expectations theory, as mentioned earlier, this is because people associate the resource advantage with competence; they assume that people with more resources are also better at most tasks than those with fewer resources. For example, in the United States, people assume that those who have more resources (money, land, wealth) are believed to be more competent than those with fewer resources (Berger et al. 1985). Is this true? No, but people assume that this connection is so—or at least assume that other people in general think that this is so. As a result, these resource-advantaged people act more leaderlike and appear more competent, thus creating a correspondence between the difference in a social characteristic and positions in the status hierarchy. In a sufficient number of encounters, it is the case that those individuals with more resources also tend to be of one category (such as men) who interact with people with fewer resources charaterized by another category (such as women). These are called doubly dissimilar encounters. As a result, people begin to associate individuals from one category as more competent than those in the other category. Once this occurs, As (say, men) and Bs (say, women) in the population will carry these status beliefs into future encounters, favoring As as more worthy and competent than Bs.

Because more people develop beliefs favoring As than favoring Bs as repeated interactions continue, people who hold beliefs that favor As are more likely to have their beliefs supported in future encounters than people who hold contrary beliefs. As a result of this systematic advantage, status beliefs favoring As over Bs are likely to diffuse widely and become roughly consensual in the population. Once widely held status beliefs develop, they confer independent status value on the A/B characteristic so that As are advantaged over Bs across situations. That is, people believe that most people believe that people in Category A are more competent in general than people in Category B. This advantage occurs even in interactions where Bs are just as economically or otherwise resource privileged as As. Importantly, status beliefs become part of the implicit, taken-for-granted social framework of beliefs that individuals bring into encounters to frame their behavior. People operate as if these assumptions are true. Empirical evidence supports these arguments (Ridgeway and Correll 2006; Ridgeway et al. 1998; Ridgeway et al. 2009).

Brezina and Winder (2003) apply status construction theory to the case of race in the United States. They argue that there is an unequal distribution of economic resources between racial categories in the population; they focus specifically on whites and blacks. In the United States, whites, on average, have higher incomes and have abundantly more wealth (e.g., owning more property and earning more interest on mutual funds and stocks due to historical and legal reasons, such as inheritance laws) than blacks. In addition, the population is easily identified along the characteristic of race. People at least assume that they can identify the race of individuals in interaction. Finally, there is a correlation between resource level and race, where there is an "overrepresentation of blacks among the resource-poor" (Brezina and Winder 2003:406). Importantly, members of the population continually "see" the association between black skin color and resource poverty, both through interactions and through third parties, such as television news and other programs (Ridgeway and Erickson 2000). In fact, people tend to overestimate this correlation, but it is the *perception* of this relationship between black skin color and poverty that matters. As a result, blacks inherit the relatively low status that is often assigned to resource-poor individuals. People associate blacks with being resource-poor and then associate blacks in general as less worthy and competent than whites.

Brezina and Winder (2003) show that, as a result, there is persistent negative racial stereotyping in the United States, even though traditional racial beliefs have declined in recent decades. Specifically, they find that, "The larger the perceived economic gap between whites and blacks—with blacks seen as relatively disadvantaged—the greater the whites' tendency to stereotype blacks as lazy as opposed to hard-working" (Brezina and Winder 2003:415). The implication here is that if racial or economic inequalities were reduced, that would also decrease the perceived correlation between being black and low levels of competence. Racial stereotyping could be reduced by "(1) reducing media distortion, which tends to exaggerate the extent of economic failure among blacks, and (2) increasing awareness of structural barriers to economic success" (Brezina and Winder 2003:416).

Segue: Status and Power

In an innovative study, Taylor (2014) examines whether men and women who lose social influence in a group are likely to have a physiological stress response as a result. One of the author's ideas is that achieving social influence in groups is also a way to achieve "masculinity." When men do not achieve social influence, particularly with other men, they may experience stress because they fail to achieve masculinity by losing social influence. She refers to this as the "stigma of failed masculinity" (Taylor 2014:58).

Demonstrations of social influence and power are ways of enacting masculinity in everyday interaction (Ridgeway and Correll 2004). As you recall, men have higher status than women in society as discussed in this chapter, and masculinity is more highly valued in society than femininity (see Chapter 4). Taylor (2014) argues that sociologists can study the effects of loss of social influence by measuring cortisol response. Cortisol is a stress hormone that has been shown to be related to threats to social influence and status. Taylor found that men who lost social influence while working on a task with other men exhibited stress measured by a cortisol response. Women, on the other hand, did not have a cortisol response to loss of social influence when they worked on a task with other women or other men. And men who worked on a task with women also did not exhibit a cortisol response. These results show that loss of influence is important to men, especially men interacting with other men. In addition, Taylor (2015:57) notes, "When men's social influence, and thus masculinity, is compromised they are at risk of stigmatization because masculinity in the U.S. is associated with status, power, and competence."

In the next chapter, we examine power processes and their link to status processes. Status structures clearly have an impact on behavior in groups, but so do power relations among group members. We all experience power in our relationships, but what is power, and what are the consequences of using power? In the next chapter, we define power and power use and then look at the effects of power relations on behavior in relationships.

Suggested Readings

Biagas, David E., Jr., and Alison J. Bianchi. 2016. "The Latin Americanization Thesis: An Expectation States Approach." *Social Forces* 94:1335–58.

Correll, Shelley J., Erin L. Kelly, Lindsey Trimble O-Connor, and Joan C. Williams. 2014. "Redesigning, Redefining Work." *Work and Occupations* 41:3–17.

King, Ryan D., and Brian D. Johnson. 2016. "A Punishing Look: Skin Tone and Afrocentric Features in the Halls of Justice." *American Journal of Sociology* 122:90–124.

Kuwabara, Ko, Sigu Yu, Alice J. Lee, and Adam D. Galinsky. 2016. "Status Decreases Dominance in the West but Increases Dominance in the East." *Psychological Science* 27:127–37.

Lynn, Freda B., Mark H. Walker, and Colin Peterson. 2016. "Is Popular More Likeable? Choice Status by Intrinsic Appeal in an Experimental Music Market." *Social Psychology Quarterly* 79:168–80.

Rudman, Laurie A., Corinne A. Moss-Racusin, Julie E. Phelan, and Sanne Nauts. 2012. "Status Incongruity and Backlash Effects: Defending the Gender Hierarchy Motivates Prejudice against Female Leaders." *Journal of Experimental Social Psychology* 48:165–79.

Thebaud, Sarah. 2015. "Status Beliefs and the Spirit of Capitalism: Accounting for Gender Biases in Entrepreneurship and Innovation." *Social Forces* 94:61–86.

References

Allen, Vernon L., and John M. Levine. 1969. "Consensus and Conformity." *Journal of Experimental Social Psychology* 5(4):389–99. doi:10.1016/0022–1031(69)90032–8

Asch, Solomon E. 1951. "Effects of Group Pressure upon the Modification and Distortion of Judgments." Pp. 177–90 in *Groups, Leadership, and Men*, edited by H. Guetzkow. Pittsburgh, PA: Carnegie Press.

Asch, Solomon E. 1955. "Opinions and Social Pressure." *Scientific American* 193:31–5. doi:10.10 38/scientificamerican1155–31

Asch, Solomon E. 1957. "An Experimental Investigation of Group Influence." Pp. 17–24 in *Symposium on Preventative and Social Psychiatry*, Part 3, edited by Walter Army Medical Center and the National Research Council. Washington, DC: Walter Reed Army Institute of Research.

Bales, Robert F. 1950. *Interaction Process Analysis: A Method for the Study of Small Groups*. Cambridge, MA: Addison-Wesley.

Bales, Robert F. 1970. *Personality and Interpersonal Behavior*. New York: Holt, Rinehart and Winston.

Benard, Stephen, and Shelley J. Correll. 2010. "Normative Discrimination and the Motherhood Penalty." *Gender & Society* 24:616–46. doi:10.1177/ 0891243210383142

Berger, Joseph, M. Hamit Fisek, Robert Z. Norman, and Morris Zelditch. 1977. *Status Characteristics and Social Interaction: An Expectation-States Approach*. New York: Elsevier.

Berger, Joseph M., Susan J. Rosenholtz, and Morris Zelditch Jr. 1980. "Status Organizing Processes." *Annual Review of Sociology* 6:479–508. doi:10.1146/annurev. so.06.080180.002403

Berger, Joseph M., David G. Wagner, and Morris Zelditch. 1985. "Expectations States Theory: Review and Assessment." Pp. 1–72 in *Status, Rewards, and Influence: How Expectations Organize Behavior*, edited by J. Berger and M. Zelditch. San Francisco, CA: Jossey-Bass.

Blau, Peter. 1977. *Inequality and Heterogeneity: A Primitive Theory of Social Structure*. New York: Free Press.

Bond, Rod, and Peter B. Smith. 1996. "Culture and Conformity: A Meta-Analysis of Studies Using Asch's (1952b, 1956) Line Judgement Task." *Psychological Bulletin* 119:111–37. doi:10.1037/0033-2909.119.1.111

Brezina, Timothy, and Kenisha Winder. 2003. "Economic Disadvantage, Status Generalization, and Negative Racial Stereotyping by White Americans." *Social Psychology Quarterly* 66:402–18. doi:10.2307/1519837

Carli, Linda L. 1990. "Gender, Language, and Influence." *Journal of Personality and Social Psychology* 59:941–51. doi:10.1037/0022-3514.59.5.941

Carli, Linda L. 1991. "Gender, Status, and Influence." Pp. 89–114 in *Advances in Group Processes: Theory and Research*, edited by E. J. Lawler, B. Markovsky, C. Ridgeway, and H. A. Walker. Greenwich, CT: JAI Press.

Cartwright, Dorwin, and Alvin Zander. 1968. "Power and Influence in Groups: An Introduction." Pp. 215–35 in *Group Dynamics: Research and Theory*, edited by D. Cartwright and A. Zander. New York: Harper & Row.

Cohen, Elizabeth G. 1982. "Expectation States and Interracial Interaction in School Settings." *Annual Review of Sociology* 8:209–35. doi:10.1146/annurev.so.08.080182.001233

Cohen, Elizabeth G., and R. A. Lotan. 1997. *Working for Equity in Heterogeneous Classrooms*. New York: Teachers College Press.

Cohen, Elizabeth G., and S. Roper. 1972. "Modification of Interracial Interaction Disability: Application of Status Characteristics Theory." *American Sociological Review* 37:643–55. doi:10.2307/2093576

Cook, Karen S. 1975. "Expectations, Evaluations, and Equity." *American Sociological Review* 40: 372–88. doi:10.2307/2094464

Correll, Shelley J., Stephen Benard, and In Paik. 2007. "Getting a Job: Is There a Motherhood Penalty?" *American Journal of Sociology* 112:1297–338. doi:10.1086/511799

Correll, Shelley J., and Ridgeway, Cecilia L. 2003. "Expectation States Theory." Pp. 29–51 in *Handbook of Social Psychology*, edited by J. DeLamater. New York: Plenum.

Cross, Theodore. 1985. *The Black Power Imperative: Racial Inequality and the Politics of Nonviolence*. New York: Faulkner.

DeLamater, John D., and Daniel J. Myers. 2007. *Social Psychology*. 6th ed. Belmont, CA: Thomson Wadsworth.

Ettinger, Ronald F., C. J. Marino, Norman S. Endler, Sheldon H. Geller, and Taras Natziuk. 1971. "Effects of Agreement and Correctness on Relative Competence and Conformity." *Journal of Personality and Social Psychology* 19(2):204–12. doi:10.1037/h0031275

Fiske, Susan T., Amy J. C. Cuddy, Peter Glick, and Jun Xu. 2002. "A Model of (Often Mixed) Stereotype Content: Competence and Warmth Respectively Follow from Perceived Status and Competition." *Journal of Personality and Social Psychology* 82(6):878–902. doi:10.1037/0022-3514.82.6.878

Forsyth, Donelson R. 2014. *Group Dynamics*. 6th ed. Belmont, CA: Wadsworth Cengage Learning.

Foschi, Martha. 1996. "Double Standards in the Evaluation of Men and Women." *Social Psychology Quarterly* 59:237–54. doi:10.2307/2787021

Foschi, Martha. 2000. "Double Standards for Competence: Theory and Research." *Annual Review of Sociology* 26:21–42. doi:10.1146/annurev.soc.26.1.21

Griggs, Richard A. 2015. "The Disappearance of Independence in Textbook Coverage of Asch's Social Pressure Experiments." *Teaching of Psychology* 42:137–42. doi:10.1177/0098628315569939

Harrod, Wendy J. 1980. "Expectations from Unequal Rewards." *Social Psychology Quarterly* 43:126–30. doi:10.2307/3033756

Hashimoto, Hirofumi, Yang Li, and Toshio Yamagishi. 2011. "Beliefs and Preferences in Cultural Agents and Cultural Game Players." *Asian Journal of Social Psychology* 14:140–47. doi:10.1111/j.1467-839X.2010.01337.x

Hoffman, Hunter G., Pär Anders Granhag, Sheree T. Kwong See, and Elizabeth F. Loftus. 2001. "Social Influences on Reality-Monitoring Decisions." *Memory & Cognition* 29:394–404. doi:10.3758/BF03196390

Hogg, Michael A., and Joel Cooper. 2003. *The Sage Handbook of Social Psychology*. Thousand Oaks, CA: Sage.

Hysom, Stuart J. 2009. "Status Valued Goal Objects and Performance Expectations." *Social Forces* 87:1623–48. doi:10.1353/sof.0.0160

Jackson, Pamela Braboy, Peggy A. Thoits, and Howard F. Taylor. 1995. "Composition of the Workplace and Psychological Well-Being: The Effects of Tokenism on America's Black Elite." *Social Forces* 74:543–57. doi:10.2307/2580491

Janes, Leslie M., and James M. Olson. 2000. "Jeer Pressure: The Behavioral Effects of Observing Ridicule of Others." *Personality and Social Psychology Bulletin* 26:474–85. doi:10.1177/0146167200266006

Janis, Irving L. 1982. *Groupthink*. 2nd ed. Boston: Houghton Mifflin.

Kalkoff, Will, C. Wesley Younts, and Lisa Troyer. 2011. "Do Others' Views of Us Transfer to New Groups and Tasks? An Expectation States Approach." *Social Psychology Quarterly* 74:267–90. doi:10.1177/0190272511416105

Kemper, Theodore D. 1991. "Predicting Emotions from Social Relations." *Social Psychology Quarterly* 54:330–42. doi:10.2307/2786845

Kricheli-Katz, Tamar, and Tali Regev. 2016. "How Many Cents on the Dollar? Women and Men in Product Markets." *Science Advances* 2(2):e1500599. doi:10.1126/sciadv.1500599

Lickel, Brian, David L. Hamilton, Grazyna Wieczorkowska, Amy Lewis, Steven J. Sherman, and Neville A. Uhles. 2000. "Varieties of Groups and the Perception of Group Entitativity." *Journal of Personality and Social Psychology* 78:223–46. doi:10.1037/0022-3514.78.2.223

Lively, Kathryn J., and Brian Powell. 2006. "Emotional Expression at Work and at Home: Domain, Status, or Individual Characteristics?" *Social Psychology Quarterly* 69:17–38. doi:10.1177/019027250606900103

Lovaglia, Michael J., and Jeffrey A. Houser. 1996. "Emotional Reactions and Status in Groups." *American Sociological Review* 61:867–83. doi:10.2307/2096458

Lovaglia, Michael J., Jeffrey W. Lucas, Jeffrey A. Houser, Shane R. Thye, and Barry Markovsky. 1998. "Status Processes and Mental Ability Test Scores." *American Journal of Sociology* 68:464–80.

Lucas, Jeffrey W. 1999. "Behavioral and Emotional Outcomes of Leadership in Task Groups." *Social Forces* 78:747–78. doi:10.2307/3005574

Markovsky, Barry, Leroy F. Smith, and Joseph Berger. 1984. "Do Status Interventions Persist?" *American Sociological Review* 49:373–82. doi:10.2307/2095281

Melamed, David, and Scott V. Savage. 2013. "Status, Numbers and Influence." *Social Forces* 91:1085–104. doi:10.1093/sf/sos194

Pendry, Louise, and Rachael Carrick. 2001. "Doing What the Mob Do: Priming Effects on Conformity." *European Journal of Social Psychology* 31:83–92. doi:10.1002/ejsp.33

Petri, Alexandra. 2015. "Famous Quotes, The Way a Woman Would Have to Say Them during a Meeting." *Washington Post*, October 13.

Pugh, Meredith D., and Ralph Wahrman. 1983. "Neutralizing Sexism in Mixed-Sex Groups: Do Women Have to be Better than Men?" *American Journal of Sociology* 88:746–62. doi:10.1086/227731

Ridgeway, Cecilia L. 1982. "Status in Groups: The Importance of Motivation." *American Sociological Review* 47:76–88. doi:10.2307/2095043

Ridgeway, Cecilia L. 1991. "The Social Construction of Status Value: Gender and Other Nominal Characteristics." *Social Forces* 7(2):367–86.

Ridgeway, Cecilia L. 1997. "Interaction and the Conservation of Gender Inequality: Considering Employment." *American Sociological Review* 62:218–35. doi:10.2307/2657301

Ridgeway, Cecilia L. 2006. "Status Construction Theory." Pp. 301–23 in *Contemporary Social Psychological Theories*, edited by P. J. Burke. Stanford, CA: Stanford University Press.

Ridgeway, Cecilia L. 2011. *Framed by Gender: How Gender Inequality Persists in the Modern World*. New York: Oxford University Press.

Ridgeway, Cecilia L. 2014. "Why Status Matters for Inequality." *American Sociological Review* 79:1–16. doi:10.1177/0003122413515997

Ridgeway, Cecilia L., Kristen Backor, Yan E. Li, Justine E. Tinkler, and Kristan G. Erickson. 2009. "How Easily Does a Social Difference Become a Status Distinction? Gender Matters." *American Sociological Review* 74:44–62. doi:10.1177/000312240907400103

Ridgeway, Cecilia L., Elizabeth E. Boyle, Kathy Kuipers, and Dawn Robinson. 1998. "How Do Status Beliefs Develop? The Role of Resources and Interaction." *American Sociological Review* 63:331–50. doi:10.2307/2657553

Ridgeway, Cecilia L., and Shelley J. Correll. 2004. "Motherhood as a Status Characteristic." *The Journal of Social Issues* 60:683–700. doi:10.1111/j.0022-4537.2004.00380.x

Ridgeway, Cecilia L., and Shelley J. Correll. 2006. "Consensus and the Creation of Status Beliefs." *Social Forces* 85:431–53. doi:10.1353/sof.2006.0139

Ridgeway, Cecilia L., and Kristan G. Erickson. 2000. "Creating and Spreading Status Beliefs." *American Journal of Sociology* 106:579–615. doi:10.1086/318966

Ridgeway, Cecilia L., and Cathryn Johnson. 1990. "What Is the Relationship between Socioemotional Behavior and Status in Task Groups?" *American Journal of Sociology* 95:1189–1212. doi:10.1086/229426

Ridgeway, Cecilia L., and Sandra Nakagawa. 2014. "Status." Pp. 3–26 in *Handbook of the Social Psychology of Inequality*, edited by J. McLeod, E. Lawler, and M. Schwalbe. New York: Springer.

Ridgeway, Cecilia L., and Lynn Smith-Lovin. 1999. "The Gender System and Interaction." *Annual Review of Sociology* 25:191–216. doi:10.1146/annurev.soc.25.1.191

Ridgeway, Cecilia L., and Henry A. Walker. 1995. "Status Structures." Pp. 281–310 in *Sociological Perspectives on Social Psychology*, edited by K. S. Cook, G. A. Fine, and J. S. House. Boston: Allyn & Bacon.

Shackelford, Susan, Wendy Wood, and Stephen Worchel. 1996. "Behavioral Styles and the Influence of Women in Mixed Sex Groups." *Social Psychology Quarterly* 59:284–93. doi:10.2307/2787024

Sherif, Muzafer. 1935. "A Study of Some Social Factors in Perception." *Archives of Psychology* 187:60.

Sherif, Muzafer. 1936. *The Psychology of Social Norms*. New York: Harper.

Snyder, Mark, Elizabeth D. Tanke, and Ellen Berscheid. 1977. "Social Perception and Interpersonal Behavior: On the Self-fulfilling Nature of Social Stereotypes." *Journal of Personality and Social Psychology* 35:656–66. doi:10.1037/0022-3514.35.9.656

Stewart, Penni A., and James C. Moore, Jr. 1992. "Wage Disparities and Performance Expectations." *Social Psychology Quarterly* 55:78–85. doi:10.2307/2786688

Strodtbeck, Fred L., Rita M. James, and Charles Hawkins. 1957. "Social Status in Jury Deliberations." *American Sociological Review* 22:713–19. doi:10.2307/2089202

Taylor, Catherine J. 2014. "Physiological Stress Response to Loss of Social Influence and Threats to Masculinity." *Social Science & Medicine* 103:51–9. doi:10.1016/j.socscimed.2013.07.036

Troyer, Lisa, and C. Wesley Younts. 1997. "Whose Expectations Matter? The Relative Power of First- and Second-order Expectations in Determining Social Influence." *American Journal of Sociology* 103:692–732. doi:10.1086/231253

Turner, John. C., Michael A. Hogg, Penelope J. Oakes, Stephen D. Reicher, and Margaret S. Wetherell. 1987. *Rediscovering the Social Group: A Self-Categorization Theory.* Oxford, England: Blackwell.

Wagner, David G., and Joseph Berger. 1997. "Gender and Interpersonal Task Behaviors: Status Expectation Accounts." *Sociological Perspectives* 40:1–32. doi:10.2307/1389491

Wagner, David G., and Joseph Berger. 2002. "Expectation States Theory: An Evolving Research Program." Pp. 41–76 in *New Directions in Contemporary Sociological Theory*, edited by J. Berger and M. Zelditch. Lanham, MD: Rowman & Littlefield.

Wagner, David G., Rebecca S. Ford, and Thomas W. Ford. 1986. "Can Gender Inequalities be Reduced?" *American Sociological Review* 51:47–61. doi:10.2307/2095477

Webster, Murray, Jr., and James E. Driskell. 1978. "Status Generalization: A Review and Some New Data." *American Sociological Review* 43:220–36. doi:10.2307/2094700

Webster, Murray, Jr., and Martha Foschi. 1988. *Status Generalization.* Stanford, CA: Stanford University Press.

Webster, Murray, Jr., and Stuart J. Hysom. 1998. "Creating Status Characteristics." *American Sociological Review* 63:351–78. doi:10.2307/2657554

Webster, Murray, Jr., and Lisa Slattery Walker. 2014. "Emotions in Expectation States Theory." Pp. 127–53 in *Handbook of the Sociology of Emotions*, Vol. 2, edited by Jan E. Stets and Jonathan H. Turner. New York: Springer. doi:10.1007/978-94-017-9130-4_7

Webster, Murray, Jr., and James Whitmeyer. 1999. "A Theory of Second-order Expectations and Behavior." *Social Psychology Quarterly* 62:17–31. doi:10.2307/2695823

Willer, Robb. 2009. "Groups Reward Individual Sacrifice: The Status Solution to the Collective Action Problem." *American Sociological Review* 74:23–43. doi:10.1177/000312240907400102

Williams v. Florida, 399 U.S. 78 (1970).

Wood, Wendy, and Steven J. Karten. 1986. "Sex Differences in Interaction Style as a Product of Perceived Sex Differences in Competence." *Journal of Personality and Social Psychology* 50:341–47. doi:10.1037/0022-3514.50.2.341

Power Relations in Groups and Social Networks

What comes to mind when you think of power? How is the power of a president of a country similar to or different from the power of a soccer coach, a gang leader, a college professor, or a romantic partner? There are many definitions of power, but we define **power** here as the potential of an actor to carry out his or her will despite resistance from others (Weber [1924] 1978). Power often results in compliance. Actors with high power can get people to do things they may not otherwise do. For example, a manager of a restaurant instructs the host to help clean tables; a professor requires students to take exams. Power is linked to possessing resources, such as control over employees' pay and work duties. Sometimes people willingly do what another person asks them to do, but the point here is that the actor who has more power in the relationship can get others with less power to carry out his or her will.

Notice that our definition of power refers to *power potential* and not to actual *power use*. For example, a boss has the ability to impose negative sanctions (e.g., docking pay, insisting on working late) if an employee fails to do his job. The boss may never do this, but she has the potential to do so. Power use is the actual act of using power behaviorally, such as giving rewards and punishments or taking away rewards.

Are presidents, soccer coaches, gang leaders, college professors, or romantic partners powerful in and of themselves, or do they have power only in relation to other people? Power, like status, is not an attribute of an individual but a feature of a relationship and is linked to resources available in the larger social structure in which the relationship is embedded. Power is a property of the social relation and not the individual (Emerson 1962). Thus, a president is powerful in relation to the citizens, a professor is powerful only in relation to the students, and a coach is powerful only in relation to the players. Because power is relational, a person can be powerful in one relationship or context and much less powerful in another relationship or context. A professor has more power than a student within the classroom, but she has less power than a dean who oversees the faculty. Power, like status, depends on the context.

Returning to our *Harry Potter* example from the previous chapter, power dynamics abound in the story. For example, Harry has some power at Hogwarts because Dumbledore depends on him to aid him in defeating Voldemort (the fallen wizard). But Harry has very little power within his aunt and uncle's house while he lives there. That is, he has very little opportunity to exert his own will to get what he desires, such as staying out late or having freedom around the house. Dudley, the son of Harry's hateful aunt and uncle, on the other hand, is provided with unlimited resources and freedoms. In addition, even though Filch, the caretaker of Hogwarts and a squib with no magical powers, has low status, he does have quite a bit of power at Hogwarts. When he catches students breaking the rules, he has the authority to dole out punishments, an activity in which he takes great delight. Not surprisingly, Filch thought that Dolores Umbridge (who became headmistress of Hogwarts for a short while and is very nasty to Harry and the students in general) was the best thing that happened to Hogwarts because she increased his power over the students while she was in charge. Filch, then, had low status, but high power relative to the students during Umbridge's rule.

Our two goals in this chapter are the following: (1) to examine power dynamics in social exchange processes and social networks and (2) to show how power processes operate in groups and social networks to perpetuate and maintain social inequality in society (we will distinguish between groups and social networks later in the chapter). We begin our discussion of power by providing an overview of social exchange theory. Richard Emerson (1962) developed a theory about power relations among members of groups and, in the 1970s, theorized about power relations in social networks (Emerson 1972). Emerson, along with Homans (1961) and Blau (1964), is one of the early scholars of social exchange theory. In this overview, we address the following questions: (1) How is relative power determined in relationships? and (2) What are power relations in social networks?

Then, following this important foundational information, we address the following: (1) When will actors use power in social exchange relations? (2) How do commitment and trust develop in social exchange relations? (3) What is the role of emotions in social exchange relations? and (4) What is the relationship between status and power?

As you read what follows, think about your own relationships and the power dynamics exhibited and expressed within them.

Social Exchange Theory Overview

The focus of **social exchange theory** is on the *relationships among actors.* **Actors** can be individuals, groups, organizations, or even nation-states. We focus mainly on individuals here. **Relationships** include many types, such as friendships, romantic relations, parental relationships, buyer–seller relationships, and authority relationships, such as between managers and workers or patients and doctors. People benefit from and contribute to social interactions within these relationships. Much of what we need and value (e.g., food, approval, companionship, information, and love) can be obtained only from other people. We depend on each other for these valued resources and provide them to each other in the process of social exchange. When actors have possessions and capabilities that are valued by others in social relations, they are resources in that relation. **Resources** include tangible goods and services of economic exchange and socially valued outcomes such as approval, love, and status that are valued by others. "Because resources depend on their value to others, they are attributes of *relations,* not actors; i.e., what constitutes a resource for an actor in one relation may not in another" (Molm 2006:26).

Similar to the symbolic interaction perspective (Chapter 3), social exchange theory has assumptions that are neither true nor false (Blau 1964; Homans 1962; Molm and Cook 1995). First, *relationships exist because needs are met through exchange with others.* We are born into a family, which involves a web of relationships, and then we build relationships in day care, at school, in places of religious or spiritual worship, and in other activities with peers and teachers. As we grow, we are in romantic relationships and in coworker relationships at our jobs in addition to our ongoing family and friend relations. It is through relationships that we are able to fulfill our needs, from basic needs like food and shelter to intangibles such as learning skills as well as loving and being loved, touching and being touched, and having fun. Therefore, we are dependent to some degree on others to meet these needs.

Second, people in relationships try to behave in ways that *maximize the benefits or rewards that they positively value and minimize the costs that they negatively value in relationships* by seeking rewarding relationships and trying to avoid painful ones. **Benefits or rewards** are positively valued and include both material and nonmaterial things such as money, cars, prestige, love, or companionship. **Costs** are negatively valued and also include material and nonmaterial things such as fights, time, dishonesty, money, broken promises, or boredom. People exchange rewards and costs in their relationships to meet their needs, and they do so in ways that attempt to increase their benefits and decrease their costs.

Third, *to keep a relationship going, both parties must perceive that the benefits or rewards they get in the relationship outweigh the costs they incur in the relationship.* For example, if you have a friend who is continually asking for your help but does not help you in return, the relationship is becoming one-sided or off-balance. People want mutual reciprocity in their relationships. If you give, then you expect something similar in return. If the friendship continues to be imbalanced from your point of view, where the costs of staying in the relationship seem greater than the rewards you get out of the relationship, then the friendship may end or fade away over time, unless something changes.

Fourth, *benefits being exchanged are guided under a principle of satiation or diminishing marginal utility.* For example, food is more valuable to a hungry person than to one who has just eaten. Also, benefits diminish in value over a period of exchanges, but some benefits lose their value more slowly than others because they can be used to obtain other types of benefits. For example, money loses its value much more slowly than a series of watches. You can use money in many cultures to buy other goods that you value (therefore, money has *exchange value*); however, you only really need one watch (watches have simply *use value*) (Molm and Cook 1995).

Fifth, *actors in relationships consider alternative relationships to the present relationship.* Sometimes people stay in relationships even when it is obvious that it is not a healthy or balanced relationship. You may have friends who stay in relationships with other friends or with a romantic partner even though they know that they are putting much more into the relationship than the other person. Part of the reason for staying is that the available alternative relationships are perceived as worse than staying in the present relationship. Also, the alternative of being out of the relationship is perceived as worse than staying in the present relationship. It can be very complicated, as in the case of women (and sometimes men) who are abused by their partners—they may stay for a host of reasons, such as economic support or for the sake of their children even though the costs they incur are much greater than the rewards they receive. Leaving the relationship seems worse than staying in the relationship, even though it is not a positive situation.

These assumptions point to the *interdependence* between actors in social exchange. That interdependence may be further examined in terms of the relative power positions of the individuals in the relationship.

How Is Relative Power Determined in Relationships?

Think of your relationship with your parents. Who has more power in this relationship and why? Think of your relationship with your best friend(s) or with a romantic partner. Who has more power in this relationship? How is power determined in these relationships? Can a relationship ever be balanced in terms of power, or will one party always have more power than another?

Emerson (1962) provides one way to look at power in relationships in his **power dependence theory**. He complemented Weber's conception of power noted previously, stating that the power of an actor in a relationship derives from the other person's dependence on her. That is, the power of a person, say José, in relation to another person, say Tim, is based on Tim's dependence on José. Also, the power of Tim in relation to José is based on José's dependence on Tim. But what is the source of dependence?

Dependence of one Actor A on another Actor B in a relationship is based on two things: (1) how much Actor A *values* what resources Actor B can exchange with Actor A and (2) Actor A's *availability of alternative relationships* to exchange outside of the Actor A–Actor B relationship. Take the example of José and Tim, where José is Tim's boss at a retail firm. Tim's dependence on José is based on two things: (1) Tim's value for José's resources (things that José has that meets Tim's needs) and (2) Tim's availability from alterative resources where his needs can be met outside of his relationship with José (Cook, Cheshire, and Gerbasi 2006). So, in our example, Tim depends on José for his salary and being assigned stimulating projects, and these are things that are important to Tim (high value of José's resources). Tim also does not have any alternatives to this relationship because of a current economic crisis and high unemployment in his area of work (low availability of alternatives). Tim needs what José can offer him right now, and he has no other job prospects. Tim seems to be power disadvantaged (highly dependent), but we must also look at José's position. In our example, Tim also has very good skills, but José knows that Tim's skills are not critical to the company's success and, therefore, are not important to José (low value of Tim's resources). Also, José could replace Tim fairly easily because there is a large pool of available workers with Tim's skills (high availability of alternatives). In this example, Tim is more dependent on José than José is on Tim. Tim values more of what José offers than vice versa, and he also has fewer alternatives than José to meet needs. Therefore, José is more powerful (and less dependent) than Tim in the relationship. This is an example of a **power-imbalanced relationship**, where one actor has more power (less dependent) in the relationship than the other actor.

Many relationships are imbalanced. Friendship relations can be imbalanced when one person is more dependent on the friendship than the other person. For example, take a friendship between Todrick and Robin. In this friendship, Todrick values more what Robin can give to the relationship than Robin values what Todrick can provide in the relationship. He likes to spend time with her because she is witty and fun, whereas she is somewhat bored by his company. Also, Todrick has fewer friends to hang out with than Robin. Todrick, then, is more dependent (less powerful) than Robin in this friendship. You can imagine this imbalance in one-sided romantic relationships where one person is in love and the other person is not.

Who do you think has more power in the student–professor relationship? Your first reaction is probably to say the professor—and rightly so. The professor has control over grades and possesses the knowledge that students need. But do the students have something the professor needs? Professors do "need" students in order to teach their classes and earn their salaries. If no students sign up for a professor's class, this signals to the department chair and dean that there is a problem with this professor. Also, professors desire that students participate in class discussions. It is much more fun for all with highly motivated participating students! How about alternatives? Do students and professors have any alternatives to the relationship? Not really once the drop/add period is over! A professor cannot just drop a class and teach another one during the middle of the semester, and it is unlikely that all the students would drop a class simultaneously during the semester. If we look at the two dimensions of dependence, then, we could say that professors do have more power than students but maybe not as much as you initially thought.

Power-balanced relationships are possible (Emerson 1962). In these relationships, both parties are equally dependent on each other. They could be equally and highly dependent on one another and, therefore, equally highly powerful in the relationship, both strongly desiring the resources each brings to the relationship, and both not recognizing alternative sources of the desired resources. Harry, Hermione, and Ron in *Harry Potter*, for example, all had fairly power-balanced relationships with each other, in which they were all mutually and highly dependent on one another. They all valued what each other had to offer in their friendships, such as companionship and support, and did not see alternative sources for these highly valued resources (i.e., from other students at Hogwarts). This high level of dependence is more likely to lead to strong cohesion (a strong bond) between the actors, compared to low levels of dependence (Emerson 1962). Actors may also be mutually low in dependence, such as acquaintances that get together from time to time, not highly invested in the relationships, and both have other alternatives to this relationship to meet their needs.

Emerson's power-dependence theory laid the foundation for many recent developments in exploring the give-and-take that happens in social relationships. In the next section, we see how Emerson (1972) and other social exchange theorists have extended the notion of power dependence.

What Are Power Relations in Social Networks?

Up to this point, we have mainly been examining power and exchange in relationships involving two actors (i.e., exchange in dyads). Current work in social exchange, however, has extended analysis of two-party relations to emphasize those dyadic relationships in the contexts of larger exchange networks consisting of more than two actors (Molm 2006). An **exchange network** consists of a set of two or more connected exchange relations. This means that there is a system that connects three or more individuals who exchange goods or services (Cook et al. 2006). People often exchange with one another within the context of these larger social networks (Emerson 1972). Sometimes the actors in these exchanges know each other and are collectively oriented with specified norms (e.g., in groups such as student clubs), but in other cases they do not all know each other and are not collectively oriented (e.g., in networks such as one that involves consumers, car dealers, and car manufacturers where actors are individually oriented). This network of connected exchange relations defines a set of possible ties that constrain who may exchange with whom (Lawler, Thye, and Yoon 2008). Two exchange relations are connected with each other only when the frequency or value of exchange in one relation affects the frequency or value of exchange in another relation (Molm and Cook 1995). For example, if I buy a car from Dealer X, I will not be buying a car from Dealer Y.

Like actors in dyadic relationships, actors in social exchange networks are dependent on one another for things such as material goods or services such as money, for socially valued outcomes such as love or affection, and for psychological gratification. In these networks of more than two actors, individuals exchange with others in the network, potentially establishing partners with whom they exchange on a recurring basis over time. For example, imagine a tire company that needs to buy rubber in order to make tires. This company will search for producers of rubber. Eventually, it will choose a particular seller from whom to buy, to the exclusion of the other sellers. Once a sale is made, a social relationship is formed between the two companies because actors provide reciprocal benefits to one another. Often, these exchanges continue over time, and these repeated exchanges maintain this relationship. This relationship may change if the tire company decides to buy from another rubber producer instead.

To examine how power processes operate in social networks, we need to think about structural power. **Structural power** is defined as the potential that is derived from the structure of dependence of actors on one another in the network (Emerson 1972). In effect, structural power reflects the patterns of relative dependence of dyads embedded in the network. As in dyadic relationships, in larger networks all actors may be similarly dependent, in which case the actors' power is equal and the entire power structure is balanced. On the other hand, when there are inequalities in dependence, actors have unequal power, and the power structure is considered imbalanced. Within a network of connected relationships, there may be varying degrees of mutual dependence among the actors and, therefore, varying degrees of inequality.

It is important to distinguish between power structures and power use. **Power use** (as noted previously) is the actual behavioral exercise of the power potential (inherent in the network structure) by actors to reap desired outcomes in their exchanges with one another. That is, people use the power associated with their position in the process of exchange to get what they need. Also, individuals initiate exchange in the hope of receiving benefits from others, and the receipt of desired benefits ensures the continuation of the exchange (Molm 2006).

There are different forms of social exchange. The first type is referred to as **direct exchange:** Actor A gives to Actor B, and vice versa; that is, two actors exchange benefits with each other. For example, the tire company pays money in exchange for rubber from the rubber producer. In direct exchanges, there are *two types of transactions.* First, there are **reciprocal direct exchanges**; they involve performing a beneficial act for another person, without explicit negotiation and without knowledge of when, how, or in what manner the action might be reciprocated. They occur when a person does a service or provides resources for another without expectation of an explicit immediate return. The expectation of reciprocity in the future is often implicit. Examples include giving a friend a lift to work, feeding a neighbor's cat, or providing favors for a roommate (Molm and Cook 1995).

The second type is referred to as **negotiated direct exchanges**, which involve actors engaging in a joint decision-making process to determine the terms of the exchange. As in explicit bargaining, actors make, retract, and change offers with regard, for example, to setting a price for an object, dividing up tasks, or determining limits. Thus, the level and receipt of the desired benefits is known at the time of the exchange. Examples of negotiated direct exchanges are divorce settlements and labor or union contracts (Molm and Cook 1995). Think also of sports teams bargaining over the terms of a trade, while players bargain over the terms of their contracts (Lawler, Thye, and Yoon 2009).

Many network connections are **negative** in that an exchange in one relation decreases exchange in another relation. For example, when the tire company buys rubber from one producer, this means that the company will not be buying from other potential producers at that particular time (Kollock 1994; Molm and Cook 1995). Some network connections are **positive** in that an exchange in one relation increases an exchange in another. A pharmaceutical company sells prescription drugs to physicians, who provide to patients.

A second type of social exchange is **indirect exchange** where "a benefit received by A from B is not reciprocated directly from A's giving to B, but indirectly, by A's giving to another actor in the network or group" (Molm and Cook 1995:211). Donating blood and carpooling are examples of indirect exchange: An actor provides a benefit for another actor with the expectation that in the future some other actor will do the same for them. Also, the principle of "paying it forward" embodies indirect exchange.

Two other forms of exchanges, both indirect, include productive and generalized exchange. In **productive exchange**, actors contribute individually to produce a joint outcome or collective good, and they all receive benefit from the collective good. Interdependence is high, yet the actors need to coordinate to generate the common good and distribute benefits. For example, several students each contribute to a group project for a class to produce a final product. If any of the parties fail to contribute, no one benefits. Separately obtained benefits do not occur. Other examples of this type of exchange occur in team sports, a homeowners' association, or business partnerships. In **generalized exchange**, there is an indirect form of exchange that consists of three or more actors who can give to and receive from one another, but those who give and those who receive are not matched in pairs (Lawler et al. 2008). Examples include aiding a stranded motorist or opening a door for a stranger. Acts of giving are unlikely to produce much sense of shared responsibility (Lawler et al. 2008; Molm, Collett, and Schaefer 2007).

Importantly, while these four forms of exchange are separated analytically, they are often found together in relationships. For example, some exchanges between partners in romantic relationships are reciprocal, while others are negotiated.

With this overview of social exchange and social networks, we focus next on several key questions asked by social exchange theorists: (1) When will actors use power in social exchange relations? (2) How do commitment and trust develop in social exchange relations? (3) What is the role of emotions in social exchange relations?

When Will Actors Use Power in Social Exchange Relations?

When actors are in power-balanced dyads or networks, there is less opportunity for the actors to take advantage of or exploit one another because they are mutually (high or low) dependent on one another. But what happens in the more commonly occurring power-imbalanced relations in dyads or networks? Most of our discussion in this section focuses on *direct exchanges in negatively connected networks*.

Power in relationships affects the behavior of the actors in that relationship (Emerson 1962). In many power-imbalanced relations the actor with more power will tend to use it, even if they do not intend to use it. The more powerful actor will be in a position to get the other actor to do what he or she may otherwise not do.

For example, consider two people, Anita and Simone, who work at a national retail store. Anita works in management, and Simone works in the company's information technology (IT) division. They have a good working relationship in that Simone helps Anita with any computer problems, and Anita shares information with Simone and provides resources to Simone so that her division runs smoothly throughout the year. They are in a power-balanced relationship in that each has skills and resources that both value and desire, and they do not have other alternatives to meet their needs, represented here in Figure 9.1:

FIGURE 9.1 ● Power-Balanced Relationship Between Two Actors

Anita ——————————————————— Simone

Let's say that several months go by and then the company hires Tameka, also in management. Tameka learns that Simone can help Tameka when she has computer problems, and Simone learns that Tameka also has valuable information and sources of support to help Simone. Who has more power now in the Simone and Anita relationship? Simone now has another good alternative—her relationship with Tameka, in meeting her needs (high availability). Therefore, she now also has more power in the relationship with Anita because Anita does not have another alternative (low availability) and so is more dependent on Simone than vice versa, as represented here in Figure 9.2:

FIGURE 9.2 ● Power-Imbalanced Network Between Three Actors

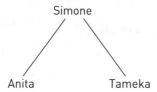

Simone is now likely, and over time, to ask Anita for more favors than Anita asks of her because she is less dependent (and therefore more powerful) in the relationship (Emerson 1962). In addition, she may not be as readily available to provide Anita with technical assistance as she was in the past. Importantly, Simone may not even be aware that she is taking advantage of Anita. Simply being in the more powerful position in a relationship often leads to using this advantage over time. Often, more powerful actors are not even fully aware of their behavior (Emerson 1962; Molm 2006). Regardless, often in power-imbalanced relations, the more powerful actors begin to impose their will to get what they want.

But can Simone continue to take advantage of Anita? What may Anita do to address this undesirable situation? Imbalanced relationships have a tendency to move toward a balanced situation (Cook et al. 2006; Emerson 1962; Molm 2006). Anita, over time, will eventually notice that she is being taken for granted or being used. As a result, she has several options to move the relationship toward balance. First, she can try to acquire more desirable information and resources that Simone wants, information that is difficult for her to get in her relationship with Tameka (this is called **status-giving by increasing value of one's own resources**, and these could be material or nonmaterial things). In this way, Anita is increasing the value of the resources she has to offer Simone. Second, Anita could try to find someone else (e.g., Rick) who has technical skills similar to Simone's so that she does not have to rely only on her. This is referred to as **extending the actor's social network** of relationships outside the Anita-Simone relationship—that is, Anita seeks out alternative relationships to meet her needs. This makes Anita less dependent because she now has increased her alternatives, as represented here in Figure 9.3:

FIGURE 9.3 ● Extending Social Network to Balance Power in a Relationship

Anita ———————— Simone
| |
| |
Rick   Tameka

Third, Anita could develop a relationship with Tameka and encourage Tameka to pool their information and resources together so that Simone has to help them equally in order to get information and support from them. Emerson called this strategy **coalition formation**. This strategy reduces Simone's available alternatives because Anita and Tameka act as a unit to exchange with Simone, as represented here in Figure 9.4:

FIGURE 9.4 ● Forming Coalition to Balance Power in a Network

Anita/Tameka ———————————————————— Simone

Finally, Anita could **withdraw** from the relationship and try to acquire her own technical skills. In this strategy, Anita is decreasing the value of what Simone has to offer. This option also breaks the imbalanced relation rather than restores balance; not surprisingly, however, it can be a difficult and unrealistic option in many situations.

These balancing techniques are used in many different types of situations. For example, workers often acquire skills to make themselves more valuable in companies or corporations. Also, sometimes they form coalitions, such as unions, so that they become more valuable to the company as a unit and become less dependent on the company compared to acting as separate individuals. These strategies, however, often come with high costs in terms of time, threats to emotional well-being, and sometimes threat of or actual physical harm. Coalitions are much easier to form in simple networks, where only a few actors in power-disadvantaged positions coalesce against one powerful actor, than in larger networks (Cook and Gilmore 1984). One reason is that it is much costlier to coordinate the activity of a large number of actors. And if some actors are left out of the coalition, this provides the more powerful actors an opportunity to seize upon their alternatives— that is, influence power-disadvantaged actors who failed to join the coalition to not join the coalition (Cook et al. 2006).

These balancing techniques can also occur in friendships or romantic relationships. For example, imagine a love triangle where Jacob and Edward are in love with Bella (yes, names are associated with the *Twilight* series—why not!). Initially, Bella and Edward fall in love with one another. They both enjoy each other's company and give to each other what each other needs. Several months later, Bella forms a close friendship with Jacob. Jacob, like Edward, is kind, loving, and generous. Eventually, Jacob falls in love with Bella. In this love triangle, Bella has more power than Edward and Jacob because she is in a position of having two alternatives, while they have only Bella. As a result, Bella could, over time, ask Edward for more favors than he asks of her. She will also have more say in the final decisions for them such as what friends they see socially and which clubs they frequent. Clearly, over time Bella will receive more benefits within the Bella–Edward or the Bella–Jacob relationship than Edward or Jacob. Eventually, though, something will need to change this unbalanced situation. For example, she may be asked to choose between them.

To complicate matters, we find out that yet another guy likes Bella: Mike. Mike, however, is dating someone else: Jessica. So, even though Mike also likes Bella, he does have another alternative to the Bella–Mike relationship. Importantly, Bella's power advantage is *structurally* determined by her strategic location in this romantic network. She has more connections in this dating network to meet her needs than Edward, Jacob, or Mike. Bella, in our example, is in the most powerful position relative to the other three actors; as a result, she will be able to exercise her will the most and receive the most benefits compared to the other actors within this network. Notice, also, that of the three guys in our network, Mike is less dependent on Bella than Edward or Jacob because he also is connected to Jessica.

The power-dependence relations created by this network structure (Bella–Edward, Bella–Jacob, Bella–Mike, and Mike–Jessica) determine not only the distribution of power but also the distribution of power use, as discussed previously (Cook and Emerson 1978; Molm 1990; Willer 1999). The relative power position in a network of exchange relations (such as in the love triangle network example), produces relative differences in the use of power and the distribution of rewards across the positions in the network (Cook and Emerson 1978; Cook et al. 2013; Markovsky, Willer, and Patton 1988). The most powerful actor relative to the other actors (i.e., the least dependent actor) in the network will use the most power and receive the most benefits or rewards relative to the other actors. Bella, in our example, will most likely receive the most favors and rewards in this network; this will be so until this network moves toward balance. For example, over time Bella may choose Edward as her sole partner, thereby breaking up the network. See Figure 9.5.

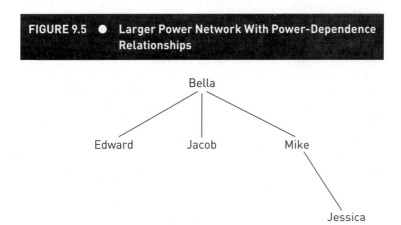

FIGURE 9.5 ● Larger Power Network With Power-Dependence Relationships

The consequences of power use in exchange networks are clear. Actors (individuals, organizations, and nations) who have more structural power are able to garner vastly more resources (wealth, income, education, political, etc.) than those who have less structural power because they can exploit the more dependent actors in the network (Cook and Emerson 1978; Molm 2006; Molm and Cook 1995). Studies show that actors in these more powerful positions acquire significantly more resources (whether money or other valuable goods) just by virtue of being in that position (Molm 2006). Social exchange principles help us explain why in many nations the rich get richer and the poor get poorer. Power-disadvantaged positions with few initial resources and more dependent ties make it very difficult for low-power actors to gain advantages.

Social exchange principles apply to macrolevel inequality patterns but also apply to your own day-to-day relationships. We often do not think about power in our relationships, but we do know when we are being taken advantage of by others. It is more difficult for us, however, to see and admit when we are taking advantage of others (we discuss this in more detail in Chapter 11 on justice).

Although a central theme of social exchange theory is to examine the distribution of power and power use and its consequences in dyads and social networks, theorists also turned their attention to other dynamics of social exchange. In the next section, we discuss how commitment to and trust in exchange relations can develop over time.

How Do Commitment and Trust Develop in Social Exchange Relations?

One of us grew up in Tacoma, Washington, a midsized city on Washington's Puget Sound, and the other grew up in Peoria, Illinois, another midsized city on the Illinois River. While we were both growing up in roughly the same time period but in different places, both of our dads would buy their cars over the years from the same car dealer in their respective towns. Coincidently, they both consistently bought Buick cars. In both situations, our dads could have potentially gotten better deals at other car dealers, but they continued to buy their cars from the same car dealers time after time. From a purely classical economics point of view, they were not acting "rationally" because they did not necessarily get the "best deal." Why did they behave this way?

Social exchange theorists provide three reasons. First, repeated exchanges with the same actor (in our example, a car dealer) can be defined as a behavioral form of commitment. **Behavioral commitment** is the extent to which pairs of actors repeatedly exchange with one another (our dads exchanging with one car dealer repeatedly over time) rather than engaging in exchanges with other members of the network (our dads exchanging with other car dealers in town over time) (Cook and Emerson 1978; Kollock 1994). Another way to think about commitment is to view it as the tendency for actors to stay with and continue to exchange with actors that they have exchanged with in the past. Why is commitment important? This behavioral commitment *reduces uncertainty* in the exchange process (Cook and Emerson 1978; Kollock 1994; Yamagishi, Cook, and Watabe 1998). Our dads knew that they would get a reliable car at a fair price at their favorite car dealer. Even though they had other options, they were not guaranteed that they would get a fair price. Buying a car is an uncertain exchange because you never know when you might be overpriced and ripped off (especially before the extensive price information found on the Internet!). Our dads bought from the car dealers with whom they had a history because this helped reduce the uncertainty in the exchange process.

Second, these repeated exchanges also build **trust** in the exchange relation. The buyers, in this case our dads, trusted these particular car dealers. Trust is the "belief that an exchange partner will not exploit or take advantage of an actor" (Molm, Schaefer, and Collett 2009:2). Our dads expected that their car dealers would treat them well as a result of their past experiences. *These expectations of trust are much more likely to develop in situations that are risky and uncertain,* such as in the case of buying a car. There is always the possibility that the buyer could end up buying a lemon because the buyer never really knows the true quality of a car until after it has been purchased and driven for a while. Over time, sellers can develop a reputation for being trustworthy (Kollock 1994), as our dads' car dealers were able to do. Social exchange, then, is not solely dependent on pure exchange principles; commitment and trust, developed under uncertainty, also fuel social exchanges (Emerson 1972; Molm 2006).

Another excellent example of the importance of uncertainty and risk in building trust in exchange relationships is provided by Kollock (1994). He discusses two types of markets in Thailand. The first market involves the selling and purchasing of rubber. Buyers of rubber cannot tell the quality of the rubber at the time of the sale. This makes this exchange relation a difficult and uncertain one. Kollock (1994:314) notes, "It is not until months later, after extensive processing, that the buyer can determine whether the grower took the extra time and expense to insure a high-quality crop." As a result, the buyer is not highly motivated to pay a high price because he does not know what the quality of the rubber will be, and the grower is also not motivated to grow high-quality goods because there is no way to show how much care he took at the time of sale. In addition, there were no regulatory agencies to oversee the exchanges. This is a situation full of uncertainty and risk. How is this problem addressed? The growers and buyers of rubber create personal long-term exchange relationships. As a result, the growers are able to establish reputations for trustworthiness.

The second market is rice—a market where uncertainty and risk are low and the need for commitment and concern for reputation is low. The quality of rice can be seen directly and at no cost by "rubbing a few grains together between blocks of wood" (Kollock 1994:315). In this market, there is certainty with little concern of reputation and, therefore, little opportunity for the emergence of commitment and trust.

Take a moment to apply these exchange principles to online buying and selling. What do you look for when you want to buy a particular item from a buyer online? You do not know them; you have never met them before, yet you are about to exchange your money for an item, such as a guitar or a French horn. How do you decide if they are trustworthy? Sellers develop reputations online, and most of us investigate this reputation that comes from other buyers with histories of buying from particular sellers. You may have the choice between buying a guitar for $300 from a seller with little to no reputation or buying it for $350 from a seller with a good reputation. Which exchange would you choose in this fairly risky situation?

Third, these repeated exchanges often lead to the development of **affective relations**, such as between our dads and the particular car dealers. That is, it feels good to have a successful exchange, and this may fuel future exchanges with the same actor. In the next section, we discuss the role of emotions in social exchange specifically.

What Is the Role of Emotions in Social Exchange Relations?

Power Relations and Emotions

How does dependence in a relationship affect the experience and expression of emotions? Let's go back to the case of José and Tim in the retail firm. José just denied Tim a pay raise, even though Tim was hoping to get one this year. Will Tim feel anger and, if so, will he express it toward José? It depends! What is the relationship between emotional responses and dependence in the relationship?

Let's say over the last 18 months Tim has acquired a distinct set of skills and, as a result, José perceives Tim's skills as unique relative to others in the retail firm. In addition, as a result of Tim's newly acquired skills, he now has many alternative job options, at least matching José's options to replace him. Tim has become less dependent on José compared to when he had fewer skills and alternatives.

Employees like Tim, who have many alternatives, are more likely to feel more intense anger and resentment and express that anger and resentment toward their boss when facing a conflict than employees who have few alternatives (because they have few job options or desired skills) (Johnson, Ford, and Kaufman 2000). The costs of displaying negative emotions toward the boss are much greater for highly dependent employees than for employees who are only minimally dependent.

Social Networks and Emotions

Recent developments in the social exchange approach focus on the emotional consequences of social exchange processes and how emotions may affect the structure of the network of exchange relations. Lawler and colleagues (Lawler and Yoon 1996, 1998; Lawler 2001, 2006; Lawler et al. 2008, 2009) argue that the power structure of a social network determines who exchanges with whom. Some actors are more likely to exchange with other actors, depending on their relative power positions within the social network. The network structure creates opportunities or constraints on these exchanges. Over time, a recurrent or repetitive pattern of exchanges occurs among two or more actors.

As a result of this consistent frequency of exchanges, actors experience **global emotions** from these interactions. For example, if the recurrent exchanges are successful, the actors are likely to experience positive global emotions, overall good feelings, such as satisfaction and pleasantness. The source of these good feelings, however, is somewhat ambiguous. As a result of this ambiguity, people search cognitively to explain these global feelings. In this process, they often attribute these positive global emotions to the exchange relationship itself. When positive emotions are attributed to the social unit (the exchange relationship), the specific emotion is **affective attachment**. As a result, they develop a sense of **solidarity toward the relationship** itself (i.e., a strong and durable relation) and, in turn, become more behaviorally committed to the relationship (Lawler 2001, 2006).

When are actors in social networks more likely to perceive the social unit as the main source of global emotions? When the exchange tasks or activities are highly **joint tasks**. Joint tasks include such tasks as child rearing for a couple, a work group in an assembly line at a factory, or an organizational merger. Here, the task fosters a sense of shared responsibility for whether the actors succeed or fail at the task. If actors perceive that they are jointly responsible for the task, they are more likely to attribute their feelings to the exchange relationship (Lawler 2006).

Using our example, in addition to building trust in their relationships, our dads also most likely experienced positive feelings of satisfaction by working with their car dealers to buy their Buicks for what they considered a good deal. As a result, over time, they may have developed positive feelings toward the relationship itself, which motivated them to continue to buy their cars from the same dealers. Positive emotions, then, led to continued behavioral commitment. You can also imagine that unsuccessful exchanges can lead to negative global emotions, attributed to the social relation, leading to a lack of solidarity, and low behavioral commitment.

Lawler and colleagues provided empirical evidence of these relationships, particularly when actors have equal power. When power is unequal, however, low-power actors seek behavioral commitment to reduce uncertainty rather than because of fondness or positive feelings for the relationship. Lawler and Yoon (1998:875) noted that "power inequality raises fairness issues in negotiated exchange (i.e., whether and how the power differences should be manifest in agreements reached), and thereby complicate the task of arriving at mutually acceptable exchanges."

In addition, productive exchange (such as in team sports) are more likely to produce recurring interactions, emotional reactions, and affective sentiments toward the social exchange relationship than any other form of exchange because the actors engage in highly joint tasks and activities more in this form than in other forms of exchange. Emerging perceptions of a "group" are also more likely to occur. The least likely to produce these strong person-to-group ties occurs in generalized exchange networks (such as reviewing for academic journals). (See Lawler, Thye, and Yoon [2015] for further developments.)

Other scholars, Molm, Takahashi, and Peterson (2000), argue for a different view of the role of emotions in social exchange processes. Their work is distinguished in two important ways from that of Lawler's. First, they argued that actors attribute their felt emotions to particular exchange partners rather than to the social relation itself (Molm 2006; Molm et al. 2000). Second, they suggest that the emotional bonds that develop between specific partners are a *result* of behavioral commitment, rather than a *producer* of behavioral commitment. Emotion, then, is an outcome of the exchange process produced mainly from commitments to the exchange relation. Molm and colleagues view structural arrangements as the key to understanding recurring exchanges in networks; emotion is an outcome of these exchanges. Lawler and colleagues, however, as stated previously, see emotions as one important causal mechanism (among others) that affects behavioral commitment in exchanges and, in turn, structural arrangements.

Molm and colleagues also found empirical evidence for their ideas. Reciprocal exchange is inherently more uncertain and risky than negotiated exchange (Molm et al. 2000). In reciprocal exchange, remember that actors risk giving benefits or goods unilaterally while receiving little to nothing in return. Their results show that because of this uncertainty, the opportunity to demonstrate commitment and trustworthiness is greater in reciprocal than in negotiated exchanges. Actors are more likely to attribute these positive experiences to the exchange partner's positive traits and intentions rather than to the social relation, and this is more likely to occur in reciprocal than in negotiated exchanges (Molm et al. 2000). In addition, actors who are disadvantaged in the exchange network are more likely to stay in the network when they have a history of reciprocal, rather than negotiated, exchange. Reciprocal exchange produces more personal attraction to the network than negotiated exchange. And, in turn, power-disadvantaged actors (more dependent actors) are more likely to view themselves as group members in reciprocal than in negotiated exchange (Savage and Sommer 2016).

In addition, in contrast to Lawler and colleagues, Molm and colleagues found that generalized exchange produces the most social solidarity among the actors (Molm et al. 2007; Molm 2010). The risk of nonreciprocity is great in generalized exchange because benefits flow unilaterally, and reciprocity in general is highly uncertain and indirect. Therefore, the opportunity for building social solidarity is much more likely in these types of exchanges.

In effect, creating perceptions of an emerging group through task jointness (Lawler et al.'s approach) and building trust through risk-taking (Molm et al.'s approach) can be seen as distinct processes, and both could be on the right track under certain conditions (Cook et al. 2013). It may be that when bilateral (two-way) exchanges are seen as a cooperative venture solidarity may be an outcome, but when they are seen as competitive, solidarity is less likely to occur (Kuwabara 2011).

By this time in the chapter, you may be trying to tease out what distinguishes status from power. After all, many times they are often associated with one another. For example, Supreme Court justices in the United States are perceived as worthy and esteemed and hold powerful positions within U.S. democracy. In our last section, we discuss the similarities and the distinctions between them as well as their relationship to one another. We also segue into our next chapter, which is on legitimacy.

What Is the Relationship Between Status and Power?

Status, discussed in the previous chapter, and power are both group processes, and they both involve inequalities in benefits or rewards and costs. People often follow the directives of actors who have high status and high power. A major distinction, however, lies in the reasons why people comply. In regard to status, people comply with a high-status person because they respect and value this person and their opinions. For example, church members may follow the directives of a deacon because they value her opinions and view her as competent. The deacon has no power over them per se in that she cannot kick them out of the church. In contrast, people often comply with a powerful actor because they may face consequences if they do not. For example, if a professor required you to take three exams, you may not want to do so, but you do it anyway because he controls your grade. Actors with high power, then, can get people to do things they might not otherwise do. This is so because power is associated with possessing resources that others want, such as control over grades, pay, and work duties. Power, therefore, is structural in that its source is in the positions that people have in relation to others, and the associated resources that come with those positions.

What are the connections between status and power in groups and in networks? Being high in status can significantly help in obtaining powerful positions. Being high in power can significantly affect acquiring status. In regard to the first situation, one reason that status can lead to power is that resources that high-status people possess are more highly valued than resources possessed by low-status people. For example, celebrity personal items, such as Elton John's wardrobe of designer labels, Lady Gaga's "meat dress," or Prince's "Yellow Cloud" electric guitar are worth much more than any clothes or musical instruments that we own. We value things that high-status people possess. As a result, high-status people have more valuable things to exchange than low-status people. They gain more power by controlling access to more "valuable" things than low-status people (Thye 2000).

In a laboratory experiment, Thye (2000) illustrates this relationship between status and power. In this study, participants exchanged resources with one another. The resources they traded had the same monetary value, but the low- and high-status participants valued the resources of the high-status people more than the resources of the low-status people. As a result, high-status participants were more sought after as exchange partners, and they received more favorable exchange rates.

And they gained power by controlling access to resources that the other actors desired. In a second study, high-status actors once again earned more than low-status actors across exchanges, and they also exerted more influence over other participants and were perceived as more competent than low-status participants (Thye, Willer, and Markovsky 2006). Status, then, is one important source of power.

Conversely, people who are in powerful positions are at an advantage of obtaining status. One reason for this opportunity is that actors in powerful positions are often thought to be more competent than those in less powerful positions (Lovaglia 1995). Reward expectations theory and status construction theory, discussed in Chapter 8, suggest this very process (Berger, Wagner, and Zelditch 1985; Ridgeway 1991). People who are more resource advantaged, such as people who earn more money or who have fancy offices, are thought to be more competent. This is consistent with our tendency to think that more expensive things are also better, even though this is often not the case. Another way that power may lead to status is when powerful actors use their resources to do favors for other people in the group or in networks. CEOs of companies, for example, may engage in corporate social responsibility activities such as sponsorship of community outreach; these activities can increase their status in the community.

Segue: Power and Legitimacy

Relative power in groups and social networks often determines who will have the potential to use power and who will benefit the most in terms of gaining more resources than others. In many contexts, power potential and power use lead to unfair situations. Powerful actors have the opportunity to abuse their power in order to get what they want, often to the detriment of low-power actors. In many situations, this power advantage leads to the unequal distribution of valuable resources such as money, wealth, food, or kindness. For example, CEOs of large companies may be paid extremely high bonuses, even in times of economic crisis, while at the same time laying off many workers or decreasing their benefits and pay. Dictators of poor countries continue to increase their own wealth while many of their citizens struggle to get adequate food and safe drinking water. In the United States, we know that inequality based on wealth and income continues to increase, such that the gap between those with few resources and those with many resources continues to increase. Is this fair? In Chapter 11, on justice, we will discuss the concept of justice; how people determine what is fair and unfair; and, in turn, how people respond to injustice.

Before we get to justice, however, the next chapter considers the idea that often power and power use by people in positions within status and power structures is viewed as legitimate. For example, the Congress of the United States uses its power within the legislative process to sign bills into law. Umpires determine calls in sports games such as baseball and soccer. Parents provide rules and boundaries for their children. Power use can be positive and seen as appropriate to a majority of people. Power in exchange relationships can also be used to legitimate a leader in his or her position. In certain contexts, then, there is some consensus that power and power use are appropriate. In the next chapter, we will look at how people, acts, and structures become legitimated—that is, perceived as appropriate and right. We will also discuss the consequences (good and bad) of legitimacy in everyday interaction.

Suggested Readings

Brescoll, Victoria L. 2011. "Who Takes the Floor and Why: Gender, Power, and Volubility in Organizations." *Administrative Science Quarterly* 56:622–41.

Harrell, Ashley, and Brent Simpson. 2016. "The Dynamics of Prosocial Leadership: Power and Influence in Collective Action Groups." *Social Forces* 94:1283–1308.

McLintock, Elizabeth Aura. 2014. "Beauty and Status: The Illusion of Exchange in Partner Selection?" *American Sociological Review* 79:575–604.

McPherson, Miller, Lynn Smith-Lovin, and Matthew E. Brashears. 2006. "Social Isolation in America: Changes in Core Discussions Networks Over Two Decades." *American Sociological Review* 71:353–75.

Schaefer, David R. 2009. "Resource Variation and the Development of Cohesion in Exchange Networks." *American Sociological Review* 74:551–72.

Sinclair, H. Colleen, Diane Felmlee, Susan Sprecher, and Brittany L. Wright. 2015. "Don't Tell Me Who I Can't Love: A Multimethod Investigation of Social Network and Reactance Effects on Romantic Relationships." *Social Psychology Quarterly* 78:77–99.

Wakslak, Cheryl J., Pamela K. Smith, and Albert Han. 2014. "Using Abstract Language Signals Power." *Journal of Personality and Social Psychology* 107:41–55.

References

Berger, Joseph M., David G. Wagner, and Morris Zelditch. 1985. "Expectations States Theory: Review and Assessment." Pp. 1–72 in *Status, Rewards, and Influence: How Expectations Organize Behavior*, edited by J. Berger and M. Zelditch. San Francisco: Jossey-Bass.

Blau, Peter M. 1964. *Exchange and Power in Social Life*. New York: Wiley.

Cook, Karen S., Coye Cheshire, and Alexandra Gerbasi. 2006. "Power, Dependence, and Social Exchange." Pp. 194–216 in *Contemporary Social Psychological Theories*, edited by P. J. Burke. Palo Alto, CA: Stanford University Press.

Cook, Karen S., Coye Cheshire, Eric R. W. Rice, and Sandra Nakagawa. 2013. "Social Exchange Theory." Pp. 61–88 in *Handbook of Social Psychology*, 2nd ed., edited by J. DeLamater and A. Ward. New York: Springer. doi:10.1007/978-94-007-6772-0_3

Cook, Karen S., and Richard M. Emerson. 1978. "Power, Equity and Commitment in Exchange Networks." *American Sociological Review* 43:721–39. doi:10.2307/2094546

Cook, Karen S., and Mary R. Gilmore. 1984. "Power, Dependence, and Coalitions." *Advances in Group Processes* 1:27–58.

Emerson, Richard M. 1962. "Power Dependence Relations." *American Sociological Review* 27:31–40. doi:10.2307/2089716

Emerson, Richard, M. 1972. "Exchange Theory, Part 2: Exchange Relations and Networks." Pp. 61–83 in *Sociological Theories in Progress*, edited by J. Berger, M. Zelditch Jr., and B. Anderson. Boston: Houghton Mifflin.

Homans, George C. 1961. *Social Behavior: Its Elementary Forms*. New York: Harcourt Brace & World.

Homans, George C. 1962. *Sentiments and Activities: Essays in Social Science*. Glencoe, IL: Free Press.

Johnson, Cathryn, Rebecca Ford, and Joanne Kaufman. 2000. "Emotional Reactions to Conflict:

Do Dependence and Legitimacy Matter?" *Social Forces* 79:107–37. doi:10.2307/2675566

Kollock, Peter. 1994. "The Emergence of Exchange Structures: An Experimental Study of Uncertainty, Commitment, and Trust." *American Journal of Sociology* 100:313–45. doi:10.1086/230539

Kuwabara, K. 2011. "Cohesion, Cooperation, and the Value of Doing Things Together: How Economic Exchange Creates Relational Bonds." *American Sociological Review* 76:560–80. doi:10.1177/0003122411414825

Lawler, Edward J. 2001. "An Affect Theory of Social Exchange." *American Journal of Sociology* 107:321–52. doi:10.1086/324071

Lawler, Edward J. 2006. "The Affect Theory of Social Exchange." Pp. 244–67 in *Contemporary Social Psychological Theories*, edited by P. J. Burke. Stanford, CA: Stanford University Press.

Lawler, Edward J., Shane R. Thye, and Jeongkoo Yoon. 2008. "Social Exchange and Micro Social Order." *American Sociological Review* 73:519–42. doi:10.1177/000312240807300401

Lawler, Edward J., Shane R. Thye, and Jeongkoo Yoon. 2009. *Social Commitments in a Depersonalized World*. New York: Russell Sage Foundation.

Lawler, Edward J., Shane R. Thye, and Jeongkoo Yoon, eds. 2015. *Order on the Edge of Chaos*. Cambridge, England: Cambridge University Press.

Lawler, Edward J., and Jeongkoo Yoon. 1996. "Commitment in Exchange Relations: A Test of a Theory of Relational Cohesion." *American Sociological Review* 61:89–108. doi:10.2307/2096408

Lawler, Edward J., and Jeongkoo Yoon. 1998. "Network Structure and Emotion in Exchange Relations." *American Sociological Review* 63:871–94. doi:10.2307/2657506

Lovaglia, Michael J. 1995. "Power and Status: Exchange, Attribution, and Expectation States." *Small Group Research* 26:400–26. doi:10.1177/1046496495263005

Markovsky, Barry, David Willer, and Travis Patton. 1988. "Power Relations in Exchange Networks." *American Sociological Review* 53:220–36. doi:10.2307/2095689

Molm, Linda D. 1990. "Structure, Action, and Outcomes: The Dynamics of Power in Social Exchange." *American Sociological Review* 53:810–37.

Molm, Linda D. 2006. "The Social Exchange Framework." Pp. 24–45 in *Contemporary Social Psychological Theories*, edited by P. J. Burke. Stanford, CA: Stanford University Press.

Molm, Linda D. 2010. "The Structure of Reciprocity." *Social Psychology Quarterly* 73:119–31.

Molm, Linda D., Jessica L. Collett, and David R. Schaefer. 2007. "Building Solidarity through Generalized Exchange: A Theory of Reciprocity." *American Journal of Sociology* 113:205–42. doi:10.1086/517900

Molm, Linda D., and Karen S. Cook. 1995. "Social Exchange and Exchange Networks." Pp. 209–35 in *Sociological Perspectives in Social Psychology*, edited by K. S. Cook, G. A. Fine, and J. S. House. Boston: Allyn & Bacon.

Molm, Linda D., David R. Schaefer, and Jessica L. Collett. 2009. "Fragile and Resilient Trust: Risk and Uncertainty in Negotiated and Reciprocal Exchange." *Sociological Theory* 27:1–32.

Molm, Linda D., Nobuyuki Takahashi, and Gretchen Peterson. 2000. "Risk and Trust in Social Exchange: An Experimental Test of a Classical Proposition." *American Journal of Sociology* 105:1396–1427. doi:10.1086/210434

Ridgeway, Cecilia L. 1991. "The Social Construction of Status Value: Gender and Other Nominal Characteristics." *Social Forces* 70:367–86. doi:10.2307/2580244

Savage, Scott V., and Zachary L. Sommer. 2016. "Should I Stay or Should I Go? Reciprocity, Negotiation, and the Choice of Structurally Disadvantaged Actors to Remain in Networks." *Social Psychology Quarterly* 79:115–35. doi:10.1177/0190272516641392

Thye, Shane R. 2000. "A Status Value Theory of Power in Exchange Relations." *American Sociological Review* 65:407–32. doi:10.2307/2657464

Thye, Shane R., David Willer, and Barry Markovsky. 2006. "From Status to Power: New Models at the Intersection of Two Theories." *Social Forces* 84:1471–95. doi:10.1353/sof.2006.0070

Weber, Max. [1924] 1978. *Economy and Society*, Vols. I and II, edited by Guenther Roth and Claus Wittich. Reprint, Berkeley: University of California Press. 1968.

Willer, David. 1999. "Network Exchange Theory: Issues and Directions." Pp. 1–22 in *Network Exchange Theory*, edited by D. Willer. Westport, CT: Praeger.

Yamagishi, Toshio, Karen S. Cook, and Motoki Watabe. 1998. "Uncertainty, Trust, and Commitment Formation in the United States and Japan." *American Journal of Sociology* 104(1):165–94. doi:10.1086/210005

Legitimacy

Shaping Behavior in Groups and Organizations

Why do the majority of U.S. citizens pay their taxes, even though some do so only begrudgingly? Why do most undergraduates take the core curriculum—specific courses every student must take as designated by their colleges and universities—even though they are often not fond of taking them? Why do most people obey their bosses at work much of the time? After reading Chapter 9, you may answer these questions by bringing up the issue of power. After all, if people do not pay taxes, they are breaking the law and may face prison; if students do not take the core requirements at their college or university, they will not graduate with their degrees; if employees do not comply with their bosses' directives, they may get a cut in pay or lose their jobs. Obviously, power processes are at play here because those with more power control desired rewards and undesired punishments for those with less power.

Does power, however, fully explain the behavior of citizens, undergraduates, and employees? After all, are citizens paying taxes only because of the threat of prison? Are students taking core courses only for fear of not graduating? Are employees following orders only because of the sanctions they may face? Indeed, many people believe that paying taxes is something citizens should do; many students believe that they should take the core requirements; and many employees believe, in principle, that they should obey their bosses. Why?

Let's take the case of students and the core curriculum requirements at colleges and universities. Although educational institutions vary on what these requirements entail, most colleges and universities require some sort of core curriculum. The core curriculum consists of specific courses that must be taken by all students regardless of major and are determined by faculty. Often, their purpose is to ensure that students are exposed to and acquire the knowledge and methodologies that characterize the social sciences, natural sciences, and arts and humanities. Described in more depth, Columbia University explains the relevance of its core curriculum to the enhancement of the mind on their website (http://www.college.columbia.edu/core), and in so doing attempts to legitimate its existence:

The Core Curriculum is the set of common courses required of all undergraduates and considered the necessary general education for students, irrespective of their choice in major. The communal learning—with all students encountering the same texts and issues at the same time—and the critical dialogue experienced in small seminars are the distinctive features of the Core. Begun in the early part of the 20th century, the Core Curriculum is one of the founding experiments in liberal higher education in the United States and it remains vibrant as it enters its tenth decade. Not only academically rigorous but also personally transformative for students, the Core seminar thrives on oral debate of the most difficult questions about human experience. What does it mean, and what has it meant to be an individual? What does it mean, and what has it meant to be part of a community? How is human experience relayed and how is meaning made in music and art? What do we think is, and what have we thought to be worth knowing? What rules should we be, are we governed by? The habits of mind developed in the Core cultivate a critical and creative intellectual capacity that students employ long after college, in the pursuit and the fulfillment of meaningful lives.

Some universities and colleges do not have the core curriculum. Rather, they have an open curriculum, which means that they have no requirements other than students must complete eight semesters and a major. Brown University's website (http://www.brown.edu/Administration/Admission/thebrowneducation/ourphilosophy.html) provides an explanation and justification of its open curriculum:

The purpose of the Brown Curriculum is to put your education in your hands. It is designed to give you the freedom to explore, the freedom to focus, the freedom to take risks, the freedom to fail, and the freedom to succeed. It encourages and develops your inherent strengths and gives you the opportunity to discover new interests and passions. As the architect of your own course of study, you will leave Brown with the intellectual tools that will allow you to adapt and succeed. Your education at Brown will be the foundation from which you engage the world.

Unlike Brown and a few others, however, most colleges and universities in the United States continue to require a core curriculum, and most undergraduates are resigned to taking these courses. Students assume that colleges and universities have the right to impose the core curriculum, whether they like it or not. Many students view this core curriculum as legitimate—that is, as something that should exist.

Just as there is a general consensus that colleges and universities have the right to impose a set of core requirements upon students, there is also a general consensus in the United States that the U.S. government has a right to impose a tax system upon its citizens. Indeed, many citizens recognize that taxes pay for services such as the following: (1) providing and repairing roads, bridges, and tunnels; (2) enforcing policies to reduce pollution, food contamination, and workplace hazards; (3) supporting medical research and cultural institutions such the National Endowment for the Arts; (4) protecting the nation's borders; and (5) providing public transportation. In addition, revenue from taxes can potentially reduce the country's debt, making life better for future generations. So, too, in most organizations there is a general consensus that bosses have the right to give orders to their employees within limits. Indeed, there is perceived consensus among a majority of people that the government, colleges and universities, and bosses or supervisors have the authority to make decisions and give orders (within limits) and that this authority is appropriate and right.

Authority refers to the ability of an actor (e.g., a government body, an organization, an individual) to issue orders to others—that is, the actor can direct, regulate, and evaluate the behavior of others because the authority has rights that are vested in the position. There are boundaries to this authority. For example, there is an explicit limit on the amount of taxes the U.S. government can impose on its citizens, just as there is a limit on how many required courses universities may impose on students. Also, bosses or supervisors do not have the right to ask employees to wash their cars! Nonetheless, supervisors, in this position, do have a range of directives that are considered appropriate, such as determining work assignments, pay, and evaluation performance criteria.

Broad consensus or social support of these rights and patterns of behavior is referred to as **legitimacy**. U.S. citizens, undergraduates, and employees perceive that in general people around them believe that legislators, faculty, and managers have this authority. Actors in authority positions, then, have **legitimate authority**. Governments, college faculty and administration, and bosses (e.g., CEOs), as legitimate authorities, elicit obedience from others (i.e., carrying out commands).

Another example of legitimate authority is the typical interaction between umpires and coaches. When an umpire tosses an unruly coach out of a baseball or softball game and orders him or her to leave the field, the umpire does not need to persuade the coach to leave. The coach may be very upset and throw his or her hat on the ground but will still comply with the umpire. Compliance (obeying even when one privately disagrees [see Chapter 8]) in this case occurs because both the umpire and coach operate within a larger social system, with its set of roles and rules that go beyond any individual. *This larger system is accepted and approved of by a majority of the social audience,* including the players, the coaches, the fans, and the administrators of that particular league. There is, then, a general consensus that the umpire has the right, in his or her role as umpire, to throw the coach out of the game when he or she is being disruptive and that the coach must obey, even if he or she personally disagrees. Imagine if there was no legitimate order in baseball or softball; chaos would ensue with every disagreement and conflict.

Similarly, there are roles and rules in a court of law that must be upheld in order to conduct judicial proceedings. Citizens and court employees approve of and support these roles and rules. In this way, *legitimacy acts as a sort of glue that holds together larger social systems in which we operate and interact with one another on a daily basis.*

In this chapter, we explore this process of legitimacy by first examining the Milgram (1963, 1974) studies on obedience and legitimate authority. These studies provide a good foundation for understanding how legitimate authority operates in interaction. We then discuss the following questions: (1) What is the process of legitimacy? (2) How does something become legitimated? and (3) What are the consequences (good and bad) of legitimacy in everyday interaction?

The Milgram Studies on Obedience and Legitmate Authority

Stanley Milgram (who was a doctoral research assistant of Solomon Asch at Harvard, whose studies are discussed in Chapter 8) created a situation in which an experimenter, who assumed the authority role, directed the participant to engage in actions that ostensibly hurt a third person (a confederate who played the role of a victim). In an initial study in the 1960s, Milgram (1963) recruited 40 male adult participants 20 to 50 years of age from various social class backgrounds, through newspaper advertisements, to participate in a study at Yale University. When the subject arrived in the laboratory, he met another person who had also supposedly responded to the advertisement; the subject was told that he would be participating in a study together with this other person. The other person was actually a confederate working for the experimenter (unbeknownst to the subject—see Chapter 2), claiming to be a 47-year-old male accountant.

The experimenter told the subject and the confederate that they were participating in a study that examined the effects of punishment, in this case electric shock, on learning. One person would be in the role of the teacher and the other person in the role of the learner. After drawing lots, the subject was assigned the role of the teacher, and the confederate the role of the learner receiving the electric shocks. In fact, this process was rigged; the subject was always the teacher and the confederate (the person working for the experimenter) was always the learner.

The learner (i.e., the confederate) was taken to an *enclosed adjacent room* where he was strapped in a chair and electrodes were then attached to his wrist. At this time, the confederate told the experimenter, in front of the subject so that she or he could hear clearly, that he had some heart trouble and was concerned about the danger of receiving electric shock. The experimenter, dressed in a white lab coat, told him that the shock would be painful but would not cause any permanent damage.

The subject and the confederate then began to work on their task. The subject in the role of teacher read pairs of words over an intercom system to the learner, and the learner was asked to memorize these pairs. After reading the entire list of pairs, the subject began the task by reading aloud the first word of each pair and four alternative words for the second word of the pair. The learner (confederate) was to choose the correct word for each item.

When the confederate got the right answer, the subject moved to the next word on the list. When the confederate was incorrect, the experimenter ordered the subject to shock the learner. The shock was administered via an electric generator that had 30 voltage levels, ranging from 15 to 450 volts. The subject was ordered to begin with the lowest voltage, with each successive incorrect answer the subject was to increase the voltage by 30, all the way up to 450. The labels on the generator indicated that 15 volts was a "slight shock"; 135 volts was a "strong shock"; 375 volts was a "danger, severe shock"; and 450 volts was marked XXX. In reality, the confederate was never shocked, but the subject thought that this was a real electric generator.

Not long after the session began, it was clear that the confederate could not remember the words well. He would get a few answers right, but most of his answers were incorrect, putting the subject in a very difficult position. The subject was ordered by the experimenter to continue to increase the voltage with every incorrect answer, knowing that the learner had heart trouble. In addition, each time he was administered a shock, the subject would hear the learner grunting loudly at first and then with each stronger voltage, shouting that the shocks were painful. By 150 volts, the learner demanded to be released from the experiment, saying, "Get me out of here! I won't be in the experiment anymore! I refuse to go on!" At 270 volts, he let out an agonizing scream. By 330 volts, there was only silence from the other room. In actuality, all the confederate's responses came from a tape recording.

Many of the subjects were very upset with the situation and asked that the experimenter check in on the learner. But the experimenter urged them to persist, saying, "The experiment must continue" or "You have no other choice, you must go on." Milgram expected that very few subjects would actually continue all the way to 450 volts. The results showed, however, that 26 of the 40 subjects (65%) went all the way, even though they could have refused to proceed. In addition, all 40 subjects did not stop before 300 volts, even though the confederate had let out screams and pleaded for the experiment to end. Clearly, most subjects were very stressed and concerned for the learner. They were not "bad" or cruel people. Many laughed nervously; others made sure that they were not responsible for the health of the learner.

Needless to say, the Milgram studies would never be conducted in the same way today because of the extreme stress experienced by the participants; they would be viewed as illegitimate scientific studies. Similar to other studies conducted at this time in the 1960s, they raised ethical concerns about exposure of risks or potential harms to participants, informed consent, and use of deception—critical ethical issues raised in Chapter 2. The obedience studies were replicated more recently and in a more acceptable way to Institutional Review Boards. Subjects participated up to the point at which they first heard the learner's verbal complaint at 150 volts. Obedience rates at this point in the studies were only slightly lower than in the early Milgram studies 45 years ago (see Burger 2009).

Yet the Milgram studies, although problematic, illustrated the incredible impact of directives from a legitimate authority on human behavior. They show a disturbing side of human behavior that we are all capable of enacting. (Indeed, we note that it is believed that Milgram had a personal interest in understanding the activities of the Third Reich of Nazi Germany during the 1930s and 1940s, which produced the Holocaust.) Most of us believe that we would never have obeyed the experimenter like "those" subjects. We may think to ourselves, How could these subjects be so cruel!? But instead of making internal (dispositional) attributions, we should be asking this: What was happening in the situation that led to this behavior by a majority of subjects? That is, what external factors lead to obedience to authority?

As the Milgram studies show, obedience to an authority is very likely when that authority is perceived as legitimate (in this case, a scientist at Yale University). Several other factors also contribute to the likelihood of obedience. First, if the person giving orders uses an *overt display of symbols,* such as a uniform, people are more likely to obey that authority (Bushman 1988). In the Milgram studies, the lab coat is an example of an overt display of authority. Uniforms worn by umpires or referees, firefighters, clergy, nurses, and physicians, for example, also symbolize the legitimate authority of the individuals in these roles.

A second factor that increases compliance by an authority *is the potential of the authority to back up his or her demands with sanctions or punishments* for noncompliance. The greater the intensity of potential punishment, the more likely people will comply (Michener and Burt 1975). Interestingly, there was very little threat of sanctions toward the subjects in the Milgram studies, showing how powerful legitimate authority can be. Imagine the pressure to obey a legitimate authority that is also backed by high threat of severe punishments.

Third, the greater the *degree of surveillance by the authority*, the more likely the subordinate will obey (Milgram 1974). Milgram examined this factor in a set of his experiments. For example, in the condition noted previously, the experimenter was only a few feet away from the subject during the study, maintaining direct surveillance. In another condition, however, after giving basic instructions, the experimenter issued orders by telephone at a different location. Subjects were three times more likely to obey in the face-to-face surveillance condition than in the remote telephone condition.

Milgram also showed that the *physical distance to the victim* affected the likelihood of obedience. When subjects were seated right next to the learner, obedience decreased substantially, compared to when the learner was located in a separate enclosed room. It was much more difficult to shock the learner when he was physically close to the subjects because the subjects were much more aware of the learner's suffering and of their individuality, and this increased their feelings of responsibility for his suffering.

Finally, Milgram performed the original study conducted at Yale in another location—a rundown warehouse in the center of a nearby city. Not surprisingly, obedience to authority was higher in the context of the prestigious Yale University than at the warehouse. Yale symbolizes higher status and legitimacy than a rundown inner-city building. Obedience, then, is more likely when the *authority is situated within a prestigious context*.

As the previous discussion shows, people allow legitimate authorities to perform certain actions within boundaries because many believe there is a general consensus about the appropriateness of the authorities' behavior. Often, legitimate authority is a good thing because it facilitates cooperation, predictability, and smooth operations. Think of the importance of following orders in an emergency room or in a military operation. Yet in other situations, it can be a bad thing for people to obey orders that are harmful and destructive to others.

Thus far, we have discussed the legitimacy of authority, but many "ways of doing things" can become legitimated (i.e., taken for granted as the right way of doing things). Practices, people, positions, and structures of positions can all be legitimated. In the next section, we examine more thoroughly the process of legitimacy.

What Is the Process of Legitimacy?

Why do many people in the United States believe that the institution of marriage is an appropriate way for heterosexual couples to form a partnership together but not for gay couples, even with the recent passing of federal laws that now allow gay couples to legally marry? Why do many people believe that being rational is better than being emotional in general and assume that emotions and rationality are not compatible? Why do many people still assume that men are much more capable of excelling in theoretical physics than women?

After reading Chapter 8 on status, you may answer these questions by bringing up the issue of status processes. After all, heterosexuality is more highly valued than homosexuality in the United States (as well as in most countries); "feminine-labeled" behaviors such as emoting are often perceived as less valued than "masculine-labeled" behaviors such as acting "rationally"; and women are still viewed as having less status in the science fields (typically perceived as masculine fields) than men (as described in Chapter 4; Correll 2004; Merolla et al. 2012). But do status processes fully explain why many people take for granted heterosexual but not gay marriage, or the gendered nature of emotions and superiority of rationality, and the sex segregation of "masculine" occupations?

Once again, legitimacy, in addition to status (and power), helps us address this question of why. That is, certain taken-for-granted practices, beliefs, and notions about individuals and groups of individuals take on a life of their own. What we see as a certain way of doing things becomes something that should be done this way. *What is becomes what ought to be* (Berger and Luckmann 1966; Homans 1962). Heterosexual people, but not gay people, should get married; women should be more emotional than men, while men should be more rational; and men should be better at theoretical physics than women. Legitimacy, then, is a socially constructed process whereby something taken for granted becomes what ought to happen.

Specifically, as stated previously, the **legitimacy** of any cultural or social object refers to the process through which patterns of behavior gain social support (Johnson, Dowd, and Ridgeway 2006; Zelditch and Walker 1984). When something has legitimacy, such as a particular practice (e.g., paying taxes or getting married), a particular person or category of person in a position (e.g., Barack Obama as U.S. president or men as physicists), a particular position (an umpire in a game), a structure of positions (e.g., a formal hierarchy in an organization), an organization (e.g., the World Bank), or a political structure (e.g., democracy), it means that there exists taken-for-granted support of it by a real or an implied social audience. Simply put, people believe that other people support the social object, be it an act, individual, position, or structure.

For example, when an employment practice, such as a family leave policy, is legitimated within an organization, its existence and prevalence are taken for granted by a social audience. In this case the social audience is the organizational members, as well as other audiences such as people in other organizations, the government that enforces this policy, etc. Thus, there is a consensus that most people support this family leave practice. Indeed, many countries, such as Nordic and European countries, require employers to provide paid time off for new parents. The United States, however, does not require this, but it does mandate unpaid parental leave. Differences in cultural beliefs about the nature of parental leave affect legitimation of this policy.

As a result of legitimacy, people feel obligated to obey the norms or rules associated with the social object, even when they personally disagree with these rules (Dornbusch and Scott 1975; Weber [1924] 1978). For example, as stated previously, the majority of people who should pay taxes do pay taxes in the United States—even those who personally disagree that they should pay taxes or at least disagree with the amount they are required to pay. Another example is evident in the Milgram studies noted previously. The experimenter, in his official position as the authority of the study at Yale University, was perceived to be legitimate in his position. There was a perceived consensus by the subjects in the study that this person was the appropriate person to conduct this experiment. Subjects consequently obeyed the experimenter's commands, even when they personally disagreed with him, and even though they believed that another person was harmed as a result of their compliance.

The previously given examples show that there are *two different aspects of legitimacy*. First, on the individual level, there is the actor's personal belief that the rules and norms of conduct are desirable, proper, and appropriate patterns of action. An individual's personal approval and support of something as proper is called **propriety** (Dornbusch and Scott 1975). For example, let's say you believe that it is appropriate for the faculty of a college or university to make and control curricular decisions, such as decisions about our core curriculum example. You personally approve of the faculty's authority in this matter.

Second, **validity** refers to an individual's belief that he or she is obliged to obey these norms even in the absence of personal approval of them (Dornbusch and Scott 1975; Zelditch and Walker 1984). For example, we may not always agree with our faculty colleagues' decisions, but we are obliged to obey them anyway because they are the legitimate body to make curricular decisions. Norms, values, beliefs, practices, and procedures are valid if they observably govern the behavior of actors in an organization. Importantly, the views of others in the social context enhance the validity of rules. That is, if an individual believes that others around her believe that the authority structure is appropriate, she expects others to act in accord with it and support it. She will also expect that others expect her to act in accord with and support it. Validity, then, acts through the expectations as well as the behavior it creates. Order, then, is greatly facilitated when individuals believe that there is *collective approval and support* in the legitimacy of the social object such as an authority structure, a person, an act, or a political structure. Collective support for friendly or generous family leave policies (e.g., maternal leave schemes with considerable time out of work) in Nordic countries is an example of this collective process.

Two key sources of legitimacy are authorization and endorsement. **Authorization** occurs when support for the rules, procedures, or authority comes from individuals who occupy higher positions within the organization or hierarchy. **Endorsement** occurs when there is support for the rules or authority from people of equal or lower positions (Dornbusch and Scott 1975). Both authorization and endorsement are external sources of collective support for the rules and the authority. In the previous example, an umpire has authorization when actions and decisions are supported by the league officials, such as the Major Baseball League or the National Softball Association. An umpire has endorsement when other umpires in the league support him in this position and players support his decisions.

Legitimacy of any aspect of social life is fundamentally a collective process rather than a question of private individual consent (Walker and Zelditch 1993; Zelditch 2006; Zelditch and Walker 1984). The authority of any person, act, position, or structure of positions rests on the cooperation from others. When the social object or pattern of behavior is strongly authorized and endorsed, individuals are more likely to comply even if they personally disagree (i.e., weak propriety) because they expect formal sanctions from superiors or informal sanctions from peers. For example, some employees may not support a family leave policy personally, but they do not protest against it because they believe that other coworkers are in favor of the policy. Over time, however, they could begin to personally accept the appropriateness of the policy. Authorization and endorsement, then, often increases an individual's personal approval (i.e., propriety).

Endorsement and authorization are two key sources of legitimacy for leaders in organizations. Recent research confirms the importance of these two sources for managers in work teams within modern Korean organizations (Yoon and Thye 2011). Modern organizations globally have adopted work teams as a means of collaboration, production, and service. In work team structures, power is more evenly spread across team members and team managers, unlike in strict hierarchical structures. This more even spread of power helps to emphasize a sense of shared responsibility among team members, as well as an environment that fosters creative solutions to problems. In a study of 56 teams across five Korean organizations, support of the team manager from upper management (i.e., authorization) and from team members (i.e., endorsement) were positively related to team members' approval of the team manager (i.e., propriety). Team members' support was more important than upper management support for team members' perceptions of their manager's legitimacy. Strong endorsement, authorization, and propriety of the manager helped to make teams more efficient and increased team member commitment to the team (Yoon and Thye 2011).

Social psychologists who study legitimacy processes in groups and organizations focus on two questions. First, how do individuals and structures become legitimated? Specifically, how do individuals in authority positions and status structures of groups become to be perceived as appropriate and right? Second, what are the consequences of the legitimation of individuals and structures? As well, they focus on the conditions under which these legitimate orders become inefficient and perpetuate inequality within groups, organizations, and society. In the next two sections of this chapter, we address these two questions.

How Do Individuals and Structures Become Legitimated?

In this section, we first discuss how individuals in authority positions become legitimated—that is, seen as the right and appropriate persons for the position. We then discuss how status structures in groups, such as in committees, boards, or task forces, acquire legitimacy.

How Do Individuals in Authority Positions Become Legitimated?

Have you ever been a member of an organization, club, or student group where you doubted the leader's right to be in that position or thought that someone else (or yourself!) would be more appropriate as the leader? Have you ever had a supervisor or boss that you strongly believed should be the boss because he or she is the right person for that position? In this section, we take a look at how leaders gain support (i.e., become legitimated) from those below them (i.e., their subordinates) and from those above them (i.e., their superiors).

Being Endorsed

There are several key factors that lead to leader support from below. First, individuals in authority positions are more likely to be legitimated by those below them when their *appointment to their positions is based on qualifications and skills* that are important to carrying out the requirements of the position, rather than based on other factors such as nepotism or random appointment (Lucas 2003).

This is not shocking—people in leadership positions should be qualified! Of course, as discussed in Chapters 5 and 8, perceptions about qualifications and competence are not always straightforward and can be biased and inaccurate.

Second and related to the first factor, *appointments based on past achievements* also signal to people below them that the authority possesses relevant abilities. This also makes sense, although again, past achievements may not be perceived or interpreted in a straightforward way. Third, individuals are more likely to be legitimated when they are *appointed to the position by an individual who already has legitimate authority*—often someone from the top of the authority structure. Therefore, leaders who are appointed and supported from those above them (i.e., are authorized) are more likely to be perceived as legitimate by people below them.

In addition to these fundamental factors, however, authorities gain legitimacy based on the ways they interact with their subordinates. The first specific way of interaction is the *use of fair procedures when making decisions* concerning the distribution of resources (Hegtvedt and Johnson 2009; Tyler 1990, 2001). Fair procedures involve being unbiased, respectful, consistent across individuals, and taking into consideration their subordinates' views (Leventhal, Karuza, and Fry 1980; Tyler and Lind 1992 [see Chapter 11]). For example, if a club president wants to do a particular fundraiser event, she solicits input from the members to talk about how this should be accomplished and who should be responsible for which tasks. She is also careful to suppress her own biases that favor some members over others.

An authority's use of fair procedures and treatment signals to the subordinates that they are respected within their group, which, in turn, increases subordinates' feelings of self-worth. Therefore, when an authority uses fair procedures to make decisions, the legitimacy of that authority is enhanced (Tyler 1990, 2001). For example, when a floor supervisor acts respectfully toward assembly line workers and treats them all consistently, those workers are more likely to see that supervisor as legitimate.

The second specific way of interaction that helps leaders gain legitimacy is the *use of benevolent power in distributing resources/rewards* (Blau 1964; Hegtvedt and Johnson 2009). Authorities gain legitimacy by providing resources to their subordinates that benefit their welfare and help them do their jobs successfully. Authorities typically have more resources than subordinates and therefore have opportunities to contribute to their subordinates' welfare by distributing rewards that assist them in being successful in their jobs. For example, managers in many organizations often have access to valuable knowledge, skills, training, and strategic information that is useful to their employees. They may also offer guidance, assistance, and advice to enhance and facilitate their subordinates' work. In addition, managers may be able to benefit them in other ways, such as allowing extra time for lunch, giving credit to employees for successful outcomes, providing bonuses, or upgrading offices. As a result, subordinates can get their work done as well as advance their own skills and position in the organization.

When authorities provide rewards that contribute to the *collective* interest of subordinates—that is, they use their power benevolently to benefit the collective—joint obligations between the authority and the subordinates emerge. Repeated successful exchanges (exchanges of rewards and cooperation) between authorities and their subordinates are likely to lead to perceptions of trust and fairness and feelings of social obligation (Lawler and Worley 2006; Molm 2006). We trust others when we experience successful, positive exchanges with others (as discussed in Chapter 9). We also are more likely to perceive that leaders who use their power benevolently, rather than play favorites, are fair-minded. In addition, we feel a sense of obligation to these leaders. As a result of this trust and feelings of obligation, we are more likely to perceive these leaders as legitimate (Blau 1964; Hegtvedt and Johnson 2009).

In summary, to the extent that leaders use fair procedures to make decisions, are given opportunities to benefit the welfare of their subordinates, *and* use these opportunities inherent in their power positions to contribute to the welfare of their subordinates, they are more likely to gain legitimacy in their positions. Subordinates are more likely to support the leader (i.e., endorsement) and believe that other subordinates support the leader.

Being Authorized

Although subordinates are likely to focus their primary attention on their own and their coworkers' exchange relationships with the leader, they are also likely to be aware of how their leader interacts with those above him or her. This begs the following question: How are leaders authorized—that is, how do they gain the support from those above them?

Authorization is a key source of legitimacy because leaders need appropriate and sufficient resources to get their jobs done, and importantly, to help their subordinates get their jobs done (Kanter 1977). People perceive authorized leaders as more competent than leaders who lack authorization. In effect, as discussed previously, authorized managers can use their power advantage to benefit their subordinates in terms of providing guidance, training, additional skills, and relevant and useful information to perform their jobs. Those who lack authorization will have fewer opportunities to use their resources to benefit their subordinates, which will negatively affect the quality of the authority–subordinate relationship (Kanter 1977; Hegtvedt and Johnson 2009).

Several keys factors lead to leader legitimacy from above. First, authorization typically stems from *perceived competence of leaders by officials above them* (Molm 1986). Leaders perceived as competent by those above them are more likely also to be supported. Perceptions of competence, however, depend on a second set of factors embodying the opportunity for leaders to do *activities that are perceived as extraordinary* (as opposed to ordinary), *visible* (as opposed to invisible), and *relevant* to the group or organization's problems or concerns. Such activities allow leaders to show they are able to offer something unique and important to the organization's goals (Kanter 1977).

For example, imagine that you work for an Internet search corporation. Obviously, one of the major goals of the business is to devote a lot of engineering time to the search engine because this is at the heart of the company's mission. But every corporation must continue to offer innovative and relevant products to the public. You are very fortunate because you happen to be working on creating new and useful web applications (apps) that have never been seen by the public before. Apps are "in," and you have the opportunity to work on making fast and responsive apps, as well as ensuring the safety and security of users' data. You, as an expert in this area, bring your exciting ideas to your boss high in the corporate structure.

She loves your ideas and provides you with the resources to create these new apps. You have accomplished something *extraordinary* in your innovative apps; very *visible*; and, importantly, highly *relevant* to your business. Your company wants to expand more into apps! Your friend, however, is not so lucky because he is stuck in a product division that is going nowhere in the company. Thus, your chances of being authorized are much higher than those of your friend.

A third factor that leaders need to gain legitimacy from their superiors is their ties and connections to other more powerful and legitimate members of the organization—or, simply, the *breadth and depth of their social networks* (Burt 1992, 1998; Kanter 1977; Smith-Lovin 2007). Legitimacy (and power) comes from social connections, especially those that are outside one's immediate group. For example, sponsors, such as teachers, coaches, or top managers, can support leaders in their positions, allow them to bypass red tape, provide them with key information, and give them status purely by association. In addition, alliances with peers allow for direct exchanges of resources such as favors, information, and challenging and visible work assignments.

Individuals with status advantages (discussed in Chapter 8), such as white men, are more likely to be given opportunities to do extraordinary, visible, and relevant activities in groups and organizations than individuals with status disadvantages. This is because they are more likely to have broader and deeper connections with key people internal and external to the organization who are knowledgeable about visible and relevant opportunities. Indeed, research shows that white men are likely to have broader network ties and more access to informal social networks than women and minorities (e.g., Ibarra, 1992, 1993, 1997; Ibarra and Hunter 2007; Ibarra, Carter, and Silva 2010; Kanter 1977). Thus, even if occupying leadership positions, women and minorities in many organizational contexts face more difficulty gaining and maintaining legitimacy than white men because their social networks are more limited. (See Taylor [2016] for an innovative study that shows that social inclusion in the workplace is a key dimension of work environments and health: men and women who are integrated into the majority express less physiological stress response—measured by cortisol response—than men and women who are socially excluded [e.g., subjected to "mircroaggressions," interactional-level discrimination, or interactional injustice].) Women, on average, face more social isolation than men, particularly in male-dominated organizations. Taylor (2016:81) concludes that "policies should focus on improving the social integration of all workers regardless of the demographic characteristics of the worker. Doing so also holds the potential for improving employee health."

Newsworthy discrimination cases over the last decade filed by female stockbrokers against several Wall Street firms illustrate these processes. Female stockbrokers reported being disadvantaged because when other stockbrokers left or retired from their firms, male, rather than female, stockbrokers were much more likely to receive the departing coworkers' clients. This pattern reflects, in part, the women's more limited social networks in the firm. The female stockbrokers were also left out of informal networks that male stockbrokers use to gain clients partly because some of the firms' business took place in strip clubs or on the golf course. When we address consequences of legitimacy in the next section, we will discuss in more depth how legitimacy processes can lead to disadvantaged leadership positions for women and minorities.

How Do Status Structures of Groups Become Legitimated?

Recall from Chapter 8, in our discussion of expectation states theory (EST), that status structures of groups are rank ordered relationships between group members and that widespread cultural beliefs indicate that individuals who have higher status in society will also have higher status in face-to-face groups. In specific groups, members who possess a more valued state of a social (diffuse) characteristic (e.g., men, whites, middle-aged, and middle or upper class) in a particular society are likely to be perceived as more competent and worthy in general than members who possess a less valued state (e.g., women, blacks, Latino/as, youth, or poor or working class). As a result of the association between states of diffuse status characteristics and general competence beliefs, these members are more likely to offer their opinions and be more influential in decision-making, and thus become high-status group members. A status structure thus forms in which some members have higher status than others. How does this status structure become legitimated—that is, how is it accepted and supported, either implicitly or explicitly, by the group members in that they believe that high-status members *should* have high status in the group?

Low- and high-status members in a group expect that those with highly valued states of characteristics will also occupy highly valued positions within the group because this is *typically* what they perceive around them. In other words, individuals with highly valued status characteristics are also likely to hold high-status positions in groups within occupational, economic, political, and religious structures in general (Correll and Ridgeway 2003; Ridgeway and Berger 1986). For example, white men are typically seen in top positions such as CEOs of S&P 500 companies. Indeed, women occupy about 4% of the CEO positions in these 500 companies (and with Ursula Burns, CEO of Xerox, stepping down in late 2016, there will be no black women leading these companies; Catalyst 2016), and there have been only 15 black CEOs on the Fortune 500 over time. In addition, brokers on Wall Street, senators in the U.S. Senate (83% male in 2010), and clergy and rabbis in religious institutions in the United States are still predominately white men.

Consequently, when individuals advantaged in terms of status characteristics become high-status members within a group, low- and high-status members tend to react to this as if this ranking should have happened this way because they, in fact, expected it. Thus, low-status members enact deferential behaviors such as giving esteem, respect, and honor (communicated verbally or nonverbally) toward high-status members. This interaction creates a process where everyone believes that everyone else supports who is more worthy and exercises more influence. Members believe that other members support the status structure. If no one challenges this pattern of deference, members will continue to act as if this should happen, and the hierarchy becomes implicitly legitimate (Correll and Ridgeway 2003; Johnson et al. 2006).

In addition, if members do not defer to high-status members in the group, they face the threat of informal sanctions from other group members. As a result, compliance with high-status members is expected and, in fact, is what typically occurs. This pattern of behavior, then, maintains the status quo (Correll and Ridgeway 2003).

Legitimation of individuals in authority positions and of status structures in groups leads to particular consequences for social relations among members in groups and organizations. In the next section, we take a look at the good and the bad in terms of the legitimacy of individuals and structures. In some situations, legitimacy helps to maintain order and prevent chaos, yet in other situations, legitimacy contributes to the perpetuation of inequality.

What Are the Consequences of Legitimation? The Good and the Bad

The Good: Maintaining Systems of Order

In many contexts, legitimate authorities and legitimate practices are beneficial for interaction. Indeed, the legitimacy of rules, hierarchies, and patterns of behavior *facilitates coordination and cooperation* among people in groups, organizations, and societies. Imagine what would happen if people did not abide by the rules, the hierarchy, and particular patterns of behavior in an emergency room! People's lives literally depend on all involved to support the ways of doing things in the emergency room. In addition, civil order is dependent upon the obedience to laws by judicial officials and the public; without it, disorder would be rampant, and many individuals would face immense suffering.

Likewise, the legitimacy of authority relations in organizations *fosters stability* in interaction among organizational members (Dornbusch and Scott 1975; Zelditch and Walker 1984). For example, legitimacy is undoubtedly a key factor in predicting managers' success with their subordinates. Subordinates who perceive their boss as legitimate are more likely to comply, defer, and cooperate with his or her requests. Subordinates perceive legitimated authorities as more effective and influential than authorities without legitimacy. Legitimated authorities also have more leeway in the directives (e.g., work assignments, evaluations or demands of performance) that subordinates accept from them, albeit these directives must fall within the scope of their authority. Effective performance, then, in work settings depends on employees following the directives of their bosses. Also, as noted earlier, legitimacy of an authority is founded on the authority's use of fair procedures and benevolent power—two positive ways to facilitate good working relations.

Although legitimacy processes can lead to positive consequences such as cooperation, productivity, and even solidarity, legitimation can also lead to patterns of inefficiency and inequality. Next, we show that this occurs by maintaining (1) inefficient and sometimes unfair practices and (2) disadvantages for women and minority leaders.

The Bad: Maintaining Inefficient and Unfair Practices Perpetuating Inequality

You have probably heard of the term *bureaucratic red tape*. It is a pejorative term, referring to a situation where strict conformity to the rules produces redundancy and inefficiency. You might have experienced this going to the DMV or trying to get a passport, or trying to get insurance to cover expenses after an accident. This "red tape" often hinders effective decision-making. Sometimes rules, procedures, and practices initially thought of as "a good and useful way of doing things" become outdated, inefficient, and even unfair to people who must abide by these practices. For example, modern personnel systems in corporations may often be a good way to hire and promote people; on the other hand, they may become very inefficient and also lead to biases in hiring and promotion. The bottom line is, *many taken-for-granted practices are actually not very good, yet they take on a life of their own* (Johnson et al. 2006). They become legitimated, perceived as the right way to do things. As a result, they remain relatively stable.

When existing practices are incompatible with the actual running of the organization or a system of organizations, people often feel tension and dissatisfaction with these practices. They question why they have to do to things a certain way even when it makes no sense. Why, then, are inefficient and unfair practices difficult to change?

Although you can imagine that there is pressure to change these practices and rules, there are also countervailing pressures due to legitimacy processes that dampen the likelihood of attempts to change the structure in which these practices are embedded (Walker and Zelditch 1993; Zelditch 2004; Zelditch and Walker 1984). First, the existing status quo that visibly governs others' behavior within the organization makes it seem as though the authority structure and associated practices appear to have support by almost everyone. *Individuals think that everyone else at least implicitly agrees with the current practices*; those at the top act as though things are in working order (authorizing the practice); those at the bottom go along too, at least implicitly (endorsing the practice). If individuals believe, and believe that others believe, that the practices are valid, then they will expect others to act in accord with them and support them. They will also expect that others will expect them to act in accord with these prescribed practices.

Second, as a result of this widespread appearance of consensus, individuals continue to engage in widespread compliance to these taken-for-granted practices, even when they privately disagree with them. Legitimacy of these practices induces a sense of obligation and cooperation; *actors often accept "the way things are"* (Johnson et al. 2006).

Third, *fear of formal sanctions from superiors and informal sanctions from peers reinforces individuals' compliance* (Zelditch and Walker 1984). Examples of formal sanctions may include low performance evaluations, undesired work assignments, or limited raises or cuts in pay. Examples of informal sanctions may be being ignored, being excluded from social networks, or being snubbed. It is difficult and energy consuming to go against what appears to be formidable support for a rule or practice. Sometimes these inefficient and unfair practices are perpetuated by unscrupulous motivations, such as greed. In other cases, there is no malicious intent behind the practices—they just take on a life of their own.

Fourth, as a consequence, people *accept nonoptimal procedures and practices as the way things should be* while new practices that may be more efficient but are not embedded in the status quo often disappear (Johnson et al. 2006; Zelditch 2004). Films, literature, and TV shows provide commentary for this taken-for-granted process, where media often make fun of ridiculous and inefficient rules that nevertheless continue to be enacted (e.g., *Brazil*, *Dilbert*, and *The Office*).

An example of inefficient, taken-for-granted practices can be found in the 2010 Deep Horizon oil spill in the Gulf of Mexico—the largest environmental disaster in U.S. history so far. Although we do not know the details of BP's set of rules and procedures for oil drilling, we do know that they were charged by the U.S. government with numerous violations in 2009. Also, the oil company did not have a contingency plan for the Deepwater Horizon oil rig explosion that occurred on

April 20, 2010. Congressional hearings revealed that BP engineers made a set of cost-cutting decisions that were contrary to the advice of key contractors in the days leading up to the rig explosion. Some senators stated that BP made decisions that increased the risk of an explosion in order to save the company time and expense. They cited five decisions made in regard to the design and completion of the well that may have led to vulnerabilities in the design. Statements by BP workers, too, indicated that warning signs of the potential of a blowout were ignored. Making decisions that cut corners that also lead to inefficient and sometimes dangerous consequences are often accepted by a majority as legitimate decisions in many organizations.

The current U.S. health care system provides another example of inefficiency, although, in this case, most people know that it is inefficient and want to see health care reform. For example, the U.S. health care system divides the population into two groups: the insiders and the outsiders. Insiders are people who have good insurance and thus are much more likely to receive the most benefits, such as the most advanced treatments of diseases like cancer and heart disease, no matter how expensive. Outsiders, those who have poor insurance or none at all, receive very little. This system does not treat everyone equally, yet it is very difficult to change, as we continue to witness the debates and battles in Congress about health care reform. It is, in part, difficult to change because of the complex power dynamics among providers (e.g., physicians, hospitals, and pharmacies), purchasers (i.e., individuals, business, and government), insurers, and suppliers (e.g., pharmaceutical companies, medical supply companies, and computer equipment; Bodenheimer and Grumbach 2016). Health care reform is also difficult to attain because all these actors are advocates for different ways to address access to health care, rising costs, and quality of health care. Unfortunately, as the debates continue across the political landscape, many people in this very wealthy country continue to go without adequate health care.

Another Bad: Leadership Disadvantages for Women and Minorities Perpetuating Inequality

Imagine an interaction between a Latina doctor and a white patient in her office. We all assume that a doctor knows more about health-related issues than a patient. But in our scenario, the patient perceives the Latina doctor as not just simply a doctor. She is a Latina doctor, and for this patient, this means that this doctor is not as competent as a white male doctor. In addition, the white patient perceives that usually doctors, at least "good" and "qualified" doctors, are typically white and male, not Latina and female. As a result of these biased perceptions, the Latina doctor does not automatically command the respect she deserves compared to her white male colleagues. For example, her patient is more likely to interrupt her and be more hesitant to listen to and follow her orders. Ultimately, the patient complies; after all, the doctor does have more expertise, but she must also justify her treatment decision more than her white male colleagues.

This example illustrates a problem with legitimacy. Although women and minorities acquire status in interactions because they possess specific skills relevant to the task at hand and therefore do achieve influence, they are also more likely to face resistance from others because they are not automatically legitimated in their positions. For example, when they are directing those below them, they are in danger of being *perceived as "too directive"* (Ridgeway 2001; Ridgeway and Smith-Lovin 1999). They are more likely to be perceived as more strong-willed, too assertive, and more uppity than men and whites exhibiting the same directive behavior (Eagly and Carli 2007; Heilman and Parks-Stamm 2007; Heilman et al. 2004). There is a *"backlash" effect* where women's highly assertive behavior is seen as "not right," given her status position (Ridgeway and Nakagawa 2014; Rudman et al. 2012). As a consequence of their lack of legitimacy in interaction, women and minorities are more limited in the range of behaviors accepted by the others. This is so because they are not perceived as the "typical" or "usual" type of people that hold and occupy high-status leader positions. They will gain influence because of their demonstrated skills, but they are more likely to face resistance when they go beyond persuasion to exercise power to direct, command, and lead (Ridgeway, Johnson, and Diekema 1994).

In addition to being seen as too directive, leaders who are not legitimated (more often women and minorities) are *less likely to receive the resources, support, and positive evaluations* they need from those above them in the hierarchy compared to their white male counterparts. Part of the reason for this is that whites and men dominate the top positions in the hierarchy, and when the organization faces uncertainty such as financial problems, individuals in top positions feel more comfortable with those who are similar to them in many types of attributes when hiring or promoting employees (Kanter 1977). These feelings of comfort may come from similarity on certain characteristics such as gender and race, but it may also come from similarities on things such as extracurricular or leisure activities, experiences, and self-presentation styles. Culturally similar employees or candidates for employment are perceived as more likely to enjoy their jobs and stay in the organization, even though there is no basis for these perceptions (Rivera 2012). And these cultural similarities are associated with characteristics such as gender and race in some situations. As a result, those who are "different" or do not "fit" the organization have less chance of being hired, and even if hired, they are likely to have *fewer opportunities to provide benefits to their subordinates*—opportunities that are important in creating trust and feelings of obligation that foster leader legitimacy.

Subordinates who have leaders with little legitimacy are more likely to use tactics such as going over their heads or forming coalitions with other coworkers when they disagree with their leader than leaders with legitimacy (Johnson and Ford 1996). This, in turn, impedes the building of trust in the relationship.

Consider a black female manager in a white-dominated company. As a result of her expertise and seniority, she has higher status than her employees and therefore is influential in many of the decisions. But the threshold for how directive she is able to be with her employees is lower than for managers advantaged in terms of status, such as white male managers. She is perceived as too directive compared to the white male managers and will not have the taken-for-granted acceptance that they enjoy because she is not perceived as the "typical" leader. In addition, she does not receive the resources she needs to get the job done or to support the employees that she supervises. As a result, she has fewer opportunities to benefit her employees and create feelings of trust and obligation needed to gain legitimacy (Hegtvedt and Johnson 2009).

There is hope, however. For example, a study by Lucas (2003) showed that when female leadership in general is legitimated in organizations—that is, when many people in the organization believe that successful groups are led by women in the organization—women leaders appointed on ability attain influence as high as men leaders appointed on ability. It takes a lot of work and determination for an organization to change the belief structure in an organization around who should be leaders, but it is possible.

In summary, legitimacy processes may lead to both good and bad consequences, depending on the situation. We are dependent on the legitimacy of social orders to maintain coordination and cooperation. Yet legitimacy processes also lead to inefficient and unfair practices that take on a life of their own and are difficult to change. Also, as a result of legitimation of status structures, women and minority leaders often find themselves limited in their leadership, facing resistance in their leadership roles.

Segue: Legitimacy and Justice

Just as individuals, practices, and group status structures become legitimated, stratified orders in societies, consisting of status and power relations between groups, also become legitimated (that is, perceived as accepted and even appropriate). In all societies, certain groups are perceived as superior and have greater access to valuable resources than other groups. Even groups who are treated poorly relative to other groups (e.g., in terms of access to quality health care, reasonably priced foods, education, and public transportation) often accept these stratified orders. Legitimation of these stratified orders leads to reproduction of inequality in societies.

Why do people in disadvantaged positions often accept their position in the stratified order? In many contexts, political, economic, and religious systems are extremely stratified (e.g., based on gender, race, ethnicity, and social class), yet people act as if these systems are legitimate structures. Obviously, individuals in disadvantaged groups are in positions where they have fewer resources, social connections, less wealth accumulation, and in some cases fewer legal rights relative to individuals in status-advantaged groups, which put them on an unequal footing in general. Also, people who live in countries with dictators are in constant fear and face life-threatening consequences if they go against the status quo. We offer three possible reasons (in addition to the already clear economic, legal, political, and social network disadvantages) for why the disadvantaged (and the advantaged) accept the status quo.

First, the material fact of the unequal distribution of resources in society is incorporated into the consciousness of the individual through day-to-day interaction so that what is (i.e., what is valid) becomes what ought to be (what is proper) (Della Fave 1980, 1986, 1991). That is, people are impressed by those who are able to control their environment, both physical and social. As a result, the wealthy and most powerful in society are the most "impressive" both to themselves and others, and this leads to a generalized image of their superiority and a corresponding image of the inferiority of the poor and less powerful.

These images of superiority and inferiority not only affect people's self-evaluations. These images also suggest that unequal wealth and power are *deserved*. Why? One reason is that many people widely accept the equity rule, where those who contribute more ought to reap more benefits compared to others who contribute less (we discuss equity theory in the next chapter). Everyday encounters that routinely result in unequal bargains due to people's unequal resources reinforces this sense of unequal deservingness. That is, wealthy members of society are able to get more valuable resources in exchanges in day-to-day interactions than the less wealthy. Such encounters make inequality seem normal and natural as well as deserved. This general acceptance of unequal exchanges and unequal distributions of benefits as the way things are leads to acceptance of inequality by members of disadvantaged groups, even when they do not privately accept its propriety (Stolte 1983).

Second, stratified orders may be maintained because legitimacy of these orders decreases individuals' emotional reactions and responses to improper treatment. For example, workers in a company who are treated poorly by a legitimated manager are less likely to feel anger and resentment than workers with managers who are not legitimated (Johnson, Ford, and Kaufman 2000). As a result, they are less likely to take specific actions to redress the situation, such as going over their managers' heads or forming coalitions for collective action to resolve the conflict. As we will see in the next chapter, perceptions of legitimacy tone down the negative emotions felt and expressed as a result of unequal distribution of resources.

Third, the legitimacy of individuals, acts, distributions of resources, or structures can suppress the reactions of individuals who feel themselves improperly treated (Thomas, Walker, and Zelditch 1986; Walker, Thomas, and Zeldtich 1986). Importantly, individuals often accept the status quo because they believe that others accept the status quo. What others think in the situation affects how individuals perceive the distribution of resources. In addition, it takes a lot of energy, courage, and resilience to resist and challenge instances of social inequality because of the inherent stability of these structures, as noted above. There are high costs in resisting the status quo, both tangible (e.g., money, resources, and sometimes threat of harm) and intangible (e.g., time, energy, and courage) costs.

Not all legitimated practices, rules, individuals, and structures remain so (Johnson et al. 2006; Walker 2014). New practices, procedures, and stratified orders emerge as the legitimacy of old ones is challenged. In the United States, the Black Lives Matter movement courageously works to question the legitimacy of the legal, economic, and political systems that practice institutional and interactional racism (we discuss this movement in the last chapter). And there is profound unrest in North African and Middle East countries where courageous people have protested against extreme inequality and injustice, stimulated by extremely high food prices, low-quality education, and widespread impoverished conditions. For example, mass protests erupted in Egypt in January 2011, on the heels of the revolution in Tunisia. After 18 days of angry protests (yet for the most part peaceful and consistently resilient), President Hosni Mubarak resigned, ending his 30 years of autocratic rule. The announcement of his resignation took place during the evening prayers in Cairo, where powerful emotions of jubilation exploded as protestors shouted, "Egypt is free!" Obviously, the transformation in politics in Egypt does not happen overnight and is always in process, and historical events and conditions led to this delegitimation of Mubarak and Zine El-Abidine Ben Ali's rule.

Another complicated situation was revealed in Brazil in 2016, as the Summer Olympics approached. President Dilma Rousseff was suspended in early May, pending a Senate impeachment trial, and Michel Temer, her vice president, assumed the role of interim leader as this chapter was written. Two thirds of the lower house voted to approve the impeachment measure—a measure that raises questions about the legitimacy (and honesty) of a political leader. She was accused of illegally borrowing from state banks to fix holes in the budget. In context, Brazil is currently suffering one of its worst economic crises in decades, with more and more citizens falling out of the middle class and into poverty. It is a complicated situation that would take pages to describe, but it is an illustration of the potential delegitimation process of a political leader.

Indeed, strategies about legitimacy are common in presidential elections. For example, as the 2016 presidential elections took place in the United States, questions of the legitimacy of the Republican's presumptive nominee, Donald Trump, repeatedly arose from Hillary Clinton, a Democratic candidate. In the news, she stated, "We are trying to elect a president, not a dictator." "Donald Trump's ideas are not just different, they are dangerously incoherent." The Clinton campaign's strategy was to delegitimize Trump as a potential leader of the United States by emphasizing that he is not fit to be the president, as well as lack of specifics in his foreign and domestic policies. For example, Clinton remarked, "He says he has foreign policy experience because he ran the Miss Universe pageant in Russia," and juxtaposed her experience as secretary of state in the same speech. Trump responded with his "crooked Hillary" reference, and incited many of his supporters to chant, "Lock her up!" You may also recall that it was Trump, among others, who tried to delegitimize Obama while he was running for office, claiming that his birth certificate from Hawaii was not legitimate. Serious questions regarding the legitimacy of now President Trump and his administration continue as we write this chapter.

In the next chapter, we examine how justice processes work in everyday interaction in groups and in organizations. Specifically, we discuss how justice shapes social interaction by investigating types of justice, how people perceive injustice, and how they respond to perceptions of injustice not only for themselves but for others who are perceived to be unfairly treated. In addition, we will see how legitimacy processes discussed in this chapter, as well as many additional key factors, affect justice processes. Understanding perceptions of and responses to injustice is fundamental to understanding intergroup relations and responses to inequality (as discussed in Chapter 12).

Suggested Readings

Kalev, Alexandra. 2014. "How You Downsize Is Who You Downsize: Biased Formalization, Accountability, and Managerial Diversity." *American Sociological Review* 79:109–35.

Rivera, Lauren A. 2014. "Hiring as Cultural Matching: The Case of Elite Professional Service Firms." *American Sociological Review* 77:999–1022.

Walker, Henry A., and David Willer. 2014. "Legitimizing Collective Action and Countervailing Power." *Social Forces* 92:1217–39.

Yoon, Jeongkoo, and Shane Thye. 2011. "A Theoretical Model and New Test of Managerial Legitimacy in Work Teams." *Social Forces* 90:639–59.

References

Berger, Peter, and Thomas Luckmann. 1966. *The Social Construction of Knowledge: A Treatise in the Sociology of Knowledge*. New York: Doubleday.

Blau, Peter M. 1964. *Exchange and Power in Social Life*. New York: Wiley.

Bodenheimer, Thomas, and Kevin Grumbach. 2016. *Understanding Health Policy: A Clinical Approach*. New York: McGraw-Hill.

Burger, Jerry M. 2009. "Replicating Milgram: Would People Still Obey Today?" *The American Psychologist* 64:1–11. doi:10.1037/a0010932

Burt, Ronald S. 1992. *Structural Holes*. Cambridge, MA: Harvard University Press.

Burt, Ronald S. 1998. "The Gender of Social Capital." *Rationality and Society* 10:5–46. doi:10.1177/104346398010001001

Bushman, Brad J. 1988. "The Effects of Apparel on Compliance: A Field Experiment with a Female Authority Figure." *Personality and Social Psychology Bulletin* 14:459–67. doi:10.1177/0146167288143004

Catalyst. 2016, June 14. *Pyramid: Women in S&P 500 Companies*. New York: Catalyst.

Correll, Shelley J. 2004. "Constraints into Preferences: Gender, Status, and Emerging Career Aspirations." *American Sociological Review* 69(1):93–113. doi:10.1177/000312240406900106

Correll, Shelley J., and Cecilia L. Ridgeway. 2003. "Expectation States Theory." Pp. 29–51 in *Handbook of Social Psychology*, edited by J. DeLamater. New York: Kluwer Academic/Plenum.

Della Fave, Richard. 1980. "The Meek Shall Not Inherit the Earth: Self-Evaluation and the Legitimacy of Stratification." *American Sociological Review* 45:955–71. doi:10.2307/2094912

Della Fave, Richard. 1986. "Toward an Explication of the Legitimation Process." *Social Forces* 65:476–500. doi:10.2307/2578683

Della Fave, Richard. 1991. "Ritual and the Legitimation of Inequality." *Sociological Perspectives* 34:21–38. doi:10.2307/1389141

Dornbusch, Sanford M., and W. Richard Scott. 1975. *Evaluation and the Exercise of Authority*. San Francisco, CA: Jossey-Bass.

Eagly, Alice Hendrickson, and Linda Lorene Carli. 2007. *Through the Labyrinth: The Truth about How Women Become Leaders*. Boston: Harvard Business School Press.

Hegtvedt, Karen, and Cathryn Johnson. 2009. "Power and Justice: Toward an Understanding of Legitimacy." *The American Behavioral Scientist* 53:376–99. doi:10.1177/0002764209338798

Heilman, Madeline E., and Elizabeth J. Parks-Stamm. 2007. "Gender Stereotypes in the Workplace: Obstacles to Women's Career Progress." Pp. 47–77 in *Advances in Group Processes: Social Psychology of Gender*, Vol. 24, edited by S. J. Correll. Bingley, England: Emerald Group Publishing. doi:10.1016/S0882-6145(07)24003-2

Heilman, Madeline E., Aaron S. Wallen, Daniella Fuchs, and Melinda M. Tamkins. 2004. "Penalties for Success: Reactions to Women Who Succeed at Male Gender-Typed Tasks." *The Journal of Applied Psychology* 89:416–27. doi:10.1037/0021-9010.89.3.416

Homans, George C. 1962. *Sentiments and Activities*. Glencoe, IL: Free Press.

Ibarra, Herminia. 1992. "Homophily and Differential Returns: Sex Differences in Network Structure and Access in an Advertising Firm." *Administrative Science Quarterly* 37:422–47. doi:10.2307/2393451

Ibarra, Herminia. 1993. "Personal Networks of Women and Minorities in Management: A Conceptual Framework." *Academy of Management Review* 18(1):56–87.

Ibarra, Herminia. 1997. "Paving an Alternative Route: Gender Differences in Managerial Networks." *Social Psychology Quarterly* 60:91–102. doi:10.2307/2787014

Ibarra, Herminia, Nancy M. Carter, and Christine Silva. 2010. "Why Men Still Get More Promotions Than Women." *Harvard Business Review* 88:80–5.

Ibarra, Herminia, and Mark Hunter. 2007. "How Leaders Create and Use Networks." *Harvard Business Review* 85(1):40.

Johnson, Cathryn, Timothy J. Dowd, and Cecilia L. Ridgeway. 2006. "Legitimacy as a Social Process." *Annual Review of Sociology* 32:53–78. doi:10.1146/annurev.soc.32.061604.123101

Johnson, Cathryn, and Rebecca Ford. 1996. "Dependence Power, Legitimacy, and Tactical Choice." *Social Psychology Quarterly* 59:126–39. doi:10.2307/2787047

Johnson, Cathryn, Rebecca Ford, and Joanne Kaufman. 2000. "Emotional Reactions to Conflict: Do Dependence and Legitimacy Matter?" *Social Forces* 79:107–37. doi:10.2307/2675566

Kanter, Rosabeth M. 1977. *Men and Women of the Corporation*. New York: Basic Books.

Lawler, Edward E., and Christopher G. Worley. 2006. "Designing Organizations That Are Built to Change." *MIT Sloan Management Review* 48(1):19.

Leventhal, Gerald S., Karuza, Jurgis, Jr., and Fry, William Rick. 1980. "Beyond Fairness: A Theory of Allocation Preferences." Pp. 167–218 in *Justice and Social Interaction*, edited by G. Mikula. New York: Springer-Verlag.

Lucas, Jeffery W. 2003. "Status Processes and the Institutionalization of Women as Leaders." *American Sociological Review* 68: 464–80. doi:10.2307/1519733

Merolla, David M., Richard T. Serpe, Sheldon Stryker, and P. Wesley Schultz. 2012. "Structural Precursors to Identity Processes the Role of Proximate Social Structures."

Social Psychology Quarterly 75(2):149–72. doi:10.1177/0190272511436352

Michener, H. Andrew, and Martha R. Burt. 1975. "Components of 'Authority' as Determinants of Compliance." *Journal of Personality and Social Psychology* 31(4):606–14. doi:10.1037/h0077080

Milgram, Stanley. 1963. "Behavioral Study of Obedience." *Journal of Abnormal and Social Psychology* 67(4):371–78. doi:10.1037/h0040525

Milgram, Stanley. 1974. *Obedience to Authority: An Experimental View*. New York: Harper and Row.

Molm, Linda D. 1986. "Gender, Power and Legitimation: A Test of Three Theories." *American Journal of Sociology* 91:1356–86. doi:10.1086/228425

Molm, Linda D. 2006. "The Social Exchange Framework." Pp. 24–45 in *Contemporary Social Psychological Theories*, edited by P. J. Burke. Stanford, CA: Stanford University Press.

Ridgeway, Cecilia L. 2001. "Gender, Status, and Leadership." *The Journal of Social Issues* 57:637–55. doi:10.1111/0022-4537.00233

Ridgeway, Cecilia L., and Joseph Berger. 1986. "Expectations, Legitimation, and Dominance Behavior in Task Groups." *American Sociological Review* 51:603–17. doi:10.2307/2095487

Ridgeway, Cecilia L., Cathryn Johnson, and David Diekema. 1994. "External Status, Legitimacy, and Compliance in Male and Female Groups." *Social Forces* 72:1051–77.

Ridgeway, Cecilia L., and Sandra Nakagawa. 2014. "Status." Pp. 3–26 in *Handbook of the Social Psychology of Inequality*, edited by Jane McLeod, Edward Lawler, and Michael Schwalbe. New York: Springer.

Ridgeway, Cecilia L., and Lynn Smith-Lovin. 1999. "The Gender System and Interaction." *Annual Review of Sociology* 25:191–216. doi:10.1146/annurev.soc.25.1.191

Rivera, Lauren A. 2012. "Hiring as Cultural Matching: The Case of Elite Professional Service Firms." *American Sociological Review* 77:999–1022. doi:10.1177/0003122412463213

Rudman, Laurie, Corrine Moss-Racusin, Julie Phelan, and Sanne Nauts. 2012. "Status Incongruity and Backlash Effects: Defending the Gender Hierarchy Motivates Prejudice against Female Leaders." *Journal of Experimental Social Psychology* 48:165–79. doi:10.1016/j .jesp.2011.10.008

Smith-Lovin, Lynn. 2007. "The Strength of Weak Identities: Social Structural Sources of Self, Situation and Emotional Experience." *Social Psychology Quarterly* 70(2):106–24. doi:10.1177/019027250707000203

Stolte, John F. 1983. "The Legitimation of Structural Inequality: Reformulation and Test of the Self-Evaluation Argument." *American Sociological Review* 48:331–42. doi:10.2307/2095226

Taylor, Catherine J. 2016. "'Relational by Nature'? Men and Women Do Not Differ in Physiological Response to Social Stressors Faced by Token Women." *American Journal of Sociology* 122:49–89. doi:10.1086/686698

Thomas, George M., Henry A. Walker, and Morris Zelditch Jr. 1986. "Legitimacy and Collective Action." *Social Forces* 65:378–404. doi:10.2307/2578679

Tyler, Tom R. 1990. *Why People Obey the Law.* New Haven, CT: Yale University Press.

Tyler, Tom R. 2001. "A Psychological Perspective on the Legitimacy of Institutions and Authorities." Pp. 416–36 in *The Psychology of Legitimacy,* edited by J. T. Jost and B. Major. New York: Cambridge University Press.

Tyler, Tom R., and E. Allan Lind. 1992. "A Relational Model of Authority in Groups." *Advances in Experimental Social Psychology* 25:115–91. doi:10. 1016/S0065-2601(08)60283-X

Walker, Henry A. 2014. "Legitimacy and Inequality." Pp. 353–79 in *Handbook of the Social Psychology of Inequality,* edited by J. McLeod, E. Lawler, and M. Schwalbe. New York: Springer.

Walker, Henry A., George M. Thomas, and Morris Zelditch Jr. 1986. "Legitimation, Endorsement and Stability." *Social Forces* 64:620–43. doi:10.2307/2578816

Walker, Henry A., and Morris Zelditch Jr. 1993. "Power, Legitimacy, and the Stability of Authority: A Theoretical Research Program." Pp. 364–81 in *Theoretical Research Programs: Studies in the Growth of Theory,* edited by J. Berger and M. Zelditch Jr. Stanford, CA: Stanford University Press.

Weber, Max. [1924] 1978. *Economy and Society,* Vols. I and II, edited by Guenther Roth and Claus Wittich, Reprint, Berkeley: University of California Press.

Yoon, Jeongkoo, and Shane Thye. 2011. "A Theoretical Model and New Test of Managerial Legitimacy in Work Teams." *Social Forces* 90:639–59. doi:10.1093/sf/sor016

Zelditch, Morris, Jr. 2004. "Institutional Effects on the Stability of Organizational Authority." Pp. 25–48 in *Legitimacy Processes in Organizations,* edited by C. Johnson. Oxford, England: JAI. doi:10.1016/S0733-558X(04)22001-8

Zelditch, Morris, Jr. 2006. "Legitimacy Theory." Pp. 324–52 in *Contemporary Social Psychological Theories,* edited by P. J. Burke. Stanford, CA: Stanford University Press.

Zelditch, Morris, Jr., and Henry A. Walker. 1984. "Legitimacy and the Stability of Authority." *Advances in Group Processes* 20:217–49. doi:10.1016/S0882-6145(03)20008-4

11

Justice Processes and Evaluations Within Groups

In 1905, Albert Einstein (1879–1955) published a series of papers that revolutionized scientific views on space, time, and matter, laying the basis for the study of modern physics. Einstein was extremely prolific, and his works earned him, among many accolades, the 1921 Nobel Prize in Physics and recognition in 1999 by *Time* magazine as the "Person of the Century." It would be hard to detract from Einstein's genius, yet some have argued that his first wife, Mileva Marić, a brilliant mathematician whom he met in 1896, may have contributed to the 1905 papers. If so, then some might claim an injustice: Einstein took all of the credit and glory for the new theories, leaving his wife's accomplishments unacknowledged and without reward. A *Stone Soup* cartoon in 2005 humorously captures this interpretation of events (see Figure 11.1).

FIGURE 11.1

Although often represented in cartoons, concerns about justice pervasive in social life are no laughing matter. Evaluations of injustice may arise in discussions of inequalities in outcomes and rewards in large and small groups, of biases in decision-making processes, and even in the lack of respect that people show each other. Three general types of justice contribute to defining a state of affairs as just or fair (see Jost and Kay 2010). **Distributive justice** (Adams 1965; Homans 1974) refers to the dispersion of benefits and burdens in a society according to agreed upon principles such as equity, equality, or needs. **Procedural justice** (Lind and Tyler 1988) involves rules of neutrality, consistency, representation, and the like that govern decision-making to ensure basic rights of individuals and groups. And **interactional justice** (Bies 2001) focuses on treating people with dignity and respect, which often engenders trust. Essentially, *a distribution, procedure, or interaction may be seen as just when it meets the expectations set up by the relevant and shared rules*, which are discussed in more detail later in the chapter.

The *Stone Soup* "Herstory Lesson" illustrates the types of justice. Val argues that Albert *and* his wife Mileva worked out the theory of relativity *together*—because both made contributions, both should be entitled to rewards. Yet Val sees an injustice because the Nobel Prize recognizes just Albert. She implies that Albert may have recognized this distributive injustice, with his excessive rewards creating feelings of guilt, which in turn propelled him to give the prize money to Mileva, as compensation for her contribution. Also implicit in Val's argument is that the largely male scientific community at the time may have favored one of their own, thereby failing to demonstrate neutrality in their decision-making. Moreover, Val makes Einstein out to be distributively unfair at the interpersonal level by leaving Mileva with the burden of raising their schizophrenic son alone and interactionally unfair by having extramarital affairs that undermine respect and trust. While the historical accuracy of the cartoon's claims may be questioned (see Pais 1994), it nonetheless exemplifies elements of justice processes.

The cartoon taps into two key suppositions about justice processes. First, *evaluations of the justness or fairness of outcomes, procedures, or interaction dynamics are* **subjective**, not objective. In other words, justice is in the eyes of the beholder. For example, Val believes that Mileva has not received a just reward for her work with Albert, yet her brother-in-law Wally had to be convinced. From his knowledge of Einstein and, perhaps, his male view, he initially believed that Einstein's sole recognition for the theory of relativity was deserved. The second idea complements the first: *what people perceive as fair* **depends upon the context** *in which they are embedded*. For instance, drawing from the discussion of legitimacy in the last chapter, we might say that women scientists were not legitimated in the late 19th century. Thus, the Nobel Prize committee was "fair" to recognize only Einstein with the award. Legitimacy of a distribution, a procedure, or mode of interaction is one contextual factor shaping subjective perceptions of fairness, which may lead to justification of inequalities or stymie injustice responses (Hegtvedt and Johnson 2000). In a subsequent section, we look at how such individual-level factors and other contextual factors affecting evaluations of and responses to various types of injustice.

This chapter generally focuses on the ways justice shapes social interaction. For example, consider the social dynamics of a family. A younger sibling may lament wearing hand-me-down clothes, being the last served at dinner, and suffering relentless teasing by older siblings. In contrast, an older sibling may ignore the younger sibling's rants as those of the "baby" of the family, spoiled by parents and getting more of everything desired (e.g., attention, privileges) and less of everything not desired (e.g., chores, curfews). Regardless of the reality of the family's resource distribution, ways of making rules, or treatment among members, cries of "it's not fair!" may chime through the home periodically. Such cries may be followed by behaviors enacted by the victim or others to redress perceived injustices. How people respond to (or ignore) the cries of unfairness may then shape subsequent interaction. The youngest child may suffer in silence and then, as an adult, rub his or her success in the face of the older siblings!

Although perceptions of justice are subjective, there are existing guidelines for judging what might constitute a just distribution, procedure, or treatment. Thus, we begin by answering this question: What is justice? The subjectivity of evaluations, however, leads us also to address a second question: How do individual and situational factors affect people's judgments about justice? And, when people truly feel that they have been treated unjustly, they may attempt to do something about it. Thus, a third question is this: How do people respond to injustice? The nature of responses to injustice, like perceptions, depends upon situational factors as well. We conclude the chapter with a discussion of how justice processes may affect dynamics between groups as well as among individuals.

What Is Justice?

When we ask our students if they have ever experienced injustice, they regale us with a variety of stories: roommates who never do any housework, lazy coworkers who fail to pull their weight but get paid the same, professors whose exam questions pertain to readings that were not assigned, being followed by store security officers because of their skin color, and the like. Sometimes they also offer evaluations of the state of society that imply injustice: the continuing existence (in 2015) of nearly 29 million Americans without health insurance, the receipt of stiffer prison sentences for black offenders than white offenders, or even the fact that (in 2012) the United States, with 4.5% of the world's population, uses about 20% of the world energy resources (while India, with 17.8% of the world's population, uses about only 5% of energy resources). Clearly, they have no difficulty in coming up with experiences of injustice. But then when asked, "What is justice?" we are met with relative silence.

Nonetheless, justice is a feature of all social groups—human and nonhuman (primates) alike. Although animals cannot communicate social ideals, through their behavior they illustrate elements contributing to the understanding of the evolution of fairness in humans (Brosnan and de Waal 2014). Members of various species readily "protest" receiving less than a partner (i.e., signaling what we might call "instances of injustice") (Brosnan 2013; Talbot, Price, and Brosnan 2016). Great apes, our closest nonhuman relatives, also try to equalize their outcomes with partners, even at the expense of getting less for themselves. Such behavior may ensure future cooperation among members of the social group, beyond that necessary for mating and kinship, and constitutes a small piece of the puzzle that led humans to discuss, at length, what justice is.

Philosophers (see Solomon and Murphy 2000) have long debated what constitutes a just society. Yet they have also offered principles of what might constitute justice in interpersonal relationships. For example, Aristotle (Book V, *Nicomachean Ethics*) admonishes that equals should be treated equally and unequals should be treated unequally. In doing so, he suggests a notion of proportionality between the rewards people receive and their contributions or statuses. Social contractarian philosophers (e.g., Thomas Hobbes and John Locke) caution of the necessity for rational people to see their way to compromising their divisive self-interests to create civil society. Justice for them means moving beyond self-interests to ensure something that enhances the well-being of *both* others and the self. More recently, Rawls (1971) and Barry (1989) have emphasized impartiality as an important guiding principle of justice that effectively suppresses unfettered self-interests as the basis of justice. Moreover, people tend to agree on distributions, procedures, or treatment if they do not reflect the biases of any one individual or group.

Typically, to assess justice, *people compare a given distribution, procedure, or treatment to the one expected on the basis of a "just" rule* (see Hegtvedt 2006). Various rules constitute distributive, procedural, and interactional justice. The rules themselves do not designate what is just in a situation, however. Within a situation, a just rule should be consistent with criteria suggested in philosophical writings. First, it must *foster social cooperation* (Deutsch 1976; Tyler and Blader 2000) as exemplified by consequences promoting collective welfare, not simply the welfare of the individual evaluator. Second, the rule should reflect a degree of *impartiality* (Frohlich and Oppenheimer 1992). As Rawls (1971) suggests, rules that are just are decided upon without knowing in advance what would serve one's personal interests. And, third, justice rules are *consensual*—people agree that they are the right rules in the situation and apply to everyone.

Application of a justice rule, of course, requires designation of the group or "moral community" to which it will apply (Opotow 1990). For instance, in a family, a distribution based on needs seems appropriate; parents buy new shoes for a child when shoes are needed. In contrast, in a college setting, giving a student an A because he or she needs good grades to apply to medical school rather than the B deserved based on work performance would be challenged as unfair. In effect, the need principle takes on one meaning in reference to children within a family and another meaning for students in a school setting. Appropriate or fair principles depend upon the meaning of the group, the situation, and the goals of both. The cluster of attitudes and moral values that define a moral community may vary across cultures and shift over time. For example, in the United States, it was once "fair" to pay women less than men for performing very similar jobs or to exclude women from performing certain jobs; today, that distribution of payment or jobs would be unfair (unlawful even) in the United States, though in a country characterized by more paternal values, it would not. Likewise, while the United States may stress the fairness of equal access to education regardless of gender, in countries characterized by religiously dictated rigid gender roles such equality would be disdained. Though we offer abstract qualities of justice, designating specific rules that capture justice, ultimately what is just is subjective and depends upon the context.

Three rules may constitute, depending on the situation, distributive justice or fairness in the distribution of positive outcomes (i.e., benefits or rewards such as pay, prestige) or negative ones (i.e., burdens or punishments such as fines, reduced access) (e.g., Deutsch 1975; Leventhal, Karuza, and Fry 1980). The **equality** rule dictates that each recipient should get an objectively equal share of the outcomes distributed. For example, a mother provides each of her children with six candies, or everyone in a specific work group receives the same percentage pay raise. The **needs** rule indicates that outcomes should be commensurate with the needs of potential recipients. For example, only the child who has outgrown his or her shoes gets new shoes in a family. In the 19th century, some companies paid employees a "family wage," assuming that breadwinners needed more money than their single counterparts. The **equity** rule stresses that outcomes should be proportional to contributions defined positively as productivity, effort, ability, merit, and status or negatively like harms and losses perpetrated by individuals. For example, a father pays $5 for each A his child brings home, or employees who work more hours get paid more.

Given multiple rules for each type of justice, you might ask, "When is a particular rule the basis for judging fairness in a situation?" The nature of social relations among potential recipients and the goals of a social system responsible for making a distribution contribute to determining which rule defines justice in a situation (Deutsch 1985; Leventhal et al. 1980). People perceive equal shares as just when they feel personally connected to each other or when the situational goal or social system promotes group harmony or cooperation. So, a group of friends at work might be more inclined to agree that everyone should get an equal share of a monetary bonus than would workers who are in little contact. Similarly, a focus on the welfare of group members and their personal development results in emphasis on needs-based distributions as just. This is, of course, what typically occurs in families and maybe even in schools with regard to children who have learning disabilities. In contrast, when social relationships are impersonal, the situational goal stresses productivity, or the system engenders competition, then the equity principle emerges as just. People who work for the same company but do not work "together" might argue that pay bonuses should be distributed according to performance level—for example, the person who had the highest sales for a given time period should get the highest bonus.

Procedural justice focuses on fairness in decision-making procedures generally and specifically on procedures used to make distributions. In the realm of conflict resolution (Thibaut and Walker 1975), people tend to believe that procedures giving themselves some control over reward distribution decisions might be fairest. But beyond notions of underlying process control, there are broader principles of procedural justice (Leventhal et al. 1980), including (1) **bias suppression**, (2) **consistency of procedures across persons and across time**, (3) **information accuracy**, (4) **correctability** (being able to change bad decisions), (5) **representativeness of the participants in a decision**, and (6) **ethicality of standards**. When our university decided to revise the first- and second-year student advising system, the dean sent the same memo to faculty and staff from all departments requesting their input (consistency and representativeness), did not voice his own opinions to avoid influencing the discussion (thus disrupting status processes and his own biases), made sure that information on the number of students to be advised and of faculty to be advisors was correct (accuracy), noted that there would be an evaluation of the new system after 3 years (correctability), and tried to guide an honest discussion of the issues of implementing various systems (ethicality). Of these rules, key to ensuring procedural justice in nearly all situations are representativeness, which is activated by giving "voice" to the opinions of the individuals affected by the decision, and consistency (Lind and Tyler 1988).

How discussions unfold in decision-making may include elements of interactional justice or fairness in treatment of subordinates by authorities or between peers. Key principles communicate information about the quality of the interpersonal relationship among interacting individuals in general and specifically in decision-making situations (Bies 2001; Tyler and Lind 1992). **Standing** refers to polite behavior; dignified treatment; and, importantly, respect for one's rights and opinions. **Neutrality** points to equal treatment of all parties and includes honesty and lack of bias. **Trust** characterizes the intentions of the decision-maker to be fair and ethical in the immediate situation and in the future. Additionally, **truthfulness** and **justification** (provision of rationale) constitute other interactional justice principles. Imagine the chaos that might ensue on a neighborhood youth soccer field if opposing team members and coaches did not treat each other and the referee in interactionally just ways. Certainly, the referee must act neutrally and demonstrate respect toward members of both teams. She may even be called upon to provide rationale for the calls (e.g., offside) that she makes. Likewise, although teammates are of course biased toward each other, they are expected to demonstrate respect toward each other by following the rules of the game (e.g., no holding or intentional tripping), stopping play when someone is injured, and lining up at the end to express sentiments of "good game" to each other.

Individuals may focus only on one type of justice in a given situation, yet all are likely to contribute to a general fairness judgment in a situation (Lind 2001). Accordingly, it becomes possible to contrast the impact of fairness concerns with other motivations or processes (e.g., status, power) to more thoroughly realize what drives interaction in social groups (Ambrose and Arnaud 2005).

How Do People Perceive Injustice?

When individuals fail to experience what is expected on the basis of rules presumed to be just in a given situation, they are likely to perceive the distribution, procedure, or treatment as unjust. For example, in a work organization, employees are likely to expect their boss to treat members of the work group consistently and politely. If the boss always singles out one person for the "choice" jobs and responds dismissively to group members' attempts get his feedback on their own work, then the employees are likely to perceive procedural and interactional injustice (though they may not use those terms!). Similarly, students expect professors to distribute grades on the basis of performance—students who do well in a course (say, average scores above 92%) are likely to look forward to an A and further anticipate that those scoring 89% or lower will get a B or worse. If the professor gives everyone in the class an A, high performers are likely to feel that their grade is unfair. Low performers, even though they benefit by the professor's grading scheme, may even feel the same because the expectation based on the agreed upon justice principle is violated. Evaluations of injustice, however, are more complicated than simply the recognition of unfulfilled expectations.

A *justice evaluation is a result of a sense-making process* (van den Bos, Lind, and Wilke 2001), which relies upon various social cognitive processes (see Chapter 5) and affective concerns (van den Bos 2003; see Chapter 7). The information that individuals take into account to make sense of situational justice elements in the situation depend on who they are as individuals (their characteristics and their beliefs) and contextual circumstances (e.g., goals, group structure, information available, amount of rewards). These factors also may shape motivations in the situation. Justice evaluators or perceivers may be people directly affected by a distribution, procedure, or treatment (i.e., "first parties"), or they may be observers of how a distribution, procedure, or treatment affects others (i.e., "third parties"). Observers attempt to make sense out of justice elements in a manner similar to that of first parties (see Skarlicki and Kulik 2005): by consciously or automatically

FIGURE 11.2

Source: Baby Blues Partnership. Distributed by Features Syndicate, Inc..

processing information in the situation, as influenced by their motivations, other individual level characteristics, and contextual factors.

These individual and contextual factors influence subjective evaluations of justice and injustice. A consequence of this subjectivity is that two people may see the same distribution, procedure, or treatment pattern differently, one assessing it as fair and the other as unfair. For example, in the *Baby Blues* cartoon, Zoe and Hammie's mother Wanda tries explicitly and carefully to divide the remaining birthday cake equally between her two children (see Figure 11.2). Then Zoe notes that her piece "has more vowels" than does Hammie's piece. Zoe's observation leads Hammie to cry, "No fair!" Although few mothers would anticipate that the vowels are valued, in this instance Zoe touts them as something special, making her cake slice "better" than Hammie's. From Hammie's point of view, equality is dashed! Zoe could have gone on to argue that she "deserves" more vowels because she is older. In doing so, she would invoke a contributions principle as just in the situation. Sometimes people have different beliefs about which rules are just in a situation. Other times they may differentially evaluate the elements that make up the distributions (e.g., the contributions and outcomes), the decision process, or the interpersonal treatment.

Next, we consider underlying motivational, cognitive, comparison, and affective processes that influence justice evaluations. While these processes occur at the individual level, they often take into account social and other information in the situation.

Underlying Processes

Think about the last time that (1) you received what you considered an unfair work performance evaluation, (2) your parents did not listen to why you wanted to do something that they forbid, or (3) your friend snubbed you at a party. These situations denote potential instances of distributive, procedural, and interactional injustice, respectively. Now, reflect back on how you came to see the example as unfair. Most likely you consciously or automatically tried to understand the situation by asking yourself questions, or you felt a negative emotion and wondered why. Maybe both things occurred simultaneously, happening so fast that you cannot recount how you arrived at the injustice evaluation. The seemingly instantaneous assessment of unfairness probably involved several steps. Sometimes the process may seem rational or calculated and other times intuitive (van den Bos 2007). Generally, subjective justice appraisals stem from combinations of (1) motivations, (2) cognitive processing, (3) social comparisons, and (4) affective processes. Individual- and group-level factors influence each element.

Motivations

Recall that justice extends beyond the individual by emphasizing impartiality, group welfare, and consensus. Sometimes people may indeed be motivated by the ideal of justice (Lerner 2003). And when people make sense out of a situation to determine whether a particular distribution, procedure, or interaction experience is just, their motivations often color their subjective evaluations. Yet these motivations may reflect something different from the justice ideal. When a child complains that it is unfair to make her wash her own dishes because her brother did not have to do so until he was older than her current age, she injects justice rhetoric to justify a largely self-interested motivation to avoid a chore. Sometimes it is difficult to discern whether justice evaluations stem from concerns truly about justice (and morality) or from concerns about one's own material or social (self) interests.

Three motivations may underlie justice perceptions and behaviors: (1) material self-interest, (2) social concerns, and (3) moral convictions (Skitka, Bauman, and Mullen 2008). Distributive justice approaches (Adams 1965; Walster, Walster, and Berscheid 1978) largely assume that individuals are economic actors, motivated by *material self-interest*. People are likely to designate as fair distributions maximizing their own and their group members' outcomes with the lowest expenditure of real or psychological costs. For example, in a work group, people who perform really well might find a contributions-based or equitable distribution of outcomes as fair because it ensures higher outcomes than an equal distribution; in contrast, low performers might suggest an equal distribution so that they are not penalized for their low performance. Similarly, the **instrumental approach** to procedural justice (Thibaut and Walker 1975) suggests that people prefer procedures that give them control over the process as a means of achieving fair outcomes. In other words, fair procedures are ones that lead to maximizing an individual's outcomes.

Alternatively, social concerns capture consideration of individuals' desire to feel valued or well-regarded by authorities (and peers), even if doing so does not maximize material outcomes (Lind and Tyler 1988; Tyler and Lind 1992). This motivation underlies the **group value approach** to procedural justice. Procedural and interactional justice rules communicate sentiments of value and regard, which in turn increase an individual's self-esteem and ultimately uphold social conventions. Essentially, being valued by group authorities and other members maximizes "outcomes" in the form of intangible, infinite social well-being (see Gillespie and Greenberg 2005). Thus, the second motivation is akin to pursuing *self-interested social rewards*. For example, imagine working as a barista at a Starbucks that announced one opening for an assistant manager. You, along with five coworkers, apply for the position, which comes with higher pay. Regardless of the outcome of the application process, you know that you will be working with these people in the future. In such case, what may be of most concern for you is how you and the others are treated in the application process. You are likely to perceive that consistent, unbiased decision-making procedures and respectful treatment of all applicants ensure that the manager has acted fairly in making a promotion decision. In emphasizing the pursuit of *social* rather than material rewards, attention is drawn to others, strengthening social relations. Such a pursuit may promote collective welfare at the heart of justice.

Likewise, the third basic motivation, pursuit of *moral convictions*, captures the essence of justice beyond the conventions of any particular group. These convictions, which represent universal and relatively objective standards of right and wrong that uphold human dignity, may be innate, leading to automatic responses to their violation (Folger, Cropanzano, and Goldman 2005; Skitka et al. 2008). For example, people are more likely to reject and fail to comply with decisions made by legitimate authorities regarding physician-assisted suicide, capital murder, or abortion policies that run counter to their moral convictions (Skitka et al. 2008). Thus, especially when others rather than oneself are directly affected, moral convictions may trump motivations rooted in normative adherence to distributive and procedural justice principles.

Of course, not all situations involving justice tap into moral convictions (Folger et al. 2005; Skitka et al. 2008). Situational conditions usually shape individuals' motivations, which in turn may affect the impact of other individual level factors and how they process information relevant to determining an injustice. When making evaluations of one's own outcomes or treatment, it is far easier for self-interested motivations to color perceptions than when evaluating a potential injustice that has befallen another person. Chapter 5 noted how motivations might affect cognitive processing. Such effects also extend to cognitions about justice situations.

Cognitive Processes

Recall being in high school and asking your parents if you can go to a party Saturday night. They might first tell you that they will not even consider the possibility until you have done your chores (i.e., clean your room, gather the recycling, unload the dishwasher). Then they might ask the following questions: Where is the party? Who is going to be there? Whose parents are going to be present? You might think that this is entirely unfair! You have to first "work" and then suffer through an inquisition. You might see your "inputs" (all of the work) as far too onerous for the simple "outcome" of permission to go to a party. Moreover, all of the questions make it seem as if they do not trust you or respect you as a thoughtful human being. In contrast, your parents might claim that the inputs are necessary and, of course, they trust you—they are just unsure whether they should trust others. In this situation, you and your parents have different perceptions of relevant inputs (how would having a clean room make you more prepared for a party?) and the meaning of objective information about the party. The cognitive processes underlying justice evaluations, as detailed in the two theoretical arguments that follow, are complex.

Uncertainty management theory (van den Bos 2005; van den Bos and Lind 2002) presumes that people make justice evaluations under conditions of uncertainty. Because of the uncertainty, individuals must look for cues in the situation to direct their evaluations. To do so, they draw on the nature of the information available in the situation. In some cases, that information may activate mental shortcuts or heuristics (see Chapter 5) that allow inferences with limited knowledge about the situation and thus simplify fairness judgments. The classic heuristic in justice situations is information on the fairness of decision-making procedures (Lind 2001; van den Bos et al. 2001). In what is labeled the **fair process effect**, people judge outcomes as more fair to the extent they believe procedures underlying the distribution decision are fair.

For example, imagine that you applied for a new job in your company and did not get it despite your qualifications. Whether you see failure to get the job as an instance of distributive injustice may depend upon how your employer went about the search process. If the employer advertised the job broadly, carefully reviewed all applications with the hiring committee, and methodically consulted references, you may not see the situation as unjust (though you may remain disappointed about not getting the job). In contrast, had you learned that the employer accepted applications but did not systematically review all of them and instead focused on the one from his brother-in-law, then you might perceive procedural injustice, owing to violations of consistency and bias suppression as well as distributive injustice. You have used hiring procedural fairness as a heuristic in judging the fairness of the outcome to yourself because you lack full information on applicants' skills, experience, and so forth to identify the strongest candidate.

Assessments of procedural justice heuristically affect those of distributive justice in the absence of information on others' contributions or outcomes (van den Bos et al. 1997). Plus, people may rely on information about one type of justice to infer fairness in another realm as well (Qin et al. 2015). For example, when procedural information is unclear, assessments of the fairness of interactional cues may extend to procedural justice evaluations. Thus, regardless of the type, fairness heuristics help to manage uncertainty along with other situational information.

While uncertainty management theory draws attention to cognitive heuristics and other types of information to aid in constructing fairness evaluations, **fairness theory** (Folger and Cropanzano 1998, 2001) relies heavily on deliberate and automatic cognitive assessments. The theory proposes that evaluators make "if only" or counterfactual statements about a decision-maker or injustice perpetrator's behavior. "If only" and counterfactual statements figuratively "undo" an event by imagining it otherwise. For example, Karen's son, Ross, grumbled that his sister, Marlis, had unjustly claimed and consumed his raspberry chocolate mousse dessert (she had eaten her own dessert of that type the day before). Ross's sense of injustice stemmed from and was fueled by the many other ways that he could have imagined the situation unfolding. He might see his outcome (no dessert) as less unfair *if only* Marlis had asked him if she could eat it or *if only* Mom had prevented her from claiming the dessert. By readily bringing to mind counterfactual statements that describe another state of affairs, the perception of injustice intensifies.

Such statements allow perceivers to locate blame for an injustice. Blame is likely when individuals believe (1) "if only" had the perpetrator acted otherwise, they *would* have been better off, (2) the perpetrator *could* have acted otherwise, and (3) the perpetrator *should* have acted otherwise. The "would" question implies the comparison at the heart of all justice evaluations between what was expected (based on a justice rule) and what actually occurred. The "could" question taps into whether the perpetrator had discretion in the distribution decision. And the "should" question introduces concerns about moral obligation and ethical conduct principles (see Hegtvedt and Scheuerman 2010; Skitka, Bauman, and Mullen 2016). Clearly, Ross knew he *would* have been better off eating his own dessert, and he believed his sister *could* have acted otherwise by refraining from indulging her sweet tooth or asking permission to devour it. And, most likely, he trusted that she *should* have acted otherwise; failure to do so breached the ongoing and shared understanding about the purchase and distribution of these special desserts. Given these beliefs, blame seems to rest with the sister for this injustice.

Both uncertainty management theory and fairness theory direct attention to the kinds of information that individuals may use as a basis for claiming an outcome, procedure, or treatment to be fair or unfair. People do fill in the gaps in their information as well as rely upon analyses of "what could have been" (e.g., Brockner et al. 2007; Colquitt and Chertkoff 2002; Nicklin 2013). An emphasis on determining blame relates to other work on cognitive processes underlying justice evaluations that specifically examines information necessary to make attributions.

Attribution processes (see Chapter 5), which involve inferences about the cause(s) of an action, inform both the assessment of injustice as well as potentially the responses to it. If you felt snubbed by a friend at a party, you might ask why before judging the friend's behavior as unfair. Indeed, van den Bos and colleagues (1999) argue that receipt of (unexpected) unfavorable outcomes or treatment is likely to stimulate a search for an explanation, activating an attribution process. People may look at the causes of inputs or contributions when they are deciding what should be taken into account in calculating fair outcomes. Consider two workers who have been randomly assigned to different tasks, one easy and one difficult; the one with the easy task gets more work done in an hour than the one with the tough task. Would it be fair to pay these two workers for the amount of work completed in an hour? Most likely not because the one with the easy task simply lucked out; she got more work done in an hour because of the nature of the task and not her ability or work ethic. If individuals presume external factors like luck are the source of inputs, they are more likely to discount those inputs as a credible basis for allocating rewards (Cohen 1982). Conversely, when people overcome constraints to ensure high contributions, those inputs (according to the augmentation principle) are attributed internally, to effort or ability, and weigh more heavily in determining outcomes. Thus, had the person with the difficult task gotten more work done, then, perhaps she should be compensated more highly than the one with the easy task.

Attributions also play a role in assessing the behavior of a person who may have perpetrated an injustice. Why did the friend snub you at the party? If you were to learn that the friend had lost his contacts and literally could not recognize your face, then you might presume that he did not intend to treat you in a manner that seemed unfair. Typically, external attributions about a perpetrator's behavior eliminate or decrease the severity of the perceived injustice, whereas internal attributions have the opposite effect (Mikula 2003; Utne and Kidd 1980). For example, Brockner et al. (2007) show that when employees receive low outcomes from a supervisor who does not use fair procedures, they are more likely to hold that authority responsible—that is, make an internal attribution—and to judge overall fairness of the situation much lower. And, as discussed further in a subsequent section, the attributions that people make for the injustice also affect how they choose to respond (or not respond) to the perceived injustice. Perceptions of and responses to injustice are also affected by the social comparisons that individuals make.

Social Comparisons

As noted previously, the key comparison underlying any justice evaluation is between what is expected based on a particular justice principle and what actually happens—what outcomes received or treatment experienced.[1] In addition, people compare themselves to others in terms of what they have contributed or received, in the case of distributive justice, or how they are treated, in the case of procedural and interactional justice. Social comparisons of various sorts help individuals make sense out of the fairness of a situation.

Some of you may have had summer jobs like tennis instructor, lifeguard, or camp counselor. Let's say that you have worked as a lifeguard at the, for example, Oakbrook Club for multiple summers. Each year you get a little boost in your pay. And you know that you make the same amount of money as other lifeguards at Oakbrook with your same level of experience. One summer, you learn that the tennis instructors at the same complex with the pool actually make $10 more an hour than you do. This gets you and your co-lifeguards to invoke the different types of comparison at the heart of distributive justice to determine the fairness of your pay.

Comparisons of your hourly pay as a lifeguard over time constitute an **internal** comparison assessing outcome levels for the same individual at multiple points in time. If your base pay was less during your second year than during your first, you might claim unfairness. In talking to another lifeguard about your hourly pay, you invoke what is called a **local** comparison. Such comparisons occur when a person compares his or her outcomes—or outcomes/inputs ratio—with that of one other individual (Adams 1965). For example, you might expect that lifeguards at your pool with two years of experience receive $10 an hour. So, with "hours" as inputs and pay as the outcome, if you worked 30 hours one week and your coworker worked 20, you would expect $300 and $200 as your respective pay levels. Adams's (1965) equity formula represents the local comparison as follows: $O_A/I_A = O_B/I_B$, where O represents the outcomes level, I indicates actors' inputs or contributions, and subscripts refer to two different actors.

If the ratios are equal, fairness exists; if they are unequal, then one actor may be underpaid or overpaid. When both lifeguards work 20 hours, if you (Actor A) receive $200 and your co-lifeguard (Actor B) gets $300, you might feel underpaid and your colleague might feel overpaid. While both underpayment and overpayment may be seen as unfair, underpayment is particularly distressful. The logic of the equity comparison can be extended to include multiple local comparisons within a group (see van den Bos et al. 1997). In contrast to the information in this example, knowledge and measurement of inputs and outcomes may be vague. In such cases, people rely on their perception of what they presume to be relevant inputs and outcomes.

Multiple local comparisons, however, fail to address "what people like us normally get." Local comparisons must be put in the context of what similar others receive. **Referential** comparisons (Berger et al. 1972) refer to abstract others with the same social characteristics and their typical outcomes. The referential comparison in the lifeguard example might be what, for example, Ansley, Inman, and Piedmont pools pay their lifeguards with 2 years of experience. The referential comparison allows assessments about whether the two local actors are individually under-rewarded, fairly rewarded, or over-rewarded. If the other pools compensate their lifeguards with the same years of experience $15/hour, you might decide that you are certainly underpaid for your 20 hours of work but your co-lifeguard is not. Had you both been underpaid vis-à-vis the referential comparison, then you could join forces to complain to management!

Recall also that the Oakbrook pool complex also hires tennis instructors who make twice as much per hour as you do. The tennis instructors are distinct from you and thus do not really constitute a referential comparison. But the two groups are necessary to successful summer revenues at Oakbrook, so it would not be surprising if lifeguards as a group compared themselves to the group of tennis instructors. The **group** comparison typically involves assessment of how one's group fared compared to another group (Markovsky 1985). Comparisons of average hourly pay across the two groups would constitute a group comparison. On the surface, your group of lifeguards might contend that their group is underpaid. However, if inputs were also included in the analysis, it may grow apparent that the work that tennis instructors do is more arduous than what lifeguards do and thus their greater inputs deserve higher pay.

Although individuals rarely have sufficient information to assess all comparison types, combinations of comparisons consistently suggesting disadvantage are likely to spur motivation to redress the situation (Törnblom 1977). And the impact of group comparisons depends greatly on how much an individual identifies with a given group (Markovsky 1985). In general, the comparisons that a person invokes in making a justice judgment are contingent upon the availability and relevance of particular comparisons (Kulik and Ambrose 1992).

Social comparisons profoundly influence evaluations of distributive fairness and play an indirect role in assessments of procedural and interactional justice (Folger and Kass 2000). To assess whether procedural principles are upheld requires comparing how authorities treat people besides oneself. For example, the Oakbrook manager should ask the scheduling preference of each lifeguard when creating the work schedule, and someone should observe whether everyone is really consulted. Also, people may use the opinions of others to construct how fair or unfair their treatment has been (Folger and Kass 2000; Hegtvedt and Johnson 2000). For example, your assessment of the fairness of your lifeguard pay may depend upon whether your coworkers think their pay is unfair. Social comparisons play a pivotal role in assessments of injustice, relying heavily on information, which to some extent affects affective processing as well.

Affective Processes

Although attempts to determine how justice judgments are formed have largely focused on the cognitive processing of information, affective feelings may be another type of information relevant to making justice evaluations (van den Bos 2003). When asked how you knew a situation was unjust, you may have recalled your emotional feelings rather than the information you took into account to assess the situation. Emotions are typically conceived of as a reaction to injustice (as discussed next), but they may also signal that an injustice has occurred.

In keeping with the cognitive models of justice evaluations, van den Bos (2003) classifies emotions or moods as a form of information. For instance, if you are feeling generally happy and someone says something insulting to you—treats you in an interactionally unjust way—what happens? You might just ignore the comment or come back with a witty remark. In contrast, if you are feeling angry already, that remark may just send you over the edge. In his study, van den Bos showed that, in the absence of social comparison information about either outcomes or procedures, study participants induced to feel happy had more positive distributive and procedural justice evaluations; those induced to feel anger had more negative justice judgments. Thus justice perceptions relied heavily on evaluators' emotional state.

Similarly, people may use the emotions displayed by others in the situation as a form of information to help make their fairness judgments (De Cremer, Van

Kleef, and Wubben 2007). Think about a referee's call at a basketball game. You may have seen the play that caused the ref to blow the whistle but not judged it as fair or unfair until the arena filled with the boos of the spectators. Their emotional expression may have led you to agree that the call was unfair.

Justice-related emotions may function diagnostically, stimulating a closer examination of what is going on in the situation and, perhaps, a cognitive appraisal regarding the source of the emotion (Chebat and Slusarczyk 2005). A similar argument stems from affect control theory (see Chapter 7), which argues that individuals experience emotion when something is out of sync with their identity, which in turn triggers cognitive processing to figure out what made them feel a particular way. An emotion based on an inconsistency with an identity related to outcome or treatment expectations would evoke an emotion that may lead to a cognitive assessment of injustice (Scher and Heise 1993). That emotion might precede information processing suggests an alternative to cognitive models and implies that sometimes justice judgments are intuitive.

Clearly, the justice evaluation is a process "in which cognitive and affective determinants often work together to produce people's judgments of what they think is just or unjust" (van den Bos 2007:63). Additionally, individual-level and contextual factors shape these processes.

Individual-Level Factors

During his first year in office, President Obama approved a stimulus package, which included money to support the U.S. auto industry during the recession. Some people thought that using taxpayer dollars to shore up an important aspect of our economy was fair, whereas others condemned it as a government giveaway and inappropriate intrusion into the marketplace. People with liberal political leanings agreed with the first interpretation, and those with conservative political inclinations agreed with the second. Possibly, more women than men may have judged the stimulus package as fair as well. Individual-level factors like age and gender, identity, political, and other beliefs directly affect justice perceptions—at least in some contexts.

Characteristics and Identity

Some people, regardless of context, tend to care more about justice than others. **Justice sensitivity** is a stable disposition that indicates such concern for justice, regardless of type (Baumert and Schmitt 2016). This personality characteristic distinguishes stable and consistent differences among people in their likeliness to perceive and respond to injustice. Individuals characterized as high in justice sensitivity tend to process situational information in a way that is more likely to result in perceived injustice (Schmitt 1996). They may think about it longer, which then contributes to the intensity of their affective and behavioral responses to injustice.

The impact of other individual level characteristics focuses on preferences for certain justice principles (see Hegtvedt and Cook 2001). Age-based patterns tap into children's levels of cognitive development and role-taking abilities. Typically, younger children opt for distributions that maximize their material benefit or simple equal ones. For example, 4-year-old Chloe might distribute 21 pieces of candy by giving 10 pieces to herself and the rest for her older siblings. Her 7- and 10-year-old brothers might complain, arguing that their age entitles them to more! Chloe, however, does not have the cognitive skills to equitably distribute by giving one candy for each year of age. Also, her undeveloped role-taking skills prevent her from realizing how upset her brothers might be with her self-interested allocation.

Now, if Chloe as a young adult was faced with a distribution of rewards in a small group, she may actually take less for herself than would the male members of the group, regardless of their actual contributions to the group. Such a pattern reflects a female tendency toward a communal orientation and emphasis on interpersonal relationships, in contrast to males' agency orientation, focused on achievement. Such orientations account for why females might pay themselves less or prefer equal distributions to maintain group harmony (Major and Adams 1983). Yet such a gendered pattern does not occur in all situations. When females and males work on tasks defined as culturally appropriate for their genders or when distribution preferences are public, males and females share similar ideas about what a just distribution would be.

What trumps the direct effects of gender in some situations is how people think about themselves in the situation. The salience of a personal identity (see Chapter 4) may influence justice judgments more than one's gender category. Although a wide array of identities may be salient in a justice situation, particular identities have been shown to be impactful. For example, environmental identity (how a person sees oneself in relation to the natural word) has a positive effect on perceptions of environmental injustice (Clayton and Opotow 2003; Parris et al. 2014).

Identity processes are clearly relevant to justice evaluations in two other ways. First, when there is an inconsistency between what is expected based on a justice principle and what happens, an identity may be disconfirmed, which sets into process various cognitions and behaviors (Stets and Osborn 2008). A disconfirmed identity increases the likelihood that the situation will be seen as unfair. For example, if you think you are an excellent baker and your offer to make cookies for a school event is declined in favor of (gasp!) store-bought cookies, your identity is challenged, and you may feel unfairly treated.

And second, as the group value model suggests, identifying with a group is an important outcome of procedural justice (Tyler and Lind 1992) and may propel other justice evaluations. People tend to distribute more outcomes to their own than to other groups and evaluate them more positively (see Tajfel and Turner 1979; see Chapter 12). Strong identification with a group also reduces preferences for self-interested allocations within the group (Wenzel 2002) and would, presumably, promote adherence to fair procedural and interactional rules. Think about fraternities or sororities to illustrate how identity with a group affects justice evaluations. Members might seek a larger share of university resources for their own organization, and within that organization they value being a "brother" or a "sister," which increases distribution, procedural, and interactional behaviors that promote social relations.

Beliefs

The sets of beliefs that individuals hold may act as filtering and interpreting devices for information that helps make sense out of the fairness of the situation. Obviously, people hold many different types of beliefs ranging from specific notions about how outcomes are linked to behaviors to more abstract notions associated with religion, political affiliation, or culture.

Individuals' **belief in a just world** (BJW) regards their sense that the outcomes that people receive are in some way deserved because of who they are or what they did (Lerner 1975, 1980, 2003; see Furnham 2003; Hafer and Bègue 2005; Hafer and Sutton 2016). A consequence of this belief is that when individuals personally receive low outcomes, they may resort to self-derogation for their misfortune and thus perceive the situation to be less unfair than it really is (Olson and Hafer 2001). And, in evaluating the outcomes of others, the belief may lead to victim derogation, a form of rationalization that involves mentally decreasing the "inputs" to justify low outcomes or emphasizing negative characteristics to decrease deservingness.

For example, if you have a strong BJW, when one of your acquaintances applies for a scholarship and does not receive it, you might say that he really was not that qualified or that he must have written a poor essay; in some way, you blame your acquaintance for not winning the scholarship. In so doing, not only are you making an internal attribution, but you also ignore other factors such as the number of applicants and maybe the potential biases of the selection committee. If you have a weak BJW, then you would be more likely to commiserate with your acquaintance. People with a strong BJW may dissociate from and derogate innocent injustice victims in the hope that a similar negative fate will not befall them (Hafer 2000), or they may call for harsh punishment of perpetrators in criminal cases (Mohr and Luscri 1995). Thus, BJW affects both the perception of the injustice and responses to it.

Likewise, political beliefs may drive analysis of fairness because liberals and conservatives differ on the extent to which they value outcome equality (Jost 2009; Jost et al. 2003). Liberals are more likely to judge as fair policies that attempt to ensure equality or that no one falls below a certain level of outcomes. Obama's stimulus package allowed for people to keep their jobs in the auto industry and for people to buy cars in a cheaper way. In contrast, conservatives tend to emphasize distributions that reflect differences in merit or contributions more generally. Despite these typical patterns, the justice judgments of liberals and conservatives are sensitive to some contextual factors (Tetlock and Mitchell 1993). For example, liberals may allocate resources more like conservatives when the setting stresses the free-market goal of efficiency and conservatives allocate resources more like liberals when they recognize that recipients are not personally responsible for their plight.

Cultural beliefs also have an impact on justice evaluations (see Bolino and Turnley 2008; Fischer 2016; Fischer and Smith 2003; Leung 2005). Although using "country" is one way of capturing cultural differences, a more useful way is to identify cultural beliefs capturing theoretical dimensions of values that may affect evaluations of justice. One typical dimension pertains to how collectivistic or individualistic a culture or country is. Typically, in more collectivistic cultures (e.g., China, Taiwan, Japan) people believe that equal distributions among in-group members are more fair than are equitable distributions; the latter is more characteristic of individualistic cultures (e.g., North America, Europe) (Leung and Bond 1984). Similarly, procedural justice—with its implications for one's social standing in a group—has a stronger impact on the reactions of recipients of low outcomes in collectivistic cultures than in individualistic ones (Brockner et al. 2000). Within cultures, however, situational factors may also affect perceptions of justice, and their effects may vary cross-culturally.

Situational Factors

A wide variety of situational factors may influence distributive, procedural, and interactional justice evaluations. And typically, to explain the expected impact of a situational factor requires consideration of underlying motivational, cognitive, comparison, and affective processes. Next, we highlight the impact of some situational factors on perceptions of justice (see Hegtvedt and Cook 2001; Jost and Kay 2010; Tyler et al. 1997).

Situational goals like group harmony and productivity and the *closeness of social relationships* shape not only what rule constitutes justice in a situation but also justice perceptions (Leventhal et al. 1980). For example, when group harmony is the goal, deviations from equal distributions are judged as more unfair than would be the case if productivity were the goal. The nature of the relationship impacts the effect of performance level on justice perceptions. Among friends, fairness is typically defined in terms of equality. Among strangers, however, performance level influences perceptions of what is just: High performers emphasize equity, whereas low performers stress equality as fair. The stronger social bond between friends may enhance group identity and suppress material self-interest in distributions (Tyler and Dawes 1993). A consequence of increased group identity may be more emphasis on interactional justice as well. In other words, justice among friends and lovers may be less about outcomes and more about treatment. For example, a wife who believes that she does the lion's share of the household tasks even though she works outside the home may tolerate this burden of inequitable outcomes as long as her spouse treats her fairly—showing how much he loves and respects her. Just as people are more likely to perceive outcomes as fair if procedures are fair, interactional justice may affect perceptions of distributive justice.

One way, then, to think about the impact of other situational factors on justice perceptions is to consider *how they make people accountable to others* for their distributions, decisions, and treatment. By facilitating attention to the consequences for others, situational factors alter the extent that material self-interest drives assessments. Such situational factors may include sharing distribution information with all group members; discussing the distribution among recipients; putting people in roles requiring responsibility for others' welfare; or limiting the amount of rewards to be distributed (e.g., Hegtvedt 1987; Kernis and Reis 1984). In such situations, people tend to perceive as fair distributions that are less materially beneficial to themselves. Such "benevolent" distributions, however, may benefit perceivers socially.

With regard to procedural or interactional justice, *explanations for decisions or behavior* play a critical role. For example, if you were fired or laid off from your job, wouldn't you want to know why? When employers provide adequate explanations for the (negative) decisions that they make, workers view the situation as less unjust and are more likely to cooperate (see Shaw, Wild, and Colquitt 2003). In contrast, inadequate explanations fuel the perception of injustice because they demonstrate a lack of respect toward workers and violate other ethical standards. "Excuses" (denying responsibility owing to an external cause but admitting that the outcome is unfavorable) are more beneficial than "justifications" (admitting responsibility but denying the negativity of the outcome and emphasizing a more important goal). Excuses present mitigating circumstances to allow for making external attributions, which tend to reduce the perceived severity of injustice. Giving adequate explanations or identifying excuses helps reduce uncertainty and may provide "answers" to the questions posed by fairness theory.

Another key situational factor affecting perceptions of justice is *legitimacy* (Chapter 10). One way to think about legitimacy is in terms of this question: What do other people think? Their thoughts might indicate consensus or social support for a particular distribution, procedure, or pattern of behavior. Individuals compare their own assessments of justice about a situation to the opinions of their peers or superiors, who represent collective sources of support and approval for a distribution, a procedure, or a treatment (Hegtvedt and Johnson 2000). For example, as a teen, how many times did you ask your friends' opinions about a punishment that your parents meted out? Imagine that you missed your curfew by 15 minutes and your parents grounded you for a month. You probably would think that punishment to be unfair—far too excessive for your infraction. If your friends too thought that the punishment was unfair, they would be supporting your own view, which might actually result in more intense feelings of injustice. But what if your friends thought it was a fair punishment? In effect, they are legitimizing your parents' action, which may give you pause and decrease the intensity of your perceived injustice.

Think about managers who evaluate their employees for promotions. Legitimacy of promotion criteria in an organization positively affects perceptions of procedural justice, which in turn enhances perceptions of distributive justice (Mueller and Landsman 2004). Thus, when peers or authorities legitimate a distribution, procedure, or treatment, people are more likely to perceive them as fair, despite personal beliefs or objective criteria suggesting otherwise.

Ultimately, what people believe is just or fair stems from their characteristics and beliefs and how they interpret the information available to them in different types of situations. The cognitive and affective processes produce subjective evaluations of justice. Despite the subjectivity, patterns of perceptions emerge for certain characteristics or contextual conditions. Sometimes these factors lead to conflicting justice perceptions (Deutsch 2000; Mikula and Wenzel 2000). We all can generate examples of when our parents, lovers, or employers treated us unfairly but did not see it that way! Resolving such conflicting views of justice may depend upon engagement in cooperative activities (Tjosvold, Wong, and Wan 2010). Yet typically the goal is to resolve the perceived injustice itself; thus we turn to responses to perceived injustice.

How Do People Respond to Perceptions of Injustice?

A graduate student feels sad yet angry when he learns that he did not get a prestigious teaching fellowship but a less qualified student did. A friend promises to help you move out of your house but reneges at the last minute to go to a bar with other friends; you rethink whether this person is really your friend. An employer repeatedly cuts worker benefits, so employees start to use work supplies for their personal purposes.

Although people respond to different types of justice, equity theory (Adams 1965) provides the basic framework to explain responses. The framework also underlies instances of procedural and interactional injustice. The focus is typically on individual responses to personal injustices, though responses may involve third parties or others similarly disadvantaged. Joining with others is potentially a means of disrupting the status quo and rectifying social inequalities.

Basic Theoretical Framework of Responses to Injustice

Two main tenets of equity theory (Adams 1965; Walster et al. 1978) are at the heart of explanations for responses to any kind of injustice. First, *people who perceive injustice are likely to experience unpleasant sensations of distress and tension.* Observation of others' injustice may also create similar, though perhaps less intense, feelings. And, second, *individuals are motivated to relieve the distress or tension by restoring justice for oneself or for others.*

Given the roots of equity theory in the social exchange approach to interaction, presumably people pursue the least costly means of redressing injustice. Specifically, they may cognitively assess the material and social costs and benefits associated with possible reactions (see van den Bos et al. 2001). The goal of redress is either to restore a psychological sense of justice or to change the situation to achieve actual justice (Tyler et al. 1997; Walster et al. 1978). For example, a woman who earns less than a man for doing the same job may perceive that her pay is unfair. She can convince herself that she really does not have the skills that her male counterpart possesses; thus, her lower wage is consistent with her lower inputs. Or she can compare herself to other female workers instead of her male counterpart; these women are likely to make the same or a lower amount, and thus her own pay will seem fair. In these ways, she has restored justice psychologically. Alternatively, she can request a pay raise to bring her salary up to that of those who do the same work and in doing so restore actual justice.

The theoretical framework for redressing justice involves two mediation processes. First, *perceptions of justice mediate between actual circumstances and any kind of reaction to injustice.* For example, Younts and Mueller (2001) show that the direct effects of actual pay or particular pay comparisons on pay satisfaction disappear when justice perceptions are taken into account. In effect, such findings provide evidence of how perceived justice acts as a mediator. And second, *distress—a form of emotional response—mediates between the perception of injustice and cognitive and behavioral responses.* Next, we describe the impact of actual conditions on emotional, cognitive, and behavioral response to injustice.

Emotional Responses to Injustice

Although Adams (1965) draws attention to the pivotal role of distress, Homans (1974) disassembles distress into specific emotions experienced by people in distributive injustice situations. Generally, he argues that unmet expectations (based on the relevant justice principle) result in negative emotions, whereas met expectations stimulate positive ones. He distinguishes reactions to unmet expectations in terms of whether the situation disadvantages or advantages an individual. Such patterns largely extend to procedural and interactional injustice as well (see Cropanzano, Stein, and Nadisic 2011; Hegtvedt and Parris 2014; Hillebrandt and Barclay 2013).

Specifically, Homans indicates that when people are paid fairly (equitably), they will not experience distress and instead feel satisfied. In contrast, those who get less than expected (the under-rewarded) are likely to feel angry, whereas those who get more than expected (the over-rewarded) may feel guilty (e.g., Hegtvedt

1990; Jost, Wakslak, and Tyler 2008; Sprecher 1992). Yet because it is easy and consistent with material self-interest to justify extra rewards, feelings of guilt are more likely when an unexpected windfall is at the expense of another person, involves a local comparison, or violates a moral standard (Clay-Warner et al. 2016; Peters, van den Bos, and Bobocel 2004).

Other types of injustice elicit a similar pattern of responses. For example, researchers explored student descriptions of injustice situations and resulting emotional responses in 37 countries (Mikula, Scherer, and Athenstaedt 1998). They found that the stories respondents provided tapped into distributive, procedural, and interactional issues, which in turn stimulated feelings of anger and to a lesser extent disgust, sadness, fear, guilt, and shame. Unjust events, compared to other emotion-eliciting events, stimulated feelings of greater intensity and duration.

Procedural justice—in the form of information accuracy, neutrality, or voice—produces positive affect (e.g., De Cremer 2004; Tyler and Blader 2003). And, while unfair procedures may produce anger or resentment independent of other factors (e.g., Barclay, Skarlicki, and Pugh 2005; Hegtvedt and Killian 1999), the effect of procedural injustice may also depend on information about outcomes. Once people experience positive or negative affect resulting from their outcome level, they may scrutinize the procedures that produced them, especially if they are lower than expected (Krehbiel and Cropanzano 2000; Weiss, Suckow, and Cropanzano 1999). As you might suspect, people grow very angry when they perceive that unfair procedures have produced unfavorable outcomes. They also feel a bit guilty if they benefit from an unfair process.

Because fair procedures reduce concerns with low outcomes, procedural concerns may have a stronger impact on affective responses than distributive injustice. In a similar vein, to the extent that individuals clearly know who has treated them unfairly, interactional injustices may exert a greater effect on emotional responses than other types of injustice. Essentially, knowing "who did that to me" intensifies emotions (Bembenek, Beike, and Schroeder 2007). For example, imagine that you get a lower grade than you expected from a course, and when you consult your professor about it, he takes little time to explain how he determined the grade and then dismisses you abruptly. The lack of procedural justice and interactional fairness are likely to feel insulting and generate even deeper anger than the unexpected low grade.

Yet sometimes people experience the emotions and yet not display them because to do so may result in negative consequences. Relative power and status of the individuals in the situation often influence how people will respond to unjust outcomes. For example, most people begrudgingly accept a judge's traffic ticket ruling, not showing their resentment even when they think they have been unfairly treated. Or workers angry over the lack of salary increases during tough economic times may stymie complaints to the boss to avoid looking uncooperative before the next round of layoffs. Legitimacy processes (see Chapter 10) likewise work to suppress expression of negative emotions. Even though unfairly compensated individuals feel anger, resentment, and frustration, they may be reluctant to display those emotions to authorities who authorized or peers who endorsed the distribution for fear of negative sanctions (Johnson et al. 2007, 2016). While people consider the nature of the context and potential consequences for displaying injustice-related emotions, such processes inhibit the possibility of changing an unfair distribution. Yet under some circumstances, experienced emotions may shape cognitive and behavioral responses to injustice that may indirectly fuel changes.

Cognitive and Behavioral Responses

Equity theory and subsequent research in procedural and interactional justice recognize cognitive and behavioral responses to injustice. Cognitive responses attempt to restore a sense of psychological justice, whereas behavioral responses intend to restore actual justice. The nature of each response, of course, depends on whether a distributive, procedural, or interactional injustice is being redressed. Typically, responses are at the individual level, but individuals may join together for collective responses as well.

With regard to distributive injustice, cognitive responses focus on perceptions of parts of the equity ratio: (1) cognitive distortion of either own inputs or own outcomes, (2) cognitive distortion of either the inputs or outcomes of another recipient, or (3) changing the object or person used in the comparison (Adams 1965; Walster et al. 1978). For example, cognitive distortion of another recipient's inputs or outcomes may take the form of derogating that actor. Lower commitment to an organization may also imply a cognitive response to unfairness.

Individual behavioral responses to inequity include (1) altering outcomes or inputs and (2) leaving the situation. Increases or decreases in inputs may involve changing a worker's productivity level to bring them in line with outcomes. A *Pearls Before Swine* (see Figure 11.3) cartoon illustrates this process (in a cynical way). The strip shows goat's attempt to get a higher salary. Because goat thinks that he is valuable to the cartoon (high inputs), he asks that his salary be doubled (high rewards); the illustrator, however, disagrees and simply lowers goat's inputs (by drawing him with dashed lines) so that his inputs and outcomes once again align. Altering outcomes could come about, for example, by requesting higher pay (as goat attempted) or through acts of sabotage or stealing.

Many variations on these five core responses exist (see Tyler et al. 1997), and actual responses depend upon situational conditions (like the power of the authority—or that of the illustrator in the *Pearls* example). Complaints, in general, may

FIGURE 11.3

Source: PEARLS BEFORE SWINE © 2004 Stephan Pastis. Reprinted by permission of ANDREWS MCMEEL SYNDICATION. All rights reserved.

be a behavioral response not fully anticipated by the categories but a means of registering concerns about any type of injustice.

Psychological and behavioral responses to procedural (see Tyler et al. 1997; Vermunt and Steensma 2016) and interactional (see Bies 2005) injustices take many forms and typically focus on organizational contexts. Psychological responses may include changes in the levels of trust in or perceived legitimacy of an authority. For example, when Mike, a manager, treats Jim, his subordinate, unfairly, he undermines Jim's trust in him. To cope with a perceived injustice, Jim may simply not do what Mike wants him to do. Noncompliance is a major, counterproductive behavioral response to procedural and interactional injustices. Other responses involve actions intended to change a particular unfair procedure or treatment (e.g., establish rules of civil behavior, create a union, or reconfigure the organization) or manage distress (e.g., weakened organizational commitment, absenteeism, intention to leave an organization). Because procedural and interactional injustices strike at people's perceptions of their value to the group, psychological responses may also include decreased feelings of self-worth (Tyler and Lind 1992).

While reactions to procedural and interactional injustice are often similar, violation of procedural fairness results in responses directed to the responsible social system such as one's work organization, whereas violation of interactional fairness stimulates responses toward a particular other, such as an authority or supervisor in an organization (e.g., Bembenek et al. 2007). People see procedural justice under the control of the system that sets up decision-making procedures; thus, to effect change, they must address the system. In contrast, interactional injustice is more interpersonal, and thus the perpetrator is identifiable and targeted for responses.

Despite the wide range of responses to different forms of injustice, generally they may be categorized as compensatory or retaliatory (Bembenek et al. 2007). **Compensatory responses** provide the sufferer of injustice with some sense that justice has been restored, without involving any punitive actions toward the perpetrator of the injustice. Getting higher outcomes in the case of a distributive injustice or being given the chance to participate in a decision in an organization to ensure procedural justice constitute compensatory responses.

In contrast, **retaliatory responses** entail making the perpetrator suffer a bit as well. You might recall the movie *Mean Girls*, in which the "queen bee" leads her clique of girls to make fun of a newcomer to their school; the newcomer feels unjustly treated and ultimately gets her revenge by convincing the queen bee that special foods will help her to lose weight—but they have the opposite effect! In effect, the newcomer has punished the queen bee. Retaliatory responses are also at the heart of what is referred to as **retributive justice**, which deals with how people should be punished for intentionally committing unjust and/ or morally wrong acts (Carlsmith and Darley 2008; Wenzel and Okimoto 2016). For example, the musical *West Side Story* illustrates how gangs redress what they perceive to be acts of injustice. When Bernardo, a member of the Puerto Rican gang the Sharks, kills the leader of the rival gang, the Jets, it sets off a chain of retribution. Jet member Tony seeks revenge for his leader's death, ultimately killing Bernardo, whose gang then sets out to kill Tony. As depicted in this musical, acts of retributive justice clearly contribute to an escalation of violence, largely fueled by intense emotions.

The nature of individuals' responses to injustice may depend upon preceding emotions and cognitions. Some of these underlying processes lead to an increase in the likelihood of a behavioral response while others dampen such responses. With regard to emotions, anger tends to lead to retaliatory and other responses more than other negative emotions such as disappointment (e.g., Bembenek et al. 2007; Khan, Quratulain, and Crawshaw 2013). In contrast, cognitive processes involving external attributions and the provision of explanations may decrease active, behavioral responses (e.g., Hegtvedt, Thompson, and Cook 1993; Sharpley 1991). For example, had Jet member Tony known that his gang leader's death had been accidental (an external attribution), he may have felt less anger and not engaged in retaliatory behavior. Thus, cognitions and emotions may mediate between perceived injustice and overt behavioral responses.

Similarly, structural power conditions and identity processes affect behavioral responses. In many instances, power-disadvantaged individuals simply cannot respond behaviorally to exchange outcome inequalities owing to the constraints of their position, whereas power-advantaged individuals—essentially observers of others' injustice—could rectify the injustice by giving more to their partners (Cook, Hegtvedt, and Yamagishi 1988). And to the extent that people strongly identify with their group, unfair behavior within the group threatens that sense of belonging, spurring more intense responses (Brockner, Tyler, and Cooper-Schneider 1992). For example, when fraternity leaders ignore the advice of their members on certain issues, those members, recognizing the unfair treatment as a source of instability in the group, may attempt to unseat leaders or change procedures to ensure equal participation.

Justice issues that arise in a group move beyond concern about the nature of the individual responses. Within groups, some members may observe the injustices that befall others, and they may also respond collectively to those injustices.

Third-Party and Collective Responses to Injustice

All types of injustice may affect an individual (i.e., personal injustices), and sometimes everyone who feels unjustly treated may join together. In addition, observers or "third parties" may step in to aid victims of injustice (see Skarlicki and Kulik 2005). By observing what happens to others, individuals learn how they may be treated or rewarded and may assist in rectifying others' injustices. For example, younger siblings often assess the fairness of the curfews and chores parents set for older siblings to know what will happen to them when they reach a certain age. Older siblings may also come to a younger brother or sister's assistance when parents unjustly mete out harsh punishment.

Although observers often lack direct control over outcomes or procedures, they can act as agents for the injustice sufferer without raising the specter of material self-interests. When they do have some control, they may seek to punish the perpetrator or compensate the victim, even at their own expense. Highly empathetic individuals tend toward compensation, whereas those lower in empathy are more likely to resort to punishing the offender (Leliveld, Van Dijk, and Van Beest 2012). Sometimes the changes that third parties effect in their response to another's injustice may benefit many in the long run. Think about how privileged, southern white people or northeastern Jews joined blacks in the civil rights movement—they expended effort and resources to right a social injustice, which in the long run changed the face of our nation.

The civil rights movement is an example of a collective response to injustice. Although such responses may involve third parties, they begin as responses by people who suffer **relative deprivation**—a subjective evaluation, resulting from a comparison of individual- or group-level rewards with another person or group (Runciman 1966; Walker and Smith 2002). Shared perceptions of the source of the injustice (Lawler and Thompson 1978), group-level deprivation (Pettigrew et al. 2008), and feelings of anger or moral outrage (Goodwin, Jasper, and Polletta 2001) help solidify a collective response. Yet as with individual-level responses, to enact a collective response also requires sufficient resources (Beaton and Deveau 2005) and, most likely, the perception that the system that produced the inequalities is illegitimate (Jost and Major 2001; see Chapter 10). For these reasons, in the course of history there have been fewer rebellions and revolutions than a relative deprivation perspective would imply.

In many instances involving individual and group-level injustice, it appears that disadvantaged individuals do *not* respond to injustice. Why would that be so? The general theoretical framework for justice implies a variety of possibilities: no perceived injustice; no intense feelings of anger; unobserved cognitive responses; and/or concerns that a behavioral response is too costly in terms of time, material expenses, social relations, or the like. Plus, behavioral responses may be dampened if the disadvantaged minimize their personal discrimination, believe in a just world thwarting the idea that injustice might befall them, and suppress resentment over deprivation for fear of greater harm (Olson and Hafer 2001).

Systems justification theory (Jost, Banaji, and Nosek 2004; Jost, Gaucher, and Stern 2015) suggests why people may not respond to perceived social (rather than personal) injustices. System justification is a form of conscious or unconscious motivation that leads people to defend and justify existing social, economic, and political systems. Both situational circumstances (e.g., system threat) and personal dispositions (e.g., need for closure, openness to experience) (Jost and Hunyady 2005; Kay and Zanna 2009) shape people's system justification motivations. The stronger the motivation, the more likely individuals will stereotype to defend the status quo and support conservative political ideologies, thereby experiencing decreased negative affect regarding systems that may be objectively unjust or morally wrong, such as slavery or the lack of social welfare safety net (see Jost and Kay 2010). For example, a strong system justification motivation might allow the stereotyping of Arabs and Pakistanis as terrorists and justify torturing jailed alleged terrorists—all in the name of justice. Ironically, then, justice processes potentially ensure both the upholding of collective welfare and the defense of unjust systems.

Segue: Justice and Intergroup Relations in Society

Emphasis on the types of justice and the antecedents and consequences of perceptions of and responses to injustice highlights many of the social psychological processes discussed in previous sections of this book—for example, identity, cognitions, emotions, and power. It also calls attention to how particular distributive, procedural, and interactional rules become legitimated as justice principles and how violation of those principles results in emotional, cognitive, and behavioral responses. And, while the focus typically is on the individual who makes an assessment and who responds (or does not) to perceived injustice, shared concerns about justice often act as the glue that holds groups together. At the same time, justice concerns have implications for the dynamics between groups.

Any group is embedded in a context of other groups. To the extent that individuals categorize themselves as members of particular groups (and not as members of other groups), they begin to identify with that group (or groups). Such categorization, of course, affects their perceptions of justice. Opotow (1990) suggests that individuals' beliefs about fairness, however, apply only within respective moral communities, presumably because the well-being of those members matters to the perceiver. A moral community may promote certain types of distributions, procedures, or treatment as fair within its boundaries and may shun or even harm people outside of the community's boundaries. For example, after the attack on Pearl Harbor during World War II, the United States was so worried about the threat from Japan that it no longer trusted Japanese living in America. As a consequence, the government legitimated the removal of Japanese Americans from their homes and the internment of them in isolated camps (Nagata 1993). Opotow (1990) refers to this as a process of moral exclusion, which is inherent in "we–they" distinctions characterizing intergroup behavior.

While most interactions between groups are not as extreme as those characterizing the U.S. response to Japanese Americans during World War II, perceived boundaries between groups—differentiated in terms of culture, education, race, neighborhood, and the like—grow more rigid during times of conflict. Thus, while there may be shared ideas of justice within a group, there may be differences in those ideas between groups. Yet justice beliefs are not the only basis for differences between groups, especially as individuals strive to solidify a positive impression of their own group. In the next chapter, we analyze the dynamics between groups, which in turn influence the perceptions and behavior of individuals within groups. In doing so, we again draw upon themes discussed in earlier chapters and provide the basis for a discussion of prejudice and discrimination.

Endnote

1. Jasso (1980) formalizes this comparison notion in her theory of distributive justice when she argues that a justice evaluation (JE) compares the actual share of outcomes received with the share that would be expected based on the application of a distributive justice principle. She represents this mathematically as JE = ln(actual share/just share). Elaborations on this formula can be found in her subsequent work (see Jasso 2002).

Suggested Readings

Clay-Warner, Jody, Dawn T. Robinson, Lynn Smith-Lovin, Kimberly B. Rogers, and Katie R. James. 2016. "Justice Standard Determines Emotional Responses to Over-Reward." *Social Psychology Quarterly* 79:44–67.

Cigueró-Escofet, Natalia, Marion Fortin, and Miquel-Angel Canela. 2014. "Righting the Wrong for Third Parties: How Monetary Compensation, Procedure Changes and Apologies Can Restore Justice for Observers of Injustice." *Journal of Business Ethics* 122:253–68.

Hogue, Mary, Lee Fox-Cardamone, and Cathy L. Z. Dubois. 2011. "Justifying the Pay System Through Status: Gender Differences in Reports of What Should Be Important in Pay Decisions." *Journal of Applied Social Psychology* 41:823–49.

Joyner, Kara. 2009. "Justice and the Fate of Married and Cohabiting Couples." *Social Psychology Quarterly* 72:61–76.

Laurin, Kristin, Gráinne M. Fitzsimons, and Aaron C. Kay. 2011. "Social Disadvantage and the Self-Regulatory Function of Justice Beliefs." *Journal of Personality and Social Psychology* 100:149–71.

Mentovich, Avital, Eunho Rhee, and Tom R. Tyler. 2014. "My Life for a Voice: The Influence of Voice on Health-Care Decisions." *Social Justice Research* 27:99–117.

References

Adams, J. Stacy. 1965. "Inequity in Social Exchange." *Advances in Experimental Social Psychology* 2:267–99. doi:10.1016/S0065-2601(08)60108-2

Ambrose, Maureen L., and Anke Arnaud. 2005. "Are Procedural Justice and Distributive Justice Conceptually Distinct?" Pp. 59–84 in *Handbook of Organizational Justice,* edited by J. Greenberg and J. A. Colquitt. Mahwah, NJ: Erlbaum.

Barclay, Laurie J., Daniel P. Skarlicki, and S. Douglas Pugh. 2005. "Exploring the Role of Emotions in Injustice Perceptions and Retaliation." *The Journal of Applied Psychology* 90:629–63. doi:10.1037/0021-9010.90.4.629

Barry, Brian. 1989. *Theories of Justice.* Berkeley: University of California Press.

Baumert, Anna, and Manfred Schmitt. 2016. "Justice Sensitivity." Pp. 161–80 in *Handbook of Social Justice Theory and Research,* edited by C. Sabbagh and M. Schmitt. New York: Springer. doi:10.1007/978-1-4939-3216-0_9

Beaton, Ann M., and Mylene Deveau. 2005. "Helping the Less Fortunate: A Predictive Model of Collective Action." *Journal of Applied Social Psychology* 35:1609–29. doi:10.1111/j.1559-1816.2005.tb02187.x

Bembenek, Alicia F., Denise R. Beike, and David A. Schroeder. 2007. "Justice Violations, Emotional Reactions, and Justice-Seeking Responses." Pp. 15–36 in *Advances of the Psychology of Justice and Affect,* edited by D. De Cremer. Charlotte, NC: Information Age Publishing.

Berger, Joseph, Morris Zelditch, Bo Anderson, and Bernard P. Cohen. 1972. "Structural Aspects of Distributive Justice: A Status Value Formulation." Pp. 119–46 in *Sociological Theories in Progress,* Vol. 2, edited by J. Berger, M. Zelditch Jr., and B. Anderson. Boston: Houghton Mifflin.

Bies, Robert J. 2001. "Interactional (In)Justice: The Sacred and the Profane." Pp. 89–118 in *Advances in Organizational Justice,* edited by

J. Greenberg and R. Cropanzano. Stanford, CA: Stanford University Press.

Bies, Robert J. 2005. "Are Procedural Justice and Interactional Justice Conceptually Distinct?" Pp. 85–112 in *Handbook of Organizational Justice*, edited by J. Greenberg and J. A. Colquitt. Mahwah, NJ: Erlbaum.

Bolino, Mark C., and William H. Turnley. 2008. "Old Faces, New Places: Equity Theory in Cross-Cultural Contexts." *Journal of Organizational Behavior* 29:29–50. doi:10.1002/job.454

Brockner, Joel, Ya-Ru Chen, Elizabeth Mannix, Kwok Leung, and Daniel P. Skarlicki. 2000. "Culture and Procedural Fairness: When the Effects of What You Do Depend Upon How You Do It." *Administrative Science Quarterly* 45:138–59. doi:10.2307/2666982

Brockner, Joel, Ariel Y. Fishman, Jochen Reb, Barry Goldman, Scott Spiegel, and Charlee Garden. 2007. "Procedural Fairness, Outcome Favorability, and Judgments of an Authority's Responsibility." *The Journal of Applied Psychology* 92:1657–71. doi:10.1037/0021-9010.92.6.1657

Brockner, Joel, Tom R. Tyler, and Rochelle Cooper-Schneider. 1992. "The Influence of Prior Commitment to an Institution on Reactions to Perceived Unfairness: The Higher They Are, The Harder They Fall." *Administrative Science Quarterly* 37:241–61. doi:10.2307/2393223

Brosnan, Sarah F. 2013. "Justice- and Fairness-Related Behaviors in Nonhuman Primates." *Proceedings of the National Academy of Sciences of the United States of America* 110(suppl. 2): 10416–23. doi:10.1073/pnas.1301194110

Brosnan, Sarah F., and Frans B. M. de Waal. 2014. "Evolution of Responses to (Un)fairness." *Science* 346:12517761 (1–7). doi:10.1126/science.1251776

Carlsmith, Kevin M., and John M. Darley. 2008. "Psychological Aspects of Retributive Justice." *Advances in Experimental Social Psychology* 40:193–236.

Chebat, Jean-Charles, and Witold Slusarczyk. 2005. "How Emotions Mediate the Effects of Perceived Justice on Loyalty in Service Recovery Situations: An Empirical Study." *Journal of Business Research* 58:664–73. doi:10.1016/j.jbusres.2003.09.005

Clayton, Susan, and Susan Opotow. 2003. "Justice and Identity: Changing Perspectives on What Is Fair." *Personality and Social Psychology Review* 7:298–310. doi:10.1207/S15327957PSPR0704_03

Clay-Warner, Jody, Dawn T. Robinson, Lynn Smith-Lovin, Kimberly B. Rogers, and Katie R. James. 2016. "Justice Standard Determines Emotional Response to Over-Reward." *Social Psychology Quarterly* 79:44–67. doi:10.1177/0190272516628299

Cohen, Ronald L. 1982. "Perceiving Justice: An Attributional Perspective." Pp. 119–60 in *Equity and Justice in Social Behavior*, edited by J. Greenberg and R. L. Cohen. New York: Academic Press. doi:10.1016/B978-0-12-2995 80-4.50010-0

Colquitt, Jason A., and Jerome M. Chertkoff. 2002. "Explaining Injustice: The Interactive Effect of Explanation and Outcome on Fairness Perceptions and Task Motivation." *Journal of Management* 28:591–610. doi:10.1177/0149206 30202800502

Cook, Karen S., Karen A. Hegtvedt, and Toshio Yamagishi. 1988. "Structural Inequality, Legitimation, and Reactions to Inequality in Exchange Networks." Pp. 291–308 in *Status Generalization: New Theory and Research*, edited by M. Webster and M. Foschi. Stanford, CA: Stanford University Press.

Cropanzano, Russell, Jordan H. Stein, and Thierry Nadisic. 2011. *Social Justice and the Experience of Emotion*. New York: Routledge.

De Cremer, David. 2004. "The Influence of Accuracy as a Function of Leader's Bias: The Role of Trustworthiness in the Psychology of Procedural Justice." *Personality and Social Psychology Bulletin* 30(3):293–304. doi:10.1177/0146167203256969

De Cremer, David, Gerben A. Van Kleef, and Maarten J. Wubben. 2007. "Do the Emotions of Others Shape Justice Effects? An Interpersonal Approach." Pp. 37–60 in *Advances in the Psychology of Justice and Affect*, edited by D. De Cremer. Charlotte, NC: Information Age Publishing.

Deutsch, Morton. 1975. "Equity, Equality, and Need: What Determines Which Value Will Be Used as the Basis for Distributive Justice?" *The Journal of Social Issues* 31:137–49. doi:10.1111/j.1540–4560.1975.tb01000.x

Deutsch, Morton. 1976. "Theorizing in Social Psychology." *Personality and Social Psychology Bulletin* 2:134–41. doi:10.1177/014616727600200214

Deutsch, Morton. 1985. *Distributive Justice: A Social-Psychological Perspective*. New Haven, CT: Yale University Press.

Deutsch, Morton. 2000. "Justice and Conflict." Pp. 141–64 in *The Handbook of Conflict Resolution: Theory and Practice*, edited by M. Deutsch and P. T. Coleman. San Francisco, CA: Jossey-Bass.

Fischer, Ronald. 2016. "Justice and Culture." Pp. 459–75 in *Handbook of Social Justice Theory and Research*, edited by C. Sabbagh and M. Schmitt. New York: Springer. doi:10.1007/978–1–4939–3216–0_25

Fischer, Ronald, and Peter B. Smith. 2003. "Reward Allocation and Culture: A Meta-Analysis. *Journal of Cross-Cultural Psychology* 34(3):251–68.

Folger, Robert, and Russell Cropanzano. 1998. *Organizational Justice and Human Resource Management*. Thousand Oaks, CA: Sage.

Folger, Robert, and Russell Cropanzano. 2001. "Fairness Theory: Justice as Accountability." Pp. 1–55 in *Advances in Organizational Justice*, edited by J. Greenberg and R. Cropanzano. Stanford, CA: Stanford University Press.

Folger, Robert, Russell Cropanzano, and Berry Goldman. 2005. "What Is the Relationship between Justice and Morality?" Pp. 215–45 in *Handbook of Organizational Justice*, edited by J. Greenberg and J. A. Colquitt. Mahwah, NJ: Erlbaum.

Folger, Robert, and Edward Eliyahu Kass. 2000. "Social Comparison and Fairness: A Counterfactual Simulations Perspective." Pp. 423–41 in *Handbook of Social Comparison: Theory and Research*, edited by J. Suls and L. Wheeler. New York: Kluwer Academic/Plenum. doi:10.1007/978–1–4615–4237–7_20

Frohlich, Norman, and Joe A. Oppenheimer. 1992. *Choosing Justice: An Experimental Approach to Ethical Theory*. Berkeley: University of California Press.

Furnham, Adrian. 2003. "Belief in a Just World: Research Progress Over the Past Decade." *Personality and Individual Differences* 34:795–817. doi:10.1016/S0191–8869(02)00072–7

Gillespie, Jennifer Z., and Jerald Greenberg. 2005. "Are the Goals of Organization Justice Self-interested?" Pp. 179–213 in *Handbook of Organizational Justice*, edited by J. Greenberg and J. A. Colquitt. Mahwah, NJ: Erlbaum.

Goodwin, Jeff, James M. Jasper, and Francesca Polletta, eds. 2001. *Passionate Politics: Emotions and Social Movements*. Chicago: University of Chicago Press. doi:10.7208/chicago/9780226304007.001.0001

Hafer, Carolyn L. 2000. "Investment in Long-Term Goals and Commitment to Just Means Drive the Need to Believe in a Just World." *Personality and Social Psychology Bulletin* 26:1059–73. doi:10.1177/01461672002611004

Hafer, Carolyn L., and Laurent Bègue. 2005. "Experimental Research on Just-World Theory: Problems, Developments, and Future Challenges." *Psychological Bulletin* 131:128–67. doi:10.1037/0033–2909.131.1.128

Hafer, Carolyn, and Robbie Sutton. 2016. "Belief in a Just World." Pp. 145–60 in *Handbook of Social Justice Theory and Research*, edited by C. Sabbagh and M. Schmitt. New York: Springer. doi:10.1007/978–1–4939–3216–0_8

Hegtvedt, Karen A. 1987. "When Rewards Are Scarce: Equal or Equitable Distributions?" *Social Forces* 66:183–207. doi:10.2307/2578907

Hegtvedt, Karen A. 1990. "The Effects of Relationship Structure on Emotional Responses to Inequality." *Social Psychology Quarterly* 53:214–28. doi:10.2307/2786960

Hegtvedt, Karen A. 2006. "Justice Frameworks." Pp. 46–69 in *Contemporary Social Psychological Theories*, edited by P. J. Burke. Stanford, CA: Stanford University Press.

Hegtvedt, Karen A., and Karen S. Cook. 2001. "Distributive Justice: Recent Theoretical Developments and Applications." Pp. 93–132 in *Handbook of Justice Research in Law*, edited by J. Sanders and V. Lee Hamilton. New York: Kluwer Academic/Plenum.

Hegtvedt, Karen A., and Cathryn Johnson. 2000. "Justice Beyond the Individual: A Future with Legitimation." *Social Psychology Quarterly* 63:298–311. doi:10.2307/2695841

Hegtvedt, Karen, and Caitlin Killian. 1999. "Fairness and Emotions: Reactions to the Process and Outcomes of Negotiations." *Social Forces* 78:269–303. doi:10.2307/3005797

Hegtvedt, Karen A., and Christie Parris. 2014. "Emotions in Justice Processes." Pp. 103–26 in *Handbook of Sociology of Emotions*, edited by J. Stets and J. Turner. New York: Springer.

Hegtvedt, Karen A., and Heather L. Scheuerman. 2010. "The Justice/Morality Link." Pp. 331–60 in *Handbook of the Sociology of Morality*, edited by S. Hitlin and V. N. Y. Stephen. New York: Springer. doi:10.1007/978-1-4419-6896-8_18

Hegtvedt, Karen, Elaine A. Thompson, and Karen S. Cook. 1993. "Power and Equity: What Counts in Explaining Exchange Outcomes?" *Social Psychology Quarterly* 56:100–19. doi:10.2307/2787000

Hillebrandt, Annika, and Laurie J. Barclay. 2013. "Integrating Organizational Justice and Affect: New Insights, Challenges, and Opportunities."

Social Justice Research 26(4):513–31. doi:10.1007/s11211-013-0193-z

Homans, George C. 1974. *Social Behavior: Its Elementary Forms*. New York: Harcourt, Brace and World.

Jasso, Guillermina. 1980. "A New Theory of Distributive Justice." *American Sociological Review* 45:3–32. doi:10.2307/2095239

Jasso, Guillermina. 2002. "Formal Theory." Pp. 37–68 in *Handbook of Sociological Theory*, edited by Jonathan H. Turner. New York: Kluwer Academic/Plenum.

Johnson, Cathryn, Karen A. Hegtvedt, Leslie M. Brody, and Krysia W. Waldron. 2007. "Feeling Injustice, Expressing Injustice: How Gender and Context Matter." *Advances in Group Processes* 24:149–86. doi:10.1016/S0882-6145(07)24007-X

Johnson, Cathryn, Karen A. Hegtvedt, Nikki Khanna, and Heather Scheuerman. 2016. "Legitimacy Processes and Emotional Responses to Injustice." *Social Psychology Quarterly* 79:95–114. doi:10.1177/0190272516645317

Jost, John T. 2009. "'Elective Affinities': On the Psychological Bases of Left-Right Differences." *Psychological Inquiry* 20:129–41. doi:10.1080/10478400903028599

Jost, John T., Mahzarin R. Banaji, and Brian A. Nosek. 2004. "A Decade of System-Justification Theory: Accumulated Evidence of Conscious and Unconscious Bolstering of the Status Quo." *Political Psychology* 25:881–919. doi:10.1111/j.1467-9221.2004.00402.x

Jost, John T., Danielle Gaucher, and Chadly Stern. 2015. "'The World Isn't Fair:' A System Justification Perspective on Social Stratification and Inequality." Pp. 317–40 in *APA Handbook of Personality and Social Psychology*, Vol. 2, edited by J. F. Dovidio and J. A. Simpson. Washington, DC: American Psychological Association.

Jost, John T., Jack Glaser, Arie W. Kruglanski, and Frank J. Sulloway. 2003. "Political Conservatism as

Motivated Social Cognition." *Psychological Bulletin* 129:339–75. doi:10.1037/0033-2909.129.3.339

Jost, John T., and Orsolya Hunyady. 2005. "Antecedents and Consequences of System-Justifying Ideologies." *Current Directions in Psychological Science* 14:260–65. doi:10.1111/j.0963-7214.2005.00377.x

Jost, John T., and Aaron C. Kay. 2010. "Social Justice: History, Theory, and Research." Pp. 1122–65 in *Handbook of Social Psychology*, Vol. 2, edited by S. T. Fiske, D. T. Gilbert, and G. Lindzey. Hoboken, NJ: Wiley. doi:10.1002/9780470561119.socpsy002030

Jost, John T., and Brenda Major, eds. 2001. *The Psychology of Legitimacy: Emerging Perspectives on Ideology, Justice and Intergroup Relations*. Cambridge, England: Cambridge University Press.

Jost, John T., Cheryl J. Wakslak, and Tom R. Tyler. 2008. "System Justification Theory and the Alleviation of Emotional Distress: Palliative Effects of Ideology in an Arbitrary Social Hierarchy and in Society." *Advances in Group Processes* 25:181–211. doi:10.1016/S0882-6145(08)25012-5

Kay, Aaron C., and Mark P. Zanna. 2009. "A Contextual Analysis of the Social and Psychological Consequences of System Justification." Pp. 158–81 in *Social and Psychological Bases of Ideology and System Justification*, edited by J. T. Jost, A. C. Kay, and H. Thoristtodor. New York: Oxford University Press. doi:10.1093/acprof:oso/9780195320916.003.007

Kernis, Michael H., and Harry T. Reis. 1984. "Self-Consciousness, Self-Awareness, and Justice in Reward Allocation." *Journal of Personality* 52:58–70. doi:10.1111/j.1467-6494.1984.tb00550.x

Khan, Abdul Karim, Samina Quratulain, and Jonathan R. Crawshaw. 2013. "The Mediating Role of Discrete Emotions in the Relationship between Injustice and Counterproductive Work Behaviors: A Study in Pakistan." *Journal of Business and Psychology* 28:49–61. doi:10.1007/s10869-012-9269-2

Krehbiel, Patricia J., and Russell Cropanzano. 2000. "Procedural Justice, Outcome Favorability, and Emotion." *Social Justice Research* 13:339–60. doi:10.1023/A:1007670909889

Kulik, Carol T., and Maureen L. Ambrose. 1992. "Personal and Situational Determinants of Referent Choice." *Academy of Management Review* 17:212–37.

Lawler, Edward J., and Martha E. Thompson. 1978. "Impact of Leader Responsibility for Inequity on Subordinate Revolts." *Social Psychology* 41:265–68. doi:10.2307/3033564

Leliveld, Marijke. C., Eric van Dijk, and Ilja Van Beest. 2012. "Punishing and Compensating Others at Your Own Expense: The Role of Empathic Concern on Reactions to Distributive Injustice." *European Journal of Social Psychology* 42:135–40. doi:10.1002/ejsp.872

Lerner, Melvin J. 1975. "The Justice Motive in Social Behavior: Introduction." *The Journal of Social Issues* 31:1–19. doi:10.1111/j.1540-4560.1975.tb00995.x

Lerner, Melvin J. 1980. *The Belief in a Just World: A Fundamental Delusion*. New York: Plenum Press.

Lerner, Melvin J. 2003. "The Justice Motive: Where Social Psychologists Found It, How They Lost It, and Why They May Not Find It Again." *Personality and Social Psychology Review* 7:388–99. doi:10.1207/S15327957PSPR0704_10

Leung, Kwok. 2005. "How Generalizable Are Justice Effects Across Cultures?" Pp. 555–86 in *Handbook of Organizational Justice*, edited by J. Greenberg and J. A. Colquitt. Mahwah, NJ: Erlbaum.

Leung, Kwok, and Michael H. Bond. 1984. "The Impact of Cultural Collectivism on Reward Allocation." *Journal of Personality and Social Psychology* 47:793–804. doi:10.1037/0022-3514.47.4.793

Leventhal, Gerald S., Jurgis Karuza Jr., and William R. Fry. 1980. "Beyond Fairness: A

Theory of Allocation Preferences." Pp. 167–218 in *Justice and Social Interaction*, edited by G. Mikula. New York: Springer-Verlag.

Lind, E. Allan. 2001. "Fairness Heuristic Theory: Justice Judgments as Pivotal Cognitions in Organizational Relations." Pp. 56–88 in *Advances in Organizational Justice*, edited by M. S. Greenberg and R. Cropanzano. Stanford, CA: Stanford University Press.

Lind, E. Allan, and Tom R. Tyler. 1988. *The Social Psychology of Procedural Justice*. New York: Plenum. doi:10.1007/978-1-4899-2115-4

Major, Brenda, and Jeffrey B. Adams. 1983. "Role of Gender, Interpersonal Orientation, and Self-Presentation in Distributive-Justice Behavior." *Journal of Personality and Social Psychology* 45:598–608. doi:10.1037/0022–3514 .45.3.598

Markovsky, Barry. 1985. "Toward a Multilevel Distributive Justice Theory." *American Sociological Review* 50:822–39. doi:10.2307/2095506

Mikula, Gerold. 2003. "Testing an Attribution-of-Blame Model of Judgments of Injustice." *European Journal of Social Psychology* 33: 793–811. doi:10.1002/ejsp.184

Mikula, Gerold, Klaus R. Scherer, and Ursula Athenstaedt. 1998. "The Role of Injustice in the Elicitation of Differential Emotional Reactions." *Personality and Social Psychology Bulletin* 24:769–83. doi:10.1177/0146167298247009

Mikula, Gerold, and Michael Wenzel. 2000. "Justice and Social Conflict." *International Journal of Psychology* 35:126–35. doi:10.1080/ 002075900399420

Mohr, Philip B., and Giuseppa Luscri. 1995. "Blame and Punishment: Attitudes to Juvenile and Criminal Offending." *Psychological Reports* 77:1091–96. doi:10.2466/pr0.1995.77.3f.1091

Mueller, Charles W., and Miriam J. Landsman. 2004. "Legitimacy and Justice Perceptions." *Social Psychology Quarterly* 67:189–202. doi:10.1177/019027250406700205

Nagata, Donna K. 1993. *Legacy of Injustice: Exploring the Cross-Generational Impact of the Japanese American Internment*. New York: Springer. doi:10.1007/978-1-4899-1118-6

Nicklin, Jessica M. 2013. "Expertise, Counter-factual, Thinking, and Fairness Perceptions: A Test of Fairness Theory." *Social Justice Research* 26:42–60. doi:10.1007/s11211-012-0173-8

Olson, James M., and Carolyn Hafer. 2001. "Tolerance of Personal Deprivation." Pp. 157–75 in *The Psychology of Legitimacy: Emerging Perspectives on Ideology, Justice, and Intergroup Relations*, edited by J. T. Jost and B. Major. Cambridge, England: Cambridge University Press.

Opotow, Susan. 1990. "Moral Exclusion and Injustice: An Introduction." *The Journal of Social Issues* 46:1–20. doi:10.1111/j.1540–4560.1990 .tb00268.x

Pais, Abraham. 1994. *Einstein Lived Here*. Oxford, England: Oxford University Press.

Parris, Christie, Karen A. Hegtvedt, Cathryn Johnson, and Lesley Watson. 2014. "Justice for All? Factors Affecting Perceptions of Environmental and Ecological Injustice." *Social Justice Research* 27:67–98. doi:10.1007/s11211-013-0200-4

Peters, Suzanne, Kees van den Bos, and Ramona Bobocel. 2004. "The Moral Superiority Effect: Self Versus Other Differences in Satisfaction with Being Overpaid." *Social Justice Research* 17:257–73. doi:10.1023/ B:SORE.0000041293.24615.f7

Pettigrew, Thomas F., Oliver Christ, Ulrich Wagner, Roel Meertens, Rolf van Dick, and Andreas Zick. 2008. "Relative Deprivation and Intergroup Prejudice." *The Journal of Social Issues* 64:385–401. doi:10.1111/j.1540–4560.2008.00567.x

Qin, Xin, Run Ren, Zhi-Xue Zhang, and Russell E. Johnson. 2015. "Fairness Heuristics and Substitutability Effects: Inferring Fairness of Outcomes, Procedures, and Interpersonal Treatment When Employees Lack Clear

Information." *The Journal of Applied Psychology* 100:749–66. doi:10.1037/a0038084

Rawls, John. 1971. *A Theory of Justice.* Cambridge, MA: Belknap Press/Harvard University Press.

Runciman, Walter G. 1966. *Relative Deprivation and Social Justice: A Study of Attitudes to Social Inequality in Twentieth-Century England.* Berkeley: University of California Press.

Scher, Steven J., and David R. Heise. 1993. "Affect and the Perception of Injustice." *Advances in Group Processes* 10:223–52.

Schmitt, Manfred. 1996. "Individual Differences in Sensitivity to Befallen Injustice (SBI)." *Personality and Individual Differences* 21:3–20. doi:10.1016/0191-8869(96)00028-1

Sharpley, Christopher F. 1991. "Giving a Reason for Unfairness: Effects of Rationale on Australian Students' Performances Within an Implicit Reward Situation." *International Journal of Psychology* 26:71–81. doi:10.1080/00207599108246850

Shaw, John C., Eric Wild, and Jason A. Colquitt. 2003. "To Justify or Excuse? A Meta-Analytic Review of the Effects of Explanations." *The Journal of Applied Psychology* 88:444–58. doi:10.1037/0021-9010.88.3.444

Skarlicki, Daniel, and Carol T. Kulik. 2005. "Third-Party Reactions to Employee (Mis)treatment: A Justice Perspective." *Research in Organizational Behavior* 26:183–229. doi:10.1016/S0191-3085(04)26005-1

Skitka, Linda J., Christopher W. Bauman, and Elizabeth Mullen. 2008. "Morality and Justice: An Expanded Theoretical Perspective and Empirical Review." *Advances in Group Processes* 25:1–27. doi:10.1016/S0882-6145(08)25001-0

Skitka, Linda J., Christopher W. Bauman, and Elizabeth Mullen. 2016. "Morality and Justice." Pp. 407–23 in *Handbook of Social Justice Theory and Research*, edited by C. Sabbagh and M. Schmitt. New York: Springer. doi:10.1007/978-1-4939-3216-0_22

Solomon, Robert C., and Mark C. Murphy, eds. 2000. *What Is Justice? Classic and Contemporary Readings.* New York: Oxford University Press.

Sprecher, Susan. 1992. "How Men and Women Expect to Feel and Behave in Response to Inequality in Close Relations." *Social Psychology Quarterly* 55:57–69. doi:10.2307/2786686

Stets, Jan E., and Shelley N. Osborn. 2008. "Injustice and Emotions Using Identity Theory." *Advances in Group Processes* 25:151–79. doi:10.1016/S0882-6145(08)25010-1

Tajfel, Henri, and John Turner. 1979. "An Integrative Theory of Intergroup Conflict." Pp. 33–47 in *Psychology of Intergroup Relations*, edited by W. G. Austin and S. Worchel. Monterey, CA: Brooks/Cole.

Talbot, Catherine F., Sara A. Price, and Sarah F. Brosnan. 2016. "Inequity Responses in Nonhuman Animals." Pp. 387–403 in *Handbook of Social Justice Theory and Research*, edited by C. Sabbagh and M. Schmitt. New York: Springer. doi:10.1007/978-1-4939-3216-0_21

Tetlock, Phillip E., and Gregory Mitchell. 1993. "Liberal and Conservative Approaches to Justice: Conflicting Psychological Portraits." Pp. 234–256 in *Psychological Perspectives on Justice: Theory and Application*, edited by B. A. Mellers and J. Baron. London, England: Cambridge University Press. doi:10.1017/CBO9780511552069.012

Thibaut, John, and Laurens Walker. 1975. *Procedural Justice: A Psychological Analysis.* Hillsdale, NJ: Erlbaum.

Tjosvold, Dean, Alfred S. H. Wong, and Paulina M. K. Wan. 2010. "Conflict Management for Justice, Innovation, and Strategic Advantage in Organizational Relationships." *Journal of Applied Social Psychology* 40:636–65. doi:10.1111/j.1559-1816.2010.00591.x

Törnblom, Kjell Y. 1977. "Magnitude and Source of Compensation in Two Situations of Distributive Injustice." *Acta Sociologica* 20(1):75–95. doi:10.1177/000169937702000105

Tyler, Tom R., and Steven L. Blader. 2000. *Cooperation in Groups: Procedural Justice, Social Identity, and Behavioral Engagement.* Philadelphia, PA: Psychology Press/Taylor & Francis.

Tyler, Tom R., and Steven L. Blader. 2003. "The Group Engagement Model: Procedural Justice, Social Identity, and Cooperative Behavior." *Personality and Social Psychology Review* 7: 349–61. doi:10.1207/S15327957PSPR0704_07

Tyler, Tom R., Robert J. Boeckmann, Heather J. Smith, and Yuen J. Huo. 1997. *Social Justice in a Diverse Society.* Boulder, CO: Westview.

Tyler, Tom R., and Robin Dawes. 1993. "Fairness in Groups: Comparing the Self-interest and Social Identity Perspectives." Pp. 87–108 in *Psychological Perspectives on Justice: Theory and Application,* edited by B. A. Mellers and J. Baron. London, England: Cambridge University Press. doi:10.1017/CBO9780511552069.006

Tyler, Tom R., and E. Allan Lind. 1992. "A Relational Model of Authority in Groups." *Advances in Experimental Social Psychology* 25:115–91. doi:10.1016/S0065-2601(08)60283-X

Utne, Mary K., and F. Robert Kidd. 1980. "Equity and Attribution." Pp. 63–93 in *Justice and Social Interaction,* edited by Gerold Mikula. New York: Springer-Verlag.

van den Bos, Kees. 2003. "On the Subjective Quality of Social Justice: The Role of Affect as Information in the Psychology of Justice Judgments." *Journal of Personality and Social Psychology* 85:482–98. doi:10.1037/0022-3514.85.3.482

van den Bos, Kees. 2005. "What Is Responsible for the Fair Process Effect?" Pp. 273–300 in *Handbook of Organizational Justice,* edited by J. Greenberg and J. A. Colquitt. Mahwah, NJ: Erlbaum.

van den Bos, Kees. 2007. "The Combined Influence of Cognitive and Affective Factors on the Justice Judgment Process." Pp. 61–84 in *Advances in the Psychology of Justice and Affect,* edited by D. De Cremer. Charlotte, NC: Information Age Publishing.

van den Bos, Kees, Jan Bruins, Henk A. M. Wilke, and Elske Dronkert. 1999. "Sometimes Unfair Procedures Have Nice Aspects: On the Psychology of the Fair Process Effect." *Journal of Personality and Social Psychology* 77:324–36. doi:10.1037/0022-3514.77.2.324

van den Bos, Kees, and E. Allan Lind. 2002. "Uncertainty Management by Means of Fairness Judgments." *Advances in Experimental Social Psychology* 34:1–60. doi:10.1016/S0065-2601(02)80003-X

van den Bos, Kees, E. Allan Lind, Riel Vermunt, and Henk A. M. Wilke. 1997. "How Do I Judge My Outcome When I Do Not Know the Outcome of Others? The Psychology of the Fair Process Effect." *Journal of Personality and Social Psychology* 72:1034–46. doi:10.1037/0022-3514.72.5.1034

van den Bos, Kees, E. Allan Lind, and Henk A. M. Wilke. 2001. "The Psychology of Procedural and Distributive Justice Viewed from the Perspective of Fairness Heuristic Theory." Pp. 49–66 in *Justice in the Workplace,* edited by R. Cropanzano. Mahwah, NJ: Erlbaum.

Vermunt, Riel, and Steensma, Herman. 2016. "Procedural Justice." Pp. 219–36 in *Handbook of Social Justice Theory and Research,* edited by C. Sabbagh and M. Schmitt. New York: Springer. doi:10.1007/978-1-4939-3216-0_12

Walker, Iain, and Heather J. Smith, eds. 2002. *Relative Deprivation: Specification, Development, and Integration.* New York: Cambridge University Press.

Walster, Elaine, G. William Walster, and Ellen Berscheid. 1978. *Equity: Theory and Research.* Boston: Allyn & Bacon.

Weiss, Howard M., Kathleen Suckow, and Russell Cropanzano. 1999. "Effects of Justice Conditions on Discrete Emotions." *The Journal of Applied Psychology* 84:786–94. doi:10.1037/0021-9010.84.5.786

Wenzel, Michael. 2002. "What Is Social about Justice? Inclusive Identity and Group Values as the Basis of the Justice Motive." *Journal of Experimental Social Psychology* 38:205–18. doi:10.1006/jesp.2001.1501

Wenzel, Michael, and Tyler G. Okimoto. 2016. "Retributive Justice." Pp. 237–56 in *Handbook of Social Justice Theory and Research*, edited by C. Sabbagh and M. Schmitt.

New York: Springer. doi:10.1007/978-1-4939-3216-0_13

Younts, C. Wesley, and Charles W. Mueller. 2001. "Justice Processes: Specifying the Mediating Role of Perceptions in Distributive Justice." *American Sociological Review* 66:125–45. doi:10.2307/2657396

Intergroup Processes

Theodor Geisel, aka Dr. Seuss, charmed young children with his imaginative characters, clever rhymes, and silly stories. Though entertaining, a number of Dr. Seuss's stories conveyed his political attitudes and his concerns about significant social issues. He captures dynamics between groups, the topic of this chapter, in his tale of the "Star-Belly" and the "Plain-Belly" Sneetches (*The Sneetches and Other Stories*; Geisel [1961] 1989). Though the stars were described as "really so small" that they should not matter at all, they did matter. Dr. Seuss chronicles how the trivial difference shapes the self-presentation, attitudes, feelings, and behaviors of individuals that ultimately have implications for the dynamics between the groups with the stars and without them.

In the opening of the story, the Star-Belly Sneetches walk on the beaches with their snoots in the air proclaiming how they are the best. They refuse to have anything to do with the Plain-Belly Sneetches. Their children learn not to let Plain-Belly children into their games and all activities are segregated. In this way, the Star-Belly Sneetches maintain their presumed superiority while the Plain-Belly Sneetches are "moping and doping alone on the beaches." The Fix-It-Up Chappie arrives, however, to disrupt the long enduring star (i.e., status) hierarchy by offering (for $3) admission to his "very peculiar machine." The Sneetches entered as Plain-Belly and when they "popped out, they had stars! . . . They had stars upon thars!" With this new branding they yelled "to the ones who had stars at the start, 'We're exactly like you! You can't tell us apart. We're all just the same, now.'" This, of course, dismayed the original Star-Belly Sneetches so much so that they then paid the Fix-It-Up Chappie $10 a piece to remove their stars. By doing so, they regained the distinction they had lost and at the same time angered the new Star-Belly Sneetches, who now wanted their stars removed! The Fix-It-Up Chappie ran his machine all day long, removing stars, adding stars "Until neither the Plain nor the Star-Bellies knew Whether this one was that one . . . or that one was this one." While the Fix-It-Up Chappie got quite rich, once he departed the Sneetches got even richer: They came to realize "that Sneetches are Sneetches and no kind of Sneetch is the best on the beaches."

This children's tale captures the social psychological topic of **intergroup relations**, which recognize differentially positioned groups whose interactions are propelled by cognitive and emotional processes. Such relations, moreover, characterize what we typically address in terms of issues of prejudice and discrimination. Thus, underlying the dynamics among individuals in groups are many of the social psychological processes discussed in earlier chapters, and dissection of those dynamics contributes to understanding larger issues of inequality in society.

Dr. Seuss reveals how individuals (Sneetches, in this case) categorize themselves as members of particular groups (and not as members of other groups) and identify with that group (or groups). With such identification, people come to compare themselves and their group to members of other groups. As described further later in this chapter, the comparisons serve as a potential way to establish a positive impression of one's own group. And that desire for a positive impression of one's own group may stimulate biased or prejudicial perceptions of members of other groups and possibly even discriminatory behavior toward them. Intergroup dynamics, thus, essentially rest upon the cognitive, affective, and behavioral actions of members of each group.

Here we begin by examining **intergroup behavior**, which refers to "how people in groups perceive, think about, feel about, act towards, and relate to people in other groups" (Hogg and Abrams 2003:407). Work in intergroup dynamics highlights the importance of cognitive elements of categorization (Chapter 5), with a focus on "sifting" people into groups characterized by visible features, situational factors, or statuses (Chapter 8). Such categorization may spur motivational and affective processes that propel the development of a **social identity**, or a sense of self based on membership in a particular group (Tajfel 1979). Social identity theory, detailed in a subsequent section, illustrates how the motivation for a positive social identity helps to maintain boundaries between groups and how certain situational conditions may undermine those boundaries. Such processes draw attention to **prejudice**, typically defined as an attitude or feeling, favorable or unfavorable, toward people owing to their membership in particular groups (Allport 1954). This cognitive or affective state may propel positive or negative actions toward members of those groups, resulting in **discrimination** that benefits those belonging to a favored or dominant group and disadvantages those belonging to a disfavored or dominated group.

This chapter begins by focusing on processes involved in intergroup behavior and then delves specifically into issues of prejudice and discrimination. In doing so, the chapter addresses this question: How does "belonging" to a particular group impact perceptions of and behavior aimed at individuals belonging to another group? Elements of the response to this question contribute to explaining the maintenance of inequality. The third part of the chapter focuses on a second question: How can negative intergroup behaviors be ameliorated? A response to that question entails the potential for social change and possibly ameliorating inequality. The chapter concludes with a reflection on how the understanding of social psychological processes detailed in this book are critical to addressing social inequality more generally.

What Processes Underlie Intergroup Behavior?

A core, underlying element of intergroup behavior is identification of the "group." Recall that in Chapter 8 we defined a group as involving interaction between at least two people who consciously recognize their membership or identify with the group and who share goals, expectations, and norms. Thus, groups may range in size from very small (e.g., a dating couple, classmates doing a joint presentation) to very large (e.g., women, African Americans). Typically, especially with larger groups, members are more likely to vary some in terms of shared goals and the like and to be aware of that variation. For example, among the Sneetches, the most distinguishing factor was whether group members possessed a star on their bellies or not. Those with a star saw themselves as belonging to one group, and those without saw themselves belonging to another group. But the actual size of the stars or exact placement on the belly might vary. Regardless of that variation, if a Sneetch had a star, then his or her "ingroup" consisted of the Star-Belly Sneetches, whose "outgroup" were those Sneetches without stars. When individuals act and react in ways influenced by their group membership, it constitutes intergroup behavior. The behaviors may be fairly tame, such as when sports fans paint their faces in the colors of their favorite team, or devastating, such as when members of one ethnic group massacre members of another ethnic group.

Two factors generally shape intergroup dynamics (see Yzerbyt and Demoulin 2010). The first factor is the *position of each group* in the social system. Position stems from both the objective level of material or symbolic resources (e.g., How much money, education, or recognition in political life does each group have?) and from the subjective perception of group members regarding those resource levels. For example, in 18th-century England, the nobility possessed both higher material resources (land!) and symbolic ones (titles!) than those in industry. The nobility's disdain for those in industry suggests a negative subjective perception of members of the rising capitalist class. Yet as manufacturing and trade took off in the 19th century, the masters of industry began to accrue vast wealth, which may have shifted, in a positive direction, the nobility's subjective perception of the merchants, thereby altering the dynamics between the groups. The second factor is the *relative standing of each group*. Resource-advantaged groups may dominate other less advantaged or subordinated groups. For example, Dr. Seuss's opening characterization of the Star-Belly Sneetches who walk with their snoots in the air to indicate that they are "best" suggests that they are the dominant group, and the moping Plain-Belly Sneetches are the dominated group. In middle school, eighth graders might be seen to be a dominant group vis-à-vis sixth and seventh graders. But once they move on to ninth grade, then that same group of students may be cast as disadvantaged or subordinate compared to the upper-class students in high school. Thus, the relative position of groups, owing to their material and symbolic resources, depends upon the context in which they are embedded.

Next, we discuss two fundamental processes—(1) social categorization and (2) social identity—that pertain to all groups and drive intergroup dynamics. These perspectives, however, recognize that the position (dominant or subordinate) of the group may affect perceptual, motivational, and affective responses, which in turn drive the nature of intergroup behavior.

Social and Self-Categorization Processes

Most of you are not middle-aged sales representatives who have lost jobs owing to the onset of the digital age, as was the case in the 2013 movie *The Internship*. Nonetheless, you might someday find yourselves at a large orientation meeting for interns at a successful Silicon Valley firm (e.g., Google). At such a meeting, the first thing you might do is take stock of who else is there in terms of their age, sex, racial, or ethnic appearance. And, as you learn more about your fellow cohort members, you might sort the individuals in terms of their background training (e.g., engineering, computer science, business, social science, humanities) or previous work experience (e.g., none, only summer jobs, years in sales). Essentially, doing so is a more elaborate form of what the Sneetches do by categorizing those with star and plain bellies.

"Categorization is the process by which individuals simplify their environment, creating categories on the basis of attributes that objects appear to have (or not to have) in common" (Yzerbyt and Demoulin 2010:1028). Chapter 5 details the need for such simplification and notes that individuals sometimes draw upon concrete exemplars of a category (e.g., characteristics of LeBron James to represent all basketball players) and other times fit together a general set of attributes derived from a variety of members of a particular category (e.g., the prototype of a basketball player stems from characteristics attached to a number of well-known players). Pieces of information are organized into individuals' schema about particular categories.

As a type of a schema, **stereotype** refers to beliefs about the features, opinions, and expected behaviors of a group that are generalized to individuals belonging to the group. There is no shortage of examples of stereotypes, which bring to mind a grouping of characteristics. For example, the stereotype of the southerner described in Chapter 5 involves characteristics like white, uncouth, poor, stupid, and lazy. The "soccer mom" stereotype includes both individual statuses (e.g., white, middle-class, suburban, female) as well as activities (e.g., driving her school-age children to their many activities in her minivan). Although the definition leaves silent whether the content of a stereotype is positive or negative, accurate or inaccurate, stereotypes are problematic because they are often negative and used to judge every member of a group in the same way (Stangor 2009). When negative stereotypes (of race, gender, religion, and the like) are linked to negative outcomes (e.g., prejudice and discrimination) and seen as fueling intergroup conflict, a presumption that stereotypes are inaccurate often also arises. Inaccuracy in stereotypes—for example, claims that blacks are lazy or that Jews are greedy—reflects historical attempts to subjugate members of a particular group or limit their types of employment. Such claims are typically false. Yet many stereotypes are relatively accurate (Jussim et al. 2009). For example, girls are often believed to do better in school than boys, and indeed, on average over a range of classes they tend to have higher GPAs.

As will be detailed in various ways, stereotyping is a means of differentiating members of groups, which may fuel intergroup dynamics. Yet given the content of and associated behavioral expectations, stereotyping also has implications for how individuals view themselves and their performances. Within society, unfavorable stereotypes characterizing particular groups may specify limitations on the competence of members (at least in particular realms). **Stereotype threat** suggests that individuals suspect that they will be judged on the basis of the (negative) stereotype of the group to which they belong (Steele 1997). Despite efforts to disconfirm negative stereotypes, such a threat undermines actual performances (Schmader, Johns, and Forbes 2008). For example, if blacks are not expected to do well on standardized tests, an African American test taker aware of the stereotype may feel disheartened and worry about confirming the expectations—all of which may disrupt concentration leading to a performance deficit. One means of remedying the ill consequences of stereotype threat is to emphasize one's unique characteristics (Martens et al. 2006) or distance oneself from the cultural stereotype of one's group (Pronin, Steele, and Ross 2004). In effect, these strategies rely upon the separation of personal and social identities, as described next.

In addition to the social categorization of individuals into different groups, intergroup processes depend heavily on an individual's view of himself or herself as a member of a particular group. **Self-categorization theory** (Turner et al. 1987) elaborates on the emergence and interplay between the personal self, which focuses on individual characteristics, and the social self, which entails categorization as member of a group, especially in comparison to an outgroup.[1] The personal self reflects idiosyncratic traits and specific interpersonal ties, unique to an individual. A social identity, in contrast, relies upon category or group memberships for definition, emphasizing shared characteristics and networks of relationships. For example, when Karen thinks of herself, she considers in concrete terms what she likes (e.g., cats, dark chocolate, pedestrians who use crosswalks), what she does (e.g., walks her dog, gardens, reads mysteries), what characterizes her personality (e.g., optimism, indecisiveness, empathy), and how she is connected to others (e.g., her spouse, kids, and next-door neighbors)—all things that make her who she is and distinct from others. But when she classifies herself as a social scientist, a social identity, a different set of characteristics come to mind, like commitment to empirical evidence to illustrate social patterns. The characteristics of her social identity may become particularly pronounced in comparison to other groups, say, humanities scholars.

Turner and his colleagues (1987) developed self-categorization theory to identify conditions that give rise to thinking about the self in terms of one's group memberships. Individuals are more likely to activate their social identities when they strongly identify with a particular social or group-based category. Also, social identities become focal when the situation stimulates accessibility to and highlights the relevance of such categories. Thus, when sitting in a college-wide faculty meeting debating whether a course in comparative literature or a basic quantitative methods course should be part of the required curriculum, Karen's social identity as a social scientist is more likely to be activated than her personal identity as a dark chocolate lover. Likewise, a member of a sorority or fraternity is unlikely to invoke that social identity when he or she is interviewing for a prestigious scholarship; in such a situation, one's personal identity as an academic achiever is likely to be foremost.

When people or Sneetches think of themselves in terms of their social category, additional cognitive processes unfold. They are likely to emphasize **intragroup similarities**, what makes their group members alike, and **intergroup differences**, what makes their group different from other groups. Star-Belly Sneetches may think of that important emblem that they possess, emphasizing how they are similar to one another and distinct from those without stars. Social scientists may emphasize how anthropologists, sociologists, and political scientists believe in bringing data to bear upon understanding social phenomena and how this approach is distinct from literary approaches. Individuals tend to self-stereotype, emphasizing how they feel and behave like other members of their group. Self-stereotyping diminishes the importance of unique personal characteristics, which leads to viewing a situation through the eyes of one's social category rather than one's unique characteristics. Self-categorization theory, thus, focuses on cognitive processes underlying intergroup dynamics captured by social identity theory.

Social Identity Processes

Imagine going off to summer camp. When you arrive, you are assigned to Hillside Cabin. You will do nearly all of your daily activities with your cabinmates: eating, swimming, practicing archery, hiking, and so forth. The same is true for the residents of another cabin, Lakeside. The two cabins are virtually identical, and neither boasts a superior view, despite their names. On the evening of the second day at camp (when you barely know the names of your cabinmates), you find yourself in a series of "challenges" against Lakeside residents: three-legged race, egg toss, and Hula-Hoop contest. The competition is fierce; those on the sidelines make up funny cheers regaling the prowess of your team. Even though less than 48 hours earlier you did not know your cabinmates, now you favor them more than you could ever have imagined. Essentially, you have developed a social identity as a resident of Hillside Cabin. And with that identity comes certain cognitions, feelings, and behaviors. **Social identity theory** (Tajfel 1979; Tajfel and Turner 1979; see also Abrams and Hogg 2010; Hogg and Abrams 1988) complements self-categorization theory by providing a critical understanding of motivational elements underlying intergroup dynamics. The theory examines how group membership impacts perceived status differences among groups and resulting behaviors, including individuals' abilities to move across group boundaries, to create positive group- and self-images, and to foment intergroup conflict.

Group membership in itself does not necessarily signal status differences. Yet that membership, resulting from categorization processes and spurring the development of a social identity, may stimulate intergroup comparisons and motivational processes that affect subsequent behaviors (Tajfel and Turner 1979). Early evidence for the emergence of status differences grew out of results from experiments focusing on **minimal groups,** where individuals are categorized into groups randomly or based on some trivial characteristic (Tajfel et al. 1971; see also Brown 2000). Even in the absence of group history, knowledge of other group members, or interaction, those categorized into a particular group demonstrate **ingroup favoritism**—discriminating in favor of their own group by, for example, allocating greater points to or more positively rating ingroup members compared to members of the "other" or outgroup. They are also likely to voice a sense of belonging and suggest similarity to other group members, even when those members remain anonymous to them. If such ingroup bias emerges in anonymous groups, without any interaction, it is no wonder that residents of different camp cabins come to promote their own even after only a brief acquaintance! Evidence suggests that ingroup favoritism may operate automatically, largely outside of conscious control (Otten and Wentura 1999). The sense of belonging to an ingroup provides individuals with not only possible material support but also psychological benefits of belonging and security (Correll and Park 2005).

Like self-categorization theory, social identity theory recognizes that behavior ranges on a continuum from interpersonal to intergroup. Identification of self and others as members of particular social categories, each consisting of multiple individuals, highlights more than the interaction between two unique people. Importantly, Tajfel and Turner (1979) assume *that individuals are intrinsically motivated to achieve a positive self-concept and that they do so by emphasizing* **positive distinctiveness**—what makes oneself or one's group special, distinct, or better— in comparison to others or to other social categories or groups. The cheering on the sideline of cabin competitions at a camp is a means of stressing the positive image of one's group. The Star-Belly Sneetches who hold their snouts in the air and look down on Plain-Belly others is another manifestation of positive distinctiveness. In effect, doing so allows the establishment or maintenance of the superiority of one's group over another, thus suggesting status differences.

The pursuit of a positive social identity may also promote uncertainty reduction (Hogg 2007). By identifying with a group, which provides prescriptions for behavior and a positive social anchor, individuals reduce their uncertainties about situations and their roles in them. A camper uncertain about his identity might cling to what being a resident of Hillside cabin means and what his cabinmates do as a way to achieve a positive self and social identity.

People, of course, may have multiple social identities—based on gender, race, the school attended, occupation, or the like. Social contexts make salient different social identities. For example, during college football season, your social identity as a student at the University of Georgia (UGA) may be more salient, especially before the big game against University of Florida. Yet when you attend your cousin's wedding in the spring, your social identity as a UGA Bulldog may not matter in the least. Situations that highlight benefits received by one group but not another or burdens affecting one group but not another may increase the salience of a particular social identity. For example, being a resident of a particular neighborhood may not be that important until the local government attempts to place a polluting incinerator very close to your home. Then one's social identity as a resident of that neighborhood grows in importance, and neighbors may cast those supporting the incinerator as members of an outgroup.

Behaviors acted upon to ensure a positive self-concept or social identity depend on (1) the strength of social identification with the group and (2) the relative structural positions of the groups within a situation. People who only weakly identify with a social group are unlikely to rely upon their group membership as a source of self-esteem. For example, even if you have lived in the South for 30 years, if you don't identify as a southerner then you are unlikely to care about the South's uniqueness compared to the North. Deriving a positive image of yourself through southern pride would be unlikely. You might, however, be embedded in a group that differs from another in terms of the amount of resources possessed or status accorded. In such situations, one group may be dominant and the other dominated. For example, the neighbors fighting city plans for an incinerator may be relatively poor, especially in comparison to those backing the incinerator plans (e.g., rich developers and officials).

U.S. history is rife with examples about the relative positioning and changes in positioning of immigrants described in terms of their ethnicity. At different historical points in time, U.S. residents descended from early Anglo immigrants dominated the Irish and Italians, who represented later waves of immigration, often arriving with fewer resources as well. Currently, within different Western nation-states, there is talk of the dominance of the "white majority" compared to the less influential minority groups, characterized by differences in skin color or religion. As these historical examples illustrate, whether one group is dominant or dominated depends upon the social situation in which they are embedded and the comparisons that emerge. These concerns go beyond shifting historical circumstances. Consider, for example, the dynamics within a high school. In the social hierarchy of the school, the jocks may reign supreme over the nerds and the delinquents. But in a comparison between the nerds and the delinquents, the former may have the edge of superiority. A major issue for social identity theory is how members of a dominated group achieve and claim a positive social identity.

According to the theory, the means by which dominated groups ensure a positive social identity depend upon the extent to which the boundaries between groups in a social hierarchy are permeable and whether the hierarchy is stable and legitimate (Tajfel and Turner 1979). **Boundary permeability** refers to the potential for social mobility between groups; in other words, a member of a low-status (dominated) group might potentially move into a high-status (dominant) group. A **stable social hierarchy** is one that is largely unchanging and, if accepted by members of both dominated and dominant groups, is considered legitimate as well. Even when group statuses are relatively stable, if the boundaries between groups are permeable, people may pursue a positive self-concept by focusing on personal or individual identities rather than social identities (see Ellemers 1993). Emphasis on individual identities tends, then, to inhibit intergroup competition and the potential for social change in the social hierarchy.

For example, the Plain-Belly Sneetches first to get imprinted with stars were opting for social mobility from their lower-status group into one claiming greater status. Similarly, Alexander Hamilton, a nearly penniless orphan from the British West Indies, immigrated (thanks to sponsorship by wealthy merchants) to seek advanced education at King's College (now Columbia University) in New York City. His education, military service, legal expertise, and authorship of papers promoting the ratification of the U.S. Constitution contributed to securing his position as the first secretary of the Treasury of the United States. While Hamilton's story of social mobility is distinctive (and has been the subject of a Broadway musical), subsequent immigrants to the United States in the 19th century likewise attempted to demonstrate their individual-level skills and determination in the hope of climbing the socioeconomic ladder, even if other members of their group remained in undesirable and low-wage jobs. Those immigrants experienced the permeability of boundaries in a way that slaves in the 18th century never could.

Status distinctions between slaves and nonslaves at that particular historical moment were stable and legitimate. Such rigidity of the social hierarchy contributes to preventing the development of a positive social identity among members of a dominated group. As a consequence, individuals might seek greater emphasis on personal identity as a source of positive esteem. For example, individuals denied the opportunity for social mobility may come to emphasize a particular skill that they possess (such as training horses, woodworking) or the type of person they are (e.g., religiously pious, warmhearted).

Alternatively, they may achieve positive distinctiveness by what Tajfel and Turner (1979) call **social creativity**. Lower-status group members may pursue social creativity to achieve positive distinctiveness by (1) changing the value assigned to attributes of their group, (2) comparing their group to the outgroup on some new dimension, or (3) choosing a different outgroup as a basis of comparison. Examples illustrate each of the means, respectively, for positive distinctiveness. During the civil rights movement of the 1960s, U.S. blacks embraced the slogan "Black is beautiful," which enhances the value of an attribute of their group compared to whites. Immigrants arriving with particular skills (e.g., stone masonry, banking) might focus on how their group is superior on that dimension to the resident population. And 19th century Irish immigrants, who were dominated by established Anglos who had long resided in the United States, may have focused on how their position was superior, at least, to that of Italian immigrants.

Beyond establishing conditions under which members of low-status groups use personal identities to enhance their esteem, social identity theory lays the groundwork for understanding the impact of salience of and commitment to a particular social identity. Threats to the social esteem of the group to which individuals belong generate cognitive, affective, and behavioral responses to intergroup dynamics (Ellemers, Spears, and Doosje 2002). Such threats and reactions ultimately may fuel prejudice and discrimination against other groups.

Cognitive Consequences

Defining oneself as a member of a particular group has implications for how one views other groups and their members. **Intergroup bias** "refers generally to the systematic tendency to evaluate one's own membership group (the in-group) or its members more favorably than a non-membership group (the out-group) or its members" (Hewstone, Rubin and Willis 2002:576). Such bias may be unjustifiable as well as considered unfair or illegitimate. Overly generalized stereotypical images of ingroups and outgroups illustrate such bias, as do attitudinal prejudices and discriminatory behaviors (as discussed in subsequent sections).

For both dominant and dominated groups, social identity theory suggests that in seeking a positive identity, group members are likely to express ingroup favoritism, as previously discussed. Additionally, they may convey **outgroup derogation**, defined as negative evaluations of people viewed as belonging to the outgroup and possibly accompanied by hostility, antagonism, or aggression. The minimal group studies demonstrate that intergroup dynamics clearly elicit positive evaluations of ingroup members but not much outgroup derogation (Brewer 2001). Ingroup favoritism extends to groups having existing affective ties or shared purpose, activity, or task. Additionally, among such existing, socially identified groups, comparisons, *especially in the context of competition, threat, or limited resources*, tend to be more likely to produce derogation of outgroup members (see Dovidio and Gaertner 2010). Thus, as a camp season progresses and ties to cabinmates crystallize, the boys belonging to different cabins might not simply voice cheers indicating the superiority of their cabinmates but over time also include more derogatory or antagonistic remarks denigrating the abilities of the opponents. As described in Upton Sinclair's *The Jungle,* which provides a fictionalized account of the strikes affecting the Chicago meat-packing industry at the turn of the 20th century, the striking immigrant groups did not simply rely on positive images of their own group when southern blacks were brought in to work at the meat processing plants to break the strike; they also cast disparaging comments on those interlopers. In effect, striking immigrant groups were threatened by southern blacks within a context of competition for jobs and conflict over wages.

Beyond appraisals of one's own group as "good" and the outgroup as "bad," intergroup dynamics affect more specific cognitions about each group. As previously indicated, through self-stereotyping, individuals note how they are similar to other ingroup members and how all fit the prototype of the group. Such a process defines the boundaries of a group and may spur other intragroup processes useful to maintaining a sense of the group, including its positive evaluation and solidarity, and its difference from other groups (Dovidio 2013).

With it comes perceptual processes that help to distinguish among group members. People tend to recall in more detail (e.g., Park and Rothbart 1982) information about ingroup members compared to outgroup members. For example, people have better memories for same-race faces than for cross-race faces (Michel, Corneille, and Rossion 2007) and, consequently, are likely to individuate faces rather than seeing them as all the same. Remembering details involves how people encode information about the positive and negative behaviors of ingroup and outgroup members. That encoding affects later descriptions of observed behavior.

For example, Maass et al. (1989) show that individuals recall positive behaviors of ingroup members in general abstract terms (e.g., "She's so kind") rather than concrete terms (e.g., "She baked cookies for the new neighbor"), but the reverse is true for such behaviors performed by outgroup members. By remembering the positive behaviors of outgroup members in concrete terms, those behaviors are easier to discount as exceptions and not as information challenging the view of the outgroup. For negative behaviors, people recall those performed by outgroup members in general terms (e.g., "He's so mean"), which allows confirmation of a stereotype, whereas they remember that of ingroup members in concrete terms (e.g., "He pushed me out of line"), which might be explained away by taking into consideration situational conditions. Thus, how people recall the behaviors of ingroup and outgroup members has implications for perpetuating stereotypes, which fuels intergroup conflict.

Taking more into consideration for ingroup members also suggests that people tend to process information about ingroup members more deeply (van Bavel, Packer, and Cunningham 2008). As a consequence, ingroup members can recognize heterogeneity within their group (after all, the Star-Belly Sneetches can see nuanced differences in the stars on their group members' bellies) even while boasting the similar features that draw ingroup members together.

Such a view contrasts with the tendency to view outgroup members as more alike. The **outgroup homogeneity effect** (e.g., Haslam et al. 1996; Judd and Park 1988) emerges when perceivers belong to one of two categories and view members of the outgroup as more similar to each other than they view individuals in their own group. This effect may stem from a cognitive process whereby ingroup members look at information about outgroup members at a more abstract level and have greater familiarity with ingroup members. It might also stem from a motivational desire to avoid threats from the outgroup (see Yzerbyt and Demoulin 2010). Regardless of the source, seeing outgroup members as homogeneous allows for greater differentiation between the ingroup and outgroup, which may fuel negative emotions and behaviors. Imagine how Nazis convinced the German population of how people who looked like them but differed in religious beliefs came to see all Jews as similar and a threat to their nation.

Affective Consequences

People function emotionally as a member of a group, in a manner similar to how they experience emotions as an individual. The perceived differences between groups stimulate different types of emotional reactions. Those responses depend upon the position of one's group, especially when groups are in competition or sharing a finite number of resources. A dominated group may be depressed about its group status, as the Plain-Belly Sneetches were when they were moping on the beaches, or may feel anger or resentment owing to perceptions of unfair treatment (see Chapter 11). While disadvantaged group members ought to feel angry (Van Zomeren, Spears, and Leach 2008), whether they express it or use it to propel collective action depends on other situational factors. Those with stronger group identification (Ellemers 1993) or perception that their group will be effective in challenging another group (Drury and Reicher 2005) may be more likely to act on that anger. Lower levels of group identification or perceived efficacy might restrain such actions, much like concerns that inhibit people's responses to injustice, noted in Chapter 11.

Encounters with the dominant group may also create anxiety (Stephan and Stephan 1985), owing to previous discriminatory contact with outgroup members, in the form of exploitation or domination, or fear of potential rejection or attack on one's opinions. For example, angry low-income minority group members who show up to contest the placement of an air-polluting incinerator in their neighborhood may worry about reprisals from other community members or from the incinerator company. Other community members and company executives may be white and of higher socioeconomic class and thus distinguished from the protesting group. Moreover, they may see great benefit from such a development and, thus, in contrast to the protestors, be experiencing positive emotions.

As the example illustrates, in contrast to members of dominated groups, members of dominant groups are more likely to experience positive emotions. The bragging of Star-Belly Sneetches attests to their feelings of happiness about their status. Indeed, as discussed in Chapter 7, the structural theory of emotions suggests that at the individual level those of higher power and status tend to have more positive emotional experiences, and this largely extends to the group level as well. Yet under certain circumstances, groups may also feel guilt or shame regarding how their members have treated another group. The experience of collective guilt is important in spurring acts of reparation, public apologies, and the like. For example, before reconciliation between the black majority and white minority could unfold in South Africa, whites had to come to recognize the harmful actions they took in apartheid. Doosje, Branscombe, and Spears (2006) show how strong identification with a group coupled with perceived illegitimacy of the superiority of one's group owing to its violation of shared moral values enhances collective guilt feelings. Without that perceived illegitimacy, however, strongly identified dominant group members may employ different strategies for avoiding feelings of guilt, such as by emphasizing variability of the ingroup, recognizing harmdoers in the group as "black sheep," or by favorably comparing the actions of one's ingroup to the actions of other groups of wrongdoers (see Yzerbyt and Demoulin 2010).

Intergroup emotion theory attempts to capture such distinct emotional reactions involving groups, not simply individual experiences of emotion (Mackie, Maitner, and Smith 2009; Smith 1993). Affective appraisals of situations unfold based on relevance to the group to which an individual belongs. When ingroup members are in a strong position, they feel more anger when outgroup members challenge their opinions (Mackie, Devos, and Smith 2000). Such anger leads to a greater likelihood of opposing the outgroup. Beyond the positioning of the ingroup, the salience of a particular social identity also impacts the experience of a group-related emotion (see Yzerbyt et al. 2006). The most important or relevant social identity provides a "lens" through which to assess a given situation. And discussion among group members of social identity–relevant issues exacerbates group-level emotions (Kuppens et al. 2013). These processes are aptly illustrated by how the 2014 shooting of unarmed Michael Brown in Ferguson, Missouri, by a white police officer enhanced the salience of racial identity in the majority-black city, stimulated the collective anger by African Americans and allies in the city and beyond, and erupted into protests, civil unrest, and a nationwide conversation about use of police force.

Although a number of factors affect the pattern of collective emotions, to the extent that groups feel a particular way about the harm they have endured or caused, they may be launched into certain actions. Those actions have implications for the reproduction of inequalities between the groups or the potential to change the situation.

Behavioral Consequences

In April 2015, Italy faced a migration crisis: Boats filled with hopeful immigrants were crossing the Mediterranean Sea from war-torn countries in North Africa. Tragedy often ensued when overloaded boats sank or broke apart, requiring swift action from coast guards and other boaters to rescue survivors. One set of survivors told of a horrific event during the risky crossing: In an overcrowded rubber boat, Muslim migrants pushed overboard 12 Christian migrants, whose only offense seemed to be profession of their faith. (Other Christians on board were threatened but created a "human chain" to thwart further attack.) History is replete with examples of how a dominant group acts to maintain its position by threatening or even attempting to decimate a dominated group (e.g., Nazi treatment of Jews in World War II; Turkish actions toward Armenians in the early 1900s; the mass genocide of Tutsi in Rwanda by members of the Hutu majority in 1994). Although behavioral consequences may be extremely severe as these examples suggest, most are more restrained or subtle.

As predicted by social identity theory, individuals are likely to favor their ingroups, especially when groups are in competition. Different behavioral responses, often accompanying cognitive and affective ones noted above, emerge. People are more likely to allocate more resources to or vote for members of their ingroup than members of outgroups (see Hewstone et al. 2002). People are also more likely to approach ingroup members and avoid members of the outgroup (Paladino and Castelli 2008), owing, in part, to negative expectations for how interaction with others perceived to be different will unfold. Thus, it is not surprising that individuals tend to be more cooperative and helpful with members of their own group than those belonging to an outgroup (see Gaertner and Dovidio 2000). "In general, individuals derive material benefit, receive valuable information, and experience a sense of belonging and security from the ingroup" (Dovidio and Gaertner 2010:1091). And toward outgroup members, both avoidance and discriminatory behaviors tend to emerge.

The cognitive and affective consequences of intergroup processes capture beliefs underlying prejudice while the behavioral consequences suggest forms of discrimination. We address those specific processes in the next section. Whether dealing with the perceptions and behaviors of Star-Belly Sneetches to those without stars or of Muslims toward Christians in competition over boat space and opportunities in a new country, intergroup processes often maintain the status quo between groups. Members of dominant groups discriminate as a means of remaining superior, whereas those in dominated groups might look for individual avenues of advancement (e.g., social mobility) or become resigned to their plight.

Prejudice and Discrimination

Around the turn of the 20th century, many former Confederate states passed laws instituting requirements for voting eligibility, such as paying a "poll tax" prior to voting, passing a literacy or comprehension test, or producing certain records (sometimes just the "receipt" for paying the poll tax). Some states made temporary exceptions if one's ancestors had previously voted, especially in elections prior to the abolition of slavery. Such laws thus disenfranchised many blacks from voting in elections while at the same time preserving the rights of (literate) whites to vote. State-sanctioned racial segregation in the South began with these laws, along with others focused on funding for public libraries, schools, and so on, and became known as Jim Crow laws.

Underlying the emergence of such laws are the social processes captured by theories related to intergroup behavior: categorization of people into groups; recognition of the dominance of one group over another, fueled by differences in access to resources; pursuit of positive social- or group-based identities through cognitive biases and the development of stereotypes to reinforce views of differences; and enactment of negative behaviors, especially by the dominant group, to maintain their position. White lawmakers expressed prejudice—their unfavorable *attitudes*—toward blacks (owing to their membership in a particular racial group) by enacting laws leading to discrimination or *behaviors* designed to increase the standing or resources of their own group while decreasing or limiting those of blacks.

Not surprisingly, the context of racial dynamics in the United States has drawn attention to the study of prejudice and discrimination. Prejudice brings together the cognitive mechanisms described previously that underlie intergroup behaviors as well as elements of attitudes and emotions (discussed in Chapters 6 and 7). Prejudices often, though not always, get translated into behavioral discrimination. Unlike the fully expressed negative attitudes and behaviors toward racial minorities during the era of Jim Crow laws, dynamics in the 21st century are subtler but nonetheless detrimental (see Bobo et al. 2012; Hunt 2007). Beyond racial dynamics, processes of prejudice and discrimination pertain to the social treatment of women, those with disabilities; religious minorities; gays, lesbians, or transgendered individuals; and others identified as members of groups who may be different, perhaps threatening, to members of a majority group. To illustrate issues of prejudice and discrimination, we focus largely on research bearing upon race.

Types and Sources of Prejudice

Defining Racism

Rooted in cognitive and affective processes, prejudice represents a form of bias (see Dovidio and Gaertner 2010). That bias may be overt and explicit, such as when people indicate that they do not "like" blacks, Muslims, gays, liberals, or other minority groups or even simply members of their outgroups. Presumably, people are aware that they possess such explicit biases and may even act to control their expression. In contrast, **implicit biases** involve biased judgments that are below the level of conscious awareness and thus not under intentional control (e.g., Dovidio, Kawakami, and Gaertner 2002; Greenwald and Banaji 1995). Such biases are automatically activated in the presence of particular stimuli and affect subsequent treatment of a negatively evaluated group (e.g., Greenwald and Krieger 2006).

Both types of biases develop through socialization as individuals learn views of others such as family, friends, and classmates and also chalk up firsthand experiences with people from different groups (Samson and Bobo 2014). Everyone holds prejudices consisting of biases against particular groups, which may range from the rather trivial and largely inconsequential (such as when people say "I don't like redheads") to the profound and highly consequential (such as that found in systems of apartheid).

Racism goes beyond individual-level biases or prejudices, to represent a system of beliefs or ideology involving the legitimation of a minority group's subordination or exploitation. Such an ideology identifies so-called inferior characteristics of a racial or ethnic group and offers norms prescribing differential treatment. The related belief system justifies the inequality between racial groups. (Likewise, sexism as an ideology prioritizes men and their actions over women and their actions, resulting in justification for unequal treatment of males and females.) While explicit group-level antipathy toward racial minorities in the United States, especially as codified in Jim Crow laws, has waned, more subtle forms of bias have emerged.

Few in the United States today openly advocate racial inequality. Instead, what has emerged is **symbolic racism** (Sears 1988; Sears and Henry 2005; known also as modern racism [McConahay 1982] or racial resentment [Kinder and Sanders 1996]). Such racism characterizes people's contention that minority group members' continuing disadvantages do not stem from discrimination but rather from their unwillingness to work hard, an all-American value upon which some argue our nation was founded. The notion of symbolic racism arose to explain the seeming paradox of whites' support for racial equality subsequent to the 1960s civil rights movement but lack of support for programs and policies designed to eradicate discrimination and achieve such equality. For example, symbolic or modern racists oppose affirmative action because they see it as violating their sense of equal opportunity, not because they are against racial equality (Sears, Sidanius, and Bobo 2000). Symbolic racism combines antiblack sentiment and beliefs that blacks fail to buy into American individualistic values of hard work, self-reliance, discipline, and delayed gratification. Such beliefs stimulate racial resentment regarding "perceived special favors to minorities, . . . demands being made by minorities, and the denial that racial discrimination remained influential" (Samson and Bobo 2014:519). Resentment, in turn, undermines whites' willingness to support government programs designed to ameliorate racial inequalities in education, home buying, employment, and so forth.

Another subtle form of racism recognizes ambivalent attitudes and expressions and ultimately underscores explicit and implicit components of bias. **Aversive racism** (Dovidio and Gaertner 2004) involves negative evaluations of minority groups, rationalized by unflattering stereotypical images, which propel avoidance of interaction with members of such groups, despite professing egalitarian beliefs. Given such beliefs, an aversive racist, even though harboring feelings of discomfort and fear, will attempt to display an unprejudiced self, which might sometimes thwart discriminatory behavior. The thwarting of racially motivated negative behaviors is likely in situations characterized by clear-cut egalitarian expectations and the lack of plausible nonracial justifications for such behavior.

For example, in their now-classic study of aversive racism, Dovidio and Gaertner (2000) showed that white, college-aged research participants recommended hiring a more qualified candidate, regardless of race, for a campus position. Yet when candidates' qualifications were ambiguous, neither particularly strong nor weak, study participants typically favored the white candidate over the black and justified the decision in terms of factors independent of race. Participants favoring the white candidate probably were unaware of their racial preference, yet their selection behavior indicates a subtle willingness to avoid nonwhite candidates. Similar studies in other arenas (e.g., college admissions, legal decisions, and teamwork) show how situational demands—like superior qualifications of a nonwhite candidate—attenuate expression of prejudice, whereas in the absence of such demands, difficult-to-control implicit biases emerge (see Dovidio and Gaertner 2004).

In addition to these subtle forms of racism, **racial apathy** suggests general indifference toward racial and ethnic inequality (Forman 2004). Such apathy stymies recognition of any differences between racial groups or forms of prejudice. By ignoring or explaining away racial inequalities, racially apathetic individuals disengage from dealing with race-related social issues. For example, Forman and Lewis (2006) describe how white Americans were utterly surprised by the images of the aftermath of Hurricane Katrina in New Orleans in 2005 documenting the overwhelming devastation of poor black neighborhoods. For so many whites, the racial inequality plaguing the landscape of New Orleans was not on their radar and thus not of their concern. Both ignorance of such inequality and not wanting to deal with it may be as harmful to minority group members as Jim Crow legislation.

Examining forms of racism and racial apathy involves challenges in measuring racial prejudices. Researchers have employed various strategies. Those that tap into explicit biases face the possibility that study participants provide socially desirable responses, thereby leading to underestimation of the extent of any type of prejudice. Other measures tackle implicit biases.

Measuring Prejudice

Traditional survey measures of prejudice or racism often tap into explicit biases and allow study participants to exert control over their responses. *Direct measures* (see Olson 2009) include disagree/agree items such as the following: "I think it is right that the black race should occupy a somewhat lower position socially than the white race"; "I would not take a black person to eat with me in a restaurant where I was well known"; or "Interracial dating should be avoided." Respondents can readily figure out that "disagreement" with such items would indicate lack of prejudice, which, given norms suppressing blatant racism, would allow them to appear nonracist. Scales involving such items are less likely to exhibit differences among individuals.

Items in the symbolic racism 2000 scale (Henry and Sears 2002) are subtle and incorporate scaling properties to reduce mindless response sets. For example, in addition to agree or disagree items like "It's really a matter of some people not trying hard enough; if blacks would only try harder they could be just as well off as whites," the scale asks "How much of the racial tension that exists in the United States today do you think blacks are responsible for creating?" (all of it, most, some, not much). Results with this scale show that it elicits differences in racial attitudes and perceptions among individuals and better predicts support for programs and policies to address racial inequality than previous measures (Sears and Henry 2005).

Beyond survey measures, which largely tap into explicit, if subtle, bias, researchers have developed means to measure nonconscious biases and prejudices. *Indirect measures* tapping implicit biases assume that concepts (e.g., black, white, straight, gay) are associated in memory with other concepts (e.g., good, bad, helpful). Such measures capture spontaneous and uncontrollable cognitive processes and thus are unaffected by attempts to control expression through socially desirable responses. Strategies for assessing implicit biases (see Olson 2009) often rely upon priming (see Chapter 5; Fazio et al. 1995), which involves very brief exposure (e.g., about a quarter of a second) to an attitude object followed by a "target" that requires a positive or negative response. For example, to assess implicit bias regarding race, the prime may be a picture of someone of another race and the target may be an adjective like awesome, wonderful, terrible, or worrisome. The respondent must indicate (by a keystroke on a computer) whether the target connotes something good or bad; the amount of time it takes for a response captures the extent of bias. "Response latency" should be shortest with compatible associations (e.g., positive category and positive words or negative category and negative words).

One well-known indirect measure of prejudice is the implicit association test (IAT) (Greenwald, McGhee, and Schwartz 1998; Nosek, Greenwald, and Banaji 2007; but see critiques by De Houwer, Beckers, and Moors 2007; Fiedler 2010). Designed to examine whites' prejudice against blacks, the IAT involves four phases, during which study participants must categorize the presented stimuli as quickly as possible. Phase 1 involves categorizing pictures of blacks and whites by pressing *e* for pictures of blacks and *i* for pictures of whites. During Phase 2, respondents classify negative and positive words, by pressing *e* and *i* respectively. The (counterbalanced) third and fourth stages involve both the two categories of race and the two types of words presented as "compatible" and "incompatible" pairs. From the viewpoint of white respondents, compatible associations between one's cultural perspective and the meaning of a word involve pairing blacks and negative words (represented by pressing *e*) and whites and positive words (indicated by pressing *i*). Incompatible pairing involves pairing of whites and negative words (with an *i* key press) and of blacks and positive words (with an *e* key press). The measure of implicit bias stems from a difference score between the average response latencies (over a series of trials) for the compatible and incompatible phases.

Faster responses to compatible pairings over incompatible ones signal an implicit negative bias toward blacks relative to whites. Using the IAT, research has demonstrated a significant preference for whites among both white and black study participants and a tendency for white respondents to show much greater implicit than explicit bias (Nosek, Banaji, and Greenwald 2002). Interestingly, in comparing explicit and implicit measures of prejudice, researchers find that while explicit measures predict controllable verbal behaviors of friendliness, implicit ones have a greater impact on nonverbal behaviors (e.g., standing further away, crossing the street to avoid an encounter with someone of a different race) that signal distancing and tension (Dovidio et al. 2002; Heider and Skowronski 2007). The lack of a strong association between explicit and implicit measures (see Greenwald et al. 2009) reinforces ideas represented by the different forms of racism: people (whites) are vested in presenting themselves as nonprejudiced and supportive of equality, yet they still hang on to negative beliefs, at times unconsciously, that denigrate members of minority groups. So what are sources of such prejudicial attitudes?

Sources of Prejudice and Racism

Early in the musical *Wicked*, Galinda sings, "Are people born wicked? Or do they have wickedness thrust upon them?" The same can be said about prejudice: Are people born that way, or do they become that way owing to the contexts in which they are embedded? A social psychological approach, of course, argues the latter. The Star-Belly Sneetches look down on the Plain-Belly Sneetches, but each has learned to do so through their interactions. As noted earlier, biases underlying prejudice emerge as individuals are socialized into the groups to which they belong. There is, in effect, a reciprocal relationship between the impact of societal level factors and processes on individual attitudes and experiences, which in turn affect patterns of racial inequality (Samson and Bobo 2014). While delving into the processes and factors contributing to socialization is beyond the scope of this chapter (but see Perez-Felkner 2013), here we focus on individual- and group-level approaches to understanding why some people are more prejudiced than others and the nature of that prejudice.

Individual-Level Approaches Some psychological research tells us who is more likely to be prejudiced (see Yzerbyt and Demoulin 2010). Individuals who lack **empathy**—the ability to take on the points of view of others and feel their emotions—tend to voice more prejudicial attitudes (e.g., Vescio, Sechrist, and Paolucci 2003). Also, researchers have investigated two sets of beliefs, sometimes referred to as "personality" types, more prone to prejudice. Post–World War II, interest focused on why people blindly submit to authority, rigidly uphold conventional standards, and act aggressively toward those who fail to meet those standards. This set of characteristics, known as **authoritarianism** (Adorno et al. 1950), morphed into what is now labeled right-wing authoritarianism (Altemeyer 1988). People characterized as high in such authoritarianism tend to be more prejudiced (Altemeyer and Hunsberger 1992). In a similar vein, the **social dominance orientation,** or SDO (Sidanius and Pratto 1999), pertains to beliefs that one's own group should be dominant while other groups remain subordinate and that inequality is acceptable. People with a strong SDO tend to be more prejudiced, especially toward members of groups that challenge the system legitimizing the superiority of their own group and advocate greater equality. While such belief sets illustrate why people may vary in levels of prejudice, to understand how such beliefs might emerge requires consideration of contextual factors.

Group-Level Approaches Absent from *Sneetches* is any backstory: Why do Star-Belly Sneetches claim superiority? Do they have more resources, more education, or higher-paying jobs? Although Dr. Seuss remains mute on such background, when we think of intergroup dynamics in most countries, we typically can look to the historical record and patterns of education, employment, land ownership, wealth, and income over time to anchor the backstory of different groups. Anchoring that backstory helps to determine the emergence of prejudice targeted against members of certain groups. **Realistic conflict theory (RCT)** argues that intergroup conflict emerges when two (or more) groups want to achieve prosperity, but resources are such that only one group can achieve its goal; consequently, they compete over scarce resources (see Sherif 1966). More specifically, situations stimulating RCT involve an opposition of interests, where one group's gains are another group's losses, or what is called a "zero-sum" situation. Under such conditions, group members may grow frustrated and develop antagonistic attitudes toward outgroup members while at the same time increasingly identify with their own group, enhancing the sense of solidarity within the group (much in the manner of processes captured by social identity theory, as previously described).

The previous examples of the dynamics between members of Hillside and Lakeside cabins were inspired by a now classic field study designed to test RCT. Sherif and colleagues (1961) observed white, middle-class boys, ages 11 and 12, at summer camp located at Robbers Cave State Park in Oklahoma. Unbeknownst to the campers, the organization of their activities during their 2-week camp stay captured elements of RCT. First, the boys largely interacted only with members of their own group and engaged in activities requiring cooperation (e.g., cooking together, carrying canoes) designed to enhance cohesion and solidarity. Each group also chose a name to represent them. Then, the groups known as the Rattlers and Eagles engaged in tournament games (i.e., baseball, tug-of-war, and a treasure hunt), where one group's victory signaled the other group's loss and the victor took home a highly valued prize. During the competitions, as your knowledge of social identity theory would lead you to expect, the boys began exhibiting unsportsmanlike behavior, stereotyping, casting derogatory comments at, and even destroying the property (banners and flags) belonging to their opponents. (Such behavior may be witnessed today by fans of competing teams in the soccer World Cup or perhaps even at local high school football games!)

When Sherif asked the boys at summer camp to identify their friends, they consistently picked members of their own groups. Such a pattern facilitated hostility and antagonism between the groups. Having set the context for the development of such prejudices, Sherif then executed activities designed, he hoped, to undo them. As discussed further later on, such activities required far more than simply increased contact between the Rattlers and Eagles. Both groups needed to be engaged in cooperative activities to achieve goals beyond each group's respective interests.

Given the havoc that competition over valued resources at camp created, extrapolate from that study to imagine the impact on prejudice of distinguishable groups competing over economic resources like jobs or housing or even intangible resources like status and respect. Previous examples regarding waves of immigrant groups to the United States or even the fictional account of the northern migration of African Americans into the meat-packing industry of Chicago, represented in *The Jungle*, illustrate contexts rife with the potential for conflict, prejudice, and ultimately discrimination. Under such conditions, the results of competition for resources fuel durable inequalities that become associated with specific racial or ethnic group identities.

Group position theory (GPT; Blumer 1958; see also Bobo 1999) casts racial prejudice as "the collective process through which racial groups define themselves and other racial groups in relation to each other," which ultimately defines the relative status of and boundaries between groups (Samson and Bobo 2014:521). The theory stresses that it is the *subjective* perception of position, shaped over time and circumstances like population size, opportunity structures, and distribution of knowledge and skills, that matters. Dominant groups define the subordinate group as inherently different, and they feel superior, entitled to tangible and symbolic resources and opportunities. Attempts by subordinate group members to encroach on the standing of dominant groups create a threat. Because the groups' perceptions are anchored in a sociohistorical context, as conditions shift over time, so too does the sense of group position. For example, the growth of the size of a minority group over time may enhance a feeling of group threat among members of the dominant group resulting in intensive negative attitudes toward the minority group (e.g., Quillian 1995; Taylor 1998). Both RCT and GPT feature social structure and group identity processes, not simply individual-level negative affect toward racial minorities. Indeed, Bobo (1983) showed that whites' opposition to busing to desegregate schools stemmed from their group interests and perceived entitlements (represented by measures tapping into attitudes toward civil rights and black politics), not simply their personal animosities.

Whenever two or more groups occupy different positions in a social structure, the potential for prejudice exists. As the foregoing illustrated, prejudice may be blatant or subtle. Sometimes people are not even fully aware of their prejudices, a phenomenon that researchers have attempted to address by devising implicit measures of racial attitudes. While some individuals may have a greater propensity toward prejudice than others, it is the sociohistorical context, especially the relative positions of different groups in respect to access to tangible and intangible resources, which potentially foments prejudice. Although prejudice may not always result in discriminatory behaviors (much like the linkage between attitudes and behavior in general—see Chapter 6), often everyday behaviors capture subtle forms of discrimination.

(Racial) Discrimination

Inspired by an assigned reading by Joe Feagin (1991), a renowned race ethnicity scholar, one of Karen's students conducted a mini experiment for his social psychology research paper. This African American young man asked four of his college friends, two blacks and two whites, all from professional families with incomes putting them in the upper-middle (if not upper) class, to be "shoppers" at an exclusive store in an upscale mall. He tried to match his four "confederates" on attractiveness, but he instructed them to dress differently. One in each racial group was to dress very casually, in shorts and a T-shirt, and appear a bit disheveled; the other in each group was to look more formal, garbed in pressed slacks and a button-down shirt, looking very neat. Thus, in addition to race of customer, he also attempted to manipulate their perceived status or social class (and, by implication, ability to purchase anything in the store). By giving them instructions about how they should "look around" the store and a loose script to follow in speaking with a salesperson, he made sure the behavior of each shopper was similar. While each confederate shopped, he observed how long it took sales personnel to approach them—if they did at all—and additional verbal interaction.

He expected, and found, that the more formally attired confederates received attention more quickly. But, also as expected, race mattered: Black confederates, regardless of how well dressed, were followed more in the store (without any verbal interaction) and the formally attired black shopper waited longer to get service than his white counterpart. While there were many limitations to the student's study (e.g., no control over the number of customers in the store, only a few "observations") for each confederate), he was disappointed (though not surprised) that in the late 20th century his racial peers received such treatment in Atlanta, the city's former mayor Andrew Young said was "too busy to hate." Even in the post–civil rights era, just as prejudice has grown subtler, so has discrimination, denoted as negative and unequal treatment of persons or groups based on their group membership. Driven by the social psychological processes involving stereotypes and prejudice (both explicit and implicit biases), as well as organizational and societal patterns (Pager and Shepherd 2008), discrimination reinforces existing inequalities.

As Allport (1954) points out, the expression of prejudice in behavioral form— discrimination—can range from simple actions on the part of members of a dominant group, like avoidance, lack of eye contact, to progressively more aggressive behaviors including exclusion, physical assaults, or even extermination. The killing of nine African Americans at a 2015 Bible study session in Emanuel African Methodist Episcopal Church in Charleston, South Carolina, by a white 21-year-old male reminds us that the extremes of discrimination—what we have come to know as hate crimes—emerge on our soil and defy the notion that the United States is a postracial society. Regardless of the cause or type of behavior, investigating patterns of discrimination by race, gender, age, sexual orientation, or the like is challenging.

Researchers have employed different strategies (see Quillian 2006; Pager and Shepherd 2008). One measure statistically analyzes trends in, for example, employment or wages to determine whether there is a "gap" between groups (e.g., males versus females; whites versus nonwhites). For example, that females earned 78.3% of what males did in 2013 represents a statistical difference between median salaries for women and men; similarly, a comparison of 2015 median hourly earnings show that black men earn 73% of what white men do (a smaller gap exists for black and white women). When such analysis takes into account factors like education level, experience, and work hours, such wage gaps close some but do not entirely disappear (e.g., Blau and Kahn 2007). What is left over—"the residual"—is often attributed to discrimination in hiring, promotion, and salaries.

Other strategies involve specifically asking perpetrators and victims alike about their experiences with discrimination. As you might imagine, given the illegality of and strong normative prescriptions against discriminatory behavior in hiring, employers rarely admit such actions. Studies using such a measurement strategy are plagued by social desirability biases and are likely to underreport the extent of discrimination. Asking victims of discrimination about their experiences may be less subject to social desirability effects, but their reports are based on perceptions and may not reflect a shared, objective reality (though, as discussed previously, individuals' perceptions and socially constructed reality shape their subsequent behaviors).

Feagin (1991; see also Feagin and Sikes 1994) used such an approach, relying on in-depth interviews with 37 middle-class African Americans. He asked questions designed to tap into the types of situations, especially those involving barriers to employment, education, and housing, that respondents generally encountered. Most of the accounts detailed public settings and interactions with strangers. The often very subtle forms of discrimination, or **microaggressions,** included behaviors such as white sales clerks failing to place change in the hands of black customers to avoid any minor physical contact; restaurant hosts making blacks wait, even in empty establishments, or routinely seating them in undesirable locations;

excessive surveillance of black shoppers in stores or of blacks walking in predominantly white neighborhoods, especially at night; talking among whites ceasing in elevators when a black walks on; and whites crossing the street to avoid encounters with blacks. Such forms of discrimination, Feagin argues, are chronic and burdensome and as a consequence take a cumulative toll on the well-being of African Americans. His study challenges the assumption that black members of the middle-class are largely free of the prejudicial and discriminatory practices inherent in behaviors governed by Jim Crow laws.

In a similar vein, "audit" studies reveal discriminatory behaviors on the part of employers. Such studies employ a quasi-experimental technique, which allows control of potentially confounding factors, in the field of employment or housing. Researchers select, match, and carefully train at least two people, who, as in the student study introducing this section, are similar in all important respects but differ in their race or ethnicity, and send them to apply for certain types of jobs or to rent an apartment. These "testers," or confederates, are equally qualified and act the same in their interactions with potential employers or landlords. Researchers then observe whether the "job applicant" was called back for an interview or offered the job or whether the "renter" was offered the apartment. A variant on the audit study is the submission of two résumés to potential employers that are identical but signal different races of applicants (for example, by varying the name of the candidate: James versus Jamal). Racial differences in callbacks, hires, or the like signal the extent of discrimination.

Pager, Western, and Bonikowski (2009) employed such a method to challenge the assumption that racial discrimination, a contributing factor in racial inequality, is a thing of the past because of racial progress in the past 20 years. The researchers focused on entry-level jobs in the low-wage labor market in New York City (e.g., restaurant worker, telemarketer, warehouse worker, movers, retail salesperson, and clerical worker). Their testers, working in two teams, each including a white, a black, and a Latino, were matched in terms of physicality, interaction styles, and physical attractiveness. Their résumés reflected the same level of educational achievement, work experience, and neighborhood residence. (One team also responded affirmatively to a typical employment question: Have you ever been convicted of a crime?) A positive response entailed getting a call back or a job offer. Such positive responses occurred 31% of the time for white applicants, 25.1% for Latino applicants, and 15.3% for black applicants. Even white applicants with a criminal record had a higher percentage of positive responses (17.2%) than black applicants with no record.

To get at processes underlying hiring decisions, the testers also wrote detailed narratives of their interactions with employers, which were used for content analysis. The confederates' accounts suggested no outward signs of strong negative feelings toward minority candidates. Nonetheless, many reports indicated forms of categorical exclusion (e.g., the employer taking aside the white and Latino candidates and explicitly saying that she did not want to talk to the equally qualified black candidate), shifting standards (e.g., ignoring the lack of experience for a particular job for white and Latino applicants but highlighting the same deficiency as a means of denying a job to a black applicant), or channeling applicants into particular jobs based on their race (e.g., hiring the white for a restaurant server position and the black as a dishwasher). These patterns represent subtle forms of employment discrimination in the absence of overt hostility.

While there are clearly methodological means of revealing acts of discrimination, sociological studies rarely also address the underlying social psychological mechanisms that propel the patterns of discrimination (Quillian 2006). For example, in the audit studies, researchers have no information on how employers process information about candidates' educational background, job skills, and employment experiences as well as racial categories. What stereotypes are employers invoking? How accurate are those stereotypes? Is outgroup homogeneity at work? Psychological work, however, attempts to relate prejudice, explicit or implicit, to discrimination to help determine the cognitive and social conditions under which the prejudice or discrimination link may be disrupted. Strategies for undermining the negative effects of prejudice and discrimination consider cognitive and affective processes as well as behavioral dynamics between members of different groups. Such strategies serve to ameliorate the ill effects of prejudice and discrimination for individual targets and the social inequality between groups.

How Can Negative Intergroup Behavior Be Ameliorated?

For the Sneetches to realize that "Sneetches are Sneetches and no kind of Sneetch is best on the beaches," the "Fix-It-Up Chappie" had to arrive on the scene. The Fix-It-Up Chappie made a small fortune removing and putting on stars, depleting the financial resources of both the Star-Belly and Plain-Belly Sneetches. In effect, the Fix-It-Up Chappie posed an external threat to the well-being of *all* of the Sneetches. He did not solve their problems but rather created a problem that by working together those with and without stars needed to overcome. Sherif et al. (1961) in resolving the hostilities between the Eagles and Rattlers likewise turned to an emphasis on the cooperative pursuit by members of both groups of a shared, overarching goal. Sherif's strategy resonates with the basic tenet of **intergroup contact theory,** originated by Allport (1954; see also classic work by Williams 1947 and a recent summary, Pettigrew and Tropp 2011), that under certain conditions, contact between different groups becomes a means by which to reduce tensions produced by prejudice and discrimination. Next, we first identify those conditions and then turn to consideration of cognitive and affective mechanisms that help to account for why intergroup contact "works" to undermine prejudice.

Contact Conditions

At the beginning of a school year, black children huddle together on the playground, shooting hoops or playing four square while their white classmates pursue kickball and tag. The separation continues in the cafeteria, where each dines with other members of each respective ingroup. The classroom, however, is a different matter. The teacher seats students alphabetically to ensure that they get to know students other than their closest friends. He assigns them randomly to work in small groups on social studies projects about the customs in different countries around the world. The principal also encourages each class to develop a way to improve the school, whether by planting a garden or putting together a skit or musical performance for others to enjoy. These school officials, as agents of the institution, are setting norms for how individuals who identify with different groups should act when they are together. Their behavior essentially sets up the first condition under which positive contact between members of different groups reduces prejudice and discrimination: *signaling the value of positive intergroup contact* (Allport 1954). (In this case, having support from superiors in the school for the value of positive intergroup contact is a form of legitimation [Chapter 10].)

Allport (1954) also specifically identifies three other conditions. Second, *the contact must be between groups holding equal status within a specific situation.* In the classroom, the children of each racial group have that sort of equality (even if, in the larger society, the groups vary in status levels). Such equal status may take the form of opportunities to participate in activities, access resources, or make decisions. Third, *members of the two groups should share common goals*, like completing a social studies project or a campus improvement effort. The fourth condition complements the third: *Members of each group must work cooperatively—in a friendly and sincere fashion—to achieve the shared goals.* Sherif et al. (1961) set up these four conditions to reduce the negative interaction between the Rattlers and the Eagles. Specifically, the two camp groups worked together to fix their water supply and to help start a truck.

The combination of these four conditions reduces hostilities and perhaps fosters friendships across a wide variety of situations, in the classroom, at camp, or in work organizations. Hundreds of studies have tested the "contact hypothesis," as it has become known. Analysis across 515 studies (Pettigrew and Tropp 2006) leaves no doubt that intergroup contact reduces intergroup prejudice, especially when Allport's conditions are all met.

While the quantity of contact is important, perhaps more so is the quality of the contact. The development of cross-group friendships shifts emphasis from simply the number of cross-group contacts to the affective quality of the contact. Pettigrew (1997) shows that the affective ties associated with friendships facilitate intergroup liking and identification with outgroup members. Less intimate contact, such as that between coworkers or neighbors, has a weaker impact than friendships. Field (e.g., Aron and McLaughlin-Volpe 2001) and experimental (e.g., Wright, Aron, and Tropp 2002) studies confirm that intergroup contact is most effective in reducing prejudice when it stimulates cross-group friendships. The teacher's strategies for increasing mixed-race ties in the previously given example may foster such friendships.

Pettigrew's reasons for why cross-group friendships may more forcefully attenuate prejudices emphasize affective components. How do such affective processes unfold? And how does cognitive processing of situations of contact also contribute to prejudice reduction?

Cognitive and Affective Mechanisms

Cognitive categorization processes, as the first part of this chapter indicates, play a fundamental role in intergroup dynamics. Accordingly, it is hardly surprising that they may also help explain why intergroup contact is an effective means of reducing prejudice. People rely upon the stereotypical images they possess of their own group and of outgroups. Thus, when positive intergroup contact occurs, it is important that the outgroup member be perceived as a "typical" representative of a larger group (see Brown and Hewstone 2005). By perceiving the typicality of the outgroup member, people are more likely to generalize to other outgroup members and thereby undermine a particular stereotype. For example, the white student who works with a black classmate and sees that person as smart and industrious is more likely to believe such positive characteristics of other blacks if she judges the classmate as typical. (In contrast, seeing the classmate as an "exception" works against changing the stereotype.)

Beyond seeing the outgroup member as typical, three types of categorization may unfold (see Dovidio and Gaertner 2010). First, categories could be de-emphasized (e.g., all Sneetches are Sneetches, regardless of the appearance of their bellies). Second, greater emphasis could be placed on categories (e.g., subgroup identification as white or black could be stressed). And, third, members of different groups could promote a superordinate category (e.g., people are people, not blacks or whites). In different ways, all of these types of categorization act as mechanisms for the positive impact of intergroup contact.

Because of fears that emphasis on group differences may exacerbate tensions and hostilities, Miller (2002) suggests people should decategorize individuals, by emphasizing variability within an outgroup and personalizing their members through attention to individual characteristics and other personally relevant information. Decategorization, presumably, will lead to less emphasis on group membership as the sole basis for response. In the absence of subgroup emphasis, tension and potential conflict may abate.

In contrast, Brown and Hewstone (2005) argue that positive contact with outgroup members ameliorates prejudice when that contact is between groups that recognize their differences. The goal of such intergroup contact is to produce positive feelings about outgroup members with whom they interact in the hope that those feelings then generalize to members who have not participated in the interaction. For example, white children who get along well with their black classmates while working on a social studies project may find themselves taking opportunities to join in the four-square games on the playground with other black children.

Development of a superordinate category allows the formation of more positive attitudes toward members previously defined as the outgroup (Gaertner and Dovidio 2000). For example, one way schools have often brought students of different backgrounds together is through the development of "school spirit" or pep rallies to promote a football or other school team. Doing so is a means to say, for example, "We are all Panthers from Dillion High School." Whites, blacks, Asians, and all other minority groups cheer alongside each other at the games. Issues of agreeing to the defining characteristics of the superordinate category and, perhaps more important, of worry that the lower status group is simply being incorporated into the higher status group (Hornsey and Hogg 2000) challenge the appropriateness of this strategy, however. Success in creating such an overarching identity may emerge over time, as individuals come to recognize their commonalities despite their differences.

In intergroup situations, individuals may fear being rejected or treated differently (Frey and Tropp 2006). People also subjectively experience the situation that brings them into contact with outgroup members and often want to maintain their unique group identities. Taking these concerns into account, categorization processes underlying successful intergroup contact may unfold sequentially. For example, Pettigrew (1998) proposes that in the initial stages of equal status, cooperative contact, diminished salience of group membership (i.e., decategorization) might reduce tensions so that individuals get to know each other. Then once relationships are established across group lines, enhanced emphasis on group membership might reemerge as a means by which to generalize positive feelings to other group members. Additionally, individuals typically want their identity as a member of a racial minority group to be respected prior to also claiming identity in a superordinate group (Huo and Molina 2006). Maintaining dual identities, both superordinate (e.g., national) and subgroup (e.g., racial or ethnic group), is a means of balancing competing demands. Superordinate categories or identities might be useful under particular conditions, for example, mobilizing social change or thwarting an external threat.

In addition to cognitive categorization processes, affective processes provide a link between actual intergroup encounters and decreases in prejudice. As already noted, cross-group friendships involving liking between parties attenuate prejudices. Liking emerges through both repeated equal status contact across a range of situations (e.g., between classmates in a course, on a team, at the local mall) and through the process of self-disclosure (Pettigrew 1998).

Self-disclosure (Derlega et al. 1993) involves revealing facts about oneself, typically beginning with superficial information (e.g., weather preferences, hometown, favorite TV programs) and progressing to more intimate details (e.g., deep-seated attitudes, aspirations, family problems) as the relationship unfolds and trust begins to build. Important especially in early stages of relationships is the reciprocity of self-disclosure among partners (Won-Doornink and Jin 1979). Imagine two students, South Asian Ashok and Latino Carlos, on the first day of class in a school new to both of them. During recess, they begin to share details about themselves. If they both provide similar details about their families (e.g., previous school, number of siblings) and interests (e.g., sports, video games), then a friendship is likely to develop that would involve revelation of more intimate details. In contrast, if only Carlos is forthcoming with such information and Ashok remains relatively silent or if Ashok begins by explaining that his father murdered his mother and now he lives with an aunt whose house is in this school district, the relationship may not unfold. Ashok is violating the rule of reciprocity by not providing similar information and by delving into intimate details too soon in the relationship. Such reciprocal self-disclosure, along with perceived partner responsiveness, contributes to greater relationship intimacy and helps to build interracial friendships (Shelton et al. 2010).

The responsiveness that cross-group friends show to each other has at least two effects. First, it signals, on the affective level, an increase in empathy, which involves the cognitive process of perspective-taking, which tends to reduce prejudice (e.g., Turner, Hewstone, and Voci 2007). Second, it may facilitate the emergence of more positive attributions for the behaviors of outgroup members because the individuals are no longer seen as "other" but as friends and thus more like oneself than different (see Wright et al. 2002).

Certain circumstances and emotions, however, may thwart cross-group friendships. Especially problematic are circumstances that involve social segregation, which limits the opportunities for members of different groups to get to know one another (Wagner et al. 2006). When circumstances allow for cross-group relationships, an additional problem, noted previously, is the emergence of uncertainty and anxiety about encounters with others belonging to a group different from one's own (Stephan and Stephan 1985). As Tropp and Molina (2012:559) suggest, "particularly during initial stages of contact, people are likely to experience anxiety regarding how they might be perceived or received by outgroup members, and this anxiety could lead to avoidance of or awkwardness during cross-group interactions." Anxiety over such interactions creates stress, which most people want to avoid. Prior positive intergroup contact and accumulating a number of cross-group friendships tends to reduce feelings of anxiety and prejudice (e.g., Paolini et al. 2004; see also Pettigrew and Tropp 2008).

Ameliorating negative intergroup behavior—reducing prejudice and potentially the discrimination that follows from it—requires contact of the sort described by Sherif, Pettigrew, and others: equal status cooperative contact to achieve mutually desirable goals. Whether such interactional conditions succeed, however, depends upon individuals' perceptions of their own and others' group identities as well as affective mediating processes, such as the development of empathy and the thwarting of anxiety. To the extent that these strategies involve self-involvement with outgroup members and connect the outgroup with positivity, implicit biases are also reduced (Lai et al. 2014). Despite the expansive research on intergroup processes, actual reduction in prejudices depends upon sociohistorical circumstances. Such circumstances shape the identities, perceptions, emotions, and evaluations of members of groups, distinguished in terms of power and status, who have different assessments of the inequalities that they face.

Conclusion: Intergroup Processes and Addressing Social Inequalities

This chapter opened with a look at the dynamics among Sneetches, those with stars on their bellies and those without. The Dr. Seuss tale, while illustrative of elements of intergroup dynamics—categorization processes, stereotypes, ingroup favoritism and outgroup derogation, emotions, behavioral discrimination, development of a superordinate identity—is also simplified. In most societies, many groups vie for resources and/or for social affirmation. And the permeability between the boundaries of coexisting groups may vary, depending on the historical, social, economic, and political contexts in which they are embedded. Despite claims to a particular social identity, within each identifiable group, individuals' identities, perceptions, attitudes, and affective experiences infuse meaning into situations and shape behaviors. Structural differences in status and power, both within and between groups, further impact unfolding interaction. Evaluations of the legitimacy or justice of particular social arrangements, whether within family or work groups or between ethnic or social class factions in a nation-state, potentially reinforce or ameliorate inequalities characterizing those social units.

As we noted in Chapter 1, social psychological processes detail the ways in which people construct their realities and ways of doing things in everyday interaction. We have reviewed theories and research relevant to helping readers of this book to understand their own social interactions and those that they observe. We have also stressed that the microlevel dynamics of individuals contribute to the larger social arrangements of groups in society. We illustrated this in our initial example of young Spelman women in the early 1960s whose new identities, perceptions, and actions, in small but significant ways, facilitated the success of the civil rights movement, designed to address inequalities facing the United States at that moment in history.

In the 50-plus years since that landmark legislation, racial dynamics in this country have changed. From a social psychological viewpoint, the different forms of prejudice described in this chapter reflect elements of those changes. The prominent shift from a focus on explicit bias to implicit bias also corresponds to developments in social psychology that increase understanding of the underpinnings and evolution of dynamics among individuals in groups. Examples of such developments, noted in various chapters, include greater emphasis on automatic processing, recognition that perceivers are motivated actors, the anchoring of cultural beliefs about status in resource distributions, the process by which status characteristics impact influence, the mechanisms by which benefits accrue to the power-advantaged from social exchanges, and the potential for differences in evaluations of fairness and the legitimacy of unequal arrangements that may stymie concerted action to rectify injustice. Consider how you can use what you have learned about social psychological processes in analyzing current tensions arising from recent high-profile incidents in which unarmed black citizens have been killed by (largely white) police officers.[2] The shooting death of Michael Brown in Ferguson, Missouri, in 2014 touched off a national protest against police brutality and the Black Lives Matter movement. In the summer of 2016, people in Dallas took to the streets in a planned event to protest police action in the early July shooting deaths of Alton Sterling (Baton Rouge, Louisiana) and Philando Castile (St. Paul, Minnesota). Micah Xavier Johnson disrupted the expected orderly march when he targeted the police present to protect the protestors, killing five officers and injuring nine others (plus two civilians).

In response to this horrific event, President Barack Obama crafted a speech (presented at the memorial for the fallen officers) identifying the differences among Americans, especially in terms of inequality and how those differences engender bias and fear. He stated that "the deepest fault lines of our democracy have suddenly been exposed, perhaps even widened. . . . Faced with this violence, we wonder if the divides of race in America can ever be bridged. We wonder if an African American community that feels unfairly targeted by police and police departments that feel unfairly maligned for doing their jobs, can ever understand each other's experience." He noted how biases on each side inhibit the building of bridges, for example: "When anyone, no matter how good their intentions may be, paints all police as biased, or bigoted, we undermine those officers that we depend on for our safety." He also said, "We also know that centuries of racial discrimination, of slavery, and subjugation, and Jim Crow; they didn't simply vanish with the law against segregation."

But President Obama also stressed how working together holds the promise of creating those bridges. Even as the attack was unfolding, one witness noted how "everyone was helping each other," regardless of race. And, Dallas mayor Rawlings and Police Chief Brown, "a white man and a black man with different backgrounds" worked "not just to restore order and support a shaken city, a shaken department, but . . . to unify a city with strength and grace and wisdom." He applauded "what's possible when we recognize that we are one American family, all deserving of equal treatment. All deserving equal respect." He concluded by imploring people to recognize that within the context of democracy that we have "space to work through our differences and debate them peacefully, to make things better," ensuring the capacity to change.

It is unlikely that President Obama intended his speech as a primer on social psychological explanations of how intergroup dynamics forge and reinforce social inequalities and what is necessary to change them. Nonetheless, his speech illustrates what we argued in the opening of this book: that the processes described in social psychology are interrelated; what individuals think, feel, and do depends upon the social context; and that those thoughts, feelings, and emotions contribute to understanding more macrophenomena like social inequality. While social psychologists use their many methods to examine specific processes, each of which may address only a slice of reality, together the theories and patterns of findings provide a basis for a more thorough understanding of our social world.

Endnotes

1. Because this terminology grew from a more psychological approach, it does not map directly on to notions of the self that are anchored in symbolic interaction (see Chapters 3 and 4). Mead (1934), of course, contends the self is social, but he does not confine it to mean categorization as a member of a group.

2. Here are two examples: in 2015, Freddie Gray (Baltimore, Maryland) and Walter Scott (North Charleston, South Carolina).

Suggested Readings

Albarello, Flavia and Monica Rubini. 2012. "Reducing Dehumanisation Outcomes towards Blacks: The Role of Multiple Categorisation and of Human Identity." *European Journal of Social Psychology* 42:875–82.

Burke, Sara E., John Dovidio, Sylvia P. Perry, Diana J. Burgess, Rachel R. Hardeman, Sean M. Phelan, Brooke A. Cunningham, Mark W. Yeazel, Julia M. Przedworski, and Michelle van Ryn. 2017. "Informal Training Experiences and Explicit Bias against African Americans among Medical Students." *Social Psychology Quarterly* 80:1–20.

Cavacho, H., A. Zick, A. Haye, R. Gonzá, J. Manzi, C. Kocik, and M. Bertl. 2013. "On the Relation between Social Class and Prejudice: The Roles of Education, Income, and Ideological Attitudes." *European Journal of Social Psychology* 43:272–85.

Herman, Melissa R. 2010. "Do You See What I Am? How Observers' Backgrounds Affect Their Perceptions of Multiracial Faces." *Social Psychology Quarterly* 73:58–78.

Kanas, Agnieszka, Peer Scheepers, and Carl Sterkens. 2015. "Interreligious Contact, Perceived Group Threat, and Perceived Discrimination: Predicting Negative Attitudes among Religious Minorities and Majorities in Indonesia." *Social Psychology Quarterly* 78:102–26.

Park, Jerry Z., Brandon C. Martinez, Ryon Cobb, Julie J. Park, and Erica Ryu Wong. 2015. "Exceptional Outgroup Stereotypes and White Racial Inequality Attitudes toward Asian Americans." *Social Psychology Quarterly* 78:399–411.

Stark, Tobias H. 2015. "Understanding the Selection Bias: Social Networks and the Effects of Prejudice on the Avoidance of Outgroup Friends." *Social Psychology Quarterly* 78:127–50

References

Abrams, Dominic, and Michael A. Hogg. 2010. "Social Identity and Self-Categorization." Pp. 179–93 in *The SAGE Handbook of Prejudice, Stereotyping and Discrimination*, edited by J. F. Dovidio, M. Hewstone, P. Glick, and V. Essess. Newbury Park, CA: Sage. doi:10.4135/9781446200919.n11

Adorno, Theodor W., Else Frenkel-Brunswik, Daniel J. Levinson, and R. Nevitt Sanford. 1950. *The Authoritarian Personality.* New York: Harper.

Allport, Gordon W. 1954. *The Nature of Prejudice.* Cambridge, MA: Perseus Books.

Altemeyer, Bob. 1988. *Enemies of Freedom: Understanding Right-Wing Authoritarianism.* San Francisco, CA: Jossey-Bass.

Altemeyer, Bob, and Bruce Hunsberger. 1992. "Authoritarianism, Religious Fundamentalism, Quest, and Prejudice." *The International Journal* for the *Psychology of Religion* 2(2):113–33. doi:10.1207/s15327582ijpr0202_5

Aron, Arthur, and McLaughlin-Volpe, Tracy. 2001. "Including Others in the Self: Extensions to Own and Partner's Group Memberships." Pp. 89–108 in *Individual Self, Relational Self, Collective Self*, edited by C. Sedikides and M. Brewer. New York: Psychology Press.

Blau, Francine D., and Lawrence M. Kahn. 2007. "The Gender Pay Gap: Have Women Gone as Far as They Can?" *The Academy of Management Perspectives* 21(1):7–23. doi:10.5465/AMP.2007.24286161

Blumer, Herbert. 1958. "Race Prejudice as a Sense of Group Position." *Pacific Sociological Review* 1(1):3–7. doi:10.2307/1388607

Bobo, Lawrence D. 1983. "Whites' Opposition to Busing: Symbolic Racism or Realistic Group Conflict?" *Journal of Personality and Social Psychology* 45:1196–210. doi:10.1037/0022-3514.45.6.1196

Bobo, Lawrence D. 1999. "Prejudice as Group Position: Micro-foundations of a Sociological Approach to Racism and Race Relations." *The Journal of Social Issues* 55:445–72. doi:10.1111/0022-4537.00127

Bobo, Lawrence D., Camille Z. Charles, Maria Krysan, and A. D. Simmons. 2012. "The Real Record on Racial Attitudes." Pp. 38–83 in *Social Trends in the United States: Evidence from the General Social Survey since 1972*, edited by P. V. Marsden. Princeton, NJ: Princeton University Press.

Brewer, Marilyn B. 2001. "Ingroup Identification and Intergroup Conflict: When Does Ingroup Love Become Outgroup Hate?" Pp. 17–41 in *Social Identity, Intergroup Conflict, and Conflict Reduction*, edited by R. D. Ashmore, L. Jussim, and D. Wilder. New York: Oxford University Press.

Brown, Rupert J. 2000. "Social Identity Theory: Past Achievements, Current Problems, and Future Challenges." *European Journal of Social Psychology* 30:745–78. doi:10.1002/1099-0992(200011/12)30:6‹745::AID-EJSP24›3.0.CO;2-0

Brown, Rupert, and Miles Hewstone. 2005. "An Integrative Theory of Intergroup Contact." *Advances in Experimental Social Psychology* 37:255–343. doi:10.1016/S0065-2601(05)37005-5

Correll, J., and Bernadette Park. 2005. "A Model of the Ingroup as a Social Resource." *Personality and Social Psychology Review* 9:341–59. doi:10.1207/s15327957pspr0904_4

De Houwer, Jan, Tom Beckers, and Agnes Moors. 2007. "Novel Attitudes Can Be Faked on the Implicit Association Test." *Journal of Experimental Social Psychology* 43(6):972–78. doi:10.1016/j.jesp.2006.10.007

Derlega, Valerian J., Sandra Metts, Sandra Pertonio, and Stephen T. Margulis. 1993. *Self Disclosure*. Newbury Park, CA: Sage.

Doosje, B., Nyla R. Branscombe, and Russell Spears. 2006. "Antecedents and Consequences of Group-Based Guilt: The Effects of Ingroup Identification." *Group Processes & Intergroup Relations* 9(3):325–38. doi:10.1177/1368430206064637

Dovidio, John F. 2013. "Bridging Intragroup Processes and Intergroup Relations: Needing the Twain to Meet." *British Journal of Social Psychology* 52(1):1–24. doi:10.1111/bjso.12026

Dovidio, John F., and Samuel L. Gaertner. 2000. "Aversive Racism and Selection Decisions: 1989 and 1999." *Psychological Science* 11(4):315–19. doi:10.1111/1467-9280.00262

Dovidio, John F., and Samuel L. Gaertner. 2004. "Aversive Racism." *Advances in Experimental Social Psychology* 36:1–52. doi:10.1016/S0065-2601(04)36001-6

Dovidio, John F., and Samuel L. Gaertner. 2010. "Intergroup Bias. *Pp. 1084–1121 in Handbook of Social Psychology*, Vol. 2, edited by S. T. Fiske, D. T. Gilbert, and G. Lindzey. Hoboken, NJ: Wiley. doi:10.1002/9780470561119.socpsy002029

Dovidio, John F., Kerry Kawakami, and Samuel L. Gaertner. 2002. "Implicit and Explicit

Prejudice and Interracial Interaction." *Journal of Personality and Social Psychology* 82(1):62–8. doi:10.1037/0022–3514.82.1.62

Drury, John, and Steve Reicher. 2005. "Explaining Enduring Empowerment: A Comparative Study of Collective Action and Psychological Outcomes." *European Journal of Social Psychology* 35(1):35–58. doi:10.1002/ejsp.231

Ellemers, Naomi. 1993. "Influence of Socio-structural Variables on Identity Enhancement Strategies." *European Review of Social Psychology* 4:27–57. doi:10.1080/14792779343000013

Ellemers, Naomi, Russell Spears, and Bertjan Doosje. 2002. "Self and Social Identity." *Annual Review of Psychology* 53:161–86. doi:10.1146/annurev.psych.53.100901.135228

Fazio, Russell H., Joni R. Jackson, Bridget C. Dunton, and Carol J. Williams. 1995. "Variability in Automatic Activation as an Unobtrusive Measure of Racial Attitudes: A Bona Fide Pipeline?" *Journal of Personality and Social Psychology* 69:1013–27. doi:10.1037/0022–3514.69.6.1013

Feagin, Joe R. 1991. "The Continuing Significance of Race: Antiblack Discrimination in Public Places." *American Sociological Review* 56:101–116. doi:10.2307/2095676

Feagin, Joe R., and M. P. Sikes. 1994. *Living with Racism: The Black Middle Class Experience.* Boston: Beacon.

Fiedler, Klaus. 2010. "The Asymmetry of Causal and Diagnostic Inferences: A Challenge for the Study of Implicit Attitudes." Pp. 75–92 in *The Psychology of Attitudes and Attitude Change,* edited by J. P. Forgas, J. Cooper, and W. D. Crano. New York: Psychology Press.

Forman, Tyrone A. 2004. "Color-blind Racism and Racial Indifference: The Role of Racial Apathy in Facilitating Enduring Inequalities." Pp. 43–66 in *The Changing Terrain of Race and Ethnicity,* edited by M. Krysan and A. Lewis. New York: Russell Sage.

Forman, Tyrone A., and Amanda E. Lewis. 2006. "Racial Apathy and Hurricane Katrina:

The Social Anatomy of Prejudice in the Post-Civil Rights Era." *Du Bois Review* 3(1):175–202. doi:10.1017/S1742058X06060127

Frey, Frances E., and Linda R. Tropp. 2006. "Being Seen as Individuals versus as Group Members: Extending Research on Metaperception to Intergroup Contexts." *Personality and Social Psychology Review* 10(3):265–80. doi:10.1207/s15327957pspr1003_5

Gaertner, Samuel L., and John F. Dovidio. 2000. *Reducing Intergroup Bias: The Common Ingroup Identity Model.* Ann Arbor, MI: Taylor & Francis.

Geisel, Theodor Seuss. [1961] 1989. *The Sneetches and Other Stories.* New York: Random House Children's Books.

Greenwald, Anthony G., and Mahzarin R. Banaji. 1995. "Implicit Social Cognition: Attitudes, Self-Esteem, and Stereotypes." *Psychological Review* 102(1):4–27. doi:10.1037/0033–295X.102.1.4

Greenwald, Anthony G., and Linda Hamilton Krieger. 2006. "Implicit Bias: Scientific Foundations." *California Law Review* 94(4):945–68. doi:10.2307/20439056

Greenwald, Anthony G., Debbie E. McGhee, and Jordan L. K. Schwartz. 1998. "Measuring Individual Differences in Implicit Cognition: The Implicit Association Test." *Journal of Personality and Social Psychology* 74(6):1464. doi:10.1037/0022–3514.74.6.1464

Greenwald, Anthony G., T. Andrew Poehlman, Eric Luis Uhlmann, and Mahzarin R. Banaji. 2009. "Understanding and Using the Implicit Association Test: III. Meta-Analysis of Predictive Validity." *Journal of Personality and Social Psychology* 97(1):17. doi:10.1037/a0015575

Haslam, Alex, Penny Oakes, John Turner, and Craig McGarty. 1996. "Social Identity, Self-categorization, and the Perceived Homogeneity of Ingroups and Outgroups: The Interaction between Social Motivation and Cognition." Pp. 182–222 in *Handbook of Motivation and Cognition: The Interpersonal Context,* Vol. 3, edited by R. Sorrentino and E. Higgins. New York: Guilford Press.

Heider, Jeremy D., and John J. Skowronski. 2007. "Improving the Predictive Validity of the Implicit Association Test." *North American Journal of Psychology* 9(1):53–76.

Henry, Patrick J., and David O. Sears. 2002. "The Symbolic Racism 2000 Scale." *Political Psychology* 23(2):253–83. doi:10.1111/0162–895X .00281

Hewstone, Miles, Mark Rubin, and Hazel Willis. 2002. "Intergroup Bias." *Annual Review of Psychology* 53(1):575–604. doi:10.1146/annurev. psych.53.100901.135109

Hogg, Michael A. 2007. "Uncertainty-identity Theory." *Advances in Experimental Social Psychology* 39:69–126. doi:10.1016/S0065– 2601(06)39002–8

Hogg, Michael A., and Dominic Abrams. 1988. *Social Identifications*. New York: Routledge.

Hogg, Michael A., and Dominic Abrams. 2003. "Intergroup Behavior and Social Identity." Pp. 407–31 in *The SAGE Handbook of Social Psychology*, edited by M. A. Hogg and J. Cooper. Thousand Oaks, CA: Sage.

Hornsey, Matthew J., and Michael A. Hogg. 2000. "Subgroup Relations: A Comparison of Mutual Intergroup Models of Prejudice Reduction." *Personality and Social Psychology Bulletin* 26:242–56. doi:10.1177/0146167200264010

Hunt, Matthew O. 2007. "African-American, Hispanic, and White Beliefs about Black/White Inequality, 1977–2004." *American Sociological Review* 72:390–415. doi:10.1177/00031224070720 0304

Huo, Yuen J., and Ludwin E. Molina. 2006. "Is Pluralism a Viable Model of Diversity? The Benefits and Limits of Subgroup Respect." *Group Processes & Intergroup Relations* 9(3):359– 76. doi:10.1177/1368430206064639

Judd, Charles M., and Bernadette Park. 1988. "Out-Group Homogeneity: Judgments of Variability at the Individual and Group Levels." *Journal of Personality and Social Psychology* 54(5):778. doi:10.1037/0022–3514.54.5.778

Jussim, Lee, Thomas R. Cain, Jarret T. Crawford, Kent Harber, and Florette Cohen. 2009. "The Unbearable Accuracy of Stereotypes." Pp. 199–228 in *Handbook of Prejudice, Stereotyping, and Discrimination*, edited by Todd D. Nelson. New York: Psychology Press.

Kinder, Donald R., and Lynn M. Sanders. 1996. *Divided by Color: Racial Politics and Democratic Ideals*. Chicago: University of Chicago Press.

Kuppens, Toon, Vincent Y. Yzerbyt, Sophie Dandache, Agneta H. Fisher, and Job van der Schalk. 2013. "Social Identity Salience Shapes Group-based Emotions through Group-based Appraisals." *Cognition and Emotion* 27:1359–77. doi:10.1080/02699931.2013.785387

Lai, Calvin K., Maddalena Marini, Steven A. Lehr, Carlo Cerruti, Jiyun-Elizabeth L. Shin, Jennifer A. Joy-Gaba, Arnold K. Ho, Bethany A. Teachman, Sean P. Wojcik, Spassena P. Koleva, Rebecca S. Frazier, Larisa Heiphetz, Eva E. Chen, Rhiannon N. Turner, Jonathan Haidt, Selin Kesibir, Carlee Beth Hawkins, Hillary S. Schaefer, Sandro Rubichi, Giuseppe Sartori, Christopher M. Dial, N. Sriram, Mahzarin R. Banaji, and Brian A. Nosek. 2014. "Reducing Implicit Racial Preferences: A Comparative Investigation of 17 Interventions." *Journal of Experimental Psychology* 143(4):1765– 85. doi:10.1037/a0036260

Maass, Anne, Daniela Salvi, Luciano Arcuri, and Gün R. Semin. 1989. "Language Use in Intergroup Contexts: The Linguistic Intergroup Bias." *Journal of Personality and Social Psychology* 57(6):981. doi:10.1037/0022–3514.57.6.981

Mackie, Diane M., Thierry Devos, and Eliot R. Smith. 2000. "Intergroup Emotions: Explaining Offensive Action Tendencies in an Intergroup Context." *Journal of Personality and Social Psychology* 79(4):602 . doi:10.1037/0022–3514.79.4.602

Mackie, Diane M., Angela T. Maitner, and Eliot R. Smith. 2009. "Intergroup Emotions Theory." Pp. 285–307 in *Handbook of Prejudice, Stereotyping, and Discrimination*, edited by T. D. Nelson. Mahwah, NJ: Erlbaum.

Martens, Andy, Michael Johns, Jeff Greenberg, and Jeff Schimel. 2006. "Combating Stereotype

Threat: The Effect of Self-Affirmation on Women's Intellectual Performance." *Journal of Experimental Social Psychology* 42(2):236–43. doi:10.1016/j.jesp.2005.04.010

McConahay, John B. 1982. "Self-Interest versus Racial Attitudes as Correlates of Anti-Busing Attitudes in Louisville: Is It the Buses or the Blacks?" *The Journal of Politics* 44(3):692–720. doi:10.2307/2130514

Mead, George H. 1934. *Mind, Self, and Society: From the Standpoint of a Social Behaviorist*, edited by C. W. Morris. Chicago: University of Chicago Press.

Michel, Caroline, Olivier Corneille, and Bruno Rossion. 2007. "Race Categorization Modulates Holistic Face Encoding." *Cognitive Science* 31:911–24. doi:10.1080/03640210701530805

Miller, Norman. 2002. "Personalization and the Promise of Contact Theory." *The Journal of Social Issues* 58:387–410. doi:10.1111/1540-4560.00267

Nosek, Brian A., Mahzarin Banaji, and Anthony G. Greenwald. 2002. "Harvesting Implicit Group Attitudes and Beliefs from a Demonstration Web Site." *Group Dynamics* 6(1):101. doi:10.1037/1089-2699.6.1.101

Nosek, Brian A., Anthony G. Greenwald, and Mahzarin R. Banaji. 2007. "The Implicit Association Test at Age 7: A Methodological and Conceptual Review." Pp. 265–92 in *Automatic Processes in Social Thinking and Behavior*, edited by J. A. Bargh. New York: Psychology Press.

Olson, Michael A. 2009. "Measures of Prejudice." Pp. 367–86 in *Handbook of Prejudice, Stereotyping, and Discrimination*, edited by T. D. Nelson. New York: Psychology Press.

Otten, Sabine, and Dirk Wentura. 1999. "About the Impact of Automaticity in the Minimal Group Paradigm: Evidence from Affective Priming Tasks." *European Journal of Social Psychology* 29(8):1049–71. doi:10.1002/(SICI)1099-0992(199912)29:8<1049::AID-EJSP985>3.0.CO;2-Q

Pager, Devah, and Hana Shepherd. 2008. "The Sociology of Discrimination: Racial Discrimination in Employment, Housing, Credit, and Consumer Markets." *Annual Review of Sociology* 34:181–209. doi:10.1146/annurev. soc.33.040406.131740

Pager, Devah, Bruce Western, and Bart Bonikowski. 2009. "Discrimination in a Low-Wage Labor Market: A Field Experiment." *American Sociological Review* 74:777–99. doi:10.1177/000312240907400505

Paladino, Maria P., and Luigi Castelli. 2008. "On the Immediate Consequences of Intergroup Categorization: Activation of Approach and Avoidance Motor Behavior toward Ingroup and Outgroup Members." *Personality and Social Psychology Bulletin* 34:755–68. doi:10.1177/0146 167208315155

Paolini, Stefania, Miles Hewstone, Ed Cairns, and Alberto Voci. 2004. "Effects of Direct and Indirect Cross-group Friendships on Judgments of Catholics and Protestants in Northern Ireland: The Mediating Role of an Anxiety-reduction Mechanism." *Personality and Social Psychology Bulletin* 30:770–86. doi:10.1177/0146167203262848

Park, Bernadette, and Myron Rothbart. 1982. "Perception of Out-Group Homogeneity and Levels of Social Categorization: Memory for the Subordinate Attributes of In-Group and Out-Group Members." *Journal of Personality and Social Psychology* 42(6):1051. doi:10.1037/0022-3514.42.6.1051

Perez-Felkner, Lisa. 2013. "Socialization in Childhood and Adolescence." Pp. 119–49 in *Handbook of Social Psychology*, edited by J. DeLamater and A. Ward. New York: Springer. doi:10.1007/978-94-007-6772-0_5

Pettigrew, Thomas F. 1997. "Generalized Intergroup Contact Effects on Prejudice." *Personality and Social Psychology Bulletin* 23:173–85. doi:10.1177/0146167297232006

Pettigrew, Thomas F. 1998. "Intergroup Contact Theory." *Annual Review of Psychology* 49:65–85. doi:10.1146/annurev.psych.49.1.65

Pettigrew, Thomas F., and Linda R. Tropp. 2006. "A Meta-analytic Test of Intergroup Contact Theory." *Journal of Personality and*

Social Psychology 90:751–83. doi:10.1037/0022–3514.90.5.751

Pettigrew, Thomas F., and Linda R. Tropp. 2008. "How Does Intergroup Contact Reduce Prejudice? Meta-analytic Tests of Three Mediators." *European Journal of Social Psychology* 38:922–34. doi:10.1002/ejsp.504

Pettigrew, Thomas F., and Linda R. Tropp. 2011. *When Groups Meet: The Dynamics of Intergroup Contact.* New York: Psychology Press.

Pronin, Emily, Claude M. Steele, and Lee Ross. 2004. "Identity Bifurcation in Response to Stereotype Threat: Women and Mathematics." *Journal of Experimental Social Psychology* 40(2):152–68. doi:10.1016/S0022–1031(03)00088-X

Quillian, Lincoln. 1995. "Prejudice as a Response to Perceived Group Threat: Population Composition and Anti-immigrant and Racial Prejudice in Europe." *American Sociological Review* 60:586–611. doi:10.2307/2096296

Quillian, Lincoln. 2006. "New Approaches to Understanding Racial Prejudice and Discrimination." *Annual Review of Sociology* 32:299–328. doi:10.1146/annurev.soc.32.061604.123132

Samson, Frank L., and Lawrence D. Bobo. 2014. "Ethno-Racial Attitudes and Social Inequality." Pp. 515–45 in *Handbook of the Social Psychology of Inequality*, edited by J. McLeod, E. Lawler, and M. Schwalbe. New York: Springer.

Schmader, Toni, Michael Johns, and Chad Forbes. 2008. "An Integrated Process Model of Stereotype Threat Effects on Performance." *Psychological Review* 115(2):336–56. doi:10.1037/0033–295X.115.2.336

Sears, David O. 1988. "Symbolic Racism." Pp. 53–84 in *Eliminating Racism: Profiles in Controversy*, edited by P. A. Katz and D. A. Taylor. New York: Plenum. doi:10.1007/978–1–4899–0818–6_4

Sears, David O., and P. J. Henry. 2005. "Over Thirty Years Later: A Contemporary Look at Symbolic Racism." *Advances in Experimental Social Psychology* 37:95–150. doi:10.1016/S0065–2601(05)37002-X

Sears, David O., Jim Sidanius, and Lawrence Bobo. 2000. *Racialized Politics: The Debate about Racism in America.* Chicago: University of Chicago Press.

Shelton, J. Nicole, Thomas E. Trail, Tessa V. West, and Hilary B. Bergsieker. 2010. "From Strangers to Friends: The Interpersonal Process Model of Intimacy in Developing Interracial Friendships." *Journal of Social and Personal Relationships* 27:71–90. doi:10.1177/0265407509346422

Sherif, Muzafer. 1966. *In Common Predicament: Social Psychology of Intergroup Conflict and Cooperation.* Boston: Houghton Mifflin.

Sherif, Muzafer, Oliver J. Harvey, B. Jack White, William R. Hood, and Carolyn W. Sherif. 1961. *Intergroup Conflict and Cooperation: The Robbers Cave Experiment.* Norman: Oklahoma Book Exchange.

Sidanius, J. Pratto, and Felicia Pratto. 1999. *Social Dominance.* Cambridge, England: Cambridge University Press. doi:10.1017/CBO9781139175043

Smith, Elliot R. 1993. "Social Identity and Social Emotions: Toward New Conceptualizations of Prejudice." Pp. 297–315 in *Affect, Cognition, and Stereotyping: Interactive Processes in Group Perception*, edited by D. M. Mackie and D. L. Hamilton. San Diego, CA: Academic Press. doi:10.1016/B978–0–08–088579–7.50017-X

Stangor, Charles. 2009. "The Study of Stereotyping, Prejudice, and Discrimination within Social Psychology: A Quick History of Theory and Research." Pp. 1–22 in *Handbook of Prejudice, Stereotyping, and Discrimination*, edited by T. D. Nelson. New York: Psychology Press.

Steele, Claude M. 1997. "A Threat in the Air: How Stereotypes Shape Intellectual Identity and Performance." *The American Psychologist* 52(6):613–29. doi:10.1037/0003–066X.52.6.613

Stephan, Walter G., and Cookie White Stephan. 1985. "Intergroup Anxiety." *The Journal of Social Issues* 41(3):157–75. doi:10.1111/j.1540–4560.1985.tb01134.x

Tajfel, Henri. 1979. "Individuals and Groups in Social Psychology." *The British Journal of Social and Clinical Psychology* 18:183–90. doi:10.1111/j.2044-8260.1979.tb00324.x

Tajfel, Henri, Michael Billig, R. P. Bundy, and Claude Flament. 1971. "Social Categorization and Intergroup Behaviour." *European Journal of Social Psychology* 1:149–78. doi:10.1002/ejsp.2420010202

Tajfel, Henri, and John C. Turner. 1979. "An Integrative Theory of Intergroup Conflict." Pp. 33–47 in *The Social Psychology of Intergroup Relations*, edited by W. G. Austin and S. Worchel. Monterey, CA: Brooks/Cole.

Taylor, Marylee. 1998. "How White Attitudes Vary with the Racial Composition of Local Populations: Numbers Count." *American Sociological Review* 63:512–35. doi:10.2307/2657265

Tropp, Linda R., and Ludwin E. Molina. 2012. "Intergroup Processes from Prejudice to Positive Relations Between Groups." Pp. 545–70 in *The Oxford Handbook of Personality and Social Psychology*, edited by Kay Deaux and Mark Snyder. New York: Oxford University Press.

Turner, John C., Michael A. Hogg, Penelope J. Oakes, Stephen D. Reicher, & Margaret S. Wetherell. 1987. *Rediscovering the Social Group: A Self-categorization Theory*. Oxford, England: Blackwell.

Turner, Rhiannon N., Miles Hewstone, and Alberto Voci. 2007. "Reducing Explicit and Implicit Outgroup Prejudice via Direct and Extended Contact: The Mediating Role of Self-disclosure and Intergroup Anxiety." *Journal of Personality and Social Psychology* 93:369–88. doi:10.1037/0022-3514.93.3.369

Van Bavel, Jay J., Dominic J. Packer, and William A. Cunningham. 2008. "The Neural Substrates of In-group Bias." *Psychological Science* 19:1131–39. doi:10.1111/j.1467-9280.2008.02214.x

Van Zomeren, Martijn, Russell Spears, and Colin Wayne Leach. 2008. "Exploring Psychological Mechanisms of Collective Action: Does Relevance of Group Identity Influence How People Cope with Collective Disadvantage?" *British Journal of Social Psychology* 47:353–72. doi:10.1348/014466607X231091

Vescio, Theresa K., Gretchen B. Sechrist, and Matthew P. Paolucci. 2003. "Perspective Taking and Prejudice Reduction: The Mediational Role of Empathy Arousal and Situational Attributions." *European Journal of Social Psychology* 33:455–72. doi:10.1002/ejsp.163

Wagner, Ulrich, Oliver Christ, Thomas F. Pettigrew, Jost Stellmacher, and Carina Wolf. 2006. "Prejudice and Minority Proportion: Contact Instead of Threat Effects." *Social Psychology Quarterly* 69:380–90. doi:10.1177/019027250606900406

Williams, Robin M., Jr. 1947. *The Reduction of Intergroup Tensions*. New York: Social Science Research Council.

Won-Doornink, Myong Jin. 1979. "On Getting to Know You: The Association between the Stage of a Relationship and Reciprocity of Self-Disclosure." *Journal of Experimental Social Psychology* 15(3):229–41. doi:10.1016/0022-1031(79)90034-9

Wright, Stephen C., Art Aron, and Linda R. Tropp. 2002. "Including Others (and Groups) in the Self: Self-expansion and Intergroup Relations." Pp. 343–63 in *The Social Self: Cognitive, Interpersonal, and Intergroup Perspectives*, edited by J. P. Forgas and K. D. Williams. Philadelphia, PA: Psychology Press.

Yzerbyt, Vincent, and Stéphanie Demoulin. 2010. "Intergroup Relations." Pp. 1024–83 in *Handbook of Social Psychology*, Vol. 2, edited by S. T. Fiske, D. T. Gilbert, and G. Lindzey. Hoboken, NJ: Wiley. doi:10.1002/9780470561119.socpsy002028

Yzerbyt, Vincent Y., Muriel Dumont, Bernard Mathieu, Ernestine Gordijn, and Daniel Wigboldus. 2006. "Social Comparison and Group-Based Emotions." Pp. 174–205 in *Social Comparison Processes and Levels of Analysis: Understanding Cognition, Intergroup Relations, and Culture*, edited by S. Guimond. Cambridge, England: Cambridge University Press.

• Index •